SAT®

2007 Edition

Premier Program

Other Kaplan Books for College-Bound Students

SAT Comprehensive Program 2007

12 Practice Tests for the SAT

SAT Strategies for Super Busy Students, 2006 Edition

Inside the SAT: 10 Strategies to Help You Score Higher, 2007 Edition

SAT 2400, 2006 Edition

SAT Critical Reading Workbook, Second Edition

SAT Math Workbook, Second Edition

SAT Writing Workbook, Second Edition

SAT Vocabulary Flashcards Flip-O-Matic, Third Edition

Extreme SAT Vocabulary Flashcards Flip-O-Matic, Second Edition

The Ring of McAllister: A Score-Raising Mystery Featuring 1,046 Must-Know SAT Vocabulary Words

Frankenstein: A Kaplan SAT Score-Raising Classic

The Tales of Edgar Allan Poe: A Kaplan SAT Score-Raising Classic

Dr. Jekyll and Mr. Hyde: A Kaplan SAT Score-Raising Classic

Wuthering Heights: A Kaplan SAT Score-Raising Classic

Domina El SAT: Prepárate para Tomar el Examen para Ingresar a la Universidad

AP Biology

AP Calculus AB/BC

AP Chemistry

AP English Language & Composition

AP English Literature & Composition

AP Macroeconomics/Microeconomics

AP Physics B & C

AP Psychology

AP Statistics

AP U.S. Government & Politics

AP U.S. History

AP World History

SAT Subject Test: Biology E/M

SAT Subject Test: Chemistry

SAT Subject Test: Literature

SAT Subject Test: Mathematics Level 1

SAT Subject Test: Mathematics Level 2

SAT Subject Test: Physics

SAT Subject Test: Spanish

SAT Subject Test: U.S. History

SAT Subject Test: World History

SAT®

2007 Edition

Premier Program

The Staff of Kaplan Test Prep and Admissions

KAPLAN PUBLISHING

New York • Chicago

Contributing Editors: Mark Ward, Annette Riffle, and Brandon Jones
Editorial Director: Jennifer Farthing
Editor: Sheryl Gordon
Production Artist: Renée Mitchell
Cover Designer: Carly Schnur

Published by Kaplan Publishing, a division of Kaplan, Inc.
888 Seventh Ave.
New York, NY 10106

Printed in the United States of America

July 2006
10 9 8 7 6 5 4 3 2 1

ISBN-13: 978-1-4195-4183-4
ISBN-10:   1-4195-4183-8

Kaplan Publishing books are available at special quantity discounts to use for sales promotions, employee premiums, or educational purposes. Please call our Special Sales Department to order or for more information at 800-621-9621, ext. 4444, e-mail kaplanpubsales@kaplan.com, or write to Kaplan Publishing, 30 South Wacker Drive, Suite 2500, Chicago, IL 60606-7481.

Table of Contents

How to Use Kaplan's SAT Premier Program

Are you ready for a totally unique test prep experience? The SAT team at Kaplan understands what you are going through.

First, you're facing perhaps the single most important test of your high school career. Second, you're dealing with a longer, more grueling exam today—3 hours and 45 minutes to be exact—testing everything from writing to reading comprehension to reasoning to advanced math. Third, you're struggling to balance your normal activities such as sports and music with SAT prep. Finally, you're a person in need of options—the option of when to study, where to study, and most of all—*how to study.*

That's why you need this Program. The SAT Premier Program contained here is *your* program—flexible and customizable. What's unique about it is that *you* control the variety and amount of study that best suits your needs. You don't have to read this book starting on page 1 and ending on page 748 if you don't want to. We encourage you to mix it up a little. And to make sure that you don't get bored with a big book of lessons and tests, we made your study time on the SAT interactive—you customize your study time by jumping among the book, the CD-ROM, the mobile prep, and the online resources.

To get you started, we've put the Diagnostic Quiz and some essay prompts online so you can get used to moving from book to computer to prepare for your test. And so you never run low on practice questions and tests, we've given you more of each on the CD-ROM. Not at your computer and don't want to carry this big book around with you? No problem—we've got you covered. Download our mobile practice files to your cell phone or PDA, and study time becomes portable—you can practice anytime, anywhere.

Finally, we know you want to keep your skills fresh, so we've included something really cool—each month, we add a brand-new SAT quiz to your online syllabus! This way, you are totally up-to-date on the SAT, and you can never run out of questions to practice!

Here's the plan, step-by-step.

STEP 1: REGISTER YOUR PROGRAM ONLINE

To register, you will need to have your book in front of you because you will be prompted for the serial number on the lower left corner of the inside back cover.

kaptest.com/SATbooksonline

The address is case sensitive, so enter it carefully.

Registration is important because:

1. It gives you access to all the SAT Program components that are not included between the covers of this book, such as your Diagnostic Quiz, essay writing practice, CD-ROM, mobile prep, new quizzes each month, and links to Kaplan's best SAT information.

2. It protects your SAT Premier Program so that your practice content remains exclusive to you.

3. It gives you access to important SAT information and developments, along with any updates and additions to this program.

Once you have registered, access your Online Companion whenever you want to. You'll see a syllabus that lists all SAT Premier Program elements—Diagnostic Quiz, book chapters, CD-ROM, online practice, updates, new quizzes each month, and more!

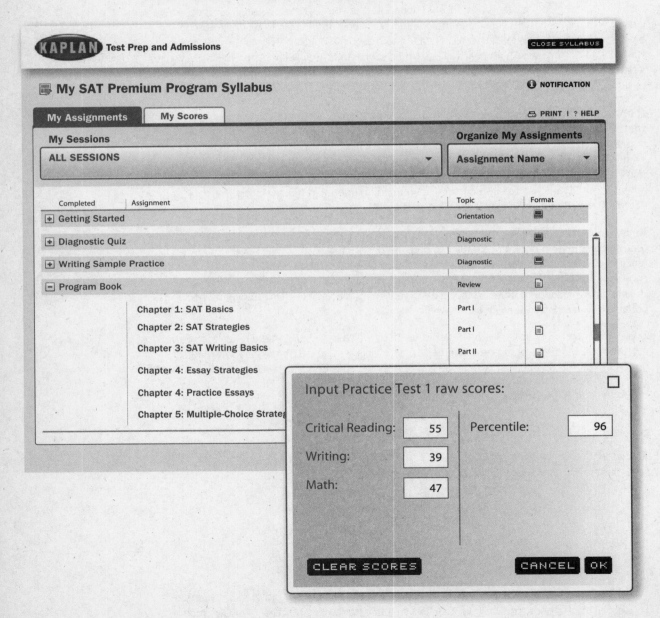

STEP 2: TAKE THE ONLINE DIAGNOSTIC QUIZ

Taking the Diagnostic Quiz is the first thing we recommend you do in this Program. It will help you to pinpoint your strengths and weaknesses. With that information, you can customize and focus your study time.

1. This half-length SAT provides you with a sample of each question type, enabling you to accurately gauge what you know and what you need to practice.

2. Review the explanation to each question to better understand where you went wrong. This is useful in helping you target your practice time to specific concepts.

STEP 3: TRY AN ONLINE ESSAY PROMPT AND HAVE YOUR WRITING SCORED

Your Online Companion includes a series of essay prompts similar to those you will see on Test Day.

1. Choose a prompt, and allow yourself 25 minutes to write your essay.

2. When you are finished, compare it to the model essays provided and check it against the scoring rubric.

3. How you have the option to have your essay scored by an online grader! Look in your Online Companion options for the special essay that can be scored by the grader. Read the prompt, and allow yourself 25 minutes to write your essay. When done, submit it to our grader with the click of a botton. Within minutes, you will have a scored essay.

How did you do? There are additional essay prompts online and on your CD-ROM. Try these over the course of your study to gauge your writing improvement.

STEP 4: IDENTIFY YOUR WEAKNESSES

Check your answers to the Diagnostic Quiz, noting how many questions you got right and how many you got wrong. Look for patterns. Did you ace reading comprehension? Did the tough math trip you up?

Don't limit your initial review to the questions you got wrong. Read all of the explanations—even those you got right—to reinforce key concepts and sharpen your skills. As time permits, go back to the question types that you aced so you can keep that material sharp.

STEP 5: CUSTOMIZE YOUR STUDY PLAN USING THE ONLINE SYLLABUS

Based on your performance on the Diagnostic Quiz (and the amount of time you have available to study), use the online syllabus to select the lessons, quizzes, and other tools online and on your CD-ROM that will constitute your customized study plan. Then stick to it—your plan works only if you follow it!

The best study plan you can build will adapt to your individual needs and should adhere to the following:

- Start with a review of content weaknesses and include quizzes on weaker topics to boost skills and understanding.
- Devote time to reinforcing content strengths through lesson reviews and practice quizzes.
- Use full-length practice tests as milestones.

1. Go back to the syllabus to help you find those concepts you need to work on, so you can chart your personalized study plan. Think about the topics on which you need to focus. Plan to read those lessons in the book and take the practice sets.

2. As time permits, go back to the question types that you aced so you can keep that material sharp.

3. Plan time to go online and practice with the essay prompts, even if writing is your best subject.

4. There are 4 full-length practice tests in this book and 5 more on your CD-ROM; don't plan on saving them all for the final weeks.

STEP 6: REVIEW, REINFORCE, AND BUILD SKILLS

Once you've made your plan, follow through. Targeted SAT study is a sure way to perform well on the test. You will maximize your study time by focusing on those areas you need to cover most.

1. Read the lessons you identified in the book, take the practice sets, and read the answer explanations. Chart your improvement by recording quiz and practice test scores in your syllabus.

2. Take time to practice your essay writing. Understanding the essay requirements and practicing periodically will help you deliver the right paragraphs on Test Day.

3. As soon as you get comfortable with the SAT question types and Target Strategies, take a full-length practice test. There are 9 in the Program, so you will be able to assess your improvement. Test yourself periodically and chart your progress on the syllabus. If your strengths and weaknesses change, adjust your plan appropriately.

ABOUT THIS PROGRAM BOOK

In addition to the online syllabus, this book has a detailed Table of Contents, so if you are away from your computer, you will still be able to navigate the Premier Program. Throughout the book, we have added icons to highlight certain points.

- The characteristics of a standardized test can be used to your advantage. The "Know the SAT" section offers management techniques and advice about which questions to answer and which to guess on.

- Section Two offers specific methods, strategies, and practice problems for every type of SAT question you're likely to see in the Writing, Critical Reading, and Math sections.

- The material in this book is up-to-date at the time of publication, but the College Board may institute changes in the test or the registration process. Be sure to read the materials you receive from the College Board carefully. Any important late-breaking developments or corrections for this book can be found posted on the Online Companion.

Icon Key

📖 A NOTE ON...	Call outs to help you focus on key concepts
➤ GO ONLINE	Find more information and practice online.
💿 AVAILABLE ON CD-ROM	Find more tests and practice on your CD-ROM
📱 MOBILE PREP	Find more practice on mobile applications.
♟ BE SMART!	Study methods that pay off on Test Day.
◎ KAPLAN'S TARGET STRATEGY	These proven strategies will help you conquer the SAT.
! SMARTPOINTS	Kaplan's exclusive strategy for scoring higher on the SAT.

ABOUT THE CD-ROM

The CD-ROM you receive with the SAT Premier Program contains and section-length practice tests for each question type plus 5 full-length practice tests.

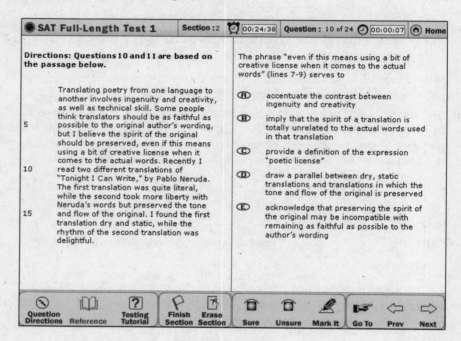

Once you've completed a test, the program scores and analyzes your results and offers comprehensive explanations to each question. We recommend alternating between the tests in your book and the tests on the CD-ROM. All tests are identified on your online syllabus.

SYSTEM REQUIREMENTS

Windows®:

Windows® 98SE, NT 4.0 (with Service Pack 6), 2000, ME, XP

Pentium®II 300 MHz or faster, 15 MB free hard disk space, 640 × 480—thousands of colors (millions recommended), SoundBlaster-compatible sound card, 4x CDROM or higher.

Note: An Internet connection is required for the web features of the program.

Macintosh®:

Macintosh® OS 8.6, OS 9.1, 9.2.2, OS 10.1.3, 10.1.5, 10.2.4, 10.2.8, 10.3, 10.3.7, 10.3.8

400 MHz Power PC®, G3, G4 or faster, 15 MB free hard disk space, 640 × 480—thousands of colors (millions recommended), 4x CDROM or higher.

Note: an Internet connection is required for the web features of the program.

INSTALLATION INSTRUCTIONS

Windows®:

Exit out of all open applications; make sure you have no applications running.

Insert the Higher Score CD into your CD-ROM drive. The installation window opens automatically if Autorun is enabled on your system.

If you have Autorun disabled on your system, from the Start Menu, choose Run and type (or browse for) d:\setup.exe (where d: is your CD-ROM drive).

Press OK and follow the prompts.

You are now ready to use the software. You must have the CD-ROM in your computer when using the software, even though you have in installed information on your hard drive. To launch the program, go to the Start Menu, choose Programs, then Kaplan and then Higher Score on the SAT or double-click the Higher Score on the SAT icon located on your desktop.

Macintosh®:

Exit out of all open applications; make sure you have no applications running.

Insert the Higher Score CD into your CD-ROM drive

Double-click the Kaplan install icon.

You will be presented with a dialog box that will let you choose where to install the program. Follow the prompts.

You are now ready to use the software. You must have the CD-ROM in your computer when using the software, even though you have in installed information on your hard drive. To launch the program, double-click the "Higher Score on the SAT" icon.

User Tips:

You can skip over the introductory music by either hitting the **ESC** key or by going into the program Preferences and checking the box labeled "Skip Intro." You can use the **ESC** key to skip over most of the audio voice-overs or videos within the program. Please be sure to have your headphones plugged in or your speakers turned on before using the program. If you are experiencing any problems installing these programs, please visit the Customer Service area of our website at www.kaptest.com/support.

ONLY KAPLAN GIVES YOU MORE

Our goal is to ensure that you reach your goals, so we've added more practice across the entire SAT Premier Program; more question in the chapter quizzes in the book, more section-length quizzes and tests on the CD-ROM, more prep to download to your PDA or cell phone, and fresh online quiz practice sets every month for the entire subscription period of your online companion. No matter where you are or what your format preference may be, Kaplan's got you covered.

SAT DATES AND REGISTRATION

SAT Test Dates

These days, more students are taking the SAT earlier in high school. Many are applying to early-decision programs, and many are taking the SAT more than once.

Here are the SAT dates for 2006–2007:

Test Date	Registration Deadlines	United States Late Registration	International Deadlines
October 14, 2006	September 12, 2006	September 20, 2006	September 12, 2006
November 4, 2006	September 29, 2006	October 11, 2006	September 29, 2006
December 2, 2006	November 1, 2006	November 9, 2006	November 1, 2006
January 27, 2007	December 20, 2006	January 4, 2007	December 20, 2006
March 10, 2007	February 2, 2007	February 14, 2007	n/a
May 5, 2007	March 29, 2007	April 11, 2007	March 29, 2007
June 2, 2007	April 27, 2007	May 9, 2007	April 27, 2007

SAT Registration

There are a few different ways to register for the SAT exam. Check out the College Board website at www.collegeboard.com for complete information about registering for the SAT and for the most up-to-date information concerning changes in dates, fees, etc. Try to register early to secure the test center of your choice and to avoid late registration fees.

Register by Mail, Online, or Telephone

- To register by mail, you'll need to get a Registration Bulletin from your high school guidance counselor and follow the instructions within.

- To register online, you'll need to visit www.collegeboard.com/sat/html/satform.html. The website contains easy, step-by-step instructions for electronically submitting your registration. Not all students are eligible to register online; read the instructions and requirements carefully.

- You may re-register by telephone if you've previously registered for the SAT and you require no special forms (like a fee waiver). If you have a touch-tone phone and a major credit card, you can re-register by calling (800) SAT-SCORE. If you need assistance, you can reach a customer service representative at (609) 771-7600. Students with disabilities can call (609) 771-7137 (TTY: (609) 882-4118) for more information regarding special testing accommodations.

Other Important Registration Information

- The basic fee for the SAT will be approximately $40 in the United States. This price includes reports for you, your high school, and up to four colleges and scholarship programs. There are additional fees for late registration, standby testing, international processing, changing test centers or test dates, rush reporting, and for additional services and products.

- You will receive an admission ticket at least a week before the test. The ticket confirms your registration at a specified date and at a specified test center. Make sure to bring it and proper identification with you to the test center. Some acceptable forms of identification include photo IDs, such as a driver's license, a school identification card, or a valid passport. Unacceptable forms of identification include a social security card, credit card, or birth certificate.

- The SAT is administered on select Saturdays during the school year. Sunday testing is available for those who cannot take the Saturday test because of religious observances.

Also …

- You might be wondering whether to take the ACT in addition to the SAT. For more information on the ACT, go to the ACT website at www.act.org/aap/.

- SAT scores will be available online approximately three weeks after the test. If you can't wait that long, you can get your scores eight days earlier with Scores by Web or Scores by Phone. Please visit www.collegeboard.com for more information.

- Check your online companion or log onto the College Board for all the latest information on the test. Every effort is made to keep the information in this book up to date, but changes may occur after the book is published.

HOW DID WE DO?

When you have completed the Premier Program and have taken your SAT, go back one last time and fill out the online survey. We want to know how you did on the exam, and how we did in helping you prepare.

Good luck!

Know the SAT

Knowing the SAT inside and out will gain you points on *every section*. Getting just one extra question right every 10 minutes translates to about 20 more correct questions over the entire test, which could boost your score by close to 200 points. Those extra points could mean a lot to an admissions officer reviewing your score.

Section One of the Kaplan SAT Premier Program is an overview of the SAT and Kaplan's strategies for doing your absolute best on the exam. The sections on Writing, Critical Reading, and Math build upon the materials in these chapters, so read Section One slowly and methodically. Be sure you understand the information it presents before you move on to Sections Two–Five.

Chapter One: **SAT Basics**

- What Components Make Up the SAT?

- How Much Time Will I Have for the SAT?

- How Is My Test Scored?

If you don't have much time to prep for the SAT, spend what time you do have reading the two chapters in this section. They cover basic information on the SAT and Kaplan's overall strategies for approaching the test—the fundamentals you need to be ready for the exam and improve your score. Knowing this information will make you feel more confident when you walk into the testing room, and the more confidence you have, the more success you will have in attaining a top score.

SAT FORMAT

The SAT is 3 hours and 45 minutes long, and there are two 10-minute breaks. The exam is mostly multiple-choice, and it's divided into three Math, three Critical Reading, and three Writing sections. There is also an experimental section, but we will discuss that section later. The essay section is always first. The multiple-choice sections can appear in *any order* on Test Day. The order is random, and your test will be different from that of the person sitting next to you.

The SAT sections are broken down like this:

Section	Length	Content	Type
1. Critical Reading	25 minutes	Sentence Completion and Reading Comprehension	Multiple-choice questions
2. Critical Reading	25 minutes	Sentence Completion and Reading Comprehension	Multiple-choice questions
3. Critical Reading	20 minutes	Sentence Completion and Reading Comprehension	Multiple-choice questions
4. Math	25 minutes	High school geometry and algebra, numbers and operations, statistics, probability, and data analysis	Multiple-choice questions and student-produced responses
5. Math	25 minutes	High school geometry and algebra, numbers and operations, statistics, probability, and data analysis	Multiple-choice questions and student-produced responses
6. Math	20 minutes	High school geometry and algebra, numbers and operations, statistics, probability, and data analysis	Multiple-choice questions
7. Writing	25 minutes	Student-written essay	Long-form essay
8. Writing	25 minutes	Identifying Sentence Errors, Improving, Sentences, Improving Paragraphs	Multiple-choice questions
9. Writing	10 minutes	Improving Sentences	Multiple-choice questions
10. Experimental	25 minutes	Math, Writing, or Critical Reading	(Anything is fair game)

SAT SCORING

You gain one point for each correct answer on the SAT and lose a fraction of a point (1/4 point, to be exact) for each wrong answer (except with Grid-ins, where you lose **nothing** for a wrong answer). You do not lose any points for questions you leave blank. This is important, so we'll repeat it:

You do not lose *any* points for questions you leave blank.

The totals for the Critical Reading, Writing, and Math questions are added up to produce three raw scores. These raw scores equal the number you got right minus a fraction of the number you got wrong. These scores are converted into scaled scores, with 200 as the lowest score and 800 the highest. Each raw point is worth approximately 10 scaled points.

The three scaled scores are added together to produce your final score of 600–2400, as follows:

Scaled Scores:	Writing	Math	Critical Reading	Total
	200–800	200–800	200–800	600–2400
For example:	650	710	620	1980

ORDER OF DIFFICULTY

In the SAT, some sections will have their multiple-choice questions arranged in order of difficulty. Here's a breakdown:

		Arranged Easiest to Hardest?
Math	Regular math	Yes
	Grid-ins	Yes
Critical Reading	Sentence Completion	Yes
	Short Reading Comprehension	No
	Long Reading Comprehension	No
Writing	Essay	N/A
	Identifying Sentence Errors	No
	Improving Sentences	No
	Improving Paragraphs	No

As you can see, all question sets in math are normally arranged in order of difficulty, as are Sentence Completion questions in the Critical Reading section. As you work through a set that is organized this way, *be aware of where you are in a set*. When working on the easy problems, you can generally trust your first impulse—the obvious answer is likely to be right. As you get to the end of the set, you need to be more suspicious of *obvious* answers, because the answer should not come easily. If it does, look at the problem again. It may be one of those distracters—a wrong answer choice meant to trick you.

GROUND RULES

These are SAT rules you can use to your advantage. Knowing these rules will keep you from asking questions and wasting precious time and from committing minor errors that result in serious penalties.

- You are NOT allowed to jump back and forth between sections.
- You are NOT allowed to return to earlier sections to change answers.
- You are NOT allowed to spend more than the allotted time on any section.
- You CAN move around within a section.
- You CAN flip through your section at the beginning to see what types of questions are coming up.

SAT COMPONENTS

Now it's time for brief summaries of each of the SAT's three components: Writing, Critical Reading, and Math.

The Writing Component

The SAT has three Writing sections. Only one of them involves actual writing.

The Essay

The Essay directions ask you to write a persuasive essay answering the assigned question, which typically asks you to respond to a quotation. Here is an example of a quote and essay prompt that you might see on the test:

> "My future starts when I wake up every morning … Everyday I find something creative to do with my life."
>
> —Miles Davis

Assignment: Are there more advantages to planning for the future than living in the moment?

We know what kind of essay the SAT graders are looking for, and we'll tell you exactly how to write one in Chapter Four.

Multiple Choice Questions

The Writing component's multiple-choice questions test your ability to spot errors in grammar, sentence structure, and paragraph structure or organization. Here's an example of a sentence structure question:

3. The lawyer advised her client to wear a suit, shave, <u>and stopping crying</u>.

    (A) and stopping crying
    (B) and crying is stopped
    (C) also stopping crying
    (D) and they should stop crying
    (E) and stop crying

We go into detail on the Writing component's multiple-choice questions in Chapter Five.

 GO ONLINE

Check out your new online essay grading option.

The Critical Reading Component

There are two kinds of questions in the Critical Reading component of the SAT. Both are multiple choice.

Sentence Completion Questions

These questions test your ability to determine how words or ideas work together to create meaning in a sentence. About half have one word missing from a sentence; the other half have two words missing. Both types test vocabulary and reasoning skills.

Here is a sample question:

> The king's ------- decisions as a diplomat and administrator led to his legendary reputation as a just and ------- ruler.
>
> (A) quick . . capricious
>
> (B) equitable . . wise
>
> (C) immoral . . perceptive
>
> (D generous . . witty
>
> (E) clever . . uneducated

Reading Comprehension Questions

These questions test your ability to understand a piece of writing. Some passages are short (100–150 words), others are long (400–850 words), and at least one passage contains two related readings. Most Reading Comprehension questions test how well you understand the information in the passage, some ask you to draw conclusions, and some test your vocabulary or your ability to determine the meaning of words in context.

Here is a sample question:

> According to lines 52–56, one difficulty of using a linear representation of time is that
>
> (A) linear representations of time do not meet accepted scientific standards of accuracy
>
> (B) prehistoric eras overlap each other, making linear representation deceptive
>
> (C) the more accurate the scale, the more difficult the map is to copy and study
>
> (D) there are too many events to represent on a single line
>
> (E) our knowledge of pre-Cambrian time is insufficient to construct an accurate linear map

The Sentence Completion questions are arranged in order of difficulty. The first few questions in a set would be fairly easy. The middle few questions are harder, and the last few are the most difficult. Keep this in mind as you work through this section of the exam.

Reading Comprehension questions are not arranged by difficulty. Whenever you find yourself spending too much time on a question in these sections, you should skip it and return to it later.

We cover Critical Reading questions in Section Three.

The Math Component

There are two kinds of questions in the Math component, broken down as follows:

Regular Math Questions

These questions are straightforward multiple-choice questions with five answer choices.

Here is a sample question:

At a diner, Joe orders three strips of bacon and a cup of warm water and is charged $2.25. Stella orders two strips of bacon and a cup of warm water and is charged $1.70. What is the price of two strips of bacon?

(A) $0.55
(B) $0.60
(C) $1.10
(D) $1.30
(E) $1.80

Grid-in Questions

Grid-in questions are not multiple choice. Instead of picking an answer choice, you write your response in a grid like the one below.

Here is a sample Grid-in answer:

Both question types cover *the same* math concepts across the full range of difficulty. Either one can ask you a geometry, algebra, or statistics question. However, Grid-ins are more challenging because you don't have answers to choose from, as in the multiple-choice questions; you are totally on your own to come up with the correct answer.

Another important difference in the two types of questions has to do with how a wrong answer is scored. A wrong multiple-choice answer loses you 1/4 point. A wrong Grid-in loses you *nothing*. Always fill in something for each Grid-in.

SAT Math is covered in detail in the SAT Premier Program's Section Four.

Experimental Section

Every SAT has an experimental section. The experimental section is used by the test developers to try out new questions before including them in upcoming SATs. The experimental section DOES NOT COUNT in your score. It can show up anywhere on the exam and will look just like a normal section. You shouldn't try to figure out which SAT section is experimental. You will fail to do so. Just treat all the sections as if they count toward your score.

These are the basics you need to know about the structure of the test before you take the SAT. You'll get more familiar with the format and setup of the SAT question types and sections as you work your way through the rest of the book.

IF YOU LEARNED ONLY FOUR THINGS IN THIS CHAPTER . . . .

1. The SAT is divided into 10 sections.
2. You gain 1 point for every question you get right.
3. You lose 1/4 points for every multiple-choice question you get wrong.
4. Order of difficulty is important to keep in mind for certain sections of the test.

ANSWERS TO THE QUESTIONS ON PAGE 3

What Components Make Up the SAT?

- 3 Critical Reading sections
- 3 Math sections
- 3 Writing sections
- 1 Experimental section

How Much Time Will I Have for the SAT?

- The SAT is 3 hours and 45 minutes.

How is My Test Scored?

- Each section is worth 200–800 points. Those scores are added to get your total score of 600–2400.

Chapter Two: **SAT Strategies**

- How Can I Make the SAT Work for Me?
- How Do I Tackle the Tough Questions?
- What Strategies Will Help Me Succeed?

SAT STRUCTURE: THE FUNDAMENTALS

The SAT is different from the tests you're used to taking in school. The good news is you can use the SAT's particular structure to your scoring advantage.

Here's an example. On a school test, you probably go through the problems in order. You spend more time on the hard questions than on easy ones because harder questions are usually worth more points. You probably often show your work because the teacher tells you that how you approach a problem is as important as getting the answer right.

None of this works on the SAT. If you use the same approach on the SAT, your score will suffer. On the SAT, you benefit from moving around within a section if you come across hard questions because the hard questions are worth the same as the easy ones. It doesn't matter how you determine the answers—only that you get them right.

When you take the SAT, you should have one clear objective in mind: to score as many points as you can. It's that simple. The rest of this book will help you achieve that goal.

The Directions Never Change

One of the easiest things you can do to help your performance on the SAT is to understand the directions before taking the test. Because the directions are always exactly the same, knowing them in advance will help keep your testing experience positive and efficient.

We provide sample SAT directions in Sections Two, Three, and Four. Learn them as you go through this book so you can just skim them during the test.

If you are not going to work through these sections, you can go to one of the practice tests and read the directions there for each question type (three times each would help).

Use *Order of Difficulty* to Your Advantage

Not all of the questions on the SAT are equally difficult. Some question types are ordered easiest to hardest.

As you work, always be aware of where you are in the set. When working on the easy problems, you can generally trust your first impulse—the obvious answer is likely to be right. As you get to the end of the set, you need to become more suspicious. The answers probably *shouldn't* come easily. If they do, look at the problem again because the obvious answer is likely to be wrong. Watch out for the answer that just *looks right*. It may be a *distracter*—a wrong answer choice meant to entice you. (We'll go into detail on the most common kinds of distracters later.)

 MOBILE PREP

Practice easy, medium, and tough questions on the go using your mobile device with Kaplan Mobile.

You Don't Have to Answer the Questions in Order

You are allowed to skip around within each section of the SAT. High scorers know this. They move through the test efficiently. They don't dwell on any one question, even a hard one, until they've tried every question at least once.

When you run into questions that look tough, circle them in your test booklet and skip them. Go back and try again after you have answered the easier ones. Remember, you don't get more points for answering hard questions. If you get two easy ones right in the time it would have taken you to get one hard one right, you just improved your score.

There's another benefit for coming back to hard ones later. On a second look, troublesome questions can turn out to be simple. By answering some easier questions first, you can come back to a harder question with fresh eyes, a fresh perspective, and more confidence.

Guessing

If you have come back to a tough question and still can't find the correct answer the second time around, consider a different approach. Begin eliminating choices that are absolutely wrong. If you can whittle the choices down to two, your chances of guessing the correct answer just increased from 20% to 50%.

Answer All Grid-ins

If you get an answer wrong on a Grid-in math question, you lose nothing. So you should write in an answer for every Grid-in. The worst that can happen is that you get zero points for the questions you guessed on. If you get just one right, that's an extra 10 points.

Answer Sheet Strategies

It sounds simple, but it's extremely important: Don't make mistakes filling out your answer grid. When time is short, it's easy to get confused going back and forth between your test book and your grid. If you know the answer, but misgrid, you won't get the points. To avoid mistakes on the answer grid, try some of these methods:

Circle the Questions You Skip

Perhaps the most common SAT disaster is filling in all of the right answers—in the wrong spots. Put a big circle in your test book around any question numbers you skip to help you locate these questions when you are ready to go back to them. Also, if you accidentally skip a box on the grid, you can always check your grid against your book to see where you went wrong.

 GO ONLINE

Check out your new practice quiz every month.

Circle Your Answers in Your Test Book

Circling your answers in the test book makes it easier to check your grid against your book. It also makes the next grid strategy possible.

Grid Five or More Answers at Once

Time is of the essence on this exam. To save time and make sure you are marking your answers in the correct bubbles, transfer your answers after every five questions, or at the end of each reading passage, rather than after every question. That way, you won't keep breaking your concentration to mark the grid. You'll end up with more time and less chance to make a mistake on your answer sheet.

Keep Track of Time

You need to be careful at the end of a section when time may be running out. You don't want to have your answers in the test booklet and not be able to transfer them to your answer grid because you have run out of time. If there are just two minutes left, and you still have a few questions to answer, you should start transferring your answers one by one to ensure that every question you answered earns credit.

Write Your Essay

If you write a terrible essay, you still get two raw points, no matter how bad it is. (We go into essay scoring in detail in Chapter Three.) If you freeze and skip the essay, you get zero. So write *something*. The essay is worth one third of your total 800-point Writing score. Even if you get the lowest possible score that you can get on your essay, that's 44 more points than zero!

Read the Question Carefully Before You Look at the Answers

On the SAT, there will always be distracters among the answer choices. Distracters are answer choices that look right but aren't, and they are easy to choose if you haven't read the question carefully. If you jump right into the answer choices without thinking first about exactly what you're looking for, you're much more likely to fall into one of these traps.

Locate Quick Points If You're Running Out of Time

Some questions can be done quickly. For instance, some reading questions will ask you to identify the meaning of a particular word in the passage. These can often be done at the last minute, even if you haven't read the passage. When you start to run out of time, try to locate and answer the questions that can earn you quick points. When you take the SAT, you should have one clear objective in mind—to score as many points as you can. It's that simple. The rest of this book will help you do that.

Use Backdoor Strategies

There are usually a number of ways to get to the right answer on an SAT question. Most of the questions on the SAT are multiple choice. That means the answer is right in front of you—you just have to find it. This makes SAT questions open to several different ways of finding the answer.

If you can't figure out the answer in a straightforward way, try other techniques. We'll talk about specific Kaplan methods such as backsolving and picking numbers in upcoming Math chapters.

IF YOU LEARNED ONLY FIVE THINGS IN THIS CHAPTER . . . .

1. The directions never change.
2. Order of difficulty can be used to your advantage.
3. Always answer all Grid-in questions.
4. Always write your essay.
5. Be diligent about keeping track of time.

ANSWERS TO THE QUESTIONS ON PAGE 13

How Can I Make the SAT Work for Me?

- Be familiar with every section, question type, and answer type on the SAT. Chapter One is a good resource for more of this information.

How Do I Tackle the Tough Questions?

- Rule out all of the impossible answers, and then guess from the remaining choices.

What Strategies Will Help Me Succeed?

- Do the easier questions first. You don't have to work through each section in order.
- When running out of time, locate the quick points.
- Fill in your answer sheet after every five questions, and circle your answers in your test booklet to avoid confusion.

How to Attack the Writing Component

Welcome to the SAT's Writing component. Section Two of the Kaplan SAT Premier Program covers this component in depth. From the essay to the three multiple-choice question types, Kaplan's got the prep you need to ace the Writing component.

Chapter Three: **SAT Writing Basics**

- What Question Types Make Up the Writing Section?
- What Should I Know About the Essay?
- What Should I Know About Multiple-Choice Questions?

BASICS

There are three Writing sections on the SAT:

Length	Content	Type
25 minutes	Student-written essay on assigned prompt	Original essay
25 minutes	Identifying Sentence Errors, Improving Sentences, and Improving Paragraphs	Multiple choice
10 minutes	Improving Sentences	Multiple choice

The essay will be the first section of the test and will count for one third of your 800-point Writing score. Your essay and multiple-choice section scores will be combined into a single scaled score that reflects the weight given to each section. This new scaled score will then be converted into a final score ranging from 200–800 points.

THE ESSAY

For the essay portion of the test, your task is to write a short, *persuasive* essay on an assigned topic. The word *persuasive* is key. You can write a compelling essay on a meaningful experience or ways to become more involved in your community, but if you have not offered good reasons to see things from a particular point of view, you won't earn a high score.

You are required to write about the topic you are given, but you don't need any specific knowledge to complete the SAT essay, and you do have a lot of freedom in what you actually write. Because the topic will be very broad in scope, you can write about what you know and what you are interested in.

Essay Directions

The College Board has stated that the directions for the essay will look like the following.

The essay gives you an opportunity to show how effectively you can develop and express ideas. You should, therefore, take care to develop your point of view, present your ideas logically and clearly, and use language precisely.

Your essay must be written in your Answer Grid Booklet—you will receive no other paper on which to write. You will have enough space if you write on every line, avoid wide margins, and keep your handwriting to a reasonable size. Remember that people who are not familiar with your handwriting will read what you write. Try to write or print so that what you are writing is legible to those readers.

You have twenty-five minutes to write an essay on the topic assigned below. DO NOT WRITE ON ANOTHER TOPIC. AN OFF-TOPIC ESSAY WILL RECEIVE A SCORE OF ZERO.

Think carefully about the issue presented in the following excerpt and the assignment below.

> "The weirder you're going to behave, the more normal you should look. It works in reverse, too. When I see a kid with three or four rings in his nose, I know there is absolutely nothing extraordinary about that person."
>
> —P. J. O'Rourke

Assignment: Does weird behavior indicate an ordinary or an extraordinary person? Plan and write an essay in which you develop your point of view on this issue. Support your position with reasoning and examples taken from your reading, studies, experience, or observations.

DO NOT WRITE YOUR ESSAY IN YOUR TEST BOOK.
You will receive credit only for what you write in your Answer Grid Booklet.

Essay Scoring

The essays will be scored quickly and holistically by two readers. Holistically means your essay gets a single score—a number—that indicates its overall quality. This number takes into account a variety of essay characteristics, including organization and development of ideas, sentence structure, vocabulary, and grammar and usage. Thus, a highly persuasive and eloquent essay that has several run-ons or other minor errors could still earn a top score because of its overall effectiveness and impact.

Each reader will assign your essay a score ranging from a high of 6 to a low of 1. These two scores are added together to get a total score ranging from a high of 12 to a low of 2. The essay score accounts for one third of your final Writing section score.

The following chart is a rubric that shows the main criteria that the graders use to score your essay.

The Essay Scoring Chart

 GO ONLINE

Go online to find more essay practice prompts, sample essays, and the chance to have your personal essay scored by an online grader.

Score	Competence	Organization	Language
6	clear and consistent competence, though it may have errors	is well organized and fully developed with supporting examples	displays consistent language facility, varied sentence structure, and range of vocabulary
5	reasonable competence, with occasional errors or lapses in quality	is generally organized and well developed with appropriate examples	displays language facility, with syntactic variety and a range of vocabulary
4	adequate competence with occasional errors and lapses in quality	is organized and adequately developed with examples	displays adequate but inconsistent language facility
3	developing competence, with weaknesses	inadequate organization or development	many errors in grammar or diction; little variety
2	some incompetence with one or more weaknesses	poor organization, thin development	frequent errors in grammar and diction; no variety
1	incompetence, with serious flaws	no organization, no development	severe grammar and diction errors obscure meaning

The next chapter will show you the SAT Premier Program's strategies for writing a top-scoring essay.

MULTIPLE-CHOICE QUESTIONS

The multiple-choice portion of the Writing section consists of 49 questions divided into three types: 18 Identifying Sentence Errors questions, 25 Improving Sentences questions, and 6 Improving Paragraphs questions.

The Identifying Sentence Errors and Improving Sentences questions are based on single, unrelated sentences on a variety of topics. The Improving Paragraphs questions are based on a brief passage. The sentences and passages upon which the questions are based will usually (but not always) contain one or more grammar, usage, or organizational errors. Your task is to spot (and sometimes fix) the mistakes in as many of the multiple-choice questions as you can in 25 and 10 minutes, respectively.

How Multiple-Choice Questions Are Scored

If you get a multiple-choice question right, you earn 1 point. If you get a multiple-choice question wrong, you lose 1/4 of a point. If you omit a multiple-choice question, you neither gain nor lose any points.

Your raw score for the multiple-choice questions is converted into a scaled score ranging from 200–800. This scaled score will account for two thirds of your total Writing score.

 **AVAILABLE ON CD-ROM**

Find even more review with Writing Practice Test 1 and Writing Practice Test 2 on your CD-ROM.

Identifying Sentence Errors Questions

Directions: The following sentences test your ability to recognize grammar and usage errors. Each sentence contains either a single error or no error at all. No sentence contains more than one error. The error, if there is one, is underlined and lettered. If the sentence contains an error, select the one underlined part that must be changed to make the sentence correct. If the sentence is correct, select choice E. In choosing answers, follow the requirements of standard written English.

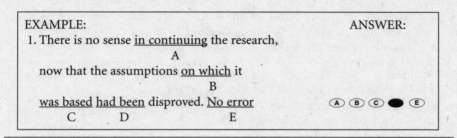

EXAMPLE:

1. There is no sense <u>in continuing</u> the research,
                          A
   now that the assumptions <u>on which</u> it
                                    B
   <u>was based</u> <u>had been</u> disproved. <u>No error</u>
       C   D   E

ANSWER:

Ⓐ Ⓑ Ⓒ ● Ⓔ

1. D

Temporarily ignoring the clause *on which it was based*, the phrase *now that* strongly suggests that the disproving has happened relatively recently. The verb should be *have been*—the present perfect, used to represent a present state as the outcome of recent past events or to express actions occurring in the past and continuing in the present.

Improving Sentences Questions

Directions: The following sentences test correctness and effectiveness of expression. Part of each sentence or the entire sentence is underlined; beneath each sentence are five ways of phrasing the underlined material. Choice A repeats the original phrasing; the other four choices are different. If you think the original phrasing produces a better sentence than any of the alternatives, select choice A; if not, select one of the other choices.

In making your selection, follow the requirements of standard written English; that is, pay attention to grammar, choice of words, sentence construction, and punctuation. Your selection should result in the most effective sentence—clear and precise, without awkwardness or ambiguity.

EXAMPLE: ANSWER:

2. The choreographer Katherine Dunham <u>having trained as an anthropologist, she studied</u> dance in Jamaica, Haiti, and Senegal and developed a distinctive dance method.

(A) having trained as an anthropologist, she studied   Ⓐ Ⓑ Ⓒ ● Ⓔ

(B) was a trained anthropologist, having studied

(C) was a trained anthropologist and a student of

(D) was a trained anthropologist who studied

(E) training as an anthropologist, she studied

---

2. D

The original sentence turns the whole first part of the sentence into an elliptical clause. It's awkward, and the chronology becomes muddled. (B), (C), and (E) all start the same but then diverge after *anthropologist*. (B) implies that Dunham's development of a *distinctive dance method* was part of her training as an anthropologist, but that's not very likely. (C) links so many ideas with *and* that it's hard to follow the direction of the sentence. (E) muddies the chronology and other links among various parts of the sentence.

Improving Paragraphs Questions

Directions: The following passage is an early draft of an essay. Some parts of the passage need to be rewritten.

Read the passage and select the best answer for each question that follows. Some questions are about particular sentences or parts of sentences and ask you to improve sentence structure or word choice. Other questions ask you to consider organization and development. In choosing answers, follow the conventions of standard written English.

Questions 3–5 are based on the following essay.

(1) Our urban public schools need to be smaller. (2) In an environment where streets are crowded and sometimes unsafe, it's necessary that schools offer an intimate sense of community so that students can learn in a nurturing atmosphere.

(3) Some people argue that creating smaller schools will be expensive. (4) We don't have to spend lots of money to achieve this vision. (5) A school building that already exists can be partitioned into two or three smaller schools. (6) And depleting funds by buying state-of-the-art equipment won't be necessary. (7) School boards can find other ways to get supplies. (8) A private business or bank can donate anything from money to computers. (9) And such donations would be beneficial for both parties involved. (10) The bank or business would gain valuable publicity by investing in the community, and the schools would get the products they need. (11) Parents can play a more active role in the school system, and then chaperone for school trips or volunteer to teach.

(12) We need to change the way our schools are built because students need a sense of community in our large cities. (13) Such a reformation might be difficult, but if we work together and we would have invested our time and energy, we can improve the schools for good.

3. In context, which of the following is the best way to revise the underlined wording in order to combine sentences 3 and 4?

    Some people argue that creating smaller schools <u>will be expensive. We don't have to spend</u> lots of money to achieve this vision.

    (A) is expensive, and we don't have to spend

    (B) will be expensive, so we don't have to spend

    (C) will be expensive, but we don't have to spend

    (D) are expensive, but we don't have to spend

    (E) are expensive, yet we will not be spending

4. In terms of context, which version of the underlined section of sentence 11 is the clearest?

    Parents can play a more active role <u>in the school system, and then chaperone for school trips or volunteer to teach.</u>

    (A) by chaperoning in the school system for school trips and volunteering to teach

    (B) in the school system, as a chaperone for school trips or volunteer to teach

    (C) in the school system, then chaperoning for school trips and volunteering to teach

    (D) in the school system by chaperoning for school trips or volunteering to teach

    (E) as chaperones for school trips or volunteers to teach in the school system

5. Which of the versions of the underlined section of sentence 13 (reproduced below) is best?

    Such a reformation might be difficult, <u>but if we work together and we would have invested</u> our time and energy, we can improve the schools for good.

    (A) (As it is now)

    (B) and if we work together and we invest

    (C) but if we work together and invest

    (D) furthermore, if we work together, also investing

    (E) although if we are working together and will be investing

3. C

The first sentence includes the word *expensive,* and the second sentence states *we don't have to spend lots of money.* Clearly, there is a contrast established between the two sentences. Choices (C) and (D) include the correct transition of contrast, but. However, only choice (C) keeps the verb phase in the correct tense.

4. D

As it is written, this sentence is unnecessarily wordy. The second part of the sentence should clarify how parents can play a more active role. Choice (D), *in the school system by chaperoning for school trips or volunteering to teach* is clear and eliminated wordiness and unnecessary punctuation.

5. C

As it is written, this sentence contains an error in verb tense, and it is unnecessarily wordy. The correct answer should include a verb in the same tense as the rest of the sentence and eliminate the wordiness of the original. Although choice (B) might look like the correct answer, the context of the sentence establishes a contrast from the first part of the sentence *might be difficult* to the second part of the sentence. Only choice (C), with the transition *but,* achieves this meaning and clarity.

IF YOU LEARNED ONLY THREE THINGS IN THIS CHAPTER . . . .

1. The Writing component is 60 minutes long and includes three tested sections.
2. If you write your essay on a different topic than what is given, you will get a zero.
3. The essay is worth 1/3 of your total Writing score.

ANSWERS TO THE QUESTIONS ON PAGE 21

What Question Types Make Up the Writing Section?

- The Essay
- Identifying Sentence Errors
- Improving Sentences
- Improving Paragraphs

What Should I Know About the Essay?

- You will be asked to write a persuasive essay on a general topic given in the form of a quote and accompanying topic prompt.
- Two graders score the Essay, each giving a score of 1—6.

What Should I Know About Multiple-Choice Questions?

- The multiple-choice questions test your grammar and vocabulary skills.
- You lost 1/4 point for each question you answer incorrectly.

Chapter Four: **The Essay**

- What Elements Equal a High-Scoring Essay?
- What Skills Will Help Me to Include Those Elements Successfully?
- How Can I Acquire Those Skills?

There are three important elements to master to succeed on the essay.

Content

You will be given a quote, or a pair of quotes, and a prompt that is related to the content of the quote. It is the prompt that will guide your essay topic; the quote is there just to get your creative juices flowing. The graders will be looking for whether your subject matter is relevant to the prompt, whether your stance is insightful, and whether your essay is persuasive. It is very important that you take a firm stance in your essay and stick to it.

Furthermore, if you remember nothing else from this review, remember that your essay needs to be *persuasive*. You are trying to convince your reader to see something from your point of view, and the bulk of your essay should be used to explain *why* you have taken your chosen stance. Also, if the topic allows, it's a good idea to include references to current events, history, and literature in your essay. You don't have to do this to get a high score, but it couldn't hurt either.

Why? These essays are graded by high school teachers and college professors. They want to know if the things they have taught you are sinking in. They'll be impressed by an essay that goes beyond your personal experience to make interesting and meaningful connections.

Please also note that grammar and punctuation are a part of a successful essay and will be looked at by the graders, but errors in these areas will not be the most important factors influencing your grade. Naturally, you want as few errors as possible, but you can still achieve a high score with some mistakes, so don't stress yourself out worrying about grammar and punctuation if they are not your strongest skills.

Length

It's true that the content and quality of your essay are two important aspects of achieving a high score, but there is also a certain expectation from the essay graders concerning the length of a well-written essay. Specifically, your essay should range between 300–400 words if you want to receive a 5 or 6. If your essay is too short, no matter how well written, it could mean the difference between a low 3 or 4 and a 5 or 6, which would have a considerable impact on your overall Writing score. That is not to say that a wordy essay will grab the top score either or that you should spend time counting each word. You will have to use your judgement as to which parts of your essay actually help and which parts are there to fill space. Just keep in mind that your essay should at least be *long enough* to put you in the running for a good score.

Another aspect of length is the space in which you will write your essay. You will only receive two pages with 46 lines, and you must use a pencil.

When you begin to write your essay, try to remember the following:

- a high-scoring essay will be approximately 300–400 well-written words
- small, yet legible, handwriting will conserve space

Neatness

Your essay must be readable. If you edit what you've written, do it neatly. If you add a word, change a phrase, or cross out a sentence, do it carefully. It may sound silly, but neatness matters—a lot.

Why? The graders have tons of essays to read and grade in a short amount of time. That means they don't have much time to spend reading your essay (about a minute, on average), and they aren't going to read an essay three or four times in order to decipher illegible hand writing. So if the handwriting in your essay is messy and hard to follow, graders may conclude that the content itself is, too. A good essay may not get the score it deserves because it is shabbily presented.

You're not expected to produce a perfect piece of writing. The graders know that you only have 25 minutes to think about, write, and proofread your work. What they expect is an organized and readable piece of writing that makes an argument supported by real examples. The rest of this chapter will show you how to accomplish this worthy task.

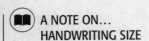 **A NOTE ON… HANDWRITING SIZE**

How large or small you write will affect the length of your essay. You get two pages on which to write—no more. Just filling up the lines with large letters and not focusing on writing a well-developed argument will not earn you more points. Practice using smaller handwriting before the test so you don't run out of space and waste time rewriting on test day.

HOW TO WRITE A HIGH-SCORING SAT ESSAY

The directions for the essay are as follows:

The essay gives you an opportunity to show how effectively you can develop and express ideas. You should, therefore, take care to develop your point of view, present your ideas logically and clearly, and use language precisely.

Your essay must be written in your Answer Grid Booklet—you will receive no other paper on which to write. You will have enough space if you write on every line, avoid wide margins, and keep your handwriting to a reasonable size. Remember that people who are not familiar with your handwriting will read what you write. Try to write or print so that what you are writing is legible to those readers.

You have twenty-five minutes to write an essay on the topic assigned below. DO NOT WRITE ON ANOTHER TOPIC. AN OFF-TOPIC ESSAY WILL RECEIVE A SCORE OF ZERO.

Think carefully about the issue presented in the following excerpt and the assignment below.

> "When I played pro football, I never set out to hurt anybody deliberately … unless it was, you know, important, like a league game or something."
>
> —Dick Butkus
>
> "Pro basketball has turned into Wrestlemania, which is why I like college basketball and high school basketball. Actually, it's why I like baseball."
>
> —Frank Layden

Assignment: Have professional sports influenced the values of American society? Plan and write an essay in which you develop your point of view on this issue. Support your position with reasoning and examples taken from your reading, studies, experience, or observations.

DO NOT WRITE YOUR ESSAY IN YOUR TEST BOOK.
You will receive credit only for what you write in your Answer Grid Booklet.

◎ **KAPLAN'S TARGET STRATEGY FOR ESSAY WRITING**

We have developed a system that we think will make writing the essay that much easier—Kaplan's 4Ps Strategy.

Prompt—know it and understand it

Plan—collect your ideas

Produce—write your essay

Proofread—read for consistency and errors

Here is a minute-by-minute run down of Kaplan's 4Ps Strategy:

Minutes 1–2: Prompt—Know It and Understand It

This step takes two minutes. That leaves you 23 minutes to plan, produce, and proofread your essay. We suggest that you wait to write anything down during these two minutes and just brainstorm. There's plenty of time for writing later. But if it helps you to jot notes down while you think, then go for it.

Let's say that you get the following quote:

> "A man walking down a crowded street noticed a dog lying by the side of the road that looked like it might be injured; but since everyone else just passed by, the man was satisfied to assume that the dog was fine. The next day he learned that the dog had been hit by a car and lay injured for two hours before a concerned man stopped and took it to the vet. The animal recovered, but the man never forgave himself for leaving it for someone else to help."
>
> —Narawhal Bherundi, *Autobiography*

Assignment: What is your view on individual responsibility in a situation in which many people could have reacted?

Then the assignment asks you to take a specific example from your personal experience, from current events, or from history, literature, or any other discipline and develop it to support your persuasive argument, using the quote as a guidepost.

The most important aspect of this step is to fully understand what you need to write about and how you will develop your essay based on that.

Minutes 3–7: Plan—Collect Your Ideas

Pick a Stance

In this essay, you must decide what your stance will be concerning individual responsibility. For example, if you believe that human beings do not have any obligation to help others, then you will want to build your argument around a particular story or experience explaining just that. Or you might believe that everyone is responsible for the welfare of others, even strangers, and thus, you would write to persuade the reader in that respect. What's important is that you take a position and state how you feel. It is not important what other people might think, just what you think, so avoid statements such as "some people feel …" or "a lot of people think…." Get the picture?

Choose Your Examples

Once you have picked your stance, you must choose examples that back up your argument. Think up two to three specific examples that you can write about intelligently and passionately. You could use an example from history, such as Mother Teresa and her life's work of helping others. You could use the scenario of a bystander witnessing a mugging. You could use an example from your life, like how you were stranded on the side of a road, and no one would stop to see if you needed help.

Use Specific Evidence

You've got to cite evidence to support your examples. When you are thinking of your examples, also think about one piece of evidence for each of them. Remember, arguing your point of view without having a good reason is not convincing and won't get you your highest essay score. For instance, you could site the many visits Mother Teresa made to impoverished countries as evidence for the before-mentioned example.

After you have your argument, your examples, and your evidence in your head, it's time to organize your paragraphs. Use the scratch paper that is provided for you. Here is one way that your essay paragraphs could be organized:

First Paragraph

Clearly state your argument, and briefly mention the evidence that you're going to cite in support of that argument.

Middle Paragraphs (2–3 paragraphs)

Explore and explain your evidence in detail. These paragraphs explain how the evidence supports the argument.

Last Paragraph

Briefly summarize your argument.

 BE SMART!

Your essay must be written with an attempt to persuade. To build your argument, choose a distinct side to write about.

Let's try it out. We'll go with humans having an obligation to help others.

> **"A man walking down a crowded street noticed a dog lying by the side of the road that looked like it might be injured; but since everyone else just passed by, the man was satisfied to assume that the dog was fine. The next day he learned that the dog had been hit by a car and lay injured for two hours before a concerned man stopped and took it to the vet. The animal recovered, but the man never forgave himself for leaving it for someone else to help."**

—Narawhal Bherundi, *Autobiography*

Assignment: What is your view on individual responsibility in a situation in which many people could have reacted?

P1. Humans should take initiative to help/individual can have an effect.

P2. Shirking responsibility/sister stuck on side of road/no one stopped/had to make a dangerous walk.

P3. Personal experience/girl lost/walked her to class/made a new friend.

P4. Everyone has a responsibility to help, even if others don't.

SMARTPOINTS

When you have a good Plan, writing the essay is just a matter of turning your notes into full, descriptive sentences.

Minutes 8–22: Produce: Write Your Essay

The writing step of your essay should take about 15 minutes. That's plenty of time to write three to five solid paragraphs if you work from a prepared outline.

To write your strongest essay, follow your outline. You spent five minutes learning the prompt and planning your essay, so stick to it! Don't panic and write from the opposing point-of-view. However, if you come up with the perfect example halfway through your essay, replace it in your outline, see how it works, then continue. But *try try try* not to erase and rewrite any big chunks of text. Trust yourself.

You also need to write clearly, write concisely, write complete sentences, and use proper grammar. But you only have 15 minutes. So write fast. Here is a quickly written essay (a draft version, you might say) about responsibility:

An individual can have a major effect on another individual or situation. In the example above, an individual save a dog's life. A group of people ignored the situation but an individual man actually did something. He stepped out of the mob mentality. Everyone else conformed to each other and walked by. This man stopped and saved the dog.

However, the primary man in the example did not do so. He conformed and walked by. He shirked his responsibility. This is like that one time my sister needed help and didn't get it. On her way home from college, she had car trouble and was stranded on the side of the road at night. Many cars passed by but no one stopped to see if they could give her a hand. After waiting for forever, she ended up having to walk to the nearest gas station two miles away, which is not safe for a young girl to do by herself. Here, no individual took responsibility to help her, and this refusal of responsibility could have led to more severe consequences.

On a lighter but related note, I had personal experience with individual responsibility. At the beginning of last year, I was walking to first period science class when I noticed a confused, nervous girl standing in the hallway. She looked like she was about to cry as everyone rushed past her. She was obviously lost, but no one who knew the way took responsibility to help her. I felt badly so approached her and asked if I could help. It turned out that she had just moved from another part of the country and knew no one at my high school. She couldn't find her science class, which turned out to be my science class, and was too shy to ask for help. I walked with her to science class, made a new friend, and took the responsibility to help someone.

At the end of the day, everyone has the responsibility not to conform in a situation in which many people can react. Each person should be the individual who takes action and helps. No one should assume that someone else will take responsibility, because maybe no one will.

Minutes 23–25: Proofread: Read for Consistency and Errors

This step takes three minutes. It involves proofreading and fixing your essay. Hopefully, all you'll need to do is fix minor grammatical or spelling errors, change a few words here and there, and, maybe, add a sentence or two for clarity's sake.

If you spend the bulk of the 25 minutes thinking about, planning, and writing the essay, the repair step should entail nothing more than putting the finishing touches on an already strong essay.

Here is our fixed up essay:

An individual can have a major effect on another individual or situation. In the example above, an individual <u>saved</u> a dog's life. A group of people ignored the <u>situation, but</u> an individual man actually did something. He stepped out of the mob mentality. Everyone else conformed to each other and walked by. This man stopped and saved the dog.

However, <u>the man</u> in the example did not do so. He conformed and walked by. He shirked his responsibility. <u>This relates to a situation that my sister experienced.</u> On her way home from college, she had car trouble and was stranded on the side of the road at night. Many cars passed <u>by, but</u> no one stopped to see if they could give her a hand. After waiting for <u>over an hour,</u> she ended up having to walk to the nearest gas station two miles away, which is not safe for a young girl to do by herself. Here, no individual took responsibility to help her, and this refusal of responsibility could have led to more severe consequences.

On a lighter but related note, I <u>had a personal</u> experience with individual responsibility. At the beginning of last year, I was walking to first period science class when I noticed a confused, nervous girl standing in the hallway. She looked like she was about to cry as everyone rushed past her. She was obviously lost, but no one who knew the way took responsibility to help her. I <u>felt badly for her, so I approached</u> her and asked if I could help. It turned out that she had just moved from another part of the country and knew no one at my high school. She couldn't find her science class, which turned out to be my science class, and was too shy to ask for help. I walked with her to science class, made a new friend, and took the responsibility to help someone.

At the end of the day, everyone has the responsibility not to conform in a situation in which many people can react. Each person should be the individual who takes action and helps. No one should assume that someone else will take responsibility, because maybe no one will.

Okay, now it's your turn. Let's go through each of the steps.

Practice with Prompts

We're going to give you three sample statements. Look at your watch. Spend exactly two minutes understanding the prompt and thinking about how you are going to write a persuasive essay for each of them. Don't write! Think.

GO ONLINE

Find more practice writing essays in the online companion. More prompts and sample essays are provided in the syllabus to further your preparation.

Essay Prompt One: 2 minutes

Is an individual's financial status the most important factor governing their quality of life?

Essay Prompt Two: 2 minutes

Do you have to be brave to do something courageous?

Essay Prompt Three: 2 minutes

Does the media have too much influence on the young adult population?

Planning Practice

Read the essay directions below and try to outline an essay based on the prompt. In your outline, you will want to try to include the stance you're taking, the evidence that supports your stance, and how this information will be arranged in 3–5 paragraphs.

The essay gives you an opportunity to show how effectively you can develop and express ideas. You should, therefore, take care to develop your point of view, present your ideas logically and clearly, and use language precisely.

Your essay must be written in your Answer Grid Booklet—you will receive no other paper on which to write. You will have enough space if you write on every line, avoid wide margins, and keep your handwriting to a reasonable size. Remember that people who are not familiar with your handwriting will read what you write. Try to write or print so that what you are writing is legible to those readers.

You have twenty-five minutes to write an essay on the topic assigned below. DO NOT WRITE ON ANOTHER TOPIC. AN OFF-TOPIC ESSAY WILL RECEIVE A SCORE OF ZERO.

Think carefully about the issue presented in the following excerpt and the assignment below.

> "A man walking down a crowded street noticed a dog lying by the side of the road that looked like it might be injured; but since everyone else just passed by, the man was satisfied to assume that the dog was fine. The next day he learned that the dog had been hit by a car and lay injured for two hours before a concerned man stopped and took it to the vet. The animal recovered, but the man never forgave himself for leaving it for someone else to help."
>
> —Narawhal Bherundi, Autobiography

Assignment: What is your view on individual responsibility in a situation in which many people could have reacted? Plan and write an essay in which you develop your point of view on this issue. Support your position with reasoning and examples taken from your reading, studies, experience, or observations.

DO NOT WRITE YOUR ESSAY IN YOUR TEST BOOK.
You will receive credit only for what you write in your Answer Grid Booklet.

Use this page to plan your paragraphs. Remember that on the SAT, you will plan your essay by using space on the test booklet, and your essay MUST be written on the lined pages of your answer sheet.

_____

_____

_____

_____

_____

_____

_____

_____

_____

_____

_____

_____

_____

_____

_____

_____

_____

_____

_____

_____

The way the paragraphs are organized on page 36 is just one method. If you feel like you need more detail and structure, you could make a full-length outline. A sample outline appears below. We've used the same quote and prompt to demonstrate that there is more than one right answer. At the end of this chapter, you'll have more opportunities to improve your outlining.

I. Introduction

    A. General argument: A person should take responsibility, as a member of a community, in a group situation to help those in need.

    B. Examples:

        1. Given example of man and injured dog.

        2. My mom's experience in the grocery store.

II. Body

    A. Given example of man and injured dog.

        1. Man assumes that others would help if it was really needed.

        2. Ignores his instinct to help and conforms to others' actions.

        3. Feels guilty for not acting.

    B. My mom's experience in the grocery store.

        1. People assumed she was crazy and weird.

        2. Others didn't help because no one else was.

        3. Not helping could have been matter of life or death.

III. Conclusion

    A. It's easy to just walk by and do what everyone else does.

    B. As a part of a community, everyone is responsible for the well-being of others.

 BE SMART!

A good outline will help you write a better essay and save time. Always take the time to prepare a detailed outline.

Producing Practice

This outline is more in-depth than the previous outline and may lend to a more complete and organized essay. It is also a little different than the first way we went about answering this question. This proves our point—there is not *one way* to write these essays. You have to use *your* knowledge and *your* experiences.

Now that you're done with your outline, you're ready to start writing. Start your practice with the essay topic that you just outlined. Write your essay on the next two pages.

Write your essay here.

_____

_____

_____

_____

_____

_____

_____

_____

_____

_____

_____

_____

_____

_____

_____

_____

_____

_____

_____

_____

Proofreading Practice

When you are done, take two minutes to proofread for spelling, grammar, and any other glaring errors. Some things to look for are comma splices, run-on sentences, misspelled or skipped words, ideas that are not sufficiently developed, vague references to the elements in the essay, e.g., *this* is a good example, *that* is important because, etc., and making sure you have taken a clear stance and have explained that stance persuasively.

HOW YOUR ESSAY IS GRADED

To help you get a sense of how your essay might be graded, we have included a sample high-scoring essay. Compare your essay to the one below using the following criteria, and you'll get a sense of how well you've done.

- My essay has a clear stance on the given issue.
- I provided specific support using examples and evidence.
- I have logical organization.
- I have used appropriate transitions between ideas.
- I have used variety in my sentence structure and vocabulary.
- My sentences are clear and have an even tone.

Now lets look at the Grade 6 essay.

Grade 6 Essay (Almost Perfect)

A person should take responsibility in a group situation. A group is made up of individuals, after all. People hide too much behind others' actions and don't think for themselves. Rather than hiding, they should be proactive.

The first man in the example had a responsibility, as did everyone on the sidewalk, to help the dog. He saw the dog, the potential bad situation, and instead of following his instinct to check out the problem, he decided to walk by because no one else was helping. He consciously decides to walk by, assuming that if the dog were really that hurt, someone else would take care of it. It doesn't occur to him that everyone is thinking the same thing and doing nothing. He feels badly because he knows he was persuaded by the actions of others and ignored his responsibility toward another living creature.

Something similar happened to my mother in a grocery store. There was a puddle of something in one of the aisles, and she slipped, fell to the ground, and hit her head. Unfortunately, no one saw what happened, so when people came around the corner and saw her lying on the floor, they just kept going past thinking that she was crazy or weird. Others came down the aisle, too, but did nothing because they saw that the people in front of them did nothing. She remained dizzy and injured on the floor until her husband came down the aisle and found her on the ground. It is sad that no one took the responsibility to help an injured woman. Someone should have called for help or at least asked her if she was OK, especially because it could have been a matter of life or death.

It's very easy to just walk by, to do what everyone else in the group does. Everyone could just look the other way and not listen to the pleas for help. But that is not how a community is run, and as humans who share this planet, we are entitled to act as a community, and that entails having a responsibility to help.

PRACTICE ESSAY

This is your chance to put the 4 Ps to work. Give yourself 25 minutes to go through this target strategy:

Prompt—know it and understand it

Plan—collect your ideas

Produce—write your essay

Proofread—read for consistency and errors

After you finish, read the three sample essays—a strong essay, a mediocre essay, and a weak essay—and the sample grader comments. Use these essays and comments to judge the quality of your own essays.

The essay gives you an opportunity to show how effectively you can develop and express ideas. You should, therefore, take care to develop your point of view, present your ideas logically and clearly, and use language precisely.

Your essay must be written in your Answer Grid Booklet—you will receive no other paper on which to write. You will have enough space if you write on every line, avoid wide margins, and keep your handwriting to a reasonable size. Remember that people who are not familiar with your handwriting will read what you write. Try to write or print so that what you are writing is legible to those readers.

You have twenty-five minutes to write an essay on the topic assigned below. DO NOT WRITE ON ANOTHER TOPIC. AN OFF-TOPIC ESSAY WILL RECEIVE A SCORE OF ZERO.

Think carefully about the issue presented in the following excerpt and the assignment below.

> "Don't flatter yourself that friendship authorizes you to say disagreeable things to your intimates. The nearer you come into relation with a person, the more necessary do tact and courtesy become. Except in cases of necessity, which are rare, leave your friend to learn unpleasant things from his enemies; they are ready enough to tell them."
> –Oliver Wendell Holmes,
> *The Autocrat of the Breakfast-Table*
>
> "A good friend can tell you what is the matter with you in a minute. He may not seem such a good friend after telling."
> –Arthur Brisbane, *The Book of Today*

Assignment: Should friends be honest with each other, even if a truthful comment could be hurtful? Plan and write an essay in which you develop your point of view on this issue. Support your position with reasoning and examples taken from your reading, studies, experience, or observations.

DO NOT WRITE YOUR ESSAY IN YOUR TEST BOOK.
You will receive credit only for what you write in your Answer Grid Booklet.

Organize your paragraphs here.

_____

_____

_____

_____

_____

_____

_____

_____

_____

_____

_____

_____

_____

_____

_____

_____

_____

_____

_____

_____

_____

Write your essay here.

_____

_____

_____

_____

_____

_____

_____

_____

_____

_____

_____

_____

_____

_____

_____

_____

_____

_____

_____

_____

_____

_____

SAMPLE ESSAYS

Grade 6 Essay

One of the defining qualities of a good friendship is that both friends can be completely honest with each other. This does not mean that the two friends don't consider each others feelings or blurt out comments without thinking, but it does mean that each person can rely on the other to tell the truth, even if the truth can sometimes be awkward or hurtful.

My sister and I have always been close friends, even when we were younger. When my sister was in junior high school and I was in elementary school, she decided to get her hair permed because all of her friends were doing the same thing. Unfortunately, the treatment didn't work well on her hair and she ended up with a big, frizzy clump of curls that stuck out on the sides. Most of her friends didn't have the courage to tell her that it didn't look good. Instead, they just made fun of her behind her back. So it was up to me to tell her the truth. I was a bit scared to confront my older sister, because I knew that she would be upset. But I also knew that she would be more upset if no one dared to be honest with her. A few years earlier, we were in the opposite roles, and she had gently but firmly advised me against a choice that I later realized would have been embarrassing for me when I started school.

Although my sister was hurt when I told her that the perm didn't look good, she was more hurt to learn that some of her other friends had thought the same thing but hadn't said anything to her. She was angry with me at first for making a negative comment, but in the end she was glad I had told her so that she could go back to the hair stylist to fix the problem. Since my sister was very concerned about her appearance and personal style at that time in her life, she appreciated my honesty because it helped her get through a tough situation and our friendship grew stronger as a result of this experience.

In the years since this incident, my sister and I have both continued to be honest and upfront with each other, and we value this aspect of our relationship. After all, friendly honesty is far better than hostile honesty, so being a good friend involves telling the truth, no matter what the circumstances. Honesty truly is an essential component of a good friendship.

(388 words)

Grader's Comments: The author begins this essay with a clear statement based on the prompt, showing that she has clearly understood the topic. The remainder of the essay presents and develops an example to support her opinion. The example provided is relevant to multiple aspects of the prompt—the importance of honesty in friendship as well as the possibility that being honest can be difficult in certain situations.

The essay is well organized, with a clear narrative flow framed by a cohesive introduction and conclusion. The structure of the essay reflects that the author took time to plan before writing and carefully followed her plan as she composed her essay. Although the vocabulary used in the essay is not very sophisticated, the author's ideas are communicated effectively. Finally, there are few grammatical or spelling errors *others* instead of *other's* in the first paragraph; a couple of sentences lacking commas in the second and third paragraphs. This author clearly managed her time effectively so that she could proofread her essay.

Grade 4 Essay

Being honest is part of being a good friend. However, their are times when you shouldn't be completely honest because what you say might hurt your friend's feelings.

For example, imagine that your best friend tells you his parents are getting divorced. He is obviously upset by this even though you know his parents haven't been getting along well because he constantly complained about their fights and even joked about hoping they'd get a divorce so he wouldn't have to listen to them anymore. In this situation, reminding your friend of his earlier comments or pointing out that his parents will be happier apart isn't the right thing to do because at a time like this you're friend doesn't need you to tell him the harsh truth, he needs you to by sympathetic and supportive. It's pretty likely that he'll hear all about the negative things from other people or even from his parents, so your job as his best friend is to try not to say or do anything unpleasant.

Another example could be if you're friend has bought something that she's really excited about. You might not agree that she's made a good choice or you might not like what she bought, but you don't need to spoil her enthusiasm by making a negative comment. Again, this is a time when you should keep quiet about your own opinion so that your friend can be happy.

There are certain situations when it's okay not to tell the complete truth to your friends. You should never lie to your friends, but an important part of being a good friend is knowing when to be totally honest and when to keep silent because a truthful comment could do more harm than good.

(292 words)

Grader's Comments: The author introduces his essay with a clear statement of his opinion, showing that he has understood the prompt. His two examples provide decent support for the topic, but the second example is vague and not well developed. The author would have a stronger essay if he expanded upon the prompt and provided additional details for the first example rather than trying to include a weak second example. Having a clear plan could help to accomplish this change in structure.

The essay is fairly well organized, with several keywords (*However, For example, Another example, Again*) that add structure to the author's argument. The weakest parts of this essay are some simplistic language and awkward sentences: in the second paragraph, the second sentence is long and wordy, and the third sentence is a run-on sentence and is very difficult to follow, so the author's meaning almost gets obscured by the effort it takes to decipher his thoughts. There are also a few usage/spelling errors: *their* instead of *they're* in the first paragraph; *you're* instead of *your* in the second and third paragraphs. The author needs to be more deliberate when writing the essay and needs to proofread to catch these spelling errors and prevent run-on sentences or awkward sentence structure.

Grade 2 Essay

No matter what, friends should tell each other the truth. That's the whole point of having friends, so you have some people around you that you can trust and talk to and that you know will tell you everything.

Friends can tell you negative things in a kind way so you can here the truth even if its not so good. Enemies tell you the same negative things in a mean way because their trying to hurt you. But friends can accomplish this in a nicer way.

Its important to know and learn the truth even if its about yourself or its something you don't want to face. You need honest friends to tell you the truth, because they do it out of love not hate like enemies.

(128 words)

Grader's Comments: This author starts strongly with a clear statement of her opinion, which is directly related to the topic of the prompt. However, the author continues with a series of generalizations, none of which are specific examples to support her opinion. She needs to spend more time planning her essay to make sure that she's got at least one strong example to include to support her argument.

This essay does not follow an organized structure, and it lacks good transitions and key-words. To improve this part of her writing, the author should make an outline during her planning stage and should focus on using several keywords while she writes, which will give her essay a stronger and clearer structure.

The author's language is simplistic and repetitive. The essay contains several grammatical and spelling errors: *that* twice instead of *whom/who* when referring to *people* in the first paragraph; *here* and *their* are misused for *hear* and *they're* in the second paragraph; *its* is misused numerous times for *it's* in the second and third paragraphs. The author should study the SAT grammar materials to improve this aspect of her writing and should also be sure to proofread to avoid careless errors.

IF YOU LEARNED ONLY FOUR THINGS IN THIS CHAPTER . . . .

1. Good handwriting can make the difference between a 6 and a 3.
2. A good essay should be between 300 and 400 words.
3. You only get 48 lines on which to write your essay. Keep your handwriting small.
4. Taking time to plan your essay before writing will make the process easier and faster.

ANSWERS TO THE QUESTIONS ON PAGE 31

What Elements Equal a High-Scoring Essay?

- Content (address the topic, and write to persuade)
- Length (should include at least three paragraphs: introduction, supportive elements, and conclusion)
- Neatness (if they can't read it, you'll get a low score)

What Skills Will Help Me to Include Those Elements Successfully?

- **Prompt**—know it and understand it
- **Plan**—collect your ideas
- **Produce**—write your essay
- **Proofread**—read for consistency and errors

How Can I Acquire Those Skills?

- Practice, practice, practice!

Chapter Five: **The Multiple-Choice Questions**

- **What Are the Three Types of Multiple-Choice Questions?**

- **What Rules Should I Know to Answer These Questions?**

- **What Strategies Will Help Me Be Successful Answering These Questions?**

The Writing section's multiple-choice questions are like a mini-SAT all to themselves. The Writing section uses three different types of multiple-choice questions to test three different writing skills, but each question type works basically the same way: You need to determine what mistake (if any) has been made in the sentences or paragraphs in question. For two of the three types, you will also need to determine the best way to correct those mistakes. Throughout this chapter, we'll show you the kinds of writing mistakes the SAT wants you to catch and how you can catch them.

Note: This is a long chapter. It might be helpful to treat it like three short chapters, one for each multiple-choice question type:

- Identifying Sentence Errors
- Improving Sentences
- Improving Paragraphs

Tackle just one question type in a single study session.

IDENTIFYING SENTENCE ERRORS QUESTIONS

The word *usage* means the customary or standard way in which words are used. The Identifying Sentence Errors questions on the SAT cover four main areas of written English:

- Basic grammar
- Sentence structure
- Choice of words (diction)
- Idiomatic expressions

That sounds like a lot of ground to cover, but as you'll see, most Identifying Sentence Errors questions only test a few key grammar and usage concepts. We'll show you the kind of grammar the SAT usually tests and help you become an expert at the SAT's spot-the-mistake questions.

Remember, the Writing section measures your ability to recognize acceptable and unacceptable uses of *written* English. Standard *written* English is a bit more formal than the average person's spoken English, and it is what professors will expect you to use on college papers. That's why it is being tested on the SAT.

THE FORMAT

Get comfortable with the directions; It will save you time on test day.

Directions: The following sentences test your ability to recognize grammar and usage errors. Each sentence contains either a single error or no error at all. No sentence contains more than one error. The error, if there is one, is underlined and lettered. If the sentence contains an error, select the one underlined part that must be changed to make the sentence correct. If the sentence is correct, select choice E. In choosing answers, follow the requirements of standard written English.

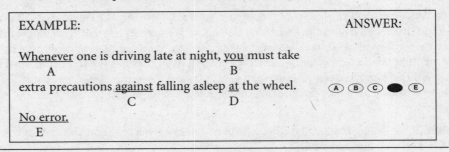

Spot the Mistake

All Identifying Sentence Errors questions are *spot-the-mistake* questions. You're given a sentence with four words or phrases underlined. The underlined parts are labeled (A) through (D). One of the underlined pieces may contain a usage error. Your task is to spot the error and fill in the corresponding oval on your grid. If the sentence is error-free, the correct answer is (E), No error. Also, you should assume that the parts of the sentence not underlined are correct. Here's an example.

<u>Although</u> the number of firms declaring
   A

bankruptcy <u>keep</u> growing, the mayor <u>claims that</u> the
        B   C

city <u>is thriving</u>. <u>No error</u>
    D   E

We'll use Kaplan's Target Strategy for answering Identifying Sentence Errors questions to show you how to find the correct answer to this question.

◎ **KAPLAN'S TARGET STRATEGY FOR IDENTIFYING────**
SENTENCE ERRORS

To tackle Identifying Sentence Errors questions, Kaplan's test experts
have devised a Target Strategy that will guide you in answering these
types of questions. The four steps are as follows:

Step 1. Read the whole sentence, listening for the mistake.

Step 2. If you clearly hear the mistake, choose it and move on.

Step 3. If not, read each underlined choice, and eliminate choices
that contain no errors.

Step 4. Choose from the remaining choices.

──

Try this out on our earlier example. Start by reading it to yourself.

<u>Although</u> the number of firms declaring
   A

bankruptcy <u>keep</u> growing, the mayor <u>claims that</u> the
      B   C

city <u>is thriving</u>. <u>No error</u>
    D   E

Did you hear the mistake? If so, your work is done. Fill in the appropriate oval, and move
on. If you didn't hear the mistake on the first reading, go back, read each underlined
part, and start eliminating underlined parts that are right.

The word *although* seems fine in this context. The word *keep* is a plural verb, but its
subject is *number*, which is singular. That seems to be a mistake. The phrase *claims that*
sounds all right; it has a singular verb for a singular subject, *mayor*. Similarly, *is thriving*
sounds all right, and it too provides a singular verb for the singular subject *city*. Choice
(B) contains the mistake, so (B) is the correct answer.

This is a classic example of subject-verb agreement, which is a common question type
in the Writing section. You'll learn more about the most common errors in the following
pages, which offer a quick reference to the most frequently made and tested grammatical
mistakes. It's much easier to spot errors when you know what to look for.

Please keep in mind that not all the Identifying Sentence Errors questions on the Writing
section contain errors. When you're reading each sentence just to spot mistakes, you
may fall into the trap of spotting mistakes where there are none.

Remember, choice (E), No error, is the correct answer to Identifying Sentence Errors
questions about ONE in FIVE times. If you find that you have chosen (E) only once or
twice, chances are you're spotting mistakes that aren't there.

▶ **GO ONLINE**

Check out your new practice quiz
every month.

BE SMART!

Being familiar with the most common mistakes that test takers make will give you confidence on test day to tackle the Identifying Sentence Errors questions.

COMMON MISTAKES

Although the SAT Writing questions will test your knowledge of grammar and usage, you won't have to recite any rules on the exam. In fact, you don't have to know all the rules *per se*; you just have to be able to recognize when something is *not* correct. So instead of trying to review all of the rules, we'll show you the top sixteen errors you need to watch out for on the SAT. Once you are used to seeing these Identifying Sentence Errors mistakes, you'll have an easier time spotting them on test day.

Common Mistake 1: Subject-Verb Agreement—When Subject Follows Verb

Singular subjects call for singular verbs. Plural subjects call for plural verbs. In certain situations, subject-verb agreement can be tricky because it is not obvious what the subject of the sentence is.

For example, it's tricky when the subject comes after the verb, as it does in a clause beginning with the word *there*. Take a look at the following:

> Despite an intensive campaign to encourage conservation, there is many Americans who have not accepted recycling as a way of life.

This sentence demonstrates one of *the most common* of all subject-verb agreement errors found on the Writing section. It generally occurs once or twice on each test. The subject of the sentence is not *there*. The subject is *Americans*, which is plural. Therefore, the singular verb is incorrect; *is* should be replaced by the plural verb *are*.

Here's another example in which the subject follows the verb.

> High above the Hudson River rises the gleaming skyscrapers of Manhattan.

This sentence is tricky because there is a singular noun, *the Hudson River*, before the verb *rises*. But the later noun *skyscrapers* is actually the subject. Think about it. What's doing the rising? Not the river, the skyscrapers. The subject is plural, and so the verb should be *rise*.

Common Mistake 2: Subject-Verb Agreement—When Subject and Verb Are Separated

The SAT has another way to complicate a subject-verb agreement. They insert some additional information about the subject before the verb appears.

Expect to see at least one question like this on the Writing section.

> The local congressman, a reliable representative of both community and statewide interests, are among the most respected persons in the public sector.

The way to determine whether the verb agrees with the subject is to identify the subject of the sentence. You see the plural *community and statewide interests* right in front of the verb *are*, but that's not the subject. It's part of the modifying phrase that's inserted between the subject *congressman*, which is singular, and the verb, which should also be singular, *is*.

Don't let intervening phrases fool you! In the example above, the commas were a tip-off that the verb was separated from the subject. Another tip-off is a preposition such as *of*:

> The collection of paintings entitled "Clammy Clam Clams" are one of the most widely traveled exhibits in recent years.

Again, you should first find the subject of the sentence. The subject is *collection*. The phrases that follow the subject, e.g., *of paintings* and *entitled "Clammy Clam Clams*," merely modify (or describe) the subject. The true subject is singular, and so the verb should be *is*.

The SAT writers like this type of question because the intervening modifying phrases or clauses can cause you to lose track of the subject. These phrases simply modify the subject they follow, without changing its number. Don't be fooled by the placement of these intervening phrases.

Common Mistake 3: Subject-Verb Agreement—When the Subject Seems Plural

Sometimes the sentence includes what seems to be, but in fact is not, a plural subject. Here's an example.

> Neither ambient techno nor trance were a part of mainstream listening habits in the United States 10 years ago.

This sentence is tough because it has two subjects, but these two singular subjects do not add up to a plural subject. When the subject of a sentence is in the form *neither* _____ *nor* ____ or in the form *either* _____ *or* ____. and the nouns in the blanks are singular, the verb should be singular. In the sentence above, it's as if *ambient techno* and *trance* act as subjects one at a time. Thus, the verb should be the singular *was*. If the nouns in a *neither-nor* or *either-or* construction are plural, then a plural verb is correct.

Here are some other constructions that seem to make plural (compound) subjects but actually don't.

_____	along with	_____
_____	as well as	_____
_____	in addition to	_____

In these constructions, the noun in the first blank is the true subject and what follows is, grammatically speaking, just an intervening modifying phrase. If the first noun is singular, the verb should be singular. Look at this sentence, for example.

> Poor pitching, along with injuries and defensive lapses, are among the problems that plagued last year's championship team.

The phrase *along with injuries and defensive lapses* is a modifying phrase that separates the subject *poor pitching* from the verb *are*. This sentence is tricky because there seem to be three problems that plagued the baseball team. But, in fact, phrases like *along with* or *in addition to* do not work in the same way as the conjunction *and* does. If the above sentence had begun *Poor pitching, injuries, and defensive lapses*, the plural verb *are* would have been correct. However, as written, the sentence has only one subject, *poor pitching*, and its verb should be *is*.

So beware of fake compound subjects. Check for compound subject constructions and intervening phrases.

Common Mistake 4: Confusion of Simple Past and Past Participle

A typical error tested on the Writing section is confusion between the simple past and the past participle forms of a verb. A past participle form may be substituted for the simple past form, as in this sentence.

> Several passersby seen the bank robber leaving the scene of his crime.

The verb form *seen* is the past participle and should be used only with a helping verb, such as *have* or *be*. This sentence requires the simple past form *saw*.

The Writing section will almost always have a Identifying Sentence Errors question in which the simple past is used with a helping verb or in which the past participle is used without a helping verb. Therefore, these are good mistakes to be able to spot.

For regular verbs, the simple past and past participle are identical, ending in *-ed*. But irregular verbs like *see* usually have two different forms for simple past and past participle. The following is a list of irregular verbs that have appeared on the SAT. These are the simple past and past participle forms that are most often confused. Instead of listing them alphabetically, we have grouped them by pattern.

Irregular Verbs

Infinitive	Simple Past	Past Participle
break	broke	broken
speak	spoke	spoken
freeze	froze	frozen
forget	forgot	forgotten
get	got	gotten
ride	rode	ridden
rise	rose	risen
arise	arose	arisen
drive	drove	driven
write	wrote	written
eat	ate	eaten
fall	fell	fallen
give	gave	given
take	took	taken
shake	shook	shaken
see	saw	seen
ring	rang	rung
sing	sang	sung
sink	sank	sunk
shrink	shrank	shrunk
drink	drank	drunk
begin	began	begun
swim	swam	swum
run	ran	run
come	came	come
become	became	become
do	did	done
go	went	gone
blow	blew	blown
grow	grew	grown
know	knew	known
throw	threw	thrown
fly	flew	flown
draw	drew	drawn

Note the patterns. Verb forms that end in *-oke, -oze, -ot, -ode, -ose, -ove, -ote, -ang, -ank, -an, -an, -am, -ame, -ew,* or *-ook* are simple past. Verb forms that end in *-en, -wn, -ung, -unk, -un, -um, -ome,* and *-one* are past participles. Train your ear for irregular verb forms that aren't already second nature to you.

Common Mistake 5: Confusion of Infinitive and Gerund

Some questions test your sense of idiomatic use of English. *Idiomatic use* means combinations of words that sound right or words that sound right in particular contexts.

For example, there is generally at least one Identifying Sentence Errors question in which the infinitive is used where a gerund would be appropriate, or vice versa, as in the following example.

> Team officials heralded Cap Day as an attempt at attracting
> a larger turnout of fans.

This sentence is not idiomatic. There's no grammar rule that explains why it's wrong to say *an attempt at attracting*. But if you have a good sense of idiom, your ear tells you it should be *an attempt to attract*. This sentence confuses the *-ing* gerund form with the *to + verb infinitive* form. Here's another sentence.

> Surveillance cameras are frequently placed in convenience
> stores to prevent customers to shoplift.

After *prevent* you don't use the infinitive but rather the word *from* plus the gerund. The sentence should end *to prevent customers from shoplifting*.

Why? There's no real grammatical reason. That's just the way we say and write it in English. You have to trust yourself on these. Whereas there are some general patterns, there are no hard and fast rules that determine when to use an infinitive or gerund, and there are so many possible combinations that there's no way to list all that could possibly appear on the Writing section. But don't worry. You don't need to see every possible combination in advance. Just remember to prick up your ears whenever an infinitive or gerund is underlined on the test.

Common Mistake 6: Nonidiomatic Preposition After Verb

The Writing section also tests your recognition of prepositions that idiomatically combine with certain verbs. Here's a sentence that uses the wrong preposition.

> City Council members frequently meet until the early
> morning hours in order to work in their stalemates.

 GO ONLINE

You can find 18 common writing rules on your downloadable Study Sheet for study on the go.

It's not always wrong to write *work in*. You might use it to speak about the field one *works in* or the place one *works in*. But this combination does not correspond to the meaning of this sentence. The writer means to say *work through* or *work out*—that is, overcome—the stalemates.

Here's another sentence with the wrong preposition.

> The rapper's new CD was frowned at by many parents because of its violent lyrics.

That's just not the way we say it in English. The preferred verb-preposition combination is *frowned upon*. That's the idiomatic expression. Once again, this is an area where you'll have to trust your ear. Just remember to pay attention and think for a moment when you see an underlined preposition after a verb.

Here are some more verb-preposition idioms.

Commonly Tested Verb-Preposition Combinations

abide by	contribute to	participate in
accuse of	count (up)on	prevent from
agree to	cover with	prohibit from
agree with	decide (up)on	protect against
agree on	depend (up)on	protect from
apologize for	differ about	provide for
apply to	differ from	provide with
apply for	differ over	recover from
approve of	differ with	rely (up)on
argue with	discriminate against	rescue from
argue about	distinguish from	respond to
arrive at	dream of	stare at
believe in	dream about	stop from
blame for	escape from	subscribe to
care about	excel in	substitute for
care for	excuse for	succeed in
charge for	forget about	thank for
charge with	forgive for	vote for
compare to	hide from	wait for
compare with	hope for	wait on
complain about	insist (up)on	work with
consist of	object to	worry about

Common Mistake 7: Wrong Word

The English language contains many pairs of words that sound alike but are spelled differently and have different meanings. Expect to encounter ONE or TWO Identifying Sentence Errors questions that test your ability to distinguish between these problematic word pairs. Here are some examples.

ACCEPT/EXCEPT To *accept* is to take or receive something that is offered. *Dad said he would accept my apology for putting a dent in his new car, but then he grounded me for two weeks.*

To *except* is to leave out or exclude. *The soldier was excepted from combat duty because he had poor field vision.* Except is usually used as a preposition meaning, with the exception of, excluding. *When the receptionist found out that everyone except him had received a raise, he demanded a salary increase as well.*

ADAPT/ADOPT To *adapt* is to change (oneself or something) to become suitable for a particular condition or use. *Fred tried to adapt his Volkswagen for use as a submarine by gluing the windows shut and attaching a periscope to the roof.*

To *adopt* is to make something one's own. *My neighbors decided to adopt a child.*

AFFECT/EFFECT To *affect* (verb) is to have an influence on something. *Al refused to let the rain affect his plans for a picnic, so he sat under an umbrella and ate potato salad. Affect* as a noun is only used as a psychology term meaning an emotion or a desire.

To *effect* is to bring something about or to cause something to happen. *The young activist received an award for effecting a change in her community.* An *effect* (noun) is an influence or a result. *The newspaper article about homeless animals had such an effect on Richard that he brought home three kittens from the shelter.*

AFFLICT/INFLICT To *afflict* is to torment or distress someone or something. It usually appears as a passive verb. *Jeff is afflicted with severe migraine headaches.*

To *inflict* is to impose punishment or suffering on someone or something. *No one dared displease the king, for he was known to inflict severe punishments on those who upset him.*

ALLUSION/ILLUSION An *allusion* is an indirect reference to something, a hint. *I remarked that Sally's boyfriend was unusual looking; this allusion to his prominent tattoos did not please Sally.*

An *illusion* is a false, misleading, or deceptive appearance. *A magician creates the illusion that something has disappeared by hiding it faster than the eye can follow it.*

EMIGRATE/IMMIGRATE To *emigrate* is to leave one country for another country and is usually used with the preposition *from. Many people emigrated from Europe in search of better living conditions.*

To *immigrate* is to enter a country to take up permanent residence there and is usually used with the preposition *to*. *They immigrated to North America because land was plentiful.*

EMINENT/IMMINENT Someone who is *eminent* is prominent or outstanding. *The eminent archeologist Dr. Wong has identified the artifact as prehistoric in origin.*

Something that is *imminent* is likely to happen soon or is impending. *After being warned that the hurricane's arrival was imminent, beachfront residents left their homes immediately.*

LAY/LIE To *lay* is to place or put something, and this verb usually does have a *something*, a direct object, following it. One form, *laid*, serves as the simple past and the past participle of *lay*. *Before she begins her pictures, Emily lays all of her pencils, brushes, and paints on her worktable to avoid interruptions while she draws and paints*, and *He can never remember where he laid his keys.*

To *lie* is to recline, to be in a lying position, or to be at rest. This verb never takes a direct object: you do not *lie* anything down. The simple past form of *lie* is *lay*; the past participle is *lain*. Notice that the past form of *lie* is identical with the present form of *lay*. This coincidence complicates the task of distinguishing the related meaning of *lay* and *lie*. *Having laid the picnic cloth under the sycamore, they lay in the shady grass all afternoon.*

LEAVE/LET To *leave* is to depart, to allow something to remain behind after departing, or to allow something to remain as it is. The irregular verb form *left* serves as both the simple past and the past participle. *I boarded my plane and it left, leaving my baggage behind in Chicago.* When *leave* is used in the third sense—to allow something to remain as it is—and followed by *alone*, this verb does overlap with *let*. *If parents leave (or let) a baby with a new toy alone, she will understand it as quickly as if they demonstrated how the toy works.*

To *let* is to allow or to rent out. These are the verb's core meanings, but it also combines with several different prepositions to produce various specific senses. *Let* is irregular. One form (*let*) serves as present, past, and past participle. *The French border police would not let the Dutch tourist pass without a passport.*

RAISE/RISE To *raise* is to lift up or to cause to rise or grow, and it usually has a direct object: You raise dumbbells, roof beams, tomato plants, and children. *Raise* is a completely regular verb. *The trade tariff on imported leather goods raised the prices of Italian shoes.*

To *rise* is to get up, to go up, and to be built up. This verb never takes a direct object: You do not rise something; rather, something rises. The past and past participle forms are irregular; *rose* is the simple past, *risen* the past participle. *Long-distance commuters must rise early, often before the sun has risen.*

SET/SIT The difference between *set* and *sit* is very similar to the difference between *lay* and *lie* and the difference between *raise* and *rise*. To *set* is to put or place something, to settle it, or to arrange it. But *set* takes on other specific meanings when it combines with several different prepositions. *Set* is an irregular verb in that one form (*set*) serves as present, past, and past participle. *Set* usually takes a direct object: You set a ladder against the fence, a value on family heirlooms, or a date for the family reunion. *The professor set the students' chairs in a semicircle to promote open discussion.*

To *sit* is to take a seat or to be in a seated position, to rest somewhere, or to occupy a place. This verb does not usually take a direct object, although you can say, *The usher sat us in the center seats of the third row from the stage*. The irregular form *sat* serves as past and past participle. Usually, no direct object follows this verb. *The beach house sits on a hill at some distance from the shoreline.*

Common Mistake 8: Wrong Tense

Here's a sentence with a verb in the wrong tense.

> Over the last half-century, the building of passenger airliners had grown into a multibillion-dollar industry.

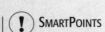

SMARTPOINTS

Knowing your verb tenses means you can eliminate at least one wrong answer choice in approximately 90% of all Writing questions.

In a one-verb sentence like this one, time-descriptive phrases help you determine what the time frame of a sentence is. The action being described is a process that began during the last half-century and that is continuing to the present day. Any action starting in the past and continuing today is expressed by a verb in the present perfect tense. The present perfect form of this verb is *has grown*. Using the verb *had* makes it seem that passenger airliners aren't being made anymore. That can't be! The key is to pay attention to the time cues in the sentence. With practice, you'll be able to spot mistakes like this with confidence.

Another type of sentence might have two verbs and an unnecessary or confusing shift in tense. Here's an example.

> Many superb tennis players turn professional at an alarmingly early age, but because of their lack of physical stamina, suffered early in their careers.

When there are two verbs in a sentence, first study the time relation between the verbs, and determine whether it is logical as presented. In this sentence, the verb in the first clause of this sentence is *turn*, a present tense verb. The action is not occurring at any specified occasion but in the general present. The verb *suffered* is in the simple past, but it should remain in the general present, even though the phrase *early in their careers* may suggest a past time. Be sure that there is a logical relation between the verbs when two are presented in the same sentence.

Common Mistake 9: Number Agreement Problems

The Writing section also tests number agreement between the singular or plural noun and the phrase or word describing it. For instance, a noun may be plural while a phrase describing the noun belongs with a singular noun. That sounds complicated, but fortunately, you don't need to be able to explain the grammar involved; you just need to be able to spot this type of mistake. Here's an example.

> The advertisement in the newspaper requested that only persons with a high school diploma apply for the position.

Nouns in a sentence must have logical number relations. The noun in question, the subject of the second clause of this sentence, is *persons*, a plural noun. However, the noun *diploma* is singular. Because the phrase *with a high school diploma* is singular, it seems to say that *persons* share one diploma, when in fact each person has his own diploma. The phrase should read *with high school diplomas*.

Here's an example of number disagreement in which a singular noun is coupled with a plural subject.

> Mary's rose gardens are considered by many to be the symbol of beauty in the neighborhood.

Again, identify the subject of the sentence, *gardens*. The noun that corresponds to the subject is *symbol*, a singular noun. There is no agreement in number between *gardens* and *symbol*. Each individual garden is a symbol; many gardens would not be a single symbol. The plural form, *symbols*, makes this sentence grammatically correct. Make sure that the nouns in a sentence logically agree in number.

Common Mistake 10: Pronoun in the Wrong Number

You'll be tested on your ability to tell whether or not a noun and the pronoun that refers to that noun agree in number. A singular pronoun should be used to refer to a singular noun; a plural pronoun should be used with a plural noun. In the following examples, the pronoun does not match the noun to which it refers in number.

> The typical college student has difficulty adjusting to academic standards much higher than those of their school.

The pronoun *their* should refer to a plural noun, but in this sentence, it refers back to *student*, a singular noun. Therefore, the pronoun should be the singular form *his* or *hers*, and not the plural form *their*. Look for the same kind of mistake in the next sentence.

> Most infants, even unusually quiet ones, will cry with greater intensity when it begins teething.

The error in this sentence is just the opposite from that in the first example. The subject is *infants*, a plural noun. But the pronoun that refers back to this plural noun is *it*, a singular form. The correct form of the pronoun is *they*, referring back to the plural subject. Be sure that a pronoun agrees with its antecedent in number.

Common Mistake 11: Pronoun in the Wrong Case in Compound Noun Phrases

An incorrect pronoun case is an error of the *between you and I* variety. Pronouns can either be *subjects* performing actions (I went, you saw, he ate, they sang, etc.) or objects receiving actions or *objects* (with me, give you, see her, stop them, etc.). Usually the choice of pronoun is obvious, but when pronouns are in a compound noun phrase, it's easier to make a mistake. Can you identify the compound phrase in the sentence below and the error in the choice of pronoun?

> Him and the rest of the team stopped by the malt shop for milkshakes after the game.

In this sentence, the compound subject is *Him and the rest of the team.* To identify the error, isolate the pronoun from the compound. Take away the second part of the compound subject (*and the rest of the team*), and you are left with *him*. As you can see, *him* is incorrect because *him* wouldn't stop by the malt shop; *he* would. The correct pronoun case for this sentence is *he*, the subject form.

Can you identify and isolate the incorrect pronoun in the following sentence?

> Uncle John and Aunt Rosie join my parents and I for dinner every Thursday.

In this sentence, the compound noun phrase in question is *my parents and I*, the object of the verb. Ignoring the phrase *my parents*, you can now read the sentence: *Uncle John and Aunt Rosie join I for dinner every Thursday*. The pronoun *I* is the incorrect form of the personal pronoun; the correct form is *me*, the object form.

Common Mistake 12: Pronoun Shift

Pronoun shift is a switch in pronoun person or number within a given sentence. Here's an example.

> One cannot sleep soundly if you exercise vigorously before retiring to bed.

The subject in the first clause is *one*, and the subject in the second clause is *you*. These two pronouns refer to the same performer of two actions, so they should be consistent in person and number. The sentence should not shift to the second person *you* form.

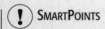 **SMARTPOINTS**

You may see a question about the pronoun "one" on the SAT; be sure this pronoun and all other pronouns are used consistently.

Look for another kind of pronoun shift in the next sentence.

> If someone loses his way in the airport, they can ask any
> employee for directions.

The subject is *someone* in the first clause, but *they* in the second clause. Clearly, both pronouns refer to the same agent; the performer of both actions, losing and asking, is the same. This switch in number from singular to plural is not grammatical. In creating such a sentence, SAT writers play on a common logical confusion. In English, singular words like *one*, *someone*, and *a person* can represent people in general. So can plural words like *people* or *they*. Be on the lookout when general statements use pronouns because this is one of the most common mistakes made in the English language, and consider whether these pronouns are consistent.

Common Mistake 13: Pronoun with Ambiguous Reference

There are two ways the Writing section might test your ability to recognize an ambiguous pronoun reference. First, a sentence may be given in which it is impossible to determine what noun the pronoun refers. Take a look at this example.

> The United States entered into warmer relations with
> China after its compliance with recent weapons
> agreements.

To which country does the pronoun *its* refer? Grammatically and logically, either country could be the antecedent of the pronoun. With the limited information provided by this sentence alone, you simply can't determine which country the pronoun stands in for. The reference is ambiguous.

Pronoun reference can also be ambiguous if the pronoun's antecedent is not explicitly stated in the sentence.

> After the derailment last month, they are inspecting trains
> for safety more often than ever before.

The question to ask about this sentence is *who* is *they*? There is no group of people identified in this sentence to whom the pronoun could refer. You can logically infer that *they* refers to agents of a railroad safety commission, but because these inspectors are not explicitly mentioned in the sentence, the personal pronoun cannot be clear. Be sure to locate the antecedent of any pronoun in Identifying Sentence Errors sentences.

Common Mistake 14: Faulty Comparison

Most faulty comparisons happen when two things that logically cannot be compared are compared. A comparison can be faulty either logically or grammatically. Look for the faulty comparison in the following sentence.

> A Nobel Peace Prize winner and the author of several
> respected novels, Elie Wiesel's name is still less well known
> than last year's Heisman Trophy winner.

 BE SMART!

Be wary of vague subject references such as *its*, *their*, *they*, and *those*. If you can't tell what the pronoun refers to, something is missing from the sentence.

In every sentence, you should first identify what things or actions are being compared. In this sentence, Elie Wiesel's *name* is compared to last year's Heisman Trophy winner. This comparison is faulty because a person's name is compared to another person. If the first item were *Elie Wiesel,* then the comparison would be valid.

Try to identify the faulty comparison in the next sentence.

> To lash back at one's adversaries is a less courageous course
> than attempting to bring about reconciliation with them.

The comparison in this sentence is logically correct in that two actions are compared. But the problem lies in the grammatical form of the words compared. An infinitive verb, *to lash*, expresses the first action, but a gerund, *attempting*, expresses the second action. These verb forms should match to make the comparison parallel. If *lashing* replaced *to lash*, the comparison would be grammatically parallel and logically valid. Check all comparisons for logic and grammatical consistency.

Common Mistake 15: Misuse of Adjective or Adverb

These questions test your ability to recognize misuses of one-word modifiers. Keep in mind that adjectives modify nouns and adverbs modify verbs, adjectives, and other adverbs. Now ask yourself what the underlined word is intended to modify as you look at the sentence below.

> The applicants for low-interest loans hoped to buy <u>decent</u>
> built houses for their families.

The word *decent* is an adjective. However, this modifier describes an adjective, explaining how the houses were built. A word that modifies an adjective like *built* is an adverb. So the word needed in this sentence is the adverb *decently*. Notice also that this adverb ends in *-ly*, the most common adverbial ending.

Now take a look at the second sentence.

> The critics who reviewed both of Dave Eggers's novels like
> the second one best.

The word *best* is a superlative modifier. Superlative adverbs and adjectives (adverbs and adjectives ending in *-est* (such as biggest, loudest, fastest, etc.) should express comparisons between three or more things or actions. Comparative adverbs and adjectives end in *-er* (bigger, louder, faster, etc.) and express comparisons between two things or actions. This sentence compares critics' responses to only two novels by Dave Eggers. Thus, instead of the superlative *best*, this sentence needs the comparative modifier *better*.

Remember that some adjectives and adverbs, usually those of two or more syllables, form the comparative with *more* instead of the *-er* ending, and *most* instead of the *-est* ending converts some modifiers to superlatives.

Trust your ear to distinguish adjectives from adverbs in Writing section Identifying Sentence Errors questions, but do *listen* carefully. Pay close attention when you decide whether a sentence needs a comparative or superlative modifier.

Common Mistake 16: Double Negative

In standard written English, it is incorrect to use two negatives together unless one is intended to cancel out the other. Notice the two negative words in this sentence.

> James easily passed the biology exam without hardly studying his lab notes.

Without is a negative, as is any word that indicates absence or lack. *Hardly* is a less familiar negative; it also denotes a scarcity of something, but perhaps not a total absence. With these two negatives, the sentence is incorrect.

Now look at the next sentence.

> In the history of the major leagues, barely no one has maintained higher than a .400 batting average for an entire season.

Clearly, *no one* is a negative, but so is *barely*. Just like *hardly* does, this word indicates a scarcity of something or an almost total absence. In Identifying Sentence Errors questions, be on the lookout for negatives that are not obviously negative, such as *hardly*, *barely*, and *scarcely*.

IMPROVING SENTENCES QUESTIONS

Just like Identifying Sentence Errors questions, most Improving Sentences questions relate to a small number of grammatical issues. Here's the main difference between the two question types: Whereas the errors in the Identifying Sentence Errors questions consist of single words or short phrases, the errors in the Improving Sentences questions generally involve the structure of the whole sentence. As a result, they can be a little harder to identify than the errors in the Identifying Sentence Errors section.

THE FORMAT

The directions for Improving Sentences questions are as follows. You will be well prepared by becoming very familiar with these.

Directions: The following sentences test correctness and effectiveness of expression. Part of each sentence or the entire sentence is underlined; beneath each sentence are five ways of phrasing the underlined material. Choice A repeats the original phrasing; the other four choices are different. If you think the original phrasing produces a better sentence than any of the alternatives, select choice A; if not, select one of the other choices.

In making your selection, follow the requirements of standard written English; that is, pay attention to grammar, choice of words, sentence construction, and punctuation. Your selection should result in the most effective sentence—clear and precise, without awkwardness or ambiguity.

Fix the Mistake

Remember our *spot-the-mistake* strategy from the Identifying Sentence Errors section of this chapter? We've got a similar strategy for Improving Sentences questions. We call Improving Sentences questions *fix-the-mistake* questions because, in addition to finding the mistake in each sentence, you have to pick the answer choice that best corrects it. Like we said, it's a little harder.

In each of these questions, you're given a sentence, part or all of which is underlined. There are five answer choices; the first one reproduces the underlined part of the sentence exactly, and the other four rephrase the underlined portion in various ways.

Here's an example.

> The Emancipation Edict freed the Russian serfs <u>in 1861; that being four years</u> before the Thirteenth Amendment abolished slavery in the United States.
>
> (A) in 1861; that being four years
> (B) in 1861 and is four years
> (C) in 1861 and this amounts to four years
> (D) in 1861, being four years
> (E) in 1861, four years

You have to pick the best choice to replace the underlined portion of the sentence. The correct answer must produce a sentence that's not only grammatically correct, but also effective: It must be clear, precise, and free of awkward verbiage (using more words than necessary to get your point across).

Here is Kaplan's Target Strategy for answering these questions. We'll use the example on the previous page to show you how it works.

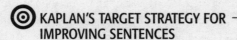 **KAPLAN'S TARGET STRATEGY FOR**
IMPROVING SENTENCES

Step 1. Read the sentence carefully and listen for a mistake.

Step 2. Identify the error or errors.

Step 3. Predict a correction.

Step 4. Look for a match that doesn't introduce a new error.

Let's use the method on the previous example.

Step 1. Read the Sentence Carefully, and Listen for a Mistake

The stem sentence (sentence in question) in the example doesn't sound right.

Step 2. Identify the Error or Errors

The semicolon and phrase *that being* sound like the wrong way of joining the two parts of the sentence.

Step 3. Predict a Correction

The semicolon and the phrase *that being* seem unnecessary. Joining the two sentence fragments with a simple comma would probably work. (Plus, as you'll learn later, answer choices that contain the word *being* are usually wrong.) Plug in your choice to be sure it sounds best.

Step 4. Look for a Match that Doesn't Introduce a New Error

Choice (E) has just a comma. Is that enough? All the answer choices begin with *in 1861* and end with *four years*, so you have to look at what comes in between to see what forms the best link. Scan the choices, and you'll find that *and is* in (B), *and this amounts to* in (C), and *being*, preceded by a comma, in (D) are no better than (A) because they are wordy and awkward phrases.

Choice (E) is the best way to rewrite the underlined portion of the sentence, so (E) is the correct answer.

Remember, not every sentence contains an error. Choice (A) is correct about one fifth of the time. In any event, because you should begin by reading the original sentence carefully, you should never waste time reading choice (A).

COMMON MISTAKES

As you work through the Improving Sentences section, *read each sentence carefully*. We can't say that often enough. The error, if there is one, will often be obvious to you in the first reading.

If it isn't, remember that only a rather limited range of grammar rules is tested. Once your ear has become attuned to the Improving Sentences section's favorite grammar mistakes, you'll have an easier time spotting them on test day.

Here are five classic Improving Sentences mistakes.

Common Mistake 1: Run-On Sentences

The Improving Sentences questions on the Writing section usually include one or two run-on sentences. In a typical run-on sentence, two independent clauses, each of which could stand alone as a complete sentence, are erroneously joined together, either with no punctuation or, most often, with just a comma. Here's an example.

> The decrease in crime can be attributed to a rise in the number of police officers, more than 500 joined the force in the last year alone.

Both clauses in this sentence are independent; each could stand alone as a sentence. So, it's incorrect to join them with a comma. There are several ways to correct run-on sentences. One way is simply to change the comma into a period, producing two separate sentences:

> The decrease in crime can be attributed to a rise in the number of police officers. More than 500 joined the force in the last year alone.

A second way is to change the comma into a semicolon. A semicolon can be described as a *weak period*. It's used to indicate that two clauses are grammatically independent but that the ideas expressed are not so independent as to warrant separate sentences. Substituting a semicolon for the comma would make this sentence correct and show that the two ideas are equally important and closely related.

> The decrease in crime can be attributed to a rise in the number of police officers; more than 500 joined the force in the last year alone.

This is a popular correction choice for test makers to use, so be on the lookout for semi-colons in place of commas.

But there are other ways to join two independent clauses. In the next example, the two clauses are independent, but one is logically subordinate to (of lesser importance than) the other. To make the correction, you can convert the independent clause expressing the subordinate idea into a grammatically subordinate, or dependent, clause. For example, identify the two independent clauses in the run-on sentence that follows.

> Litigation against chicken farms continues to increase year
> after year, farmers are now introducing organic and free-
> range chickens.

Although the clauses in this sentence are grammatically independent, they are not unrelated. Logically, the second clause depends on the first one; it seems to express a response to what is described in the first clause. The farmers are introducing these chickens *because* the number of litigations against them is great. So, a good way to correct the error in this sentence would be to make the second clause grammatically dependent on the first clause, as follows:

> Because litigation against chicken farms continues to
> increase year after year, farmers are now introducing organic
> and free-range chickens.

A fourth way to correct a run-on sentence is simply to compress the two independent clauses to one. This can be done in sentences in which the independent clauses have the same subject, as in the sentence below.

> The Humber Bridge in Britain was completed in 1981, it is
> the longest single-span suspension bridge in the world.

In this sentence, the subject of the second clause is the pronoun *it*, which refers to the subject of the first clause, *the Humber Bridge*. Thus, both clauses share the same subject. To correct this run-on sentence, remove both the comma and the pronoun *it*, and insert the coordinating conjunction *and*. The sentence now reads:

> The Humber Bridge in Britain was completed in 1981 and
> is the longest single-span suspension bridge in the world.

Now the sentence consists of one independent clause with a compound predicate and only one subject.

Common Mistake 2: Sentence Fragments

The Improving Sentences section usually includes one or two sentence fragments. Sentence fragments come in many forms, but they all share the same problem: they cannot stand alone because they have no independent clauses. A sentence must contain a subject and verb (a clause) *and* express a complete thought (be independent). What looks like a sentence on the Writing section may actually be merely a fragment. Take a look at the following example.

> Whereas many office managers are growing more and more
> dependent on facsimile machines, others resisting this latest
> technological breakthrough.

This just sounds wrong, doesn't it? Here's why. This is a sentence fragment because it has no independent clause. The first clause begins with the subordinating conjunction *whereas*, and the phrase following the comma contains the incomplete verb form *resisting*. Plus, a sentence should always have at least one clause that could stand alone, and

 SMARTPOINTS

When you see a long sentence with just a comma in the middle, suspect a run-on sentence.

here neither of the clauses can do that. The easiest way to repair this sentence is to insert the helping verb *are*.

> Whereas many office managers are growing more and more dependent on facsimile machines, others are resisting this latest technological breakthrough.

Here's another sentence fragment.

> In the summertime, the kindergarten class that plays on the rope swing beneath the crooked oak tree.

Once again, the sentence clause cannot stand alone. Here we have a fragment not because something is missing, but because something is included that makes the clause dependent. The word *that* makes everything after the comma a dependent clause. Simply remove the word *that*, and look at what you get.

> In the summertime, the kindergarten class plays on the rope swing beneath the crooked oak tree.

Now you have a grammatically complete sentence that is shorter than the fragment.

Common Mistake 3: Misplaced Modifiers

A modifier is a word or group of words that gives the reader more information about a noun or verb in the sentence. To be grammatically correct, the modifier must be positioned so it is clear which word is being modified. The best place to put a modifier is as close as possible to the word it modifies. Here is an example of a misplaced modifier like those you may see on the Writing section.

> Flying for the first time, the roar of the jet engines intimidated the small child, and he grew frightened as the plane roared down the runway.

The modifying phrase above is found at the beginning of the sentence: *Flying for the first time*. A modifying phrase that begins a sentence should relate to the sentence's subject. Usually, a comma sets off this kind of introductory modifier, and then the subject immediately follows the comma.

Logically, in this example, you know that it is the child who is flying for the first time. But because of the grammatical structure of the sentence (the placement of the modifier), the sentence actually states that it is the *roar* that is flying for the first time. Of course, this doesn't make sense: roars don't fly for the first time (or the second time or the third time). The sentence needs to be revised so that the modifier is as close as possible to the noun it modifies.

> Flying for the first time, the small child was intimidated by the roar of the jet engines and grew frightened as the plane roared down the runway.

Here's another example of a sentence with a misplaced modifying modifier.

> An advertisement was withdrawn by the producer of the
> local news program that was considered offensive by the
> city's minority communities.

Grammatically, the phrase *that was considered offensive by the city's minority communities* refers to *the local news program*, because this is the nearest noun. Is that what the writer means? Is it the local news program or the advertisement that was offensive to the minority communities? If the writer means to say that the advertisement was deemed offensive, she should rewrite the sentence as follows to make her idea clear.

> The producer of the local news program withdrew an
> advertisement that was considered offensive by the city's
> minority communities.

The same goes with this next sentence.

> The despondent little girl found her missing doll playing in
> the back yard under the swing.

The position of the modifying phrase *playing in the back yard under the swing* suggests that the girl's *missing doll* was playing in the yard, not the despondent little girl. Once again, the modifier is misplaced; it is not near enough to the noun it is intended to modify (girl) to prevent confusion. Here's how the sentence should be revised.

> Playing in the back yard under the swing, the despondent
> little girl found her missing doll.

Common Mistake 4: Faulty Parallelism

Certain sets of words in a sentence, or the general design of a sentence, often require a parallel construction—that is, the words or phrases must share the same grammatical structure. If they don't, the sentence will be off balance. For example, compare these two sentences.

> My hobbies include swimming, gardening, and to read
> science fiction.

> My hobbies include swimming, gardening, and reading
> science fiction.

In the first sentence, two of the hobbies use the *–ing* gerund form, but the third uses a different structure—the infinitive. The sentence is not parallel. In the second version, all three hobbies correctly use the same *–ing* form, creating a balanced sentence.

 BE SMART!

Use parallel structure with connective phrases such as *neither ... nor* and lists.

Two kinds of parallel construction errors are used over and over again on the Writing section. The first occurs in sentences with pairs of connective words that require parallelism. These connective words include those in the following list.

neither . . . nor

either . . . or

both . . . and

the better . . . the better

the more . . . the more (or less)

not only . . . but also

In the sentence below, look at that first pair of words, *neither . . . nor*, and the phrases that follow both words.

> Nineteenth-century nihilists were concerned with neither the origins of philosophical thought nor how societal laws developed.

The phrases following the words *neither* and *nor* must be parallel in grammatical structure. That is, if a noun phrase (*the origins of philosophical thought*) follows *neither*, then a noun phrase must follow *nor*, too. But here *nor* is followed by *how societal laws developed*—a dependent clause. The two parts of the sentence are not grammatically parallel.

In this example, the dependent clause must be rewritten as a noun phrase (*nor the development of societal laws*) to make the sentence parallel. Now both connective words are followed by a noun and a prepositional phrase. The sentence now has proper parallel construction.

Another situation that demands parallel grammatical structure occurs when a sentence contains a list of two or more items. That list can comprise two or more nouns or noun phrases, verbs or verb phrases, or dependent clauses. Any kind of list calls for grammatically parallel items. Look for the faulty parallelism in the following sentence.

> To run for a seat in the United States Senate, a candidate must be an adult at least 30 years of age, a citizen of the United States, and is to reside in the state to be represented.

This sentence lists three requirements of running for United States Senate. The first two phrases in the list *an adult at least 30 years of age* and *a citizen of the United States*, are both nouns modified by prepositional phrases. The third phrase in the list *is to reside in the state* is a verbal phrase (the present tense form *is* plus the infinitive form *to reside*).

Two noun phrases + One verbal phrase = Bad parallelism!

To correct this error, transform the verbal phrase into a noun phrase so it matches the structure of the other two items on the list. Thus, if a person is to live in a state to be elected to the Senate, he or she must be a *resident of the state*.

Common Mistake 5: Faulty Coordination/Subordination

These two kinds of errors occur when sentence clauses are joined incorrectly. Faulty coordination and faulty subordination are closely related, but they require separate explanations.

Coordination between two clauses is faulty if it doesn't express the logical relation between the clauses. Often, this error involves a misused conjunction. A conjunction is a connective word joining two clauses or phrases in one sentence. The most common conjunctions are as follows:

and

but

because

however

for

or

Identify the conjunction in the following sentence. Why does it fail to connect the clauses logically?

> Ben Franklin was a respected and talented statesman, and he was most famous for his discovery of electricity.

To identify and correct the faulty coordination, determine what the relationship between the sentence's two clauses really is. Does the conjunction *and* best express the relationship between the two facts the writer states about Ben Franklin? *And* normally expresses a consistency between two equally emphasized facts. However, the fact that Franklin is best known for his discovery of electricity is presented in contrast to the fact that he was a talented statesman. Thus, the use of *and* is an error in coordination.

A better way to connect these two contrasting ideas would be to use the conjunction *but*, which indicates some contrast between the two clauses. In this sentence, *but* points to a common expectation. An individual usually distinguishes herself or himself in one field of accomplishment—in politics or in science—but not in both. So Franklin's distinction in two diverse fields seems to contradict common expectations and calls for a *but*.

Faulty subordination is most often found on the Writing section in a group of words that contains two or more subordinate, or dependent, clauses but no independent clause. There are several connective words that, when introducing a sentence or clause, always indicate that the phrase that follows is dependent, or subordinate. They are as follows:

since

because

so that

if

Whenever a dependent clause begins a sentence, an independent clause must follow somewhere in the sentence. Look at the group of words below and identify the faulty subordination.

> Since the small electronics industry is one of the world's fastest growing sectors, because demand for the computer chip continues to be high.

Since indicates that the first clause in the group of words is subordinate and needs to be followed by an independent clause. But *because* in the second clause indicates that the second clause is also subordinate. The sentence is faulty because there is no independent clause to make the group of words grammatically complete. Result: two sentence fragments. The second connective word *because* should be eliminated to make the group of words a complete and logical sentence. With this revision, the *since* clause expresses a cause, and the independent clause expresses an effect or result.

Wordiness: How to Avoid It

Before moving on to the Improving Paragraphs questions, we should mention one more key to performing successfully on the Writing section. A common flaw in many sentences and paragraphs is wordiness.

Many people make the mistake of writing *at the present time* or *at this point in time* instead of the simpler *now* and *take into consideration* instead of simply *consider* in an attempt to make their prose seem more scholarly or more formal. It doesn't work. Instead, their prose ends up seeming inflated and pretentious.

Wordy:

I am of the opinion that the aforementioned managers should be advised that they will be evaluated with regard to the utilization of responsive organizational software for the purpose of devising a responsive network of customers.

Concise:

We should tell the managers that we will evaluate their use of flexible computerized databases to develop a customer's network.

IMPROVING PARAGRAPHS QUESTIONS

Improving Paragraphs questions follow short essays. The essays can be about any topic. You do not have to know anything about the topic to answer the questions correctly. The sentences in each passage will be numbered.

Most Improving Paragraphs questions ask you to clean up awkward and ambiguous sentences. The most important element to consider in these questions is their context. You can't determine the best way to repair poor or unclear sentences without knowing what comes before and after them.

A few Improving Paragraphs questions will also ask you about the overall organization of the essay. Again, context is critical. You can't, for example, decide which of five sentences best concludes an essay without knowing what the essay is all about.

THE FORMAT

Review the directions for this type of question.

Directions: The following passage is an early draft of an essay. Some parts of the passage need to be rewritten.

Read the passage and select the best answer for each question that follows. Some questions are about particular sentences or parts of sentences and ask you to improve sentence structure or word choice. Other questions ask you to consider organization and development. In choosing answers, follow the conventions of standard written English.

THE THREE KINDS OF IMPROVING PARAGRAPHS QUESTIONS

There are three basic types of Improving Paragraphs questions.
- General organization questions
- Revising sentences questions
- Combining sentences questions

General Organization Questions

If you've got a firm grasp of the essay after you first read through it, you should jump right to the general organization questions first. Do these questions while the essay is fresh in your mind.

However, if your grasp of the essay is a bit shaky, work on general organization questions last. Start with questions that ask you to revise or combine sentences: Doing so should improve your grasp of the overall essay, making it easier for you to tackle the general organization questions later.

Revising Sentence Questions

Take a look at the following paragraph and question. The question focuses on a single word in one sentence, but to answer this typical example of a revision question, you'll need to reread the entire paragraph.

(1) The Spanish-American War was one of the shortest and most decisive wars ever fought. (2) The postwar settlement, the Treaty of Paris, reflected the results of the fighting. (3) Under its terms, Spain was compelled to cede large territories in North America and the Pacific. (4) The United States gained control over some of these territories, including Puerto Rico and Guam. (5) It was reduced in status from a major to a minor power. (6) The United States, in contrast, emerged from the war as a world power, and would soon go on to become a major participant in Asian and European affairs.

In context, which is the best version of the underlined part of sentence 5?

It was reduced in status from a major to a minor power.

(A) (As it is now)

(B) Spain was reduced

(C) The war caused Spain to be reduced

(D) As a result of the war, it had been reduced

(E) It had now been reduced

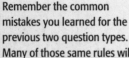

A NOTE ON...
COMMON MISTAKES

Remember the common mistakes you learned for the previous two question types. Many of those same rules will apply to Improving Paragraphs questions.

Sentence 5 refers to Spain's status. That much should have been clear to you by reading sentences 2, 3, 4, and 6. However, the pronoun *it* makes sentence 5 ambiguous. What does *it* refer to? To make this sentence less ambiguous, it should be changed to the noun *Spain*. That leaves (B) and (C) as possible correct answers. Because (B) is a more concise and less awkward construction than (C), (B) is correct.

Combining Sentences Questions

Take a look at the following paragraph and question.

(6) Albert Einstein was a great physicist. (7) He won a Nobel Prize in Physics. (8) He got the prize for his research into the photoelectric effect. (9) Later physicists demonstrated the validity of Einstein's ideas.

Which of the following is the best way to combine sentences 7 and 8?

He won a Nobel Prize in Physics. He got the prize for his research into the photoelectric effect.

(A) The Nobel Prize in Physics that he won was for his research into the photoelectric effect.

(B) Having researched the photoelectric effect, he won a Nobel Prize in Physics.

(C) He won a Nobel Prize in Physics for his research into the photoelectric effect.

(D) He got the prize in physics, the Noble Prize in Physics, for his research into the photoelectric effect.

(E) Because of his research into the photoelectric effect he got the Nobel Prize in Physics.

Did you choose (C)? It's the best written and most economical of the choices. Whether you're asked to revise or combine sentences, the correct answer will often (but not always) be the shortest answer. Good writing is concise.

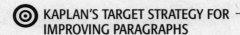 **KAPLAN'S TARGET STRATEGY FOR IMPROVING PARAGRAPHS**

Kaplan's Target Strategy works for all three kinds of Improving Paragraphs questions.

Step 1. Skim the passage for the overall idea and tone.

Step 2. Read the question.

Step 3. Reread relevant portion and its context.

Step 4. Predict the correction.

Step 5. Check for a match that doesn't introduce a new error.

Step 1. Skim the Passage for the Overall Idea and Tone

Read the entire essay quickly. Get a sense of the essay's overall main idea, as well as the main idea of each paragraph. This will come in handy when you're asked to answer questions about the essay as a whole.

Step 2. Read the Question

Now read the question closely. Make sure that you understand exactly what you're asked to do. Questions that require you to revise or combine sentences will supply you with the sentence numbers. Questions that ask about the entire essay generally won't refer to specific sentences.

Step 3. Reread the Relevant Portion and its Context

Go back and reread that sentence or two that the question is about. But don't stop there. This next part is very important! Also *reread the sentences before and after the target sentence(s)*. This will provide you with the context (the surrounding ideas or information) for the sentence(s). Context helps you to choose the best answer from the answer choices.

Note: For those questions about the essay as a whole, skim quickly over the entire essay to re-familiarize yourself with its contents.

Step 4. Predict the Correction

Say in your head what you think the correct sentence or answer should be.

Step 5. Check for a Match that Doesn't Introduce a New Error

Go to the answer choices and pick the choice that best matches the sentence or idea in your head. Make sure the one you pick doesn't introduce a new mistake if you are correcting a sentence.

So, to summarize: read the essay quickly; read the question; reread the target sentences and the sentences that surround them; make up a sentence that would eliminate the mistake; and choose the answer choice that best matches your sentence.

The practice set at the end of this chapter will help you get a handle on this approach.

PRACTICE

Use everything you have learned about Identifying Sentence Errors questions, Improving Sentences questions, and Improving Paragraphs questions to answer the questions in the practice set that follows. All of the questions are similar to the ones that will be on the SAT.

For the questions you get wrong, re-read the part of this chapter that covers the specific question type. Make sure you understand all the strategies from this chapter.

1. Since the government <u>was</u> bankrupt, many of
                          A

    the soldiers <u>which</u> were sent <u>to quell</u> the riots
                   B   C

    had <u>not been</u> paid in months. <u>No error</u>
          D   E

2. Although <u>the two had been</u> political rivals on
                     A

    <u>more than one</u> occasion, John Adams
         B

    <u>remained</u> one of Thomas Jefferson's closest
         C

    friends until <u>his</u> death. <u>No error</u>
                    D   E

3. Even <u>those who</u> profess <u>to care</u> about "green"
             A   B

    issues often fail to consider <u>how</u> their daily
                                      C

    choices <u>effect</u> the environment. <u>No error</u>
              D   E

4. Ants, <u>which</u> have inhabited the earth for at
             A

    least 100 million years, <u>are without doubt</u> the
                                       B

    <u>more successful</u> of all the social insects of the
         C

    Hymenoptera, an order <u>that also</u> includes
                               D

    wasps and bees. <u>No error</u>
                       E

5. For my sister and <u>I</u>, the trip to Paris was the
                       A

    <u>fulfillment</u> of a lifelong wish we <u>had scarcely</u>
         B   C

    <u>dared to express</u>. <u>No error</u>
         D   E

6. The volunteers, <u>upon discovering</u> that
                          A

    <u>a large number</u> of the village children <u>were</u>
         B   C

    infected by parasites <u>from</u> unclean drinking
                              D

    water, decided to make the well-digging

    project their highest priority. <u>No error</u>
                                       E

7. Although farmers complained that the

    company's new product was expensive,

    malodorous, and <u>dangerous to handle</u>,
                          A

    <u>there was</u> few who <u>would dispute</u> its
         B   C

    effectiveness <u>as</u> an insecticide. <u>No error</u>
                    D   E

8. In the wake <u>of</u> recent thefts, the town's
           A

   wealthier residents <u>have installed</u> gates, alarm
                     B

   systems, and even video surveillance

   equipment in their neighborhoods, hoping

   <u>that it will</u> prevent <u>further burglaries</u>. <u>No error</u>
     C   D   E

9. <u>To repair</u> the damage <u>that</u> time and the
     A   B

   elements <u>had wrought</u> on the ancient fresco,
           C

   the restorer used a simple mixture <u>from</u>
                         D

   plaster, pigment, and a little water. <u>No error</u>
                            E

10. Opponents of the Act <u>argued that</u> the
                    A

    legislation <u>was not only</u> vaguely formulated
              B

    and unconstitutional, but also impossible

    <u>to enforce</u> in an international <u>and virtually</u>
      C   D

    unregulated arena. <u>No error</u>
                  E

11. One reason that a growing number of people

    <u>have no</u> family doctor <u>may be that</u> fewer and
      A   B

    fewer medical students <u>are choosing to train</u> as
                    C

    <u>a general practitioner</u>. <u>No error</u>
        D   E

12. <u>That</u> J. L. Solomon's first novel <u>was selected for</u>
      A   B

    several major literary prizes <u>was surprising to</u>
                          C

    no one who had read his <u>previous</u> collections
                    D

    of short stories, poems, and essays. <u>No error</u>
                          E

13. Citizens <u>protesting</u> the planned demolition of
            A

    the historic YMCA building claim <u>that without</u>
                          B

    the YMCA, many young people in the town

    <u>would of</u> grown up <u>with no</u> access to sports
      C   D

    facilities and no place for after-school

    recreation. <u>No error</u>
            E

14. When questioned, <u>a surprising</u> number of
                    A

    fifth-graders said that telling the truth—even

    <u>if it</u> meant <u>being</u> punished—was preferable
      B   C

    <u>than living</u> with a lie. <u>No error</u>
       D   E

15. <u>Though</u> Patricia's résumé was <u>not nearly as</u>
      A   B

    long and impressive as <u>the other applicant</u>,
                    C

    her personal charisma was <u>so great that</u> Mr.
                    D

    Alvarez hired her on the spot. <u>No error</u>
                      E

16. <u>Under</u> the proposed law, which many <u>deem</u>
      A   B

    too harsh, any motorist <u>convicted of</u> drunk
                                      C

    driving would spend thirty days in prison and

    lose <u>their license</u> for five years. <u>No error</u>
            D   E

17. When <u>it became apparent</u> to Clive that not one
              A

    of the remaining jurors <u>were going to</u> believe
                              B

    his <u>client's</u> alibi, he began to reconsider the
          C

    District Attorney's <u>offer of</u> a plea bargain.
                       D

    <u>No error</u>
      E

18. <u>If only</u> the factory owners <u>had conducted</u>
      A   B

    regular safety inspections <u>of</u> their equipment,
                           C

    the horrible accident of 1969 <u>may have been</u>
                                D

    averted. <u>No error</u>
            E

19. The symphony <u>had not</u> hardly begun <u>when</u> a
                A   B

    group of schoolchildren, who <u>had been forced</u>
                                 C

    to attend, began irritating the rest of the

    audience <u>by talking loudly</u> and kicking the
                 D

    seats. <u>No error</u>
          E

20. The gods of Greek mythology, who

    <u>were neither</u> omniscient nor <u>particularly</u>
         A   B

    ethical, amused themselves <u>by taking on</u>
                              C

    disguises and <u>meddling in</u> the affairs of
                    D

    mortals. <u>No error</u>
             E

21. Fast food chains are <u>among the most</u> ubiquitous
                       A

    restaurants in our town; <u>they welcome</u> everyone
                         B

    with no <u>distinction between</u> <u>you and me</u>, teachers
                 C   D

    and students, or parents and kids. <u>No error</u>
                             E

22. <u>Like other</u> gourmet restaurants, M. Dubois creates
      A

    magnificent meals <u>in which</u> <u>he likes</u> <u>to use</u> only
                  B   C   D

    the finest ingredients. <u>No error</u>
                   E

23. *High Fidelity*, a successful book and film, <u>became</u>
                                    A

    <u>successful as</u> a cult classic because of its sharp wit
      B

    and <u>by presenting</u> a quirky main character, Rob,
          C

    <u>as a common man</u>. <u>No error</u>
        D   E

24. Often <u>believed to be</u> <u>dangerous and dirty places</u>
          A   B

    where tourists <u>were</u> always mugged, New York
              C

    City <u>has been reforming</u> its image radically with
            D

    dropping crime rates over the past few years.

    <u>No error</u>
      E

25. <u>To understand</u> the current Russian government,
        A
    <u>we have to be</u> <u>highly aware</u> of the theory and
        B   C
    history of communism, whether or not one

    <u>agrees with</u> its tenets. <u>No error</u>
        D   E

26. Bill <u>had hoped</u> to go to the baseball game
              A
    <u>that night</u>, but as the afternoon wore on, he
        B
    realized he <u>would have to work</u> late <u>to meet</u> his
                      C   D
    deadline. <u>No error</u>
                    E

27. The process <u>of learning new languages</u> <u>require</u> a
                          A   B
    commitment to memorization and pronunciation

    practice, <u>even if</u> progress <u>seems slow</u>. <u>No error</u>
                  C   D   E

28. Jane Eyre <u>could not marry</u> Mr. Rochester <u>until</u> the
                      A   B
    <u>fateful</u> night when Grace Poole <u>set</u> the mansion
        C   D
    ablaze. <u>No error</u>
                  E

29. <u>Widely divergent</u> opinions <u>could be heard</u> from
        A   B
    the audience as the planning commission unveiled

    <u>their</u> proposal <u>for a remodeled</u> city square.
        C   D
    No error
        E

30. The advisory board <u>cautioned</u> employees that the
                            A
    <u>existing</u> program of <u>health benefits</u> <u>were</u> likely to
        B   C   D
    be eliminated. <u>No error</u>
                        E

31. <u>The runners coming this far, they</u> decided to push
    through the very strenuous final miles of the
    marathon.

    (A) The runners coming this far, they
    (B) Although they came this far, the runners
    (C) Having come this far, the runners
    (D) To come this far, the runners
    (E) The runners came this far; so that they

32. <u>Our English teacher handed out the worksheet,
    and we started filling in the answers quickly, and
    we continued to do so until the bell rang.</u>

    (A) Our English teacher handed out the work-
         sheet, and we started filling in the answers
         quickly, and we continued to do so until
         the bell rang.
    (B) Upon starting to fill in the answers quickly
         after we were given the worksheet by our
         English teacher, we continued to do so
         until the bell rang.
    (C) Following our English teacher's giving us the
         worksheet, we started filling in the answers
         quickly and continued doing just that until
         the bell rang.
    (D) After our English teacher gave us the work-
         sheet, we filled in the answers quickly until
         the bell rang.
    (E) We filled in the answers quickly until the bell
         rang when the worksheet had been given to
         us by our English teacher.

33. Some of the classes taught in American <u>class-rooms are interpretations of lessons used worldwide, particularly those in European history</u>.

    (A) classrooms are interpretations of lessons used worldwide, particularly those in European history

    (B) classrooms, there are interpretations of lessons used worldwide, particularly European history

    (C) classrooms, and in particular European history, is an interpretation of lessons used worldwide

    (D) classrooms, particularly in European history, are interpretations of lessons used worldwide

    (E) classrooms being interpretations, European history in particular, of those used worldwide

34. <u>Olga Korbut, a Soviet gymnast, whose fame as an athlete</u> on the Olympic stage almost equals that of Nadia Comaneci.

    (A) Olga Korbut, a Soviet gymnast, whose fame as an athlete

    (B) Olga Korbut, who was a Soviet gymnast and whose fame as an athlete

    (C) A Soviet with fame as an Olympic athlete, Olga Korbut

    (D) Olga Korbut was a Soviet gymnast whose fame as an athlete

    (E) A Soviet, Olga Korbut who was a gymnast and whose fame

35. Many parents believe that extreme sports are too <u>dangerous, consequently, some of those parents do not allow</u> their children to bungee jump.

    (A) dangerous, consequently, some of those parents do not allow

    (B) dangerous, therefore, some of those parents do not allow

    (C) dangerous; consequently, some do not allow

    (D) dangerous, some people do not allow

    (E) dangerous, and therefore not allowing

36. <u>Although its being fictional in form</u>, the new book on America raises many historical questions.

    (A) Although its being fictional in form

    (B) Despite its fictional form

    (C) Whereas it was fictional in form

    (D) Its form being fictional

    (E) Even though fictional form was there

37. The novels of Louisa May Alcott are sought out by each new generation of readers <u>considering that her books blend both wild youthfulness and a rational side</u>.

    (A) considering that her books blend both wild youthfulness and a rational side

    (B) considering that her books blend both wild youthfulness and rationality

    (C) because her books blend wild youthfulness and rationality

    (D) because her books will blend not only wild youthfulness but also a rational side

    (E) being that her books will blend both wild youthfulness and rationality

38. Joann, the newest student at Leon Blum High School, has been portrayed as <u>the brightest student and also the most unruly of them</u>.

    (A) the brightest student and also the most unruly of them

    (B) not only the brightest student, but also more unruly than any

    (C) the brightest student at the same time as she is the most unruly student

    (D) at once the brightest and also the most unruly of them

    (E) the brightest and yet the most unruly of students

39. Anaelle's parents explained that she was promoted to head journalist <u>for the reason that her articles were mindful always for both sides of the issues.</u>

    (A) for the reason that her articles were mindful always for both sides of the issues

    (B) since her articles for issues were always mindful of both sides

    (C) because her mindfulness of both sides of the issues was always in her articles

    (D) for the fact being that her articles were always mindful about both sides of the issues

    (E) because her articles were always mindful of both sides of the issues

40. Of all the countries in the UN Security Council, <u>the representative of China was the only one to speak</u> to the General Assembly today.

    (A) the representative of China was the only one to speak

    (B) making the representative from China the only one to speak

    (C) China's representative only spoke

    (D) China's governor spoke only

    (E) China was the only one whose representative spoke

41. Patients with Alzheimer's disease typically exhibit symptoms such as confusion, memory loss, <u>and their language skills are impaired.</u>

    (A) and their language skills are impaired

    (B) and it also impairs their language skills

    (C) and impaired language skills

    (D) besides their language skills being impaired

    (E) in addition to their language skills being impaired

42. <u>Upon entering the jail, the prisoners' personal belongings are surrendered to the guards.</u>

    (A) Upon entering the jail, the prisoners' personal belongings are surrendered to the guards.

    (B) Upon entering the jail, the prisoners surrender their personal belongings to the guards.

    (C) The prisoners' personal belongings having been surrendered to the guards upon entering the jail.

    (D) Upon entering the jail, the guards are to whom the prisoners surrender their personal belongings.

    (E) Upon entering the jail, the prisoners will have been surrendering their personal belongings to the guards.

43. <u>The albatross has a broad wingspan, it is graceful in the air but ungainly on dry land.</u>

    (A) The albatross has a broad wingspan, it is graceful in the air but ungainly on dry land.

    (B) The albatross, with its broad wingspan, is graceful in the air but ungainly on dry land.

    (C) Having a broad wingspan, the albatross is graceful in the air, however it is ungainly on dry land.

    (D) The albatross, which has a broad wingspan, graceful in the air but ungainly on dry land.

    (E) The albatross, although having a broad wingspan, is graceful in the air but ungainly on dry land.

44. King John of England is remembered not so much for his administrative successes <u>but for failing in military engagements</u>.

    (A) but for failing in military engagements
    (B) but more for the fact that he failed in military engagements
    (C) than he was for having failed militarily
    (D) the reason being that he failed in military engagements
    (E) as for his military failures

45. According to older fishermen, cod and haddock were once plentiful in the North Sea, but years of over-fishing and pollution have <u>had a negative overall impact on the fish stocks</u>.

    (A) had a negative overall impact on the fish stocks
    (B) impacted the fish stocks negatively
    (C) the result that the fish stocks are diminished
    (D) depleted the fish stocks
    (E) been depleting the fish stocks overall

46. <u>During the winter months, several feet of snow cover the narrow mountain pass, which is the only route to the monastery.</u>

    (A) During the winter months, several feet of snow cover the narrow mountain pass, which is the only route to the monastery.
    (B) The only route to the monastery, several feet of snow cover the narrow mountain pass during the winter months.
    (C) Several feet of snow cover the narrow mountain pass during the winter months which is the only route to the monastery.
    (D) Several feet of snow cover the narrow mountain pass, which is the only route to the monastery during the winter months.
    (E) During the winter months, covering the narrow mountain pass which is the only route to the monastery is snow.

47. The Townshend Acts, a piece of British legislation enacted on June 29, 1767, <u>were intended for the raising of revenue, to tighten customs enforcement, and assert</u> imperial authority in America.

    (A) were intended for the raising of revenue, to tighten customs enforcement, and assert
    (B) were intended to raise revenue, tighten customs enforcement, and assert
    (C) were with the intention of raising revenue, tightening customs enforcement, and assert
    (D) had for their intention the raising of revenue, tightening of customs enforcement, and asserting
    (E) were intended to raise revenue, also to tighten customs enforcement and assert

48. The border crossing proved more unpleasant than the two American reporters had <u>expected, having their cameras seized</u> and their tape recorders smashed by belligerent soldiers.

    (A) expected, having their cameras seized
    (B) expected, their cameras being seized
    (C) expected: their cameras were seized
    (D) expected; when their cameras were seized
    (E) expected and so their cameras had been seized

49. <u>Were it not for the warming effects of the Gulf Stream, England's climate would resemble that of Greenland.</u>

  (A) Were it not for the warming effects of the Gulf Stream, England's climate would resemble that of Greenland.

  (B) Had the Gulf Stream not such warming effects, England's climate would resemble Greenland.

  (C) Without the warming effects of the Gulf Stream, England's climate were resembling Greenland's.

  (D) If not for the warming effects of the Gulf Stream, therefore England's climate would have resembled that of Greenland.

  (E) If the Gulf Stream would not have had its warming effects, England's climate would resemble that of Greenland.

50. Perhaps best known for his portrayal of T. E. Lawrence in the film *Lawrence of Arabia*, <u>Peter O'Toole's distinguished acting career spans nearly five decades.</u>

  (A) Peter O'Toole's distinguished acting career spans nearly five decades

  (B) Peter O'Toole has a distinguished acting career spanning nearly five decades

  (C) Peter O'Toole spans nearly five decades in his distinguished acting career

  (D) Peter O'Toole's distinguished acting career will have spanned nearly five decades

  (E) nearly five decades have been spanned by Peter O'Toole's distinguished acting career

51. In their haste to complete the new stadium before the Olympic games, the contractors disregarded safety <u>codes, thereby they endangered the lives of thousands of spectators</u>.

  (A) codes, thereby they endangered the lives of thousands of spectators

  (B) codes they have endangered the lives of thousands of spectators

  (C) codes and thus endangered the lives of thousands of spectators

  (D) codes; thus the lives of thousands of spectators endangered

  (E) codes, they endangered the lives of thousands of spectators as a result

52. When Dr. Park presented an abridged version of his paper at the conference, <u>several tantalizing theories about the origins of life on earth were introduced, but these were not fully developed by him.</u>

  (A) several tantalizing theories about the origins of life on earth were introduced, but these were not fully developed by him

  (B) he introduced several tantalizing theories about the origins of life on earth but they had not been fully developed

  (C) several tantalizing theories about the origins of life were introduced by him and not fully developed

  (D) several tantalizing theories about the origins of life on earth were introduced, but he did not fully develop these

  (E) he introduced, but did not fully develop, several tantalizing theories about the origins of life on earth

Questions 53–57 are based on the following essay, which is a response to an assignment to write a letter to a local newspaper protesting cuts in funding for after-school sports programs.

(1) I disagree with the editor's view that after-school sports programs should be cut in our city government's search for ways to reduce spending. (2) The editor argues that extra-curricular sports play a less important role than academic studies, distracting students from the opportunity to increase their knowledge after school is out. (3) However, I myself believe that playing sports enhances students' academic performance. (4) Why is sports so effective in this regard? (5) The main reason is that sports teaches people to excel. (6) It gives students the chance to strive for greatness. (7) It shows them that it takes courage and discipline to succeed in competition with others. (8) Top athletes such as Michael Jordan become role models for young people everywhere, inspiring them with his brilliant individual performances. (9) In addition to these personal attributes, playing in team sports show young people how to interact with each other, achieving shared goals. (10) Such principles have a direct impact on how students perform in their academic studies. (11) I know that being selected for the school lacrosse team taught me many valuable lessons about working with others. (12) Not only that, friendships which I have made there were carried into the rest of my school life. (13) In summary, I would urge the editor to strongly reconsider his stance on extra-curricular sports. (14) There are doubtless other ways of city government saving the money they require.

53. Which of the following is the best way to revise the underlined portion of sentence 3 (reproduced below)?

    However, I myself believe that playing sports enhances students' academic performance.

    (A) However, I myself believe that playing sports should enhance

    (B) Playing sports, however, I believe enhances

    (C) However, I personally believe that playing sports enhances

    (D) I believe, however, that playing sports enhances

    (E) However, I myself believe that to play sports is to enhance

54. Which of the following is the best way to revise and combine sentences 6 and 7 (reproduced below)?

    It gives students the chance to strive for greatness. It shows them that it takes courage and discipline to succeed in competition with others.

    (A) Although it gives students the chance to strive for greatness, it also shows them that it takes courage and discipline to succeed in competition with others.

    (B) While it gives students the chance to strive for greatness, also showing them that it takes courage and discipline to succeed in competition with others.

    (C) It gives students the chance to strive for greatness, showing them that it takes courage and discipline to succeed in competition with others.

    (D) Because it gives students the chance to strive for greatness, they are shown that it takes courage and discipline to succeed in competition with others.

    (E) It gives students the chance to strive for greatness and show them that it takes courage and discipline to succeed in competition with others.

55. In the context of the second paragraph, which of the following is the best version of the underlined portion of sentence 8 (reproduced below)?

    Top athletes such as Michael Jordan become role models for young people everywhere, inspiring them with his brilliant individual performances.

    (A) (As it is now)
    (B) inspiring him with their
    (C) inspiring them with their
    (D) to inspire them with his
    (E) inspiring him with his

56. Which of the following is the best way to revise the underlined portion of sentence 12 (reproduced below)?

    Not only that, friendships which I have made there were carried into the rest of my school life.

    (A) And,
    (B) Moreover,
    (C) Nevertheless,
    (D) Sequentially,
    (E) Finally,

57. The author could best improve sentence 14 (reproduced below) by

    There are doubtless other ways of city government saving the money they require.

    (A) making an analogy to historical events
    (B) taking alternative points of view into account
    (C) including a personal anecdote about her participation in team sports
    (D) speculating about the motivations of those advocating cuts
    (E) providing examples of other areas in which spending could be reduced

Questions 58–61 are based on the following passage.

(1) Until recently, I was convinced I had no musical ability whatsoever. (2) In grade school, I could hardly keep my voice in tune with other singers around me. (3) I thought that I would never play a musical instrument or become a rock star. (4) I really enjoyed music, just no one thought I had any talent at all.

(5) When I entered junior high I took music classes with our teacher, Mr. Daniels. (6) At first he seemed really stern and strict. (7) He gave us lots of warnings that even though he had a reputation for being harsh around school, the reality was ten times worse. (8) But after a couple of weeks, he started encouraging us to get into musical ensembles. (9) At first I was disinterested, thinking that I would be ridiculed as to my contribution. (10) Mr. Daniels kept insisted that everyone had to play some kind of instrument, so I chose his handbell choir. (11) Other kids thought handbells were stupid, but I liked the sound they made—it was so much purer than the electric guitar. (12) Mr. Daniels coached us regular after school. (13) Not only did the group actually start to sound good, but also I discovered that I had some rhythmic talents that no one had suspected. (14) Maybe I will be a rock star yet! (15) The whole experience showed me that with encouragement and a sense of adventure you can overcome your limitations. (16) As our former First Lady Eleanor Roosevelt once said, sometimes "you must do that which you think you cannot do."

58. Which of the following versions of sentence 4 (reproduced below) is best?

    I really enjoyed music, just no one thought I had any talent at all.

    (A) (As it is now)
    (B) Even though I really enjoyed music, just no one thought I had any talent at all.
    (C) I really enjoyed music, and therefore no one thought I had any talent at all.
    (D) Although I really enjoyed music, no one thought I had any talent at all.
    (E) The music was enjoyable to me, however no one thought I had any talent at all.

59. Which of the following sentences, if added after sentence 4, would best link the first paragraph with the rest of the essay?

    (A) As a result, I learned that other people's opinions are irrelevant.

    (B) However, I soon met an inspiring person who disproved this assumption.

    (C) This was why no one thought I would become a rock star.

    (D) Nevertheless, I knew all along that I possessed a form of musical genius.

    (E) I have held these beliefs about my musical ability for many years.

60. In the context of the second paragraph, which of the following is the best version of the underlined portion of sentence 11 (reproduced below)?

    Other kids thought handbells were stupid, but I liked the sound they made—it was so much purer than the electric guitar.

    (A) (As it is now)

    (B) it was so much more pure than the electric guitar

    (C) the sound of it was so much purer than the electric guitar

    (D) compared to the electric guitar, its sound was so much purer

    (E) it was so much purer than the sound of the electric guitar

61. Which of the following is the best version of the underlined portion of sentence 13 (reproduced below)?

    Not only did the group actually start to sound good, but also I discovered that I had some rhythmic talents that no one had suspected.

    (A) (As it is now)

    (B) The group actually started

    (C) While the group actually started

    (D) Not only was the group actually starting

    (E) Although the group was actually starting

Questions 62–67 are based on the following passage.

(1) Despite his early death at 35, Austrian composer Wolfgang Amadeus Mozart is one the most famous musicians in history for three reasons. (2) He was extraordinarily talented, he was exposed to music at an early age, and his love of it. (3) Mozart's talent showed early. (4) At age seven, he was already writing sonatas for the harpsichord. (5) He could improvise music at the keyboard and played any piece of music in any style—even when blindfolded!

(6) Mozart was always encouraged and even driven by his father. (7) Leopold Mozart was a composer, and Wolfgang learned to play and read music when he was a small child. (8) To establish his son early and build a path for his future career, he lost no time showing him off to audiences. (9) He arranged for six-year-old Wolfgang to play in the palaces of most of the major European cities. (10) Leopold Mozart determining that his gifted son should reap the rewards his talent deserved.

(11) And Mozart loved music. (12) As a child, Leopold was often surprised with tunes his son had written. (13) Some of these little pieces were so technically challenging that although Wolfgang could play them easily, his father's adult friends and colleagues could not play them at all! (14) He once wrote that composing music was such a delight to him that he could not describe it in words.

62. In context, what is the best way to revise and combine sentences 1 and 2 (reproduced below)?

    Despite his early death at 35, Austrian composer Wolfgang Amadeus Mozart is one the most famous musicians in history for three reasons. He was extraordinarily talented, he was exposed to music at an early age, and his love of it.

    (A) Despite his early death at 35, Austrian composer Wolfgang Amadeus Mozart is one the most famous musicians in history for three reasons: he was extraordinarily talented, he was exposed to music at an early age, and he loved it.

    (B) Despite his early death at 35, Austrian composer Wolfgang Amadeus Mozart is one the most famous musicians in history for three reasons, this is because he was extraordinarily talented, he was exposed to music at an early age, and his love of it.

    (C) Despite his early death at 35 years of age, Austrian composer Wolfgang Amadeus Mozart is one the most famous musicians in history for the following three reasons: he was extraordinarily talented, he was exposed to music at an early age, and he loved it.

    (D) Despite his death at 35, which was early, Austrian composer Wolfgang Amadeus Mozart is one the most famous musicians in history for three reasons: that he was extraordinarily talented, that he was exposed to music at an early age, and that he had a love of it.

    (E) Despite his early death at 35, Austrian composer Wolfgang Amadeus Mozart is one the most famous musicians in history for three reasons: he was extraordinarily talented, he was exposed to music at an early age, and his love of it.

63. In context, which revision is needed in sentence 5?

    (A) No revision is needed
    (B) Replace "He" with "Mozart"
    (C) Replace "could improvise" with "could have improvised"
    (D) Replace "played" with "play"
    (E) Eliminate the phrase "in any style"

64. In context, which is the best version of sentence 8 (reproduced below)?

    To establish his son early and build a path for his future career, he lost no time showing him off to audiences.

    (A) (As it is now)
    (B) To establish his son early and build a path for his future career, Leopold Mozart lost no time showing him off to audiences.
    (C) To establish Wolfgang early and build a path for his future career, he lost no time showing him off to audiences.
    (D) To establish his son early and build a path for his future career, he lost no time showing Wolfgang off to audiences.
    (E) To establish his son early and build a path for his future career, Mozart lost no time showing him off to audiences.

65. In context, what revision is necessary in sentence 10?

    (A) No revision is necessary
    (B) Change "determining" to "determines"
    (C) Change "determining" to "was determined"
    (D) Change "determining" to "having determined"
    (E) Change "should reap" to "should be reaping"

66. In context, what is the best version of sentence 12 (reproduced below)?

    As a child, Leopold was often surprised with tunes his son had written

    (A) As a child, the tunes his son had written often surprised Leopold.
    (B) As a child, his son often surprised Leopold with tunes he had written.
    (C) As a child, surprising Leopold with tunes he had written was his son.
    (D) Leopold was often surprised with tunes that, as a child, his son had written.
    (E) Tunes written by his son as a child often surprised Leopold.

67. Sentence 14 would make the most sense if placed after

    (A) sentence 1
    (B) sentence 2
    (C) sentence 11
    (D) sentence 12
    (E) sentence 13

IF YOU LEARNED ONLY FOUR THINGS IN THIS CHAPTER . . . .

1. You will be tested on basic grammar, sentence structure, word choice, and idiomatic expressions.
2. You should be familiar with the 16 common errors that Identifying Sentence Errors questions test.
3. You should be familiar with the 5 common errors that Improving Sentences questions test.
4. Understanding context is important to answer Improving Paragraph questions.

ANSWERS TO THE QUESTIONS ON PAGE 53

What Are the Three Types of Multiple-Choice Questions?

- Identifying Sentence Errors
- Improving Sentences
- Improving Paragraphs

What Rules Should I Know to Answer These Questions?

- Identifying Sentence Errors questions are all Spot-the-Mistake questions.
- Improving Sentences questions are all Fix-the-Mistake questions.
- Improving Paragraphs questions are General Organization, Revising Sentences, or Combining Sentences questions.

What Strategies Will Help Me Be Successful Answering These Questions?

- Kaplan's Target Strategy for Identifying Sentence Errors
  - Step 1. Read the whole sentence, listening for the mistake.
  - Step 2. If you clearly hear the mistake, choose it and move on.
  - Step 3. If you don't hear the mistake immediately, eliminate each underlined choice that contains no error.
  - Step 4. Choose from the remaining choices.

- Kaplan's Target Strategy for Improving Sentences
  - Step 1. Read the sentence carefully, listening for the mistake.
  - Step 2. Identify the error or errors.
  - Step 3. Predict a correction.
  - Step 4. Check the choices for a match that doesn't introduce a new error.

- Kaplan's Target Strategy for Improving Paragraphs
    - Step 1. Read the passage for the overall idea and tone.
    - Step 2. Read the question.
    - Step 3. Reread the relevant portion and its context.
    - Step 4. Predict the correction.
    - Step 5. Check for a match that doesn't introduce a new error.

ANSWERS AND EXPLANATIONS

Identifying Sentence Errors Questions

1.   B

The relative pronoun *which* refers to the soldiers, but *which* cannot be used to refer to people, only to things. The sentence should use the word *who* instead.

2.   D

Another pronoun error: in this sentence, it is not clear whether *his* refers to Adams or to Jefferson; hence this sentence contains a vague pronoun reference.

3.   D

Affect and *effect* are commonly confused words. Here, *affect* (meaning *to influence* or *to have an effect on*) would be the correct word, not *effect*.

4.   C

Faulty comparison: ants are being compared to all the other social insects in the *Hymenoptera* order. Since this order includes far more than two insect species, the superlative *most successful* should be used instead of the comparative *more successful*.

5.   A

Take out the words *my sister and*, and the error of pronoun case becomes obvious—you wouldn't say *for I*. Since this pronoun is the object of the preposition *for*, it should be in the objective case: for my sister and *me*.

6.   E

The sentence contains no error.

7.   B

In the second half of the sentence, the verb *was* does not agree with its subject, *few*. *Few* is a plural noun, so the sentence should read *there were few*.

8.   C

If you look for the antecedent of the pronoun *it* here, you won't find it—this is a case of ambiguous pronoun reference.

9.   D

This is an example of an idiom error. The correct preposition should be *a mixture of, not a mixture from*.

10.   E

The sentence contains no error.

11.   D

Number agreement problems: since *students* is a plural noun, the second part of the sentence should also be plural: *as general practitioners*.

12.   E

The sentence contains no error, although the phrasing may have sounded strange to your ear.

13.   C

Nonidiomatic preposition after verb: *would of* is not standard written English, and it makes no sense. The sentence should read *would have grown up*.

14   D

The correct idiom here should be *preferable to*, not *preferable than*.

15.   C

The way it's written, *Patricia's résumé* is being compared to the *other applicant*, which is not parallel. *Patricia's résumé* should be compared to the *other applicant's résumé*.

16.   D

The pronoun *their* is plural and does not agree in number with its singular antecedent, *motorist*. The sentence should read *his or her license*.

17. B

The subject *one* takes a singular verb: *not one* of the jurors *was* going to believe the alibi.

18. D

The context makes it clear that the accident was *not* averted; hence the sentence is describing a situation that is contrary to fact. When you know that something *did* happen (but would likely have been avoided if things had been different), *might* is the correct word to use. *May have* suggests that you are not sure whether a thing happened or not: e.g., "I will try Dr. Miller's office, but she may have left already."

19. A

Not hardly is a double negative.

20. E

The sentence contains no error.

21. E

(A) properly uses *among* and *most* in a comparison of more than two items. (B) is the appropriate plural pronoun with the antecedent *fast food chains*. (C) correctly uses *between* to compare two items. (Each compound object of this preposition is separate. Remember, only the conjunction *and* can form a compound; *or* cannot.) (D) correctly uses the objective pronoun form.

22. A

Here, *M. Dubois* is being compared to *other gourmet restaurants*. To form a correct comparison, (A) should read "Like chefs in other." (B) uses the correct pronoun form as the object of the preposition. In (C), *he* is the proper pronoun to refer to M. Dubois, and the verb agrees with its singular subject. (D) makes appropriate use of the infinitive verb form.

23. C

Its sharp wit and *by presenting* should have parallel structures, so (C) is incorrect. *High Fidelity* is already a classic, so (A) is correctly in the past tense. (B) properly uses an adjective to modify *High Fidelity*, and (D) is appropriate idiomatic usage.

24. B

Dangerous and dirty places in (B) refers to the singular subject in the second clause, *New York City*. Therefore, *places* should also be singular. (A) is correct usage of both the past tense and the infinitive in context. (C) agrees with its plural subject *tourists*. (D) is the appropriate verb tense, since the action is in the recent past and is still occurring (*over the past few years* indicates this).

25. B

The singular pronoun *one* used in the third clause and, since it is not underlined, cannot be changed. Therefore, the underlined pronoun *we* must be changed because it is inconsistent; the error is in (B). (A) is appropriate use of the infinitive. (C) properly uses an adverb to modify an adjective. (D) uses the appropriate preposition in context.

26. E

(A) is correct use of the past perfect to refer to one past action (*Bill had hoped*) that preceded another (*he realized*). (B) is correct idiomatic usage. (C) is an appropriate verb phrase in context. (D) is proper use of the infinitive.

27. B

Even though *languages* is closer to the verb *require*, its subject is actually the singular *process*; the error is in (B). (A) and (C) are correct idiomatic usage. (D) is consistent present tense verb use, and properly uses the adjective *slow* to modify the noun progress.

28. E

This sentence is correct as written. (A) is an appropriate verb phrase in context. (B) is correct preposition usage. (C) properly uses an adjective to modify *night*. (D) agrees with its singular subject *Grace Poole*.

29. C

Although a commission is made up of a number of people, the noun itself is singular; (C) should be "its." (A) appropriate uses an adverb to modify an adjective, and an adjective to modify the noun *opinions*. (B) is an appropriate verb phrase in context. (D) uses the idiomatically correct preposition, and an adjective to describe *city square*.

30. D

Although *benefits* is the closest noun to the verb *were*, the subject of the verb is actually the singular *program*; (D) should be "was." (A) uses an appropriate verb tense in context. (B) appropriately modifies the noun *program*. (C) is a correctly used prepositional phrase.

Improving Sentences Questions

31. C

As written, this is a run-on sentence. (C) corrects this by making the first clause subordinate. (B) and (D) use transition words that are inappropriate in context. (E) misuses the semicolon splice.

32. D

As written, this sentence is unnecessarily wordy, and the conjunction *and* merely strings the ideas together, without relating them in any way. (D) corrects both errors. (B) is awkward and introduces the passive voice unnecessarily. (C) is even wordier than the original sentence. (E) is awkward and still too wordy.

33. D

As written, it is unclear what noun *particularly those in European history* is intended to modify. (D) corrects this error without adding any other ones. (B) is grammatically incorrect. The singular verb is in (C) does not agree with its subject *Some*, which is grammatically plural. (E) is a sentence fragment.

34. D

As written, this sentence is a fragment. (D) adds a predicate verb without introducing any additional errors. (B) and (E) do not address the error. (C) is incorrect grammatical structure.

35. C

As written, this is a run-on sentence. Both clauses are independent, so a comma cannot join them. (C) corrects this error by using a semicolon splice. (B) and (D) do not address the error. (E) leaves the meaning of the second clause incomplete.

36. B

The underlined selection here is awkward and wordy. (B) expresses the same idea more clearly and concisely. (C) introduces an inconsistent verb tense. (D) does not express the correct relationship between the clauses. (E) is awkward and unnecessarily wordy.

37. C

The transition words *considering that* do not accurately express the cause and effect relationship between the clauses. Both (C) and (D) correct this error with the *because*. However, (D) uses a verb tense that is incorrect in context; *will blend* indicates a future action, but Louisa May Alcott's books were written in the past. (B) does not address the error. (E) also uses the future tense.

38. E

The preposition *as* here has a compound object; (E) is the only choice that puts *brightest and…most unruly* in parallel form. (B), (C), and (D) do not address the error.

39. E

As written, this sentence is overly wordy. Additionally, *mindful…for* is idiomatically incorrect; in English, we are "mindful of." (E) corrects both errors. In (B), *for* is the incorrect preposition in context. (C) and (D) are even wordier than the original sentence, and *for the fact being* in (D) is incorrect grammatical structure.

40. E

As written, this sentence calls *the representative of China* one of *the countries on the UN Security Council.* Although it's slightly longer than some of the other choice, only (E) is correct in context. (B), (C), and (D) do not address the error.

41. C

For the sake of parallelism, all three things in this list must be in the same grammatical form. *Confusion* and *memory loss* are both nouns, so *impaired language skills* is the best choice to complete the sentence.

42. B

Upon entering the jail is an introductory phrase that describes the prisoners (they are the ones entering the jail). As the sentence is worded, it sounds as though the prisoners' personal belongings are entering the jail. (B) and (E) are the only two choices that place *the prisoners* right next to the phrase that describes them. (B) is the best choice; (E) puts the verb in an awkward and incorrect tense.

43. B

Choice (B) is the best way to rephrase this run-on sentence; it expresses, in an economical and graceful way, the logical connection between these two pieces of information about the albatross.

44. E

So much should be followed by the preposition *as*. (E) completes the comparison and conforms to the rules of parallelism; *administrative successes* (an adjective-noun pair) is balanced by *military failures*.

45. D

The underlined portion of the sentence is wordy and awkward. (D) is a concise and correct rephrasing (note that it is also the shortest answer choice).

46. A

The sentence contains no error. Choices (B) through (E) are all awkward or grammatically incorrect.

47. B

The three items in this list should be in parallel grammatical form. The best way to correct the error is to rephrase all three as infinitive verbs. (Note, again, that the correct answer is also the shortest and most concise.)

48. C

The second half of the sentence is an explanation of the first half, and a colon best expresses this logical connection. (A), (B), and (D) all introduce sentence fragments, and (E) uses the wrong verb tense and incorrectly presents the camera seizure as a consequence (not an explanation) of the first half of the sentence.

49. A

The sentence contains no error and is not wordy or awkward.

50. B

The sentence contains a misplaced modifier: it sounds as though O'Toole's *career* is known for his portrayal of T. E. Lawrence. The introductory phrase describes *Peter O'Toole* (the man, not his career); hence, Peter O'Toole should come directly after it. Only choices (B) and (C) begin correctly, and (C) is poorly worded.

51. C

The best way to repair this run-on sentence while preserving the logical relationship between the two halves of the sentence is with choice (C), which correctly presents the second half of the sentence as a consequence of the first. (A), (B), and (E) are all run-ons, and (D) makes *spectators* the subject of *endangered*.

52. E

The underlined portion of this sentence is passive, wordy, and awkward. A good rephrasing will begin with *he* and will be in the active voice. (B) and (E) are possibilities, but (B) is still somewhat awkward and puts the verb into the past perfect for no apparent reason. (E) is clear and concise.

Improving Paragraphs Questions

53. D

The key to this problem is realizing that *I myself* is redundant—if the author has already used *I*, there's no need to add *myself* to clarify. (D) provides the best fix here—notice that it's also the shortest, most straightforward answer. Choices (A) and (E) still include *myself*. (C) substitutes another redundancy—the word *personally*. (B) is unnecessarily convoluted and is missing a comma following *I believe*.

54. C

The context here suggests a strong link between the two sentences—the idea is that sports provide students with the chance to strive for greatness by showing them it takes courage. Choice (C) is the best answer. (A) introduces an illogical contrast. (B) creates a sentence fragment. (D) uses the passive voice unnecessarily. In (E), the verb *show* doesn't agree with the subject *it*.

55. C

The key to this sentence is spotting a subject-verb agreement problem—the subject in the sentence is *top athletes*, not *Michael Jordan*—he's only introduced as an example of a top athlete. So the underlined pronouns should be *them* (to agree with *young people*) and *their* (to agree with *top athletes*).

56. B

To fix this ambiguous introductory phrase, you're looking for a conjunction that expresses the idea of listing an *additional benefit* of participation in team sports. (B) *moreover* does this effectively. (A)'s *and* is not an idiomatic conjunction with which to begin a sentence. (C) creates an unnecessary contrast. In (D), *sequentially* means in order, not *consequently*. (E), *finally*, is wrong because this sentence describes the second item in a list of two.

57. E

Sentence 14 provides a weak ending to the passage because it refers to *other ways of the city government saving money*, without suggesting what these might be. So the best improvement to sentence 14 might be (E) to provide examples of alternative areas for cuts. (A) would be an odd solution—historical events haven't been mentioned thus far in the passage. (B) would weaken the essay just at the point at which the author needs to strengthen it. (C) would be repetitive—the author has already included a personal anecdote. Finally, (D) would simply offer a digression at this point.

58. D

The word *just* creates a run-on sentence here that needs fixing. To combine both clauses in a logical manner, you need to remove *just* and add conjunctions that express the idea of *contrast—in spite of* the author's enjoyment of music, everyone thought he had no talent. (D) is the best

answer here. (B)'s wrong because it still includes *just*. (C)'s not logical—why would people conclude the author was talentless if he enjoyed music? (E)'s *however* is the wrong conjunction—it expresses contrast, but it doesn't link the two phrases to fix the run-on.

59. B

A good setup for paragraph 2 would be a sentence that leads into the author's discovery that he had musical ability and introduces Mr. Daniels. (B) accomplishes this. (A)'s illogical because Mr. Daniel's opinion soon persuades the author to try playing music. (C) and (E) are *non sequiturs*—they don't lead into paragraph 2 in any way. (D)'s too extreme and a bit premature—the author doesn't discover his talent until mid-paragraph 2.

60. E

The key here is realize that sentence 11 contains an illogical comparison. The *sound of the handbell* cannot be purer than the *electric guitar*—it has to be purer than the *sound of the electric guitar*, as (E) suggests. None of the other choices fixes this problem.

61. A

There is no error in this sentence—*Not only… but also* is a common and perfectly idiomatic expression.

62. A

There are two problems here. The sentences are choppy as written, and the items in the second sentence's list are not parallel. (A) does the best job of combining the sentences and corrects the parallelism error. (B) creates a run-on sentence: two independent clauses combined with a comma splice. (C) and (D) address the errors, but unnecessarily add additional words and phrases, making the sentence wordier than it needs to be. (E) correctly combines the sentences, but fails to address the parallelism problem.

63. D

The conjunction "and" requires that the two verbs in the compound predicate be in parallel form, which they are not here ("He could improvise...and played..."). (D) makes the two verbs parallel. (B) is unnecessary—the pronoun "He" clearly refers to Mozart. (C) introduces an inconsistent verb tense. (E) alters the meaning of the sentence.

64. B

This sentences uses the pronouns "his," "he," and "him." Sometimes the pronoun refers to the elder Mozart, sometimes it refers to Wolfgang, so the reader is likely to lose track of which person is being referred to. (B) is best because none of the pronouns is ambiguous. (C) and (D) still leave some pronoun usage unclear. (E) is confusing because "Mozart" could refer to either of the men.

65. C

As written, this sentence is actually a fragment. (Remember, the *–ing* verb form can never be a predicate verb.) Changing "determining" to "was determined" corrects the problem. (B) and (E) introduce verb tenses that are inappropriate in context. (D) does not correct the error.

66. B

Leopold was not a child when he was surprised by his son's tunes; his son was. (B) corrects the error without introducing any additional issues. In (A), the phrase "As a child," is modifying "tunes." (C) and (E) introduce the passive voice unnecessarily. (D) is awkwardly worded.

67. C

The best choice here is (C), because the pronoun "he" in sentence 14 refers to "Mozart," and the ideas make sense in sequence. (A) is incorrect because sentence 14 does not give the three reasons referred to in sentence 1. Placing it after sentence 2, as (B) suggests, does not make sense in context. (D) is wrong because sentences 12 and 13 deal with the same specific detail and should not be separated. (E) is incorrect because the pronoun reference would be unclear and the ideas in sentence 14 do not follow as logically from sentence 13 as they do from sentence 11.

How to Attack the Critical Reading Component

Section Three of the Kaplan SAT Premier Program covers the two Critical Reading question types on the exam: Sentence Completion questions and Reading Comprehension questions. The Reading Comprehension questions are based on two kinds of reading passages—short passages and long passages.

Chapter Six: **SAT Critical Reading Basics**

- **What Question Types Make Up the Critical Reading Component?**
- **What Should I Know About Sentence Completion Questions?**
- **What Should I Know About Reading Comprehension Questions?**

There are three Critical Reading sections on the SAT.

Length	Content	Type
25 minutes	Sentence Completion and Reading Comprehension (short and long)	Multiple choice
25 minutes	Sentence Completion and Reading Comprehension (short and long)	Multiple choice
20 minutes	Sentence Completion and Reading Comprehension (short and long)	Multiple choice

The Critical Reading component of the SAT is designed to test three basic skills:

- Vocabulary—both the breadth of your vocabulary and your ability to determine meaning from context
- Reasoning skills—including your ability to determine the relationship between words and ideas
- Reading skills—how well you understand what you read (main idea, tone, etc.)

The Critical Reading section of the SAT includes two types of questions.

1. Sentence Completion questions
2. Reading Comprehension questions

To do well on SAT Critical Reading, you need to be systematic in your approach to each question type. We'll describe each type in more detail in a moment.

Sentence Completion questions are the fastest question type of the three because there is no passage to read—just a sentence with one or two blanks that you need to fill in. You can earn points faster on these questions than on Reading Comprehension questions, which require you to read anywhere from one to three paragraphs. Thus, you should do these first, even if they are the last questions in the section.

You might want to do the Reading Comprehension questions based on the shorter passages right after that. Why? It takes less time to read a short passage than it does to read a long one, so the short passage points can be accumulated faster. By working on the long passage questions last, you won't run the risk of getting bogged down on the longer passages and leaving yourself only a few minutes for the short passages and Sentence Completion questions.

Now that you know what order to work through the Critical Reading section, let's take a look the question types. (We go into detail in the chapters that follow.)

 GO ONLINE

Check out your new practice quiz every month.

SENTENCE COMPLETION QUESTIONS

The Sentence Completion question sets are arranged in order of difficulty. The first few questions in a set might be fairly straightforward and manageable. The middle few questions will be a little harder, and the last few questions should be the most difficult. Keep this in mind as you work.

Sentence Completion questions look like this:

> Although this small and selective publishing house is famous for its -------
> standards, several of its recent novels have appealed to the general population.
>
> (A) proletarian
> (B) naturalistic
> (C) discriminating
> (D) imitative
> (E) precarious

To answer this type of question, you must choose the word that best completes the sentence. We have specific strategies for tackling this question type in Chapter Seven. In case you're curious, the answer for this question is C, *discriminating*.

READING COMPREHENSION QUESTIONS

As we mentioned, there are two kinds of Reading Comprehension passages: short and long. Short passages are approximately 100–150 words long. They are typically followed by two questions. Long passages are approximately 400–850 words long and are typically followed by 8–13 questions.

The passages and questions are predictable. The topics are drawn from the humanities, social sciences, natural sciences, and fiction. The questions ask about the overall tone and content of a passage, the details used, and what the author's overall meaning may be. You will also have one or more *paired-passage* question sets consisting of two related excerpts. Those questions will ask you to compare and contrast the two passages. (You'll see an example of this in Chapter Nine.)

Reading Comprehension questions are not arranged by difficulty. That means easy, medium, and hard questions can appear in any order. Any time you find yourself spending too much time on a question, skip it and return to it later.

Reading Comprehension questions are covered in detail in Chapters Eight and Nine.

 **AVAILABLE ON CD-ROM**

With 5 more full-length practice tests on the CD-ROM, you'll be ready to master the Critical Reading component on Test Day.

IF YOU LEARNED ONLY THREE THINGS IN THIS CHAPTER . . . .

1. The Critical Reading component tests vocabulary, reasoning, and reading skills.
2. Sentence Completion questions are arranged by order of difficulty.
3. Reading Comprehension questions are not arranged by order of difficulty.

ANSWERS TO THE QUESTIONS ON PAGE 107

What Question Types Make Up the Critical Reading Component?

- Sentence Completion questions
- Long-Passage Reading Comprehension questions
- Short-Passage Reading Comprehension questions

What Should I Know About Sentence Completion Questions?

- These questions require you to fill in either one or two blanks in a sentence from a list of words.

What Should I Know About Reading Comprehension Questions?

- These questions ask about the overall tone and content of a passage, the details used in the passage, and the author's main point in the passage.
- Some passages may be paired passages that ask about the differences and similarities between the passages.

Chapter Seven: **Sentence Completion Strategies**

- **What is the Best Strategy for Acing Sentence Completion Questions?**
- **How Can I Learn to Use Clue Words and Predict the Answer?**
- **What Should I Do When I Come Across a Hard Sentence Completion Question?**

Sentence Completion questions are probably the Critical Reading section's most student-friendly question type. Unlike the Reading Comprehension questions that make up the bulk of this section, Sentence Completion questions require you to pay attention to just one sentence at a time.

THE FORMAT

Sentence Completion questions are basically fill-in-the-blank questions. The instructions for Sentence Completion questions are as follows.

Directions: Each sentence below has one or two blanks, each blank indicating that something has been omitted. Beneath the sentence are five words or sets of words labeled A through E. Choose the word or set of words that, when inserted in the sentence, best fits the meaning of the sentence as a whole.

> EXAMPLE:
>
> Today's small, portable computers contrast markedly with the earliest electronic computers, which were -------.
>
> (A) effective
> (B) invented
> (C) useful
> (D) destructive
> (E) enormous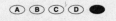

In this example, the new, small, portable computers are contrasted with old computers. You can infer that old computers must be the opposite of small and portable, so (E), *enormous*, is the answer.

As you can see, you need to determine how the parts of the sentence relate to each other first in order to figure out how to fill in the blank. We'll show you how to do this.

WHAT ARE CLUE WORDS?

Clue words tell you how the parts of a sentence fit together to create meaning. Structural clues help you to get a fix on whether the sentence will continue along in the same line or shift directions and contrast with the rest of the sentence. Be on the lookout for structural clues such as the following:

Continuations:

- ; (a semicolon)
- and
- because
- also
- consequently

Contrasts:

- but
- however
- although
- despite
- yet

The more clues you uncover, the clearer the sentence becomes, and the better you can predict what goes in the blanks. Take a look at this example.

> Though some have derided it as -------, the search for extraterrestrial intelligence has actually become a respectable scientific endeavor.

Here, *though* is a clue word. *Though* sets up a contrast between the way some have *derided* (belittled or ridiculed) the search for extraterrestrial intelligence and the fact that the scientific endeavor has become respectable. Another important clue is *actually*. *Actually* completes the contrast: Though some think the endeavor ridiculous, the reality is that it has become respectable.

These clues tell you that whatever goes in the blank must complete the contrast implied by the word *though*. Therefore, to fill in the blank, you need a word that would be used to describe the opposite of *a respectable scientific endeavor*. *Foolish* or *trivial* would be good predictions for the blank.

◎ **KAPLAN'S TARGET STRATEGY FOR SENTENCE COMPLETION QUESTIONS**

This is Kaplan's powerful Target Strategy for tackling Sentence Completion questions. If you can master this strategy, you will be on your way to a higher score on Sentence Completion questions.

Step 1.   Read the sentence for clue words.

Step 2.   Predict the answer.

Step 3.   Select the best match.

Step 4.   Plug your answer choice back into the sentence.

Step 1. Read the Sentence for Clue Words

Read the sentence. Now think about the sentence for five seconds. Take special note of the clue words. A clue word like *but* tells you to expect a CONTRAST in the next part of the sentence; a clue word like *moreover* tells you that what follows is a CONTINUATION of the same idea. Clue words such as *and, but, such as, however*, and *although* tell you how the parts of the sentence will relate to each other.

▶ **GO ONLINE**

Check out your new practice quiz every month.

Step 2. Predict the Answer

Decide what sort of word should fill the blank or blanks. Do this before looking at the answer choices. You don't have to guess the *exact* word; a rough idea of the *kind* of word you'll need will do. It's often enough to simply predict whether the missing word is positive or negative. But often you will be able to go farther. For example, you may be able to predict whether you need a pair of synonyms to fill in the blanks or two words that contrast.

Step 3. Select the Best Match

Compare your prediction to each answer choice. Read every answer choice before deciding which answer best completes the sentence.

Step 4. Plug Your Answer Choice into the Sentence

Put your answer choice in the blank (or blanks). Only one choice should really make sense. If you've gone through the four steps and more than one choice still looks good, eliminate the choice(s) that you can, guess from the remaining choices, and move on. If all of the choices look great or all of the choices look terrible, circle the question and come back to it when you've finished the section.

Let's unleash the powers of Kaplan's Target Strategy for Sentence Completion Questions on a sample question.

> The king's ------- decisions as a diplomat and admin-
> istrator led to his legendary reputation as a just and
> ------- ruler.
>
> (A) quick . . capricious
> (B) equitable . . wise
> (C) immoral . . perceptive
> (D) generous . . witty
> (E) clever . . uneducated

Step 1. Read the Sentence for Clue Words

The clues here are the phrase *led to* and the word *just*. You know that the kind of decisions the king made *led to* his having a reputation as a just and ------- ruler. So whatever goes in both blanks must be consistent with *just*.

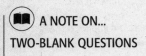

A NOTE ON...

TWO-BLANK QUESTIONS

Another approach for two-blank Sentence Completion questions is to take them one blank at a time. Choose the easier blank, cross out any choices that clearly don't fit, and finish by checking ONLY the remaining choices for the other blank.

Step 2. Predict the Answer

Both blanks must contain words that are similar in meaning. Because of his ------- decisions, the king is viewed as a just and ------- ruler. So if the king's decisions were good, he'd be remembered as a good ruler, and if his decisions were bad, he'd be remembered as a bad ruler.

Just, which means *fair*, is a positive-sounding word; therefore, you can predict that both blanks will be similar in meaning and that both will be positive words. You can write a plus sign in the blanks or over the columns of answer choices to remind you.

Step 3. Select the Best Match

One effective way to choose the best answer is to determine which answer choices have the kinds of words you predicted—in this case, words that are both positive and synonymous. In (A), *quick* and *capricious* are not necessarily positive, and they are not similar in meaning. (*Capricious* means erratic or fickle.) In (B), *equitable* means fair. *Equitable* and *wise* are similar, and they're both positive. When you plug them in, they make sense, so (B) looks right. But check out the others to be sure. In (C), *immoral* and *perceptive* are not similar at all; moreover, *perceptive* is positive, but *immoral* is not. In (D), *generous* and *witty* are both positive, but they are not very similar, and they don't make sense in the sentence. In (E), *clever* and *uneducated* aren't similar, and *clever* is positive, but *uneducated* isn't. Thus, (B) is the best match.

Step 4. Plug Your Answer Choice into the Sentence

The king's equitable decisions as a diplomat and administrator led to his legendary reputation as a just and wise ruler. Choice (B) is the correct answer.

GETTING THE HARD QUESTIONS AT THE END RIGHT

Sentence Completion questions will go from easiest to hardest, though some sections will start with medium-difficulty questions. The higher the question number, the harder the question, so the last few Sentence Completion questions in a set will be the most difficult.

If you find yourself getting stuck, we have a few techniques to pull you through:

- Avoid tricky wrong answers.
- Take apart tough sentences.
- Work around tough vocabulary.

Avoid Tricky Wrong Answers

Toward the end of a set, watch out for tricky answer choices. Avoid the following:

- Opposites of the correct answer
- Words that sound right just because they're hard
- Two-blankers in which one word fits but the other doesn't

Take a look at the following example.

> Granted, Janyce is extremely --------; still, it is
> difficult to imagine her as a professional comedian.
>
> (A) dull
> (B) garrulous
> (C) effusive
> (D) conservative
> (E) witty

 BE SMART!

Before picking a word that you don't know the meaning of, be sure to look at the other choices to eliminate those words for which you do know the meanings.

Read this sentence carefully or you may get tricked. If you read too quickly, you might think, "If Janyce is hard to imagine as a comedian, she's probably extremely dull or conservative. So I'll pick either (A) or (D)." But the sentence is saying something else.

Remember to pick up the clues. The key here is the clue word *granted*, which is another way of saying *although*. So the sentence means, "Sure Janyce is funny, but she's no professional comedian." Therefore, the word in the blank must resemble *funny*. That means (E), *witty*, is correct. *Still* is another important clue word that emphasizes the contrast between how Janyce is (witty) and imagining her as a comedian.

Now don't pick an answer just because it sounds hard. *Garrulous* means talkative, and *effusive* means overly expressive. You might be tempted to pick one of these simply because they sound impressive. But they're put on the test just to trick you. Don't choose them without good reason.

Now let's look at a two-blank sentence.

> When the state government discovered that thermal pollution was killing valuable fish, legislation was passed to ------- the dumping of hot liquid wastes into rivers and to ------- the fish population.
>
> (A) discourage . . decimate
> (B) regulate . . quantify
> (C) facilitate . . appease
> (D) discontinue . . devastate
> (E) prohibit . . protect

Look at all the choices. Check out the first blank first. Legislation was not passed to *facilitate* dumping, so that eliminates choice (C). The other four are all possible.

Now check the second blanks. The legislature wouldn't pass a law to *decimate*, *quantify*, or *devastate* the fish population, so (A), (B), and (D) are wrong. Only choice (E), *prohibit . . protect*, fits for both blanks. The legislature might well pass a law to *prohibit* dumping hot liquids and to *protect* fish.

Take Apart Tough Sentences

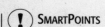 **SMARTPOINTS**

Some sense of the charge of a word—the general positive, negative, or neutral connotation of a word—will often suffice for eliminating a few answer choices.

Some sentences are difficult because they seem to lack the context you need to determine the correct answer. Let's look again at a previously used example.

> Although this small and selective publishing house is famous for its -------standards, several of its recent novels have appealed to the general public.
>
> (A) proletarian
> (B) naturalistic
> (C) discriminating
> (D) imitative
> (E) precarious

In this sentence, the parts of the sentence surrounding the blank seem a little vague, and the word choices are advanced adjectives. What sort of publishing house is it? The answer here is not clear right off the bat. But what if you were stumped and had no idea which word to pick or what the meaning of all of the words were? Sometimes the only thing to do in this situation is to plug in the answer choices and make the best guess based on which word you think gives the most information. Here, we are looking for a word that describes standards that would keep them from publishing books that appeal to the general public.

(A) *Proletarian* standards? Hmmm . . . doesn't seem appropriate. Proletarian means characteristic of the average citizen or working class, so, in fact, it's the opposite of what we need.

(B) *Naturalistic* standards? Not great. It doesn't seem to contrast with the idea of popular appeal.

(C) *Discriminating* standards? Seems to fit. If they are discriminating, they are very selective and would probably not publish books that are popular with the general public.

(D) *Imitative* standards? Sounds weird and doesn't really make sense.

(E) *Precarious* standards? Nope. Again, it doesn't make sense in the context of the sentence, whatever kind of publisher it is.

Choice (C) sounds best and is correct. Although the small publishing house has *discriminating*, or picky, standards, several of its recent novels appeal to a general audience.

 MOBILE PREP

Keep your Sentence Completion questions review on the fast track—practice on the go with Kaplan Mobile.

Now try a complex sentence with two blanks. Use these two important guidelines:

- Try the easier blank first.
- Save time by eliminating all choices that won't work for one blank.

The following example is the fifth question out of a nine-problem set, so it would be considered of medium difficulty.

> These latest employment statistics from the present administration are so loosely documented, carelessly explained, and potentially misleading that even the most loyal senators will ------- the ------- of the presidential appointees who produced them.
>
> (A) perceive . . intelligence
> (B) understand . . tenacity
> (C) recognize . . incompetence
> (D) praise . . rigor
> (E) denounce . . loyalty

It's not so easy to see what goes in the first blank, so try the second blank. You need a word to describe presidential appointees who produced the *loosely documented, carelessly explained,* and *misleading* statistics. Based on these key words, we know that the second blank must be negative. The only second-word answer choice that's definitely negative is (C), *incompetence,* or inability to perform a task. Now try *recognize* in the first blank. It fits, too. (C) must be correct. See how much time you save? This step safely eliminates all choices except the correct answer.

Work Around Tough Vocabulary

Fortunately, you can often figure out enough context to get the correct answer, even if you don't know all of the vocabulary words in the sentence. That's because test developers often provide other clues to help you figure out the intended meaning. Look at the following sentence as an example.

 BE SMART!

Review the word list in Resource Four to become more familiar with SAT vocabulary words.

> Despite her ------- of public speaking experience, the student council member was surprisingly cogent, and expressed the concerns of her classmates persuasively.
>
> (A) hope
> (B) depth
> (C) method
> (D) lack
> (E) union

If you don't know what *cogent* means, work around it. From the sentence, especially the clue word *and*, you know that *cogent* goes with *expressed the concerns of her classmates persuasively*. So you don't have to worry about what *cogent* means. All you need to know is that the student council member was persuasive despite a ------- of speaking experience. *Surprisingly* is another clue. It suggests that the student was not expected to express herself so effectively because she did not have much public-speaking experience. Further, two of the answer choices don't really make sense if you insert them in the blank—a *method* or *union* of speaking experience? Can't be.

Only (D), *lack*, fits the context. *Despite her lack of public speaking experience, the student council member expressed the concerns of her classmates persuasively*. (By the way, *cogent* means convincing, believable, roughly the same as *expressing concern persuasively*.)

Let's look at another Sentence Completion question. This time the tough vocabulary is in the answer choices.

> Advances in technology occur at such a fast pace that dictionaries have difficulty incorporating the ------- that emerge for new inventions.
>
> (A) colloquialisms
> (B) euphemisms
> (C) compensations
> (D) neologisms
> (E) clichés

Whatever goes in the blank has to describe the *new inventions*. If you don't know what all of these words mean, don't give up. Rule out as many choices as you can, and guess among the remaining ones.

You can eliminate (C) and (E)—words that you are probably familiar with—right off the bat. They don't describe new inventions and wouldn't be put in a dictionary. Now you can make an educated guess. Remember, educated guessing will help your score more than guessing blindly or skipping the question. So use your knowledge of prefixes, suffixes, word roots, and foreign languages to try to rule out one or more of the remaining choices.

For example, you might know that *neo* means *new*, so the word *neologisms* might be the best choice for something that gets put in a dictionary and describes new inventions. In fact, it's the right answer. *Neologisms* are newly coined words.

If All Else Fails—Guess!

If you're really stumped, don't be afraid to guess. Eliminate all answer choices that can't possibly be right, and guess from the remaining choices. If you have eliminated at least one or two choices, the chance to gain points outweighs the possibility of losing points for incorrect answers.

Now take a deep breath before you go on to practice the strategies you've learned on this Sentence Completion problem set.

 GO ONLINE

You can find word roots on your downloadable Study Sheet for study on the go.

PRACTICE

Select the lettered word or set of words that best completes the sentence.

1. The stranger was actually smaller than I thought; his stature was ------- by the alarm he caused as he loomed up suddenly in the dark alley.

   (A) worsened

   (B) magnified

   (C) disparaged

   (D) disfigured

   (E) admonished

2. Although the risk of a major accident remained -------, the public's concern about such an accident gradually -------.

   (A) steady . . waned

   (B) acute . . persisted

   (C) unclear . . shifted

   (D) obvious . . endured

   (E) pressing . . remained

3. Prior to the American entrance into World War I, President Woodrow Wilson strove to maintain the ------- of the United States, warning both sides against encroachments on American interests.

   (A) involvement

   (B) belligerence

   (C) versatility

   (D) magnanimity

   (E) neutrality

4. The graceful curves of the colonial-era buildings that dominated the old part of the city contrasted sharply with the modern, ------- subway stations and made the latter appear glaringly out of place.

   (A) festive

   (B) grimy

   (C) angular

   (D) gigantic

   (E) efficient

5. The discovery of the Dead Sea Scrolls in the 1940s quickly ------- the popular imagination, but the precise significance of the scrolls is still ------- by scholars.

   (A) impressed . . understood

   (B) alarmed . . obscured

   (C) troubled . . perceived

   (D) sparked . . disputed

   (E) eluded . . debated

6. In Kafka's characteristically surreal story "The Hunger Artist," the main character "entertains" the public by starving himself until he is too ------- to survive.

   (A) glutted

   (B) lachrymose

   (C) emaciated

   (D) superfluous

   (E) satiated

7. Recent editions of the Chinese classic *Tao Te Ching*, based on manuscripts more authoritative than those hitherto available, have rendered previous editions -------.

   (A) incomprehensible
   (B) interminable
   (C) inaccessible
   (D) obsolete
   (E) illegible

8. Despite their outward resemblance, the brothers could not be more ------- temperamentally; while one is quiet and circumspect, the other is brash and -------.

   (A) inimical . . timid
   (B) passionate . . superficial
   (C) dissimilar . . audacious
   (D) different . . forgiving
   (E) alike . . respectful

9. Her scholarly rigor and capacity for ------- enabled her to undertake research projects that less ------- people would have found too difficult and tedious.

   (A) fanaticism . . slothful
   (B) comprehension . . indolent
   (C) analysis . . careless
   (D) negligence . . dedicated
   (E) concentration . . disciplined

10. It was difficult to tell what the auditor was thinking, as his expression was -------.

    (A) palpable
    (B) salient
    (C) titular
    (D) impassive
    (E) bilious

11. As a result of being confined to the rim of the excavation site, the archeologist found it difficult to surmise exactly what the ------- chamber might hold.

    (A) potable
    (B) fulsome
    (C) insensate
    (D) beatific
    (E) subterranean

12. Casey's creative writing teacher praised his story but said it was somewhat ------- and suggested that he ------- it a bit.

    (A) adept…declaim
    (B) gauche…filibuster
    (C) verbose…pare
    (D) contiguous…diffuse
    (E) abortive…abscond

13. Dr. Fowler's compact disc collection clearly revealed his ------- for early jazz recordings.

    (A) penchant
    (B) tenet
    (C) confluence
    (D) phalanx
    (E) hegemony

KAPLAN

14. If all world leaders were to ------- violent solutions to problems, there would soon be a ------- of war.

    (A) emulate...tutelage
    (B) condole...paean
    (C) eschew...cessation
    (D) becloud...demagogue
    (E) mitigate...recidivism

15. The austere life of a medieval monk required sleeping in a ------- cell.

    (A) variegated
    (B) specious
    (C) Spartan
    (D) inchoate
    (E) intransigent

16. The corrupt judge's ------- insistence on his honesty was belied by his ------- unfair rulings.

    (A) colloquial...amorphously
    (B) disingenuous...blatantly
    (C) macabre...morosely
    (D) saturnine...stringently
    (E) opprobrious...truculently

17. The chess-playing computer Big Blue is a ------- opponent, as it never makes a careless mistake.

    (A) illusory
    (B) formidable
    (C) circuitous
    (D) novel
    (E) temporal

18. The leader of the minority party met with members of the business ------- to devise an economic reform package.

    (A) caucus
    (B) aerie
    (C) milieu
    (D) rostrum
    (E) interregnum

19. Because of her ------- the cat burglar was finally caught, when she showed a neighbor her ------- of stolen jewels.

    (A) hubris...cache
    (B) pseudonym...fodder
    (C) yen...vernacular
    (D) calumny...onus
    (E) kismet...platitude

20. One who betrays the trust of a close-knit group is likely to be shunned by his former compatriots, as when, for example, a whistle blower becomes a ------- within her organization.

    (A) exponent
    (B) pariah
    (C) sybarite
    (D) potentate
    (E) paragon

21. Gerald felt his history assignment was not well defined; in fact, he found it rather -------.

    (A) prosaic
    (B) importunate
    (C) epochal
    (D) nebulous
    (E) febrile

22. Just as a criminal could ------- honesty in order to dupe a victim, likewise a superhero might fake ------- in order to trick a villain.

    (A) burnish...histrionics
    (B) ingratiate...aplomb
    (C) feign...duplicity
    (D) aver...sinecure
    (E) thwart...convergence

23. By choosing to live in a relatively impoverished country, Mr. Jones enjoyed a ------- lifestyle, despite having a rather ------- income by European standards.

    (A) replete...squalid
    (B) lavish...paltry
    (C) licentious...obstinate
    (D) cumulative...complacent
    (E) winsome...tortuous

24. Later, it was hard for Maia to say which had been more frightening: the tyrant's ------- stare or his ------- words.

    (A) mawkish...wry
    (B) gamely...imperious
    (C) tenuous...sanctimonious
    (D) incarnadine...implacable
    (E) malevolent...virulent

IF YOU LEARNED ONLY FOUR THINGS IN THIS CHAPTER . . . .

1. Clue words tell you whether the missing word contrasts with or is a continuation of the ideas in the question sentence.

2. Choosing the easier blank first in two-blank questions makes it easier to eliminate answer choices without spending time on the second blank.

3. A knowledge of prefixes, suffixes, word roots, and foreign languages is helpful in determining the meaning of the answer choices.

4. Don't pick answer choices because they sound hard. They are often there to trick you.

ANSWERS TO THE QUESTIONS ON PAGE 111

What is the Best Strategy for Acing Sentence Completion Questions?

- Kaplan's Target Strategy for Sentence Completion Questions

    Step 1. Read the sentence for clue words.

    Step 2. Predict the answer.

    Step 3. Select the best match.

    Step 4. Plug your answer choice back into the sentence.

What are Clue Words, and How Do They Help Predict the Answer?

- Clue words will tell you whether the parts of the sentence are related to or contrasting with each other.

- Knowing whether you are looking for a word to contrast or continue the idea of the sentence will help you predict what type of word you are looking for.

What Should I Do When I Come Across a Hard Sentence Completion Question?

- Keep your eyes open for answer choices given just to trick you, plug in the answer choices to see which best fits the context, or break apart the vocabulary words to get at their meanings.

ANSWERS AND EXPLANATIONS

1. B

The clue here is the phrase *was actually smaller than I thought*. The missing word has to mean *made larger* or *made to seem larger*. Choice (B), *magnified*, is the answer. *Disparaged* (C) means belittled. *Admonished* (E) means scolded. (A) and (D) do not make sense in the context. The stranger's stature cannot be *worsened* because it was never suggested that it was bad in the first place, and a *disfigured* stature would cause alarm, not be caused by alarm.

2. A

The word *although* indicates contrast. The contrast is between the risk and the public's concern. Choice (A) is the only one that presents a clear contrast: the risk didn't decrease, but the public's concern did.

3. E

The phrase *warning both sides against encroachments on American interests* indicates that Wilson was attempting to prevent each side from taking an action that would force the United States to get involved in the war. Choice (E), *neutrality*, gets this point across. *Involvement* (A) suggests the opposite of the correct answer. *Belligerence* (B) is the quality of being warlike; *versatility* (C) means being able to handle a variety of different situations; *magnanimity* (D) is generosity.

4. C

You're specifically told that there's a contrast between the buildings and the subway stations. Checking the answer choices for a word that contrasts in meaning with *graceful curves*, you find that the answer is (C), *angular*, which means *jagged* or *angled*.

5. D

The word *but* indicates contrast. If you plug in the answer choices, (D) makes the most sense with the word *imagination* and completes the contrast: the public became quickly excited about the issue, but agreement among experts as to the significance of the scrolls has been slower in coming. None of the other choices provides a clear contrast of ideas. In addition, *still* suggests a lack of understanding, so (A) and (C) cannot be correct.

6. C

The missing word describes people who starve themselves and become malnourished. Choice (C), *emaciated*, which means extremely thin, is the only choice that really fits. (A) and (E) are the exact opposites of what's needed, and *lachrymose* (B) means tearful. (D), *superfluous*, means unnecessary, which would be a comment on the person's social, not physical, status.

7. D

If new editions of this book are based on *more authoritative*, or more accurate, manuscripts, previous editions would be rendered out-of-date, or *obsolete* (D)—scholars wouldn't use the old editions because the new ones are markedly superior. However, the new edition wouldn't render the old edition *incomprehensible* (A), *interminable* (B), *inaccessible* (C), or *illegible* (E).

8. C

The clue word *despite* indicates that the brothers must have different temperaments—making *dissimilar* (C) and *different* (D) both possibilities. The second word has to contrast with *quiet and circumspect* and be similar in tone to *brash*; *audacious*, or bold, is the only choice that makes sense, so (C) is correct.

9. E

It's easier to start with the second blank. You need a word that goes with *rigor* and contrasts with finding things *difficult and tedious*. *Slothful* (A) and *indolent* (B) both mean lazy, so they're the opposite of what you need. Only *dedicated* (D) and *disciplined* (E) fit. Eliminate the other choices and try (D) and (E) in the first blank. The correct choice will be a quality held by a dedicated, rigorous scholar, so *concentration* (E) is the answer. *Negligence* (D) is the opposite of what you're looking for.

10. D

The key to this question is the word *as*, which signals a cause and effect relationship. You must look for a word that tells you why "it was difficult to tell what the auditor was thinking." *Impassive* means expressionless, revealing nothing. (A), *palpable*, means obvious or easily perceived. *Salient*, (B), means prominent. Choice (C), *titular*, refers to having a title, often in name only. *Bilious*, (E), means sickly or ill humored, both with a connotation of too much bile.

11. E

The logical relationship within this sentence is cause and effect, signaled by the phrase *as a result of*. The archeologist cannot determine what the chamber holds because of being *confined to the rim of the excavation site*. On the rim of a hole, one could not see what is underground, the meaning of *subterranean* (*sub*, below, and *terranean* from *terre*, meaning earth). (A), *potable*, means fit to drink. *Fulsome*, (B), means abundant, often with a connotation of insincerity, as in the phrase *fulsome praise*. (C), *insensate*, means unconscious or lacking awareness. *Beatific*, (D), means showing joy and calmness.

12. C

The second part of the sentence, after *but*, contrasts with the first part, in which Casey's teacher praises his story. Therefore, you are looking for a word for the first blank that denotes a flaw in the writing. The key word for the second blank is *suggested*. That means you are looking for a second word that will correct the flaw noted in the first blank. *Verbose* means wordy, while to *pare* is to trim or cut, in this case words. (A) is incorrect, as *adept* is a positive word meaning skilled. To *declaim* is to recite or speak, usually vehemently. In (B), *gauche* means lacking in social polish, though it's an adjective appropriate to a human, not to writing. To *filibuster* is to delay through speech making. (D), *contiguous* and *diffuse* are in the relationship of possible flaw and remedy, but *contiguous* means touching or adjacent without a break, while *diffuse* means to spread out; so the choices don't fit the sentence. (E)'s choices, *abortive* and *abscond*, mean fruitless or imperfectly developed (abortive) and to flee and hide oneself (abscond), which are extreme choices for a bit of good, though somewhat flawed writing.

13. A

The word *revealed* is the key to this question. It directs you to look for the word that connects *Dr. Fowler's compact disc collection* to *early jazz recordings*. *Penchant* means a definite liking. (B), *tenet*, refers to a belief of doctrine or principle. *Confluence*, choice (C), means a gathering or flowing together, either literal or figurative. (D), *phalanx*, is a close-knit group of people, often used in reference to troops or guards. (E), *hegemony*, refers to the dominance of one nation over others.

14. C

The logical relationship in this sentence is cause and effect, an *if…then* relationship, although in this case the *then* is implied. To *eschew* is to forego or avoid. *Cessation* refers to stopping or ceasing. Avoiding violence, the sentence says, would stop war. (A) is incorrect because to *emulate* is to strive to equal or surpass through imitation, while *tutelage* is instruction or guardianship, from the same root as *tutor*. The words in (B), *condole* and *paean*, are incorrect because *condole* means to feel or express sympathy for another, while *paean* means joyful praise, as a hymn. In (D), *becloud* and *demagogue* mean to obscure or cover, as with clouds (becloud), and a popular leader who appeals to the emotions of the people (demagogue). At first, (E) seems as though it could be correct: to *mitigate* is to alleviate or moderate; but *recidivism* is a relapse into previous bad behaviors, often applied to repeat criminals, and so does not fit the sense of the sentence.

15. C

The verb *required* is the key to this sentence. The *austere life* of a monk *required sleeping in* what kind of cell? *Spartan*, from the Greek city of Sparta, means simple or frugal, in other words, austere. (A), *variegated*, means characterized by variety, especially of color. *Specious*, (B), refers to something that is false, though it has the appearance of truth. (D), *inchoate*, means in an early, imperfect, state of development. (E), *intransigent*, means extreme and uncompromising.

16. B

The correct answer can be determined by the context of the sentence. *Corrupt* is a keyword, as are *honesty* and *belied* (shown to be false, and thus a relationship of contrast), so look for words that relate to honesty, or corruption. *Disingenuous* means not straightforward; *blatantly* means obviously offensive, without any effort to conceal. In other words, the judge misrepresented his honesty, but his obviously unfair rulings showed his representation to be false. In (A), *colloquial* means conversation-like in its informality, and *amorphously* means shapeless or lacking form. In (C), *macabre* means gruesomely horrifying or reminiscent of death, and *morosely* means in a sullen or melancholy manner. *Saturnine* in (D) means tending to be bitter or sardonic in manner, while *stringently* means rigorous or severe. In (E), *opprobrious* means either scornful and abusive, or disgraceful and shameful, so it could possibly fit in the first blank. *Truculently*, however, means bitterly or violently opposed and does not fit the sentence.

17. B

This sentence includes a logical restatement in its structure, signaled by the word *as*. Ask yourself what kind of opponent never makes a careless mistake. *Formidable* means difficult to defeat, thus inspiring awe and dread. (A), *illusory*, means deceptive, as in the word *illusion*. (C), *circuitous* means roundabout, as in *circuit*. *Novel*, (D), means new and different, when it's not referring to a literary form. (E), *temporal*, means limited by time, as is the material world.

18. A

This question must be answered by looking at context. First, note the words that are clues, such as *minority party*, *members*, and *business*, as well as *economic reform package*. You are looking for a term that is used in politics to apply to a group with members. *Caucus* means a group with a special focus within a larger group or party. *Aerie*, (B), is a nest or a house built on a high place. (C), *milieu*, is an environment or setting. *Rostrum*, (D), is an elevated platform for public speaking. (E), *interregnum*, refers to the interruption of the usual functions of government.

19. A

This sentence contains a cause and effect relationship, signaled by the word *because*. The second part of the sentence sheds more light on the chain of cause and effect. *Hubris* is another word for excessive pride. It was the cat burglar's pride that led her to show her neighbor her *cache*, her concealed store, of jewels. In (B), *pseudonym* means alias or assumed name. *Fodder* is food or raw material. *Yen*, (C), means desire; and *vernacular* means everyday, informal language. (D), *calumny* and *onus*, mean slander or false statements and burden or blame, respectively. *Kismet* and *platitude* (E) mean fate or fortune (kismet) and cliché statement (platitude).

20. B

The logical form of this question is one of comparison, as the phrase *for example* tells you. A *pariah* is a social outcast, one who is shunned by a community. (A), *exponent*, in the non-mathematical sense, is one who advocates or speaks for. (C), *sybarite*, refers to a person devoted to

pleasure. *Potentate*, (D), means one who exercises extensive power. *Paragon*, (E), refers to a model of excellence, even perfection.

21. D

The words *in fact* signal a restatement. The logical form of this sentence directs you to look for a restatement of the phrase *not well defined*. *Nebulous* means vague, i.e. not well defined. (A), *prosaic*, from the same root as the word *prose*, means straightforward, lacking in imagination. *Importunate*, (B), means urgent and persistent in requesting. (C), *epochal*, means significant or momentous. *Febrile*, (E), means feverish, either literally or figuratively.

22. C

The relationship signaled in this sentence by *just as* and *likewise* is one of comparison. The comparison is inverted by the choice of the two subjects, the criminal and the superhero. The words *dupe* and *trick* are synonyms that help you see the comparison. When inserted into the blanks, the words *feign* and *duplicity* work by aligning with their counterparts *fake* (feign) and *honesty* (duplicity). Though *fake* and *feign* are synonyms, *honesty* and *duplicity* (deception) are antonyms, which makes sense because a criminal and a superhero would be faking, or feigning, opposite traits. In (A), *burnish* means to make smooth or glossy by rubbing, and *histrionics* is exaggerated emotional behavior. *Ingratiate* in (B) means to seek the good graces of another, and *aplomb* is self-confidence or assurance. To *aver* (D) is to declare or affirm, and a *sinecure* is a job that requires little or no effort to secure or maintain. In (E), to *thwart* is to frustrate or prevent the realization of plans, and *convergence* means meeting or coming together from different directions.

23. B

The logical relationship in this sentence is one of contrast, signaled by the word *despite*. You want to make sure that the first word, an adjective describing *lifestyle*, contrasts with the adjective that describes *income*. Then you also want to look at the introductory clause that tells you Mr. Jones has chosen to live in an impoverished country and ask yourself why someone would make that choice in relation to lifestyle and income. The word *lavish* means abundant, even extravagant; while *paltry* means lacking in worth or trivial. In (A), *replete* means abundantly supplied and *squalid* means dirty and wretched, as from poverty. These words fit the general sense of the sentence but their use is idiomatically incorrect here. *Licentious* in (C) means lacking restraint, especially in sexual connotations; and *obstinate* means stubborn. *Cumulative* (D) means enlarged by successive additions, and *complacent* means unconcerned due to self-satisfaction. *Winsome* (E) means charming, often in a childish way, and *tortuous* means devious and not straightforward, either literally or figuratively.

24. E

In this sentence, the colon indicates an elaboration on the word *frightening*. The word *tyrant* reinforces this concept, so you are looking for words that could express frightening qualities of a tyrant's stare and words. *Malevolent* means exhibiting ill will, and *virulent* means hostile, harmful, or poisonous. The other answer choices can be eliminated, as they do not have the same connotations. *Mawkish* (A) means sickeningly sentimental, and *wry* means dryly humorous. In (B), *gamely* means bravely and *imperious* means arrogantly overbearing. *Tenuous* (C) means having little substance, literally or figuratively, and *sanctimonious* means feigning righteousness. In (D), *incarnadine* means flesh or blood colored, and *implacable* means impossible to appease or satisfy.

Chapter Eight: **Reading Comprehension Strategies—Short Passages**

- What Are the Different Categories of Reading Comprehension Questions?

- What is the Best Strategy for Acing Reading Comprehension Questions?

- How Can I Learn to Read Actively?

LONG AND SHORT PASSAGES

The Reading Comprehension questions are divided into two types—short passages and long passages. We'll cover the short passages in this chapter and then look at the longer passages in Chapter Nine. Just remember that the two types are more alike than they are different. Everything you learn in this chapter will also help you tackle the longer passages.

As we have mentioned, the topics you will see will be based on the humanities, social sciences, natural sciences, and fiction. In order to do well on these, you must read actively and analyze information. You will not, however, need to have any previous knowledge about a topic to answer the questions. Everything you need to know will be right there in front of you.

THE FORMAT

Reading Comprehension instructions tell you to answer questions based on what is stated or implied in the accompanying passage or passages. As with other question types, you should get familiar enough with the format so you can just skim the directions again on the day of the test.

The instructions for the Critical Reading section are simple and are as follows:

Directions: The passages below are followed by questions based on their content; questions following a pair of related passages may also be based on the relationship between the paired passages. Answer the questions on the basis of what is <u>stated</u> or <u>implied</u> in the passages and in any introductory material that may be provided.

THE DIFFERENT CATEGORIES OF READING COMPREHENSION QUESTIONS

When you read passages on the SAT, you're reading for a specific purpose: to be able to correctly answer as many questions as possible. Fortunately, the SAT tends to use the same kinds of Reading Comprehension questions over and over again, so whatever the passage is about and however long it may be, you can expect the same four basic question categories:

- Big Picture
- Little Picture
- Inference
- Vocabulary-in-Context

You can expect slightly more than half of the questions to be Little Picture and Inference questions; fewer (approximately 30%–40%) will be about Big Picture issues and Vocabulary.

Big Picture Questions

Big Picture questions test how well you understand the passage as a whole. They ask about:

- The main point or purpose of a passage or individual paragraphs
- The author's overall attitude or tone
- The logic underlying the author's argument
- How ideas relate to each other in the passage

If you're stumped on a Big Picture question, even after reading the passage, do the Little Picture questions first. They can help you fill in the Big Picture. Big Picture questions will usually be at the end of the question set anyway, so you can often use the question order to help you get a deeper understanding of the whole passage.

Here are two sample Big Picture questions.

> Based on the passage, the author believes that extra-terrestrial life
>
> (A) exists only in science fiction
> (B) is abundant throughout the universe
> (C) will not be discovered in our lifetime
> (D) is physically impossible
> (E) may never be discovered because life may take vastly different forms in other galaxies

The author describes his experience as a grocery store clerk and waiter in order to

(A) show that you should always treat others as you want to be treated
(B) explain why he became a writer
(C) suggest that believing in yourself is the key to success
(D) demonstrate the value of hard work
(E) emphasize the importance of a good education

Little Picture Questions

About a third of Critical Reading questions are Little Picture questions that ask about localized bits of information—usually specific facts or details from the passage. These questions often give you a line reference—a clue to where in the passage you'll find your answer. Beware of answer choices that seem to reasonably answer the question in the stem but that don't make sense in the context of the passage or that are true but refer to a different section of the text.

Little Picture questions test:

- Whether you understand significant information that's stated in the passage
- Your ability to locate information within a text
- Your ability to differentiate between main ideas and specific details

 BE SMART!

Little Picture questions are usually easier to answer than Big Picture questions. Keep this in mind if you're short on time.

Sometimes the answer to a Little Picture question will be directly in the line or lines that are referenced. Other times, you might need to read a few sentences before or after the referenced line(s) to find the correct answer. When in doubt, use the context (surrounding sentences) to confirm the right choice.

Here are some sample Little Picture questions.

The inspiration for Mary Shelley's "monstrous creation" (line 17) came from

(A) a ghost story popular at the time
(B) a tale she remembered from her early childhood
(C) a nightmare she had
(D) a conversation with Lord Byron
(E) a story in the local newspaper

In the phrase "hideous progeny" (line 18), Shelley is referring to

(A) her daughter
(B) her novel
(C) her editor
(D) herself
(E) the reader

Inference Questions

To *infer* is to draw a conclusion based on reasoning or evidence. For example, if you wake up in the morning and there's three feet of fresh snow on the ground, you can infer that school will be canceled.

Often, writers will use suggestion or inference rather than stating ideas directly. But they will also leave you plenty of clues so you can figure out just what they are trying to convey. Inference clues include word choice (diction), tone, and specific details. For example, say a passage states that a particular idea *was perceived as revolutionary*. You might infer from the use of the word *perceived* that the author believes the idea was not truly revolutionary but only *perceived* (or seen) that way.

Thus, Inference questions test your ability to use the information in the passage to come to a logical conclusion. The key to inference questions is to stick to the evidence in the text. Most inference questions have pretty strong clues, so avoid any answer choices that seem far-fetched. If you can't find any evidence in the passage, then it probably isn't the right answer.

Here are two sample Inference questions.

> The author suggests that Henry Ford's experience working on his father's farm
>
> (A) was traumatic
>
> (B) inspired Ford to become an engineer
>
> (C) turned Ford away from his desire to be a
>   farmer
>
> (D) was uneventful
>
> (E) gave him the courage to try out some of his
>   inventions

> It can be inferred from the passage that the author
>
> (A) agrees with Ford that the present is the only
>   thing that matters
>
> (B) believes that Ford placed too much emphasis
>   on success
>
> (C) thinks Ford's industrial revolution under-
>   mined basic human values
>
> (D) believes we should be less dependent upon
>   automobiles
>
> (E) believes Americans are too materialistic

Make sure you read Inference questions carefully. Some answer choices may be true, but if they can't be inferred from the passage, then they can't be the correct answer.

GO ONLINE

Keep Kaplan's Target Strategy for Reading Comprehension Questions fresh in your mind with your downloadable Study Sheet for study on the go.

Vocabulary-in-Context Questions

Vocabulary-in-Context questions ask about the usage of a single word. These questions do not test your ability to define hard words like *archipelago* and *garrulous*. Instead, they test your ability to infer the meaning of a word from context.

Words tested in SAT questions are usually fairly common words with more than one definition. But that's the trick! Many of the answer choices will be definitions of the tested word, but only one will work in context. Vocabulary-in-Context questions almost always have a line reference, and you should always use it!

Sometimes one of the answer choices will jump out at you. It will be the most common meaning of the word in question—but it's RARELY right. You can think of this as the *obvious* choice. Say *curious* is the word being tested. The obvious choice is *inquisitive*. But curious also means *odd*, and that's more likely to be the answer.

Using context to find the answer will help keep you from falling for this kind of trap. But you can also use these obvious choices to your advantage. If you get stuck on a Vocabulary-in-Context question, you can eliminate the obvious choice and guess from the remaining answers.

Here's our strategy for Vocabulary-in-Context questions: Once you find the tested word in the passage, treat the question like a Sentence Completion question. Pretend the word is a blank in the sentence. Read a line or two around the imaginary blank if you need to. Then predict a word for that blank. Check the answer choices for a word that comes close to your prediction.

Here's a sample Vocabulary-in-Context question.

> The word "abandon" as used in line 32 most nearly means
>
> (A) without restraint or control
> (B) to leave alone
> (C) to surrender
> (D) to move on
> (E) unusual or abnormal

 BE SMART!

Everything you need to answer SAT questions is provided in the material. Take the time to review the surrounding sentences of Vocab-in-Context words to have the most success possible.

HOW TO READ A PASSAGE

Contrary to what you might expect, to answer each question correctly, you don't need to read the passage word-for-word. Instead, your best bet is to carefully *skim* the passage.

Serious Skimming

Each Reading Comprehension passage is written for a purpose: The author wants to make a point, describe a situation, or convince you of his or her ideas. As you're reading, ask yourself the following questions:

- What is this passage about?
- What is the point of this passage?
- What is the author trying to say?
- Why did he or she write this?
- What are the two or three most important things in this passage?

This is active reading, and it's the key to staying focused on the page.

Active reading does not necessarily mean reading the passage word-for-word. In this case, it means reading lightly but with a focus—in other words, *serious skimming*. This way, you can quickly find the main ideas and identify the tone of the passage. The questions themselves will help you fill in the details by directing you back to important information and specific details in the passage.

Getting hung up on details is a major Reading Comprehension pitfall. You need to grasp the outline, but you don't need to get all the fine features.

Components of the Serious Skimming Technique

- Skim the passage to get the writer's drift. Don't read the passage thoroughly. It's a waste of time.
- As you skim, search for important points. Don't wait for important information to jump out at you.
- Don't get caught up in details. The questions will often supply them for you or tell you exactly where to find them.

⦿ KAPLAN'S TARGET STRATEGY FOR ─────── READING COMPREHENSION QUESTIONS

Serious skimming is a vital component of Kaplan's Target Strategy for attacking Reading Comprehension questions. Once you have seriously skimmed the passage, here's how to attack the questions:

Step 1. Read the question stem.

Step 2. Locate the material you need.

Step 3. Predict the answer.

Step 4. Select the best answer choice.

Step 1. Read the Question Stem

This is the place to really read carefully. Make sure you understand exactly what the question is asking. Is it a Big Picture question? Little Picture? Inference? Vocabulary? Are you looking for an overall main idea or a specific piece of information? Are you trying to determine the author's attitude or the meaning of a particular word?

Step 2. Locate the Material You Need

If you are given a line reference, read the material surrounding the line mentioned. It will clarify exactly what the question is asking and provide you with the context you need to answer the question correctly.

If you're not given a line reference, scan the text to find the place where the question applies, and quickly reread those few sentences. Keep the main point of the passage in mind.

Step 3. Predict the Answer

Don't spend time making up a precise answer. You need only a general sense of what you're after so you can recognize the correct answer quickly when you read the choices.

Step 4. Select the Best Answer Choice

Scan the choices, looking for one that fits your idea of the right answer. If you don't find an ideal answer, quickly eliminate wrong choices by checking back to the passage. Rule out choices that are too extreme or go against common sense. Get rid of answers that sound reasonable but don't make sense in the context of the passage or the question. Don't pick farfetched inferences, and make sure there is evidence for your inference in the passage. Remember, SAT inferences tend to be strongly implied in the passage.

PRACTICE

Try Kaplan's Target Strategy on the passage and question that follow.

Question 1 refers to the following passage.

Recently, at my grandmother's eightieth birthday party, my family looked at old photographs. In one of them, I saw a scared little boy holding tightly to his mother's skirt, and I scarcely recognized myself. My foremost memory of that
(5) time is simply being cold—the mild Vietnamese winters that I had known couldn't prepare me for the bitter winds of the American Midwest. The cold seemed emblematic of everything I hated about my new country—we had no friends, no extended family, and we all lived together in a
(10) two-room apartment. My mother, ever shrewd, remarked that selling heat in such a cold place would surely bring fortune, and she was right. My parents now own a successful heating supply company.

1. The author's attitude toward the "scared little boy" mentioned in line 3, indicates that the author

   (A) is unsure that the photograph is actually of his family

   (B) believes that the boy is likely overly dependent on his mother

   (C) feels that he has himself changed considerably since childhood

   (D) regards his mother's strategy to sell heating supplies as clever

   (E) regrets his family's move to the United States

AVAILABLE ON CD-ROM

Get even more Reading Comprehension review with Critical Reading Practice Tests 1–4 on your CD-ROM.

Step 1. Read the Question Stem

In this case, the question is straightforward: what does the author think about the little boy? It asks you to make an inference about the author's attitude.

Step 2. Locate the Material You Need

You're given a line reference, so be sure and go back to that line. But don't read just that specific line—read the line or two before and after as well. When you do, you see that the author says that he scarcely recognizes himself. From this, you know that the boy in the picture is the author when he was younger.

Step 3. Predict the Answer

Why would the author say that he scarcely recognizes himself? The implication is that the author (now grown) is so different from that frightened little boy that it's hard to believe they're the same person. So, look for an answer choice that matches this prediction.

Step 4. Select the Best Answer Choice

(A) is too literal—the author is speaking figuratively when he says he scarcely recognizes the boy.

(B) goes too far in making an inference. Although the boy is sticking close to his mother in the picture, there's no evidence that the author thinks this is a bad thing.

(C) is a great match for your prediction and is the correct answer.

(D) might be a true statement, but it comes later in the passage. It has nothing to do with the author's attitude toward the boy in the picture.

(E) like (B), is too great a leap and can't safely be inferred from the information in the passage.

Now try Kaplan's Target Strategy on the remaining questions for the passages. Question 2 uses the same passage that we used for question 1; we've reprinted the passage below. (Answers are on page 147. We also show you there how to apply the Target Strategy to questions 3 and 4.)

Question 2 refers to the following passage.

Recently, at my grandmother's eightieth birthday party, my family looked at old photographs. In one of them, I saw a scared little boy holding tightly to his mother's skirt, and I scarcely recognized myself. My foremost memory of that
(5) time is simply being cold—the mild Vietnamese winters that I had known couldn't prepare me for the bitter winds of the American Midwest. The cold seemed emblematic of everything I hated about my new country—we had no friends, no extended family, and we all lived together in a
(10) two-room apartment. My mother, ever shrewd, remarked that selling heat in such a cold place would surely bring fortune, and she was right. My parents now own a successful heating supply company.

2. Lines 10–13 ("My mother . . . heating supply company") suggest that the author's mother regarded the cold of the American Midwest as

(A) more drastic than that of Vietnam

(B) an opportunity for economic success

(C) an obstacle to familial happiness

(D) symbolic of other challenges and problems

(E) unimportant to the family's future

Questions 3–4 refer to the following passage.

Many mammals instinctively raise their fur when they are cold—a reaction produced by tiny muscles just under the skin which surround hair follicles. When the muscles contract, the hairs stand up, creating an increased air space
(5) under the fur. The air space provides more effective insulation for the mammal's body, thus allowing it to retain more heat for longer periods of time. Some animals also raise their fur when they are challenged by predators or even other members of their own species. The raised fur makes
(10) the animal appear slightly bigger, and, ideally, more powerful. Interestingly, though devoid of fur, humans still retain this instinct. So, the next time a horror movie gives you "goosebumps," remember that your skin is following a deep-seated mammalian impulse now rendered obsolete.

3. The "increased air space under the fur" mentioned in lines 4–5 serves primarily to

   (A) combat cold
   (B) intimidate other animals
   (C) render goosebumps obsolete
   (D) cool over-heated predators
   (E) make mammals more powerful

4. Based on the passage, the author would most likely describe "goosebumps" in humans as

   (A) an unnecessary and unexplained phenomenon
   (B) a harmful but necessary measure
   (C) an amusing but dangerous feature
   (D) a useless but interesting remnant
   (E) a powerful but infrequent occurrence

Questions 5–6 refer to the following passage.

Elizabeth Barrett Browning, a feminist writer of the Victorian Era, used her poetry and prose to take on a wide range of issues facing her society, including "the woman question." In her long poem *Aurora Leigh*, she explores this
(5) question as she portrays both the growth of the artist and the growth of the woman within. Aurora Leigh is not a traditional Victorian woman—she is well educated and self-sufficient. In the poem, Browning argues that the limitations placed on women in contrast to the freedom men
(10) enjoy should incite women to rise up and effect a change in their circumstances. Browning's writing, including *Aurora Leigh*, helped to pave the way for major social change in women's lives.

5. It can be inferred from the passage that the author believes the traditional Victorian woman

   (A) wrote poetry

   (B) was portrayed accurately in *Aurora Leigh*

   (C) fought for social change

   (D) was not well educated

   (E) had a public role in society

6. As used in line 10, "effect" most nearly means

   (A) imitate

   (B) result

   (C) cause

   (D) disturb

   (E) prevent

Questions 7–8 refer to the following passage.

Each passing evening brings more frustration. Tonight I spent an hour in front of the typewriter staring at the silent keys, listening to the girl upstairs play the piano and sing. I'd never noticed her ability before; she is remarkable. It

(5) seems everything she plays is of her own spontaneous creation, an absolute movement of feeling. Her music is a painting, the lines so intense and coloring that it manages to exist above the realm of the material, impressing a desolate image of the pianist upon my mind. But even the

(10) beauty of this pure work of art failed to inspire me, and after she stopped I was again without refuge.

7. In lines 2–3 the phrase "silent keys" implies that the narrator

   (A) can't play the piano

   (B) is suffering from writer's block

   (C) is tone deaf

   (D) is searching for clues

   (E) is annoyed by the girl upstairs

8. The narrator uses the description of the girl's playing in lines 4–6 (It seems … feeling) mainly to

   (A) contrast it with his inability to write

   (B) illustrate her talents as a musician

   (C) compare it with painting

   (D) criticize her lack of skill

   (E) indicate his inferiority as an artist

Questions 9–10 refer to the following passage.

Bear Mountain State Park opened in 1916 and rapidly became a popular weekend destination for many New Yorkers looking for an escape from the city grind. The ensuing unnaturally high volume of visitors to the area
(5)   caused an upsurge in traffic, and it was soon apparent that the ferry services used to cross the Hudson were insufficient. In 1922, the New York State Legislature introduced a bill that authorized a group of private investors led by Mary Harriman to build a bridge across the river. The
(10)   group, known as the Bear Mountain Hudson Bridge Company, was allotted thirty years to construct and maintain the bridge, after which the span would be handed over to New York State.

9.   In context, "volume," (line 4) most closely means

    (A) loudness

    (B) pollution

    (C) resentment

    (D) capacity

    (E) quantity

10. According to the passage, which is true about the bridge?

    I. It was originally constructed by New York State

    II. It opened to the public in 1916

    III. It was necessitated by inadequate ferry services

    (A) Statement II

    (B) Statement III

    (C) Statements I and II

    (D) Statements I and III

    (E) Statements II and III

Questions 11–12 refer to the following passage.

Like the writers of the Beat Generation almost a half-century before, many of the original grunge musicians who helped give birth to a movement were horrified at the final result of their efforts. Grunge music and culture was
(5) spawned in Seattle in the late 1980s as an underground revolt against the shallow values of the time. But with Nirvana's 1991 release of *Nevermind*, and the successive popularity of other Seattle bands like Pearl Jam and Soundgarden, the once-countercultural grunge movement
(10) skyrocketed into popular consciousness. Many aspects of the culture that were originally forms of rebellion, such as the hairstyles and fashions worn by grunge musicians, found its way into the most mainstream of places.

 GO ONLINE

Check out your new practice quiz every month.

11. In line 7, the author invokes the Beat Generation in order to

   (A) detail an earlier movement in music
   (B) introduce the topic by illustrating a similarity
   (C) imply the insignificance of grunge
   (D) recall an important time in American cultural history
   (E) emphasize grunge's influence upon today's music

12. As used in line 3, "movement" most closely means

   (A) an organized attempt at change
   (B) a specific manner of moving
   (C) the changing of location or position
   (D) a rhythmic progression or tempo
   (E) a mainstream belief

Questions 13–14 refer to the following passage.

Bovine spongiform encephalopathy (BSE) is a fatal, transmissible, neurological disorder found in cattle that slowly attacks a cow's brain cells, forming what resembles sponge-like holes in its brain. As the disease progresses, the
(5)   cow begins to behave abnormally, hence BSE's more common name, "Mad Cow Disease."

On December 23, 2003, the first case of BSE in the U.S. was detected in a cow from Washington State. The ensuing national hysteria was largely unfounded; years earlier, in
(10)   response to the previous epidemics abroad, the USFDA had implemented preventative measures to contain an outbreak of the disease before it could spread. These measures were in place for a good reason: there is a causal link between eating BSE-infected meat and the development of a fatal
(15)   human brain disorder known as new variant Creutzfeldt-Jakob Disease (nvCJD).

13. The first paragraph mostly serves to

(A) explain the origin of the term "Mad Cow Disease"

(B) introduce background information on BSE

(C) warn of BSE's transmissibility to humans

(D) dissuade people from eating meat

(E) provide in-depth description of BSE's different stages

14. Which of the following best describes the "national hysteria" in line 9 of the passage?

(A) totally justified

(B) necessary for USFDA policy change

(C) rooted in misinformation about BSE's harmfulness

(D) completely inexcusable

(E) understandable, but unnecessary

Questions 15–16 refer to the following passages.

Ann's footsteps crunching upon the fallen leaves are
amplified by the pre-dusk serenity that is quickly setting
upon the forest. The path before her is quickly dissolving
into the growing shadows, yet the fear that would normally
(5) be creeping into her chest is absent. Somewhere secretly
inside she finds the prospect of disappearing into the
woods exhilarating. Liberated, all her daily burdens would
go as the daylight goes, replaced with only the empty night,
spattered with benevolent stars. But as the trail opens onto
(10) her backyard, Ann is surprised to find herself breaking into
a trot, eager to return to the familiar warmth of her home.

15. Ann's absence of fear (lines 4–5) suggests that she

  (A) is brave in the face of danger
  (B) doesn't realize she is lost
  (C) is an apathetic person.
  (D) longs for a change in her life
  (E) knows exactly where she is

16. In line 8, "the empty night" is symbolic of

  (A) everyday life
  (B) a lack of responsibility
  (C) being lost
  (D) loneliness
  (E) death

IF YOU LEARNED ONLY FOUR THINGS IN THIS CHAPTER . . . .

1. The two most important skills for Reading Comprehension questions are to read with a purpose and use the context of the passage to decipher unfamiliar words.

2. Reading Comprehension passages are not ordered by difficulty.

3. It is better to seriously skim the passages than to read every word.

4. The main idea of most passages is mentioned in the first paragraph.

ANSWERS TO THE QUESTIONS ON PAGE 129

What Are the Different Categories of Reading Comprehension Questions?

- Big Picture questions
- Little Picture questions
- Inference questions
- Vocabulary-in-Context questions

What is the Best Strategy for Acing Reading Comprehension Questions?

- Kaplan's Target Strategy for Reading Comprehension Questions
  - Step 1. Read the question stem.
  - Step 2. Locate the material you need.
  - Step 3. Predict the answer.
  - Step 4. Select the best answer choice.

How Can I Learn to Read Actively?

- As you read the passage, ask yourself the following questions:
  - What is the passage about?
  - What is the point of this?
  - What is the author trying to say?
  - Why did he or she write this?
  - What are the two or three most important things in this passage?

ANSWERS AND EXPLANATIONS

1. C

Explanation on pages 136–137.

2. B

Context clues from lines 10–13 include the word *shrewd* and the inference that selling heat would *surely bring fortune*. Although choice (A) is certainly true of the passage, it is not specifically referred to in the lines cited. There was no mention of the cold being an obstacle (C) or of it being unimportant (E), so choice (B) is the correct answer.

3. A

Question 3 is a Little Picture question. Here's how you could solve it with the Five-Step Method.

> The "increased air space under the fur" mentioned in lines 4–5 serves primarily to
>
> (A) combat cold
> (B) intimidate other animals
> (C) render such measures obsolete
> (D) cool over-heated predators
> (E) make mammals more powerful

Step 1. Read the Question Stem

Because the question is asking about a particular detail (it's just about the increased air space, not the passage as a whole), you know that this is a Little Picture question.

Step 2. Locate the Material You Need

When you go back to the referenced line, you find that the increased air space *provides more effective insulation … allowing it to retain more heat*.

Step 3. Predict the Answer

It looks like the increased air space helps keep the animal warm.

Step 4. Select the Best Answer Choice

> (A) looks perfect.
> (B) is tempting because the raised fur also serves to make the animals look bigger and more intimidating.
> (C) doesn't make too much sense in this context and seems to be a distortion of the idea that goosebumps are obsolete.
> (D) is actually the opposite of what you're looking for. This kind of wrong answer choice appears fairly often on the test.
> (E) is also a distortion. Raised fur makes animals *appear* more powerful, but they are not actually more powerful.

You're left with (A) and (B). Be careful, though! The question is specifically asking about the increased air space, not raised fur in general. (A) refers to the air space, whereas (B) is more general. So, (A) is correct. Challenging Reading Comprehension questions force you to make *very* subtle distinctions.

4. D

Question 4 is a Big Picture question. Here's how you might answer it with Kaplan's Five-Step Method.

> Based on the passage, the author would most likely describe "goosebumps" in humans as
>
> (A) an unnecessary and unexplained phenomenon
> (B) a harmful but necessary measure
> (C) an amusing but dangerous feature
> (D) a useless but interesting remnant
> (E) a powerful but infrequent occurrence

Step 1. Read the Question Stem

Seems simple enough: What does the author think about goosebumps?

Step 2. Locate the Material You Need

This is a Big Picture question—to answer it correctly, you need to understand the passage as a whole and the author's attitude toward the subject. Because you're asked about the overall point, you probably don't need to go back to a specific part of the passage. Instead, quickly summarize the author's point, as though you wanted to explain it to a younger brother or sister. (This can get you to boil everything down to the simplest possible terms.)

Step 3. Predict the Answer

You might say something like, "Goosebumps are left over from when people had fur."

Step 4. Select the Best Answer Choice

   (A) *unnecessary* fits, but *unexplained* is wrong. (The whole passage was written to explain goosebumps.)

   (B) goosebumps seem to do no harm and don't seem to be necessary in people, so this one's doubly wrong.

   (C) *amusing* maybe, but *dangerous* doesn't fit.

   (D) looks very good. (The author must think it's pretty interesting or she wouldn't have written the passage in the first place.)

   (E) the passage never talks about the frequency, and *powerful* doesn't really fit.

Only (D) fits, so that's your answer.

5. D

The answer to this question can be found in lines 6–8. The author writes, *Aurora Leigh is not a traditional Victorian woman—she is well educated and self-sufficient.* This statement sets up the contrast between Aurora, who is well-educated, and the traditional Victorian woman, who is not well-educated.

6. C

The word *effect* is both a noun and a verb, so you must look at its use in the sentence to determine its part of speech and meaning. The word is used in the phrase *to rise up and effect a change.* If you are unclear of the meaning, try inserting the answer choices in the sentence to see if it makes sense: to *imitate* a change, to *result* a

change, to *cause* a change, to *disturb* a change, to *prevent* a change. Although you may have been tempted to choose (B), *result*, thinking that effect is a noun, the only answer choice that makes sense in the context of the sentence is choice (C), *cause.*

7. B

The "silent keys' referred to in the passage are the keys of a typewriter, and the fact that they are described as "silent" implies that they are not in use. Using what the author offered you in the first sentence about his mounting frustration, you are looking for the choice that best reflects what conclusions can be drawn from this phrase. (A) is a distortion; the silent keys are those of a typewriter, not a piano. The author never mentions whether or not he can play the piano. (C) is the opposite of what you're looking for. The author's detailed description of the music upstairs proves that he is obviously not *tone deaf.* (D) is out of scope. The narrator may be searching for clues to break his writer's block, but this implication makes no sense within the scope of the paragraph. (E) is also opposite. The girl's playing does not annoy the narrator; in fact, in the paragraph's final sentence he admits that he found "refuge" in it. (B) is the best answer.

8. A

The narrator's description of the piano player has one overarching function in the paragraph—the ease with which she plays the piano offers a stark contrast to the narrator's writer's block, thus highlighting his frustration. (B) and (C) are distortions. Although the description does serve to *illustrate her talents* (B), it's true function in the paragraph is to emphasize the author's frustration with his own writer's block. Also, the author compares the piano player's music to a painting (C) in the sentence that follows the one in question. (D) is the opposite of what you're looking for. The narrator describes the girl's playing as "remark-able." (E) is out of scope; nowhere in the passage does the author offer a critique of his own skills, he simply tells of his frustration at not being able to employ them. (A) is a solid match with your prediction.

9. E

Often, the simplest way to answer a vocabulary-in-context problem is to replace the word in question with each of the given answer choices to see which fits best in the context of the sentence. Look for the word that could best be linked to "an upsurge in traffic" and "insufficient." (A) is a distortion; this synonym of volume might have been a product of "the upsurge in traffic," but it is unlikely to have been the cause of it. (B) and (C) are both out of scope. *Pollution* is an effect of traffic, but this makes no sense in context, and *resentment* is never alluded to in the passage. (D) is also a distortion. Although exceeding the *capacity* for cars in an area is the cause of traffic, this definition of "volume" does not work in terms of the sentence's structure. (E) is an excellent match for your prediction.

10. B

Don't let the Roman numeral statements affect your approach, this is a simple detail question whose answer is specifically based in the facts of the passage. Verify each given statement, and find the answer choice that corresponds with the statement or statements to you validated. (A) is a distortion. Bear Mountain State Park opened in 1916. The bridge opened later, but the date is not is mentioned. You can thus assume that (C) and (E) are incorrect, as well. (D) is also a distortion. Statement III is true, but I is false: New York State did not build the bridge, "it introduced a bill that authorized a group of private investors" to build it. (B) is the best answer.

11. B

The author uses the similar experiences of the Beat writers and grunge musicians to establish the main idea of the passage. Look for the choice that best illustrates this statement. (A) is a distortion. The first sentence clearly establishes that the Beats were writers, not musicians. (C) is out of scope. The author never implies that the grunge movement was insignificant. By invoking the Beats, the author is recalling *an important time in American cultural history* (D), but this is not the purpose for the author's doing so. (E) is also out of scope. The author only mentions *grunge's influence* upon mainstream culture of the early '90s.

12. A

In line 3, the author describes the movements of the Beat writers and Grunge musicians as "efforts," and then in line 6 characterizes the grunge movement as a "revolt." Look for the choice that contains the best definition of what both of these words could imply.

(B) is out of scope. This alternate definition of "movement" makes no sense in the context of the passage. (C) is also out of scope. Again, this definition makes no sense in context. (D) is a distortion. The definition of "movement" used in the passage refers to the efforts of musicians, not a "rhythmic progression or tempo" in music. (E) is the opposite of what you're looking for. A movement is usually an organized effort by an individual or group to change a *mainstream belief.* (A) is the best choice.

13. B

The author uses the first paragraph to brief the reader on the basic facts about BSE, and then uses the second paragraph to explore the subject a bit further. You are looking for the choice that best fits the first paragraph's role in the author's use of structure. (A) is a distortion. This is only a supporting detail of the first paragraph—you are looking for the paragraph's overall purpose in the passage. (C) and (E) are also distortions; the transmissibility of BSE to humans (C) is not established until the second paragraph, and the quick summary of BSE's stages hardly amounts to *in-depth description* (E). (D) is out of scope. Although this first paragraph certainly may dissuade some from eating meat, that is not the intended function of the paragraph or the passage. (B) is an excellent match for your prediction.

14. E

The answer to this question lies in one important detail of the passage: the use of the word *largely* (line 9). The author describes the "national hysteria" as *largely* unfounded because while the USFDA was well prepared for such a scenario, the dire consequences of the disease should not be overlooked. (A) is the opposite of what the answer is. By definition, the word "hysteria" implies going a bit overboard in terms of response or emotion. (B) and (C) are distortions; the details of the passage clearly state that the USFDA had effected BSE policy change (B) long before the first case in the country, and (C) suggests that the hysteria was largely unfounded because BSE is not particularly harmful. (D) is too extreme; BSE is a fatal, transmissible disease. (E) is the best choice.

15. D

The passage states that rather than fear, Ann secretly feels exhilarated by the "prospect of disappearing into the woods" because she would be "liberated" from "all her daily burdens." You are looking for the choice that best conveys what these statements suggest about Ann. (A) is a distortion; the passage states that "normally," Ann would be scared by the prospect of being lost in the woods at night. (B) is also a distortion. Ann is not lost; the passage deals only with the prospect of her losing her way in the woods. (C) is the opposite of the correct answer. The fact that Ann could find something "exhilarating" (line 7) proves that she is not *apathetic*. The fear would come from the prospect of Ann losing her way on the path as the darkness sets in, but the author never suggests that she does not know where she is on the path (E). (D) is the best choice.

16. B

Like the "daylight" (line 8), Ann wants her burdens to disappear into the night. Using this comparison, the answer is the choice that best expresses what the empty night represents with respect to her "daily burdens." (A) is the opposite of the best answer; in the passage, "the empty night" is symbolic of what Ann hopes would replace in her *everyday life*. (C) and (D) are distortions. Don't be fooled by (C); *being lost* could be a literal representation of the empty night, but you're looking for the symbolic meaning. Although "empty night" may invoke images of *loneliness* (D), the author never suggests that Ann is lonely. (E) is also opposite of the correct choice. The passage deals with themes of life, not *death*. (B) is a solid choice.

Chapter Nine: **Reading Comprehension Strategies—Long Passages**

- What Are the Strategies Specific to Long Passages?
- What Tools Do I Need to Succeed on These Question Types?

You use the same skills and strategies to tackle long passages as you do short passages—specifically, *serious skimming* and Kaplan's Target Strategy. The subject matter and questions are also about the same for both passage types.

The difference? With longer passages, you need to work harder to stay focused and organized. Here's how.

LONG PASSAGE STRATEGIES

There are a few things to keep in mind when you read the long passages. Consider these as strategies that will help you master the section.

Question Order

Although Reading Comprehension questions are not arranged by degree of difficulty, they do have a specific order for longer passages. In general, the questions correspond to the passage, so the first few questions ask about the beginning of the passage, the middle questions about the middle, and the last few questions about the end. The last couple of questions are likely to be Big Picture questions that ask you about the overall main idea of the passage.

Introduction

Each long passage begins with a brief introduction that tells you what the passage is about. This is an important part of the question set and should not be skipped. The introduction helps you focus your reading by preparing you for the kind of information and ideas to come.

Map It

Longer passages cover many aspects of a topic. For example, the first paragraph might introduce the subject, the second paragraph might present one viewpoint, and the third paragraph might argue for a different viewpoint. Within each of these paragraphs, there are several details that help the author convey a message.

Because there is a lot to keep track of, you need to mark up long passages as follows:

- Write simple notes in the margin as you read.
- Write down the purpose of each paragraph.
- Underline key points.
- Concentrate on places where the author expresses an opinion. Most Reading Comprehension questions hinge on opinions and viewpoints, not facts.

These notes are your *passage map*. The passage map helps you find the part of the passage that contains the information you need. The process of creating your passage map also forces you to read actively. This is especially helpful in the SAT's second and third hour when your energy is flagging. Because you are constantly trying to identify the author's viewpoint and the purpose of each sentence and paragraph, you will be working hard to understand what's happening in the passage. This translates into points on the test.

PASSAGE MAP PRACTICE

Write a passage map of this sample SAT passage using the guidelines we just provided.

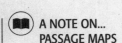

**A NOTE ON...
PASSAGE MAPS**

A good passage map should:

- Contain short words or phrases, not whole sentences (e.g., "what author now believes")
- Include markings in the passage like underlined and circled words
- Concentrate on viewpoints and opinions
- Note places where opinions other than the author's are expressed
- Avoid specific details

What a marvelous and celestial creature was Leonardo da Vinci. As a scientist and engineer, his gifts were unparalleled. But his accomplishments in these capacities were hindered by the fact that he was, before all else, an artist. As

(5) one conversant with the perfection of art, and knowing the futility of trying to bring such perfection to the realm of practical application, Leonardo tended toward variability and inconstancy in his endeavors. His practice of moving compulsively from one project to the next, never bringing

(10) any of them to completion, stood in the way of his making any truly useful technical advances.

When Leonardo was asked to create a memorial for one of his patrons, he designed a bronze horse of such vast proportions that it proved utterly impractical—even impossi-

(15) ble—to produce. Some historians maintain that Leonardo never had any intention of finishing this work in the first place. But it is more likely that he simply became so intoxicated by his grand artistic conception that he lost sight of the fact that the monument actually had to be cast.

(20)   Similarly, when Leonardo was commissioned to paint the *Last Supper*, he left the head of Christ unfinished, feeling incapable of investing it with a sufficiently divine demeanor. Yet, as a work of art rather than science or engineering, it is still worthy of our greatest veneration, for

(25) Leonardo succeeded brilliantly in capturing the acute anxiety of the Apostles at the most dramatic moment of the Passion narrative.

Such mental restlessness, however, proved more problematic when applied to scientific matters. When he turned

(30) his mind to the natural world, Leonardo would begin by inquiring into the properties of herbs and end up observing the motions of the heavens. In his technical studies and scientific experiments, he would generate an endless stream of models and drawings, designing complex and unbuild-

(35) able machines to raise great weights, bore through mountains, or even empty harbors.

It is this enormous intellectual fertility that has suggested to many that Leonardo can and should be regarded as one of the originators of modern science. But Leonardo was not

(40) himself a true scientist. "Science" is not the hundred-odd principles or *pensieri* that have been pulled out of his *Codici*. Science is comprehensive and methodical thought.

Granted, Leonardo always became fascinated by the intricacies of specific technical challenges. He possessed the

(45) artist's interest in detail, which explains his compulsion with observation and problem solving. But such things alone do not constitute science, which requires the working out of a systematic body of knowledge—something Leonardo displayed little interest in doing.

Now take a look at our passage map notes on the next page. Did you highlight similar parts of the passage? Did you concentrate on the author's views? Look carefully at your mark up. How would you summarize the author's main idea?

What a marvelous and celestial creature was Leonardo da Vinci. As a scientist and engineer, his gifts were unparalleled. But his accomplishments in these capacities were hindered by the fact that he was, before all else, an artist. As
(5) one conversant with the perfection of art, and knowing the futility of trying to bring such perfection to the realm of practical application, Leonardo tended toward variability and inconstancy in his endeavors. His practice of moving compulsively from one project to the next, never bringing
(10) any of them to completion, stood in the way of his making any truly useful technical advances.

When Leonardo was asked to create a memorial for one of his patrons, he designed a bronze horse of such vast proportions that it proved utterly impractical—even impossi-
(15) ble—to produce. Some historians maintain that Leonardo never had any intention of finishing this work in the first place. But it is more likely that he simply became so intoxicated by his grand artistic conception that he lost sight of the fact that the monument actually had to be cast.
(20) Similarly, when Leonardo was commissioned to paint the *Last Supper*, he left the head of Christ unfinished, feeling incapable of investing it with a sufficiently divine demeanor. Yet, as a work of art rather than science or engineering, it is still worthy of our greatest veneration, for
(25) Leonardo succeeded brilliantly in capturing the acute anxiety of the Apostles at the most dramatic moment of the Passion narrative.

Such mental restlessness, however, proved more problematic when applied to scientific matters. When he turned
(30) his mind to the natural world, Leonardo would begin by inquiring into the properties of herbs and end up observing the motions of the heavens. In his technical studies and scientific experiments, he would generate an endless stream of models and drawings, designing complex and unbuild-
(35) able machines to raise great weights, bore through mountains, or even empty harbors.

It is this enormous intellectual fertility that has suggested to many that Leonardo can and should be regarded as one of the originators of modern science. But Leonardo
(40) was not himself a true scientist. "Science" is not the hundred-odd principles or *pensieri* that have been pulled out of his *Codici.* Science is comprehensive and methodical thought. Granted, Leonardo always became fascinated by the intricacies of specific technical challenges. He possessed
(45) the artist's interest in detail, which explains his compulsion with observation and problem solving. But such things alone do not constitute science, which requires the working out of a systematic body of knowledge—something Leonardo displayed little interest in doing.

KEY:

OP = opinion

Ex = example

L = Leonardo

Margin annotations:

OP— L is great

MainPoint—L is genius, but never stuck w/1 thing long enuf 2B a "scientist"

OP – L underachieved

Ex #1 – horse

alt. opinion

OP – L is a genius but impractical

Ex #2 – last Sup

MainPoint L gets caught up in idea, forgets actual work

OP – switching from art to science here

Ex #1 – Natural

Ex #2 – technical

MainPoint: L's short attention span bad for science

alt. opinion

OP

back?

MainPoint—L is genius and a compulsive problem-solver, but no scientist

L not good at

PAIRED PASSAGES

The SAT will include at least one long paired passage and one short paired passage. Paired passages are two separate passages that relate to the same topic. Questions following paired passages are generally ordered the same way. The first few questions relate to the first passage, the next few to the second passage, and the final questions ask about the passages as a pair.

Don't let the paired passages intimidate you—they're not twice as hard as the single-passage reading selections. In fact, students often find the paired passages the most interesting selections on the test.

 **KAPLAN'S TARGET STRATEGY FOR PAIRED PASSAGES**

The Target Strategy for Paired Passages is as follows:

Step 1. Skim passage 1, looking for the general idea (as you would with a single passage).

Step 2. Do the question or questions that relate to passage 1.

Step 3. Skim passage 2, looking for the general idea and thinking about how it relates to passage 1.

Step 4. Do the question or questions that relate to passage 2.

Step 5. Do the questions that ask about the relationship between the two passages.

 SMARTPOINTS

Answering the Passage 1 questions helps you to get a fix on the first passage before reading Passage 2.

Because you have to keep track of two different viewpoints with paired passages, it's especially important to read actively and create a map for each passage. Remember to ask yourself, "What are these passages about? What is each author's point? What is similar about the two passages? What is different?"

WHEN TIME IS RUNNING OUT

We told you to save long passages for last, so you may find yourself racing against the clock. It's always best to skim the passage before you hit the questions. But if you only have a few minutes left, here's how to score fast points.

You can answer Vocabulary-in-Context questions and many Little Picture questions without reading the passage. If the question has a line reference, locate the material you need to find your answer and follow the Target Strategy as usual. You won't have the overall picture to guide you, but you might be able to reach the correct answer just by focusing on the little picture and using the context around a particular word or line.

Also, remember to skip around within the section if you need to. You can tackle the passages in any order you like within the same section. So if you can see from the introductions that one passage will be much easier for you than the others, work through that one first. But don't skip around after you've already read most or all of a passage. You've already invested your time reading, so try all the questions that go with it before you move to another text.

PRACTICE

Test your reading skills on the following sample long passage, keeping our tips in mind. Remember to read actively and construct a Passage Map. Then, use the Target Strategy to answer the questions that follow. Answers and explanations are on page 169. We also show you how we used the Target Strategy to answer question 1.

Questions 1–8 refer to the following passage.

In this essay, the author writes about her childhood on a Caribbean island that was an English colony for many years.

When I saw England for the first time, I was a child in school sitting at a desk. The England I was looking at was laid out on a map gently, beautifully, delicately, a very special jewel; it lay on a
(5) bed of sky blue, its yellow form mysterious, because though it looked like a leg of mutton*, it could not really look like anything so familiar as a leg of mutton because it was England. England was a special jewel all right, and only special peo-
(10) ple got to wear it. The people who got to wear England were English people. They wore it well and they wore it everywhere: in jungles, in deserts, on plains, in places where they were not welcome, in places they should not have been. When my
(15) teacher had pinned this map up on the black-board, she said, "This is England"—and she said it with authority, seriousness, and adoration, and we all sat up. We understood then—we were meant to understand then—that England was to be our
(20) source of myth and the source from which we got our sense of reality, our sense of what was mean-ingful, our sense of what was meaningless—and much about our own lives and much about the very idea of us headed that last list.
(25)   At the time I was a child sitting at my desk see-ing England for the first time, I was already very familiar with the greatness of it. Each morning before I left for school, I ate a breakfast of half a grapefruit, a bowl of oat porridge, bread and but-
(30) ter and a slice of cheese, and a cup of cocoa. The can of cocoa was often left on the table in front of me. It had written on it the name of the company, the year the company was established, and the words "Made in England." Those words, "Made in
(35) England," were written on the box the oats came in too. The shoes I wore were made in England; so

were my socks and cotton undergarments and the satin ribbons I wore tied at the end of two plaits of my hair. My father, who might have sat next to
(40) me at breakfast, was a carpenter and cabinet maker. The shoes he wore to work would have been made in England, as were his khaki shirt and trousers, his underpants and undershirt, his socks and brown felt hat. Felt was not the proper mate-
(45) rial from which a hat that was expected to provide shade from the hot sun should be made, but my father must have seen and admired a picture of an Englishman wearing such a hat in England. As we sat at breakfast a car might go by. The car, a
(50) Hillman or a Zephyr, was made in England. The very conception of the meal itself, breakfast, and its substantial quality and quantity was an idea from England; we somehow knew that in England they began the day with this meal called breakfast
(55) and a proper breakfast was a big breakfast.
    At the time I saw this map—seeing England for the first time—I did not say to myself, "Ah, so that's what it looks like," because there was no longing in me to put a shape to those three words
(60) that ran through every part of my life, no matter how small; for me to have had such a longing would have meant that I lived in a certain atmos-phere, an atmosphere in which those three words were felt as a burden. But I did not live in such an
(65) atmosphere. My father's brown felt hat would develop a hole in its crown, the lining would sepa-rate from the hat itself, and six weeks before he thought that he could not be seen wearing it—he was a very vain man—he would order another hat
(70) from England. And my mother taught me to eat my food in the English way: the knife in the right hand, the fork in the left, my elbows held still close to my side. When I had finally mastered it, I overheard her saying to a friend, "Did you see how
(75) nicely she can eat?" But I knew then that I enjoyed my food more when I ate it with my bare hands, and I continued to do so when she wasn't looking.

And when my teacher showed us the map, she asked us to study it carefully, because no test we
(80) would ever take would be complete without this statement: "Draw a map of England."

I did not know then that the statement "Draw a map of England" was something far worse than a declaration of war. I did not know then that this
(85) statement was part of a process that would result in my erasure, not my physical erasure, but my erasure all the same. I did not know then that this statement was meant to make me feel in awe and small whenever I heard the word "England": awe
(90) at its existence, small because I was not from it. I did not know very much of anything then—certainly not what a blessing it was that I was unable to draw a map of England correctly.

*the flesh of a sheep

1. According to the author, England could not really look like a leg of mutton (lines 6–8) because

    (A) maps generally don't give an accurate impression of what a place looks like
    (B) England was too grand and exotic a place for such a mundane image
    (C) England was an island not very different in appearance from her own island
    (D) the usual metaphor used to describe England was a precious jewel
    (E) mutton was one of the few foods familiar to her that did not come from England

2. The author's reference to felt as "not the proper material" (line 44) for her father's hat chiefly serves to emphasize her point about the

    (A) extremity of the local weather
    (B) arrogance of island laborers
    (C) informality of dress on the island
    (D) weakness of local industries
    (E) predominance of English culture

3. The word "conception" as used in line 51 means

    (A) beginning
    (B) image
    (C) origination
    (D) notion
    (E) plan

4. The word "substantial" in line 52 means

    (A) important
    (B) abundant
    (C) firm
    (D) down-to-earth
    (E) materialistic

5. In the third paragraph, the author implies that any longing to put a shape to the words "Made in England" would have indicated

    (A) a resentment of England's predominance
    (B) an unhealthy desire to become English
    (C) an inability to understand England's authority
    (D) an excessive curiosity about England
    (E) an unfamiliarity with English customs

6. The author cites the anecdotes about her father and mother in lines 65–75 primarily to convey their

   (A) love for their children
   (B) belief in strict discipline
   (C) distaste for anything foreign
   (D) reverence for England
   (E) overemphasis on formal manners

7. For the author, the requirement to "Draw a map of England" (lines 81–83) represented an attempt to

   (A) force students to put their studies to practical use
   (B) glorify one culture at the expense of another
   (C) promote an understanding of world affairs
   (D) encourage students to value their own heritage
   (E) impart outmoded and inappropriate knowledge

8. The word "erasure" (line 86) as used by the author most nearly means

   (A) total annihilation
   (B) physical disappearance
   (C) sense of insignificance
   (D) enforced censorship
   (E) loss of freedom

Questions 9–15 refer to the following passage.

The following is adapted from a biology textbook.

Blood, a connective tissue, is a sticky fluid that has multiple functions. It transports oxygen, nutrients, and other solutes to cells; carries away metabolic wastes and secretions; and helps stabi-
(5) lize internal pH. Plasma, red blood cells, white blood cells, and platelets are its components.

Plasma, which is mostly water, functions as a transport medium for blood cells and platelets. It also serves as a solvent for ions and molecules,
(10) including hundreds of different kinds of plasma proteins. Some of the plasma proteins transport lipids and fat-soluble vitamins through the body. Others have roles in blood clotting or in defense against pathogens. Collectively, the concentration
(15) of plasma proteins affects the blood's fluid volume, for it influences the movement of water between blood and interstitial fluid.

Erythrocytes, or red blood cells, are biconcave disks, like doughnuts with a squashed-in center
(20) instead of a hole. They transport the oxygen used in aerobic respiration and carry away some carbon dioxide wastes. When oxygen diffuses into blood, it binds with hemoglobin, the iron-containing pigment that gives red blood cells their color.
(25) Mature red blood cells no longer have their nucleus, nor do they require it. They have enough hemoglobin, enzymes, and other proteins to function for about 120 days. At any time, phagocytes are engulfing the oldest red blood cells or the ones
(30) already dead, but ongoing replacements keep the cell count fairly stable.

Leukocytes, or white blood cells, arise from stem cells in bone marrow. They function in daily housekeeping and defense. Many patrol tissues,
(35) where they target or engulf damaged or dead cells and anything chemically recognized as foreign to the body. Many others are massed together in the lymph nodes and spleen. There they divide to produce armies of cells that battle specific viruses,
(40) bacteria, and other invaders.

White blood cells differ in size, nuclear shape, and staining traits. There are five categories: neutrophils, eosinophils, basophils, monocytes, and lymphocytes. The neutrophils and monocytes are
(45) search-and-destroy cells. The monocytes follow chemical trails to inflamed tissues where they develop into macrophages that can engulf invaders and debris. Two classes of lymphocytes, B cells and T cells, make highly specific defense
(50) responses.

Some stem cells in bone marrow give rise to giant cells called megakaryocytes. These shed fragments of cytoplasm enclosed in a bit of plasma membrane. The membrane-bound fragments are
(55) platelets, which initiate blood clotting. Each platelet only lasts five to nine days, but hundreds of thousands are always circulating in blood.

9. The passage is primarily concerned with

  (A) blood function
  (B) plasma and platelets
  (C) blood components
  (D) blood
  (E) the circulatory system

10. According to the passage, plasma is

  (A) a biconcave disk
  (B) composed of ions and molecules
  (C) interstitial fluid
  (D) mostly water
  (E) hemoglobin

11. In line 17, "interstitial" most nearly means

  (A) situated within an organ
  (B) within the blood
  (C) small space
  (D) erythrocytes
  (E) a lattice

12. According to the passage, what gives blood its red color?

    (A) hemoglobin

    (B) oxygen

    (C) iron

    (D) the nucleus

    (E) hemoglobin, enzymes, and other proteins

13. The author's use of the words "defense" and "patrol" (line 34) and "armies" and "battle" (line 39) implies that

    (A) white blood cells serve as protection against invaders

    (B) white blood cells differ in size, shape, and traits

    (C) white blood cells are violent

    (D) B and T cells are highly specific

    (E) phagocytes attack old red blood cells

14. In line 46, "inflamed" most nearly means

    (A) on fire

    (B) under attack

    (C) engulfed

    (D) irritated

    (E) healthy

15. Megakaryocytes are

    (A) plasma

    (B) giant cells that shed cytoplasm

    (C) giant cells that are platelets

    (D) giant cells that initiate blood clotting

    (E) platelets that last five to nine days

Questions 16–22 refer to the following passage.

A renaissance is a rebirth. The Harlem Renaissance of the 1920s was a time when African-American art and literature flourished. Blacks migrating from the south brought with
(5) them a key element to the thriving Harlem area; jazz. The rhythms of this music set the stage for a new kind of literature and a new kind of art. But the vitality was not just exhibited in the fine arts; it was also present in the politics of the era.
(10) Inevitably, it changed African-Americans and America through the power of its legacy.

Inspired by the freedom that jazz construction provided, poet Langston Hughes began writing riffs that contained the elements of jazz and blues
(15) but maintained the structure of poetry. However, it was the language in his writing that was truly revolutionary. Instead of the highly stylized, theatrical black voice used at the time, Hughes wrote in the everyday language he heard around him. It
(20) was the language of musicians, workers, and servants and it became a poetic revolution.

Likewise, African-American art was revitalized. The works of Aaron Douglas could be seen throughout New York City. He was a prolific
(25) muralist and graphic illustrator. His subjects were rendered in the art deco style that was popular at the time. His murals depicted jazz musicians and singers posing heroically above the cityscape. No major literary work from the Harlem Renaissance
(30) was published without his design gracing its cover. Other notable artists, like Archibald Motley Jr. and Malvin Gray Johnson, gave African-American subjects dignity and grace that were considered radical in the America of 1920.
(35) At the same time, African-American scholars, like W.E.B. Du Bois, urging racial pride, were publishing magazines. Activist Marcus Garvey campaigned against the colonization of Africa and started an organization called the Universal Negro
(40) Improvement Association to further the goal of racial pride. This was a reformation; an intellectual rebellion shouting out that the black voice in America would be heard.

And heard it was, not just in America but
(45) around the world. Paris, considered the cultural capital of the world, was quick to assimilate the sounds, textures and words that were coming out of Harlem. The sound of Duke Ellington and the songs of Bessie Smith swung from the Cotton
(50) Club in Harlem to the nightclubs of Paris. The world was taking notice of the artists, activists, and writers of Harlem. This meant that the world was also taking note of black Americans, their struggles and their achievements
(55) 1920s Harlem, with its intellectuals and artists, its activists and musicians, inspired generations. Its influence can be seen in the novels of Toni Morrison, the music of Wynton Marsalis, the films of Spike Lee and, perhaps most importantly, the
(60) politics of Malcolm X and Martin Luther King, Jr. Inspired by the art and politics of the time, African-Americans redefined themselves and the world had to take notice.

16. Renaissance and rebirth are synonymous. Why were the intellectuals and artists of 1920s Harlem considered to be part of a renaissance?

(A) They studied the revival of art and learning from the 14th, 15th, and 16th centuries in Europe.

(B) They underwent a religious transformation.

(C) Their work is the basis of all African-American art and politics today.

(D) Their works are still considered masterpieces today.

(E) Their collective works of art and thought were instrumental in changing the perception of African-Americans at the time and continue to influence attitudes today.

17. What impact did the migration of blacks from the south have on the Harlem Renaissance?

    (A) More black people in New York City allowed Harlem to flourish.

    (B) Southern thought and art was superior to that found in the north.

    (C) African-Americans from the south brought their musical sensibilities which influenced the writings, art, and thought of the 1920s.

    (D) Southern African-Americans were not interested in music so more time could be spent on writing, painting and politics.

    (E) Duke Ellington played in Paris thus allowing African-American music to gain acceptance.

18. In paragraph 2, lines 17–19, the author describes Langston Hughes as writing in a voice very different than the *highly stylized, theatrical* style accepted at the time. What characterized the difference between the two styles?

    (A) Shakespearean English was the only acceptable literary voice of the time.

    (B) Langston Hughes wrote in the language of ordinary people instead of the artificial voice that identified the style of the time.

    (C) Southern dialects became important in Langston Hughes work but were not important to the elite New Yorker of the 1920s.

    (D) The use of literary devices like similes and metaphors were common in the poetry of Langston Hughes but not in mainstream America.

    (E) The preferred voice of the time was less affected than that of Langston Hughes.

19. In paragraph 4, line 41, the word *reformation* is used. Which of the following is the best description of the meaning of this word in the context of the passage?

    (A) The act of reshaping an object or thing.

    (B) An act of civil disobedience to further a cause.

    (C) A decision made by a group of people to form a committee to investigate a community need.

    (D) A vote taken directly to the people to decide an issue.

    (E) A transformation that corrects and betters the current condition.

20. In the last sentence of paragraph 3, the author states that the subjects of African-American artists were depicted with dignity and grace. This would indicate which of the following:

    (A) That previous depictions of African-American subjects were largely based on stereotypical biases present at the turn of the century.

    (B) All African-American artwork prior to the Harlem Renaissance was unflattering.

    (C) African-American artists were working with inferior supplies and were unable to create artwork that reflected their subjects in a respectful manner.

    (D) Art Deco, by virtue of the stylistic approach, created an air of nobility and culture to the subject matter.

    (E) The artistic atmosphere created by the Harlem Renaissance allowed for a more realistic portrayal of African-Americans, which resulted in a more dignified and tasteful depiction of the subject.

21. The author states that the Harlem Renaissance changed the political climate of the time and that both Martin Luther King Jr. and Malcolm X were influenced by the activists of the 1920s. In what way might these two very different leaders have been affected?

    (A) The pioneers of racial political activism infused their message with pride in one's heritage.

    (B) Both W.E.B. DuBois and Marcus Garvey organized large numbers of like-minded people, both black and white, in demonstrations across the country.

    (C) W.E.B. DuBois and Marcus Garvey instructed Malcolm X and Martin Luther King Jr.

    (D) The Harlem Renaissance was an intellectual movement that resulted in a large body of work of which Martin Luther King Jr. and Malcolm X must surely have been aware.

    (E) Marcus Garvey organized a bus strike in New York City that Martin Luther King later emulated in the South.

22. In paragraph 2, line 14, the author states that Langston Hughes was writing *riffs*. This word is not normally associated with writing. Why would the author choose this particular word?

    (A) The use of this word indicates that Langston Hughes was an angry poet.

    (B) *Riff* is a term for a passage in a jazz performance. The author used the word to illustrate the close connection between Hughes' poetry and jazz.

    (C) The word *riff* is actually synonymous with verse.

    (D) This is a shortened version of the word riff-raff, which further illustrates his revolutionary poetic voice.

    (E) The use of this word indicates that his poetry was vital and teeming with imagery of the Harlem of his day.

Questions 23–29 refer to the following passage.

The following passage is about a form of expression called conceptual art.

Conceptual "art" is a relatively recent artistic movement that began in the 1960s. After abstract impressionism and minimalism, artists were left at a dead end as far as finding new inroads into
(5) abstraction; there was nowhere left to go with traditional artistic media. Those who wished to further pursue abstraction to its absurd end became conceptual artists.

Conceptual artists were heavily influenced by
(10) the French dadaist/surrealist artist Marcel Duchamp, who maintained that the most important part of a work of art is its idea, rather than its physical expression. A 1970s bumper sticker capitalized on this idea and made fun of it: "If you like
(15) conceptual art, think about honking."

Conceptual art, for the most part, completely left behind a physical representation and relied only on the concept of the work that might (or might not) result. For example, Sol LeWitt created
(20) a *Wall Drawing* series that was composed only of a set of instructions for creating the drawings—that is to say, a blueprint for the eventual work. No physical representation of the ideas ever resulted. On a slightly different track, the contemporary
(25) conceptual artist Adib Fricke deals with language; his company The Word Company produces and distributes "words that do not yet exist" (*protonyms*). Similarly, performance art was a natural outgrowth of the idea of conceptual art, and
(30) visual one-time events became popular in the 1960s. They were often documented by pictures or narrative statements, but the actual work could not be preserved: only its idea.

This type of "art" stretches the limits of credibil-
(35) ity; the bumper sticker referenced previously shows the slanted light in which many view conceptual art. Abstract art blurs the boundaries between "art" and "not art" nearly to unrecognizability, but conceptual art obliterates this distinction
(40) completely. It is thus a way to avoid having to undertake the effort and exhibit the skill necessary to produce a lasting physical work of art. The author Leo Tolstoy created intricate plot outlines on the walls of the room in which he wrote. If he
(45) had left only the outlines and had never made them into books, would he still receive the same acclaim he now receives for works such as *War and Peace*?

23. In lines 1–2 "Conceptual 'art' is a relatively recent artistic movement that began in the 1960s," the quotation marks around *art* serve to

   (A) show that the author is about to define *art*

   (B) no purpose

   (C) set the tone for the passage

   (D) indicate that the author is especially fond of conceptual art

   (E) emphasize the importance of art

24. In line 11, the word "maintained" most nearly means

   (A) repaired

   (B) asserted

   (C) kept up

   (D) argued

   (E) disputed

25. An appropriate title for this passage might be

   (A) "Conceptual Art: An Important Advance"

   (B) "Marcel Duchamp: Life and Times"

   (C) "Bumper Stickers and Art"

   (D) "Conceptual Art: A Negative Opinion"

   (E) "All Art Is Absurd"

26. *Protonyms* are

   (A) words that do not yet exist

   (B) subatomic particles

   (C) words that sound alike

   (D) prototypical sounds

   (E) a type of visual art

27. All of the following statements are true EXCEPT

    (A) Adib Fricke uses language as a medium for conceptual art

    (B) Leo Tolstoy's outlines are an example of conceptual art

    (C) a work of conceptual art can exist with no physical representation

    (D) according to the author, conceptual art is the lazy way out

    (E) conceptual art is an extension of abstract art

28. The author of this passage would probably view a work of art that consisted only of a description of how to create a sculpture (rather than of an actual sculpture)

    (A) with sadness

    (B) with architectural curiosity

    (C) with anger

    (D) with joy

    (E) with disdain

29. This passage serves mainly to

    (A) provide a history of conceptual art

    (B) describe Leo Tolstoy's literary methods

    (C) convince the reader that conceptual art is unimportant

    (D) introduce the work of Adib Fricke

    (E) compare and contrast conceptual and abstract art

Questions 30–33 refer to the following passages.

Passage 1

In 1984, great fanfare and optimism accompanied the funding of an ecosystem research project called "Biosphere 2." The project's mission was to create an airlock-sealed habitat that could support
(5) a human crew for several years without contact with or resources from the outside world. Less than a decade later, however, enthusiasm for the project had almost entirely eroded after serious questions were raised about adherence to that
(10) mission. Media scrutiny began with reports that the mission's managers had quietly supplied the crew with goods from the outside, and this scrutiny intensified when these same administrators denied having tampered with the project. As an unfortu-
(15) nate result, doubts regarding the integrity of all the scientific data generated by the project began to surface.

Passage 2

Consistently propped up by the press since its inception, Biosphere 2 came to be regarded during
(20) the late 1980s as an indicator of the possibility of human habitation in space. Even as many scientists worked to quench such lofty goals, the press was dubbing Biosphere 2 the most exciting scientific project undertaken since the moon landing.
(25) Then, as the project's first crew emerged from a supposed two-year isolation to be greeted by a swirl of negative attention and controversy, the publications that had trumpeted the project quickly reversed direction. Frustrated with their
(30) conception's failures, the project's financiers fired their management team and, in a reversal of their own, lashed out at the same press they had once courted.

30. The word "quietly" as it is used in line 11 most nearly means

(A) gingerly
(B) easily
(C) meekly
(D) secretly
(E) carelessly

31. In the second sentence of Passage 2 (lines 21–24), the author implies that

(A) the media's expectations for the project were probably unrealistic
(B) many scientists thought that aeronautical projects should not have ambitious goals
(C) some scientists found the Biosphere 2 project more exciting than the moon landing
(D) the project's management team should have heeded the advice of scientists
(E) few could have predicted how controversial the project would become

32. Both authors agree that the Biosphere 2 project

(A) failed to produce any useful data
(B) became more scientifically valuable over time
(C) neglected to supply the crew properly
(D) was comparable to the moon landing
(E) resulted in disappointment

33. The two passages differ in their approaches to the topic of the Biosphere 2 project in that

(A) Passage 1 emphasizes both the successes and failures of the project, while Passage 2 focuses primarily on the project's disappointments
(B) Passage 1 indicates that the goal of the project was to create a self-sufficient habitat, while Passage 2 states that the project was only intended to explore space habitation
(C) Passage 1 is supportive of the financiers, while Passage 2 is critical of the financiers' anger with the media
(D) Passage 1 focuses on how excitement for the project declined, while Passage 2 focuses largely on the media's relationship to the project
(E) Passage 1 concludes that the management team ruined the project, while Passage 2 indicates that the media caused its failure

Questions 34–45 refer to the following passages.

Passage 1

There are approximately 90 different elements that occur naturally, but most of the things we encounter are made up of combinations of only about one third of them. Like most things in life,
(5) elements are each unique and, yet, can be grouped into classifications with other elements because of similarities. Thus, elements can be grouped according to whether they are highly reactive, somewhat reactive, or inert.
(10) Each element is made up of atoms. Within each atom is a certain number of protons and a matching number of electrons. This balance is necessary to keep each atom electrically neutral. An atom contains a nucleus with shells around it. The inner
(15) shell contains a maximum of two electrons. The next shell contains a maximum of eight electrons. Large atoms have a third shell that can contain a maximum of 32 electrons. As a general rule, if the outer shell is complete, it will seldom react with
(20) anything. If the outer shell still has room for several electrons, it is considered somewhat reactive. However, an atom that only needs one or two electrons to fill its outer shell will grab an electron or two from another atom. It is then considered
(25) highly reactive.

Table salt, which is the combination of sodium and chlorine, is an example of two highly reactive elements coming together. Sodium loses an electron from its outer shell, and chlorine gains that
(30) electron. This makes an ionic bond. One is negatively charged, the other is positively charged. This "opposites attract" bond is very strong.

Another kind of bond is a covalent bond. This is a bond in which elements come together and
(35) share electrons. Oxygen has six electrons in its outer shell. It thus needs two more. Hydrogen has one in its outer shell. So, when two hydrogens meet one oxygen, the one electron in the outer shell of each hydrogen fills in the two missing in
(40) oxygen to complete it to eight. However, they simply share the electrons. It is a nice sharing bond.

There are six elements that usually do not combine with others. These are called inert gases. They have the maximum number of electrons in their
(45) outer shells so they are not looking to find another element to bond with. Four of these elements are helium, argon, neon, and krypton.

Passage 2

It is often said that all is fair in love and war. That is used to explain the seemingly unlikely
(50) pairings done in the name of love. From years of observing couples, I have found that they can be classified into three main types. One pairing I call the sharing the relationship type. Another I term separate, but equal. The final type is what I call
(55) the odd couples.

In the first type, the people are true partners. They are together because they choose to share resources, space, and their lives. Sometimes, she is in charge. Sometimes, he is in charge. They take
(60) turns being the caregiver and the receiver. Some months, he writes out the bills. Other months, she does.

The second type is separate, but equal. Each member of the couple lives a separate life. They
(65) may have married because of society's expectation or because of a particular need, such as having children. They may live in the same household. But, overall, they have not bonded in an emotional sense.
(70) The third type, the odd couples, fall into the "opposites attract" category. She is attracted to him because he has characteristics she doesn't see in herself. Likewise, he is attracted to her because she displays traits he knows he will never have.
(75) Examples of this type of couple are the shy, quiet, studious librarian who is married to the life of the party.

34. What is the main idea of Passage 1?

    (A) one third of the elements are common

    (B) the ninety elements

    (C) the classification of elements according to bonding preference

    (D) bonds versus elements

    (E) the periodic table

35. According to Passage 1, most common items are composed of

    (A) approximately thirty separate elements

    (B) combinations of approximately thirty separate elements

    (C) approximately ninety different elements

    (D) combinations of approximately ninety different elements

    (E) the passage does not address this

36. The author of Passage 1 uses the phrase *As a general rule* (line 18) to indicate

    (A) that most elements will combine with other elements given the right environment

    (B) that most elements have two missing electrons in their outer shell

    (C) that elements with full outer shells are not reactive

    (D) how table salt is made

    (E) the reactivity of hydrogen

37. In looking at Passage 1, which of the following is true?

    (A) there are only four inert gases

    (B) inert gases are elements that do not combine with other elements easily

    (C) the six inert gases are helium, argon, neon, and krypton

    (D) verification of inert gases has never been done

    (E) inert gases are more readily able to combine with other elements than are sodium and chlorine

39. What is the main idea of Passage 2?

    (A) people choose strange partners because of love

    (B) all is fair in love and war

    (C) pairings of people can be classified into three types

    (D) true partners versus infatuation

    (E) couples can be observed

39. The use of the sentence, *Other months, she does.* (lines 61–62), in Passage 2 is used

    (A) to show that the woman is in charge in this type of pairing

    (B) as a part of an example demonstrating the true partners type

    (C) to indicate that women can have equal rights in a relationship

    (D) to introduce one of the types of pairings

    (E) to allow the reader into the insight of the author

40. According to Passage 2, which of the following statements is true?

    (A) The odd couples are the same as the opposites attract pairings.

    (B) The separate but equal pairings are similar to the true partners.

    (C) The opposites attract couples usually evolve into becoming separate but equal pairings.

    (D) The opposites attract pairings often become true partners over time.

    (E) Most of the odd couples end up being in failed marriages.

41. In Passage 2, the term *resources* (line 58) most likely refers to

    (A) land, air, and water

    (B) emotional closeness

    (C) children and pets

    (D) relatives, including the extended family

    (E) shelter, money, and possessions

42. In terms of person, which is true concerning these two passages?

    (A) Passage 1 is first person; Passage 2 is third person

    (B) both are in first person

    (C) both are in third person

    (D) Passage 1 is in third person; Passage 2 is in first person

    (E) Passage 1 is in first person; Passage 2 is in second person

43. The ionic bonds in Passage 1 are most like

    (A) the odd couples in Passage 2

    (B) the couples who share resources, but do not share their emotions in Passage 2

    (C) the separate, but equal partners in Passage 2

    (D) the true partners described in Passage 2

    (E) the partners who are unhappily married, as described in Passage 2

44. The passages differ in tone in that Passage 1 is

    (A) informational but Passage 2 is not

    (B) expository but Passage 2 is not

    (C) less formal than is Passage 2

    (D) more formal in its presentation of material while Passage 2 is more informal in its presentation

    (E) friendly and Passage 2 is businesslike

45. The reason for pairing these two passages is to show that

    (A) couples are made up of elements like everything else in life

    (B) elements can be classified in similar classifications to those of classifying people

    (C) people combine into couples in ways that are similar to the ways that elements combine

    (D) ionic bonds are different from covalent bonds

    (E) true partners in life cannot be separated once they have combined, be they either elements or people

IF YOU LEARNED ONLY THREE THINGS IN THIS CHAPTER . . . .

1. Stay focused while reading long passages.

2. The questions for long passages will always follow the content flow in the passage.

3. Paired passages contain two passages on one topic. Approach them the same way you approach single passages.

ANSWERS TO THE QUESTIONS ON PAGE 151

What Are the Strategies Specific to Long Passages?

- Always read the introduction to the passage.
- If time is running out, answer Vocabulary-in-Context and Little Picture questions first.

What Tools Do I Need to Succeed on These Question Types?

- Create a Passage Map that includes:
  - Notes in the margin
  - The purpose of each paragraph
  - Key points underlined
  - Author opinions pointed out

ANSWERS AND EXPLANATIONS

1. B

Here's how you might use your passage map and the Five-Step Method to answer question 1.

> According to the author, England could not really look like a leg of mutton (lines 6–8) because
>
> (A) maps generally don't give an accurate impression of what a place looks like
>
> (B) England was too grand and exotic a place for such a mundane image
>
> (C) England was an island not very different in appearance from her own island
>
> (D) the usual metaphor used to describe England was a precious jewel
>
> (E) mutton was one of the few foods familiar to her that did not come from England

Step 1. Read the Question Stem

There's no mystery about what the question is asking: Why couldn't England really look like a leg of mutton? (Notice that mutton is defined at the end of the passage—you aren't expected to know the meaning of unfamiliar terms.)

Step 2. Locate the Material You Need

Here's where active reading and your passage map come into play. In the margin by the first paragraph, you might have written "England = big deal." You might also have underlined *England was to be our source of myth and the source from which we got our sense of reality.* All that information around the cited lines helps you make a prediction.

Step 3. Predict the Answer

A good prediction might be, *England was too special to look like a familiar leg of mutton*.

Step 4. Scan the Answer Choices

Choice (B) comes close to the ideal—it might have jumped out. But if you weren't sure, you could have quickly eliminated the other choices. Thinking of the main idea would have helped you eliminate (A) and (C)—ideas that are not discussed in the passage. England was

precious—like a jewel—but the author doesn't imply that England was usually compared to a *jewel* (D), and you never learn where mutton *comes from* (E).

Step 5. Select Your Answer

Choice (B) is the only one that works here. By reading the material surrounding the line reference and putting an answer into your own words, you should have been able to choose (B) with confidence.

2. E

To find the correct answer, you must read the context of the statement referenced in the question. When the author states that felt is *not the proper material*, you may be tempted to choose answer (B) which mentions *arrogance*, or (C), *informality*. Refer back to the passage. Lines 44–46 mention that felt was not proper because it could not provide protection from the sun. This may cause you to think that choice (A) is correct because of the comment about the weather. However, if you keep reading, the author mentions that her *father must have seen and admired…an Englishman wearing such a hat in England*. This supports choice (E) as the correct answer.

3. D

Use context clues to determine the answer. Refer back to the passage and, if necessary, replace *conception* with the answer choices to find the best meaning of the word. *The very conception of the meal itself, breakfast, [...] was an idea from England*. Although *beginning* and *origination* seem to fit in the context of the sentence, only *notion*, or idea, most nearly means *conception*.

4. B

For this question, try replacing *substantial* as it is used in the sentence, with each of the answer choices. For example, [...] *its substantial quality and quantity was an idea from England*: its *important* quality, its *abundant* quality, its *firm* quality, its *down-to-earth* quality, or its *materialistic* quality. Even if you don't know the meaning of the word *abundant*, this answer choice makes the most sense in the context of the sentence.

5. B

You should re-read the third paragraph to get a sense of the tone of the question. If you scan the answer choices, most of them imply something negative: resentment, unhealthy, inability, excessive, unfamiliarity. In lines 63–64, the author states, *those three words were felt as a burden*. Lines 75–76 also mention that she *enjoyed [her] food more when I ate it with my bare hands*. These things imply that the author did not have a desire to become English.

6. D

Throughout the passage, the author is commenting on her parents' love for England and its traditions. The anecdotes refer to their behavior relating to English custom, so the author is conveying her parents' *reverence* for England.

7. B

Drawing a map of England did not promote an understanding of world affairs, encourage students to value their own heritage, or give them inappropriate knowledge. Although you might be tempted by choice (A), within the context of the passage, drawing a map of England was a way of glorifying one culture at the expense of another.

8. C

Read the lines referenced in the question. The author talks about a *process that would result in my erasure, no my physical erasure, but my erasure all the same*. The context eliminates choices (A) and (B) since she is not *being destroyed* or *physically disappearing*. The context mentions nothing of *censorship* or *freedom*. Therefore, the best choice is (C), *her sense of insignificance*.

9. C

Carefully read the opening paragraph and notice that the topic becomes more detailed as the paragraph progresses. The topics mentioned are blood, blood attributes, blood function, and blood components. (A) is a misused detail; although the *function* of blood is discussed, the overall passage focuses on the components of blood and the attributes of those components. (C), although similar, is a better answer. *Plasma and platelets* (B) are discussed, but they are not the main concern of the entire passage. (D) and (E) are both out of scope. The passage is concerned with *blood* (D) but focuses on a more detailed topic, and

although blood is a component of *the circulatory system* (E), this is never mentioned in the passage. (C) is the best choice.

10. D

The detail of plasma being *mostly water* (D) is set apart by commas, which should alert the reader that the author recognizes this attribute as important and wants it to be noted. (A) is a misused detail; red blood cells, not plasma, are biconcave disks. (B) is a distortion; plasma serves as a solvent for ions and molecules, but the passage does not state that it is composed of them. (C) and (E) are both too extreme; plasma interacts with the movement of water between blood and interstitial fluid (C) but is not itself *interstitial fluid*. Likewise, the passage does not say that plasma is *hemoglobin* (E), which is mentioned in the next paragraph pertaining to red blood cells. (D) is the only answer supported in the passage.

11. A

Notice that interstitial fluid is separated from blood and plasma in this sentence. Where would other fluids be located in the body? (B) is opposite of what you are looking for; plasma affects the water between blood and interstitial fluid, thus signifying that blood is not the same as this fluid. (C) and (E) are misused details; (C) relies on the assumptions of the reader and not the context of the passage. Interstices are indeed small spaces, but interstitial in this context is descriptive of the fluid. (E) relies on the assumption of the reader. Although a lattice is often used as a metaphor for interstitial space, this metaphor is not mentioned in the passage at hand. (D) is too extreme. Erythrocytes are red blood cells, which are not related to the topic of plasma in this sentence. (A) is the best answer choice.

12. C

Notice that many elements are responsible for eventually coloring blood red. Oxygen must bind with hemoglobin, and the iron (C) in hemoglobin is mentioned as giving "red blood cells their color," making choice (A) a distortion of what is stated in the passage. (B) is also a distortion; *oxygen* binds with hemoglobin and plays a part in coloring red blood cells, but the passage provides more details than that. (D) is too extreme; mature red blood cells no longer have their nucleus, and the nucleus does not color them.

Hemoglobin, enzymes, and other proteins (E) help in red blood cell function, but this fact is not detailed enough to discern what colors the red blood cells.

13. A

Writers use metaphor to better illustrate their argument. Consider what patrols and armies do, and picture what that role would be within the blood system and body. (B) is a misused detail; these are attributes of white blood cells, but the author's metaphors do not apply to them.

(C) is too extreme because although white blood cells may be considered violent by the invader's standpoint, the passage implies that they must be provoked before acting. Indeed, *B and T cells are highly specific* (D), combative cells, but this is too detailed an answer given the broad range of the question. Like (C), (E) is also too extreme; phagocytes engulf old red blood cells, and these metaphors do not pertain to red blood cells but rather white blood cells. (A) is the best choice.

14. B

The sentence states that macrophages "engulf invaders and debris" at the site of "inflamed tissues." It can therefore be inferred that "inflamed" describes the state of being attacked, or choice (B). (A) is out of scope; although flame can be found in inflamed, this answer solely relies on the assumptions of the reader and not the context of the sentence. (C) and (D) are distortions; macrophages engulf the invaders, which are responsible for inflaming the tissue, and *irritated* (D) is often synonymous with *inflamed*. However, the reader should extricate the meaning of inflamed from the context of the sentence, which points out that inflammation is the result of invaders and debris. (E) is too extreme; an inflamed tissue is clearly not healthy but is one in need of rescue.

15. B

The introduction to the passage names platelets as a blood component that would be discussed. Carefully read the paragraph on platelet production, and find the role megakaryocytes play in their development. (A) is a misused detail; megakaryocytes work with *plasma* to produce platelets. (C) and (D) are distortions; megakaryocytes are giant cells responsible for the development of *platelets* (C), but they are not platelets. Likewise, megakaryocytes are giant cells indirectly responsible for *blood clotting* (D),

which is the role of platelets. (E) is opposite of the correct answer; megakaryocytes are responsible for the development of platelets, and their life span is not mentioned in the passage. (B) is the best choice.

16. E

A rebirth indicates a dramatic and lasting change. With that in mind, how did the intellectuals and artists of the 1920s make dramatic or lasting changes? (A) and (B) are out of scope; the author never talks about the European Renaissance (A) or a religious transformation (B). (C) is too extreme; the author does not say that all contemporary African-American artists and politicians were influenced by the Harlem Renaissance. (D) is a distortion; the artists and intellectuals of 1920s Harlem certainly created some masterpieces, but this would not constitute a renaissance. (E) speaks of a lasting change that would characterize a *rebirth or renaissance*, and thus, is the correct answer.

17. C

The first two paragraphs of this passage are describing the musical influence inherent in the roots of the Harlem Renaissance. Where did these musical styles originate? (A) is a distortion; it could be inferred that there were more black people living in New York, but this does not explain the flourishing of arts and ideas that characterized the Harlem Renaissance. (B) is out of scope; there is nothing in the passage that would indicate that southern thought and art was superior. (D) is opposite of what the correct answer should be. The first paragraph clearly states that African-Americans from the south brought jazz to the north, which clearly influenced the works of the Harlem writers, artists, and intellectuals. (E) is a misused detail; Duke Ellington is mentioned in the passage, but this is unrelated to the question being asked. (C) most closely reflects the author's intention.

18. B

The author is asking you to contrast two styles. Which of the above answers best shows a contrast? (A) is out of scope; there is no mention of Shakespeare in this passage. (C) is a distortion; it could be inferred that southern dialects were present in the Harlem of 1920, but there is nothing in the passage to indicate that Hughes was influenced by them or that the elite found the dialects unimportant. (D) is also out of scope; there is no mention of similes or metaphors in the passage. (E) is opposite; a voice that is *highly stylized and theatrical* would be more affected than the voice of ordinary people used by Hughes. (B) best contrasts two different styles; the voice of ordinary people versus the accepted artificial voice.

19. E

Reformation has been used to describe any movement that alters the status quo and moves a group towards a specified goal. Which of the above definitions best fits with the historical use of the word? While reform can mean to reshape something (A), this definition does not make sense in the context of the passage. There is no indication of *civil disobedience* (B) being a part of the Harlem Renaissance, so this answer cannot be correct. (C) does not make sense in the context of the sentence or passage. Community need does not come into play here. (D) is the definition of a referendum, not a reformation. (E) is the best fit in the context of the sentence. It is used to show that social reform was necessary to bring about change and better the current conditions.

20. E

The author talks about Langston Hughes' poetry as revolutionary because it used the language of the people he encountered instead of the stylized voice common at the time. Can you make any assumptions about other art forms based on this theme? (A) is out of scope; while this may be true, it is not addressed in the passage. There is no indication in the passage that African-American art was *unflattering* (B). (C) is also out of scope; there is no mention in the passage about what kind of art supplies were used by the artists of the time. *Art Deco* (D) is mentioned as a style used by one of the artists. It does not indicate that all Art Deco works were, by virtue of the style, imbued with an air of dignity and grace. (E) best fits the overall mood of the Harlem Renaissance that allowed for a more realistic depiction of the African-American life of the 1920s.

21. A

There are a couple of answers that may be correct, but only one answer is directly addressed by the author. (A) is the only answer that is directly written about in the passage. (B) is out of scope; there is no mention of either man organizing demonstrations in this passage. Also, the passage does not substantiate the claim that Martin Luther

King Jr. and Malcolm X ever met W.E.B. Dubois or Marcus Garvey (C). (D) is a distortion; it is probably true that both Martin Luther King Jr. and Malcolm X were aware of the works from the Harlem Renaissance. This awareness does not answer the question of how they might have been influenced by what they read. Finally, the passage does not state that there was any such bus strike mentioned in answer choice (E).

22. B

The question states that this word is not normally associated with writing. Which of the answers would show an association to another area or art form? (A) cannot be correct because the passage never speaks to his mental state or any thematic anger. (C) If *riff* were synonymous with verse, it would certainly be associated with writing and is, therefore, incorrect. (D) does not make sense in the context of the sentence. (E) would not meet the criteria that it was a word that was not normally associated with writing. (B) meets all the qualifications of the question and is, therefore, correct.

23. C

To answer this question, decide what the overall goal of the passage is. How does this introductory sentence serve to further this goal? How do the quotation marks around *art* help with this goal? (A) seems possible, but the author never attempts to define art itself. (B) is incorrect because it is usually good to assume that in test question passages, literary and typographical devices do serve a purpose. (C) is correct because the quotation marks around *art* indicate that the author questions the classification of conceptual art as art (this is an *ironic* sense of quotation marks). This indicates a negative view toward conceptual art, and because in the passage the author states the opinion that conceptual art is not a worthwhile medium, this minimal typographical detail alerts the reader about what is likely to follow. (D) is opposite of what you're looking for; the passage indicates that the author is NOT fond of conceptual art. (E) is out of scope; the importance of art in general is not discussed in this passage.

24. B

Several wrong answer choices reflect a more common meaning of *maintain*. Eliminate these, and try the others in the sentence, paying close attention to the surrounding context; can you guess which is the best answer? The correct answer is (B) "asserted." *Maintain* most often means "repair" or "keep up," but as always, don't reactively select the first answer choice that looks as if it might be correct. Choices (D) and (E) make sense in the sentence, but not with its surrounding context (no dispute or argument is involved).

25. D

Skim the passage, and try to understand how the author seems to feel about the topic. Is there an answer choice that reflects your impression? (A) is opposite; the author clearly does not believe that conceptual art is important and, in fact, calls it *absurd*. (B) is a misused detail; Marcel Duchamp is mentioned in the passage but only as a supporting detail. It would therefore be inappropriate to title the passage accordingly. (C) is also a misused detail; one bumper sticker is referenced in the passage, but again, this is only a supporting detail and not worthy of inspiring a title for the passage. (E) is too extreme; the word *all* should alert you that this may be an extreme answer choice, but, in addition, the passage does not attempt to describe *all art* or make any value judgments about it. The passage is written to explain what conceptual art is and why the author dislikes it. The last paragraph, in particular, makes it very clear that the author holds a negative opinion of this type of art, which makes (D) correct.

26. A

This word is defined immediately before it appears. The correct answer is (A) (line 27: *"words that do not yet exist"*).

27. B

Answering this question requires you to make several inferences and then exclude each answer choice that can be supported by the passage. (A) is supported by lines 24–25, "the contemporary conceptual artist Adib Fricke deals with language." (C) is supported by lines 16–19, "Conceptual art, for the most part, completely left behind a physical representation...." (D) is supported by the lines 40–42, "It is thus a way to avoid having to undertake the effort and exhibit the skill necessary to produce a lasting physical work of art." (E) is supported by lines 6–8, "Those who wished to further pursue abstraction to its absurd end became conceptual artists." Tolstoy's outlines are actually given as an example that is NOT conceptual art, and thus choice (B) is the correct answer.

28. E

To answer this question, you must first use your inference skills to determine how the author feels about this type of art. The correct answer is (E) *with disdain*. This inference can be made on the basis of the author's example about Leo Tolstoy; the rhetorical question in the last sentence, as well as the clearly stated opinion about this type of art, show that author's main feeling toward conceptual art is disdain.

29. C

The author has a strong opinion on the topic of the passage. What is it? (A) is a distortion; the middle paragraphs do describe the history of conceptual art, but this is not the main point of the passage. (B) is a misused detail; Tolstoy's literary methods are described in order to support the author's opinion about conceptual art; however, this is not the main subject or goal of the passage. From the first line of the passage (in which *art* is placed in quotation marks to cue the reader that the author has a disparaging opinion of the subject matter) to the last paragraph (in which the author states outright that conceptual art is "a way to avoid having to undertake the effort and exhibit the skill necessary to produce a lasting physical work of art"; lines 40–42), the author attempts to convince the reader that conceptual art is undeserving of attention as a real art form. (D) is also a misused detail; Adib Fricke's work with The Word Company is treated in the passage as a way to clarify what conceptual art consists of. Still, this is a supporting detail and is not the main point of the passage. (E) is out of scope. Abstract art is mentioned, but it is neither compared nor contrasted with conceptual art.

30. D

Because the cited line describes an act that caused people to question the project's adherence to its mission of self-sufficiency, you can infer that the managers would probably have tried to be secretive about any supplies they were providing to the crew. Look for a choice that reflects the undercover or illicit nature of the activity. Doing something *gingerly* (A) means doing it in a cautious, tentative way. While this comes close to capturing the meaning of the cited word, it does not express the idea that the managers' actions were not intended to be seen or discovered.

The context of the passage does not indicate how difficult it was for the managers to supply the crew with outside goods, thus (B) is incorrect. Whereas a quiet person might be meek or submissive, *meekly* (C) does not fit the context. Whereas you might infer that the managers were careless because they got caught, (E) is not a meaning of the cited word. (D) nicely matches your prediction.

31. A

The sentence tells you that many scientists were trying to suppress or extinguish the "lofty goals" or overly high expectations for the project, suggesting that the scientists thought such goals were unrealistic. Since it was the press that was "dubbing" the project as so exciting, this indicates that the unrealistic expectations were put forth or perpetuated by the media. (B) is out of scope; the passage only discusses the Biosphere 2 project, not projects dealing with aircraft or flight. (C) is a distortion; the passage only suggests that the *press* believed the project was *as* exciting as the moon landing, not that scientists found it more exciting. The author makes no recommendations regarding what the management team (D) should or should not have done, and the passage does not mention whether the management team consulted scientists. While (E) may be accurate given all the hype about the project, the cited sentence does not support this statement.

32. E

Whereas the focus in the two passages is different, both authors discuss changes in how the project was viewed. Passage 1 states that it began with "great fanfare and optimism" that later became "almost entirely eroded," and Passage 2 notes that the project was initially seen as "exciting" but eventually caused frustration. Both passages, then, discuss how high expectations were let down. (A) is too extreme; both passages suggest that the project failed to achieve its main goal, but they do not rule out the possibility that some useful data were produced. (B) is out of scope; neither passage explores changes over time in the scientific value of the project. (C) misinterprets a statement in Passage 1 about managers sneaking outside supplies to the crew. (D) is also out of scope; Passage 1 does not mention the moon landing. (E) is the best answer choice.

33. D

Passage 1 focuses on how and why enthusiasm for the project declined, while Passage 2 focuses on the media's role in portraying the project. You are looking for a choice that captures this difference. (A) is out of scope; neither passage emphasizes successes of the project. (B) is a

distortion; Passage 2 does not state that exploring space habitation was the project's only goal. (C) is also a distortion; Passage 1 does not express an opinion of the financiers, and Passage 2 describes but does not evaluate the financiers' anger with the media. (E) is too extreme; both characterizations are too strong given the rather objective tone of the passages. Thus, (D) is the best answer.

34. C

This passage describes the fact that elements can be classified into three types based on their likelihood of forming bonds.

Although (A) and (B) are both mentioned in the first paragraph, these are simply establishing details. They are not the main ideas of the passage. (D) is not accurate because of the *versus*. This passage discusses elements and bonds, but they are not in a *versus* relationship. Although the periodic table is indeed where the classification of the elements could be found, the table itself is not the main idea of the passage. Thus, (E) is not correct.

35. B

The passage states that there are approximately 90 elements, but most things are made up of combinations of approximately one third of those. That would be approximately 30. Answers (A) and (C) are not correct because most things are not made up of single elements. (D) is not correct because most common things involve only about one third of the ninety elements. (E) is not correct because, whereas the passage does not say it directly, it can be inferred using the evidence from the passage that there are approximately *90 elements* and *most things* are made up of combinations of *one third* of them.

36. C

This is using the heuristic introductory element to give a simplistic rule of thumb that explains a natural occurrence. None of the other answers are correct because this introductory element precedes a statement about elements with full outer shells and the fact that they are not reactive.

37. B

This is a specific detail question answered by the evidence offered in the first two sentences in the last paragraph.

Although there are only four inert gases listed, there are actually six inert gases. Thus, answer (A) is not correct.

Answer (C) is not correct because it uses the number six, but then only lists four.

Answer (D) is not correct because it is not addressed in the passage, and it is not true.

Answer (E) is not correct because inert gases, as stated in the final paragraph, do not combine readily with other elements.

38. C

This entire passage is about the idea of classifying couples into three distinct types.

(A) is not correct because it does not address the entire passage. (B) is simply a statement that is used to introduce the topic but certainly is not the main idea of the entire passage. (D) is not accurate because infatuation is not discussed in the passage at all. (E) is not correct because, whereas indeed the couples had to be observed in order for the author to come to the conclusions she did, the idea that this observation took place is not the main idea being expressed.

39. B

This sentence corresponds with the sentence before it and is a part of the example that explains how a couple classified as true partners conduct their relationship. (A) is not accurate because the woman in this type of pairing is in charge some of the time, but at other times, she is not. (C) is not correct because the purpose of the statement is simply to exemplify the type, not to make a political statement about male/female relationships. (D) is not correct because the statement is a part of an example, rather than a part of an introduction of a classification. (E) is not correct because the statement is simply showing an example rather than insight into the thinking of the author.

40. A

In the first sentence of the final paragraph, the author names couples in the third classification as both odd couples and as opposites who are attracted to one another. (B) includes one type from the second classification and one type from the first classification. They are not similar. (C) and (D) are not accurate because the passage does not state anything about one classification type evolving into another type. (E) is not accurate because the passage does not discuss any aspect of failed marriages.

41. E

Because the passage is discussing couples and the things they share, it can be inferred that the resources are shelter, money, and possessions. (A) is about natural resources, but it would not make sense to choose it in this context. (B) is not correct because the author chooses to include *their lives* in the same series. The emotional closeness is probably inferred there rather than in the term *resources*. (C) and (D) are not correct because they do not describe items that are normally thought of as resources.

42. D

Passage 1 is written using the objective voice of third person. Because of the usage of "I" in Passage 2, we can determine that it is written in first person. The other answers are not accurate because none of them indicate this correct identification.

43. A

This inference question asks you to consider how the three classifications in the first passage correlate with the three classifications in the second passage. The correlations are: 1) ionic bonds correlate with the odd couples; 2) covalent bonds correlate with the true partners; and 3) inert gases correlate with the separate, but equal partners. Thus, (A) is the only one that shows the correct correlation.

44. D

Passage 1 is written as straight information, using third person. It is expository in nature and formal. Passage 2 is also expository, but because it is written in first person, it is less formal. (A) and (B) are not correct because both passages are expository (informational). (C) is not correct because Passage 1 is actually more formal than Passage 2. (E) is not correct because neither of the passages fall into the category of "friendly."

45. C

This describes the correlation of the two passages. (A) is not correct because, whereas the statement is true, it does not show the correlation of the passages. (B) is not correct because the second passage is not about classification of people, but rather is about classification of couples. (D) is not correct because it only mentions bonds discussed in Passage 1. (E) describes only one type of bond in each passage. However, there are two other types of bonds in each of the passages.

Chapter Ten: **Vocabulary-Building Strategies**

- What Are the Types of Words I'm Going To See on the SAT?

- What Strategies Will Help Me Learn the Right Vocabulary Words?

- What Skills Will Help Me Succeed with the Tough SAT Vocabulary Words?

A good score on the Critical Reading component depends, in part, upon your ability to work with unfamiliar words. You will often need to have a sense of their meaning to answer both the Sentence Completion and Reading Comprehension questions.

If you have only a week or two to prepare for the SAT, either go straight to the "Decoding Strange Words on the Test" section of this chapter and master those skills, or, if you are really pressed for time, just skim that section to learn our most basic SAT vocabulary strategies.

Otherwise, read on.

HARD SAT WORDS

There are two types of hard SAT words:

- Unfamiliar words
- Familiar words with secondary meanings

Some words are hard because you haven't seen them before. The words *scintilla* and *circumlocution*, for instance, are probably not part of your everyday vocabulary. But they might pop up on your SAT.

Easy words, such as *recognize* or *appreciation*, can also trip you up on the test because they have secondary meanings that you aren't used to. Reading Comprehension, in particular, will throw you familiar words with unfamiliar meanings.

To get a sense of your vocabulary strength, we've provided a representative list of words you might find on the SAT. Take a couple of minutes to work through it and see how many you know. How many words can you define? Write your answer right in the book. Give yourself one point for each word you know. (The answers follow, so don't cheat by looking at them. As authority figures like to say: you'll only be hurting yourself.)

irritate _____

truthful _____

conquer _____

passionate _____

inactive _____

eliminate _____

benevolent _____

elocution _____

irk _____

pragmatic _____

breadth _____

rectify _____

duplicity _____

impartial _____

abandon (n.) _____

vie _____

overt _____

august (adj.) _____

laud _____

voluble _____

flag (v.) _____

perspicacity _____

maladroit _____

sonorous _____

doleful _____

serpentine _____

rail (v.) _____

quiescence _____

idiosyncrasy _____

kudos _____

Here are the definitions:

irritate	to annoy, bother
truthful	honest, straightforward, trustworthy
conquer	to defeat, overthrow
passionate	emotional, ardent, enthusiastic
inactive	not active, not moving
eliminate	to get rid of
benevolent	generous, kind
elocution	the study and practice of public speaking
irk	to irritate, anger, annoy
pragmatic	practical; moved by facts rather than abstract ideal
breadth	broadness, wideness
rectify	to correct
duplicity	deception, dishonesty, double-dealing
impartial	fair, just, unbiased, unprejudiced
abandon (n.)	total lack of inhibition
vie	to compete, contend
overt	apparent, unconcealed
august (adj.)	dignified, awe-inspiring, venerable
laud	to praise, applaud, honor
voluble	speaking much and easily, talkative; glib
flag (v.)	to droop, lose energy; to signal, to mark
perspicacity	shrewdness, astuteness, keenness of wit

maladroit	clumsy, tactless
sonorous	producing a full, rich sound
doleful	sad, mournful
serpentine	serpentlike; twisting, winding
rail (v.)	to scold with bitter or abusive language
quiescence	inactivity, stillness
idiosyncrasy	peculiarity of temperament, eccentricity
kudos	fame, glory, honor

10 or fewer

If you got 10 definitions or fewer right, you should probably work on building your vocabulary. The techniques and tools in this chapter will help you improve your word base and make the most out of what you do know about words.

10–20 correct

If you got between 10 and 20 right, your vocabulary is about average. If you're willing to put in the time, using these techniques and tools can help you improve your vocabulary and your score on the exam.

20 or more correct

If you got 20 or more right, your vocabulary is in great shape. You can polish it further, but you don't have to. If time is short, learn the strategies in the "Decoding Strange Words" section and concentrate on other aspects of the SAT that you find difficult.

 BE SMART!

Even if you think your vocabulary skills are great, you can always benefit from reviewing the Vocabulary List in the Resources at the end of this book.

⊚ **KAPLAN'S TARGET STRATEGY FOR ———— LEARNING VOCABULARY**

A great vocabulary can't be built overnight, but it can be improved in a relatively short period of time with a minimum amount of pain. But you need to study wisely. Be strategic. How well you use your time between now and the day of the test is just as important as how much time you spend prepping.

Here's our three-step plan for building your vocabulary for the SAT:

Step 1. Learn words strategically.

Step 2. Learn word roots and prefixes.

Step 3. Personalize your vocabulary study.

Step 1. Learn Words Strategically

The best words to learn are words that have appeared often on the SAT. The test makers are formulaic in test creation, so the test is consistent from one administration to the next, thus words that have appeared frequently are likely bets to show up again.

The word list in Resource Four give you a jump on some common SAT words. Learn a few words each day from these lists, spreading them over the time remaining before the SAT. Keep reviewing those you've already studied.

Step 2. Learn Word Roots and Prefixes

Most SAT words are made up of prefixes and roots that can get you at least part way to a definition. Often, that's all you need to get a right answer. Use the word root list in Resource Two to pick up the most valuable SAT roots. Target these words in your vocabulary review. Learn a few new roots a day, familiarizing yourself with the meaning and sample words.

Word families may also be of some use. A word family is a group of words that shares a similar meaning. For example, *loquacious, verbose,* and *garrulous* all mean *wordy, talkative*. *Taciturn, laconic, terse, concise,* and *pithy* all mean *not talkative, not wordy*. Instead of learning just one of these words, learn them all together—you get eight words for the price of just two definitions.

 GO ONLINE

Learn word roots daily with your downloadable Study Sheet for study on the go.

Step 3. Personalize Your Vocabulary Study

There isn't just one *right* way to study vocabulary. Figure out a study method that works best for you and stick to it. Here are some proven strategies:

- Use flashcards. Write down new words or word groups and run through them whenever you have a few spare minutes. Put one new word or word group on one side of a 3 × 5 index card and a short definition on the back.

- Make a vocabulary notebook. List words in one column and their meanings in another. Test yourself. Cover up the meanings, and see what words you can define from memory. Make a sample sentence using each word in context.

- Make a vocabulary tape. Record yourself saying unknown words and their definitions. Pause for a moment before you read the definition. This will give you time to define the word in your head when you play back the tape. Quiz yourself. Listen to your tape in your portable cassette player. Play it in the car, on the bus, or whenever you have a few spare moments.

- Think of hooks that lodge a new word in your mind: Create visual images of words. For example, to remember the verb form of *flag*, you can picture a flag drooping or losing energy as the wind dies down.

- Use rhymes and other devices that help you remember the words. For example, you might remember that a *verbose* person uses a lot of verbs.

It doesn't matter which techniques you use, as long as you learn words steadily and methodically. Doing so over several months with regular reviews is ideal.

DECODING STRANGE WORDS ON THE TEST

Trying to learn every word that could possibly appear on the SAT is like trying to memorize the license plate number of every car on the road. There are just too many to commit to memory.

No matter how much time you spend with flashcards, vocabulary tapes, or word lists, you're bound to face some mystery words on your SAT. Just as you can use your basic multiplication skills to find the product of even the largest numbers, you can use what you know about words to focus on likely meanings of tough vocabulary words.

Remember Where You've Heard the Word Before

If you can recall a phrase in which the word appears, that may be enough to eliminate some answer choices or even zero in on the right answer.

> Between the two villages was a ---- through which passage was difficult and hazardous.
>
> (A) precipice
> (B) beachhead
> (C) quagmire
> (D) market
> (E) prairie

To answer this question, you need to know whether or not to eliminate the word *quagmire*. You may remember *quagmire* from news reports referring to "a foreign policy *quagmire*" or "a *quagmire* of financial indebtedness." If you can remember how *quagmire* was used, you'll have a rough idea of what it means, and you'll see it fits. You may also be reminded of the word *mire*, as in "We got *mired* in the small details and never got to the larger issue." Sounds something like stuck, right? You don't need an exact definition. A *quagmire* is a situation that's difficult to get out of, so (C) is correct. Literally, a *quagmire* is a bog or swamp.

Decide Whether the Word Has a Positive or Negative Charge

Simply knowing that you're dealing with a positive or negative word can earn you points on the SAT. For example, look at the word *cantankerous*. Say it to yourself. Can you guess whether it's positive or negative? Often words that sound harsh (such as *irk*) have a negative meaning, whereas smooth-sounding words (such as *benevolent*) tend to have positive meanings. If *cantankerous* sounded negative to you, you were right. It means *ill-tempered, disagreeable,* or *difficult to handle.*

Prefixes and roots can suggest a word's charge. *Mal, de, dis, un, in, im, a,* and *mis* often indicate a negative, whereas *pro, ben,* and *magn* are often positives.

Not all words sound positive or negative; some sound neutral. But if you can define the charge, you can probably eliminate some answer choices on that basis alone. Here's an example.

> He seemed at first to be honest and loyal, but before long it was necessary to ---- him for his ---- behavior.
>
> (A) admonish . . steadfast
> (B) extol . . conniving
> (C) reprimand . . scrupulous
> (D) exalt . . insidious
> (E) castigate . . perfidious

All you need to know to answer this question is that negative words are needed in both blanks. Then you can scan the answer choices for one that contains two clearly negative words. Even if you don't know what all the words mean, you can use your sense of positive or negative charge to eliminate answers. Choice (E) is right. *Castigate* means *punish* or *scold harshly*, and *perfidious* means *treacherous*.

Use Your Foreign Language Skills

Many of the roots you'll encounter in SAT words come from Latin. Spanish, French, and Italian also come from Latin and have retained much of it in their modern forms. English is also a cousin to German and Greek. That means that if you don't recognize a word, try to remember if you know a similar word in another language. Look at the word *carnal*. Unfamiliar? What about *carne*, as in *chili con carne*? *Carn* means *meat* or *flesh*, which leads you straight to the meaning of *carnal*—pertaining to the flesh.

You could decode *carnivorous* (meat-eating) in the same way. You can almost always figure out something about strange words on the test. Chances are that few words on the SAT will be totally new to you, even if your recollection is more subliminal than vivid.

When All Else Fails

If you feel totally at a loss in determining the exact meaning of the word, eliminate choices that are clearly wrong and make an educated guess from the remaining choices. A wrong answer won't hurt you much, but a right answer can help you a lot.

IF YOU LEARNED ONLY TWO THINGS IN THIS CHAPTER . . . .

1. Learning vocabulary takes time. Start now and continue throughout your preparation.
2. The best words to learn are words that have appeared often on the SAT.

ANSWERS TO THE QUESTIONS ON PAGE 179

What are the Types of Words I'm Going To See on the SAT?

- Unfamiliar words
- Familiar words with secondary meanings

What Strategies Will Help Me Learn the Right Vocabulary Words?

- Kaplan's Target Strategy for Learning Vocabulary Words
  - Step 1. Learn words strategically.
  - Step 2. Learn word roots and prefixes.
  - Step 3. Personalize your vocabulary study.

What Skills Will Help Me Succeed with the Tough SAT Vocabulary Words?

- Decode tough vocabulary words by:
  - Using your instinct about where you've heard the word before.
  - Decide whether the word has a positive or negative charge.
  - Think if you've seen a similar word in another language.

How to Attack the Math Component

Many students fear the Math section more than they do the Writing and Critical Reading sections. But there is no reason to feel that way. Just as in the other sections, there are proven Kaplan strategies for approaching the different kinds of SAT Math questions.

Section Four of the SAT Premier Program attacks the SAT Math sections. We approach the Math sections differently than we approached the Writing and Critical Reading sections. Chapter Eleven shows you our test-taking strategies for solving SAT-style math problems. Chapters Twelve and Thirteen are specifically structured around the different math concepts you will encounter on the SAT and provides examples, practice sets, and content-specific strategies for solving everything from simple ratios to the qualitative behavior of graphs and functions. Chapter Fourteen shows you the SAT's favorite math traps and how to recognize them and avoid falling for them on test day.

Chapter Eleven: **SAT Math Basics and Strategies**

- What Question Types Make Up the Math Component?
- What Do I Need to Know About Each Question Type?
- What Strategies Will Help Me Succeed on the Math Component?

There are three Math sections on the SAT. They can appear anywhere during the test, except section 1, in any order. They are:

Length	Content	Type
25 minutes	High school geometry and algebra, numbers and operations, statistics, probability, and data analysis	Multiple choice and student-produced responses*
25 minutes	High school geometry and algebra, numbers and operations, statistics, probability, and data analysis	Multiple choice and student-produced responses*
20 minutes	High school geometry and algebra, numbers and operations, statistics, probability, and data analysis	Multiple choice

Questions in the Math sections are arranged to gradually increase in difficulty. Be aware of the difficulty level as you go through a question set. The harder the question seems, the more traps you will have to avoid.

*Grid-ins will appear in one of the two 25-minute sections.

MATH COVERED IN THE SAT

The tested math concepts on the SAT are as follows:

- Numbers and operations
- Algebra I, II, and functions
- Geometry
- Statistics, probability, and data analysis

We will cover them all in detail in upcoming chapters.

MULTIPLE-CHOICE QUESTIONS

The multiple-choice question setup in the Math section is the same as in the other two sections. You will be given five answers from which to choose the best one. Thus, certain techniques will help you eliminate answer choices and make the problems more manageable. We will go over those techniques later in this chapter.

Directions

Read these directions through carefully. By test day, you will want to know these directions by heart so you won't waste precious time trying to decipher their meaning.

Directions: For this section, solve each problem and decide which is the best of the choices given. Fill in the corresponding oval on the answer sheet. You may use any available space for scratchwork.

Notes:

(1) Calculator use is permitted.

(2) All numbers used are real numbers.

(3) Figures are provided for some problems. All figures are drawn to scale and lie in a plane UNLESS otherwise indicated.

(4) Unless otherwise specified, the domain of any function f is assumed to be the set of all real numbers x for which $f(x)$ is a real number.

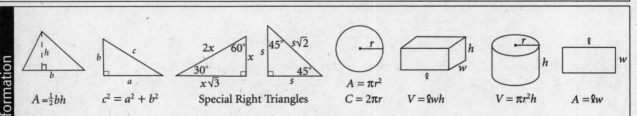

$A = \frac{1}{2}bh$ $c^2 = a^2 + b^2$ Special Right Triangles $A = \pi r^2$ $C = 2\pi r$ $V = \ell wh$ $V = \pi r^2 h$ $A = \ell w$

The sum of the degree measures of the angles in a triangle is 180.
The number of degrees of arc in a circle is 360.
A straight angle has a degree measure of 180.

GRID-IN QUESTIONS

The Grid-in section on the SAT is more like the math tests you're used to taking at school. Rather than choosing your answer from five choices provided by the test makers, you have to work through the problem and write whatever answer you came up with in grid boxes on the answer sheet. Some Grid-in questions only have one correct answer, whereas others have several correct answers. *There is no penalty for wrong answers on the Grid-in section.*

Directions

Each Grid-in question provides four boxes and a column of ovals, or bubbles, to write your answer in. The elements of your answer, that is, the digits, decimal points, or fraction signs, should be written in a separate box for each part. The corresponding bubbles underneath should be shaded in to match the box at the top of the column. There are limitations to what you may grid and what will not be counted.

Each of the remaining 10 questions requires you to solve the problem and enter your answer by marking the ovals in the special grid, as shown in the example below. You may use any available space for scratch work.

Answer: 1.25 or $\frac{5}{4}$ or 5/4

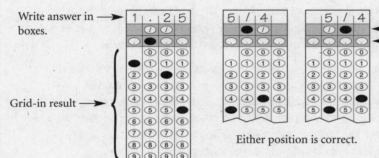

Write answer in boxes.

Grid-in result

Fraction line
Decimal point

Either position is correct.

You may start your answers in any column, space permitting. Columns not needed should be left blank.

- It is recommended, though not required, that you write your answer in the boxes at the top of the columns. However, **you will receive credit only for darkening the ovals correctly**.

- Grid only one answer to a question, even though some problems have more than one correct answer.

- Darken no more than one oval in a column.

- No answers are negative.

- **Mixed numbers** cannot be gridded. For example: the number $1\frac{1}{4}$ must be gridded as 1.25 or 5/4.

(If 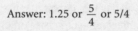 is gridded, it will be interpreted as $\frac{11}{4}$ not $1\frac{1}{4}$.)

- <u>Decimal Accuracy:</u> Decimal answers must be entered as accurately as possible. For example, if you obtain an answer such as 0.1666…, you should record the result as .166 or .167. **Less accurate values such as .16 or .17 are not acceptable.**

Acceptable ways to grid $\frac{1}{6}$ = .1666…

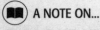 **A NOTE ON...**

GRID-INS AND MIXED NUMBERS

To grid a mixed number, you must first convert it to an improper fraction or decimal and then grid that new value. For example, $2\frac{1}{2}$ will be read as $\frac{21}{2}$ if gridded as a mixed number. Thus, gridding it as $\frac{5}{2}$ or 2.5 will ensure that your answer will be correct.

You cannot grid:

- Negative answers
- Answers with variables (x, y, w, etc.)
- Answers greater than 9,999
- Answers with commas (write 1000, not 1,000)
- Mixed numbers (such as $2\frac{1}{2}$)

We discuss Grid-ins more in this chapter and other chapters in this section.

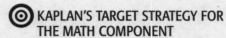 **KAPLAN'S TARGET STRATEGY FOR THE MATH COMPONENT**

It is not enough to know about the types of math questions on the test and how many you will have to answer. If it were, we could end this section right now. To maximize your score on the Math section, you will need to work systematically. Just like the Critical Reading and Writing questions, the key to working systematically on Math questions is to think about the question before you look for the answer.

On the more basic questions, you may find that you know the answers right away and are able to work through them quickly. However, when working through the harder problems, a few extra seconds spent looking for traps, thinking about your approach, and deciding whether to work on the problem immediately or to come back to it later is very important and will help you accrue more points.

Kaplan's Target Strategy is a good system for tackling *all* SAT Math problems. If you can quickly conjure up these steps on test day, you will find that the questions will seem manageable and that you are using your time efficiently. The steps are as follows:

Step 1. Estimate the question's difficulty.

Step 2. Read the question.

Step 3. Skip or do.

Step 4. Look for fastest approach.

We will now show you how our Target Strategy works as we use it to answer this sample SAT question:

> At a diner, Joe orders three strips of bacon and a cup of coffee and is charged $2.25. Stella orders two strips of bacon and a cup of coffee and is charged $1.70. What is the price of two strips of bacon?
>
> (A) $0.55
> (B) $0.60
> (C) $1.10
> (D) $1.30
> (E) $1.80

Step 1. Estimate the Question's Difficulty

SAT Math questions are arranged in order of difficulty. Keep this in mind as you work through a set. In a math set, the first few questions are basic, the middle few are moderately difficulty, and the last few are hard. The question above is a moderately difficult word problem.

On difficult questions, watch out for math traps (see Chapter Fourteen). Hard questions are often written to be misleading, containing one or two answers that will seem to be right at first glance. Be careful of these easy answers for hard questions. They are there specifically to trick you. Make sure you always know what's being asked.

Step 2. Read the Question

If you try to start solving the problem before reading the question all the way through, you may end up doing unnecessary work. The question above looks straightforward, but read through it carefully, and you will see a slight twist. You're asked to find the cost of two strips of bacon, not one. Many people will find the price of a single bacon strip and forget to double it. Don't make this mistake.

Step 3. Skip or Do

If a problem renders you clueless, circle it in your test booklet and move on. Spend your time on the problems you can solve; if there's still time at the end of the section, come back to the ones you had trouble with then. It is better to get two points from two less challenging problems than spend the same amount of time on one tricky question you are unsure of.

 GO ONLINE

Check out your new practice quiz every month.

Step 4. Look for the Fastest Approach

On an easy question, all the information you need to solve the problem may be provided in the question stem or in a diagram. Harder questions often hide the information that will help you solve the problem. For instance, for a question like the one on the previous page that would appear in the middle of the question set, you would want to be suspicious of easy answers and cautious in your approach to it. If you get the answer too easily, you may have missed something. (In this case, you're asked to find the price of two strips of bacon, not one.)

Look for shortcuts. Sometimes the obvious way of doing a problem is the long way. If the method you choose involves lots of calculating, look for another route. There's usually a shortcut you can use that won't involve tons of arithmetic.

Again, in the sample question, the cost of bacon and coffee could be translated into two distinct equations using the variables b and c. You could find c in terms of b, and then plug this into the other equation. But if you think carefully, you'll see there's a quicker way. The difference in price between three bacon strips and a cup of coffee and two bacon strips and a cup of coffee is the price of one bacon strip. So one bacon strip costs $2.25 − $1.70 = $0.55.

(Remember, you have to find the price of two strips of bacon. Twice $0.55 is $1.10.)

Chapters Twelve and Thirteen provide strategies for specific problem types that help you get to the right answer fast. You can also use Kaplan's alternate techniques, such as picking numbers and backsolving, which we will get to in this chapter.

ALTERNATIVE TECHNIQUES

Kaplan's Target Strategy for the Math Component will help you save time and avoid mistakes on the SAT. But sometimes you won't know how to do the Math needed to find the answer or doing so will simply be too time-consuming. Luckily, there are several methods for working through math problems. There are two techniques, in particular, that can be useful when you don't know where to start: picking numbers and backsolving.

Picking Numbers

Sometimes you get stuck on a Math question just because it's too general or abstract. A good solution to this problem is to substitute particular numbers for the equation variables.

This picking numbers strategy works especially well with even/odd questions.

> If a is an odd integer and b is an even integer, which of the following must be odd?
>
> (A) $2a + b$
>
> (B) $a + 2b$
>
> (C) ab
>
> (D) a^2b
>
> (E) ab^2

 BE SMART!

When picking numbers, keep it simple. Choose small numbers that are easier to work with than larger numerals.

Rather than trying to wrap your brain around abstract variables, simply pick numbers for a and b. When you are adding, subtracting, or multiplying even and odd numbers, you can generally assume that what happens with one pair of numbers generally happens with similar pairs of numbers. Let's say, for the time being, that $a = 3$ and $b = 2$. Plug those values into the answer choices, and there's a good chance that only one choice will be odd:

> (A) $2a + b = 2(3) + 2 = 8$
>
> (B) $a + 2b = 3 + 2(2) = 7$
>
> (C) $ab = (3)(2) = 6$
>
> (D) $a^2b = (3^2)(2) = 18$
>
> (E) $ab^2 = (3)(2^2) = 12$

Choice (B) is the only odd answer for $a = 3$ and $b = 2$; thus, it is fair to assume that it must be the only odd answer choice, no matter what odd numbers you plug in for a and b. The answer is (B).

Another good situation for picking numbers is when the answer choices to percent problems are all percents. Look at the following example.

> From 1985 to 1990, the berry production of bush x increased by 20 percent. From 1990 to 1995, the berry production increased by 30 percent. What was the percent increase in the berry production on the bush over the entire ten-year period from 1985–1995?
>
> (A) 10%
>
> (B) 25%
>
> (C) 50%
>
> (D) 56%
>
> (E) 60%

Rather than attempting to solve this problem in the abstract, choose a number for the berry production in 1985 and see what happens. There's no need to pick a realistic number. You're better off picking a number that's easy to work with. In percent problems, the number that's easiest to work with is almost always 100.

 KAPLAN

Now that we have our number, let's plug it into the problem. The number of berries on the bush in 1985 was 100. What would the 1990 berry production be? Twenty percent more than 100 is 120. Now, if 1990's berry production was 120, what would the number of berries in 1995 be? What's 30 percent more than 120? Be careful. Don't just add 30 to 120. You need to find 30 percent of 120 and add that number on.

Thirty percent of 120 is $(.30)(120) = 36$. Add 36 to 120, and you get 156 berries in 1995. What percent greater is 156 than 100? That's easy—that's why we picked 100 to start with. It's a 56 percent increase. The answer is (D).

A third problem ideal for picking numbers is when the answer choices to a word problem are algebraic expressions.

> If n sunglass lenses cost p dollars, then how many dollars would q sunglass lenses cost?
>
> (A) $\dfrac{nq}{q}$
>
> (B) $\dfrac{nq}{p}$
>
> (C) $\dfrac{pq}{n}$
>
> (D) $\dfrac{n}{pq}$
>
> (E) $\dfrac{p}{nq}$

The hard thing about this question is it uses variables instead of numbers. So, make it real. Pick numbers for the variables. Pick numbers that are easy to work with. Let's say that $n = 2$, $p = 4$, and $q = 3$. The question then becomes: "If two sunglass lenses cost $4.00, how many dollars would three sunglass lenses cost?" That's easy—$6.00. When $n = 2$, $p = 4$, and $q = 3$, the correct answer should equal 6. Plug those values into the answer choices and see which ones yield 6:

$$\text{(A) } \frac{np}{q} = \frac{(2)(4)}{3} = \frac{8}{3}$$

$$\text{(B) } \frac{nq}{p} = \frac{(2)(3)}{4} = \frac{6}{4} = \frac{3}{2} = 1\frac{1}{2}$$

$$\text{(C) } \frac{pq}{n} = \frac{(4)(3)}{2} = \frac{12}{2} = 6$$

$$\text{(D) } \frac{n}{pq} = \frac{2}{(4)(3)} = \frac{2}{12} = \frac{1}{6}$$

$$\text{(E) } \frac{p}{nq} = \frac{4}{(2)(3)} = \frac{4}{6} = \frac{2}{3}$$

Choice (C) is the only one that yields 6, so it must be the correct answer.

When picking numbers for an abstract word problem like this one, try all five answer choices. Sometimes more than one choice will yield the correct result. When that happens, pick another set of numbers to eliminate the coincidences. *Avoid picking 0 and 1.* These often give several *possibly correct* answers.

Backsolving

Sometimes it is not possible simply to pick numbers and solve the problem. In these cases, the answer choices become your tools, and you can work backward to find the right choice. We call this backsolving, which essentially means plugging the choices back into the question until you find the one that fits. Backsolving works best when:

- The question is a complex word problem, and the answer choices are numbers
- The alternative is setting up multiple algebraic equations

Backsolving is not ideal:

- If the answer choices include variables
- On algebra questions or word problems that have ugly answer choices, such as radicals and fractions (plugging them in takes too much time)

Complex Question, Simple Answer Choices

Sometimes backsolving is faster than setting up an equation. For example:

> A music club draws 27 patrons. If there are seven more musicians than singers in the club, how many patrons are musicians?
>
> (A) 8
> (B) 10
> (C) 14
> (D) 17
> (E) 20

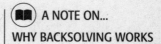
A NOTE ON...
WHY BACKSOLVING WORKS

The answer choices on the SAT are arranged in order, either descending or ascending, from (A) to (E). Choosing choice (C) first will guide your next step in solving the problem. For example, if plugging in choice (C) into the equation gives you too small of a value, then either (A) and (B) or (D) and (E) can be eliminated, depending on which values are smaller than (C).

The five answer choices represent the possible number of musicians in the club, so try them in the question stem. The choice that gives a total of 27 patrons, with seven more musicians than singers, will be the correct answer.

When backsolving, start with answer choice (C). For example, plugging in (C) gives you 14 musicians in the club. Because there are seven more musicians than singers, there are seven singers in the club. But 14 + 7 < 27. The sum is too small, so there must be more than 14 musicians; thus, you can eliminate answer choices (A), (B), and (C) just like that.

Either (D) or (E) will be correct. Plugging in (D) gives you 17 musicians in the club; 17 − 7 equals 10 singers, and 17 + 10 = 27 patrons total. Answer choice (D) is correct.

Algebra Problems with Multiple Equations

If $a + b + c = 110$, $a = 4b$, and $3a = 2c$, then $b =$

(A)   6

(B)   8

(C)   9

(D) 10

(E) 14

You're looking for b, so plug in the answer choices for b in the question and see what happens. The choice that gives us 110 for the sum $a + b + c$ must be correct.

Start with the midrange number, 9, choice (C).

If $b = 9$, then $a = 4 \times 9 = 36$.

$2c = 3a = 3 \times 36 = 108$

$c = 54$

$a + b + c = 36 + 9 + 54 = 99$

Because this is a smaller sum than 110, the correct value for b must be larger. Therefore, eliminate answer choices (A), (B), and (C). Now, plug in either (D) or (E), and see which answer works.

Short on time? Try guessing between (D) and (E). But guess intelligently. Because (C) wasn't that far off the correct answer, you want to choose a number just slightly bigger than 9. That's choice (D).

GRID-IN STRATEGIES

The Grid-in section is special. Grid-in questions are not multiple choice, and there is no penalty for wrong answers. You have to solve the equation in the question yourself and fill in your answer on a special grid.

Write Your Answers in the Number Boxes

This doesn't get you points by itself, but you will make fewer mistakes if you write your answers in the number boxes. You may think that gridding directly will save time, but writing first then gridding helps guarantee accuracy, which means more points.

Always Start Your Answer in the First Column Box

Of course you can start in any column you choose, but if you go in order, you will avoid any confusion. If you always start with the first column, even if your answer has only one or two figures, your answers will always fit. However, there is no oval for 0 in the first column, so you will need to grid an answer with 0 in any other column.

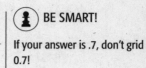

BE SMART!

If your answer is .7, don't grid 0.7!

In a Fractional Answer, Grid (/) in the Correct Column

The sign (/) separates the numerator from the denominator. It appears only in columns two and three. A fractional answer with four digits—like 31/42—won't fit and will need to be converted. This will be discussed more later in the chapter.

Change Mixed Numbers to Decimals or Fractions Before You Grid

If you try to grid a mixed number, it will be read as a fraction and be counted wrong. For example, $4\frac{1}{2}$ will be read as the fraction $\frac{41}{2}$, which is $20\frac{1}{2}$. So, first change mixed numbers to fractions or decimals; then grid in. In this case:

- Change $4\frac{1}{2}$ to $\frac{9}{2}$ and grid in the fraction; or

- Change $4\frac{1}{2}$ to 4.5 and grid in the decimal.

Watch Where You Put Your Decimal Points

A few pointers:

- For a decimal less than 1, such as .127, enter the decimal point in the first box.
- Only put a zero before the decimal point if it is part of the answer, as in 20.5—don't put one there (if your answer is, say, .5) just to make your answer look more accurate.
- Never grid a decimal point in the last column.

With Long or Repeating Decimals

Grid the first three digits only, and plug in the decimal point where it belongs. Say three answers are .45454545, 82.452312, and 1.428743. Grid .454, 82.4, and 1.42, respectively. You could round 1.428743 up to the nearest hundredth (1.43), but it's not required, and you could make a mistake. Note that rounding to an even shorter answer—1.4—would be incorrect.

More than One Right Answer? Choose One and Enter It

Say you're asked for a two-digit integer that is a multiple of 2, 3, and 5. You might answer 30, 60, or 90. Whichever you grid would be right.

Some Grid-ins Have a Range of Possible Answers

Suppose you're asked to grid a value of m where $1 - 2m < m$ and $5m - 2 < m$.

Solving for m in the first inequality, you find that $\frac{1}{3} < m$. Solving for m in the second inequality, you find that $m < \frac{1}{2}$. So, $\frac{1}{3} < m < \frac{1}{2}$. Grid in any value between $\frac{1}{3}$ and $\frac{1}{2}$. (Gridding in $\frac{1}{3}$ or $\frac{1}{2}$ would be wrong.) When the answer is a range of values, it's often easier to work with decimals: $.333 < m < .5$. This way, you can quickly grid .4 (or .35 or .45, etc.) as your answer.

USING YOUR CALCULATOR (OR NOT)

You've read about all of our techniques for finding the answers to Math questions using just your pencil and your mind. However, there are times when you can get some extra help and make life a little easier.

You are allowed to use a calculator on the SAT. However, that doesn't mean that you should always use your calculator on the SAT. Yes, you can do computations faster, but you may be tempted to waste time using a calculator on questions that shouldn't involve lengthy computation. Remember, you never need a calculator to solve an SAT problem. If you ever find yourself doing extensive calculations—elaborate division or long drawn-out multiplication—stop. You probably missed a shortcut.

Should I Just Leave My Calculator at Home?

No. Bring it. By zeroing in on the parts of problems that need calculation, you can increase your score and save yourself time on the SAT by using your calculator.

What Kind of Calculator Should I Bring?

One that you're comfortable with. If you don't have a calculator now, buy one right away, and practice using it between now and test day. You can use just about any small calculator; however, there are a few restrictions you must abide by. You may not bring:

- Calculators that print out your calculations
- Handheld minicomputers or laptop computers
- Any calculators with a typewriter keypad
- Calculators with an angled readout screen
- Calculators that require a wall outlet
- Calculators that make noise

When Should I Use My Calculator?

Calculators help the most on Grid-ins. Because Grid-ins don't give you answer choices to choose from, it's especially important to be positive about your results, and calculators can help you check your work and avoid careless errors.

Remember, a calculator can be useful when used selectively and strategically. Not all parts of a problem will necessarily be easier with a calculator. Consider this problem:

> If four grams of peanuts can make 32 Peanut Joy candy bars, how many Peanut Joy candy bars could be produced from 86 grams of peanuts?

This word problem has two steps. Step one is to set up the following proportion:

4 g of peanuts = 32 bars

A little algebraic engineering tells you that:

1 g of peanuts = 8 bars

Here's where you whip out that calculator. This problem has now been reduced down to pure calculation:

$86 \times 8 = 688$

When Should I Avoid My Calculator?

You may be tempted to use your calculator on every problem, but many questions will be easier without it. Look at this example:

If $x \neq \frac{1}{3}$ and $\frac{51}{3x - 1} = \frac{51}{29}$, then what is the value of x?

One way of answering this question would be to cross-multiply and then isolate x:

$$(51)(29) = (3x - 1)(51)$$

$$1{,}479 = 153x - 51$$

$$1{,}530 = 153x$$

$$\frac{1{,}530}{153} = x$$

$$10 = x$$

Notice how much more quickly you'll arrive at the answer if, rather than reflexively reaching for your calculator, you invest a few moments in thinking about the question—specifically what you're given and what you're asked for. Notice that after you cross-multiplied the equation above, you were left with $(51)(29) = (3x - 1)(51)$. Simply cancel out (51) from both sides. You are now left with the following equation:

$$3x - 1 = 29$$

$$3x = 30$$

$$x = 10$$

Common Calculator Mistake #1: Calculating Before You Think

On the Grid-in problem below, how should (and shouldn't) you use your calculator?

The sum of all the integers from 1 to 44, inclusive, is subtracted from the sum of all the integers from 7 to 50, inclusive. What is the result?

The Wrong Approach

1. Grab calculator.
2. Punch in all the numbers.
3. Put down answer and hope you didn't hit any wrong buttons.

You might be tempted to punch in all the numbers from 1 to 44, find their sum, do the same for the numbers 7 through 50, and then subtract the first sum from the second. But doing that means punching 252 keys. The odds are you'll hit the wrong key somewhere and get the wrong answer. Even if you don't, punching in all those numbers takes too much time.

The Kaplan Approach

1. Think first.
2. Decide on the best way to solve the problem.
3. Only then, use your calculator.

The right approach is to *think first*. The amount of computation involved in directly solving this tells you that there must be an easier way. You'll see this if you realize that both sums contain the same number of consecutive integers. Each integer in the first sum has a corresponding integer 6 digits greater than it in the second sum:

```
  1   7
+ 2 + 8
+ 3 + 9
 . .
 . .
 . .
+ 42 + 48
+ 43 + 49
+ 44 + 50
 =    =
```

As you'll see in the Math Traps chapter, the way to find the number of integers in a consecutive series is to subtract the smallest from the largest and add 1 ($44 - 1 = 43$; $43 + 1 = 44$ or $50 - 7 = 43$; $43 + 1 = 44$). So there are 44 pairs of integers that are 6 apart.

Therefore, the total difference between the two sums will be the difference between each pair of integers times the number of pairs. Now take out your calculator, punch $6 \times 44 =$, and get the correct answer of 264 with little or no time wasted.

Common Calculator Mistake #2: Forgetting the Order of Operations

Even when you use your calculator, you can't just enter numbers in the order they appear on the page—you have to follow the order of operations. This is a very simple error, but it can cost you lots of points. The order of operations is PEMDAS, which stands for:

Parentheses first, then deal with

Exponents, then

Multiplication and

Division, and finally

Addition and

Subtraction

 BE SMART!

If you're just punching keys instead of thinking, you're approaching the problem the wrong way.

That means you do whatever is in parentheses first, then deal with exponents, then multiplication and division (from left to right), and finally addition and subtraction (from left to right). For example, say you want to find the value of the expression $\frac{x^2 + 1}{x + 3}$ when $x = 7$.

If you just punched in $7 \times 7 + 1 \div 7 + 3 =$ you would get the wrong answer.

The correct way to work it out is:
$$(7^2 + 1) \div (7 + 3) = (7 \times 7 + 1) \div (7 + 3) = (49 + 1) \div 10 = 50 \div 10 = 5$$

Combining a calculator with an understanding of when and how to use it can help you boost your score.

GOOD GUESSING ON SAT MATH

The SAT's regular Math sections, like its Critical Reading and Writing multiple-choice sections, are scored to discourage random guessing. For every question that you get right, you earn a whole point. For every question you get wrong, you lose a fraction of a point. So, if you guess at random on a number of questions, the points you lose on incorrect guesses could cancel out the points you gain from correct guesses.

But you *can* and *should* make *educated* guesses. If you can eliminate one or more wrong answer choices, it increases your odds of guessing correctly. This increases your score, which is a good thing. We'll show you how.

The exception to the guessing penalty rule is the Grid-in section. You lose no points for wrong answers on Grid-in questions; therefore, you should ALWAYS fill something in the grid on these questions.

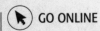
GO ONLINE

You can find the most helpful math rules on your downloadable Study Sheet for study on the go.

The Four Strategies for Educated Guessing

To make an educated guess, you need to eliminate answer choices that you know are wrong and guess from what's left. The more answer choices you can eliminate, the better chance you have of guessing the correct answer from what's left over. You do this by:

- Eliminating unreasonable answer choices
- Eliminating the obvious on hard questions
- Eyeballing lengths, angles, and areas on geometry problems
- Finding the range on Grid-ins—then guessing

Eliminating Unreasonable Answer Choices

Before you guess, think about the problem, and decide which answers don't make sense.

> The ratio of celebrities to agents in a certain room
> is 13:11. If there are 429 celebrities in the room,
> how many agents are there?
>
> (A) 143
> (B) 363
> (C) 433
> (D) 507
> (E) 792

The ratio of celebrities to agents is 13:11, so there are more celebrities than not. Because there are 429 celebrities, there must be fewer than 429 agents. You can eliminate choices (C), (D), and (E). The answer must be either (A) or (B), so guess. The correct answer is (B).

Eliminating the Obvious on Hard Questions

On the hard questions late in a set, obvious answers are usually wrong. So eliminate them when you guess. This strategy does not hold true for easier questions that may appear at the beginning of the math set, when the obvious answer could be right. In the following difficult problem, found late in a question set, which obvious answer would you eliminate?

> A number x is increased by 30 percent, and then
> the result is decreased by 20 percent. What is the
> final result of these changes?
>
> (A x is increased by 10 percent
> (B) x is increased by 6 percent
> (C) x is increased by 4 percent
> (D x is decreased by 5 percent
> (E) x is decreased by 10 percent

 MOBILE PREP

Put these math strategies to the test anytime, anywhere with Kaplan Mobile.

If you picked (A) as the obvious choice to eliminate, you'd be right. Most people would combine the decrease of 20 percent with the increase of 30 percent, getting a net increase of 10 percent. That's the easy, obvious answer, but not the correct answer. If you must guess, avoid (A). The correct answer is (C).

Eyeballing Lengths, Angles, and Areas on Geometry Problems

Use diagrams that accompany geometry problems to help you eliminate wrong answer choices. First, double check for specific instructions involving whether or not the diagram is drawn to scale. Diagrams are always drawn to scale unless there's a note like this: Note: Figure not drawn to scale. If it's not drawn to scale, you cannot use this strategy. If it is, estimate quantities or eyeball the diagram, then eliminate answer choices that are way too large or too small.

Length–When a geometry question asks for a length, use the given lengths to estimate the unknown length. Measure off the given length by making a nick in your pencil with your thumbnail. Then hold the pencil against the unknown length on the diagram to see how the lengths compare. Try it.

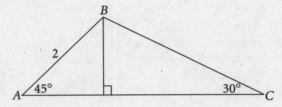

In the figure above, what is the length of *BC*?

(A) $\sqrt{2}$

(B) 2

(C) $2\sqrt{2}$

(D) 4

(E) $4\sqrt{2}$

- *AB* is 2, so measure off this length on your pencil.
- Compare *BC* with this length.
- *BC* appears almost twice as long as *AB*, so *BC* is approximately 4.
- Because $\sqrt{2}$ is approximately 1.4, and *BC* is clearly longer than *AB*, choices (A) and (B) are too small.
- Choice (E) is greater than 4, so eliminate that.
- Now guess between (C) and (D). The correct answer is (C).

Angles–You can also eyeball angles. To eyeball an angle, compare the angle with a familiar angle, such as a straight angle (180 degrees), a right angle (90 degrees), or half a right angle (45 degrees). The corner of a piece of paper is a right angle, so use that to see if an angle is greater or less than 90 degrees.

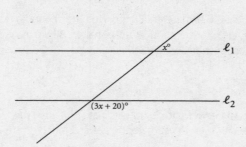

In the figure above, if $\ell_1 \parallel \ell_2$, what is the value of x?

(A) 40

(B) 50

(C) 80

(D) 100

(E) 130

- You see that x is less than 90 degrees, so eliminate choices (D) and (E).
- Because x appears to be much less than 90 degrees, eliminate choice (C).
- Now pick between (A) and (B). In fact, the correct answer is (A).

Areas—Eyeballing an area is similar to eyeballing a length. You compare an unknown area in a diagram to an area that you do know.

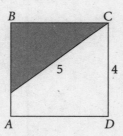

In square $ABCD$ above, what is the area of the shaded region?

(A) 4

(B) 6

(C) 8

(D) 9

(E) 10

Because *ABCD* is a square, it has the area 4^2, or 16. The shaded area is less than one half the size of the square, so its area must be less than 8. Eliminate answer choices (C), (D), and (E). The correct answer is (B).

Finding the Range on Grid-ins—Then Guessing

On Grid-ins, there are no answer choices to eliminate, but you won't lose points for guessing. So if you are stuck, try to estimate the general range of the answer and guess.

PRACTICE

Regular Math

1. A certain pump can drain a full 375-gallon tank in 15 minutes. At this rate, how many more minutes would it take to drain a full 600-gallon tank?

    (A) 9
    (B) 15
    (C) 18
    (D) 24
    (E) 25

2. A gardener plants flowers in the following order: carnations, daffodils, larkspurs, tiger lilies, and zinnias. If the gardener planted 47 flowers, what kind of flower did he plant last?

    (A) carnation
    (B) daffodil
    (C) larkspur
    (D) tiger lily
    (E) zinnia

3. How many different positive two-digit integers are there such that the tens' digit is greater than 5 and the units' digit is odd?

    (A) 10
    (B) 12
    (C) 15
    (D) 20
    (E) 25

4. If a and b are positive integers, what is a percent of b percent of 200?

    (A) $\dfrac{ab}{100}$
    (B) $\dfrac{ab}{50}$
    (C) ab
    (D) $50ab$
    (E) $100ab$

5. A 7.5-L mixture of water and molasses is 60 percent molasses. If 1.5 L of water is added, approximately what percent of the new mixture is molasses?

    (A) 40%
    (B) 50%
    (C) 63%
    (D) 64%
    (E) 68%

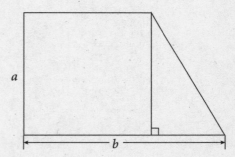

6. The figure above is formed from a square and a right triangle. What is its area?

    (A) $\dfrac{a(a + b)}{2}$
    (B) $\dfrac{a^2 + b^2}{2}$
    (C) $\dfrac{a(b - a)}{2}$
    (D) $a^2 + b^2$
    (E) $a^2 + \dfrac{ab}{2}$

Grid-ins

7. If the three-digit number $11Q$ is a prime number, what digit is represented by Q?

9. A triangle has one side of length 3 and another of length 7. If the length of the third side is a solution to the equation $x^2 - 2x = 63$, what is the length of the third side?

8. The sum of five consecutive odd integers is 425. What is the greatest of these integers?

IF YOU LEARNED ONLY FOUR THINGS IN THIS CHAPTER . . . .

1. Math questions are arranged by order of difficulty.

2. All figures are drawn to scale unless otherwise indicated.

3. Mixed numbers must be converted to improper fractions or decimals for Grid-in answers.

4. Calculators should not automatically be used to solve an equation. Often there is an easier path to the answer.

ANSWERS TO THE QUESTIONS ON PAGE 189

What Question Types Make Up the Math Component?

- Multiple-choice questions
- Grid-in questions

What Do I Need to Know About Each Question Type?

- You lose 1/4 point for incorrect multiple-choice answers.
- You don't lose any points for incorrect Grid-in answers.
- You have to calculate and write out your own answers for Grid-in questions.

What Strategies Will Help Me Succeed on the Math Component?

- Kaplan's Target Strategy for the Math Component
    - Step 1. Estimate the question's difficulty.
    - Step 2. Read the question.
    - Step 3. Skip or do.
    - Step 4. Look for the fastest approach.
- Picking numbers is a good strategy for abstract questions.
- Backsolving is a good strategy for complex word problems or questions requiring numerous algebraic equations.
- The four strategies for educated guessing are as follows:
    - Eliminating unreasonable answer choices.
    - Eliminating the obvious on hard questions.
    - Eyeballing lengths, angles, and areas.
    - Finding the range on Grid-ins.

ANSWERS AND EXPLANATIONS

1. A

You're given that a pump can drain a 375-gallon tank in

15 minutes. Therefore, the rate of the pump is

$\frac{375 \text{ gallons}}{15 \text{ minutes}}$, or 25 gallons per minute. At this rate, the

pump will drain a 600-gallon tank in $\frac{600}{25}$, or 24 minutes.

So it will take 24 − 15, or 9 more minutes to drain the

600-gallon tank.

2. B

You're looking for the 47th flower in a repeating pattern. Since there are five different flowers in the pattern, the last flower in the pattern corresponds to a multiple of 5. So the 5th, 10th, . . . , and 45th flowers will be zinnias. But there will also be two *remainders,* and so the 46th will be the first flower in the pattern and the 47th will be the second flower, which is a daffodil.

3. D

Simply count all the possibilities. If the numbers must have a tens' digit greater than 5, they must be 60 or greater. Since they are two-digit numbers, they must be less than 100. Since the units' digit is odd, they must be odd. So you need to count all the odd numbers between 60 and 100. Well, there are five such numbers with a tens' digit of 6: 61, 63, 65, 67, and 69. Similarly, there will be five more numbers with a tens' digit of 7, five more with a tens' digit of 8, and another five with a tens' digit of 9. That's 5 + 5 + 5 + 5, or 20 such numbers.

4. B

In this percent word problem, since *percent* means *hundredths,* a percent = $\frac{a}{100}$ and b percent = $\frac{b}{100}$. So a

percent of b percent of 200 = $\frac{a}{100} \times \frac{b}{100} \times 200 =$
$\frac{200ab}{10,000} = \frac{ab}{50}$

5. B

First find the amount of molasses in the original mixture.

There are 7.5 L of the mixture, of which 60% is molasses,

so there are $\frac{60}{100} \times 7.5 = 4.5$ L of molasses. An additional

1.5 L of water is added, so now the mixture is 7.5 + 1.5

= 9 L, of which 4.5 L is molasses. Percent = $\frac{\text{Part}}{\text{Whole}} \times$

100%, so in this case, $\frac{4.5}{9} \times 100\% = .5 \times$

100% = 50%.

6. A

To find the area, add the dimensions of the square and the triangle. First relabel the diagram as follows:

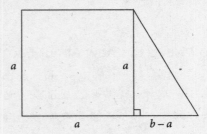

The area of a square is the length of a side squared, so

the area of this square is a^2. The area of this right triangle

is $\frac{1}{2}(\text{leg}_1 \times \text{leg}_2) = \frac{1}{2}(a)(b-a) = \frac{ab}{2} - \frac{a^2}{2}$. So the

combined area is:

$$a^2 + \frac{ab}{2} - \frac{a^2}{2} = \frac{2a^2}{2} - \frac{a^2}{2} + \frac{ab}{2}$$

$$= \frac{a^2}{2} + \frac{ab}{2}$$

$$= \frac{a^2 + ab}{2}$$

$$= \frac{a(a+b)}{2}$$

7.   3

Because Q is a digit, it must be one of the integers 0 through 9. Eliminate all the even digits because they are divisible by 2. Also, eliminate 5 because any number ending with 5 is divisible by 5. You can also eliminate 1 and 7 because they are divisible by 3 (the digits add up to a multiple of 3). You are left with 3 and 9 to pick between. The correct answer is 3.

8.   89

Because the integers are consecutive, they are all about the same size. So the number we are looking for is an odd number around $425 \div 5$, which is 85. The right answer is 89.

9.   9

Even if you can't solve that quadratic equation, you know that one side of a triangle has to be less than the sum and greater than the difference of the other two sides. Therefore, the third side is less than $7 + 3$, or 10, and greater than $7 - 3$, or 4. Because solutions to SAT quadratics are usually integers, pick an integer from 5 to 9. If you picked 9, you'd be right.

Chapter Twelve: **Basic Math Concepts**

- **What Are the 10 Basic Math Concepts Tested Most?**
- **What Methods Can I Use to Solve Each Concept?**

BASIC MATH

The SAT Math section has always tested certain topics of basic math. When you are confident that you understand these basic math concepts, the SAT Math section gets a whole lot easier. This chapter reviews these basic math concepts and explains how the SAT tests them. We also teach you our techniques for solving these problems and how these techniques will work with both types of SAT Math questions: regular math and Grid-ins.

Remainders

Remainder questions can be easier than they seem. Many students believe that the key to solving a remainder question is to find the value of a variable, which takes up a lot of time and causes confusion. However, that type of problem solving is usually not necessary. For example, look at the following remainder problem.

> When n is divided by 7, the remainder is 4. What is the remainder when $2n$ is divided by 7?
>
> (A) 0
> (B) 1
> (C) 2
> (D) 3
> (E) 4

This question doesn't depend on knowing the value of n. In fact, n has an infinite number of possible values. The easy way to solve this kind of problem is to pick a number for n. Because the remainder when n is divided by 7 is 4, pick any multiple of 7 and add 4. The easiest multiple to work with is 7. So, $7 + 4 = 11$. Plug 11 in for n and see what happens:

What is the remainder when $2n$ is divided by 7?

. . . the remainder when $2(11)$ is divided by 7?

. . . the remainder when 22 is divided by 7?

$$\frac{22}{7} = 3 \text{ remainder } 1$$

The remainder is 1 when $n = 11$. So the answer is (B). The remainder will also be 1 when $n = 18$, 25, or 46.

Averages

Instead of giving you a list of values to plug into the average formula $\frac{\text{Sum of Terms}}{\text{Number of Terms}}$, SAT average questions often put a spin on the problem, like so:

> The average weight of five amplifiers in a guitar shop is 32 pounds. If four of the amplifiers weigh 25, 27, 19, and 35 pounds, what is the weight of the fifth amplifier?
>
> (A) 28 pounds
> (B) 32 pounds
> (C) 49 pounds
> (D) 54 pounds
> (E) 69 pounds

This problem tells you the average of a group of terms and asks you to find the value of a missing term. To get the answer, you need to work with the sum. Let the variable $x =$ the weight of the fifth amplifier. Plug this into the average formula:

$$\text{Average} = \frac{\text{Sum of Terms}}{\text{Number of Terms}}$$

$$32 = \frac{25 + 27 + 19 + 35 + x}{5}$$

$$32 \times 5 = 25 + 27 + 19 + 35 + x$$

The average weight of the amplifiers times the number of amplifiers equals the total weight of the amplifiers. The new formula is:

$$\text{Average} \times \text{Number of Terms} = \text{Sum of Terms}$$

Remember this version of the average formula so you can find the total sum whenever you know the average of a group of terms and the number of terms. Now you can solve for the weight of the fifth amplifier as follows:

$32 \times 5 = 25 + 27 + 19 + 35 + x$

$\qquad 160 = 106 + x$

$\qquad 54 = x$

The weight of the fifth amplifier is 54 pounds, choice (D).

Ratios

SAT test makers often write ratio questions in a way that tricks you into setting up the wrong ratio. For instance, try to work through the question below.

> Out of every 50 CDs produced in a certain factory, 20 are scratched. What is the ratio of unscratched CDs produced to scratched CDs produced?
>
> (A) 2:5
> (B) 3:5
> (C) 2:3
> (D) 3:2
> (E) 5:2

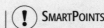 **SmartPoints**

Step back and focus on the right prize. Do you want a part:part or a part:whole ratio?

You need to find the parts and the whole in this problem. In this case, the total number of CDs is the whole, and the numbers of unscratched CDs and scratched CDs, respectively, are the parts that make up this whole. You're given a part-to-whole ratio (the ratio of scratched CDs to all CDs) and asked to find a part-to-part ratio (the ratio of unscratched CDs to scratched CDs).

If 20 CDs of every 50 are scratched, the remaining 30 CDs must be OK. So, the part-to-part ratio of good-to-scratched CDs is 30:20, or 3:2, choice (D). If you hadn't identified the part and the whole first, it would have been easy to become confused and compared a part to the whole, like the ratios in answer choices (A), (B), and (E).

This approach also works for ratio questions where you need to find actual quantities. Here's an example.

> Of every 5 CDs produced in a certain factory, 2 are scratched. If 2,200 CDs were produced, how many were scratched?

(Note: This is a Grid-in, so there are no answer choices.)

Here you need to find a quantity: the number of defective CDs. If you're looking for the actual quantities in a ratio, set up and solve a proportion. You're given a part-to-whole ratio (the ratio of scratched CDs to all CDs) and the total number of CDs produced. You can find the answer by setting up and solving a proportion:

$$\frac{\text{Number of scratched CDs}}{\text{Total number of CDs}} = \frac{2}{5} = \frac{x}{2,200}$$

$x =$ number of scratched CDs

$5x = 4,400$ (by cross-multiplying $\frac{2}{5} = \frac{x}{2,200}$)

$x = 880$ (by dividing both sides by 5)

> 🛈 **BE SMART!**
>
> Remember that ratios compare only relative size; they don't tell you the actual quantities involved. Distinguish clearly between the parts and the whole in ratio problems.

Rates

A rate is a ratio that compares quantities represented by different units. In the following problem, the units are dollars and the number of headphones.

> If 8 headphones cost a dollars, b headphones would cost how many dollars?
>
> (A) $8ab$
>
> (B) $\dfrac{8a}{b}$
>
> (C) $\dfrac{8}{ab}$
>
> (D) $\dfrac{a}{8b}$
>
> (E) $\dfrac{ab}{8}$

This rate problem at first seems difficult because of the variables. It's hard to get a clear picture of what the relationship is between the units. You need to pick numbers for the variables to find the context of that relationship.

Pick numbers for a and b that will be easy for you to work with in the problem.

Let $a = 16$. Then 8 headphones will cost $16. So the cost per headphone at this rate is $\dfrac{\$16}{8 \text{ headphones}} = \$2$ per headphone. Let $b = 5$. Therefore, the cost of 5 headphones at this rate will be 5 headphones $\times$ \$2 per headphone $= \$10$.

Now plug in $a = 16$ and $b = 5$ into the answer choices to see which one gives you a value of 10.

(A) $8 \times 16 \times 5 = 640$. Eliminate.

(B) $\dfrac{8 \times 16}{5} = \dfrac{128}{5}$. Eliminate.

(C) $\dfrac{8}{16 \times 5} = \dfrac{1}{10}$. Eliminate.

(D) $\dfrac{16}{8 \times 5} = \dfrac{2}{5}$. Eliminate.

(E) $\dfrac{16 \times 5}{8} = 10$

Because (E) is the only one that gives the correct value, it is the correct answer.

Percents

In percent problems, you're usually given two pieces of information and asked to solve for a third value, as in the following question.

> Last year Aunt Edna's annual salary was $20,000. This year's raise brings her to an annual salary of $25,000. If she gets a raise of the same percentage every year, what will her salary be next year?
>
> (A) $27,500
> (B) $30,000
> (C) $31,250
> (D) $32,500
> (E) $35,000

When you see a percent problem, remember the following formulas:

If you are solving for a percent: $\dfrac{\text{Part}}{\text{Whole}} = \text{Percent}$

If you need to solve for a part: $\text{Percent} \times \text{Whole} = \text{Part}$

This problem asks for Aunt Edna's projected salary for next year—that is, her current salary plus her next raise. You know last year's salary ($20,000), and you know this year's salary ($25,000), so you can find the difference between the two salaries: $25,000 - $20,000 = $5,000 = her raise.

Now, your next step is to find the percent this raise represents by using the formula $\text{Percent} = \dfrac{\text{Part}}{\text{Whole}}$. Because Aunt Edna's raise was calculated on last year's salary, divide by $20,000. Be sure you know which *whole* to plug in. Here, you're looking for a percentage of $20,000, not of $25,000.

Percent $\dfrac{\$5,000}{\$20,000} = \dfrac{1}{4}$, or 25%

You know Aunt Edna will get the same percent raise next year, so solve for the part. Use the formula Percent × Whole = Part. Make sure you change the percent to either a fraction or a decimal before beginning calculations.

Her raise next year will be 25% × $25,000 = $\dfrac{1}{4}$ × 25,000 = $6,250. Add that amount to this year's salary and you have her projected salary: $25,000 + $6,250 = $31,250, or answer (C).

Combinations

Combination problems ask you to find the different possibilities that can occur in a given situation. The order of events is not important.

> If Alice, Betty, and Carlos sit in three adjacent empty seats in a movie house, how many different seating arrangements are possible?
>
> (A) 3
> (B) 4
> (C) 5
> (D) 6
> (E) 8

 GO ONLINE

Stay familiar with essential math rules on your downloadable Study Sheet for study on the go.

To solve this question, you need to find the number of possibilities by listing them in a quick but systematic way. Let the first letter of each name stand for that person. First, find all the combinations with Alice in the first seat as follows:

ABC

ACB

Use the same system, putting Betty in the first seat, and then Carlos. You get the combinations:

BAC

BCA

CAB

CBA

At this point, we've exhausted every possibility. There are six possible arrangements, so (D) is the correct answer. Some problems set up conditions that limit the possibilities somewhat. Some may ask for the number of distinct possibilities, meaning that if the same combination shows up twice in different forms, you should count it only once. Consider the following problem.

Set I: {2, 3, 4, 5}

Set II: {1, 2, 3}

If x is a number generated by multiplying a number from Set I by a number from Set II, how many possible values of x are greater than 5?

(A) 3

(B) 4

(C) 5

(D) 6

(E) 7

Again, list the possibilities in a systematic way, pairing off each number in the first set with each number in the second set, so every combination is included. The following list is a good example of how this strategy works.

$2 \times 1 = 2$ $4 \times 1 = 4$

$2 \times 2 = 4$ $4 \times 2 = 8$

$2 \times 3 = 6$ $4 \times 3 = 12$

$3 \times 1 = 3$ $5 \times 1 = 5$

$3 \times 2 = 6$ $5 \times 2 = 10$

$3 \times 3 = 9$ $5 \times 3 = 15$

Always write down the possibilities as you organize them, so you can count them accurately, and so you don't count the same combination twice. How many of these values are greater than 5? Going down the list: 6, 6, 9, 8, 12, 10, and 15. Although there are seven answers for x that are greater than 5, two of them are the same. There are six different values of x greater than 5, not seven. The answer is (D). Here, it would have been very easy to quickly take seven as the correct answer and miss the last step. Be sure you carefully consider every possibility before moving on. We will teach you how to recognize and avoid traps like this one in Chapter Fourteen.

Simultaneous Equations

To get a numerical value for each variable in a simultaneous equation, you need as many different equations as there are variables. So, if you have two variables, you need two distinct equations. Let's look at the following example.

If $p + 2q = 14$ and $3p + q = 12$, then $p =$

(Note: This is a Grid-in, so there are no answer choices.)

You could tackle this problem by solving for one variable in terms of the other and then plugging this expression into the other equation. But the simultaneous equations that appear on the SAT can usually be handled in an easier way. Combine the equations, by adding or subtracting them, to cancel out all but one of the variables. You can't eliminate p or q by adding or subtracting the equations in their present forms. But if you multiply the second equation by 2, you'll have this equation:

$$2(3p + q) = 2(12)$$
$$6p + 2q = 24$$

With this new equation, subtracting one equation from the other is easier because the q's will cancel out, so you can solve for p:

$$6p + 2q = 24$$
$$-[p + 2q = 14]$$
$$5p + 0 = 10$$

If $5p = 10$, $p = 2$. On the answer sheet, you would grid in the answer 2.

Symbols

You should be quite familiar with the arithmetic symbols $+$, $-$, $\times$, and $\div$. Finding the value of $10 + 2$, $18 - 4$, 4×9, or $96 \div 16$ is easy. However, on the SAT, you may come across bizarre symbols. You may even be asked to find the value of $10 \star 2$, $5 ❋ 7$, $10 ✳ 6$, or $65 ❤ 2$.

The SAT puts strange symbols in questions to confuse or unnerve you. Don't let them succeed. The question stem always tells you what the strange symbol means. Although this type of question may look difficult, it is really an exercise in plugging in numbers. Look at the following example:

> If $a \star b = \sqrt{a + b}$ for all non-negative numbers, what is the value of $10 \star 6$?
>
> (A)   0
> (B)   2
> (C)   4
> (D)   8
> (E)   16

To solve, just plug in 10 for a and 6 for b into the expression $\sqrt{a + b}$. That equals $\sqrt{10 + 6}$, or $\sqrt{16} = 4$, choice (C). Don't get confused by the symbol; just plug in the numbers, and you'll be fine.

Special Triangles

Look for the special triangles in geometry problems. Special triangles contain a lot of information. For instance, if you know the length of one side of a 30-60-90 triangle, you can easily work out the lengths of the others. Special triangles allow you to transfer one piece of information around the whole figure.

The following are the special triangles you should look for on the SAT. You don't have to memorize the ratios (they're listed in the instructions), but you should be able to recognize them when you see them.

Equilateral Triangles

All interior angles are 60 degrees, and all sides have equal length.

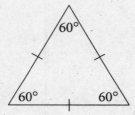

Isosceles Triangles

Two sides have equal length, and the angles facing these sides are equal.

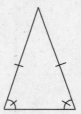

Right Triangles

These contain a 90-degree angle. The sides are related by the Pythagorean theorem: $a^2 + b^2 = c^2$, where a and b are the legs and c is the hypotenuse.

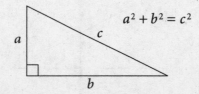

$$a^2 + b^2 = c^2$$

The *Special* Right Triangles

Many triangle problems contain *special* right triangles in which the side lengths always come in predefined ratios. If you recognize them, you won't have to use the Pythagorean theorem to find the value of a missing side length.

The 3-4-5 Right Triangle

(Be on the lookout for multiples of 3-4-5 as well.)

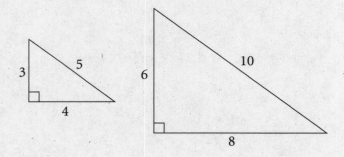

The Isosceles Right Triangle

(Note the side ratio: 1 to 1 to $\sqrt{2}$.)

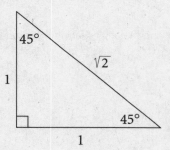

The 30-60-90 Right Triangle

(Note the side ratio: 1 to $\sqrt{3}$ to 2, and which side is opposite which angle.)

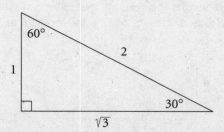

Now that we've gone through all the special triangles, try this problem.

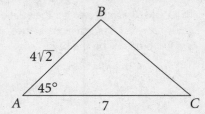

Note: Figure not drawn to scale.

In the triangle above, what is the length of side *BC*?

(A) 4

(B) 5

(C) $4\sqrt{2}$

(D) 6

(E) $5\sqrt{2}$

You can drop a vertical line from *B* to line *AC*. This divides the triangle into two right triangles. That means you know two of the angles in the triangle on the left: 90° and 45°. The third angle must also be 45°, so this is an isosceles right triangle, with sides in the ratio of 1 to 1 to $\sqrt{2}$.

The hypotenuse here is $4\sqrt{2}$, so both legs have length 4. Filling this in, you have the following:

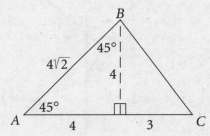

Now you can see that the legs of the smaller triangle on the right must be 4 and 3, making this a 3-4-5 right triangle, and the length of hypotenuse *BC* is 5. So choice (B) is correct.

Multiple and Strange Figures

In a problem that combines figures, you have to look for the relationship between the figures. Look for pieces the figures have in common. For instance, if two figures share a side, information about that side will probably be the key.

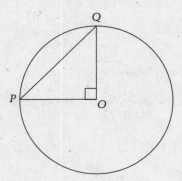

In the figure above, if the area of the circle with center O is 9π, what is the area of triangle POQ?

(A) 4.5

(B) 6

(C) 9

(D) 3.5π

(E) 4.5π

In this case, the figures don't share a side, but the triangle's legs are important features of the circle—they are radii. You can see that $PO = OQ =$ the radius of circle O. The area of the circle is 9π. The area of a circle is πr^2, where $r =$ the radius. So $9\pi = \pi r^2$, $9 = r^2$, and the radius $= 3$.

The area of a triangle is $\frac{1}{2}(\text{base} \times \text{height})$. Therefore, the area of $\triangle POQ$ is

$\frac{1}{2}(\text{leg}_1 \times \text{leg}_2) = \frac{1}{2}(3 \times 3) = \frac{9}{2} = 4.5$, answer choice (A).

But what if, instead of a number of familiar shapes, you are given something like this?

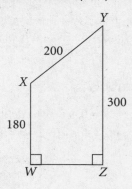

What is the perimeter of quadrilateral *WXYZ*?

(A)   680

(B)   760

(C)   840

(D)   920

(E) 1,000

 GO ONLINE

Check out your new practice quiz every month.

Try breaking the unfamiliar shape into familiar ones. Once you do this, you can use the same techniques that you would for multiple figures. Perimeter is the sum of the lengths of the sides of a figure, so you need to find the length of *WZ*. Drawing a perpendicular line from point *X* to side *YZ* will divide the figure into a right triangle and a rectangle. Call the point of intersection *A*.

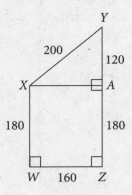

Opposite sides of a rectangle have equal length, so *WZ = XA* and *WX = ZA*. *WX* is labeled as 180, so *ZA* = 180. Because *YZ* measures 300, *AY* is 300 − 180 = 120. In right triangle *XYA*, hypotenuse *XY* = 200, and leg *AY* = 120; you should recognize this as a multiple of a 3-4-5 right triangle. The hypotenuse is 5 × 40, one leg is 3 × 40, so *XA* must be 4 × 40 or 160. (If you didn't recognize this special right triangle, you could have used the Pythagorean theorem to find the length of *XA*.) Because *WZ = XA* = 160, the perimeter of the figure is 180 + 200 + 300 + 160 = 840, answer choice (C).

 KAPLAN

PRACTICE

We have labeled the following questions by the math concept they test. If you get stumped, go back to the appropriate part of this chapter and refresh your memory on how to solve that kind of problem. There is no time limit for this practice set.

Remainders

1. When z is divided by 8, the remainder is 5. What is the remainder when $4z$ is divided by 8?

   (A) 1
   (B) 3
   (C) 4
   (D) 5
   (E) 7

Ratios

2. The ratio of right-handed pitchers to left-handed pitchers in a certain baseball league is 11:7. What fractional part of the pitchers in the league is left-handed?

   (A) $\dfrac{6}{7}$

   (B) $\dfrac{6}{11}$

   (C) $\dfrac{7}{11}$

   (D) $\dfrac{7}{18}$

   (E) $\dfrac{11}{18}$

Symbols

3. If $x \neq 0$, let $\neg x$ be defined by $\neg x = x - \dfrac{1}{x}$. What is the value of $\neg 2 - \neg \dfrac{1}{2}$?

Combinations

4. A three-digit code is made up of three different digits from the set {2, 4, 6, 8}. If 2 is always the first digit in the code, how many three-digit codes can be formed if each digit is used only once?

   (A) 6
   (B) 8
   (C) 10
   (D) 12
   (E) 16

Averages

5. The average (arithmetic mean) of six numbers is 16. If five of the numbers are 15, 37, 16, 9, and 23, what is the sixth number?

   (A) −20
   (B) −4
   (C)   0
   (D)   6
   (E) 16

Multiple and Strange Figures

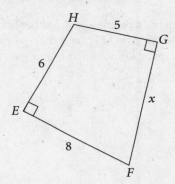

6. What is the value of x in the figure above?

   (A) 4
   (B) $3\sqrt{3}$
   (C) $3\sqrt{5}$
   (D) $5\sqrt{3}$
   (E) 9

Rates

7. If David paints at the rate of h houses per day, how many houses does he paint in d days, in terms of h and d?

   (A) $\dfrac{h}{d}$
   (B) hd
   (C) $h + \dfrac{d}{2}$
   (D) $h - d$
   (E) $\dfrac{d}{h}$

Percents

8. What is 25 percent of 25 percent of 72?

Simultaneous Equations

9. If $x + y = 8$ and $y - x = -2$, then $y =$

   (A) −2
   (B)   3
   (C)   5
   (D)   8
   (E) 10

Special Triangles

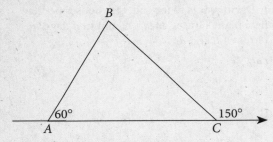

Note: Figure not drawn to scale.

10. In triangle *ABC* above, if *AB* = 4, then *AC* =

(A)   6

(B)   7

(C)   8

(D)   9

(E)   10

Remainders

11. When *n* is divided by 12, the remainder is 0. What is the remainder when 2*n* is divided by 6?

Averages

12. Bart needs to buy five gifts with $80. If two of the gifts cost a total of $35, what is the average (arithmetic mean) amount Bart can spend on each of the remaining three gifts?

(A) $10

(B) $15

(C) $16

(D) $17

(E) $45

Ratios

13. In a group of 24 people who are either homeowners or renters, the ratio of homeowners to renters is 5:3. How many homeowners are in the group?

(A)   8

(B)   9

(C) 12

(D) 14

(E) 15

Rates

14. Bill has to type a paper that is *p* pages long, with each page containing *w* words. If Bill types an average of *x* words per minute, how many hours will it take him to finish the paper?

(A) $60wpx$

(B) $\dfrac{wx}{60p}$

(C) $\dfrac{60wp}{x}$

(D) $\dfrac{wpx}{60}$

(E) $\dfrac{wp}{60x}$

Percents

15. Eighty-five percent of the members of a student organization registered to attend a certain field trip. If 16 of the members who registered were unable to attend, resulting in only 65 percent of the members making the trip, how many members are in the organization?

Special Triangles

16. In the coordinate plane, point *R* has coordinates (0, 0) and point *S* has coordinates (9, 12). What is the distance from *R* to *S*?

Simultaneous Equations

17. If $4a + 3b = 19$ and $a + 2b = 6$, then $a + b =$

Symbols

18. If $r \heartsuit s = r(r - s)$ for all integers *r* and *s*, then $4 \heartsuit (3 \heartsuit 5)$ equals

(A) −8

(B) −2

(C) 2

(D) 20

(E) 40

Combinations

19. Five people attend a meeting. If each person shakes hands once with every other person at the meeting, what is the total number of handshakes that take place?

Multiple and Strange Figures

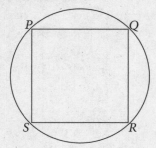

20. In the figure above, square *PQRS* is inscribed in a circle. If the area of square *PQRS* is 4, what is the radius of the circle?

    (A) 1
    (B) $\sqrt{2}$
    (C) 2
    (D) $2\sqrt{2}$
    (E) $4\sqrt{2}$

Averages

21. The average (arithmetic mean) of five numbers is 8. If the average of two of these numbers is −6, what is the sum of the other three numbers?

    (A) 28
    (B) 34
    (C) 46
    (D) 52
    (E) 60

Rates

22. If Seymour drove 120 miles in *x* hours at constant speed, how many miles did he travel in the first 20 minutes of his trip?

    (A) $60x$
    (B) $3x$
    (C) $\dfrac{120}{x}$
    (D) $\dfrac{40}{x}$
    (E) $\dfrac{6}{x}$

Symbols

23. $c \star d = \dfrac{(c - d)}{c}$, where $c \neq 0$.

    $12 \star 3 =$

    (A) −3
    (B) $\dfrac{1}{4}$
    (C) $\dfrac{2}{3}$
    (D) $\dfrac{3}{4}$
    (E) 3

Ratios

24. Magazine *A* has a total of 28 pages, 16 of which are advertisements and 12 of which are articles. Magazine *B* has a total of 35 pages, all of them either advertisements or articles. If the ratio of the number of pages of advertisements to the number of pages of articles is the same for both magazines, then Magazine *B* has how many more pages of advertisements than Magazine *A*?

    (A) 2
    (B) 3
    (C) 4
    (D) 5
    (E) 6

Remainders

25. A bracelet is made of colored beads in the repeated sequence red, orange, yellow, green, blue, indigo, and violet. If the first bead in the bracelet is red and the last is yellow, then the total number of beads in the bracelet could be

(A) 48
(B) 49
(C) 50
(D) 51
(E) 52

Simultaneous Equations

26. If $m - n = 5$ and $2m + 3n = 15$, then $m + n =$

(A) 1
(B) 6
(C) 7
(D) 10
(E) 15

Percents

27. If a sweater sells for $48 after a 25 percent markdown, what was its original price?

(A) $56
(B) $60
(C) $64
(D) $68
(E) $72

Special Triangles

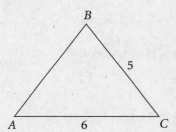

28. If the perimeter of triangle *ABC* above is 16, what is its area?

(A) 8
(B) 9
(C) 10
(D) 12
(E) 15

Multiple and Strange Figures

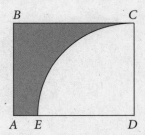

Note: Figure not drawn to scale.

29. In the figure above, the quarter circle with center *D* has a radius of 4 and rectangle *ABCD* has a perimeter of 20. What is the perimeter of the shaded region?

(A) $20 - 8\pi$
(B) $10 + 2\pi$
(C) $12 + 2\pi$
(D) $12 + 4\pi$
(E) $4 + 8\pi$

Symbols

30. $x \star y = \dfrac{(x - y)}{x}$, where $x \neq 0$.

    If $9 \star 4 = 15 \star k$, then $k =$

    (A) 3
    (B) 6
    (C) $\dfrac{20}{3}$
    (D) $\dfrac{25}{3}$
    (E) 9

Combinations

31. Three people stop for lunch at a hot dog stand. If each person orders one item and there are three items to choose from, how many different combinations of food could be purchased? (Assume that order doesn't matter; e.g., a hot dog and two sodas are considered the same as two sodas and a hot dog.)

    (A) 6
    (B) 9
    (C) 10
    (D) 18
    (E) 27

ANSWERS TO THE QUESTIONS ON PAGE 215

What Are the 10 Basic Math Concepts Tested Most?

1. Remainders
2. Averages
3. Ratios
4. Rates
5. Percents
6. Combinations
7. Simultaneous Equations
8. Symbols
9. Special Triangles
10. Multiple and Strange Figures

What Methods Can I Use to Solve Each Concept?

1. Remainders—Pick a number for the variable.
2. Averages—Use the average formula, and work with the sum.
3. Ratios—Identify the parts and the whole.
4. Rates—Pick numbers for the variables to make the relationship between units clear.
5. Percents—Make sure you know which whole to plug in.
6. Combinations—Be systematic and organized when listing possible combinations.
7. Simultaneous Equations—Combine equations by adding or subtracting them to cancel out all but one variable.
8. Symbols—Use the symbols as a map of where to plug in numbers.
9. Special Triangles—Know the predefined ratios for special triangles.
10. Multiple and Strange Figures—Find the parts that the different figures have in common.

ANSWERS AND EXPLANATIONS

Remainders

1. C

Let $z = 13$ and plug in $4z = 4(13) = 52$, which leaves a remainder of 4 when divided by 8.

Ratios

2. D

The parts are the number of right-handed pitchers (11) and the number of left-handed pitchers (7). The whole is the total number of pitchers (right-handed + left-handed), which is 11 + 7, or 18. So:

$$\frac{\text{part}}{\text{whole}} = \frac{\text{left-handed}}{\text{total}} = \frac{7}{11 + 7} = \frac{7}{18}.$$

Symbols

3. 3

Identify the value of $\neg 2$ and then of $\neg\frac{1}{2}$, and then subtract the second value from the first:

$$\neg 2 = 2 - \frac{1}{2} = 1\frac{1}{2} = \frac{3}{2}$$

$$\neg\frac{1}{2} = \frac{1}{2} - \frac{\frac{1}{2}}{2} = \frac{1}{2} - 2 = -1\frac{1}{2} = -\frac{3}{2}$$

$$\neg 2 - \neg\frac{1}{2} = \frac{3}{2} - \left(-\frac{3}{2}\right) = \frac{3}{2} + \frac{3}{2} = \frac{6}{2} = 3$$

Combinations

4. A

Every code starts with 2, so the last two digits determine the number of possibilities. The last two digits could be: 46, 48, 64, 68, 84, and 86. That makes six combinations that fit the conditions.

Averages

5. B

Average × Number of Terms = Sum of Terms

$$16 \times 6 = 15 + 37 + 16 + 9 + 23 + x$$
$$96 = 100 + x$$
$$-4 = x$$

Multiple and Strange Figures

6. D

Draw a straight line from point H to point F to divide the figure into two right triangles.

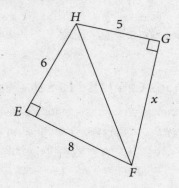

ΔEFH is a 3-4-5 right triangle with a hypotenuse of length 10. Use the Pythagorean theorem in ΔFGH to find x:

$$x^2 + 5^2 = 10^2$$
$$x^2 + 25 = 100$$
$$x^2 = 75$$
$$x = \sqrt{75}$$
$$x = \sqrt{25}\sqrt{3}$$
$$x = 5\sqrt{3}$$

Rates

7. B

Pick numbers for h and d. Let $h = 2$ and $d = 3$; that is, suppose he paints two houses per day and he paints for three days, so in three days he can paint six houses. You multiply the rate (h) by the number of days (d). The only answer choice that equals 6 when $h = 2$ and $d = 3$ is choice (B).

Percents

8.   4.5

"25 percent of 25 percent" means (.25)(.25), so (.25)(.25)(72) = 4.5.

Simultaneous Equations

9.   B

When you add the two equations, the x's cancel out and you find that $2y = 6$, so $y = 3$.

Special Triangles

10.   C

Angle BCA is supplementary to the angle marked 150°, so angle $BCA = 180° - 150° = 30°$. Because the sum of interior angles of a triangle is 180°, angle A + angle B + angle $BCA = 180°$, so angle $B = 180° - 60° - 30° = 90°$. So triangle ABC is a 30-60-90 right triangle, and its sides are in the ratio $1 : \sqrt{3} : 2$. The side opposite the 30°, AB, which we know has length 4, must be half the length of the hypotenuse, AC. Therefore, $AC = 8$, and that's answer choice (C).

Remainders

11.   0

If there's no remainder when n is divided by 12, then n is a multiple of 12, as is $2n$. Anything that's a multiple of 12 is a multiple of factors of 12, so $2n$ is a multiple of 6. Thus, the remainder is 0 when $2n$ is divided by 6. Picking numbers highlights this. Say n is 24. $2n$ is 48, and there's a remainder of 0 when 48 is divided by 6.

Averages

12.   B

Bart has $80 and spent $35 on two gifts; therefore, he has $45 left to spend on the remaining three. So,

$$x = \frac{\$45}{3}$$

$$x = \$15$$

Ratios

13.   E

The parts are the number of homeowners (5) and the number of renters (3). The whole is the total (homeowners + renters).

So: $\dfrac{\text{part}}{\text{whole}} = \dfrac{\text{homeowners}}{\text{homeowners} + \text{renters}} = \dfrac{5}{5 + 3} = \dfrac{5}{8}$.

Because there are 24 people in the group, $\dfrac{5}{8} = \dfrac{x}{24}$ making $x = 15$.

Rates

14.   E

Pick numbers for p, w, and x that work well in the problem. Let $p = 3$ and let $w = 100$. So there are three pages with 100 words per page, or 300 words total. Say he types five words a minute, so $x = 5$. Therefore, he types 5×60, or 300 words an hour. It takes him one hour to type the paper. The only answer choice that equals 1 when $p = 3$, $w = 100$, and $x = 5$ is choice (E).

Percents

15.   80

You need to solve for the Whole, so identify the Part and the Percent. If 85 percent planned to attend and only 65 percent did, 20 percent failed to attend, and you know that 16 students failed to attend.

Percent $\times$ Whole = Part

$$\frac{20}{100} \times \text{Whole} = 16$$

$$\text{Whole} = 16 \times \frac{100}{20}$$

$$\text{Whole} = 80$$

Special Triangles

16. 15

Draw a diagram. Because *RS* isn't parallel to either axis, the way to compute its length is to create a right triangle with legs that are parallel to the axes, so their lengths are easy to find. If the triangle formed is not a special triangle, we can then use the Pythagorean theorem to find the length of *RS*.

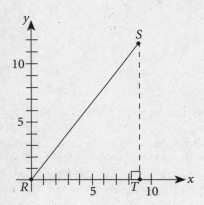

Because *S* has a *y*-coordinate of 12, it's 12 units above the *x*-axis, so the length of *ST* must be 12. Also, because *T* is the same number of units to the right of the *y*-axis as *S*, given by the *x*-coordinate of 9, the distance from the origin to *T* must be 9. So we have a right triangle with legs of 9 and 12. You should recognize this as a multiple of the 3-4-5 triangle. $9 = 3 \times 3$; $12 = 3 \times 4$; so the hypotenuse *RS* must be 3×5, or 15.

Simultaneous Equations

17. 5

Adding the two equations, you find that $5a + 5b = 25$. Dividing by 5 shows that $a + b = 5$.

Symbols

18. E

Start in the parentheses and work out: $(3 \heartsuit 5) = 3(3 - 5) = 3(-2) = -6$; $4 \heartsuit (-6) = 4 [4 - (-6)] = 4(10) = 40$.

Combinations

19. 10

Be careful not to count each handshake twice. Call the five people A, B, C, D, and E. We can pair them off like this:

A with B, C, D, and E (four handshakes)

B with C, D, and E (three more—note that we leave out A because the handshake between A and B is already counted)

C with D and E (two more)

D with E (one more)

The total is $4 + 3 + 2 + 1$, or 10 handshakes.

Multiple and Strange Figures

20. B

Draw in diagonal *QS* and you will notice that it is also a diameter of the circle.

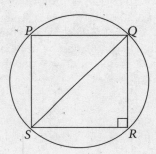

Because the area of the square is 4, its sides must each be 2. Think of the diagonal as dividing the square into two isosceles right triangles. Therefore, the diagonal $= 2\sqrt{2} =$ the diameter; the radius is half this amount, or $\sqrt{2}$.

Averages

21. D

Average × Number of Terms = Sum of Terms

The sum of all five numbers is

$8 \times 5 = 40$

The sum of two of these numbers is

$(-6) \times 2 = -12$

So, the difference of these two sums, $40 - (-12) = 52$, is the sum of the other numbers.

Rates

22. D

Let $x = 4$. That means that he drove 120 miles in four hours, so his speed was $\frac{120 \text{ miles}}{4 \text{ hours}}$, or 30 miles per hour. Because 20 minutes $= \frac{1}{3}$ of an hour, the distance he traveled in the first 20 minutes is $\frac{1}{3}$ hours $\times$ 30 miles per hour $= 10$ miles. The only answer choice that equals 10 when $x = 4$ is choice (D).

Symbols

23. D

Plug in 12 for c and 3 for d: $\frac{12 - 3}{12} = \frac{9}{12} = \frac{3}{4}$.

Ratios

24. C

The $\frac{part}{whole}$ ratio of advertisements (16) to total pages (28) in Magazine A is $\frac{16}{28}$, or $\frac{4}{7}$. Magazine B has the same ratio, so if there are 35 pages in Magazine B, $\frac{4}{7} \times 35$—or 20 pages—are advertisements. Therefore, there are four more pages of advertisements in Magazine B than in Magazine A.

Remainders

25. E

The sequence contains seven terms: R, O, Y, G, B, I, and V. So V will be every seventh bead, that is, the 7th, 14th, 28th, 35th beads, and so on. Another way of saying this is that all the multiples of 7 will always be V. Y is three beyond V, so it's three beyond a multiple of 7. (E) is the only choice that's three more than a multiple of 7.

Simultaneous Equations

26. C

Multiply the first equation by 2, then subtract the first equation from the second to eliminate the m's and find that $5n = 5$, or $n = 1$:

$$2m + 3n = 15$$
$$\underline{-2m + 2n = -10}$$
$$5n = 5$$
$$n = 1$$

Plugging this value for n into the first equation shows that $m = 6$:

$m - n = 5$

$m - 1 = 5$

$m = 6$

So $m + n = 7$:

$m + n = 6 + 1 = 7$

Choice (C) is correct.

Percents

27. C

We want to solve for the original price, the Whole. The percent markdown is 25 percent, so $48 is 75 percent of the whole.

Percent $\times$ Whole $=$ Part

75 percent $\times$ original price $= \$48$

original price $= \frac{\$48}{0.75} = \$64$

Special Triangles

28. D

To find the area you need to know the base and height. If the perimeter is 16, then $AB + BC + AC = 16$, that is, $AB = 16 - 5 - 6 = 5$. Because $AB = BC$, this is an isosceles triangle. If you drop a line from vertex B to AC, it will divide the base in half. This divides up the triangle into two smaller right triangles:

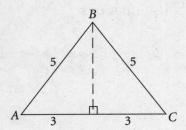

These right triangles each have one leg of 3 and a hypotenuse of 5; therefore, they are 3-4-5 right triangles. The missing leg (which is also the height of triangle *ABC*) must have a length of 4. We now know that the base of *ABC* is 6, and the height is 4, so the area is $\frac{1}{2} \times 6 \times 4$, or 12, answer choice (D).

Multiple and Strange Figures

29. C

The perimeter of the shaded region is *BC* + *AB* + *AE* + arc *EC*. The quarter circle has its center at *D*, and point *C* lies on the circle, so side *DC* is a radius of the circle and equals 4.

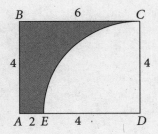

Opposite sides of a rectangle are equal, so *AB* is also 4. The perimeter of the rectangle is 20, and because the two short sides account for 8, the two longer sides must account for 12, making *BC* and *AD* each 6. To find *AE*, subtract the length of *ED*, another radius of length 4, from the length of *AD*, which is 6; *AE* = 2.

Because arc *EC* is a quarter circle, the length of the arc *EC* is $\frac{1}{4}$ of the circumference of a whole circle with radius 4: $\frac{1}{4} \times 2\pi r = \frac{1}{4} \times 8\pi = 2\pi$. So the perimeter of the shaded region is $6 + 4 + 2 + 2\pi = 12 + 2\pi$.

Symbols

30. C

Plug in on both sides of the equation:

$$\frac{9-4}{9} = \frac{15-k}{15}$$

$$\frac{5}{9} = \frac{15-k}{15}$$

Cross-multiply and solve for *k*:

$75 = 135 - 9k$

$-60 = -9k$

$$\frac{-60}{-9} = k$$

$$\frac{20}{3} = k$$

Combinations

31. C

To find the number, let's call the three items they can purchase A, B, and C. The possibilities are as follows:

All three order the same thing: AAA, BBB, CCC

Two order the same thing: AAB, AAC, BBA, BBC, CCA, CCB

All three order something different: ABC

There are 10 different ways the three items could be ordered.

Chapter Thirteen: **Advanced Math Concepts**

- What Are the 20 Tested Advanced Math Concepts?

- What Methods Can I Use to Solve Each Concept?

In this chapter, we review the advanced math concepts tested on the SAT. This list is extensive and may seem overwhelming. But remember, your goal should not be to memorize each concept and method, but rather to familiarize yourself with the review of each concept so you will know what to expect on test day.

ADVANCED MATH

The SAT covers the following advanced math topics:
- Sequences involving exponential growth
- Sets
- Absolute value
- Rational equations and inequalities
- Radical equations
- Manipulation with integer and rational exponents
- Direct and inverse variation
- Function notation and evaluation
- Concepts of domain and range
- Functions as models
- Linear functions—equations and graphs
- Quadratic functions—equations and graphs
- Geometric notation
- Problems in which trigonometry can be used as an alternative method of solution
- Properties of tangent lines
- Coordinate geometry
- Qualitative behavior of graphs and functions
- Transformations and their effect on graphs of functions
- Data interpretation, scatterplots, and matrices
- Geometric probability

As in Chapter Twelve, the techniques we give for solving these problems will work with both types of SAT Math questions: regular math and Grid-in questions.

Sequences Involving Exponential Growth

The name sounds like a mouthful, but relax: sequences involving exponential growth, also known as geometric sequences, are a tough but manageable area of SAT math.

What is a geometric sequence, and what does it take to ace questions about them on the SAT? A geometric sequence of numbers is simply one in which a constant ratio exists between consecutive terms. Questions about geometric sequences are likely to hinge on this formula:

If r is the ratio between consecutive terms, a_1 is the first term, and a_n is the nth term, then $a_n = a_1 r^{n-1}$.

Now take a look at how the SAT might ask a question about geometric sequences.

> If the first term in a geometric sequence is 4, and
> the fifth term is 64, what is the eighth term?
>
> (A)   512
> (B)   864
> (C) 1,245
> (D) 13,404
> (E) 22,682

First, use the formula to solve for r:

$$64 = 4r^4$$
$$16 = r^4$$
$$r = 2$$

Now, using $r = 2$, solve for a_8:

$$a_8 = 4(2)^7$$
$$a_8 = 512$$

The correct answer is (A).

BE SMART!

Remember that if r is the ratio between consecutive terms, a_1 is the first term, and a_n is the nth term, then $a_n = a_1 r^{n-1}$. Most questions concerning geometric sequences will involve this formula.

Sets

Most questions about geometric sequences are likely to appear in the middle or end of an SAT Math section because such questions tend to be hard for most students. Sets, on the other hand, are slightly easier and are more likely to show up in the beginning or middle of a section.

The things in a set are called *elements* or *members*. The union of sets, sometimes expressed with the symbol ∪, is the set of elements that are in either or both of the different sets you start with. Think of the union set as what you get when you merge sets. For example, if Set $A = \{1, 2\}$ and Set $B = \{3, 4\}$, then $A \cup B$ $\{1, 2, 3, 4\}$.

The intersection of sets, sometimes expressed with the symbol ∩, is the set of elements common to the respective sets you start with. For example, if Set $A = \{1, 2, 3\}$ and Set $B = \{3, 4, 5\}$, then $A \cap B = \{3\}$.

Try to work through the following example.

> If Set R contains 6 distinct numbers and Set S contains 5 distinct letters, how many elements are in the union of the two sets?
>
> (A) 1
> (B) 5
> (C) 6
> (D) 8
> (E) 11

In this question, because Set R and Set S contain different kinds of elements, no element is in both sets. So the union set of S and R—$S \cup R$—contains everything in each: $6 + 5 = 11$. The correct answer is (E).

Absolute Value

The absolute value of a number is the distance between that number and zero on the number line. Because absolute value is a distance, it is always positive. The absolute value of 7 is 7; this is expressed as $|7| = 7$. Similarly, the absolute value of −7 is 7: $|-7| = 7$. Every positive number is the absolute value of two numbers: itself and its negative counterpart. The diagram below helps to illustrate this point.

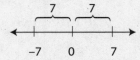

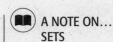 A NOTE ON...
SETS

Think of the union of sets as what you get when you merge the sets. Think of the intersection of sets as the overlap of the sets.

As you'll see in the following example, the SAT sometimes connects the concept of absolute value to the concept of inequalities.

If $|r + 7| < 2$, which of the following statements are true?

    I. $r < -9$
   II. $r < -5$
  III. $r > -9$

(A) I only

(B) II only

(C) III only

(D) I and II only

(E) II and III only

 GO ONLINE

Check out your new practice quiz every month.

You can solve this problem algebraically, as shown below, or you can think about what the inequality would look like on a number line. You can express $|r + 7| < 2$ *as the difference between r and −7 is less than* 2 and determine that r must be between −5 and −9:

$r + 7 < 2$ and $-r - 7 < 2$

$r < -5$ and $-r < 9$

$r < -5$ and $r > -9$

The correct answer here is (E).

Rational Equations and Inequalities

A rational equation or inequality is one that contains at least one fraction in which the numerator and denominator are polynomials. Rational equations and inequalities follow the same rules as simpler-looking equations, and they are just as susceptible to Kaplan strategies, such as picking numbers, as the following illustration shows.

For all values of x not equal to −2 or 3,

$$\frac{x^4 - 5x^3 - 2x^2 + 24x}{x^2 - x - 6} \text{ is equal to}$$

(A) $x^2 - 4x$

(B) $x^2 - 5x - 2$

(C) $x + 24$

(D) x

(E) $x - 4$

Picking numbers is the easiest way to solve this problem. Say $x = 2$:

$$\frac{2^4 - 5(2^3) - 2(2^2) + 24(2)}{2^2 - 2 - 6} = \frac{16 - 5(8) - 2(4) + 24(2)}{4 - 2 - 6} = \frac{16 - 40 - 8 + 48}{-4} =$$

$$\frac{16}{-4} = -4$$

Now find the choice that has a value of -4 when $x = 2$. Only (A) works:

$2^2 - 4(2) =$

$4 - 8 = -4$. So, (A) is the correct answer.

Radical Equations

Like rational equations, radical equations—ones with at least one variable under a radical sign—follow the same rules as other kinds of algebraic equations, so solve them accordingly. What makes radical equations special is that the last step in isolating the variable is often to square both sides of the equation. Look at the following example.

If $4 - \sqrt{n} = -1$, what is the value of n?

(A)   3

(B)   5

(C)   9

(D) 25

(E)   81

Apply the same algebraic steps here as you would in any other question involving an equation, isolating the variable step by step. Just remember to square both sides of the equation as your last step. (Notice that (B) is a trap for test takers who forget to do so. We will cover math traps in more detail in the next chapter.)

$$4 - \sqrt{n} = -1$$
$$5 = \sqrt{n}$$
$$(5)^2 = (\sqrt{n})^2$$
$$25 = n$$

Answer choice (D) is correct.

Manipulation with Integer and Rational Exponents

Not every exponent on the SAT is a positive integer. Numbers can be raised to a fractional or negative exponent. Although such numbers follow their own special rules, they adhere to the same general rules of exponents with which you've probably worked before.

If $x = \dfrac{1}{4}$, $x^{-4} =$

(A) $\dfrac{-1}{256}$

(B) $\dfrac{-1}{16}$

(C) 4

(D) 16

(E) 256

(📖) A NOTE ON...

EXPONENTIAL EQUIVALENTS

$x^{-a} = \dfrac{1}{x^a}$

$x^{\frac{p}{q}} = \sqrt[q]{x^p}$

To find the value of a number raised to a negative power, simply rewrite the number, without the negative sign in front of the exponent, as the bottom of a fraction with 1 as the numerator of the fraction: $3^{-2} = \dfrac{1}{3^2} = \dfrac{1}{9}$. In this case:

$$x^{-4} = \dfrac{1}{x^4} = \dfrac{1}{\left(\dfrac{1}{4}\right)^4} = \dfrac{1}{\left(\dfrac{1}{256}\right)} = 256, \text{ or answer choice (E)}.$$

Direct and Inverse Variation

In direct variation, $y = kx$, where k is a nonzero constant. In direct variation, the variable y changes directly as x does. If a unit of Currency A is worth 2 units of Currency B, then $A = 2B$. If the number of units of B were to double, the number of units of A would double, and so on for halving, tripling, etc.

In inverse variation, $xy = k$, where x and y are variables and k is a constant. A famous inverse relationship is *rate* $\times$ *time* $=$ *distance*. Imagine having to cover a distance of 24 miles. If you were to travel at 12 miles per hour, you'd need 2 hours. But if you were to cut your rate in half, you would have to double your time. This is just another way of saying that rate and time vary inversely. The following is an example of direct variation.

If the length of a sea turtle is directly proportional to its age, and a 2-year-old sea turtle is 3 inches long, how many feet long is an 80-year-old sea turtle?

(A) 10

(B) 12

(C) 100

(D) 120

(E) 144

Relate the length of the turtle to its age. Use the equation to find the length of an 80-year-old sea turtle in inches; then convert from inches to feet. Because length is directly proportional to age, you can represent their relationship as $l = ka$, where l is length, a is age, and k is a constant:

$3 = k(2)$

$1.5 = k$

$l = 1.5(80) = 120$ inches $= 10$ feet

(A) is the correct answer.

Function Notation and Evaluation

A few questions on test day will probably focus on functions and use standard function notation such as $f(x)$. Evaluating a function sounds fancy, but it mostly involves substitution of numbers for variables—a skill you should already be familiar with.

For example, to evaluate the function $f(x) = 5x + 1$ for $f(3)$, replace x with 3 and simplify: $f(3) = 5(3) + 1 = 15 + 1 = 16$

 **AVAILABLE ON CD-ROM**

Need more help with function notation and evaluation? Your CD-ROM features 5 full-length practice tests and section-length practice tests for each SAT component. More math practice is at your fingertips.

The example below presents a slightly more complex variation: a composition of functions. $h(g(a))$ requires you to first evaluate $g(a)$, and then apply h to the result.

> If $g(a) = (a + 4)^2$ and $h(b) = 2b - 7$, then what is the value of $h(g(2))$?
>
> (A)   1
> (B)   36
> (C)   45
> (D)   65
> (E)   79

Follow the order of operations:

$g(2) = (2 + 4)^2 = 6^2 = 36$

$h(36) = 2(36) - 7 = 72 - 7 = 65$

The correct answer is choice (D).

Concepts of Domain and Range

The domain of a function is the set of values for which the function is defined. For example, the domain of $f(x) = \dfrac{1}{1 - x^2}$ is all values of x except 1 and -1, because for those values, the denominator has a value of 0 and the fraction is therefore undefined. The range of a function is the set of outputs or results of the function. For example, the range of $f(x) = x^2$ is all numbers greater than or equal to zero because x^2 cannot be negative. Try the following sample question.

> If $f(a) = a^2 + 7$ for all real values of a, which of the following is a possible value of $f(a)$?
>
> (A) -2
> (B) 0
> (C) $\sqrt{5}$
> (D) $\sqrt{7}$
> (E) $100\sqrt{3}$

If a is a real number, then a^2 must be positive or equal to zero. Think about how this limits the range of $f(a)$: If $a = 0$, then $f(a) = 7$. All other values of a result in a higher value of $f(a)$. Only (E) is greater than 7 and is the correct answer.

Functions as Models

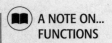
The SAT might challenge your ability to relate functional relationships to real-life situations. For example, consider the question below, in which you're asked to interpret data about the relationship between the selling price of a car and the number of cars that sell at that price.

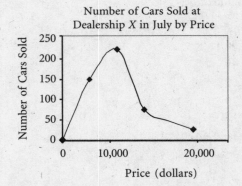

Number of Cars Sold at Dealership X in July by Price

The above graph represents the number of cars sold at Dealership X in July. If the dealer wants to sell the maximum number of cars possible in August, at what price should he set the cars, based on his sales in July?

(A) 5,000
(B) 10,000
(C) 15,000
(D) 20,000
(E) 22,500

Make sure to read your graphs carefully, knowing what each axis represents. If you are not careful, you may choose the incorrect answer that is meant as a trap.

Use the graph of July to figure out which price point sold the most cars. The peak value is $10,000, which sold 225 cars. Based on this information, the dealer should price cars at $10,000 in August and hope to sell the maximum number of cars that he can in that month. Answer choice (B) is correct.

Linear Functions—Equations and Graphs

You'll most likely see a question or two on the SAT involving equations and graphs of linear functions. A linear function is simply an equation whose graph is a straight line. The following question is an example of what could appear on the SAT.

> Which of the following equations describes a line perpendicular to the line $y = 7x + 49$?
>
> (A) $y = -7x - 49$
>
> (B) $y = -\frac{1}{7}x + 10$
>
> (C) $y = \frac{1}{7}x + 7$
>
> (D) $y = 7x - 49$
>
> (E) $y = 7x + 14$

If two lines are perpendicular, then the slope of one is the negative reciprocal of the slope of the other. These lines are written in the form $y = mx + b$, where m is the slope and b is the y-intercept, or the value of y when $x = 0$. In this case, the negative reciprocal of 7 is $-\frac{1}{7}$. The only equation with this slope is (B), the correct answer.

Quadratic Functions—Equations and Graphs

Quadratic functions are closely related to linear functions. A quadratic function is one that takes the form $f(x) = ax^2 + bx + c$. Rather than take the form of a straight line as, you'll recall, a linear function does, the graph of a quadratic function is a parabola. As the following question illustrates, a quadratic function question could be similar to a quadratic equations question.

> If $x^2 - 7x + 12 = 0$, what is the sum of the two possible values of x?
>
> (A) −4
> (B) −1
> (C) 3
> (D) 4
> (E) 7

Factor:

$x^2 - 7x + 12 = 0$

$(x - 4)(x - 3) = 0$

$x = 4$ or $x = 3$

$4 + 3 = 7$

You should have come up with (E) as the correct answer.

Geometric Notation for Length, Segments, Lines, Rays, and Congruence

You should expect SAT geometry questions to use the symbols $\leftrightarrow$, $-$, and $\cong$.

$\leftrightarrow$ signifies a line. $\overleftrightarrow{XY}$ is the line that passes through points X and Y.

$-$ signifies a line segment: $\overline{XY}$ is the line segment whose endpoints are X and Y.

$\cong$ symbolizes congruence. If two triangles are congruent, they coincide exactly when superimposed. You may want to think of two congruent figures as identical twins.

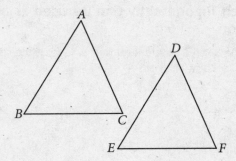

Note: Figure not drawn to scale.

$\angle CAB \cong \angle FDE$ and $\angle ABC \cong \angle DEF$. Which of the following must be true?

   I. $\triangle ABC \cong \triangle DEF$

  II. Triangles ABC and DEF are similar.

 III. $\overline{AB} = \overline{DE}$

(A) II only

(B) III only

(C) I and III

(D) II and III

(E) I, II, and III

 GO ONLINE

Stay familiar with advanced math rules on your downloadable Study Sheet for study on the go.

When a figure is not drawn to scale, it is most likely drawn in a misleading way. The figure on the previous page certainly looks as though *ABC* and *DEF* are identical and that all their parts are congruent, but you can't assume that based on the information in the problem. You may want to draw your own diagrams to think about some of the different possibilities. All we know about these triangles is that they have two pairs of corresponding angles that are congruent. Therefore, the third angle of each triangle must also be congruent. This tells us that the triangles are similar because their angles are the same. However, we know nothing about the lengths of the sides—one triangle could be much smaller than the other; thus, choice (A) is the correct answer.

Problems in Which Trigonometry Can Be Used as an Alternative Method of Solution

Now more than ever, the SAT will reward test takers who recall the special relationships in 45-45-90 and 30-60-90 right triangles:

The Isosceles Right Triangle

(Note the side ratio—$1:1:\sqrt{2}$)

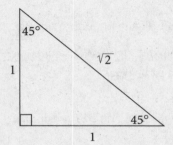

The 30-60-90 Right Triangle

(Note the side ratio—$1:\sqrt{3}:2$, and which side is opposite which angle.)

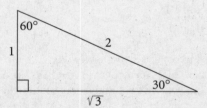

Try the following question.

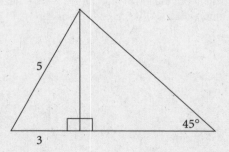

What is the total area of the figure above?

To find the area of a triangle, you need its height and the length of its base. Think about the information presented in the figure. What other data can you derive from it? The triangle on the left is a special triangle with side lengths of 3, 4, and 5. (You could also find the missing side using the Pythagorean theorem.) The triangle on the right is a 45-45-90 triangle, so its base must also equal 4. The total area of the figure is then $\frac{1}{2}(3 + 4)(4) = 14$.

Properties of Tangent Lines

When a line is tangent to a circle, the radius of the circle is perpendicular to the line at the point of contact. Look at the following example.

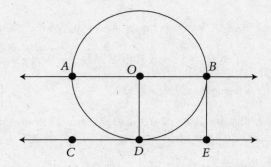

In the figure above, $\overline{AB}$ is a diameter of the circle, and $\overleftrightarrow{CE}$ is tangent to the circle at point D. $\overline{AB}$ is parallel to $\overleftrightarrow{CE}$. If the area of quadrilateral $OBED$ is 16 cm^2, what is the area of the circle whose center is at O?

(A)   4 cm^2
(B)   4π cm^2
(C)   8π cm^2
(D) 16π cm^2
(E) 256 cm^2

 GO ONLINE

Review the most common formulas on your downloadable Study Sheet for study on the go.

Because there's a circle in this problem, you can be sure you'll need the radius at some point. To figure out how to get that from the area of quadrilateral $OBED$, you'll need to use the rest of the information in the question stem. It may be helpful to add a few angles to the figure—for instance, because $\overleftrightarrow{CE}$ is tangent to the circle at point D, it is perpendicular to the radius of the circle at that point. The information given in the first two sentences of the question stem tells you that $\overline{OD}$ is perpendicular to $\overleftrightarrow{CE}$ and therefore also to $\overline{AB}$. $\overline{OD}$ and $\overline{OB}$ are both radii of the circle, so quadrilateral $OBED$ is a square. The area of $OBED$ is 16, so each side has a length of 4. This is also the radius of the circle. $4^2\pi = 16\pi$ is the area of the circle, so you should have chosen answer (D).

Coordinate Geometry

Coordinate geometry questions on the SAT tend to focus on the properties of straight lines. The equation of a straight line is $y = mx + b$, where y and x are the infinite number of coordinated (x, y) pairs that fall on the line. Variable b is the y-intercept, or the value of y when $x = 0$. Variable m is the slope of the line and is expressed $\frac{\Delta Y}{\Delta X}$, or $\frac{y_2 - y_1}{x_2 - x_1}$. What this means, exactly, is that the slope or steepness of a line is the change in y-values in relation to the change in corresponding x-values. Positive slopes tilt upward to the right. Negative slopes tilt downward to the right. A horizontal line has a slope of zero. A vertical line has an undefined slope. Parallel lines have equal slopes.

Perpendicular lines have negative reciprocal slopes.

As the question below illustrates, the SAT may also ask you to identify the midpoint of a line segment or the distance between two points.

> If point P is at $(8, 10)$ and point Q is at $(0, 4)$, what is the midpoint of PQ?
>
> (A) $(0, 10)$
> (B) $(4, 2)$
> (C) $(4, 5)$
> (D) $(4, 7)$
> (E) $(9, 2)$

The midpoint of a line segment whose ends are at the points (x_1, y_1) and (x_2, y_2) is the point $\left(\frac{x_1 + x_2}{2}, \frac{y_1 + y_2}{2} \right)$. Now plug in the numbers from the question.

$$x = \frac{8 + 0}{2} = \frac{8}{2} = 4$$

$$y = \frac{10 + 4}{2} = \frac{14}{2} = 7$$

The midpoint is $(4, 7)$, or choice (D).

Qualitative Behavior of Graphs and Functions

The SAT will likely ask you to show an understanding of a general or particular property of a complex graph, such as the one in the example problem below.

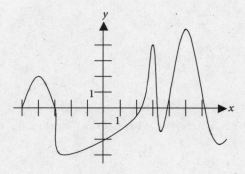

The figure above shows the graph of $f(x)$. At how many values of x does $f(x)$ equal 4?

(A) 0
(B) 1
(C) 2
(D) 3
(E) 4

The value of $f(x)$ is measured on the y-axis. Find 4 on the y-axis, and then see how many points on the graph have a y-value of 4. The points are approximately (3, 4), (4.7, 4), and (5.4, 4). So your answer here is 3, or choice (D).

Transformations and Their Effect on Graphs of Functions

A transformation is an alteration in a function. An SAT question might present a graph and ask you to identify a specific transformation, such as in the question on the next page.

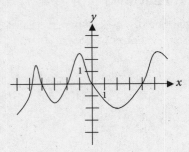

The figure above shows the graph of the function $r(x)$. Which of the following figures shows the graph of the function $r(x - 2)$?

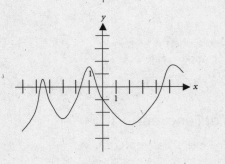

(A)

(D)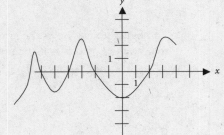

(B)

(E)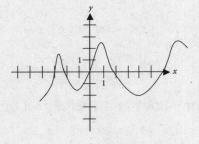

(C)

The graph of $r(x - 2)$ will look like the graph of $r(x)$ shifted two units to the right. You can check this by plugging in a few points. For example, $r(-1) = 2.5$, so $r(1 - 2)$ should equal 2.5. This is only true of answer (E).

Data Interpretation, Scatterplots, and Matrices

Some SAT questions focus on the test taker's ability to interpret, evaluate, and draw conclusions from data presented in matrices or, like those below, in scatterplots.

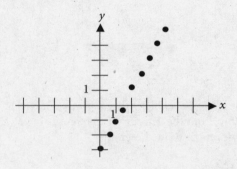

Which of the following equations best fits these points?

(A) $y = 3x + 2$

(B) $y = 3x - 2$

(C) $y = 2x + 3$

(D) $y = 2x - 3$

(E) $y = x - 3$

 SMARTPOINTS

Before answering the questions, invest about 10 seconds acquainting yourself with the subject matter, units of measurement, and data points on a graph or chart.

Try to figure out what sort of line would fit these points. What should the slope be? What should the y-intercept be? Remember that the standard equation for a line is in the form $y = mx + b$, where m is the slope and b is the y-intercept.

If you think visually, you might want to try sketching the line described by each answer choice to see which one fits the closest to the points on the graph. If you're more comfortable working with numbers, you could try plugging a few points from the graph into each possible equation to see which one works. The y-intercept of this graph is at -3. The slope is around 2 because the graph is raised about 2 units for every 1 unit it moves along the x-axis. The correct answer to this question is (D).

Geometric Probability

Geometric probability questions are those geometry questions that contain a final step in which you're asked to calculate a probability. At this final stage, use the formula

$$\text{probability} = \frac{\text{desired outcome}}{\text{possible outcomes}}.$$ Try this formula on the following question.

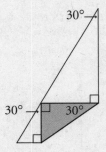

What is the probability that a point selected at random from the interior of the figure above will fall within the shaded region?

(A) $\dfrac{\sqrt{3}}{13}$

(B) $\dfrac{3}{13}$

(C) $\dfrac{6}{13}$

(D) $\dfrac{1}{3}$

(E) $\dfrac{1}{2}$

The probability that a randomly selected point will fall into the shaded region is equal to the area of the shaded region divided by the area of the entire figure. The figure is made up of three 30-60-90 triangles, so you can calculate the ratio of the lengths of the bases and heights of the various triangles and then find their areas.

This will be easier if you pick a number to be the length of the base of the smallest triangle. The lengths of the sides of a 30-60-90 triangle are in the ratio $x: x\sqrt{3} :2x$. If the length of the smallest triangle is 1, its height is $\sqrt{3}$. This is also the length of the base of the middle triangle. The height of the middle triangle is $\sqrt{3} \times \sqrt{3} = 3$, which is also the length of the base of the largest triangle. The height of the largest triangle is $3\sqrt{3}$.

Area of smallest triangle: $\frac{1}{2}(1)(\sqrt{3}) = \frac{\sqrt{3}}{2}$

Area of middle triangle: $\frac{1}{2}(\sqrt{3})(3) = \frac{3\sqrt{3}}{2}$

Area of largest triangle: $\frac{1}{2}(3)(3\sqrt{3}) = \frac{9\sqrt{3}}{2}$

Probability that a point will lie in the shaded region: $\dfrac{\dfrac{3\sqrt{3}}{2}}{\dfrac{\sqrt{3}}{2} + \dfrac{3\sqrt{3}}{2} + \dfrac{9\sqrt{3}}{2}} = \dfrac{\dfrac{3\sqrt{3}}{2}}{\dfrac{13\sqrt{3}}{2}} = \dfrac{3}{13}$

Use the techniques and knowledge you just gained to work through the practice set. Be sure to go over the concepts that you struggled with.

PRACTICE

We have labeled the following questions by the math concept they test. If you get stumped, go back to the appropriate part of this chapter and refresh your memory on how to solve that kind of problem.

Sequences Involving Exponential Growth

1. A scientist is running an experiment with two species of bacteria that grow exponentially. If species A doubles in population every 2 days, species B doubles in population every 5 days, and each species began the experiment with a population of 50 bacteria, what will the difference be between the populations of the two species after 10 days?

   (A) 200
   (B) 800
   (C) 1,200
   (D) 1,400
   (E) 1,500

Sets

2. If Set $A = \{2, 3, 5, 7, 10\}$ and Set $B = \{3, 4, 5, 6, 7\}$, how many elements are in the intersection of the two sets?

   (A) 2
   (B) 3
   (C) 5
   (D) 7
   (E) 10

Absolute Value

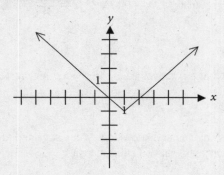

3. Which of the following equations best represents the graph above?

   (A) $y = |x|$
   (B) $y = |x| - 1$
   (C) $y = |x - 1|$
   (D) $y = |x - 1| - 1$
   (E) $y = |x - 2|$

Rational Equations and Inequalities

4. If $\dfrac{x^3 - 4x}{x^3 - 5x^2 + 6x} = 0$, and $x \neq 0$, 2, or 3, what is the value of x?

   (A) -3
   (B) -2
   (C) 0
   (D) 1
   (E) 4

Radical Equations

5. If $\sqrt{x + 2y} - 2 = 15$, what is the value of y in terms of x?

   (A) $\dfrac{289 - x}{2}$

   (B) $289 - x$

   (C) $\dfrac{17 - x}{2}$

   (D) $17 - x$

   (E) 289

Manipulation with Integer and Rational Exponents

6. What is the value of $4^{\frac{1}{2}} + 4^{\frac{3}{2}}$?

   (A) 4

   (B) 8

   (C) 10

   (D) 16

   (E) 64

Direct and Inverse Variation

7. The rate at which a certain balloon travels is inversely proportional to the amount of weight attached to it. If the balloon travels at 10 inches per second when there is a 2-gram weight attached to it, approximately how much weight must be attached to the balloon for it to travel 18 inches per second?

   (A) 0.4 grams

   (B) 1.0 gram

   (C) 1.1 grams

   (D) 3.6 grams

   (E) 10.0 grams

Function Notation and Evaluation

8. If $f(x) = \dfrac{(x^2 - 9)}{(x + 3)}$, what is the value of $f(-4)$?

   (A) -7

   (B) $-\dfrac{1}{4}$

   (C) 0

   (D) $\dfrac{1}{4}$

   (E) 7

Concepts of Domain and Range

9. If $g(x) = 2 - \sqrt{x - 7}$, and $g(x)$ is a real number, which of the following cannot be the value of x?

   (A) 4

   (B) 7

   (C) 11

   (D) 102

   (E) 496

Functions as Models

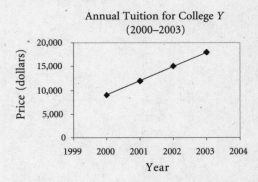

10. The graph represents the annual tuition for college Y from 2000–2003. Based on the graph, what was most likely the tuition for college Y in 1999?

    (A) $6,000

    (B) $9,000

    (C) $15,000

    (D) $18,000

    (E) $21,000

KAPLAN

Linear Functions—Equations and Graphs

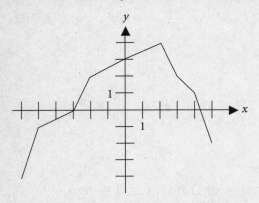

11. The graph shows the function $g(x)$. What is the value of $g(0)$?

   (A) −1

   (B) $-\dfrac{1}{2}$

   (C) 0

   (D) 1

   (E) 3

Quadratic Functions—Equations and Graphs

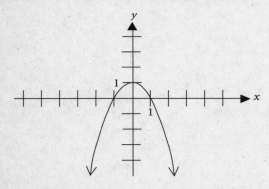

12. Which of the following equations best describes the curve above?

   (A) $y = x^2 + 4$

   (B) $y = x^2 - 1$

   (C) $y = -x^2 + 4$

   (D) $y = -x^2 + 1$

   (E) $y = -x^2 - 1$

Geometric Notation for Length, Segments, Lines, Rays, and Congruence

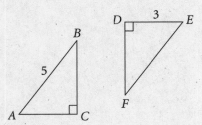

13. In the figure above, $\triangle ABC \cong \triangle EFD$. What is the area of $\triangle ABC$?

   (A) 6

   (B) 7.5

   (C) $6\sqrt{2}$

   (D) $6\sqrt{3}$

   (E) 12

Problems in Which Trigonometry Can Be Used as an Alternative Method of Solution

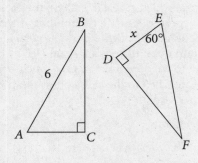

14. In the figure above, $\triangle ABC \cong \triangle EFD$. What is the value of x?

   (A) 3

   (B) 4

   (C) 5

   (D) 6

   (E) 7

Properties of Tangent Lines

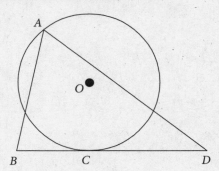

Note: Figure not drawn to scale.

15. In the figure above, $\overline{BD}$ is 8 units long and tangent to the circle at point C. $\overline{AC}$ is a diameter of the circle. If the circumference of the circle is 6π, what is the area of $\triangle ABD$?

    (A)   9
    (B)   12
    (C)   24
    (D) 9π
    (E) 10π

Coordinate Geometry

16. If point R is $(2, 4)$ and point S is $(7, 7)$, what is the length of $\overline{RS}$?

    (A) 2
    (B) $\sqrt{7}$
    (C) $\sqrt{34}$
    (D) 9
    (E) $\sqrt{202}$

Qualitative Behavior of Graphs and Functions

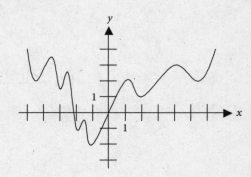

17. The figure above shows the graph of $g(x)$. What is the largest value of $g(x)$ shown in this figure?

    (A)   −2
    (B)   2
    (C)   4
    (D)   6
    (E)   6.5

Transformations and Their Effect on Graphs of Functions

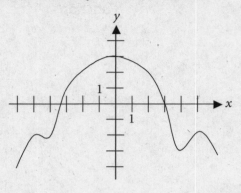

18. The figure above shows the graph of the function $h(x)$. Which of the following figures shows the graph of the function $h(x + 1)$?

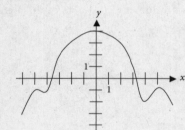

(A)

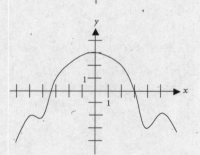

(D)

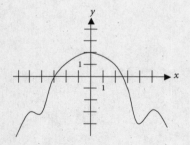

(B)

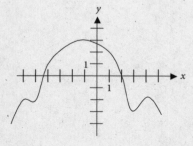

(E)

(C)

Data Interpretation, Scatterplots, and Matrices

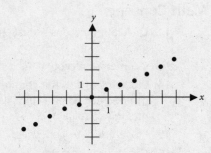

19. Which of the following equations best fits these points?

    (A) $y = \dfrac{1}{2}x$

    (B) $y = \dfrac{1}{2}x + 4$

    (C) $y = x$

    (D) $y = 2x - 4$

    (E) $y = 2x$

Geometric Probability

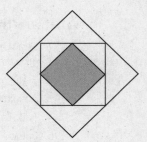

20. The figure above shows a square inscribed in a square inscribed in another square. What is the probability that a point selected at random from the interior of the largest figure will fall within the shaded region?

    (A) $\dfrac{1}{5}$

    (B) $\dfrac{1}{4}$

    (C) $\dfrac{1}{3}$

    (D) $\dfrac{4}{9}$

    (E) $\dfrac{1}{2}$

ANSWERS TO THE QUESTIONS ON PAGE 241

What Are the 20 Tested Advanced Math Concepts?

1. Sequences involving exponential growth
2. Sets
3. Absolute value
4. Rational equations and inequalities
5. Radical equations
6. Manipulation with integer and rational exponents
7. Direct and inverse variation
8. Function notation and evaluation
9. Concepts of domain and range
10. Functions as models
11. Linear functions—equations and graphs
12. Quadratic functions—equations and graphs
13. Geometric notation
14. Problems in which trigonometry can be used as an alternative method of solution
15. Properties of tangent lines
16. Coordinate geometry
17. Qualitative behavior of graphs and functions
18. Transformations and their effect on graphs of functions
19. Data interpretation, scatterplots, and matrices
20. Geometric probability

What Methods Can I Use to Solve Each Concept?

1. Sequences Involving Exponential Growth—If r is the ratio between consecutive terms, a_1 is the first term, and a_n is the nth term, then $a_n = a_1 r^{n-1}$.

2. Sets—Think of the union of sets as what you get when you merge the sets. Think of the intersection of sets as the overlap of the sets.

3. Absolute Value—Absolute value is the distance of a number from zero on the number line.

4. Rational Equations and Inequalities—When an expression looks especially complex, try to simplify it by factoring.

5. Radical Equations—Remember that $\sqrt{}$ refers only to the positive root of a number. If $\sqrt{25} = x$, then $x = 5$. But if $x^2 = 25$, then $x = \pm 5$.

6. Manipulation with Integer and Rational Exponents—$x^{-a} = \dfrac{1}{x^a}$ and $x^{\frac{p}{q}} = \sqrt[q]{x^p}$

7. Direct and Inverse Variation—direct variation is $y = kx$, where y changes as x does. Inverse variation is $xy = k$, where x and y change differently based on their relationship in the equation.

8. Function Notation and Evaluation—evaluating functions is simply substituting numbers for the variables.

9. Concepts of Domain and Range—The domain of a function is the set of values for which the function is defined. The range of a function is the set of possible values of the function.

10. Functions as Models—Be sure to understand the relationship and value of each part of a graph or chart.

11. Linear Functions—Equations and Graphs—Parallel lines have equal slopes. Perpendicular lines have negative reciprocal slopes.

12. Quadratic Functions—These functions take the shape of a parabola and the form $f(x) = ax^2 + bx + c$. Solve them like you would a quadratic equation.

13. Geometric Notation for Length, Segments, Lines, Rays, and Congruence—If two figures are similar, they have the same shape. If two figures are congruent they're identical. Any two 45-45-90 triangles are similar, even though they one might be much larger than the other. Only if they are identical in size as well as proportion are they congruent.

14. Problems in which Trigonometry can be Used as an Alternative Method of Solution— know the special relationships between 45-45-90 and 30-60-90 right triangles.

15. Properties of Tangent Lines—the radius of a circle is perpendicular to a tangent line at the point of contact.

16. Coordinate Geometry—The midpoint of two points is simply the average of the x-values and the average of the y-values.

17. Qualitative Behavior of Graphs and Functions—know the values for the x-axis and y-axis.

18. Transformations and their Effect on Graphs of Functions—a transformation is merely an adjustment to a function equation. Treat them similarly.

19. Data Interpretation, Scatterplots, and Matrices—sketch the shape given in the equation, and try plugging in some data points into that equation.

20. Geometric Probability—Probability $= \dfrac{\text{desired outcome}}{\text{possible outcome}}$

ANSWERS AND EXPLANATIONS

Sequences Involving Exponential Growth

1. D

Not every question about geometric sequences requires the application of a formula. Consider how this question, which looks at geometric sequences from a more everyday, applied perspective, really tests whether you grasp the concept of exponential growth.

Both species are growing exponentially, which means that the population at any point in time can be described by the equation $n = n_0 2^{\frac{t}{x}}$, where n_0 is the initial population, t is the number of days that have passed since the start of the experiment, and x is the number of days in which the population doubles. You don't have to know this equation to solve the problem—you could just double the original number of bacteria as many times as required to find the population of each species after 10 days, and then find the difference between them:

Population of species A:

$(50)2^{\frac{10}{2}} = (50)2^5 = (50)32 = 1{,}600$

Population of species B:

$(50)2^{\frac{10}{5}} = (50)2^2 = (50)4 = 200$

$1{,}600 - 200 = 1{,}400$, choice (D).

Sets

2. B

Focus on the overlap of the sets, which share three numbers: 3, 5, and 7. The correct answer is 3, choice (B).

Absolute Value

3. D

If you're not sure what these transformations of the graph look like, try plugging a few points from the graph into each equation to see which one is correct. Some good points to try are (0, 0) and (1, −1).

$|0 - 1| - 1 = 1 - 1 = 0$

$|1 - 1| - 1 = 0 - 1 = -1$

(D) is the correct answer.

Rational Equations and Inequalities

4. B

In general, try to simplify problems with complex rational equations like this by factoring the numerator and denominator to see whether any parts cancel out. In this case, you need only to focus on the numerator. You know the fraction has a value of zero, so the numerator must equal zero:

$x^3 - 4x = 0$

$x(x^2 - 4) = 0$

$x(x - 2)(x + 2) = 0$

$x = 0, 2, \text{ or } -2$

The question stem states that $x \neq 0$ or 2, so the answer must be $x = -2$, choice (B).

Radical Equations

5. A

$\sqrt{x + 2y} - 2 = 15$

$\sqrt{x + 2y} = 17$

$\left(\sqrt{x + 2y}\right)^2 = 17^2$

$x + 2y = 289$

$2y = 289 - x$

$y = \dfrac{289 - x}{2}$

The correct answer is (A). This is an example designed to illustrate that squaring both sides is not always the *last* step.

Manipulation with Integer and Rational Exponents

6. C

If x is a positive real number and a is a nonzero integer, then $x^{\frac{1}{a}} = \sqrt[a]{n}$. So $4^{\frac{1}{2}} = \sqrt[2]{4} = 2$. If p and q are integers, then $x^{\frac{p}{q}} = \sqrt[q]{x^p}$. So $4^{\frac{3}{2}} = \sqrt[2]{4^3} = \sqrt{64} = 8$. Therefore, $2 + 8 = 10$, and answer choice (C) is correct.

Direct and Inverse Variation

7. C

To find the exact amount of weight required, set up a relationship between the height of the balloon and the weight attached to it. Because these quantities vary inversely, you can express that relationship as $h = \dfrac{k}{w}$, where h is the rate of travel of the balloon, w is the weight attached to it, and k is a constant. First, use the given values of h and w to find k, and then use the equation to find the amount of weight required to make the balloon travel at 18 inches per second.

$$10 = \frac{k}{2}$$

$$k = 20$$

$$18 = \frac{20}{w}$$

$w = \dfrac{20}{18} = \dfrac{10}{9} = 1.\overline{11}$, which is approximately 1.1, choice (C).

Function Notation and Evaluation

8. A

Substitute -4 wherever you see x:

$$f(x) = \frac{(x^2 - 9)}{(x + 3)}$$

$$f(-4) = \frac{[(-4)^2 - 9]}{(-4 + 3)}$$

$$f(-4) = \frac{(16 - 9)}{(-1)}$$

$$f(-4) = \frac{7}{-1}$$

$f(-4) = -7$, choice (A).

Concepts of Domain and Range

9. A

If $g(x)$ is a real number, then $\sqrt{x - 7}$ must be a real number. Therefore, $x - 7$ must be zero or a positive number: $x - 7 \geq 0$, and so $x \geq 7$. Any number less than 7, such as choice (A), is outside the domain of the function, which is why it is the correct answer.

Functions as Models

10. A

Making inferences from a linear graph can be difficult, but remember that you can write in your test booklet. Use a straight surface or your free hand to extend the line on the graph. By looking at the graph, we can see that each year the tuition of college Y increases. In 2000, tuition was $9,000. So, we know that in 1999 it should be less than that. The only option is choice (A).

Linear Functions—Equations and Graphs

11. E

One question on test day might require you to evaluate the graph of a linear function, perhaps by indicating the value of y for a given value of x. This question essentially asks you to identify which value of y corresponds to an x-value of 0. Locate $x = 0$; then locate the corresponding y-value. In this case, that value is 3, or (E).

Quadratic Functions—Equations and Graphs

12. D

If you encounter a question about the graph of a quadratic function, it's likely to ask you merely to evaluate a particular point on the graph or, as this question asked, to describe the graph as a whole.

Plug in some points from the graph into each equation to see which ones fit. Good points to test on this graph include (0, 1) and (1, 0):

$$1 = -(0^2) + 1$$
$$0 = -(1^2) + 1$$

Both points work with $y = -x^2 + 1$, choice (D), so it is correct.

Geometric Notation for Length, Segments, Lines, Rays, and Congruence

13. A

Because the two triangles are congruent, you can combine the information given about each triangle. That is, because $DE = 3$, CA also equals 3. Combining the information from the two triangles gives you:

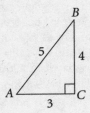

The height can be found by the Pythagorean theorem, $a^2 + b^2 = c^2$. In this case,

$$3^2 + b^2 = 5^2.$$
$$9 + b^2 = 25$$
$$b^2 = 16$$
$$b = 4$$

The area of the triangle is $\frac{1}{2}(3)(4) = \frac{1}{2}(12) = 6$, so choice (A) is correct.

Problems in Which Trigonometry Can Be Used as an Alternative Method of Solution

14. A

If two triangles are congruent, they are identical. Each angle or length in one triangle is equal to the corresponding angle or length in the other triangle. Combine the information in the two triangles to get the following triangle:

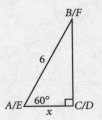

This is a 30-60-90 special triangle, so $x = \frac{1}{2}(6) = 3$, choice (A).

Properties of Tangent Lines

15. C

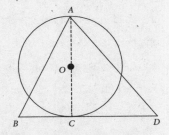

Note: Figure not drawn to scale.

When you see a figure that is not drawn to scale, you can often assume that it has been drawn to be deliberately misleading. Be careful not to assume anything from the apparent positions or lengths of any parts of the figure. Rely instead on the information in the question stem. You may wish to draw your own figure to incorporate that information. This figure includes a circle. Anytime you see a circle, you're going to want its radius at some point. How is the radius of the circle related to the triangle?

Using the circumference formula and the known circumference of the circle:

$6\pi = 2\pi r$

$r = 3$

The diagram below has been corrected to include the information in the question stem. Note that because $\overline{BD}$ is tangent to the circle at point C, it is perpendicular to $\overline{OC}$. Because $\overline{AC}$ is a diameter of the circle, it must pass through the center of the circle.

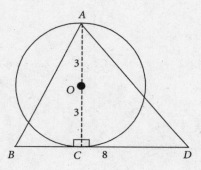

The area of a triangle is one half the length of the base times the height. The height of this triangle is $\overline{AC}$:3 + 3 = 6. The area is $\frac{1}{2}(8)(6) = 24$, choice (C).

Coordinate Geometry

16. C

The distance between two points (x_1, y_1) and (x_2, y_2) can be found by using the distance formula:

$\sqrt{(x_2 - x_1)^2 + (y_2 - y_1)^2}$. Plug in the numbers from the question.

$\sqrt{(7 - 2)^2 + (7 - 4)^2} = \sqrt{5^2 + 3^2} = \sqrt{25 + 9} = \sqrt{34}$

The correct answer is choice (C).

Qualitative Behavior of Graphs and Functions

17. C

The value of $g(x)$ is the y-value of the graph. Don't worry about how much of the x-axis is shown; it isn't relevant. The largest value of $g(x)$ shown in the figure is 4, at the points (−5, 4) and (6.5, 4), so (C) is the correct answer.

Transformations and Their Effect on Graphs of Functions

18. C

The graph of $h(x + 1)$ is the graph of $h(x)$ shifted one unit to the left. If you're not sure what that would look like, try comparing a few points from each graph:

$h(3) = h(2 + 1) = 0$

$h(0) = h(-1 + 1) = 3$

Data Interpretation, Scatterplots, and Matrices

19. A

Try to figure out what sort of line would fit these points. What should the slope be? What should the y-intercept be? A line through these points would cross the y-axis at or near 0. Its slope is positive but less than 1. Choice (A) fulfills both these criteria. You might want to check your answer by plugging a few points from the graph into the equation to make sure they work.

Geometric Probability

20. B

There are several different ways to approach this problem, but they all require some knowledge of triangles. The most important thing to notice about the figure is that all the triangles in it are 45-45-90 triangles. This allows you to either calculate the ratios between their sides or break them up further as shown below.

Adding two lines to this figure makes it much easier to work with.

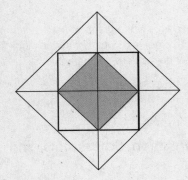

Note that every triangle in this new figure is identical. At this point, you can count the number of shaded triangles and divide by the total number of triangles.

$\frac{4}{16} = \frac{1}{4}$, choice (B).

Chapter Fourteen: **SAT Math Traps**

- What Are the Most Common Math Traps?
- What Skills Do I Need to Work Around Tricky Answer Choices to Solve the Problem?

As we've mentioned several times, Math sets are arranged in order of difficulty, with the easiest problems coming first and the hardest problems coming last. Knowing this leads you, the test taker, to treat question #3 differently from question #14. This is where SAT Math traps come into play.

If you arrive at an answer choice to a hard Math problem without too much effort, be suspicious; that answer is probably a math trap. Learning how to recognize and avoid common SAT Math traps will help you be more successful on the Math sections. There are 10 common Math traps on the SAT. We'll show you the trap, the wrong answer the trap wants you to choose, how to avoid that answer, and how to solve the problem quickly and correctly.

TRAP TEST

The following 10 questions have one thing in common—
they all have traps. Take 12 minutes to try to work through
all of them. Then check your answers on the next page.

1. Sammy purchased a new car in 2000. Three years
   later, he sold it to a dealer for 40 percent less than
   he paid for it in 2000. The dealer then added 20
   percent onto the price he paid and resold it to
   another customer. The price the final customer
   paid for the car was what percent of the original
   price Sammy paid in 2000?

   (A) 40%

   (B) 60%

   (C) 72%

   (D) 80%

   (E) 88%

2. In a class of 27 plumbers, the average (arithmetic
   mean) score of the male plumbers on the final
   exam was 83. If the average score of the 15 female
   plumbers in the class was 92, what was the average
   of the whole class?

   (A) 86.2

   (B) 87.0

   (C) 87.5

   (D) 88.0

   (E) 88.2

3. Mammo's coin collection consists of quarters,
   dimes, and nickels. If the ratio of the number of
   quarters to the number of dimes is 5:2, and the
   ratio of the number of dimes to the number of
   nickels is 3:4, what is the ratio of the number of
   quarters to the number of nickels?

   (A) 5:4

   (B) 7:5

   (C) 10:6

   (D) 12:7

   (E) 15:8

4. What is the least positive integer that is divisible
   by both 2 and 5 and leaves a remainder of 3 when
   divided by 11?

   (A) 30

   (B) 32

   (C) 33

   (D) 70

   (E) 80

5. What number is $33\frac{1}{3}$% less than 9?

6. The ratio of two quantities is 3:4. If each of the
   quantities is increased by 1, what is the ratio of
   these two new quantities?

   (A) $\frac{9}{16}$

   (B) $\frac{2}{3}$

   (C) $\frac{3}{4}$

   (D) $\frac{4}{5}$

   (E) It cannot be determined from the information given.

7. If $n \neq 0$, then which of the following must be true?

   I. $n^2 > n$

   II. $2n > n$

   III. $n + 1 > n$

   (A) I only
   (B) II only
   (C) III only
   (D) I and III only
   (E) I, II, and III

8. At a certain restaurant, the hourly wage for a waiter is 20 percent more than the hourly wage for a dishwasher, and the hourly wage for a dishwasher is half as much as the hourly wage for a cook's assistant. If a cook's assistant earns $8.50 per hour, how much less than a cook's assistant does a waiter earn each hour?

   (A) $2.55
   (B) $3.40
   (C) $4.25
   (D) $5.10
   (E) $5.95

9. A car traveled from *A* to *B* at an average speed of 40 mph and then immediately traveled back from *B* to *A* at an average speed of 60 mph. What was the car's average speed for the roundtrip in miles per hour?

   (A) 45
   (B) 48
   (C) 50
   (D) 52
   (E) 54

10. The tickets for a certain raffle are consecutively numbered. If Louis sold the tickets numbered from 75 to 148 inclusive, how many raffle tickets did he sell?

    (A) 71
    (B) 72
    (C) 73
    (D) 74
    (E) 75

HERE ARE THE ANSWERS:

1.(C) 2.(D) 3.(E) 4.(E) 5.(6) 7.(C) 8.(B) 9.(B) 10.(D)

KAPLAN

Unless you made a calculation error, chances are your incorrect answers are an indication that you got caught in a trap. The same traps occur again and again on the SAT. If you learn how they work and how to avoid them, dealing with even the hardest traps will become manageable, and you'll do much better on the harder math questions. To see how they work, let's take another look at the ten sample questions. Each contains one of the Top Ten Math Traps.

TRAP 1: PERCENT INCREASE/DECREASE

Sammy purchased a new car in 2000. Three years later, he sold it to a dealer for 40 percent less than he paid for it in 2000. The dealer then added 20 percent onto the price he paid and resold it to another customer. The price the final customer paid for the car was what percent of the original price Sammy paid in 2000?

(A) 40%

(B) 60%

(C) 72%

(D) 80%

(E) 88%

The Wrong Answer

The increase/decrease percentage problems usually appear at the end of a section and invariably contain a trap. Most students will figure that taking away 40 percent and then adding 20 percent will give them an overall loss of 20 percent, and they'll pick choice (D), 80 percent, as the correct answer. Those students would be wrong.

The Trap

When a quantity is increased or decreased by a percentage more than once, you can't simply add and subtract the percentages to get the answer. In this kind of percentage problem, the first change is a percentage of the starting amount, but the second change is a percentage of the new amount.

Avoiding the Trap

Don't blindly add and subtract percentages. They can only be added and subtracted when they are of the same amount.

Finding the Right Answer

We know:

- The *40 percent less* that Sammy got for the car is 40 percent of his original price.

- The *20 percent* the dealer adds on is 20 percent of what the dealer paid, which is a much smaller amount.

- Adding 20 percent of that smaller amount is *not* the same thing as adding back 20 percent of the original price.

Solving the Problem Fast

Use 100 for a starting quantity, even if it's not plausible in the real situation. The problem asks for the relative amount of change. So you can take any starting number and compare it with the final result. Because you're dealing with percentages, 100 is the easiest number to work with.

- If Sammy paid $100 for the car, what is 40 percent less?

- In the case of $100, each percent equals $1, so $100 - 40 = 60$. Sammy sold the car for $60.

- If the dealer charges 20 percent more than his purchase price, she's raising the price by 20 percent of $60, which is $60 \times 0.20 = \$12$. (Not 20 percent of $100, which would be $20!).

- Therefore, the dealer sold the car again for $60 + $12, or $72.

- Finally, what percent of the starting price ($100) is $72? It's 72%. So the correct answer here is choice (C).

TRAP 2: WEIGHTED AVERAGES

In a class of 27 plumbers, the average (arithmetic mean) score of the male plumbers on the final exam was 83. If the average score of the 15 female plumbers in the class was 92, what was the average of the whole class?

(A) 86.2

(B) 87.0

(C) 87.5

(D) 88.0

(E) 88.2

The Wrong Answer

Some students will rush in and simply average 83 and 92 to come up with 87.5 as the class average. Those students will be wrong.

The Trap

You cannot combine averages of different quantities by taking the average of those original averages. In an averages problem, if one value occurs more frequently than others, it is *weighted* more. Remember, the average formula calls for the sum of all the terms divided by the total number of terms.

Avoiding the Trap

Don't just take the average of the averages; work with the sums.

Finding the Right Answer

If 15 of the 27 plumbers are female, the remaining 12 must be male. We can't just add 83 to 92 and divide by two. In this class, there are more females than males, and therefore, the females' test scores are *weighted* more—they contribute more to the class average. So the answer must be either (D) or (E).

To find each sum, multiply each average by the number of terms it represents. After you have found the sums of the different terms, find the combined average by plugging them into the average formula.

$$\text{Total class average} = \frac{\text{Sum of females' scores} + \text{Sum of males' scores}}{\text{Total number of students}}$$

$$= \frac{(\text{\# of females} \times \text{females' average score}) + (\text{\# of males} \times \text{males' average score})}{\text{Total number of students}}$$

$$= \frac{15(92) + 12(83)}{27} = \frac{1{,}380 + 996}{27} = 88$$

So the class average is 88, answer choice (D).

Important

Notice how using a calculator helps in this problem.

TRAP 3: RATIO:RATIO:RATIO

Mammo's coin collection consists of quarters, dimes, and nickels. If the ratio of the number of quarters to the number of dimes is 5:2, and the ratio of the number of dimes to the number of nickels is 3:4, what is the ratio of the number of quarters to the number of nickels?

(A) 5:4
(B) 7:5
(C) 10:6
(D) 12:7
(E) 15:8

The Wrong Answer

If you chose 5:4 as the correct answer, you fell for the classic ratio trap.

The Trap

Parts of different ratios don't always refer to the same whole. In the classic ratio trap, two different ratios each share a common part that is represented by two different numbers. However, the two ratios do not refer to the same whole, so they are not in proportion to each other.

To solve this type of problem, restate both ratios so that the numbers representing the common part (in this case *dimes*) are the same. Then all the parts will be in proportion and can be compared to each other.

AVAILABLE ON CD-ROM

With 5 full-length practice tests and 4 section-length practice tests for math, you'll be a pro at avoiding math traps on Test Day.

Avoiding the Trap

Restate ratios so that the same number refers to the same quantity. Make sure the common quantity in both ratios has the same number in both.

Finding the Right Answer

To find the ratio of quarters to nickels, restate both ratios so that the number of dimes is the same in both. You are given two ratios:

quarters to dimes = 5:2   dimes to nickels = 3:4

- The number corresponding to dimes in the first ratio is 2.
- The number corresponding to dimes in the second ratio is 3.
- To restate the ratios, find the least common multiple of 2 and 3.
- The least common multiple of 2 and 3 is 2 × 3, or 6.

Restate the ratios with the number of dimes as 6:

quarters to dimes = 15:6 (which is the same as 5:2)

dimes to nickels = 6:8 (which is the same as 3:4)

The ratios are still in their original proportions, but now they can be compared easily because dimes are represented by the same number in both. The ratio of quarters to dimes to nickels is 15:6:8, so the ratio of quarters to nickels is 15:8, which is answer choice (E).

TRAP 4: "LEAST" AND "GREATEST"

What is the least positive integer that is divisible by both 2 and 5 and leaves a remainder of 3 when divided by 11?

(A) 30

(B) 32

(C) 33

(D) 70

(E) 80

The Wrong Answer

(A) is the choice not to go for here.

The Trap

In questions that ask for the *least, minimum,* or *smallest* something, the choice offering the smallest number is rarely right. In questions that ask for the *greatest, maximum,* or *largest* something, the choice offering the largest number is very rarely right.

Avoiding the Trap

Consider the constraints and requirements that the nature of the question has placed upon the possible answer. Don't leap to conclusions. In fact, if you ever need to guess on questions asking about the least number, the one place not to go is to the smallest choice and vice versa for questions asking about the largest number.

Finding the Right Answer

If the integer is divisible by both 2 and 5, it is a multiple of 2 × 5, or 10, so eliminate (B) and (C). If it leaves a remainder of 3 when divided by 11, it is 3 more than a multiple of 11. In (A), 30 − 3 = 27, which isn't a multiple of 11. In (D), 70 − 3 = 67, which isn't a multiple of 11. In (E), 80 − 3 = 77, which is a multiple of 11, and the correct answer.

TRAP 5: PERCENT "OF" VERSUS PERCENT "LESS" OR "GREATER"

What number is $33\frac{1}{3}$% less than 9?

The Wrong Answer

Three.

The Trap

Reading too quickly or with insufficient care could lead a test taker to mistake $33\frac{1}{3}$% less than 9 for $33\frac{1}{3}$% of 9, which is $\frac{1}{3} \times 9 = 3$.

Avoiding the Trap

Be on the lookout for subtleties of wording, especially in questions appearing in the middle or end of a section. Consciously and actively distinguish these three things whenever percent questions arise:

1. *a* percent *of b*;
2. *a* percent *less than b*;
3. *a* percent *greater than b*.

For example:

1. 25 percent *of* 8 means $\left(\frac{1}{4}\right)(8) = 2$;

2. 25 percent *less than* 8 means $8 - \left(\frac{1}{4}\right)(8) = 8 - 2 = 6$;

3. 25 percent *greater than* 8 means $8 + \left(\frac{1}{4}\right)(8) = 8 + 2 = 10$.

Finding the Right Answer

$33\frac{1}{3}$% less than 9 means $9 - \left(\frac{1}{3}\right)(9) = 9 - 3 = 6$.

TRAP 6: RATIO VERSUS QUANTITY

The ratio of two quantities is 3:4. If each of the quantities is increased by 1, what is the ratio of these two new quantities?

(A) $\dfrac{9}{16}$

(B) $\dfrac{2}{3}$

(C) $\dfrac{3}{4}$

(D) $\dfrac{4}{5}$

(E) It cannot be determined from the information given.

The Wrong Answer

(D) is a trap.

The Trap

If all you have is a ratio, you cannot simply add to or subtract from the parts at will. Test takers unfamiliar with this rule would probably add 1 to 3 and to 4, coming up incorrectly with the ratio of 4:5.

Avoiding the Trap

Avoid this trap by remembering the rule that you can multiply or divide a ratio or part of a ratio, but you cannot add to or subtract from a ratio or part of a ratio. Consider some examples. Imagine that at a meeting, the ratio of women to men is 6:5. If the number of women doubles, the new ratio of women to men is 12:5. In other words, you can multiply a ratio or part of a ratio. Similarly, you can divide a ratio or part of a ratio. Given the original ratio of women to men as 6:5, you can conclude that if the number of women at the meeting were cut in half, the new ratio of women to men at the meeting would be 3:5.

However, you cannot add to or subtract from a ratio or part of a ratio because knowing the ratio doesn't tell you the actual quantities associated with it. To clearly understand what we mean, we will explain two scenarios. Again considering a meeting at which the ratio of women to men is 6:5, assume that in situation I, the actual quantities of women and men are 12 and 10, respectively. Assume that in situation II, the actual quantities of women and men are 18 and 15, respectively. Now assume that one woman and one man enter the meeting. In situation I, the new ratio of women to men is 13:11.

In situation II, the new ratio of women to men is 19:16. It is obvious in this example that $\frac{13}{11} \neq \frac{19}{16}$; thus, this inequality demonstrates how it is possible to have the same ratio and get different results depending on the quantities with which you begin.

Finding the Right Answer

For students on the lookout for violations of the rule we've been discussing, this question means quick points. Once you realize that the ratio of the new quantities depends on the actual original quantities—not simply their ratio—you'll quickly recognize that the answer cannot be determined from the information provided. The correct answer is (E).

TRAP 7: NOT ALL NUMBERS ARE POSITIVE INTEGERS

If $n \neq 0$, then which of the following must be true?

   I. $n^2 > n$
  II. $2n > n$
 III. $n + 1 > n$

(A) I only
(B) II only
(C) III only
(D) I and III only
(E) I, II, and III

 GO ONLINE

Check out your new practice quiz every month.

The Wrong Answer

In the example above, if you considered only positive integers greater than 1 for the value of n, you would assume that all three statements are true. However, that is not the case.

The Trap

Not all numbers are positive integers. Don't forget there are negative numbers and fractions as well. This is important because negative numbers and fractions between 0 and 1 behave very differently from positive integers.

Avoiding the Trap

When picking numbers for variables, consider fractions and negative numbers.

Finding the Right Answer

Looking at statement I, you can assume that squaring a number will give a larger number as a result. For example, $4^2 = 16$, or $10^2 = 100$. However, when you square a fraction between 0 and 1, the result is quite different. $\left(\frac{1}{2}\right)^2 = \frac{1}{4}$ and $\left(\frac{1}{10}\right)^2 = \frac{1}{100}$. So, when you square a fraction, the resulting fraction will be a smaller number.

In statement II, what happens when you multiply a number by 2? $7 \times 2 = 14$; $25 \times 2 = 50$. Multiplying any positive number by 2 doubles that number, so you get a larger result. However, if you multiply a negative number by 2, your result is smaller than the original number. For example, $-3 \times 2 = -6$.

Finally, look at statement III. What happens when you add 1 to any number? Adding 1 to any number gives you a larger number as a result. For example, $5 + 1 = 6$; $\frac{1}{2} + 1 = 1\frac{1}{2}$; and $-7 + 1 = -6$.

Therefore, only statement III must be true, so choice (C) is correct. If you didn't consider fractions or negative numbers, you would have fallen into the trap and answered the question incorrectly.

TRAP 8: HIDDEN INSTRUCTIONS

At a certain restaurant, the hourly wage for a waiter is 20 percent more than the hourly wage for a dishwasher, and the hourly wage for a dishwasher is half as much as the hourly wage for a cook's assistant. If a cook's assistant earns $8.50 per hour, how much less than a cook's assistant does a waiter earn each hour?

(A) $2.55

(B) $3.40

(C) $4.25

(D) $5.10

(E) $5.95

The Wrong Answer

To solve this problem, you must find the hourly wage of the waiter. The cook's assistant earns $8.50 per hour. The dishwasher earns half of this—$4.25 per hour. The waiter earns 20 percent more than the dishwasher—$4.25 × 1.2 = $5.10. So the waiter earns $5.10 per hour, and your automatic reaction might be to fill in answer choice (D). But (D) is the wrong answer.

The Trap

A small clue, easily overlooked, can mean the difference between a right and wrong answer. In this case, the word *less* is that small clue. After spending all this time finding the waiter's hourly wage, in their moment of triumph, many students skip right over the vital last step. They overlook that the question asks not what the waiter earns, but how much less than the cook's assistant the waiter earns.

Avoiding the Trap

Make sure you answer the question that's being asked. Watch out for hidden instructions.

Finding the Right Answer

You have figured out that the waiter earns $5.10 per hour, and the cook's assistant earns $8.50 per hour. To find out how much less the waiter earns than the cook's assistant, subtract the waiter's hourly wage from the cook's assistant's hourly wage. The correct answer is (B).

TRAP 9: AVERAGE RATES

A car traveled from A to B at an average speed of 40 mph and then immediately traveled back from B to A at an average speed of 60 mph. What was the car's average speed for the roundtrip in miles per hour?

(A) 45

(B) 48

(C) 50

(D) 52

(E) 54

The Wrong Answer

Do you see which answer choice looks too good to be true? The temptation is simply to add 40 and 60 and divide by two. The answer is *obviously* 50 (C). But 50 is wrong.

The Trap

To get an average speed, you can't just average the rates. Why is the average speed not 50 mph? Because the car spent more time traveling at 40 mph than at 60 mph. Each leg of the round trip was the same distance, but the first leg, at the slower speed, took more time.

Avoiding the Trap

You can solve almost any average rate problem with this general formula:

$$\text{Average rate} = \frac{\text{Total distance}}{\text{Total time}}$$

Use the given information to figure out the total distance and the total time. But how can you do that when many problems don't specify the distances?

Finding the Right Answer

In our sample above, we are told that a car went from *A* to *B* at 40 mph and back from *B* to *A* at 60 mph. In other words, it went half the total distance at 40 mph and half the total distance at 60 mph.

How do you use the formula:

$$\text{Average rate} = \frac{\text{Total distance}}{\text{Total time}}?$$

If the total distance is not provided, pick a number! Pick any number you want for the total distance. Divide that total distance into half distances. Calculate the time needed to travel each half distance at the different rates.

Make sure to pick a number that's easy to work with. A good number to pick here would be 240 miles for the total distance because you can figure in your head the times for two 120-mile legs at 40 mph and 60 mph:

$$A \text{ to } B: = \frac{120 \text{ miles}}{40 \text{ mph}} = 3 \text{ hours}$$

$$B \text{ to } A: = \frac{120 \text{ miles}}{60 \text{ mph}} = 2 \text{ hours}$$

Total time = 5 hours

Now plug "total distance = 240 miles" and "total time = 5 hours" into the general formula:

$$\text{Average rate} = \frac{\text{Total distance}}{\text{Total time}} = \frac{240 \text{ miles}}{5 \text{ hours}} = 48 \text{ mph}$$

Correct answer: (B).

TRAP 10: COUNTING NUMBERS

The tickets for a certain raffle are consecutively numbered. If Louis sold the tickets numbered from 75 to 148 inclusive, how many raffle tickets did he sell?

(A) 71
(B) 72
(C) 73
(D) 74
(E) 75

The Wrong Answer

If you subtract 75 from 148 and get 73 as the answer, you are wrong.

The Trap

Subtracting the first and last integers in a range will give you the difference of the two numbers. It won't give you the number of integers in that range.

Avoiding the Trap

To count the number of integers in a range, subtract and then add 1. If you forget the rule, pick two small numbers that are close together, such as 1 and 4. Obviously, there are four integers from 1 to 4, inclusive. But if you had subtracted 1 from 4, your remainder would have been 3.

Finding the Right Answer

In the problem above, subtract 75 from 148. The result is 73. Add 1 to this difference to get the number of integers. That gives you 74. The correct answer is (D). The word *inclusive* tells you to include the first and last numbers given. So, for example, the integers from 5 to 15 inclusive would include 5 and 15. Questions always make it clear whether you should include the outer numbers or not because the correct answer hinges on this point.

PRACTICE

Directions: Identify the trap in each problem (and solve the problem correctly). Answers are found on page 291.

1. If x is 300 percent of 25 and y is 25 percent more than 40, then x is what percent of y? (Disregard the % sign when you grid your answer.)

2. In the figure above, what is the maximum number of nonoverlapping regions into which the shaded area can be divided using exactly two straight lines?

(A) 3
(B) 4
(C) 5
(D) 6
(E) 7

3. A certain school event was open only to juniors and seniors. Half the number of juniors who had planned to attend actually attended. Double the number of seniors who had planned to attend actually attended. If the ratio of the number of juniors who had planned to attend to the number of seniors who had planned to attend was 4 to 5, then juniors were what fraction of attendees?

(A) $\dfrac{1}{6}$

(B) $\dfrac{1}{5}$

(C) $\dfrac{4}{19}$

(D) $\dfrac{4}{15}$

(E) It cannot be determined from the information given.

4. If $p - q = 4$ and r is the number of integers less than p and greater than q, then which of the following could be true?

    I. $r = 3$
    II. $r = 4$
    III. $r = 5$

(A) I only
(B) II only
(C) III only
(D) I and II
(E) I, II, and III

5. Pump 1 can drain a 400-gallon water tank in 1.2 hours. Pump 2 can drain the same tank in 1.8 hours. How many minutes longer than pump 1 would it take pump 2 to drain a 100-gallon tank?

   (A) 0.15
   (B) 1.2
   (C) 6
   (D) 9
   (E) 18

6. Volumes 12 through 30 of a certain encyclopedia are located on the bottom shelf of a bookcase. If the volumes of the encyclopedia are numbered consecutively, how many volumes of the encyclopedia are on the bottom shelf?

   (A) 17
   (B) 18
   (C) 19
   (D) 29
   (E) 30

7. A reservoir is at full capacity at the beginning of summer. By the first day of fall, the level in the reservoir is 30 percent below full capacity. Then during the fall, a period of heavy rains increases the level by 30 percent. After the rains, the reservoir is at what percent of its full capacity?

   (A) 60%
   (B) 85%
   (C) 91%
   (D) 95%
   (E) 100%

8. Two classes, one with 50 students and the other with 30, take the same exam. The combined average of both classes is 84.5. If the larger class averages 80, what is the average of the smaller class?

   (A) 87.2
   (B) 89.0
   (C) 92.0
   (D) 93.3
   (E) 94.5

9. In a pet shop, the ratio of puppies to kittens is 7:6, and the ratio of kittens to guinea pigs is 5:3. What is the ratio of puppies to guinea pigs?

   (A) 7:3
   (B) 6:5
   (C) 13:8
   (D) 21:11
   (E) 35:18

10. A typist typed the first n pages of a book, where $n > 0$, at an average rate of 12 pages per hour and typed the remaining n pages at an average rate of 20 pages per hour. What was the typist's average rate in pages per hour for the entire book?

   (A) 14
   (B) 15
   (C) 16
   (D) 17
   (E) 18

IF YOU LEARNED ONLY TWO THINGS IN THIS CHAPTER . . . .

1. If an answer to a hard math question comes too easily, it is probably a trap.
2. Knowing where you are in a section will help you decipher which questions are more likely to contain traps.

ANSWERS TO THE QUESTIONS ON PAGE 273

What Are the Most Common Math Traps?

The SAT uses traps on harder math problems. The ten most common traps are:

- Trap 1: Percent Increase/Decrease
- Trap 2: Weighted Averages
- Trap 3: Ratio:Ratio:Ratio
- Trap 4: "Least" and "Greatest"
- Trap 5: Percent "of" Versus Percent "Less" or "Greater"
- Trap 6: Ratio Versus Quantity
- Trap 7: Not All Numbers Are Positive Integers
- Trap 8: Hidden Instructions
- Trap 9: Average Rates
- Trap 10: Counting Numbers

What Skills Do I Need to Work Around Tricky Answer Choices to Solve the Problem?

- Picking numbers and backsolving (discussed at length in Chapter Eleven) are helpful tools when a tricky answer choice is presented.

ANSWERS AND EXPLANATIONS

Did You Fall for the Traps?

Each wrong answer represents one trap you need to work on. Go back and reread the section on that trap. Then look at the practice set's problem again. Do you see the trap now?

1. 150	**6. C**
(Trap 5)	(Trap 10)
2. C	**7. C**
(Trap 4)	(Trap 1)
3. A	**8. C**
(Trap 6)	(Trap 2)
4. D	**9. E**
(Trap 7)	(Trap 3)
5. D	**10. B**
(Trap 8)	(Trap 9)

How to Prepare for Test Day

You've worked through your comprehensive program, and Test Day is fast approaching. If you haven't taken three out of four of your practice tests, take another one now. Go to your syllabus and note your scores and progress. Link to the official test site and check for any late-breaking information. Prepare yourself for a positive SAT experience.

Here are Kaplan's strategies for the three days leading up to the test.

Chapter Fifteen: **Test Day Strategies**

THREE DAYS BEFORE THE TEST

Take a full-length practice test under timed conditions. Use the techniques and strategies you've learned in this book. Approach the test strategically, actively, and confidently.

We don't recommend taking a full practice SAT if you have fewer than 48 hours left before the test. Doing so will probably exhaust you and hurt your score on the actual test. Remember, the SAT is a marathon, and you are a runner. Runners don't run a marathon the day before the real thing.

TWO DAYS BEFORE THE TEST

Go to your syllabus online to view the results of your practice tests. It's likely that you will see clear improvement, but don't worry too much about your scores or about whether you got any specific question right or wrong. The practice tests don't count. But do flip through your answer keys to examine your performance on specific questions with an eye to how you might get through each one faster and better on the test to come.

THE NIGHT BEFORE THE TEST

Our advice is to not do any studying on this day. Get together an *SAT Kit* containing the following items:

- A calculator with fresh batteries
- A watch
- A few No. 2 pencils (pencils with slightly dull points fill the ovals better)
- Erasers
- Photo ID card (e.g., passport, driver's license, or student ID)
- Your admission ticket from ETS
- A snack—there are breaks, and you'll probably get hungry
- SAT Premier Program Study Sheet

Know exactly where you're going, exactly how you're getting there, and exactly how long it takes to get there. It's probably a good idea to visit your test center sometime before the day of the test so that you know what to expect—what the rooms are like, how the desks are set up, and so on.

Relax the night before the test. Do some relaxation and visualization techniques. Read a magazine, take a long hot shower, or watch something on TV. Get a good night's sleep. Go to bed early, and leave yourself extra time in the morning.

 GO ONLINE

Print out a fresh Study Sheet to review your Target Strategies before the test.

THE MORNING OF THE TEST

First, wake up. After that:

- Eat breakfast. Make it something substantial but not anything too heavy or greasy.
- Don't drink a lot of coffee if you're not used to it. Bathroom breaks cut into your time, and too much caffeine may make you jittery.
- Dress in layers so that you can adjust to the temperature of the testing room.
- Read something. Warm up your brain with a newspaper or a magazine. You shouldn't let the SAT be the first thing you read that day.
- Be sure to get there early. Allow yourself extra time for traffic, mass transit delays, or detours.

DURING THE TEST

Don't be shaken. If you find your confidence slipping, remind yourself how well you've prepared. You know the structure of the test; you know the instructions; you've had practice with—and have learned strategies for—every question type.

If something goes really wrong, don't panic. If the test booklet is defective—two pages are stuck together or the ink has run—raise your hand, and tell the proctor you need a new book. If you accidentally misgrid your answer page or put the answers in the wrong section, raise your hand and tell the proctor. He or she might be able to arrange for you to regrid your test after it's over when it won't cost you any time.

Remember, don't think about which section is experimental. You never know for sure which section won't count. Besides, you can't work on any other section during that section's designated time slot.

AFTER THE TEST

Congratulate yourself.

Now, you might walk out of the SAT thinking that you blew it. This is a normal reaction. Lots of people—even the highest scorers—feel that way. You tend to remember the questions that stumped you, not the ones that you knew.

You can always call ETS within 24 hours to find out about canceling your score, but there's usually no good reason to do so. Remember, colleges typically accept your highest SAT score, and no test experience is going to be perfect. If you were distracted by a weird smell or a particularly loud test proctor this time around, next time you may be even more distracted by construction noise, a cold, or a particularly hot room. Carefully consider your performance before canceling your score.

However, we're positive that you performed well and scored your best on the exam because you followed the our SAT Premier Program. Be confident that you were prepared, and celebrate in the fact that the SAT is a distant memory.

If you want more help or just want to know more about the SAT, college admissions, or Kaplan prep courses for the SAT, give us a call at 1-800-KAP-TEST or visit us at www.kaptest.com. We're here to answer your questions and to help you in any way we can. Also, be sure to return one last time to your online syllabus and complete our survey. We're only as good as our successful students.

Practice Tests and Explanations

Before taking this practice test, find a quiet room where you can work uninterrupted for 3 hours 45 minutes. Make sure you have a comfortable desk and several No. 2 pencils. Use the answer sheet on the following page to record your answers. (You can tear it out or photocopy it.)

Once you start this practice test, do not stop until you have finished. Remember, you may review any questions within a section, but you may not go back or forward a section.

When you have finished taking your practice test, you can go on to the section that follows Practice Test Four to calculate your score.

Good luck!

SAT Practice Test One
Answer Sheet

Remove (or photocopy) the answer sheet and use it to complete the practice test. See the answer key following the test when finished. The "Compute Your Score" section on page 611 will show you how to find your score.

Start with number 1 for each section. If a section has fewer questions than answer spaces, leave the extra spaces blank.

SECTION

1

Section One is the writing section's essay component.
Lined pages on which you will write your essay can be found in that section.

SECTION

2

1. Ⓐ Ⓑ Ⓒ Ⓓ Ⓔ
2. Ⓐ Ⓑ Ⓒ Ⓓ Ⓔ
3. Ⓐ Ⓑ Ⓒ Ⓓ Ⓔ
4. Ⓐ Ⓑ Ⓒ Ⓓ Ⓔ
5. Ⓐ Ⓑ Ⓒ Ⓓ Ⓔ
6. Ⓐ Ⓑ Ⓒ Ⓓ Ⓔ
7. Ⓐ Ⓑ Ⓒ Ⓓ Ⓔ
8. Ⓐ Ⓑ Ⓒ Ⓓ Ⓔ
9. Ⓐ Ⓑ Ⓒ Ⓓ Ⓔ
10. Ⓐ Ⓑ Ⓒ Ⓓ Ⓔ

11. Ⓐ Ⓑ Ⓒ Ⓓ Ⓔ
12. Ⓐ Ⓑ Ⓒ Ⓓ Ⓔ
13. Ⓐ Ⓑ Ⓒ Ⓓ Ⓔ
14. Ⓐ Ⓑ Ⓒ Ⓓ Ⓔ
15. Ⓐ Ⓑ Ⓒ Ⓓ Ⓔ
16. Ⓐ Ⓑ Ⓒ Ⓓ Ⓔ
17. Ⓐ Ⓑ Ⓒ Ⓓ Ⓔ
18. Ⓐ Ⓑ Ⓒ Ⓓ Ⓔ
19. Ⓐ Ⓑ Ⓒ Ⓓ Ⓔ
20. Ⓐ Ⓑ Ⓒ Ⓓ Ⓔ

21. Ⓐ Ⓑ Ⓒ Ⓓ Ⓔ
22. Ⓐ Ⓑ Ⓒ Ⓓ Ⓔ
23. Ⓐ Ⓑ Ⓒ Ⓓ Ⓔ
24. Ⓐ Ⓑ Ⓒ Ⓓ Ⓔ
25. Ⓐ Ⓑ Ⓒ Ⓓ Ⓔ
26. Ⓐ Ⓑ Ⓒ Ⓓ Ⓔ
27. Ⓐ Ⓑ Ⓒ Ⓓ Ⓔ
28. Ⓐ Ⓑ Ⓒ Ⓓ Ⓔ
29. Ⓐ Ⓑ Ⓒ Ⓓ Ⓔ
30. Ⓐ Ⓑ Ⓒ Ⓓ Ⓔ

31. Ⓐ Ⓑ Ⓒ Ⓓ Ⓔ
32. Ⓐ Ⓑ Ⓒ Ⓓ Ⓔ
33. Ⓐ Ⓑ Ⓒ Ⓓ Ⓔ
34. Ⓐ Ⓑ Ⓒ Ⓓ Ⓔ
35. Ⓐ Ⓑ Ⓒ Ⓓ Ⓔ
36. Ⓐ Ⓑ Ⓒ Ⓓ Ⓔ
37. Ⓐ Ⓑ Ⓒ Ⓓ Ⓔ
38. Ⓐ Ⓑ Ⓒ Ⓓ Ⓔ
39. Ⓐ Ⓑ Ⓒ Ⓓ Ⓔ
40. Ⓐ Ⓑ Ⓒ Ⓓ Ⓔ

right in
Section 2

wrong in
Section 2

SECTION

3

1. Ⓐ Ⓑ Ⓒ Ⓓ Ⓔ
2. Ⓐ Ⓑ Ⓒ Ⓓ Ⓔ
3. Ⓐ Ⓑ Ⓒ Ⓓ Ⓔ
4. Ⓐ Ⓑ Ⓒ Ⓓ Ⓔ
5. Ⓐ Ⓑ Ⓒ Ⓓ Ⓔ
6. Ⓐ Ⓑ Ⓒ Ⓓ Ⓔ
7. Ⓐ Ⓑ Ⓒ Ⓓ Ⓔ
8. Ⓐ Ⓑ Ⓒ Ⓓ Ⓔ
9. Ⓐ Ⓑ Ⓒ Ⓓ Ⓔ
10. Ⓐ Ⓑ Ⓒ Ⓓ Ⓔ

11. Ⓐ Ⓑ Ⓒ Ⓓ Ⓔ
12. Ⓐ Ⓑ Ⓒ Ⓓ Ⓔ
13. Ⓐ Ⓑ Ⓒ Ⓓ Ⓔ
14. Ⓐ Ⓑ Ⓒ Ⓓ Ⓔ
15. Ⓐ Ⓑ Ⓒ Ⓓ Ⓔ
16. Ⓐ Ⓑ Ⓒ Ⓓ Ⓔ
17. Ⓐ Ⓑ Ⓒ Ⓓ Ⓔ
18. Ⓐ Ⓑ Ⓒ Ⓓ Ⓔ
19. Ⓐ Ⓑ Ⓒ Ⓓ Ⓔ
20. Ⓐ Ⓑ Ⓒ Ⓓ Ⓔ

21. Ⓐ Ⓑ Ⓒ Ⓓ Ⓔ
22. Ⓐ Ⓑ Ⓒ Ⓓ Ⓔ
23. Ⓐ Ⓑ Ⓒ Ⓓ Ⓔ
24. Ⓐ Ⓑ Ⓒ Ⓓ Ⓔ
25. Ⓐ Ⓑ Ⓒ Ⓓ Ⓔ
26. Ⓐ Ⓑ Ⓒ Ⓓ Ⓔ
27. Ⓐ Ⓑ Ⓒ Ⓓ Ⓔ
28. Ⓐ Ⓑ Ⓒ Ⓓ Ⓔ
29. Ⓐ Ⓑ Ⓒ Ⓓ Ⓔ
30. Ⓐ Ⓑ Ⓒ Ⓓ Ⓔ

31. Ⓐ Ⓑ Ⓒ Ⓓ Ⓔ
32. Ⓐ Ⓑ Ⓒ Ⓓ Ⓔ
33. Ⓐ Ⓑ Ⓒ Ⓓ Ⓔ
34. Ⓐ Ⓑ Ⓒ Ⓓ Ⓔ
35. Ⓐ Ⓑ Ⓒ Ⓓ Ⓔ
36. Ⓐ Ⓑ Ⓒ Ⓓ Ⓔ
37. Ⓐ Ⓑ Ⓒ Ⓓ Ⓔ
38. Ⓐ Ⓑ Ⓒ Ⓓ Ⓔ
39. Ⓐ Ⓑ Ⓒ Ⓓ Ⓔ
40. Ⓐ Ⓑ Ⓒ Ⓓ Ⓔ

right in
Section 3

wrong in
Section 3

Remove (or photocopy) this answer sheet and use it to complete the practice test.

Start with number 1 for each section. If a section has fewer questions than answer spaces, leave the extra spaces blank.

SECTION 4

1. Ⓐ Ⓑ Ⓒ Ⓓ Ⓔ   11. Ⓐ Ⓑ Ⓒ Ⓓ Ⓔ   21. Ⓐ Ⓑ Ⓒ Ⓓ Ⓔ   31. Ⓐ Ⓑ Ⓒ Ⓓ Ⓔ
2. Ⓐ Ⓑ Ⓒ Ⓓ Ⓔ   12. Ⓐ Ⓑ Ⓒ Ⓓ Ⓔ   22. Ⓐ Ⓑ Ⓒ Ⓓ Ⓔ   32. Ⓐ Ⓑ Ⓒ Ⓓ Ⓔ
3. Ⓐ Ⓑ Ⓒ Ⓓ Ⓔ   13. Ⓐ Ⓑ Ⓒ Ⓓ Ⓔ   23. Ⓐ Ⓑ Ⓒ Ⓓ Ⓔ   33. Ⓐ Ⓑ Ⓒ Ⓓ Ⓔ
4. Ⓐ Ⓑ Ⓒ Ⓓ Ⓔ   14. Ⓐ Ⓑ Ⓒ Ⓓ Ⓔ   24. Ⓐ Ⓑ Ⓒ Ⓓ Ⓔ   34. Ⓐ Ⓑ Ⓒ Ⓓ Ⓔ
5. Ⓐ Ⓑ Ⓒ Ⓓ Ⓔ   15. Ⓐ Ⓑ Ⓒ Ⓓ Ⓔ   25. Ⓐ Ⓑ Ⓒ Ⓓ Ⓔ   35. Ⓐ Ⓑ Ⓒ Ⓓ Ⓔ
6. Ⓐ Ⓑ Ⓒ Ⓓ Ⓔ   16. Ⓐ Ⓑ Ⓒ Ⓓ Ⓔ   26. Ⓐ Ⓑ Ⓒ Ⓓ Ⓔ   36. Ⓐ Ⓑ Ⓒ Ⓓ Ⓔ
7. Ⓐ Ⓑ Ⓒ Ⓓ Ⓔ   17. Ⓐ Ⓑ Ⓒ Ⓓ Ⓔ   27. Ⓐ Ⓑ Ⓒ Ⓓ Ⓔ   37. Ⓐ Ⓑ Ⓒ Ⓓ Ⓔ
8. Ⓐ Ⓑ Ⓒ Ⓓ Ⓔ   18. Ⓐ Ⓑ Ⓒ Ⓓ Ⓔ   28. Ⓐ Ⓑ Ⓒ Ⓓ Ⓔ   38. Ⓐ Ⓑ Ⓒ Ⓓ Ⓔ
9. Ⓐ Ⓑ Ⓒ Ⓓ Ⓔ   19. Ⓐ Ⓑ Ⓒ Ⓓ Ⓔ   29. Ⓐ Ⓑ Ⓒ Ⓓ Ⓔ   39. Ⓐ Ⓑ Ⓒ Ⓓ Ⓔ
10. Ⓐ Ⓑ Ⓒ Ⓓ Ⓔ   20. Ⓐ Ⓑ Ⓒ Ⓓ Ⓔ   30. Ⓐ Ⓑ Ⓒ Ⓓ Ⓔ   40. Ⓐ Ⓑ Ⓒ Ⓓ Ⓔ

☐ # right in Section 4

☐ # wrong in Section 4

SECTION 5

1. Ⓐ Ⓑ Ⓒ Ⓓ Ⓔ   11. Ⓐ Ⓑ Ⓒ Ⓓ Ⓔ   21. Ⓐ Ⓑ Ⓒ Ⓓ Ⓔ   31. Ⓐ Ⓑ Ⓒ Ⓓ Ⓔ
2. Ⓐ Ⓑ Ⓒ Ⓓ Ⓔ   12. Ⓐ Ⓑ Ⓒ Ⓓ Ⓔ   22. Ⓐ Ⓑ Ⓒ Ⓓ Ⓔ   32. Ⓐ Ⓑ Ⓒ Ⓓ Ⓔ
3. Ⓐ Ⓑ Ⓒ Ⓓ Ⓔ   13. Ⓐ Ⓑ Ⓒ Ⓓ Ⓔ   23. Ⓐ Ⓑ Ⓒ Ⓓ Ⓔ   33. Ⓐ Ⓑ Ⓒ Ⓓ Ⓔ
4. Ⓐ Ⓑ Ⓒ Ⓓ Ⓔ   14. Ⓐ Ⓑ Ⓒ Ⓓ Ⓔ   24. Ⓐ Ⓑ Ⓒ Ⓓ Ⓔ   34. Ⓐ Ⓑ Ⓒ Ⓓ Ⓔ
5. Ⓐ Ⓑ Ⓒ Ⓓ Ⓔ   15. Ⓐ Ⓑ Ⓒ Ⓓ Ⓔ   25. Ⓐ Ⓑ Ⓒ Ⓓ Ⓔ   35. Ⓐ Ⓑ Ⓒ Ⓓ Ⓔ
6. Ⓐ Ⓑ Ⓒ Ⓓ Ⓔ   16. Ⓐ Ⓑ Ⓒ Ⓓ Ⓔ   26. Ⓐ Ⓑ Ⓒ Ⓓ Ⓔ   36. Ⓐ Ⓑ Ⓒ Ⓓ Ⓔ
7. Ⓐ Ⓑ Ⓒ Ⓓ Ⓔ   17. Ⓐ Ⓑ Ⓒ Ⓓ Ⓔ   27. Ⓐ Ⓑ Ⓒ Ⓓ Ⓔ   37. Ⓐ Ⓑ Ⓒ Ⓓ Ⓔ
8. Ⓐ Ⓑ Ⓒ Ⓓ Ⓔ   18. Ⓐ Ⓑ Ⓒ Ⓓ Ⓔ   28. Ⓐ Ⓑ Ⓒ Ⓓ Ⓔ   38. Ⓐ Ⓑ Ⓒ Ⓓ Ⓔ
→ 9. Ⓐ Ⓑ Ⓒ Ⓓ Ⓔ   19. Ⓐ Ⓑ Ⓒ Ⓓ Ⓔ   29. Ⓐ Ⓑ Ⓒ Ⓓ Ⓔ   39. Ⓐ Ⓑ Ⓒ Ⓓ Ⓔ
10. Ⓐ Ⓑ Ⓒ Ⓓ Ⓔ   20. Ⓐ Ⓑ Ⓒ Ⓓ Ⓔ   30. Ⓐ Ⓑ Ⓒ Ⓓ Ⓔ   40. Ⓐ Ⓑ Ⓒ Ⓓ Ⓔ

☐ # right in Section 5

☐ # wrong in Section 5

If section 5 of your test book contains math questions that are not multiple choice, continue to item 9 below. Otherwise, continue to item 9 above.

9. | 10. | 11. | 12. | 13.

14. | 15. | 16. | 17. | 18.

Remove (or photocopy) this answer sheet and use it to complete the practice test.

Start with number 1 for each section. If a section has fewer questions than answer spaces, leave the extra spaces blank.

SECTION 6

1. Ⓐ Ⓑ Ⓒ Ⓓ Ⓔ	11. Ⓐ Ⓑ Ⓒ Ⓓ Ⓔ	21. Ⓐ Ⓑ Ⓒ Ⓓ Ⓔ	31. Ⓐ Ⓑ Ⓒ Ⓓ Ⓔ
2. Ⓐ Ⓑ Ⓒ Ⓓ Ⓔ	12. Ⓐ Ⓑ Ⓒ Ⓓ Ⓔ	22. Ⓐ Ⓑ Ⓒ Ⓓ Ⓔ	32. Ⓐ Ⓑ Ⓒ Ⓓ Ⓔ
3. Ⓐ Ⓑ Ⓒ Ⓓ Ⓔ	13. Ⓐ Ⓑ Ⓒ Ⓓ Ⓔ	23. Ⓐ Ⓑ Ⓒ Ⓓ Ⓔ	33. Ⓐ Ⓑ Ⓒ Ⓓ Ⓔ
4. Ⓐ Ⓑ Ⓒ Ⓓ Ⓔ	14. Ⓐ Ⓑ Ⓒ Ⓓ Ⓔ	24. Ⓐ Ⓑ Ⓒ Ⓓ Ⓔ	34. Ⓐ Ⓑ Ⓒ Ⓓ Ⓔ
5. Ⓐ Ⓑ Ⓒ Ⓓ Ⓔ	15. Ⓐ Ⓑ Ⓒ Ⓓ Ⓔ	25. Ⓐ Ⓑ Ⓒ Ⓓ Ⓔ	35. Ⓐ Ⓑ Ⓒ Ⓓ Ⓔ
6. Ⓐ Ⓑ Ⓒ Ⓓ Ⓔ	16. Ⓐ Ⓑ Ⓒ Ⓓ Ⓔ	26. Ⓐ Ⓑ Ⓒ Ⓓ Ⓔ	36. Ⓐ Ⓑ Ⓒ Ⓓ Ⓔ
7. Ⓐ Ⓑ Ⓒ Ⓓ Ⓔ	17. Ⓐ Ⓑ Ⓒ Ⓓ Ⓔ	27. Ⓐ Ⓑ Ⓒ Ⓓ Ⓔ	37. Ⓐ Ⓑ Ⓒ Ⓓ Ⓔ
8. Ⓐ Ⓑ Ⓒ Ⓓ Ⓔ	18. Ⓐ Ⓑ Ⓒ Ⓓ Ⓔ	28. Ⓐ Ⓑ Ⓒ Ⓓ Ⓔ	38. Ⓐ Ⓑ Ⓒ Ⓓ Ⓔ
9. Ⓐ Ⓑ Ⓒ Ⓓ Ⓔ	19. Ⓐ Ⓑ Ⓒ Ⓓ Ⓔ	29. Ⓐ Ⓑ Ⓒ Ⓓ Ⓔ	39. Ⓐ Ⓑ Ⓒ Ⓓ Ⓔ
10. Ⓐ Ⓑ Ⓒ Ⓓ Ⓔ	20. Ⓐ Ⓑ Ⓒ Ⓓ Ⓔ	30. Ⓐ Ⓑ Ⓒ Ⓓ Ⓔ	40. Ⓐ Ⓑ Ⓒ Ⓓ Ⓔ

right in Section 6

wrong in Section 6

SECTION 7

1. Ⓐ Ⓑ Ⓒ Ⓓ Ⓔ	11. Ⓐ Ⓑ Ⓒ Ⓓ Ⓔ	21. Ⓐ Ⓑ Ⓒ Ⓓ Ⓔ	31. Ⓐ Ⓑ Ⓒ Ⓓ Ⓔ
2. Ⓐ Ⓑ Ⓒ Ⓓ Ⓔ	12. Ⓐ Ⓑ Ⓒ Ⓓ Ⓔ	22. Ⓐ Ⓑ Ⓒ Ⓓ Ⓔ	32. Ⓐ Ⓑ Ⓒ Ⓓ Ⓔ
3. Ⓐ Ⓑ Ⓒ Ⓓ Ⓔ	13. Ⓐ Ⓑ Ⓒ Ⓓ Ⓔ	23. Ⓐ Ⓑ Ⓒ Ⓓ Ⓔ	33. Ⓐ Ⓑ Ⓒ Ⓓ Ⓔ
4. Ⓐ Ⓑ Ⓒ Ⓓ Ⓔ	14. Ⓐ Ⓑ Ⓒ Ⓓ Ⓔ	24. Ⓐ Ⓑ Ⓒ Ⓓ Ⓔ	34. Ⓐ Ⓑ Ⓒ Ⓓ Ⓔ
5. Ⓐ Ⓑ Ⓒ Ⓓ Ⓔ	15. Ⓐ Ⓑ Ⓒ Ⓓ Ⓔ	25. Ⓐ Ⓑ Ⓒ Ⓓ Ⓔ	35. Ⓐ Ⓑ Ⓒ Ⓓ Ⓔ
6. Ⓐ Ⓑ Ⓒ Ⓓ Ⓔ	16. Ⓐ Ⓑ Ⓒ Ⓓ Ⓔ	26. Ⓐ Ⓑ Ⓒ Ⓓ Ⓔ	36. Ⓐ Ⓑ Ⓒ Ⓓ Ⓔ
7. Ⓐ Ⓑ Ⓒ Ⓓ Ⓔ	17. Ⓐ Ⓑ Ⓒ Ⓓ Ⓔ	27. Ⓐ Ⓑ Ⓒ Ⓓ Ⓔ	37. Ⓐ Ⓑ Ⓒ Ⓓ Ⓔ
8. Ⓐ Ⓑ Ⓒ Ⓓ Ⓔ	18. Ⓐ Ⓑ Ⓒ Ⓓ Ⓔ	28. Ⓐ Ⓑ Ⓒ Ⓓ Ⓔ	38. Ⓐ Ⓑ Ⓒ Ⓓ Ⓔ
9. Ⓐ Ⓑ Ⓒ Ⓓ Ⓔ	19. Ⓐ Ⓑ Ⓒ Ⓓ Ⓔ	29. Ⓐ Ⓑ Ⓒ Ⓓ Ⓔ	39. Ⓐ Ⓑ Ⓒ Ⓓ Ⓔ
10. Ⓐ Ⓑ Ⓒ Ⓓ Ⓔ	20. Ⓐ Ⓑ Ⓒ Ⓓ Ⓔ	30. Ⓐ Ⓑ Ⓒ Ⓓ Ⓔ	40. Ⓐ Ⓑ Ⓒ Ⓓ Ⓔ

right in Section 7

wrong in Section 7

SECTION 8

1. Ⓐ Ⓑ Ⓒ Ⓓ Ⓔ	11. Ⓐ Ⓑ Ⓒ Ⓓ Ⓔ	21. Ⓐ Ⓑ Ⓒ Ⓓ Ⓔ	31. Ⓐ Ⓑ Ⓒ Ⓓ Ⓔ
2. Ⓐ Ⓑ Ⓒ Ⓓ Ⓔ	12. Ⓐ Ⓑ Ⓒ Ⓓ Ⓔ	22. Ⓐ Ⓑ Ⓒ Ⓓ Ⓔ	32. Ⓐ Ⓑ Ⓒ Ⓓ Ⓔ
3. Ⓐ Ⓑ Ⓒ Ⓓ Ⓔ	13. Ⓐ Ⓑ Ⓒ Ⓓ Ⓔ	23. Ⓐ Ⓑ Ⓒ Ⓓ Ⓔ	33. Ⓐ Ⓑ Ⓒ Ⓓ Ⓔ
4. Ⓐ Ⓑ Ⓒ Ⓓ Ⓔ	14. Ⓐ Ⓑ Ⓒ Ⓓ Ⓔ	24. Ⓐ Ⓑ Ⓒ Ⓓ Ⓔ	34. Ⓐ Ⓑ Ⓒ Ⓓ Ⓔ
5. Ⓐ Ⓑ Ⓒ Ⓓ Ⓔ	15. Ⓐ Ⓑ Ⓒ Ⓓ Ⓔ	25. Ⓐ Ⓑ Ⓒ Ⓓ Ⓔ	35. Ⓐ Ⓑ Ⓒ Ⓓ Ⓔ
6. Ⓐ Ⓑ Ⓒ Ⓓ Ⓔ	16. Ⓐ Ⓑ Ⓒ Ⓓ Ⓔ	26. Ⓐ Ⓑ Ⓒ Ⓓ Ⓔ	36. Ⓐ Ⓑ Ⓒ Ⓓ Ⓔ
7. Ⓐ Ⓑ Ⓒ Ⓓ Ⓔ	17. Ⓐ Ⓑ Ⓒ Ⓓ Ⓔ	27. Ⓐ Ⓑ Ⓒ Ⓓ Ⓔ	37. Ⓐ Ⓑ Ⓒ Ⓓ Ⓔ
8. Ⓐ Ⓑ Ⓒ Ⓓ Ⓔ	18. Ⓐ Ⓑ Ⓒ Ⓓ Ⓔ	28. Ⓐ Ⓑ Ⓒ Ⓓ Ⓔ	38. Ⓐ Ⓑ Ⓒ Ⓓ Ⓔ
9. Ⓐ Ⓑ Ⓒ Ⓓ Ⓔ	19. Ⓐ Ⓑ Ⓒ Ⓓ Ⓔ	29. Ⓐ Ⓑ Ⓒ Ⓓ Ⓔ	39. Ⓐ Ⓑ Ⓒ Ⓓ Ⓔ
10. Ⓐ Ⓑ Ⓒ Ⓓ Ⓔ	20. Ⓐ Ⓑ Ⓒ Ⓓ Ⓔ	30. Ⓐ Ⓑ Ⓒ Ⓓ Ⓔ	40. Ⓐ Ⓑ Ⓒ Ⓓ Ⓔ

right in Section 8

wrong in Section 8

Remove (or photocopy) this answer sheet and use it to complete the practice test.

Start with number 1 for each section. If a section has fewer questions than answer spaces, leave the extra spaces blank.

SECTION

9

1. Ⓐ Ⓑ Ⓒ Ⓓ Ⓔ   11. Ⓐ Ⓑ Ⓒ Ⓓ Ⓔ   21. Ⓐ Ⓑ Ⓒ Ⓓ Ⓔ   31. Ⓐ Ⓑ Ⓒ Ⓓ Ⓔ
2. Ⓐ Ⓑ Ⓒ Ⓓ Ⓔ   12. Ⓐ Ⓑ Ⓒ Ⓓ Ⓔ   22. Ⓐ Ⓑ Ⓒ Ⓓ Ⓔ   32. Ⓐ Ⓑ Ⓒ Ⓓ Ⓔ
3. Ⓐ Ⓑ Ⓒ Ⓓ Ⓔ   13. Ⓐ Ⓑ Ⓒ Ⓓ Ⓔ   23. Ⓐ Ⓑ Ⓒ Ⓓ Ⓔ   33. Ⓐ Ⓑ Ⓒ Ⓓ Ⓔ
4. Ⓐ Ⓑ Ⓒ Ⓓ Ⓔ   14. Ⓐ Ⓑ Ⓒ Ⓓ Ⓔ   24. Ⓐ Ⓑ Ⓒ Ⓓ Ⓔ   34. Ⓐ Ⓑ Ⓒ Ⓓ Ⓔ
5. Ⓐ Ⓑ Ⓒ Ⓓ Ⓔ   15. Ⓐ Ⓑ Ⓒ Ⓓ Ⓔ   25. Ⓐ Ⓑ Ⓒ Ⓓ Ⓔ   35. Ⓐ Ⓑ Ⓒ Ⓓ Ⓔ
6. Ⓐ Ⓑ Ⓒ Ⓓ Ⓔ   16. Ⓐ Ⓑ Ⓒ Ⓓ Ⓔ   26. Ⓐ Ⓑ Ⓒ Ⓓ Ⓔ   36. Ⓐ Ⓑ Ⓒ Ⓓ Ⓔ
7. Ⓐ Ⓑ Ⓒ Ⓓ Ⓔ   17. Ⓐ Ⓑ Ⓒ Ⓓ Ⓔ   27. Ⓐ Ⓑ Ⓒ Ⓓ Ⓔ   37. Ⓐ Ⓑ Ⓒ Ⓓ Ⓔ
8. Ⓐ Ⓑ Ⓒ Ⓓ Ⓔ   18. Ⓐ Ⓑ Ⓒ Ⓓ Ⓔ   28. Ⓐ Ⓑ Ⓒ Ⓓ Ⓔ   38. Ⓐ Ⓑ Ⓒ Ⓓ Ⓔ
9. Ⓐ Ⓑ Ⓒ Ⓓ Ⓔ   19. Ⓐ Ⓑ Ⓒ Ⓓ Ⓔ   29. Ⓐ Ⓑ Ⓒ Ⓓ Ⓔ   39. Ⓐ Ⓑ Ⓒ Ⓓ Ⓔ
10. Ⓐ Ⓑ Ⓒ Ⓓ Ⓔ   20. Ⓐ Ⓑ Ⓒ Ⓓ Ⓔ   30. Ⓐ Ⓑ Ⓒ Ⓓ Ⓔ   40. Ⓐ Ⓑ Ⓒ Ⓓ Ⓔ

right in
Section 9

wrong in
Section 9

 GO ONLINE

Be sure to add your scores to your syllabus.

Practice Test One

SECTION 1
Time—25 Minutes
ESSAY

The essay gives you an opportunity to show how effectively you can develop and express ideas. You should, therefore, take care to develop your point of view, present your ideas logically and clearly, and use language precisely.

Your essay must be written in your Answer Grid Booklet—you will receive no other paper on which to write. You will have enough space if you write on every line, avoid wide margins, and keep your handwriting to a reasonable size. Remember that people who are not familiar with your handwriting will read what you write. Try to write or print so that what you are writing is legible to those readers.

You have twenty-five minutes to write an essay on the topic assigned below.
DO NOT WRITE ON ANOTHER TOPIC. AN OFF-TOPIC ESSAY WILL RECEIVE A SCORE OF ZERO.

Think carefully about the issue presented in the following excerpt and the assignment below.

> "Everything comes if a man will only wait."
> –Benjamin Disraeli, *Tancred*
>
> "Destiny is not a matter of chance, it is a matter of choice; it is not a thing to be waited for, it is a thing to be achieved."
> –William Jennings Bryan, *Memoirs*

Assignment: Should we wait for good things to come, or is destiny not something we can wait for? Plan and write an essay in which you develop your point of view on this issue. Support your position with reasoning and examples taken from your reading, studies, experience, or observations.

DO NOT WRITE YOUR ESSAY IN YOUR TEST BOOK.
You will receive credit only for what you write in your Answer Grid Booklet.

GO ON TO THE NEXT PAGE

KAPLAN

_____

_____

_____

_____

_____

_____

_____

_____

_____

_____

_____

_____

_____

_____

_____

_____

_____

_____

_____

_____

IF YOU FINISH BEFORE TIME IS CALLED, YOU MAY CHECK YOUR WORK ON THIS SECTION ONLY. DO NOT TURN TO ANY OTHER SECTION IN THE TEST.

SECTION 2

Time—25 Minutes
24 Questions

Directions: For each of the following questions, choose the best answer and darken the corresponding oval on the answer sheet.

Each sentence below has one or two blanks, each blank indicating that something has been omitted. Beneath the sentence are five words or sets of words labeled A through E. Choose the word or set of words that, when inserted in the sentence, best fits the meaning of the sentence as a whole.

EXAMPLE:

Today's small, portable computers contrast markedly with the earliest electronic computers, which were -------.

(A) effective
(B) invented
(C) useful
(D) destructive
(E) enormous

1. More insurers are limiting the sale of property insurance in coastal areas and other regions ------- natural disasters.

   (A) safe from
   (B) according to
   (C) despite
   (D) which include
   (E) prone to

2. Roman legions ------- the mountain ------- of Masada for three years before they were able to seize it.

   (A) dissembled . . bastion
   (B) assailed . . symbol
   (C) besieged . . citadel
   (D) surmounted . . dwelling
   (E) honed . . stronghold

3. Unlike his calmer, more easygoing colleagues, the senator was -------, ready to quarrel at the slightest provocation.

   (A) whimsical
   (B) irascible
   (C) gregarious
   (D) ineffectual
   (E) benign

4. Although historians have long thought of Genghis Khan as a ------- potentate, new research has shown he was ------- by many of his subjects.

   (A) tyrannical . . abhorred
   (B) despotic . . revered
   (C) redundant . . venerated
   (D) jocular . . esteemed
   (E) peremptory . . invoked

5. Jill was ------- by her employees because she often ------- them for not working hard enough.

   (A) deified . . goaded
   (B) loathed . . berated
   (C) disregarded . . eulogized
   (D) cherished . . derided
   (E) execrated . . lauded

GO ON TO THE NEXT PAGE

6. Reconstructing the skeletons of extinct species like dinosaurs is ------- process that requires much patience and effort by paleontologists.

   (A) a nascent

   (B) an aberrant

   (C) a disheveled

   (D) a worthless

   (E) an exacting

7. Nearly ------- by disease and the destruction of their habitat, koalas are now found only in isolated parts of eucalyptus forests.

   (A) dispersed

   (B) compiled

   (C) decimated

   (D) infuriated

   (E) averted

8. Deep ideological ------- and internal power struggles ------- the government.

   (A) disputes . . facilitated

   (B) similarities . . protracted

   (C) distortions . . accelerated

   (D) agreements . . stymied

   (E) divisions . . paralyzed

GO ON TO THE NEXT PAGE

KAPLAN

Directions: The passages below are followed by questions based on their content; questions following a pair of related passages may also be based on the relationship between the paired passages. Answer the questions on the basis of what is <u>stated</u> or <u>implied</u> in the passages and in any introductory material that may be provided.

Questions 9–12 refer to the following passages.

Passage 1

Musicologists and linguists argue about the relationship between music and language. Prominent ethno musicologist Bruno Nettl has concluded that like language, music is a "series of
(5) symbols." However, music has traditionally been used purely to express emotions while language has also been used for more functional, prosaic tasks. This distinction was especially evident in the Romantic era of western music, when many
(10) composers and critics felt that music could stand by itself to connote emotions without any extra-musical references.

Passage 2

The fundamental building blocks of both lan-guage and music are quite similar, as are the man-
(15) ners in which these components are combined to form a cohesive whole. In the same way that an entire piece of music can be divided into phrases, and further subdivided into specific notes, lan-guage can be subdivided into paragraphs, sen-
(20) tences, and words. A single note can have differ-ent meanings depending on the piece; a lone word can have different meanings depending on the context in the sentence. Words and notes are also similar in that they have little intrinsic meaning,
(25) but instead act as symbols to convey larger ideas.

9. The author of Passage 1 most likely cites the "Romantic era of western music" (line 9) in order to establish that

   (A) our modern perception of Romantic music is different from that held in the Romantic era

   (B) unlike language, Romantic music is not used functionally

   (C) composers of Romantic music always used music to express emotion

   (D) in the Romantic era it was commonly thought that music alone could convey emotion

   (E) music of the Romantic era is compromised because it contains no extra-musical references

10. In lines 11–12, the term "extra-musical" most nearly means

    (A) especially musical

    (B) non-musical

    (C) more than musical

    (D) better than musical

    (E) classically musical

11. In both passages, the authors state that music and language are

    (A) symbols

    (B) subdivided sections

    (C) functional parts

    (D) clues

    (E) conveyers of emotion

12. About which of the following statements would the author of Passage 1 and the author of Passage 2 most likely disagree?

    (A) Music and language can both be subdivided into several parts.

    (B) Although significantly similar, music and lan-guage have several fundamentally distinct aspects.

    (C) A group of notes used in a musical composi-tion has the same meaning in a piece by a different composer.

    (D) Language is not an effective means to express emotions.

    (E) The meaning of a particular word is solely dependent on context.

GO ON TO THE NEXT PAGE

Questions 13–24 refer to the following passage.

In the following passage, a 19th-century American writer recalls his boyhood in a small town along the Mississippi River.

My father was a justice of the peace, and I supposed he possessed the power of life and death over all men and could hang anybody that offended him. This was distinction enough for me as a gen-
(5) eral thing; but the desire to be a steamboatman kept intruding, nevertheless. I first wanted to be a cabin boy so that I could come out with a white apron on and shake a tablecloth over the side, where all my old comrades could see me. Later I
(10) thought I would rather be the deck hand who stood on the end of the stage plank with a coil of rope in his hand, because he was particularly conspicuous.

But these were only daydreams—too heavenly
(15) to be contemplated as real possibilities. By and by one of the boys went away. He was not heard of for a long time. At last he turned up as an apprentice engineer or "striker" on a steamboat. This thing shook the bottom out of all my Sunday-
(20) school teachings. That boy had been notoriously worldly, and I had been just the reverse—yet he was exalted to this eminence, and I was left in obscurity and misery. There was nothing generous about this fellow in his greatness. He would always
(25) manage to have a rusty bolt to scrub while his boat was docked at our town, and he would sit on the inside guard and scrub it, where we could all see him and envy him and loathe him.

He used all sorts of steamboat technicalities in
(30) his talk, as if he were so used to them that he forgot common people could not understand them. He would speak of the "labboard" side of a horse in an easy, natural way that would make you wish he was dead. And he was always talking about "St.
(35) Looy" like an old citizen. Two or three of the boys had long been persons of consideration among us because they had been to St. Louis once and had a vague general knowledge of its wonders, but the day of their glory was over now. They lapsed into
(40) a humble silence and learned to disappear when the ruthless "cub" engineer approached. This fellow had money, too, and hair oil, and he wore a showy brass watch chain, a leather belt, and used no suspenders. No girl could withstand his
(45) charms. He "cut out" every boy in the village. When his boat blew up at last, it diffused a tranquil contentment among us such as we had not known for months. But when he came home the next week, alive, renowned, and appeared in
(50) church all battered up and bandaged, a shining hero, stared at and wondered over by everybody, it seemed to us that the partiality of Providence for an undeserving reptile had reached a point where it was open to criticism.

(55) This creature's career could produce but one result, and it speedily followed. Boy after boy managed to get on the river. Four sons of the chief merchant, and two sons of the county judge became pilots, the grandest position of all. But
(60) some of us could not get on the river—at least our parents would not let us.

So by and by I ran away. I said I would never come home again till I was a pilot and could return in glory. But somehow I could not manage
(65) it. I went meekly aboard a few of the boats that lay packed together like sardines at the long St. Louis wharf and very humbly inquired for the pilots but got only a cold shoulder and short words from mates and clerks. I had to make the best of this
(70) sort of treatment for the time being, but I had comforting daydreams of a future when I should be a great and honored pilot, with plenty of money, and could kill some of these mates and clerks and pay for them.

GO ON TO THE NEXT PAGE

KAPLAN

13. The author makes the statement that "I supposed he . . . offended him" (lines 1–4) primarily to suggest the

 (A) power held by a justice of the peace in a frontier town

 (B) naive view that he held of his father's importance

 (C) respect in which the townspeople held his father

 (D) possibility of miscarriages of justice on the American frontier

 (E) harsh environment in which he was brought up

14. As used in line 4, the word "distinction" most nearly means

 (A) difference

 (B) variation

 (C) prestige

 (D) desperation

 (E) clarity

15. The author decides that he would rather become a deck hand than a cabin boy (lines 6–12) because

 (A) the job offers higher wages

 (B) he believes that the work is easier

 (C) he wants to avoid seeing his older friends

 (D) deck hands often go on to become pilots

 (E) the job is more visible to passersby

16. The author most likely mentions his "Sunday-school teachings" in lines 18–20 in order to emphasize

 (A) the influence of his early education in later life

 (B) his sense of injustice at the engineer's success

 (C) his disillusionment with longstanding religious beliefs

 (D) his determination to become an engineer at all costs

 (E) the unscrupulous nature of the engineer's character

17. The author most likely concludes that the engineer is not "generous" (line 23) because he

 (A) has no respect for religious beliefs

 (B) refuses to share his wages with friends

 (C) flaunts his new position in public

 (D) takes pride in material possessions

 (E) ignores the disappointment of other people's ambitions

18. The author most probably mentions the use of "steamboat technicalities" (lines 29–31) in order to emphasize the engineer's

 (A) expertise after a few months on the job

 (B) fascination for trivial information

 (C) ignorance on most other subjects

 (D) desire to appear sophisticated

 (E) inability to communicate effectively

19. The word "consideration" in line 36 most nearly means

 (A) generosity

 (B) deliberation

 (C) contemplation

 (D) unselfishness

 (E) reputation

20. According to the passage, the "glory" of having visited St. Louis (lines 37–39) was over because

 (A) the boys' knowledge of St. Louis was much less detailed than the engineer's

 (B) St. Louis had changed so much that the boys' stories were no longer accurate

 (C) the boys realized that traveling to St. Louis was not a mark of sophistication

 (D) the engineer's account revealed that the boys' stories were lies

 (E) travel to St. Louis had become too commonplace to be envied

GO ON TO THE NEXT PAGE ▷

KAPLAN

21. The author describes the engineer's appearance (lines 41–44) primarily in order to

    (A) suggest one reason why many people found the engineer impressive

    (B) convey the way steamboatmen typically dressed

    (C) emphasize the inadequacy of his own wardrobe

    (D) contrast the engineer's behavior with his appearance

    (E) indicate his admiration for fashionable clothes

22. In lines 52–54, the author's response to the engineer's survival is one of

    (A) thankfulness for what he believes is God's providence

    (B) astonishment at the engineer's miraculous escape

    (C) reflection on the occupational hazards of a steamboating career

    (D) outrage at his rival's undeserved good fortune

    (E) sympathy for the extent of the engineer's wounds

23. The major purpose of the passage is to

    (A) sketch the peaceful life of a frontier town

    (B) relate the events that led to a boy's first success in life

    (C) portray the unsophisticated ambitions of a boy

    (D) describe the characteristics of a small-town boaster

    (E) give a humorous portrayal of a boy's conflicts with his parents

24. At the end of the passage, the author reflects on

    (A) his new ambition to become either a mate or a clerk

    (B) the wisdom of seeking a job in which advancement is easier

    (C) the prospect of abandoning a hopeless search for fame

    (D) the impossibility of returning home and asking his parents' pardon

    (E) his determination to keep striving for success in a glorious career

---

IF YOU FINISH BEFORE TIME IS CALLED, YOU MAY CHECK YOUR WORK ON THIS SECTION ONLY. DO NOT TURN TO ANY OTHER SECTION IN THE TEST. STOP

SECTION 3
Time—25 Minutes
20 Questions

Directions: For this section, solve each problem and decide which is the best of the choices given. Fill in the corresponding oval on the answer sheet. You may use any available space for scratchwork.

Notes:

(1) Calculator use is permitted.

(2) All numbers used are real numbers.

(3) Figures are provided for some problems. All figures are drawn to scale and lie in a plane UNLESS otherwise indicated.

(4) Unless otherwise specified, the domain of any function f is assumed to be the set of all real numbers x for which $f(x)$ is a real number.

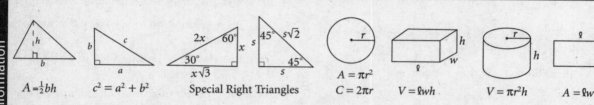

$A = \frac{1}{2}bh$ $c^2 = a^2 + b^2$ Special Right Triangles $A = \pi r^2$ $V = \ell wh$ $V = \pi r^2 h$ $A = \ell w$
$C = 2\pi r$

The sum of the degree measures of the angles in a triangle is 180.
The number of degrees of arc in a circle is 360.
A straight angle has a degree measure of 180.

1. Which of the following must be equal to 30 percent of x?

   (A) $\dfrac{3x}{1,000}$

   (B) $\dfrac{3x}{100}$

   (C) $\dfrac{3x}{10}$

   (D) $3x$

   (E) $30x$

2. $(2 \times 10^4) + (5 \times 10^3) + (6 \times 10^2) + (4 \times 10^1) =$

   (A) 2,564

   (B) 20,564

   (C) 25,064

   (D) 25,604

   (E) 25,640

3. On the number line shown above, the length of YZ is how much greater than the length of XY?

   (A) 3

   (B) 4

   (C) 5

   (D) 6

   (E) 7

4. If $2^{x+1} = 16$, what is the value of x?

   (A) 2

   (B) 3

   (C) 4

   (D) 5

   (E) 6

GO ON TO THE NEXT PAGE

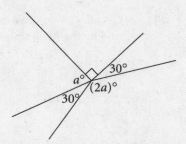

Note: Figure not drawn to scale.

5. In the figure above, what is the value of *a*?

    (A) 50
    (B) 55
    (C) 60
    (D) 65
    (E) 70

6. A machine labels 150 bottles in 20 minutes. At this rate, how many minutes does it take to label 60 bottles?

    (A)   2
    (B)   4
    (C)   6
    (D)   8
    (E) 10

7. If $x - 1$ is a multiple of 3, which of the following must be the next greater multiple of 3?

    (A) x
    (B) $x + 2$
    (C) $x + 3$
    (D) $3x$
    (E) $3x - 3$

8. When *x* is divided by 5, the remainder is 4. When *x* is divided by 9, the remainder is 0. Which of the following is a possible value for *x*?

    (A)   24
    (B)   45
    (C)   59
    (D) 109
    (E) 144

9. In triangle *ABC*, $AB = 6$, $BC = 12$, and $AC = x$. Which of the following cannot be a value of *x*?

    (A)   6
    (B)   7
    (C)   8
    (D)   9
    (E) 10

10. The average of 20, 70, and *x* is 40. If the average of 20, 70, *x*, and *y* is 50, then $y =$

    (A)   30
    (B)   60
    (C)   70
    (D)   80
    (E) 100

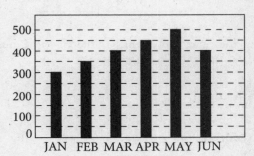

NUMBER OF BOOKS BORROWED
FROM MIDVILLE LIBRARY

11. According to the graph above, the number of books borrowed during the month of January was what fraction of the total number of books borrowed during the first six months of the year?

    (A) $\dfrac{1}{8}$

    (B) $\dfrac{1}{7}$

    (C) $\dfrac{1}{6}$

    (D) $\dfrac{3}{16}$

    (E) $\dfrac{5}{12}$

GO ON TO THE NEXT PAGE

KAPLAN

12. If 40 percent of r is equal to s, then which of the following is equal to 10 percent of r?

(A) $4s$

(B) $2s$

(C) $\dfrac{s}{2}$

(D) $\dfrac{s}{4}$

(E) $\dfrac{s}{8}$

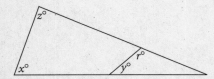

13. In the figure above, which of the following must be true?

(A) $x + r = z + y$

(B) $x + r = z - y$

(C) $x - y = z + r$

(D) $x - r = y - z$

(E) $x + y = z + r$

14. If a *prifact* number is a nonprime integer such that each factor of the integer other than 1 and the integer itself is a prime number, which of the following is a *prifact* number?

(A) 12

(B) 18

(C) 21

(D) 24

(E) 28

15. If $3x + y = 14$, and x and y are positive integers, all of the following could be the value of $x + y$ EXCEPT

(A) 4

(B) 6

(C) 8

(D) 10

(E) 12

16. A certain deck of cards contains r cards. After the cards are distributed evenly among s people, 8 cards are left over. In terms of r and s, how many cards did each person receive?

(A) $\dfrac{s}{8 - r}$

(B) $\dfrac{r - s}{8}$

(C) $\dfrac{r - 8}{s}$

(D) $s - 8r$

(E) $rs - 8$

17. If d is an integer, which of the following CANNOT be an integer?

(A) $\dfrac{d}{2}$

(B) $\dfrac{\sqrt{d}}{2}$

(C) $2d$

(D) $d\sqrt{2}$

(E) $d + 2$

GO ON TO THE NEXT PAGE

KAPLAN

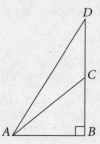

18. In the figure above, the area of triangle *ABC* is 6. If *BC* = *CD*, what is the area of triangle *ACD*?

    (A) 6
    (B) 8
    (C) 9
    (D) 10
    (E) 12

19. What is the minimum number of rectangular tiles, each 12 centimeters by 18 centimeters, needed to completely cover five flat rectangular surfaces, each 60 centimeters by 180 centimeters?

    (A) 50
    (B) 100
    (C) 150
    (D) 200
    (E) 250

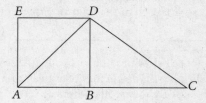

20. In the figure above, side *AB* of square *ABDE* is extended to point *C*. If *BC* = 8 and *CD* = 10, what is the perimeter of triangle *ACD*?

    (A) $18 + 6\sqrt{2}$
    (B) $24 + 6\sqrt{2}$
    (C) $26 + 6\sqrt{2}$
    (D) 30
    (E) 36

SECTION 4

Time—25 Minutes

24 Questions

Directions: For each of the following questions, choose the best answer and darken the corresponding oval on the answer sheet.

Each sentence below has one or two blanks, each blank indicating that something has been omitted. Beneath the sentence are five words or sets of words labeled A through E. Choose the word or set of words that, when inserted in the sentence, <u>best</u> fits the meaning of the sentence as a whole.

EXAMPLE:

Today's small, portable computers contrast markedly with the earliest electronic computers, which were -------.

(A) effective
(B) invented
(C) useful
(D) destructive
(E) enormous

1. The rain is so rare and the land is so ------- that few of the men who work there see much ------- in farming.

   (A) plentiful . . hope
   (B) barren . . difficulty
   (C) productive . . profit
   (D) infertile . . future
   (E) dry . . danger

2. The principal declared that the students were not simply ignoring the rules, but openly ------- them.

   (A) accepting
   (B) redressing
   (C) reviewing
   (D) flouting
   (E) discussing

3. Some critics believe that the ------- of modern art came with dadaism, while others insist that the movement was a -------.

   (A) zenith . . sham
   (B) pinnacle . . triumph
   (C) decline . . disaster
   (D) acceptance . . success
   (E) originality . . fiasco

4. She would never have believed that her article was so ------- were it not for the ------- of correspondence that followed its publication.

   (A) interesting . . dearth
   (B) inflammatory . . lack
   (C) controversial . . spate
   (D) commonplace . . influx
   (E) insignificant . . volume

5. The writings of the philosopher Descartes are -------; many readers have difficulty following his complex, intricately woven arguments.

   (A) generic
   (B) trenchant
   (C) reflective
   (D) elongated
   (E) abstruse

GO ON TO THE NEXT PAGE

Directions: The passages below are followed by questions based on their content; questions following a pair of related passages may also be based on the relationship between the paired passages. Answer the questions on the basis of what is <u>stated</u> or <u>implied</u> in the passages and in any introductory material that may be provided.

Questions 6–7 refer to the following passage.

    One of the hazards of swimming in the ocean is an unexpected encounter with a jellyfish. Contact with the poison in a jellyfish's tentacles can result in sharp, lingering pain, or even death if the person
(5) stung is highly allergic. While everyone, including the jellyfish, would like to avoid these encounters, they are not uncommon. This is hardly surprising considering that jellyfish live in every ocean in the world and have done so for more than 650 million
(10) years. The animals are likely so widespread because of their extreme adaptability—they are quite hardy and can withstand a wide range of temperatures and conditions in their environment.

6. The author uses the phrase "including the jelly-fish" (lines 5–6) in order to

(A) introduce a small note of humor to an otherwise serious discussion

(B) encourage the reader's sympathy for the jelly-fish

(C) ridicule humans' fear of jellyfish

(D) emphasize the danger that jellyfish pose for swimmers

(E) contrast the jellyfish's reaction to the encounter to that of humans

7. According to the passage, encounters between humans and jellyfish in the ocean are relatively common because jellyfish

(A) are more than 650 million years old

(B) live in all the world's oceans

(C) are extremely robust

(D) have poisonous tentacles

(E) can endure a range of temperatures

GO ON TO THE NEXT PAGE

Questions 8–9 refer to the following passage.

Connecting the northern frontier of Pakistan with Afghanistan, the Khyber Pass is one of the most noteworthy mountain passes in the world. At its narrowest point in the north, the pass is walled
(5) on either side by precipitous cliffs up to 300 meters in height, while the pass itself is only 3 meters wide. Because it is only 53 kilometers long, the Pass offers the best land route between India and Pakistan. This has led to a long and often vio-
(10) lent history—conquering armies have used the Khyber as an entry point for their invasions of India, Pakistan, and Afghanistan. Today there are two highways that snake their way through the Khyber pass, one for motor traffic and another for
(15) traditional caravans.

8. Which of the following topics is NOT addressed by the passage?

(A) the origin of the pass
(B) the countries that border the pass
(C) the length of the pass
(D) the role of the pass in history
(E) the uses of the pass today

9. In line 13, the word "snake" most directly emphasizes the

(A) function of the Khyber Pass as a means to connect two points
(B) danger of crossing the Khyber Pass
(C) Khyber Pass as a direct route through the Hindu Kush mountains
(D) relatively short length of the Khyber Pass
(E) winding quality of the Khyber Pass

GO ON TO THE NEXT PAGE

Questions 10–16 refer to the following passage.

In this excerpt, a Nobel Prize–winning scientist discusses ways of thinking about extremely long periods of time.

There is one fact about the origin of life which is reasonably certain. Whenever and wherever it happened, it started a very long time ago, so long ago that it is extremely difficult to form any realis-
(5) tic idea of such vast stretches of time. The shortness of human life necessarily limits the span of direct personal recollection.

Human culture has given us the illusion that our memories go further back than that. Before
(10) writing was invented, the experience of earlier generations, embodied in stories, myths, and moral precepts to guide behavior, was passed down verbally or, to a lesser extent, in pictures, carvings, and statues. Writing has made more pre-
(15) cise and more extensive the transmission of such information and, in recent times, photography has sharpened our images of the immediate past. Even so, we have difficulty in contemplating steadily the march of history, from the beginnings of civiliza-
(20) tion to the present day, in such a way that we can truly experience the slow passage of time. Our minds are not built to deal comfortably with periods as long as hundreds or thousands of years.

Yet when we come to consider the origin of life,
(25) the time scales we must deal with make the whole span of human history seem but the blink of an eyelid. There is no simple way to adjust one's thinking to such vast stretches of time. The immensity of time passed is beyond our ready
(30) comprehension. One can only construct an impression of it from indirect and incomplete descriptions, just as a blind man laboriously builds up, by touch and sound, a picture of his immediate surroundings.

(35) The customary way to provide a convenient framework for one's thoughts is to compare the age of the universe with the length of a single earthly day. Perhaps a better comparison, along the same lines, would be to equate the age of our
(40) earth with a single week. On such a scale the age of the universe, since the Big Bang, would be about two or three weeks. The oldest macroscopic fossils (those from the start of the Cambrian*

Period would have been alive just one day ago.
(45) Modern man would have appeared in the last 10 seconds and agriculture in the last one or two. Odysseus** would have lived only half a second before the present time.

Even this comparison hardly makes the longer
(50) time scale comprehensible to us. Another alternative is to draw a linear map of time, with the different events marked on it. The problem here is to make the line long enough to show our own experience on a reasonable scale, and yet short enough
(55) for convenient reproduction and examination. But perhaps the most vivid method is to compare time to the lines of print themselves. Let us make a 200-page book equal in length to the time from the start of the Cambrian to the present; that is,
(60) about 600 million years. Then each full page will represent roughly three million years, each line about ninety thousand years, and each letter or small space about fifteen hundred years. The origin of the earth would be about seven books ago
(65) and the origin of the universe (which has been dated only approximately) ten or so books before that. Almost the whole of recorded human history would be covered by the last two or three letters of the book.

(70) If you now turn back the pages of the book, slowly reading *one letter at a time*—remember, each letter is fifteen hundred years—then this may convey to you something of the immense stretches of time we shall have to consider. On this scale the
(75) span of your own life would be less than the width of a comma.

Cambrian: the earliest period in the Paleozoic era, beginning about 600 million years ago.
**Odysseus:* the most famous Greek hero of antiquity; he is the hero of Homer's *The Odyssey*, which describes the aftermath of the Trojan War (ca. 1200 B.C.).

GO ON TO THE NEXT PAGE

10. The phrase "to a lesser extent" in line 13, indicates that before the invention of writing, the wisdom of earlier generations was

   (A) rejected by recent generations when portrayed in pictures, carvings, or statues

   (B) passed down orally, or not at all

   (C) transmitted more frequently by spoken word than by other means

   (D) based on illusory memories that turned fact into fiction

   (E) more strongly grounded in science than in the arts

11. The author most likely describes the impact of writing (lines 14–17) in order to

   (A) illustrate the limitations of the human memory

   (B) provide an example of how cultures transmit information

   (C) indicate how primitive preliterate cultures were

   (D) refute an opinion about the origin of human civilization

   (E) explain the difference between historical facts and myth

12. The word "ready" in line 29 most nearly means

   (A) set

   (B) agreeable

   (C) immediate

   (D) apt

   (E) willing

13. The analogy of the "blind man" (line 32) is presented primarily to show that

   (A) humans are unable to comprehend long periods of time

   (B) myths and legends fail to give an accurate picture of the past

   (C) human history is only a fraction of the time since life began

   (D) humans refuse to learn the lessons of the past

   (E) long periods of time can only be understood indirectly

14. In lines 40–44, the author mentions the Big Bang and the Cambrian Period in order to demonstrate which point?

   (A) The age of the Earth is best understood using the time scale of a week.

   (B) Agriculture was a relatively late development in human history.

   (C) No fossil record exists before the Cambrian Period.

   (D) Convenient time scales do not adequately represent the age of the Earth.

   (E) The customary framework for thinking about the age of the universe should be discarded permanently.

GO ON TO THE NEXT PAGE

KAPLAN

15. According to lines 52–56, one difficulty of using a linear representation of time is that

    (A) linear representations of time do not meet accepted scientific standards of accuracy

    (B) prehistoric eras overlap each other, making linear representation deceptive

    (C) the more accurate the scale, the more difficult the map is to copy and study

    (D) there are too many events to represent on a single line

    (E) our knowledge of pre-Cambrian time is insufficient to construct an accurate linear map

16. The author of this passage discusses several kinds of time scales primarily in order to illustrate the

    (A) difficulty of assigning precise dates to past events

    (B) variety of choices faced by scientists investigating the origin of life

    (C) evolution of efforts to comprehend the passage of history

    (D) immensity of time since life began on earth

    (E) development of the technology of communication

GO ON TO THE NEXT PAGE

Questions 17–24 refer to the following passage.

The following excerpt is from a speech delivered in 1873 by Susan B. Anthony, a leader in the women's rights movement of the 19th century.

Friends and fellow-citizens: I stand before you tonight under indictment for the alleged crime of having voted at the last Presidential election, without having a lawful right to vote. It shall be my
(5) work this evening to prove to you that in thus voting, I not only committed no crime, but, instead, simply exercised my citizen's rights, guaranteed to me and all United States citizens by the National Constitution, beyond the power of any State to
(10) deny.

The preamble of the Federal Constitution says: "We, the people of the United States, in order to form a more perfect union, establish justice, insure domestic tranquillity, provide for the common
(15) defense, promote the general welfare, and secure the blessings of liberty to ourselves and our posterity, do ordain and establish this Constitution for the United States of America."

It was we, the people; not we, the white male cit-
(20) izens; nor yet we, the male citizens; but we, the whole people, who formed the Union. And we formed it, not to give the blessings of liberty, but to secure them; not to the half of ourselves and the half of our posterity, but to the whole people—
(25) women as well as men. And it is a downright mockery to talk to women of their enjoyment of the blessings of liberty while they are denied the use of the only means of securing them provided by this democratic-republican government—the ballot.
(30) For any State to make sex a qualification that must ever result in the disfranchisement* of one entire half of the people is a violation of the supreme law of the land. By it the blessings of liberty are forever withheld from women and their
(35) female posterity. To them this government had no just powers derived from the consent of the governed. To them this government is not a democracy. It is not a republic. It is an odious aristocracy; a hateful oligarchy of sex; this oligarchy of sex, which
(40) makes father, brothers, husband, sons, the oligarchs over the mother and sisters, the wife and daughters of every household—which ordains all men sover-eigns, all women subjects, carries dissension, discord and rebellion into every home of the nation.
(45) Webster, Worcester and Bouvier all define a citizen to be a person in the United States, entitled to vote and hold office.

The one question left to be settled now is: Are women persons? And I hardly believe any of our
(50) opponents will have the hardihood to say they are not. Being persons, then, women are citizens; and no State has a right to make any law, or to enforce any old law, that shall abridge their privileges or immunities. Hence, every discrimination against
(55) women in the constitutions and laws of the several States is today null and void, precisely as is every one against Negroes.

disfranchisement: to deprive of the right to vote.

17. The author addresses her "fellow citizens" (line 1) primarily in order to

(A) limit her intended audience to those who are citizens

(B) establish a spirit of good-natured cooperation

(C) irritate her audience, since they do not consider her a citizen

(D) introduce an important element of one of her main arguments

(E) make it clear that she intends to address only men

18. In the first paragraph, Anthony states that her action in voting was

(A) illegal, but morally justified

(B) the result of her keen interest in national politics

(C) legal, if the Constitution is interpreted correctly

(D) an illustration of the need for a women's rights movement

(E) illegal, but worthy of leniency

GO ON TO THE NEXT PAGE

19. Which best captures the meaning of the word "promote" in line 15?

    (A) further
    (B) organize
    (C) publicize
    (D) commend
    (E) motivate

20. By saying "we, the people . . . the whole people, who formed the Union" (lines 19–21), Anthony means that

    (A) the founders of the nation conspired to deprive women of their rights
    (B) some male citizens are still being denied basic rights
    (C) the role of women in the founding of the nation is generally ignored
    (D) society is endangered when women are deprived of basic rights
    (E) all people deserve to enjoy the rights guaranteed by the Constitution

21. By "the half of our posterity" (lines 23–24), Anthony means

    (A) the political legacy passed down from her era
    (B) future generations of male United States citizens
    (C) those who wish to enjoy the blessings of liberty
    (D) current and future opponents of the women's rights movement
    (E) future members of the democratic-republican government

22. In the fourth paragraph, lines 30–47, Anthony's argument rests mainly on the strategy of convincing her audience that

    (A) any state which denies women the vote undermines its status as a democracy
    (B) women deprived of the vote will eventually raise a rebellion
    (C) the nation will remain an aristocracy if the status of women does not change
    (D) women's rights issues should be debated in every home
    (E) even an aristocracy cannot survive without the consent of the governed

23. The word "hardihood" in line 50 could best be replaced by

    (A) endurance
    (B) vitality
    (C) nerve
    (D) opportunity
    (E) stupidity

24. When Anthony warns that "no State . . . shall abridge their privileges" (lines 52–54), she means that

    (A) women should be allowed to live a life of privilege
    (B) women on trial cannot be forced to give up their immunity
    (C) every state should repeal its outdated laws
    (D) governments may not deprive citizens of their rights
    (E) the rights granted to women must be decided by the people, not the state

IF YOU FINISH BEFORE TIME IS CALLED, YOU MAY CHECK YOUR WORK ON THIS SECTION ONLY. DO NOT TURN TO ANY OTHER SECTION IN THE TEST. STOP

SECTION 5
Time—25 Minutes
18 Questions

Directions: For this section, solve each problem and decide which is the best of the choices given. Fill in the corresponding oval on the answer sheet. You may use any available space for scratchwork.

Notes:

(1) Calculator use is permitted.

(2) All numbers used are real numbers.

(3) Figures are provided for some problems. All figures are drawn to scale and lie in a plane UNLESS otherwise indicated.

(4) Unless otherwise specified, the domain of any function f is assumed to be the set of all real numbers x for which $f(x)$ is a real number.

Information

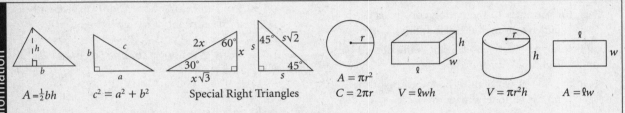

$A = \frac{1}{2}bh$ $c^2 = a^2 + b^2$ Special Right Triangles $A = \pi r^2$ $C = 2\pi r$ $V = \ell wh$ $V = \pi r^2 h$ $A = \ell w$

The sum of the degree measures of the angles in a triangle is 180.
The number of degrees of arc in a circle is 360.
A straight angle has a degree measure of 180.

---

1. If $100 + x = 100$, then $x =$

    (A) −100

    (B) −10

    (C) 0

    (D) 10

    (E) 100

2. Set X is the set of all odd numbers, and set Y is the set of all negative numbers. Which of the following represents the intersection of X and Y?

    (A) all odd numbers

    (B) all negative odd numbers

    (C) all negative numbers

    (D) all real numbers

    (E) all positive numbers

3. If $x < y < 0$, which of the following is greater than $\frac{y}{x}$?

    (A) 0

    (B) $\frac{x}{y}$

    (C) $\frac{-x}{y}$

    (D) $\frac{-y}{x}$

    (E) $\frac{y}{2x}$

GO ON TO THE NEXT PAGE

KAPLAN

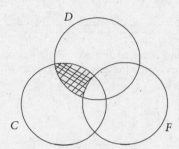

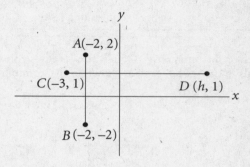

4. In the figure above, circular region D represents households with dogs, circular region C represents households with cats, and circular region F represents households with fish. What does the cross-hatched region represent?

(A) households with dogs, but no cats or fish

(B) households with cats and fish, but no dogs

(C) households with dogs, cats, and fish

(D) households with dogs and cats, but no fish

(E) households with dogs and fish, some of which may have cats

5. If $f(x) = \dfrac{(3x^2 - 9)}{(x + 1)}$, what is the value of $f(3)$?

(A) $\dfrac{3}{2}$

(B) 3

(C) $\dfrac{9}{2}$

(D) 6

(E) 9

6. In the figure above, the length of CD is twice the length of AB. What is the value of h?

(A) 2

(B) 3

(C) 4

(D) 5

(E) 6

7. The percent decrease from 12 to 9 is equal to the percent decrease from 40 to what number?

(A) 3

(B) 10

(C) 25

(D) 30

(E) 36

8. For a group of x people, Joe ordered 5 pizza pies, each of which was cut into 12 slices. Each person was originally supposed to have an equal number of slices. However, 4 people did not want any pizza, so when the pizza was distributed among the remaining people, each of them received 4 more slices. Which of the following equations could be used to find x?

(A) $x^2 - 4x - 60 = 0$

(B) $x^2 - 4x + 60 = 0$

(C) $x^2 + 4x - 60 = 0$

(D) $x^2 + 4x + 60 = 0$

(E) $x^2 - 16x - 240 = 0$

GO ON TO THE NEXT PAGE

KAPLAN

Directions: For Student-Produced Response questions 9–18, use the grids at the bottom of the answer sheet page on which you have answered questions 1–8.

Each of the remaining 10 questions requires you to solve the problem and enter your answer by marking the ovals in the special grid, as shown in the example below. You may use any available space for scratch work.

Answer: 1.25 or $\frac{5}{4}$ or 5/4

Write answer in → boxes.

Grid-in result →

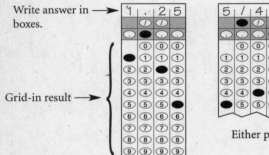

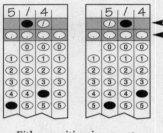

← Fraction line
← Decimal point

Either position is correct.

You may start your answers in any column, space permitting. Columns not needed should be left blank.

- It is recommended, though not required, that you write your answer in the boxes at the top of the columns. However, you will receive credit only for darkening the ovals correctly.

- Grid only one answer to a question, even though some problems have more than one correct answer.

- Darken no more than one oval in a column.

- No answers are negative.

- Mixed numbers cannot be gridded. For example: the number $1\frac{1}{4}$ must be gridded as 1.25 or 5/4.

(If 1 | 1 | / | 4 is gridded, it will be interpreted as $\frac{11}{4}$ not $1\frac{1}{4}$.)

- Decimal Accuracy: Decimal answers must be entered as accurately as possible. For example, if you obtain an answer such as 0.1666…, you should record the result as .166 or .167. **Less accurate values such as .16 or .17 are not acceptable.**

Acceptable ways to grid $\frac{1}{6}$ = .1666…

KAPLAN

9. If $A = 2.54$ and $20B = A$, what is the value of B?

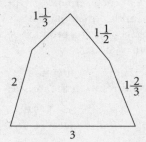

10. What is the perimeter of the figure shown above?

11. If $\dfrac{h}{3}$ and $\dfrac{h}{4}$ are integers, and if $75 < h < 100$, what is one possible value of h?

12. A retailer buys 16 shirts at \$4.50 each, and she sells all 16 shirts for \$6.75 each. If the retailer purchases more of these shirts at \$4.50 each, what is the greatest number of these shirts that she can buy with the profit she made on the 16 shirts?

13. Lines ℓ and m intersect at a point to form four angles. If one of the angles formed is 15 times as large as an adjacent angle, what is the measure, in degrees, of the smaller angle?

14. If $x = -4$ when $x^2 + 2xr + r^2 = 0$, what is the value of r?

15. Let $n \ast = n^2 - n$ for all positive numbers n. What is the value of $\dfrac{1}{4} \ast - \dfrac{1}{2} \ast$?

16. What is the area of $\triangle ABC$ shown above?

17. If x is a factor of 8,100 and if x is an odd integer, what is the greatest possible value of x?

18. In a certain class, $\dfrac{1}{2}$ of the male students and $\dfrac{2}{3}$ of the female students speak French. If there are $\dfrac{3}{4}$ as many girls as boys in the class, what fraction of the entire class speaks French?

IF YOU FINISH BEFORE TIME IS CALLED, YOU MAY CHECK YOUR WORK ON THIS SECTION ONLY. DO NOT TURN TO ANY OTHER SECTION IN THE TEST.   STOP

SECTION 6

Time—25 Minutes
35 Questions

Directions: For each question in this section, select the best answer from among the choices given and fill in the corresponding oval on the answer sheet.

The following sentences test correctness and effectiveness of expression. Part of each sentence or the entire sentence is underlined; beneath each sentence are five ways of phrasing the underlined material. Choice A repeats the original phrasing; the other four choices are different. If you think the original phrasing produces a better sentence than any of the alternatives, select choice A; if not, select one of the other choices.

In making your selection, follow the requirements of standard written English; that is, pay attention to grammar, choice of words, sentence construction, and punctuation. Your selection should result in the most effective sentence—clear and precise, without awkwardness or ambiguity.

EXAMPLE:

Every apple in the baskets <u>are ripe and labeled according to the date it was picked</u>.

ANSWER: Ⓐ ● Ⓒ Ⓓ Ⓔ

(A) are ripe and labeled according to the date it was picked
(B) is ripe and labeled according to the date it was picked
(C) are ripe and labeled according to the date they were picked
(D) is ripe and labeled according to the date they were picked
(E) are ripe and labeled as to the date it was picked

---

1. <u>Arranged as an event for funding a new wing for the art museum</u>, the museum's Board of Directors organized a fundraiser for the construction of one.

   (A) Arranged as an event to for funding a new wing for the art museum

   (B) Having been arranged as an event to fund a new wing for the art museum

   (C) A new wing for the art museum needed an event for funding

   (D) Although an event for funding a new wing for the art museum

   (E) Realizing that the art museum needed funding for a new wing

2. One of the most popular broadcasters on the evening news is a retired <u>politician; the one with nearly</u> as many fans is an executive recently retired from the film industry.

   (A) politician; the one with nearly

   (B) politician; near one with

   (C) politician, the one with nearly

   (D) politician, and also the one with near

   (E) politician; although the one with nearly

GO ON TO THE NEXT PAGE

3. Although the architects created a new earthquake-proof structural design, they <u>had refused to patent nor otherwise benefiting</u> from the design plans.

(A) had refused to patent nor otherwise benefiting

(B) had refused to patent or otherwise benefit

(C) refused to patent or otherwise benefit

(D) refuse to patent or otherwise benefit

(E) refused to patent or otherwise benefiting

4. Oscar Wilde was <u>almost as brilliant a novelist as he was at writing plays</u>.

(A) almost as brilliant a novelist as he was at writing plays

(B) almost brilliant at writing novels and plays

(C) almost equally brilliant, whether a novelist or a playwright

(D) almost as brilliant a novelist as he was a playwright

(E) a brilliant novelist, with almost as much brilliance as a playwright

5. Examining the sale offers in the catalogue, <u>the phrases</u> "while supplies last" and "get it while it's hot" are designed to encourage consumers to order the products immediately.

(A) the phrases

(B) the slogans

(C) one sees that the phrases

(D) although one saw the phrases

(E) one may have noticed phrases

6. <u>In professional soccer, players kick the ball sharply and accurately; however in other sports their technique is not quite so effective.</u>

(A) In professional soccer, players kick the ball sharply and accurately; however in other sports their technique is not quite so effective.

(B) Most professional soccer players kick the ball sharply and accurately, however in other sports their technique is not quite so effective.

(C) Although in other sports their technique is not quite so effective, most professional soccer players, however, kick the ball sharply and accurately.

(D) Most professional soccer players which kick the ball sharply and accurately do not have such effective technique in other sports.

(E) Most professional soccer players kick the ball sharply and accurately and in other sports their technique is not so effective.

7. The changing color of autumn leaves has a unique fascination for those people <u>which have an understanding of life cycles in them</u>.

(A) which have an understanding of life cycles in them

(B) who see the life cycles in them

(C) which have seen life cycles in them

(D) who understand that they have life cycles

(E) who see about them

GO ON TO THE NEXT PAGE

KAPLAN

8. The traffic rules were ignored by each of us, failing to appreciate their role in ensuring safety.

   (A) The traffic rules were ignored by each of us, failing to appreciate their role in ensuring safety.

   (B) Each of us ignored traffic rules, because we failed to appreciate their role in ensuring safety.

   (C) Traffic rules, ignored by each of us, fail to appreciate their role in ensuring safety.

   (D) Failing to appreciate their role in ensuring safety, traffic rules were ignored by each of us.

   (E) Traffic rules ignored by each of us, failing to appreciate their role in ensuring safety.

9. The meaning of his words was even more elusive in his own country than either Europe or Latin America.

   (A) either Europe or Latin America

   (B) either Europe or in Latin America

   (C) either in Europe or Latin America

   (D) in either Europe or in Latin America

   (E) in either Europe or Latin America

10. It was primarily when I visited the seashore that I felt nostalgic for my childhood home, growing up on a small island.

    (A) growing up on a small island

    (B) as I had grown up on a small island

    (C) as on a small island I grow up

    (D) which is on a small island

    (E) on a small island growing up

11. By 1975, twelve percent of the households with televisions were cable subscribers, and established hundreds of cable stations there were.

    (A) subscribers, and established hundreds of cable stations there were

    (B) subscribers, and hundreds of cable stations were established

    (C) subscribers, and there were established hundreds of cable stations

    (D) subscribers plus hundreds of cable stations established

    (E) subscribers and hundreds of cable stations

GO ON TO THE NEXT PAGE ▷

Directions: The following sentences test your ability to recognize grammar and usage errors. Each sentence contains either a single error or no error at all. No sentence contains more than one error. The error, if there is one, is underlined and lettered. If the sentence contains an error, select the one underlined part that must be changed to make the sentence correct. If the sentence is correct, select choice E. In choosing answers, follow the requirements of standard written English.

EXAMPLE:

<u>Whenever</u> one is driving late at night, <u>you</u> must take extra precautions <u>against</u>
   A   B   C

falling asleep <u>at the wheel</u>. <u>No error</u>
             D   E

(A) ● (C) (D) (E)

12. <u>As Picasso</u> matured as a painter, his <u>use of</u> shapes
     A   B
    <u>became</u> bolder, more abstract, and
    C
    <u>they can astonish people.</u> <u>No error</u>
             D   E

13. The chemical plant is already <u>such a</u> danger that
                                    A
    <u>it became</u> imperative <u>to find other ways</u> of
    B   C
    developing effective pesticides <u>for</u> use in gardens.
                                 D
    <u>No error</u>
    E

14. <u>Due to their</u> recent rapid sales growth, retail
    A   B
    stores <u>are increasing</u> their <u>stock of</u> popular items.
               C   D
    <u>No error</u>
    E

15. The <u>lyric</u> novels of Virginia Woolf <u>which eerily</u>
        A   B
    <u>hint at</u> the despair <u>of her</u> later life. <u>No error</u>
    C   D   E

16. With <u>more than</u> 150 associated countries, the
         A
    United Nations owes <u>their</u> name <u>to a</u> worldwide
                       B   C
    membership <u>that oversees</u> international treaties
                     D
    and human rights. <u>No error</u>
                     E

GO ON TO THE NEXT PAGE

KAPLAN

17. <u>Walking along</u> the empty boardwalk, I <u>could hear</u>
       A   B

    the lapping of water against the docks as <u>well as</u>
                                                 C

    the sound of Jake and Kelsey talking softly

    <u>as he approached</u>. <u>No error</u>
          D   E

18. <u>At the stoplight</u>, Hiam, <u>impatient</u> to be home on
         A   B

    that <u>rainy</u> night, drummed his fingers
         C

    <u>at the wheel</u>. <u>No error</u>
      D   E

19. If you <u>surround</u> the roots of your new rose with a
          A

    <u>generously</u> mixture of mulch and compost, you
     B

    <u>will provide</u> the roots the space to <u>grow</u> healthily.
      C   D

    <u>No error</u>
      E

20. Kelly <u>is proud of</u> <u>her</u> own abilities <u>to mediate</u>
         A   B   C

    disputes <u>more than</u> any of her other strengths.
           D

    <u>No error</u>
      E

21. We <u>had drove</u> no more than fifty yards <u>from our</u>
       A   B

    parking spot when it <u>became apparent</u> that Shelly
                      C

    <u>had left</u> her purse behind at the steakhouse.
      D

    <u>No error</u>
      E

22. <u>Most of</u> the small country stores in the United
      A

    States <u>are</u> in isolated, thinly populated areas where
         B

    there are <u>hardly no</u> supermarkets <u>within easy</u>
             C   D

    driving distance. <u>No error</u>
                 E

23. <u>Working with</u> the ease and skill of the true
        A

    professional, Lehrmann quickly outlined a <u>sketch</u>
                                      B

    of the young <u>but</u> experienced skater who was
                C

    <u>posing for</u> her. <u>No error</u>
      D   E

24. Many historians have <u>written about</u> the Roosevelt
                    A

    family, but <u>never before</u> <u>has</u> the characters of the
                 B   C

    family members been <u>so skillfully</u> evaluated.
                     D

    <u>No error</u>
      E

25. <u>No matter</u> how <u>attentive</u> Mark applies himself to
      A   B

    his studies, he <u>never seems</u> to get the grades he
                C

    <u>needs</u> to make the Dean's List. <u>No error</u>
     D   E

26. There has always been a <u>great deal of</u> antipathy
                        A

    between <u>Sarah and I</u> <u>because we</u> have opposing
         B   C

    opinions <u>about which</u> we are very outspoken.
             D

    <u>No error</u>
      E

GO ON TO THE NEXT PAGE ▷

KAPLAN

27. The extraordinary breath control <u>used by</u> students
                                        A
of meditation to control stress and pain levels <u>is</u> a
                                                   B
<u>benefit</u> to both <u>their</u> physical and mental well-
   C   D
being. <u>No error</u>
          E

28. A scientist at the institute <u>indicated that</u> an
                                     A
<u>unusually high</u> percentage of <u>their</u> funding <u>comes</u>
   B   C   D
from money donated to it by private

philanthropists. <u>No error</u>
                    E

29. The candidate, John Kallan, is of an <u>undetermined</u>
                                            A
age, <u>and</u> he <u>uses</u> this ambiguity <u>to his benefit</u>.
      B   C   D
<u>No error</u>
  E

GO ON TO THE NEXT PAGE

Directions: The following passage is an early draft of an essay. Some parts of the passage need to be rewritten.

Read the passage and select the best answer for each question that follows. Some questions are about particular sentences or parts of sentences and ask you to improve sentence structure or word choice. Other questions ask you to consider organization and development. In choosing answers, follow the conventions of standard written English.

Questions 30–35 are based on the following passage.

(1) There is a duality in ballet that most people don't see. (2) Most often, it is seen only as beautifully graceful.

(3) First, ballet is tough physically. (4) Because the human body is not designed for ballet. (5) Dancers must perform steps that come from ballet's five fundamental positions in which dancers rotate their hips and legs unnaturally. (6) This makes dancers walk funny (you can always recognize dancers by the way they walk with their feet turning out instead of facing forward). (7) Unfortunately, it also often results in permanent injury.

(8) Ballet companies' financial struggles creating fierce competition between dancers for a place in a professional company. (9) Dancers often live below the poverty line, particularly as most companies pay by the dance season, which can last for as little as twenty weeks out of the year, instead of by year. (10) In general, most people who spend years training for their jobs stay in the same career until they retire at 65. (11) Not being the case with dancers, as ballet careers hardly ever extend beyond the mid-thirties, even though the dancers have trained since they were 5 years old. (12) Few retired dancers continue as ballet teachers or choreographers. (13) The vast majority find themselves unemployed in their mid-thirties.

30. Which of the following sentences is best inserted at the end of the first paragraph, after sentence 2?

   (A) But in reality, ballet is grueling, painful, and competitive.

   (B) Yet few people really appreciate that fact.

   (C) Missing, however, the extreme athleticism it requires.

   (D) Many types of dance share this quality.

   (E) Not every ballet dancer, however, dances for this reason.

31. Which of the following is the best way to revise the underlined portions of sentences 4 and 5 (reproduced below) in order to combine the sentences?

Because the human body is not designed <u>for ballet. Dancers must perform</u> steps that come from ballet's five fundamental positions in which dancers rotate their hips and legs unnaturally.

   (A) for ballet, it is difficult for dancers to perform

   (B) for ballet; dancers must perform

   (C) for ballet, making it difficult for dancers to perform

   (D) for ballet, their difficulty in performing

   (E) for ballet; therefore dancers must perform

GO ON TO THE NEXT PAGE

32. Which is the best sentence to insert before sentence 8 to begin the third paragraph?

   (A) Second, ballet is tough financially.

   (B) Secondly, ballet is competitive.

   (C) Furthermore, ballet dancers struggle financially.

   (D) In addition, ballet companies are difficult employers.

   (E) This is not the worst consequence, however.

33. In context, which is the best version of the underlined portion of sentence 8 (reproduced below)?

   Ballet companies' financial struggles <u>*creating fierce competition*</u> *between dancers for a place in a professional company.*

   (A) (As it is now)

   (B) compiling to create fiercely

   (C) created their fierce competition

   (D) create fierce competition

   (E) had created a fierce competition

34. In context, which is the best version of the underlined portion of sentence 11 (reproduced below)?

   <u>*Not being the case with*</u> *dancers, as ballet careers hardly ever extend beyond the mid-thirties, even though the dancers have trained since they were 5 years old.*

   (A) (As it is now)

   (B) Which is not true of

   (C) That model does not apply to

   (D) But not so for

   (E) And so also for

35. Which of the following is the best way to combine sentences 12 and 13 (reproduced below)?

   Few retired dancers continue as ballet teachers or choreographers. The vast majority find themselves unemployed in their mid-thirties.

   (A) Although a few retired dancers continue as ballet teachers or choreographers, and the vast majority find themselves unemployed in their mid-thirties.

   (B) A few retired dancers continue as ballet teachers or choreographers, but the vast majority find themselves unemployed in their mid-thirties.

   (C) However, few retired dancers continued as ballet teachers or choreographers although the vast majority unemployed in their mid-thirties.

   (D) A few retired dancers continue as ballet teachers or choreographers, the vast majority find themselves unemployed in their mid-thirties.

   (E) Few retired dancers continued as ballet teachers or choreographers vastly the majority are found unemployed in their mid-thirties.

IF YOU FINISH BEFORE TIME IS CALLED, YOU MAY CHECK YOUR WORK ON THIS SECTION ONLY. DO NOT TURN TO ANY OTHER SECTION IN THE TEST. STOP

SECTION 7

Time—20 Minutes
19 Questions

Directions: For each of the following questions, choose the best answer and darken the corresponding oval on the answer sheet.

Each sentence below has one or two blanks, each blank indicating that something has been omitted. Beneath the sentence are five words or sets of words labeled A through E. Choose the word or set of words that, when inserted in the sentence, best fits the meaning of the sentence as a whole.

EXAMPLE:

Today's small, portable computers contrast markedly with the earliest electronic computers, which were -------.

(A) effective
(B) invented
(C) useful
(D) destructive
(E) enormous

1. The prisoner was ------- even though he presented evidence clearly proving that he was nowhere near the scene of the crime.

    (A) abandoned
    (B) indicted
    (C) exculpated
    (D) exhumed
    (E) rescinded

2. Many biologists are critical of the film's ------- premise that dinosaurs might one day return.

    (A) scientific
    (B) tacit
    (C) speculative
    (D) unwitting
    (E) ambiguous

3. It is ------- that people so capable of treachery and brutality should also exhibit such a tremendous capacity for heroism.

    (A) unfortunate
    (B) explicable
    (C) paradoxical
    (D) distressing
    (E) appalling

4. To ------- the seasonal migration of caribou, engineers ------- the trans-Alaska pipeline in over 500 locations to allow large animals access through the pipeline corridor.

    (A) banish . . . buried
    (B) preserve . . . elevated
    (C) admire . . . razed
    (D) prevent . . . erected
    (E) enable . . . delivered

5. Most people today think of licorice as candy; however, the ------- properties of the licorice root were once used to treat coughs, digestive problems, and insomnia.

    (A) somnolent
    (B) basic
    (C) sweet
    (D) indelible
    (E) medicinal

6. To ------- free education for children with special needs, parents have had to ------- legislation guaranteeing services and programs targeted to those children.

    (A) ensure . . . demand
    (B) prevent . . . pass
    (C) assert . . . console
    (D) alleviate . . . request
    (E) provide . . . veto

GO ON TO THE NEXT PAGE

KAPLAN

Questions 7–19 refer to the following passages.

The controversy over the authorship of Shakespeare's plays began in the 18th century and continues to this day. Here, the author of Passage 1 embraces the proposal that Francis Bacon actually wrote the plays, while the author of Passage 2 defends the traditional attribution to Shakespeare himself.

Passage 1

Anyone with more than a superficial knowledge of Shakespeare's plays must necessarily entertain some doubt concerning their true authorship. Can scholars honestly accept the idea that such master-
(5) works were written by a shadowy actor with limited formal education and a social position that can most charitably be called "humble"? Obviously, the author of the plays must have traveled widely, yet there is no record that Shakespeare ever left his
(10) native England. Even more obviously, the real author had to have intimate knowledge of life within royal courts and palaces, yet Shakespeare was a commoner, with little firsthand experience of the aristocracy. No, common sense tells us that the
(15) plays must have been written by someone with substantial expertise in the law, the sciences, classics, foreign languages, and the fine arts—someone, in other words, like Shakespeare's eminent contemporary, Sir Francis Bacon.
(20)   The first person to suggest that Bacon was the actual author of the plays was Reverend James Wilmot. Writing in 1785, Wilmot argued that someone of Shakespeare's educational background could hardly have produced works of such erudition and
(25) insight. But a figure like Bacon, a scientist and polymath* of legendary stature, would certainly have known about, for instance, the circulation of the blood as alluded to in *Coriolanus*. And as an aristocrat, Bacon would have possessed the familiarity
(30) with court life required to produce *Love's Labour's Lost*.
    Delia Bacon (no relation to Sir Francis) was next to make the case for Francis Bacon's authorship. In 1856, in collaboration with Nathaniel Hawthorne,

(35) she insisted that it was ridiculous to look for the creator of *Hamlet* among "that dirty, doggish group of players, who come into the scene [of the play Hamlet] summoned like a pack of hounds to his service." Ultimately, she concluded that the plays
(40) were actually composed by a committee consisting of Bacon, Edmund Spenser, Walter Raleigh, and several others.
    Still, some might wonder why Bacon, if indeed the plays were wholly or partly his work, would
(45) not put his own name on them. But consider the political climate of England in Elizabethan times. Given that it would have been politically and personally damaging for a man of Bacon's position to associate himself with such controversial plays, it is
(50) quite understandable that Bacon would hire a lowly actor to take the credit—and the consequences.
    But perhaps the most convincing evidence of all comes from the postscript of a 1624 letter sent to Bacon by Sir Tobie Matthew. "The most prodigious
(55) wit that I ever knew . . . is your lordship's name," Matthew wrote, "though he be known by another." That name, of course, was William Shakespeare.

*polymath—a person of wide and varied learning

Passage 2

Over the years, there have been an astonishing number of persons put forth as the "true author" of
(60) Shakespeare's plays. Some critics have even gone so far as to claim that only a "committee" could have possessed the abundance of talent and energy necessary to produce Shakespeare's thirty-seven plays. Among the individual figures most seriously pro-
(65) moted as "the real Shakespeare" is Sir Francis Bacon. Apparently, the fact that Bacon wrote most of his own work in academic Latin does nothing to deter those who would crown him the premier stylist in the English language.

GO ON TO THE NEXT PAGE ⟩

(70)   Although the entire controversy reeks of scholarly gamesplaying, the issue underlying it is worth considering: how could an uneducated actor create such exquisite works? But the answer to that is easy. Shakespeare's dramatic gifts had little to do *(75)* with encyclopedic knowledge, complex ideas, or a fluency with great systems of thought. Rather, Shakespeare's genius was one of common sense and perceptive intuition—a genius that grows not out of book-learning, but out of a deep understanding of *(80)* human nature and a keen grasp of basic emotions, passions, and jealousies.

    One of the most common arguments advanced by skeptics is that the degree of familiarity with the law exhibited in a *Hamlet* or a *Merchant of Venice* *(85)* can only have been achieved by a lawyer or other man of affairs. The grasp of law evidenced in these plays, however, is not a detailed knowledge of formal law, but a more general understanding of so-called "country law." Shakespeare was a landowner *(90)* —an extraordinary achievement in itself for an ill-paid Elizabethan actor—and so would have been knowledgeable about legal matters related to the buying, selling, and renting of real estate. Evidence of such a common understanding of land regula-*(95)* tions can be found, for instance, in the gravedigging scene of *Hamlet*.

    So no elaborate theories of intrigue and secret identity are necessary to explain the accomplishment of William Shakespeare. Scholars who have *(100)* made a career of ferreting out "alternative bards" may be reluctant to admit it, but literary genius can flower in any socioeconomic bracket. Shakespeare, in short, was Shakespeare—an observation that one would have thought was obvious to everyone.

7. In Passage 1, line 2, "entertain" most nearly means

  (A) amuse

  (B) harbor

  (C) occupy

  (D) cherish

  (E) engage

8. In Passage 1, the author draws attention to Shakespeare's social standing as a "commoner" (line 13) in order to cast doubt on the Elizabethan actor's

  (A) aptitude for writing poetically

  (B) knowledge of foreign places and habits

  (C) ability to support himself by playwriting

  (D) familiarity with life among persons of high rank

  (E) understanding of the problems of government

9. *Coriolanus* and *Love's Labour's Lost* are mentioned in Passage 1, lines 28–31 as examples of works that

  (A) only Francis Bacon could have written

  (B) exhibit a deep understanding of human nature

  (C) resemble works written by Francis Bacon under his own name

  (D) portray a broad spectrum of Elizabethan society

  (E) reveal expertise more likely held by Bacon than Shakespeare

10. In Passage 1, the quotation from Delia Bacon (lines 36–39) conveys a sense of

  (A) disdain for the disreputable vulgarity of Elizabethan actors

  (B) resentment at the way Shakespeare's characters were portrayed

  (C) regret that conditions for Elizabethan actors were not better

  (D) doubt that Shakespeare could actually have created such unsavory characters

  (E) disappointment at the incompetence of Elizabethan actors

GO ON TO THE NEXT PAGE ▷

11. The author of Passage 1 maintains that Bacon did not put his own name on the plays attributed to Shakespeare because he

    (A) regarded writing as an unsuitable occupation for an aristocrat

    (B) wished to protect himself from the effects of controversy

    (C) preferred being known as a scientist and politician rather than as a writer

    (D) did not want to associate himself with lowly actors

    (E) sought to avoid the attention that fame brings

12. In the first paragraph of Passage 2, the author calls into question Bacon's likely ability to

    (A) write in a language with which he was unfamiliar

    (B) make the transition between scientific writing and playwriting

    (C) produce the poetic language evident in the plays

    (D) cooperate with other members of a committee

    (E) single-handedly create thirty-seven plays

13. The word "premier" in Passage 2, line 68 most nearly means

    (A) earliest

    (B) influential

    (C) inaugural

    (D) greatest

    (E) original

14. In Passage 2, line 75, the word "encyclopedic" most nearly means

    (A) technical

    (B) comprehensive

    (C) abridged

    (D) disciplined

    (E) specialized

15. The author of Passage 2, cites Shakespeare's status as a landowner in order to

    (A) prove that Shakespeare was a success as a playwright

    (B) refute the claim that Shakespeare had little knowledge of aristocratic life

    (C) prove that Shakespeare didn't depend solely on acting for his living

    (D) dispute the notion that Shakespeare was a commoner

    (E) account for Shakespeare's apparent knowledge of the law

16. In Passage 2, lines 101–102, the author maintains that literary genius

    (A) is not dependent on a writer's external circumstances

    (B) must be based on an inborn comprehension of human nature

    (C) is enhanced by the suffering that poverty brings

    (D) frequently goes unrecognized among those of modest means and position

    (E) can be stifled by too much book-learning and academic training

GO ON TO THE NEXT PAGE

KAPLAN

17. The author of Passage 2 would probably respond to the speculation in the fourth paragraph of Passage 1 by pointing out that

   (A) Shakespeare's plays would not have seemed particularly controversial to Elizabethan audiences

   (B) the extent and range of Bacon's learning has been generally exaggerated

   (C) such scenarios are farfetched and unnecessary if one correctly understands Shakespeare's genius

   (D) Bacon would not have had the knowledge of the lower classes required to produce the plays

   (E) the claim implies that Shakespeare was disreputable when in fact he was a respectable landowner

18. The author of Passage 1 would probably respond to the skepticism expressed in Passage 2, lines 66–69 by making which of the following statements?

   (A) The similarities between English and Latin make it plausible that one person could write well in both languages.

   (B) Plays written in Latin would not have been likely to attract a wide audience in Elizabethan England.

   (C) The premier stylist in the English language is more likely to have been an eminent scholar than an uneducated actor.

   (D) Writing the plays in Latin would have shielded Bacon from much of the political damage he wanted to avoid.

   (E) The style of the plays is notable mostly for the clarity of thought behind the lines rather than their musicality or beauty.

19. In Passage 2, line 103, "observation" most nearly means

   (A) inspection
   (B) measurement
   (C) research
   (D) comment
   (E) memorandum

IF YOU FINISH BEFORE TIME IS CALLED, YOU MAY CHECK YOUR WORK ON THIS SECTION ONLY. DO NOT TURN TO ANY OTHER SECTION IN THE TEST. **STOP**

SECTION 8
Time—20 Minutes
16 Questions

Directions: For this section, solve each problem and decide which is the best of the choices given. Fill in the corresponding oval on the answer sheet. You may use any available space for scratchwork.

Notes:

(1) Calculator use is permitted.

(2) All numbers used are real numbers.

(3) Figures are provided for some problems. All figures are drawn to scale and lie in a plane UNLESS otherwise indicated.

(4) Unless otherwise specified, the domain of any function f is assumed to be the set of all real numbers x for which $f(x)$ is a real number.

Information

$A = \frac{1}{2}bh$ $c^2 = a^2 + b^2$ Special Right Triangles $A = \pi r^2$ $V = \ell wh$ $V = \pi r^2 h$ $A = \ell w$
$C = 2\pi r$

The sum of the degree measures of the angles in a triangle is 180.
The number of degrees of arc in a circle is 360.
A straight angle has a degree measure of 180.

1. If $p = -2$ and $q = 3$, then $p^3 q^2 + p^2 q =$

   (A) −84

   (B) −60

   (C) 36

   (D) 60

   (E) 84

A   B   C D E

Note: Figure not drawn to scale.

2. In the figure above, B is the midpoint of AC, and D is the midpoint of CE. If $AB = 5$ and $BD = 8$, what is the length of DE?

   (A) 3

   (B) 4

   (C) 5

   (D) 6

   (E) 8

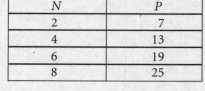

N	P
2	7
4	13
6	19
8	25

3. Which of the following equations describes the relationship of each pair of numbers (N, P) in the table above?

   (A) $P = N + 5$

   (B) $P = 2N + 3$

   (C) $P = 2N + 5$

   (D) $P = 3N + 1$

   (E) $P = 3N - 1$

GO ON TO THE NEXT PAGE

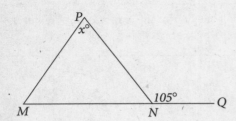

Note: Figure not drawn to scale.

4. In the figure above, MQ is a straight line. If $PM = PN$, what is the value of x?

   (A) 30
   (B) 45
   (C) 60
   (D) 75
   (E) 90

5. Marty has exactly five blue pens, six black pens, and four red pens in his knapsack. If he pulls out one pen at random from his knapsack, what is the probability that the pen is either red or black?

   (A) $\dfrac{1}{5}$

   (B) $\dfrac{1}{3}$

   (C) $\dfrac{1}{2}$

   (D) $\dfrac{2}{3}$

   (E) $\dfrac{11}{15}$

6. Two hot dogs and a soda cost $3.25. If three hot dogs and a soda cost $4.50, what is the cost of two sodas?

   (A) $0.75
   (B) $1.25
   (C) $1.50
   (D) $2.50
   (E) $3.00

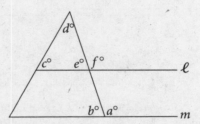

7. In the figure above, if $\ell \parallel m$, which of the following must be equal to a?

   (A) $b + c$
   (B) $b + e$
   (C) $c + d$
   (D) $d + e$
   (E) $d + f$

8. A certain phone call costs 75 cents for the first three minutes plus 15 cents for each additional minute. If the call lasted x minutes and x is an integer greater than 3, which of the following expresses the cost of the call, in dollars?

   (A) $0.75(3) + 0.15x$
   (B) $0.75(3) + 0.15(x + 3)$
   (C) $0.75 + 0.15(3 - x)$
   (D) $0.75 + 0.15(x - 3)$
   (E) $0.75 + 0.15x$

GO ON TO THE NEXT PAGE

KAPLAN

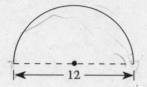

9. The figure above shows a piece of wire in the shape of a semicircle. If the piece of wire is bent to form a circle without any of the wire overlapping, what is the area of the circle?

(A) 6π

(B) 9π

(C) 12π

(D) 18π

(E) 36π

10. If $a^2 - a = 72$, and b and n are integers such that $b^n = a$, which of the following CANNOT be a value for b?

(A) -8

(B) -2

(C)   2

(D)   3

(E)   9

11. In the standard xy-coordinate plane, the midpoint of $\overline{XY}$ is $(3, 4)$. If the coordinates of point X are $(0, 2)$, what are the coordinates of point Y?

(A) $(3, 2)$

(B) $(4, 3)$

(C) $(6, 6)$

(D) $(7, 6)$

(E) $(8, 2)$

12. If $4\sqrt{2x} - 2 = 16$, then $x =$

(A) -4

(B) -2

(C)   8

(D) $\dfrac{81}{8}$

(E) $8\dfrac{1}{4}$

GO ON TO THE NEXT PAGE

KAPLAN

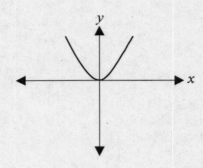

Note: Figure not drawn to scale.

13. If the above graph is $y = 3x^2$, which of the following is the graph of $y = -3x^2$?

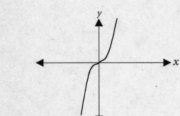

(A)

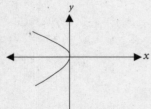

(B)

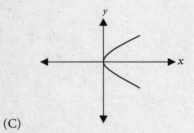

(C)

(D)

(E)

GO ON TO THE NEXT PAGE

14. What was the initial weight, in pounds, of a person who gained p pounds, then lost 8 pounds, and now weighs w pounds?

    (A) $w + p + 8$
    (B) $w + p - 8$
    (C) $w - p + 8$
    (D) $w - p - 8$
    (E) $p - w - 8$

15. If a cube has a surface area of $36n^2$ square feet, what is its volume in cubic feet, in terms of n?

    (A) $n^3\sqrt{6}$
    (B) $6n^3\sqrt{6}$
    (C) $36n^3$
    (D) $36n^3\sqrt{6}$
    (E) $216n^3$

16. The ratio of x to y to z is 3 to 6 to 8. If $y = 24$, what is the value of $x + z$?

    (A) 11
    (B) 33
    (C) 44
    (D) 66
    (E) 88

IF YOU FINISH BEFORE TIME IS CALLED, YOU MAY CHECK YOUR WORK ON THIS SECTION ONLY. DO NOT TURN TO ANY OTHER SECTION IN THE TEST. **STOP**

KAPLAN

SECTION 9

Time—10 Minutes
14 Questions

Directions: For each question in this section, select the best answer from among the choices given and fill in the corresponding oval on the answer sheet.

The following sentences test correctness and effectiveness of expression. Part of each sentence or the entire sentence is underlined; beneath each sentence are five ways of phrasing the underlined material. Choice A repeats the original phrasing; the other four choices are different. If you think the original phrasing produces a better sentence than any of the alternatives, select choice A; if not, select one of the other choices.

In making your selection, follow the requirements of standard written English; that is, pay attention to grammar, choice of words, sentence construction, and punctuation. Your selection should result in the most effective sentence—clear and precise, without awkwardness or ambiguity.

EXAMPLE:

Every apple in the baskets <u>are ripe and labeled according to the date it was picked</u>.

ANSWER: Ⓐ ● Ⓒ Ⓓ Ⓔ

(A) are ripe and labeled according to the date it was picked
(B) is ripe and labeled according to the date it was picked
(C) are ripe and labeled according to the date they were picked
(D) is ripe and labeled according to the date they were picked
(E) are ripe and labeled as to the date it was picked

---

1. The dean stated that although the teacher shortage is partly due to low salaries, <u>they did not get resolved</u> when salaries increased.

   (A) they did not get resolved
   (B) there was no resolve
   (C) resolving there was not
   (D) they did not resolve
   (E) it did not get resolved

2. Animal behaviorists are researching how bats respond to abnormalities in their environments, detect light and sound, <u>and communicate with each other</u>.

   (A) and communicate with each other
   (B) and communicating with each other
   (C) and to communicate between each other
   (D) and how they communicate with each other
   (E) and communication amongst each other

3. <u>The first truly American art movement, formed in the early nineteenth century by a group of landscape painters, called the Hudson River School.</u>

   (A) The first truly American art movement, formed in the early nineteenth century by a group of landscape painters, called the Hudson River School.
   (B) Formed in the early nineteenth century by a group of landscape painters was the first truly American art movement, called the Hudson River School.
   (C) Called the Hudson River School, it was formed in the early nineteenth century by a group of landscape painters, the first truly American art movement.
   (D) The first truly American art movement was formed in the early nineteenth century by a group of landscape painters called the Hudson River School.
   (E) By a group of landscape painters called the Hudson River School, the first truly American art movement was formed.

GO ON TO THE NEXT PAGE ⟶

4. During the rainy season, a sloth's brown fur is usually covered wih a coat of green <u>algae, which helps</u> the sloth blend with its surroundings.

   (A) algae, which helps

   (B) algae for the purpose of helping

   (C) algae; helps

   (D) algae being that it helps

   (E) algae, helping it does

5. Many researchers contend that driving while talking on a cellular phone poses essentially the same risks <u>than if you drive</u> while intoxicated.

   (A) than if you drive

   (B) than to drive

   (C) as if one drives

   (D) as driving

   (D) as it does when driving

6. Before 1988, the corporation's board of directors included 153 <u>members, none of the members were women</u>.

   (A) members, none of the members were women

   (B) members; and no women

   (C) members, none of whom were women

   (D) members, and of the members not one of them was a woman

   (E) members; none of them being women

7. <u>The client was waiting for fifteen minutes when</u> the receptionist suddenly looked up from her work, noticed him, and informed him that his appointment had been canceled.

   (A) The client was waiting for fifteen minutes when

   (B) The client, having waited for fifteen minutes, when

   (C) Already the client was waiting for fifteen minutes when

   (D) When the client waited for fifteen minutes,

   (E) The client had been waiting for fifteen minutes when

8. Banquets are frequently thrown to honor guests in a Chinese <u>home, they often feature</u> shark fin as the main dish.

   (A) home, they often feature

   (B) home; often feature

   (C) home and often feature

   (D) home and they often feature

   (E) home, these often feature

9. <u>Many wealthy taxpayers pay</u> less than ten percent of their annual incomes to the government, some middle-income taxpayers pay a much larger percentage annually.

   (A) Many wealthy taxpayers pay

   (B) However, many wealthy taxpayers pay

   (C) With many wealthy taxpayers which pay

   (D) Many a wealthy taxpayer pays

   (E) Although many wealthy taxpayers pay

10. Mysteriously beautiful, the Nepalese shrine <u>inlaid with semi-precious stones</u> rare enough to honor the spiritual essence of the Buddha.

    (A) inlaid with semi-precious stones

    (B) inlaid with semi-precious stones which are

    (C) being inlaid with semi-precious stones that are

    (D) is inlaid with semi-precious stones

    (E) inlaid with semi-precious stones, these are

GO ON TO THE NEXT PAGE

KAPLAN

11. Most western European countries have decreased their consumption of fossil <u>fuels, a number of eastern European countries, however, have</u> not done so.

   (A) fuels, a number of eastern European countries, however, have

   (B) fuels, however a number of eastern European countries have not done so.

   (C) fuels, while on the other hand a number of eastern European countries have not done so

   (D) fuels; a number of eastern European countries, however, have not done so

   (E) fuels, a number, however, of eastern European countries have not done so

12. For reasons not fully understood, nearly all children on the island <u>gifted with musical ability</u> so strong they can master any instrument in hours.

   (A) gifted with musical ability

   (B) gifted with musical ability which is

   (C) are gifted with musical ability

   (D) being gifted with musical ability that is

   (E) are gifted with musical abilities, these are

13. <u>That many people believe him to be</u> the most competent and well-informed of all the candidates currently listed on the ballot.

   (A) That many people believe him to be

   (B) Many people believe him to be

   (C) Because many people believe him to be

   (D) That many people believe he is

   (E) That many people believe him

14. Although the superintendent's proposal received crucial support from the teachers, <u>but it was rejected by</u> the school board's widespread influence.

   (A) but it was rejected by

   (B) rejecting it by

   (C) and what made its rejection possible

   (D) it was rejected by

   (E) and it was rejected by

IF YOU FINISH BEFORE TIME IS CALLED, YOU MAY CHECK YOUR WORK ON THIS SECTION ONLY. DO NOT TURN TO ANY OTHER SECTION IN THE TEST.   STOP

KAPLAN

Practice Test One: **Answer Key**

SECTION 1

Essay

SECTION 2

1. E
2. C
3. B
4. B
5. B
6. E
7. C
8. E
9. D
10. B
11. A
12. B
13. B
14. C
15. E
16. B
17. C
18. D
19. E
20. A
21. A
22. D
23. C
24. E

SECTION 3

1. C
2. E
3. A
4. B
5. E
6. D
7. B
8. E
9. A
10. D
11. A
12. D
13. D
14. C
15. A
16. C
17. D
18. A
19. E
20. B

SECTION 4

1. D
2. D
3. A
4. C
5. E
6. A
7. B
8. A
9. E
10. C
11. B
12. C

13. E
14. A
15. C
16. D
17. D
18. C
19. A
20. E
21. B
22. A
23. C
24. D

SECTION 5

1. C
2. B
3. B
4. D
5. C
6. D
7. D
8. A
9. .127
10. 9.5 or 19/2
11. 84 or 96
12. 8
13. 45/4 or 11.2 or 11.3
14. 4
15. 1/16 or .062 or .063
16. 1/8 or .125
17. 2,025
18. 4/7 or .571

SECTION 6

1. E
2. A
3. C
4. D
5. C
6. A
7. B
8. B
9. E
10. B
11. B
12. D
13. B
14. B
15. B
16. B
17. D
18. D
19. B
20. D
21. A
22. C
23. E
24. C
25. B
26. B
27. E
28. C
29. A
30. A
31. A
32. A
33. D

34. B
35. B

SECTION 7

1. B
2. C
3. C
4. B
5. E
6. A
7. B
8. D
9. E
10. A
11. B
12. C
13. D
14. B
15. E
16. A
17. C
18. C
19. D

SECTION 8

1. B
2. A
3. D
4. A
5. D
6. C
7. C
8. D
9. B
10. C
11. C
12. D
13. E
14. C
15. B
16. C

SECTION 9

1. E
2. A
3. D
4. A
5. D
6. C
7. E
8. C
9. E
10. D
11. D
12. C
13. B
14. D

Answers and Explanations

SECTION 1

6 Essay

I believe that a person's destiny is the result of hard work, not luck. One example that convinces me of this is someone I admire a lot, Michelle Kwan. I've read a lot about her and I know she has to work hard to keep in shape, develop routines, and to face the pressure of competition. She has also suffered some injuries, but she hasn't let them stop her from reaching her goals. Since the middle of the 1990s Michelle has won titles at World, National, and Olympic figure skating events. She is the only woman to lose a world title and then regain it two times. Michelle is able to acomplish all these things because she sets goals for herself and then works toward them with discipline and determination.

Probably if you have seen Michelle skate you have noticed that she always wears the same necklace. Its a Chinese good luck symbol that her grandmother gave her. Michelle will never part from it. But she wears it because of her deep feelings for her grandmother, not for luck. Even though its a good luck symbol, I don't think Michelle acomplished her goals by being lucky. Her hard work is what got her all the fame and medals.

So, as I said at the beginning, I believe that a person's destiny is the result of hard work, not luck. Since I believe this and I can see how Michelle's hard work has led to her sucess, I try to work hard, too. I set goals for myself and then put in the work that I need to, without expecting that success will be easy, or a gift from fate. Right now my goal is to get good grades and get into a good college.

Grader's Comments

All essays are evaluated on 4 basic criteria: Topic, Support, Organization, and Language. Though it is on the short side for a 6 essay, it sticks to the topic throughout. The author supports the thesis quite well by explaining how hard work has actually resulted in achieving the goals that Kwan set

for herself—a completely relevant and responsive example. This strong follow-through on an argument the writer feels strongly about raises the essay above mere technical competence.

This essay is highly organized. Paragraph 2, which could seem at first like a digression, is actually support for the author's thesis. The language is pretty good, though not exceptional. The vocabulary is straightforward and not challenging. There are a few grammatical and spelling errors, but not enough to mar the overall effect: Paragraph 1, sentence 3 is not parallel. *Accomplish* and *success* are misspelled. *Its* is misused for *it's* twice.

4 Essay

I agree that people need to work hard for their destiny and not rely on luck. When I think of people who have worked hard to get their destiny, I always think of Abraham Lincoln. He started out very poor in a log cabin in Kentucky, but he became President of the United States. He did this because he worked very hard instead of hoping good things would just happen to him.

Lincoln didn't go to school too much because his father wanted him to work on the farm. Resulting from this, Lincoln had to teach himself law by reading law books on his own. He worked hard among the people of Illinois to get into Congress. In 1860 Lincoln was elected as the 16th President of the United States. This was a result of his hard work.

Lincoln is a great example of the statement above that destiny or fate is not dependent on luck, but rather is the result of planning and effort.

Grader's Comments

All essays are evaluated on 4 basic criteria: Topic, Support, Organization, and Language. This essay is on the short side for a 4, but it sticks to the topic throughout. The essay is not very well developed. The author tends to repeat thoughts rather than develop them. He also does something that should be avoided—his final paragraph is almost entirely a repeat of the statement. This adds nothing to the author's reasoning, and uses too much of the very limited time to write. The author supports his thesis by explaining how Lincoln studied law and worked on his own. However, this is not filled in with any detail.

This essay is well organized, with each paragraph covering a separate idea. The meaning is always clear, but the author's language is sometimes below standard. For example, in paragraph 2, sentence 2 "Resulting from this" is not idiomatic. There are no misspellings in the essay.

1 Essay

For me its true that people have to work hard to get their destiny. Roger Clemons is the greatest pitcher ever and he works very hard. Someday I would like to be like Roger Clemons. I want to pitch in the majors. I practise real hard to get to do this.

On my last game I almost had a perfect no-hitter. To bad, though, that the last hitter got a single. But my coach said I did real good anyway and we did win the game. The score was 5 to 4.

In conclusion, I want to say again that as far as the statement above, I beleive its true.

Grader's Comments

All essays are evaluated on 4 basic criteria: Topic, Support, Organization, and Language. This author starts out with promise. He states his opinion and then offers an example to support his opinion. Unfortunately, he digresses to discuss his desire to succeed as a pitcher and his baseball record. The essay offers little support for the author's opinion. While this essay is fairly well organized, it's mostly off topic.

The author's language is unsophisticated and, in some cases, substandard. There are grammatical and spelling errors that break the flow of thought: "My coach said I did real good. . ." "Its" is misused for "it's" twice. "Practice" and "believe" are misspelled. "To" is misused for "too."

SECTION 2

1. E

It's easy enough to understand that insurers don't like to insure property in places where natural disasters are likely to happen. The term *prone to* in (E) means *having a tendency to*, so it is correct.

2. C

If it took Roman legions three years to seize Masada, we can predict that they spent a long time *surrounding or isolating* the mountain *fortress or stronghold* of Masada before they were finally able to take it. (C) is the best choice. (B) *assailed*, meaning *attacked*, would make sense in the first blank, and (E) *stronghold* and (A) *bastion* would fit, too. But (A), (B), and (E)'s second-position words don't make sense when plugged in.

3. B

If the senator was *unlike his calmer, more easygoing colleagues* and *ready to quarrel at the slightest provocation*, it's fair to infer that the senator was short-tempered or extremely irritable. The best choice is (B)—*irascible*.

4. B

You don't have to know that Genghis Khan was a violent dictator to get this question right. What's important to know is that the first word of the sentence, *although*, implies that the two blanks have to contain words that contrast with each other. (B) is the best choice—although historians had thought that Genghis Khan was a *despotic* potentate, new research shows that many of his subjects nevertheless *revered* him. Although (A) *tyrannical* is synonymous with *despotic*, (A)'s second-blank choice, *abhorred*, doesn't provide the predicted contrast. Choice (C) *venerated* doesn't really contrast with *redundant*. And in (E), it doesn't make sense to say that Khan's subjects *invoked* him despite his *peremptory* reputation.

5. B

The word *because* in the middle of the sentence lets us know that the words in the blanks will be consistent in meaning, which means that they will share the same type of charge. We can predict two positive words, like *Jill was appreciated by her employees because she often forgave the fact that they were lazy*, or two negative words like *Jill*

*was disliked by her employees because she often scolded
them* for being lazy. (B) matches the latter prediction—Jill
was *loathed* by her employees because she often *berated*
them for not working hard enough. No other choice
besides (B) contains two like charges.

6.   E

If *reconstructing the skeletons of extinct species like
dinosaurs . . . requires much patience and effort by
paleontologists*, we can predict that such an activity is a
painstaking or tough, demanding process. (E) *exacting* is
our best choice.

7.   C

Because of disease and the destruction of their habitat,
koalas are now found only in isolated parts of eucalyptus
forests. The word in the blank must mean something like
killed off or *destroyed*, since things like *disease and habitat destruction* are destructive processes. (C) is our best
choice—*nearly decimated or wiped out by disease and
habitat destruction*, koalas are now found only in isolated
parts of eucalyptus forests. (A) *dispersed,* meaning *scattered,* may have been a little tempting, but there's no reason to assume that the koalas were scattered around the
forests due to *disease and habitat destruction.*

8.   E

Looking at the first blank first, if there were *internal power
struggles* in the government, then it's likely that the government had something like *deep ideological differences
or conflicts*. For the second blank, we can predict that
these conflicts and power struggles harmed or crippled the
government. Although choice (C)'s first-blank choice, *distortions,* sounds negative, like *differences or conflicts,*
choices (A) and (E) make more sense. We can easily
imagine *deep ideological disputes* or *deep ideological divisions* going hand in hand with *internal power struggles,*
but it's hard to imagine ideological *distortions.* Now we can
turn to (A)'s and (E)'s second-blank choices. (A) doesn't
make sense given the context of the sentence—why would
*deep ideological disputes and internal power struggles
facilitate the government*? (E) is the best choice—*deep
ideological divisions and internal power struggles paralyzed the government.*

Music and Language Passages

9.   D

The author includes lines 8–9 as evidence that in the
Romantic era, folks believed that music by itself could sig-
nify emotion (D). There is no evidence in the Passage 1 to
support choice (A). While you know what the perception
was during the Romantic era, the author doesn't mention
the current perception, so you can't support this choice.
Although the author states that language is used functionally as opposed to music, this claim is not made specifically
for Romantic music in these lines, (B). (C) is too
extreme—the author is not saying that Romantic music
composers always used music to connote emotions. (E)
expresses a negativity absent from the passage.

10. B

The prefix "extra" covers a lot of ground. Look at the context.
The sentence is about music "standing by itself" so "extra-
musical references" must be information from non-musical
sources. (A) is the common meaning. Nothing in the context suggests the author would consider them better than
music (D), just different.

11. A

Both authors mention the symbolic nature of music and
language (A). In Passage 1, the author says, . . .*Nettl has
concluded that like language, music is a 'series of symbols.'* The author of Passage 2 says something similar in the
last line of the passage. Only the author of Passage 2
compares both to subdivided sections, (B). Only the author
of Passage 1 compares both to functional parts, (C). Clues
are never mentioned, (D). (E) fits Passage 2 pretty well,
but Passage 1 never links emotions and language.

12. B

Remember that the wrong answer here will be something
that the authors agree on, or something that is not mentioned at all in one of the passages. Author 1 would agree
with (B), whereas author 2 would disagree. Author 2
would agree with (A) and (E), but you don't know how
author 1 would feel; she might agree, or she might disagree. Author 2 would probably disagree with (C) since
context is so important, but there's no telling what author
1 would think about the statement. (D) is too extreme—
you don't know that author 1 would agree with this.

The Twain Passage

This excerpt from Mark Twain's *Life on the Mississippi* should be amusing and easy to read. All the humor comes from the same technique—using deadpan, matter-of-fact language to describe the exaggerated daydreams and jealousies of a boy's life. The central point here is the author's envy of the engineer, and many of the questions focus on this. The author starts with his own glamorous ideas about steamboating, then spends most of the passage on the show-off engineer. The passage finishes with the author's own failure to find work as a pilot. The slightly old-fashioned style isn't hard to follow, but several questions focus on the author's figurative use of words.

13. B

The key word in the sentence is *supposed*. Of course, a justice of the peace *doesn't* possess unlimited power, but because of inexperience, the author *supposed* he did. (B) accurately uses *naive* (inexperienced, gullible) to characterize the author's misconception. Three of the wrong choices assume that the father really *did* have unlimited powers and explain this in different ways—frontier justice (A and D) and public support (C). (E) mistakenly views the boy's description of his father as an indication that the boy's childhood environment was harsh.

14. C

Distinction has several meanings, including those in (A), (B), (C), and (E). The key to its use here is context: In the previous sentence the author is talking about his naive ideas of his father's great power. *Prestige,* (C), suggesting high status and honor, fits this context; the other three don't. (D) is not a meaning of *distinction* at all.

15. E

This question asks about the literal meaning of the sentence, but inference and context help, too. The sentence explains that the author wanted the job because a deck hand was *conspicuous*, or easily seen. The previous sentence stresses standing *where all my old comrades could see me*, so you can deduce that the author wants to be seen and admired in what he imagines is a glamorous profession (E). (A) and (B) invent advantages that are not mentioned and miss the humor by suggesting common-sense economic motivations. (C) assumes that if the author could be seen by his *old comrades* in the first job,

he must want not to be seen by them in a different job; but this is false, since he'd be *conspicuous* in the second job, too. (D) brings in an ambition—becoming a pilot—that the author doesn't develop until the end of the passage.

16. B

Again, context helps you to figure out the answer to the question. The *Sunday-school* reference is explained in the next sentence. The engineer had been *worldly*—which is what Sunday-school probably taught students not to be—and the author had been *just the reverse*. In other words, the author followed his Sunday-school teachings and the engineer didn't—yet the engineer gets the glory. The underlying idea is that this was unjust, choice (B). (A) is never mentioned. (C) takes the Sunday-school reference literally and misses the humorous tone. (D) invents an ambition that the author never mentions; his reaction is pure envy, not frustrated ambition. (E) misconstrues the reference to the engineer as *worldly*; it means he didn't take Sunday-school seriously, not that he was *unscrupulous* (dishonest or crooked).

17. C

To get this question, you need to read the sentence that follows. The engineer was not generous because he sat about where *we all could see him and envy him*. The implication is that great people should be generous by not showing off or (C) *flaunting* their success. (A) refers to the Sunday-school comment, but that was about undeserved greatness, not lack of generosity. (B) and (D) interpret generous in the literal sense of not caring for money, but the author is using the word figuratively. (E) relates to the author's unfulfilled desire to work on a steamboat, but the engineer is not thinking about the author, he is just showing off.

18. D

The engineer does everything for the purpose of showing off. He talks the jargon of the trade to make himself look knowledgeable, or (D) sophisticated. Reading between the lines, we realize he's not an expert (A), and doesn't care about knowledge for its own sake (B). His (C) ignorance on other subjects is not mentioned; in fact, he has a working knowledge of St. Louis. (E) takes literally the phrase about how the engineer *forgot common people could not understand*—he couldn't communicate effectively. But the author says the engineer talked *as if* he forgot common people. In other words, he didn't fail to communicate, he chose not to, to impress others.

19. E

The first four choices are all common meanings of *consideration,* but the context makes it clear that the figurative use in (E) is meant. The boys had *consideration* because they knew something about St. Louis, but their glory is over because the engineer knows much more. Prestige, respect, or (E) *reputation* supplies the meaning that fits. Boys are not likely to have the qualities of *generosity, deliberation, contemplation,* or *unselfishness* as a result of knowing a little about St. Louis.

20. A

The context makes it clear that the engineer had, or at least seemed to have, much more familiarity with St. Louis than the other boys with their *vague knowledge;* their *glory* is ended because he can talk rings around them about St. Louis (A). There's no indication that (B) *St. Louis has changed* or that the boys had been lying—their knowledge was *vague,* not false (D). Reading between the lines, it's clear that travel to St. Louis was still rare enough to seem enviable (E). As for choice (C), the passage implies just the opposite.

21. A

With his *hair oil . . . showy brass watch chain, [and] leather belt,* the engineer was obviously out to impress (A). The next sentence confirms that, telling us *no girl could withstand his charms.* The author never says the young man's dress is typical (B). (C) and (E) are both wrong; the emphasis here is on the engineer's charms, not the author's wardrobe or fashion ideas. (D) won't work because the engineer's behavior is as showy and superficial as his clothes.

22. D

As often in these questions, wrong choices give flatfooted, literal interpretations where the author is being humorous. (A) misunderstands the reference to Providence—the author is criticizing Providence, not thanking it, because it has spared an *undeserving reptile,* the engineer. So the author feels resentment, or (D) *outrage,* because the engineer's good luck seems *undeserved.* Choice (B) sounds believable at first, but the passage doesn't emphasize the

lucky escape—it focuses on people's sense that the engineer got better than he deserved. (C) and (E) are never mentioned.

23. C

The passage focuses on the author's ambition to work on a steamboat and his envy of the engineer. This makes (C) and (D) the strongest choices, so you need to decide between them. Looking at (D), the passage certainly emphasizes the engineer's *boastfulness,* but only within the framework of the author's dreams and ambitions (paragraphs 1 and 5) and the author's reactions to the engineer. So (C) describes the *whole* passage whereas (D) describes only the long central paragraphs. In a *major purpose/major focus* question, the answer that sums up the *whole* passage will be correct. The life of the town (A) is barely suggested. (B) is wrong because the passage's events don't end in success—although in reality, Mark Twain did go on to become a pilot. The author's *conflict with his parents* (E) is mentioned only briefly, toward the end of paragraph 4.

24. E

The last paragraph discusses the author's failed attempts to become a pilot and his daydreams that he will still become one, so (E) works best. Mates and clerks are mentioned as ignoring the author, but he never considers becoming either a mate or a clerk (A), looking for some other job (B), giving up his aim of being a pilot (C), or asking for his parents' forgiveness (D).

SECTION 3

1. C

Use the formula Percent × Whole = Part.

30 percent is $\frac{30}{100}$, or $\frac{3}{10}$. So $\frac{3}{10} \times x =$ part, and choice (C) is correct.

2. E

$2 \times 10^4 = 20{,}000$. $5 \times 10^3 = 5{,}000$. $6 \times 10^2 = 600$. $4 \times 10^1 = 40$. So the sum is 25,640.

3. A

Find the length of each segment, and then subtract the length of XY from the length of YZ. Y is at 3 on the number line and Z is at 8, so the length of YZ is $8 - 3 = 5$. X is at 1 on the number line and Y is at 3, so the length of XY is $3 - 1 = 2$. So the length of YZ is $5 - 2 = 3$ greater than the length of XY.

4. B

To find the value of x, you need to change 16 into a power of 2: $16 = 2^4$. Therefore, $2^{x+1} = 2^4$. So $x + 1 = 4$, or $x = 3$.

5. E

The number of degrees around a point is 360. Therefore:

$$90 + 30 + 2a + 30 + a = 360$$
$$150 + 3a = 360$$
$$3a = 210$$
$$a = 70$$

6. D

If a machine labels 150 bottles in 20 minutes, it labels 15 bottles every 2 minutes. To label 60, or 4×15, bottles would take 4×2, or 8 minutes.

7. B

To find the next multiple of 3, simply add 3 to the expression: $x - 1 + 3 = x + 2$, choice (B).

If this is unclear, pick a number for x. If $x = 4$, $4 - 1 = 3$; the next greatest multiple of 3 is 6. Plugging 4 for x into each answer choice, we find that only choice (B) gives us 6.

8. E

Since x leaves a remainder of 4 when divided by 5, it must end in either a 4 or a 9, so choice (B) can be eliminated. Since x leaves no remainder when divided by 9, it is evenly divisible by 9. Of the remaining choices, only 144 is divisible by 9.

9. A

The sum of the lengths of any two sides of a triangle must be greater than the length of the third side. So $AB + AC$ must be greater than BC; $6 + x > 12$. If $x = 6$, $6 + 6 = 12$ is not greater than 12, so x cannot equal 6.

10. D

Number of terms × average = sum of the terms. For the first group, $3 \times 40 = 120$, so the sum of 20, 70, and x is 120. For the second group, $4 \times 50 = 200$, so $20 + 70 + x + y = 200$. Since the sum of the first three terms is 120, $120 + y = 200$, $y = 80$.

11. A

Looking at the graph, you can see that the number of books borrowed in January was 300. To find the total number of books borrowed during the first six months of the year, add the values of each bar: $300 + 350 + 400 + 450 + 500 + 400 = 2,400$ books. So the number of books borrowed in January is $\frac{300}{2,400}$ or $\frac{1}{8}$ of the total number of books borrowed during the first six months of the year.

12. D

We're told that 40% of $r = s$. The value of 40% of r is 4 times the value of 10% of r, so 10% of $r = \frac{1}{4} \times s = \frac{s}{4}$.

An alternative method is to pick numbers. Since you're dealing with percents, let $r = 100$. 40% of $r = s$, so 40% of $100 = 40 = s$. You're asked which answer choice is equal to 10% of r; 10% of $100 = 10$. Now plug the value for s into the answer choices to see which ones give you 10:

(A) $4s = 4 \times 40 = 160$. Eliminate.

(B) $2s = 2 \times 40 = 80$. Eliminate.

(C) $\frac{s}{2} = \frac{40}{2} = 20$. Eliminate.

(D) $\frac{s}{4} = \frac{40}{4} = 10$. Works!

(E) $\frac{s}{8} = \frac{40}{8} = 5$. Eliminate.

Since (D) is the only choice that produces the desired result, it is the correct answer. But remember, when picking numbers you need to check all the answer choices; if more than one works, pick new numbers and plug them in until only one answer choice works.

13. D

The two overlapping triangles share a common angle, which we can label $p°$. Since the interior angles of any triangle add up to 180°, we have two equations: $x + z + p = 180$ and $y + r + p = 180$. Subtracting p from both sides of each equation, we have $x + z = 180 − p$ and $y + r = 180 − p$. Since $x + z$ and $y + r$ both equal the same quantity, $x + z$ and $y + r$ must be equal to each other. Rearranging $x + z = y + r$, we get $x − r = y − z$, which matches choice (D).

14. C

Check the answer choices. If a number has even one factor (not including 1 and itself) that is not a prime number, eliminate that choice:

(A) 12: 4 is not prime. Eliminate.

(B) 18: 6 is not prime. Eliminate.

(C) 21: 3 and 7 are its only other factors, and both are prime. Correct!

(D) 24: 6 is not prime. Eliminate.

(E) 28: 4 is not prime. Eliminate.

15. A

Try different possible values for x and y, eliminating the incorrect answer choices. Since x is multiplied by 3, let's begin with the smallest positive integer value for x: 1. If $3(1) + y = 14$, then $y = 11$, and $x + y = 12$. So choice (E) is out.

If $3(2) + y = 14$, then $y = 8$, and $x + y = 10$. So choice (D) is out. If $3(3) + y = 14$, then $y = 5$, and $x + y = 8$. So choice (C) is also out. If you're really clever, you'll see at this point that answer choice (A) is impossible (which makes it the right choice). After all, the next smallest possible value of x is 4, and since x and y must both be positive integers, neither one can equal 0. (Zero is *not* positive—or negative.) So the sum of x and y must be greater than 4. (Sure enough, if $x = 4$, then $y = 2$, and $x + y = 6$, eliminating choice (B) as well.)

16. C

When the r cards are distributed, there are 8 left over, so the number of cards distributed is $r − 8$. Divide the number of cards distributed by the number of people. Since there are s people, each person gets $\frac{r − 8}{s}$ cards.

Another approach is to pick numbers. Let $r = 58$ and $s = 10$; if $58 − 8$ or 50 cards were distributed evenly among 10 people, each would receive 5 cards. Plug the values you picked for r and s into the answer choices to see which ones give you 5:

(A) $\frac{s}{8 − r} = \frac{10}{8 − 58} = −\frac{1}{5}$. Eliminate.

(B) $\frac{r − s}{8} = \frac{58 − 10}{8} = 6$. Eliminate.

(C) $\frac{r − 8}{s} = \frac{58 − 8}{10} = 5$. Works!

(D) $s − 8r = 10 − (8 \times 58) = −454$. Eliminate.

(E) $rs − 8 = (58 \times 10) − 8 = 572$. Eliminate.

Since (C) is the only answer choice that gives you 5, it is the correct answer. But be sure to check all the answer choices when picking numbers.

17. D

Check each answer choice to see which doesn't work:

(A) $\frac{d}{2}$: If d is an even integer, say 2, then $\frac{d}{2} = \frac{2}{2} = 1$ is an integer. Eliminate.

(B) $\frac{\sqrt{d}}{2}$: If d is a perfect square with an even square root, say $d = 4$, then $\frac{\sqrt{4}}{2} = \frac{2}{2} = 1$ is an integer.

Eliminate.

(C) $2d$: This will always produce an even integer; if $d = 3$, $2d = 2 \times 3 = 6$ is an integer. Eliminate.

(D) $d\sqrt{2}$ CANNOT produce an integer. An integer would result if $\sqrt{2}$ is multiplied by another multiple of $\sqrt{2}$, which is impossible because d must be an integer. So (D) is correct.

Let's check (E) just to make sure.

(E) $d + 2$: This will always produce an integer; if $d = 5$, $d + 2 = 5 + 2 = 7$ is an integer. Eliminate.

18. A

The area of a triangle $\frac{1}{2}$(base × height). Since the area of

$\triangle ABC$ is 6, $\frac{1}{2}(AB \times BC) = 6$. If you consider CD as the base

of $\triangle ACD$, you will notice that its height is represented by

altitude AB. So the area of $\triangle ACD = \frac{1}{2}(CD \times AB)$. Since

$CD = BC$, the area of $\triangle ACD$ can be expressed as

$\frac{1}{2}(BC \times AB)$, which you know equals 6.

19. E

Each of the five surfaces is 60 by 180 centimeters, so tiles measuring 12 by 18 centimeters can be laid down in 5 rows of 10 to exactly cover one surface. There are 5 surfaces so $5 \times 5 \times 10 = 250$ tiles are needed.

20. B

The perimeter of triangle $ACD = AD + AB + BC + CD$. You are given the lengths of BC and CD, so you need to find the lengths of AD and AB. Angle DBC is a right angle because it is supplementary to angle DBA, one of the 4 right angles of square $ABDE$. Since right triangle DBC has sides of length 8 and 10, you should recognize it as a 6-8-10 right triangle (a multiple of the 3-4-5 right triangle) and realize that $BD = 6$. (If you didn't recognize this, you could have used the Pythagorean theorem to find the length of BD.) BD is also a side of the square, and since all sides of a square are equal, $AB = 6$.

So triangle DBA is an isosceles right triangle with sides in the ratio of $1:1:\sqrt{2}$. That means hypotenuse AD is equal to the length of a side times $\sqrt{2}$, so $AD = 6\sqrt{2}$. Now you can find the perimeter of triangle ACD: $6\sqrt{2} + 6 + 8 + 10 = 24 + 6\sqrt{2}$.

SECTION 4

1. D

The use of the word *and* tells us that we're looking for a word to fill the first blank which is consistent with *scarcity of rain*—a word like *dry*. We can, therefore, eliminate (A) and (C) at once. Since farming conditions are *bad*, our second blank should express the idea that there's no point in trying to work there. By that criterion, choices (B) and (E) can be eliminated. This leaves us with (D) *future*. (D)'s first word, *infertile*, also fits perfectly, so (D) is the correct answer.

2. D

The structural clue in this sentence is *not simply . . . but*, which suggests that the students were doing something even worse than ignoring the rules. The only word that fits here is *flouting*, choice (D).

3. A

The word *while* following the comma in the second part of the sentence tells us that there will be a contrast between what some critics believe about dadaism and what *others* "insist the movement was." The best choice is (A)—"some critics believe that the *zenith* of modern art came with dadaism, while others insist the movement was a *sham*." Other choices have single words that would make sense in one of the blanks, but none of the pairs except (A) expresses the contrast that is implied by the sentence.

4. C

In this question you are asked to make a logical connection between two parts of a sentence. It is clear that the content of the journalist's article either had no impact, in which case there was little or no response from the public, or it attracted a great deal of attention and was followed by a lot of correspondence. (C) is the correct answer. The author would never have thought her article was *controversial* were it not for the *spate* of correspondence. The other answer choices are wrong because they sound contradictory when plugged into the sentence. For example, in choice (A), if the article were *interesting*, one would expect it to be followed by a lot of correspondence—not by a *dearth*, or lack of it. In choice (D), if the article were *commonplace* (ordinary), why would an *influx* of letters follow its publication?

5.   E

If many readers have difficulty following Descartes's complex, intricately woven arguments, then it's likely that his writings are something like *complicated, esoteric,* or *obscure.* The best choice is (E) *abstruse.*

Jellyfish

6.   A

Since it's clear that a jellyfish couldn't have any feelings about its encounter with humans, the author is apparently using this image to make the reader smile (A). (Even if you don't think it's funny, you should note that this is the author's intent.) The author doesn't ask us to feel sympathy for either the jellyfish or humans (B), and doesn't discuss whether or not humans are afraid of jellyfish (C). Although the author does discuss the danger of jellyfish, the quote in question doesn't accomplish that purpose. The passage never discusses how humans or jellyfish react to these encounters (E).

7.   B

The third and fourth sentences contains the key to answering this question. You learn there that the relatively common encounters are not surprising because jellyfish *live in every ocean in the world* (B). (A), (C), (D), and (E) are all details from the passage, but none of them help to explain why encounters are so common.

Khyber Pass

8.   A

For this question, eliminate everything that *does* appear, and you'll be left with the answer. The passage answers (B) (Pakistan and Afghanistan), (C) (53 kilometers), (D) (was used in several wars), and (E) (two roads pass through today). The origin of the pass (A), is never mentioned.

9.   E

Function questions ask you to consider what a statement adds to the author's reasoning. To find the answer, consider what claim or argument the phrase relates to and what it adds to the author's argument. Here, the word *snake* implies a twisting, turning path, like a snake (E). Although the Khyber Pass connects two points, the word *snake*

implies a winding path (A). Although crossing the Khyber Pass may be dangerous (B), that doesn't follow from the word *snake.* (C) is the opposite of what you're looking for; the word implies that the pass is anything but direct. (D) comes from the wrong part of the passage. The short length of the Khyber Pass is mentioned earlier in the passage, but this is not why the author stated that the path *snakes.*

The Time Passage

Next up is a fairly abstract science passage. This particular passage is perhaps a little bit harder than the ones you're going to encounter on the test—but don't be intimidated by the subject matter. Even if your passage is written by a Nobel Prize winner, it's going to contain ideas that you can relate to and probably some ideas that you've seen before. The topic of the passage is how difficult it is to comprehend long stretches of time. Paragraph 2 tells us that our minds aren't built to handle the idea of thousands of years passing. We have some conception of the past through the art, writing, and photography of previous generations, but the scale of longer time periods eludes us. Paragraphs 4 and 5 attempt to bridge this gap by providing a few everyday yardsticks; the time the human race has been around is compared to a few seconds in a week, or a few letters in a book. Essentially, that's all you need to take from your first reading of the passage; you can come back to the details later.

10. C

Before writing, we're told, the wisdom of generations was passed down in two ways—verbally, and *to a lesser extent,* in pictures, carvings, and statues. This means that the wisdom of the past was transmitted less frequently by nonverbal means and thus (C) *more frequently by the spoken word than by other means.* Choices (A) and (B) *distort* this idea. Nowhere are we told that wisdom was rejected, and since spoken words *and* pictures were both used, it was obviously not an all or nothing proposition. (E) doesn't make much sense. How could there be an emphasis on science before writing existed? (D), finally, makes no sense at all—the author never says that all ancient wisdom was fiction.

11. B

This is a Little Picture question asking about the purpose of a detail. The question asks why the author discusses the impact of writing. Looking at the lines around the line reference given, we're told that writing has made the transmission of information about the past a lot more precise and extensive. Pictures and photography are also mentioned as ways in which the experience of the past has been passed down. So choice (B)'s correct here—writing is mentioned as an *example* of how cultures record knowledge about the past. (A) is a distortion—the author is showing us something about the past, not why we remember hardly anything. He never implies any criticism of preliterate cultures, so choice (C) is out too. Choices (D) and (E) are wrong because the author never mentions them in the context referred to or in the whole passage.

12. C

Another Vocabulary-in-Context question. The word *ready* can mean several things—choices (A), (C), (D), and (E) are all possible meanings. In this context, however, it most nearly means *immediate,* choice (C). In the sentence before the cited line, the author says *there is no simple way* to understand vast stretches of time. In the sentence following the cited line, the author compares the way we understand time to the way a blind man *laboriously* constructs a picture of his surroundings. This implies that our understanding of time is a difficult and time-consuming task, not something we can do *readily* or *immediately.*

13. E

Another question asking about the *purpose behind* part of the author is argument. Give the context a quick scan. Once again, the author's talking about how difficult it is to understand vast stretches of time. We're told that it's like a blind man building up a sensory picture of his surroundings. This is an *indirect* process, so choice (E) is right. Choice (C) is dealt with later in paragraph 4, so you can eliminate it right away. (A) is too sweeping. The author never says that human beings are *completely unable to comprehend time.* (B) and (D) have nothing to do with the passage.

14. A

Inference skills are required here. What is the author's underlying point in mentioning the Big Bang and the Cambrian Period? The author *introduces* this discussion in the cited passage by saying that *a week* provides a better yardstick for the age of the Earth than a day. The Big Bang

and the Cambrian Period are used as examples to support this point. So (A) is right—it's the point about the time scale that the author's trying to demonstrate. Choices (D) and (E) both distort the point in different ways. The author is not suggesting that the time scale of a day should be totally abandoned—just that the week is a better scale. The development of (B) *agriculture* is another supporting example like the Big Bang and the Cambrian Period, but it's not the author's central point here. Finally, *fossils* have nothing to do with the question at hand, so (C) is easily eliminated.

15. C

A more straightforward comprehension question this time. When we go back to the lines referred to, we're told about the problem with linear maps: When you produce one that's big enough to show us on it, the map becomes too big to study and reproduce conveniently. (C) gets the right paraphrase here. Notice especially the match up in synonyms for *convenient reproduction* and *examination*. (A), (B), and (E) aren't supported here—there's nothing about *overlapping* periods, *scientific standards,* or ignorance about *pre-Cambrian times* in the passage. (D) doesn't address the problem. The question is about getting our human experience on the map.

16. D

What's the overall point the author is trying to prove? The big picture is that life started on Earth so long ago that it is difficult for us to comprehend. Everything that follows is meant to illustrate this point, including the time scales. Don't let the material confuse you. The point is (D)—*the immensity of time* since the origin of *life.* (C) is tricky to reject because it's an aspect of the larger argument, but it's not the whole point. The other wrong choices mention issues that the author hardly touches on. In paragraphs 4–6, the author's *not* concerned with getting dates right (A), the question of how life actually began (B), or the (E) development of communication.

The Susan B. Anthony Passage

This humanities passage is from a speech by Susan B. Anthony, a 19th-century women's rights leader. Anthony admits at the outset that she was recently charged with the *crime* of voting. Her intention is to prove that her vote was no crime, but rather the exercise of her Constitutional rights, which no state should be allowed to impinge upon. This generates the passage's big idea: that Anthony—and by extension all women—should be allowed to vote. You may have found Anthony's style a little dated or confusing. Don't worry; the questions will help you focus on specific details.

17. D

To answer this question, you have to consider the entire context of the speech. Anthony reasons that all citizens automatically have the right to the vote, so the word is a part of her principal argument, and her audience would recognize that as soon as the word was spoken. Since she wants to persuade her audience on an issue of great importance to her, she wouldn't be starting out by trying to irritate or offend them (C). But the other choices don't reflect the context at all.

18. C

The important thing here is to see what exactly Anthony is saying. The question stem is keyed to the first paragraph. In the second sentence she states that she *not only committed no crime, but . . . simply exercised my citizen's rights, guaranteed me . . . by the National Constitution.* The words *no crime* are the first important clue. You can immediately rule out (A) and (E) because they say she believes the act was illegal. The second part of the line discusses the Constitution, so (C) is clearly a restatement of her argument. (B) and (D) both make sense, but she does not state these points in the first paragraph. Therefore, they are wrong.

19. A

The most common meaning of *promote* is to move up to a higher position, rank, or job. This doesn't make sense, though, in the phrase *promote the general welfare.* *General welfare* means the good of all people, so (A), *further*, makes the most sense. (B) *organize* and (C) *publicize* both could apply to the general welfare but not as well as (A). They refer more to promotion as you would do with a concert or sports event. (D) *commend* means *praise*, which seems silly in the context given, as does (E) *motivate.*

> **Hint:** In Vocabulary-in-Context questions, the right answer is usually not the most common meaning of the given word. Be sure to reread the context.

20. E

Anthony points out that no subgroup was excluded by the wording of the preamble of the Constitution. *. . . we formed it . . . to secure [the blessings of liberty]; not to the half of ourselves . . . but to . . . women as well as men.* Therefore, (E) is correct. *All people deserve to enjoy the rights* of the *Constitution.* Anthony never claims that the Founding Fathers plotted to deny women their rights (A). (B) is incorrect because the author's concern is women's rights and not rights of any other group. Although *some male citizens may still be denied basic rights,* (B) goes against the gist of what is being said. (C) is like (A) in that it's a claim Anthony never makes. Finally, though (D) is a point that Anthony does make, she doesn't make it until the next paragraph.

21. B

We're still looking at the same part of the passage. Look at the structure of the quoted sentence: *We didn't do it only for X, but for X and Y. Posterity* means *future generations*, which would include men and women. So the *X*, the *half of our posterity*, refers to the posterity of those who already enjoy the blessings of liberty. In other words, men. (B) is the right choice. (A) has nothing to do with what Anthony is discussing. Since the construction of the sentence makes it clear that the *half of our posterity* is not the whole of those who want to vote, (C) is out. There's no way of saying that one-half of the people are and will be opponents of women's rights, so (D) is wrong. (E) wrongly suggests that in the future, one half of the country's population will be members of government.

22. A

Reread the keyed paragraph. Anthony is saying that a state that prohibits women from voting violates federal law—the Constitution. Therefore, it becomes *an odious aristocracy, a hateful oligarchy.* Neither of these things is a democracy. (A) is the correct answer. Anthony mentions rebellion, but she doesn't mean the kind of violent rebellion (B) talks about. (C) is wrong because of the word *remain.* The nation is not and never has been an aristocracy. (D) plays off the same sentence as (B) does, but instead of going too far, it doesn't go far enough. Anthony wants the laws against women voting repealed; she doesn't want them merely discussed. (E) is totally wrong because at no point is Anthony arguing that an aristocracy should be preserved.

23. C

You might readily associate *hardihood* with (A) *endurance* and (B) *vitality,* but a quick check back in context shows you these aren't correct. Anthony says she doesn't believe her opponents would have the ---- to say women aren't *persons.* Saying such an offensive thing would take a lot of *nerve,* choice (C). It might also take a lot of *stupidity* (E), but that's too strong a word, considering Anthony's diplomatic tone.

24. D

The stem keys you to the second to last sentence of the passage. *Abridge* means *deprive,* so Anthony is saying that no state can deprive citizens of their rights. (D) states exactly this. In (A), *privilege* means *luxury,* but voting is a basic right, not a luxury. (B) comes out of nowhere; there's no discussion of courts in this passage. (C) plays off Anthony's reference to *any old law.* She's not talking about *any* outdated laws in this passage; she means any law *that prohibits women from voting.* Anthony never addresses how the laws will be changed, but only that they must be changed, so (E) is out.

SECTION 5

1. C

Subtract 100 from both sides of the equation to find $x = 0$.

2. B

The intersection of X and Y is the set of elements common to X (odds) and to Y (negatives).

3. B

If x and y are both negative numbers and x is less than y, then $\frac{y}{x}$ is a number greater than zero and less than one.

For example, assume that $x = -2$ and $y = -1$. Then $\frac{y}{x} = \frac{1}{2}$. Since $\frac{y}{x}$ must be a positive number, we know that is it greater than zero, so (A) is incorrect. (C) and (D)

are also incorrect, as they are negative and therefore smaller than the positive $\frac{y}{x}$. (E) would be exactly half of $\frac{y}{x}$ and is therefore smaller and incorrect. The only remaining option is (B), which is larger than $\frac{y}{x}$. (Returning to our earlier example, $\frac{x}{y}$ would be 2, which is larger than $\frac{1}{2}$.)

4. D

The small region in the middle represents households with dogs, cats, and fish. The crosshatched region includes all households with dogs and cats except those that also have fish.

5. C

Like many questions about functions, this one looks complex but really just boils down to straightforward substitution. Plug in 3 wherever you see x:

$$f(x) = \frac{(3x^2 - 9)}{(x + 1)}$$
$$f(3) = \frac{(3(3)^2 - 9)}{(3 + 1)}$$
$$f(3) = \frac{(3(9) - 9)}{4}$$
$$f(3) = \frac{(27 - 9)}{4}$$
$$f(3) = \frac{18}{4}$$
$$f(3) = \frac{9}{2}$$

6. D

First, we need to find the length of the line segment AB. It is a vertical line stretching from $(-2, 2)$ to $(-2, -2)$, so its length is $2 - (-2) = 4$. CD is twice this length, so it is $4 \times 2 = 8$ units long. CD stretches from $(-3, 1)$ to $(h, 1)$, so it is a horizontal line. If it is 8 units long, $h - (-3) = 8$. Subtract 3 from each side of this equation to get $h = 5$.

7. D

Percent change is actual change over original amount. The change from 12 to 9 is 3. The amount being changed from is 12, so $\frac{3}{12}$, or 25% is the percent decrease. 25% of 40 is $40(.25) = 10$, so the percent decrease from 40 to $40 - 10 = 30$ is the same as the percent decrease from 12 to 9. Another way to solve this problem is to set up a proportion: $\frac{12}{9} = \frac{40}{x}$, where x is the number we are looking for. Cross multiply to find $12x = 360$, then divide by 12 to find $x = 30$.

8. A

There are $5 \times 12 = 60$ slices of pizza. If these are equally distributed among x people, each person gets $\frac{60}{x}$ slices of pizza. When the same number of slices are distributed among four fewer people, each person got $\frac{60}{x} + 4$ slices of pizza. You can also describe this number of slices as $\frac{60}{x - 4}$. So you have an equation you can use to find x: $\frac{60}{x} + 4 = \frac{60}{x - 4}$. This looks nothing like the answer choices, so you'll have to play with it a bit. Multiply both sides by x to get $60 + 4x = \frac{60x}{x - 4}$, then multiply both sides by $x - 4$ to get $(x - 4)(60 + 4x) = 60x$. Distribute and simplify to get $60x + 4x^2 - 240 - 16x = 60x$, $4x^2 - 16x - 240 = 0$, and $x^2 - 4x - 60 = 0$.

9. .127

If $A = 2.54$ and $20B = A$, then $20B = 2.54$. So $B = \frac{2.54}{20}$ or .127.

10. 9.5 or $\frac{19}{2}$

The perimeter of the figure is equal to the sum of the lengths of its sides: $2 + 1\frac{1}{3} + 1\frac{1}{2} + 1\frac{2}{3} + 3 = 9\frac{1}{2}$, which is $\frac{19}{2}$ expressed as an improper fraction, or 9.5 expressed as a decimal.

11. 84 or 96

If $\frac{h}{3}$ and $\frac{h}{4}$ are both integers, then h must be a multiple of 3×4, or 12. Since it's given that h is between 75 and 100, h must be 84 or 96.

12. 8

The profit made by the retailer on the shirts is equal to the difference between the selling price and the cost for each shirt multiplied by the number of shirts: $(\$6.75 - \$4.50) \times 16 = \$2.25 \times 16 = \$36.00$ profit. To find the number of $4.50 shirts that can be bought for $36.00, you need to divide $36.00 by $4.50, and $\frac{36}{4.5} = 8$.

13. $\frac{45}{4}$ or 11.2 or 11.3

Draw a diagram and label it according to the given information:

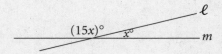

Let the smaller angle measure $x°$. Since the other angle formed is 15 times as large, label it $(15x)°$. Notice that these two angles are supplementary, that is, they add up to 180°. Therefore:

$$x + 15x = 180$$
$$16x = 180$$
$$x = \frac{45}{4}$$

So the smaller angle is $\frac{45}{4}$ degrees, which can also be gridded in decimal form as 11.2 or 11.3.

14. 4

Before you plug in −4 for x, you should factor the given equation:

$$x^2 + 2xr + r^2 = 0$$
$$(x + r)(x + r) = 0$$
$$(x + r)^2 = 0$$

Now plug in −4 for x to solve for r: $(-4 + r)^2 = 0$, $-4 + r = 0$, and $r = 4$.

15. $\frac{1}{16}$ or .062 or .063

Plug the values into the given definition:

$$\frac{1}{4} \ast = \left(\frac{1}{4}\right)^2 - \frac{1}{4}$$
$$= \frac{1}{16} - \frac{1}{4}$$
$$= \frac{1}{16} - \frac{4}{16}$$
$$= \frac{-3}{16}$$

$$\frac{1}{2} \ast = \left(\frac{1}{2}\right)^2 - \frac{1}{2}$$
$$= \frac{1}{4} - \frac{1}{2}$$
$$= \frac{-1}{4}$$

So:

$$\frac{1}{4} \ast - \frac{1}{2} \ast = \frac{-3}{16} - \left(\frac{-1}{4}\right)$$
$$= \frac{-3}{16} - \left(-\frac{4}{16}\right)$$
$$= \frac{1}{16}$$

This can also be gridded as .062 or .063.

16. $\frac{1}{8}$ or .125

You should recognize that right $\triangle ABC$ is a 45-45-90 triangle, with side lengths in a ratio of $1:1:\sqrt{2}$. Therefore, the length of the two equal legs AB and AC is $\frac{1}{2}$.

To find the area of the triangle, plug the values of the base and height (the lengths of the two equal legs) into the area formula:

$$\text{Area of a triangle} = \frac{1}{2}(\text{base} \times \text{height})$$
$$= \frac{1}{2}\left(\frac{1}{2}\right)^2$$
$$= \frac{1}{2}\left(\frac{1}{4}\right)$$
$$= \frac{1}{8}, \text{ or } .125$$

17. 2,025

You're given that x is a factor of 8,100 and it's an odd integer. To find the greatest possible value of x, begin factoring 8,100 by using its smallest prime factor, 2, as one of the factors. Continue factoring out a 2 from the remaining factors until you find an odd one as shown below:

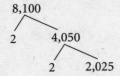

8,100

2 × 4,050

2 × 2 × 2,025

Since 2,025 is odd, you can stop factoring; it is the greatest odd factor of 8,100.

18. $\frac{4}{7}$ or .571

Translate the problem into math: Let b = number of boys; let g = number of girls. So $b + g$ = total number of students in the class.

$\frac{1}{2}$ of the boys speak French, so $\frac{1}{2}b$ = the number of boys who speak French.

$\frac{2}{3}$ of the girls speak French, so $\frac{2}{3}g$ = the number of girls who speak French.

Therefore, $\frac{1}{2}b + \frac{2}{3}g$ = total French speakers.

So the fraction of the class that speaks French

$$= \frac{\frac{1}{2}b + \frac{2}{3}\left(\frac{3}{4}b\right)}{b + g}$$

Since there are $\frac{3}{4}$ as many girls as boys in the class, $g = \frac{3}{4}b$. Plug in $\frac{3}{4}b$ for g into the fraction above.

Fraction of the class that speaks French:

$$= \frac{\frac{1}{2}b + \frac{2}{3}\left(\frac{3}{4}b\right)}{b + \frac{3}{4}b}$$

$$= \frac{\frac{1}{2}b + \frac{1}{2}b}{\frac{7}{4}b}$$

$$= \frac{b}{\frac{7}{4}b}$$

$$= \frac{4}{7} \text{ or } .571$$

SECTION 6

1. E

The introductory phrase doesn't modify the correct noun. The fundraiser is *arranged as an event*, not the Board of Directors. Also, the words *for funding* repeat information provided in the main clause. You need an introductory phrase that modifies the correct noun—the museum's Board of Directors. Only (E) does that. (B) and (D) don't correct the modification problem. (C) creates a run-on with a comma splice.

2. A

Don't forget that about 20% of Sentence Correction questions are correct as written. This sentence correctly uses a semicolon to connect two independent clauses, but (B) changes the meaning. (C) is a run-on sentence with a comma splice. (D) is a complete sentence because it adds the conjunction *and*, but it is wordy and incorrectly changes *nearly* to *near*. (E) should use a comma because it adds *although*, which subordinates the second clause.

3. C

Pay close attention to the sequence of events. The architects first made the design plans, then refused to copyright or benefit from them. The action *refused to patent* happened after, not before, the plans had been made, requiring the simple past tense. (C) and (E) make that change but only (C) makes *patent* and *benefit* parallel. (B) keeps the past perfect tense. (D) uses the present tense, even though the entire sentence is in the past.

4. D

The comparison between Wilde's novel writing and play writing must be logical. (C), (D), and (E) correctly compare *novelist* and *playwright*. However, only (D) retains the original meaning. (C) doesn't show that Wilde is a more brilliant playwright than novelist. (E) reverses the meaning, making him a more brilliant novelist than playwright. (B) changes the meaning as well, making Wilde *almost brilliant*.

5. C

The introductory phrase doesn't modify the correct noun. You need a subject that can logically examine the sale offers. (C), (D) and (E) provide that subject (*one*). Only (C) uses the present tense. (D) and (E) switch to the past tense. (D) also illogically uses the contrasting transition word *although*; (E) incorrectly omits *the* from *the phrases*. (B) doesn't address the modification problem.

6. A

This sentence is correct as written. (A) is your answer. (B) is incorrect because *however*, when used as a conjunction between two independent clauses, must be preceded by a semicolon. (C) is redundant, using two conjunctions *although* and *however*. (D) uses the relative pronoun *which* instead of *who* to refer to people. (E) loses the contrast between the two clauses (indicated by *however* in the original sentence).

7. B

The sentence uses the pronoun *which* to refer to people and includes the wordy intervening phrase *which have an understanding of.* (B) correctly changes *which* to *who* and makes the sentence more concise. (D) and (E) also use *who* but (D) introduces the ambiguous pronoun *they*, which could refer to the people or the leaves and (E) omits the fact that people understand the life cycles in leaves. (C) doesn't correct the original pronoun problem.

8. B

Be sure you understand the logic of the sentence: the traffic rules are the *they* and their role was not appreciated. (B) puts all these ideas into clear order by introducing the transition word *because* instead of relying on a modifier. (C) distorts the meaning of the sentence. (D) creates a misplaced modifier problem—the traffic rules fail to appreciate their role. (E) is a fragment, with no verb in an independent clause.

9. E

There are two pairs of parallel structures: *even more elusive in…than in* and *either….or*. In the original sentence the first pair is not parallel. (D) and (E) correctly add *in* to make the phrases *in his own country* and *in Europe or Latin America* parallel, but (D) introduces a new error by repeating *in*. (B) and (C) do not correct the parallel problem.

10. B

My old home is not *growing up*. There is a modification problem. (B) and (C) correct the modification problem by adding the transition word *as* but only (B) doesn't introduce

new errors. (C) uses the present tense *grow up* and inserts a preposition at the end of the sentence. (D) loses the idea that the author grew up on the island. (E) doesn't correct the modification problem.

11. B

The use of *there were* in the sentence is very awkward, which rules out (A) and (C). (D) and (E) do not have logical sentence structures. (B) is the only choice that makes sense and has good sentence structure.

12. D

The pronoun *they* doesn't clearly refer to anything and *they can astonish people* is not parallel to *bolder* and *more abstract*. (D) should be changed to *astonishing*. The phrases *as Picasso* (A) and *use of* (B) are idiomatically correct. The verb *became* (C) is correctly in the past tense.

13. B

The sentence begins in present tense, but then changes to past tense. This must be incorrect. The chemical plant *is* a danger, at the present moment. *It became imperative* is past tense, which does not agree with the rest of the sentence. It should be changed to *it has become imperative*. Note that you could also simply substitute *is* to form *it is imperative*. *Such a* (A) is standard written English, as is *to find other ways* (C). *For* (D) is the correct preposition for *garden*.

14. B

The main clause of this sentence contains two plural nouns: *retail stores* and *popular items*. The pronoun *their* might refer to either, and must be clarified. The transition phrase *due to* (A) establishes a cause in the first clause and a logical result in the second clause. The verb *are increasing* (C) is correctly in the present tense. *Stock of* (D) uses the correct preposition.

15. B

This is a sentence fragment; we need a verb. The phrase *which eerily hint at* in (B) and (C) should read *eerily hint at*, adding a verb and creating a complete sentence. The adjective *lyric* (A) agrees with the noun *novels*. The adverb *eerily* (B) agrees with the correct verb *hint at*. The phrase *of her later life* (D) is idiomatically correct.

16. B

The pronoun *their* refers to the United Nations. Because the United Nations is a singular proper noun, the correct pronoun is *its*. (B) is incorrect. (A) correctly uses the comparative form and *than* is idiomatically correct. (C) is the correct preposition with owes. (D) correctly uses *that* and the present tense.

17. D

Each pronoun in a sentence should agree in gender and number with the word or words to which it refers. You will note that (A) is an appropriate modifier for the subject *I*. (B) is an appropriate verb tense. (C) is a correct idiom. (D) is the right answer. In this phrase, the pronoun refers to *Jake and Kelsey* and therefore it should be the plural *they*.

18. D

Be sure that each word means precisely what the writer intended to say. (A) is an appropriate phrase modifying the subject *Hiam*. (B) is an adjective, also appropriately modifying *Hiam*. (C) is another adjective, here correctly modifying the noun *night*. (D) uses the wrong preposition for the intended meaning; the writers meant *on* or *against*.

19. B

Adverbs and adjectives can be easily mixed-up. Check the sentence again to be sure there is no confusion. (A) uses the correct verb tense and the verb agrees with the subject *you*. (B) shows an adverb used in place of an adjective *generous*. Therefore, (B) is the right answer. (C) shows a correct verb tense and (D) shows an idiom used correctly to mean *flourish*.

20. D

Does the subordinate clause fit within the context of the sentence? (A) uses the correct verb tense, and the verb agrees with the subject *Kelly*. (B) shows the correct feminine singular pronoun, referring to *Kelly*. (C) shows the correct infinitive form of the verb *mediate*.

21. A

Irregular verbs do not follow the usual pattern in their past tense forms. Check the sentence carefully to be sure that the verbs are written correctly. (A) is the correct tense for an action that occurred before the action in the second

part of the sentence: *became apparent*. However, it uses an incorrect past participle of the verb *drive*. The correct form is *driven*. (B) uses the correct preposition *from*. (C) is the correct verb tense and idiomatic expression. (D) is appropriate tense for another action that was completed before the action in the prior clause.

22. C

Check sentences for common usage errors. *Hardly no* is a double negative. You need to replace *no* with *any* to fix it.

23. E

Don't hypercorrect the sentences. All the elements in this sentence are correct.

24. C

Look for subjects that follow verbs—a common SAT trap. The verb *has* precedes its subject—*characters*. Because *characters* is plural, the verb has to be changed to the plural *have*.

25. B

Remember that adverbs modify verbs and adjectives modify nouns, adverbs and other adjectives. *Attentive* is an adjective, but it is modifying the verb *applies* so it has to be changed to the adverb *attentively*.

26. B

Know the difference between when to use nouns in the subjective case and the objective case. Any noun or pronoun that is part of a prepositional phrase must be in the objective case. Here the prepositional phrase is between *Sarah and I*. This is incorrect because *I* is a subjective case noun. To correct this sentence you need to change *I* to *me*.

27. E

Don't be distracted by phrases and clauses that come between a subject and its verb. The verb *used* and the preposition *by* (A) are used correctly. The subject *control* and its verb *is* (B) agree. *Benefit* (C), which means *aid* or *advantage*, is correctly used in this sentence. The pronoun *their* (D) agrees with its antecedent *students*.

28. C

Let the parts of the sentence not underlined help you identify the errors that are underlined. The pronoun *it* is used at the end of the sentence to refer to *the institute*, but the other pronoun that refers to *the institute,* in (C), is *their*. You need to make the pronouns consistent and correct. *The institute* is a collective noun, which means it's made up of many people, but is treated in a sentence as a single entity, so any pronouns that refer to it should be singular.

29. A

This sentence confuses *undetermined* (which means not decided) with indeterminate. You can see that this makes no sense. The word needed is *indeterminate* which means you can't tell his age by looking at him. Notice how this meaning works well with the rest of the sentence—he takes advantage of the ambiguity or uncertainty about his age. (B) The conjunction *and*, which indicates additional, related information is correctly used. (C) The present tense is correct since it expresses something that the candidate does regularly. (D) is the correct preposition in this context.

30. A

The passage begins by stating that ballet has a *duality* and the second sentences introduces the most common view of ballet. What follows should be a sentence that identifies the contrast suggested by the first sentence: the idea that ballet is *grueling, painful, and competitive*, as expressed in (A). This also gives a more clear transition to paragraphs 2 and 3, which talk about the difficulties of dancing. Although it starts appropriately with a contrast word, (B) goes off track; it even seems to contradict sentence 2. (C) is a fragment; it can't be correct even though it seems to follow the right line of reasoning. (D) and (E), like (B), go off the logical track. These would be digressions in this passage, which focuses only on the qualities of ballet.

31. A

To combine these two sentences we must first determine their relationship. It is a causal relationship—because of the first clause (the human body is not designed for ballet) it is difficult for dancers to do the second clause (perform ballet steps). (A) correctly establishes this relationship and creates a complete sentence. (B) and (E) incorrectly use a semicolon to connect a dependent and an independent clause. (C) combines the sentences into one big fragment by adding the gerund *making*. (D) is also a fragment and introduces another error—*their* is an ambiguous pronoun.

32. A

To determine what sentence should begin paragraph 3, we must understand the passage's organization. Paragraph 1 introduces the topic. Paragraph 2 describes the first negative aspect of ballet (physical injury). Paragraph 3 describes the second negative aspect (financial problems). (A) both indicates that paragraph 3 is the second aspect and that the paragraph relates to financial problems. The sentence is also identical in construction to the first sentence of paragraph 2. (B) changes *second* to *secondly* and only mentions a part of paragraph 3, not the entire subject. (C) and (D) use transition words that do not indicate that this is the second portion of the passage. (E) incorrectly indicates that the financial consequences are worse than the physical—the author never makes such a comparison.

33. D

As it is now, the sentence is a fragment; we need a subject and verb in an independent clause. (D) replaces the gerund *creating* with the present tense *create*. This works in context because the rest of the paragraph is in present tense. (B) simply substitutes the gerund *compiling* for the gerund *creating*. The sentence is still a fragment. (C) and (E) are incorrectly in the past tense; (C) uses the pronoun *they*, which would mean that the financial struggles were competitive instead of the dancers; and (E) changes the meaning to one competition.

34. B

Look at the context of sentence 11—how does it relate to sentence 10? Sentence 11 contrasts dancers' experience with that of *most people*. (D) uses the contrasting transition word *but* and also makes sentence 11, which was a fragment, a complete sentence. (B) has the right intention—it contrasts the two sentences—but the pronoun *which* makes sentence 11 a dependent clause (on sentence 10) instead of a sentence. (C) is incorrect because sentence 10 doesn't give us a *model*, just a fact. (E) incorrectly uses the transition word *and*.

35. B

What is the relationship of this pair of sentences to what came before? We've been told in sentences 10 and 11 that people in most occupations retire at 65, but that isn't true of dancing. Now we're told a few dancers continue in related careers, but most are simply unemployed.

Sentence 12 continues what preceded it, but contrasts with sentence 13. (B) captures this best. (A) confuses the contrast between these two sentences by offering transition words suggesting both contrast ("although") and continuity ("and"). (C) offers too many contrast words and needlessly changes tense. (D) is a run-on sentence. (E) also changes tense and distorts some of the meaning.

SECTION 7

1. B

The phrase *even though* indicates contrast. So, *even though* the prisoner "presented evidence clearly proving that he was nowhere near the scene of the crime," he was *indicted* or formally charged with committing the crime.

2. C

A *premise* is a proposition which is used as the basis for an argument—or a story. If scientists are critical of the premise for a movie, we can infer that they are so because they consider it to be unscientific, without basis in fact, or *speculative*. (C) is therefore the correct answer. (A) is wrong, because if the premise, or underlying argument, were *scientific* then it would hardly be open to criticism by scientists. (B) is wrong because there's no reason to think that the theme of the return of the dinosaurs is unexpressed in the movie.

3. C

In this sentence we find a description of two contradictory characteristics that exist in the same group of people. On the one hand, they are brutal; on the other, they are heroic. Such an occurrence is termed a *paradox* and therefore (C) *paradoxical* is the correct answer. Choices (A), (D), and (E) are wrong; it is *unfortunate, distressing,* and *appalling* that they are brutal—but not that they are heroic.

4. B

The second part of the sentence tells you that the engineers did something that allowed the movement of animals around the pipeline. You can, therefore, predict that this action would *help* the seasonal migration of caribou. This prediction eliminates choices (A) and (D) for the first blank. (B) and (E) both fit the first blank nicely.

When you try the second blank, (B) describes how the pipeline could be designed to accommodate the passage of animals. (D) refers not to the pipeline but to the oil *delivered* through the pipeline. (C) does not fit either blank. Be sure not to misread *razed* ("demolished, leveled to the ground"), as *raised*.

5. E

The word *however* signals a contrast between licorice as candy and its use in earlier times when licorice root was used to treat a variety of medical problems. A good prediction for the blank would be *medical* or *healing*. (E) matches the prediction. (A) is too narrow because licorice root treated conditions other than insomnia. (C) describes candy but not medicine. The remaining choices do not match the prediction. Be sure not to misread *indelible* as *inedible* ("unfit to be eaten").

6. A

In this sentence, parents are doing something to legislation that guarantees programs and services. The first part of the sentence tells you that education is one of those services. You're looking for a word like "assure" in the first blank.

(A) and (E) work for the first blank. Now look at the second blank. (A) works well. (E) would deny education to the children and can, therefore, be eliminated. To ensure free education for children with special needs, parents have had to demand legislation guaranteeing services and programs targeted to those children. (A) works for both blanks.

The Shakespeare Passages

These paired passages present two opposing arguments on a single subject, the subject here being *Who Really Wrote Shakespeare's Plays?* The author of the first passage maintains that Francis Bacon actually wrote the plays, basing that conclusion on the assertion that Shakespeare didn't have the education and social experience necessary to create such sophisticated plays. The author of the second passage takes issue with that, claiming that Shakespeare's genius grew out of a deep understanding of human nature rather than any wide learning or arcane knowledge.

7. B

Here we're asked the definition of the word *entertain* in line 2, where it is used in the phrase *entertain some doubt*. Well, when you entertain doubt, or entertain an idea, you are holding it in your head. You are *harboring* it, in the sense of *to harbor* as *to be host to*. So choice (B) is correct. The other choices are all acceptable dictionary definitions of the verb *entertain*, but none fits the context as well as choice (B) does. (A) *amuse* is a common synonym for *entertain*, but how does one amuse doubt? (C) *occupy* and (E) *engage* are closer, but they don't fit the sentence either. One's *mind* is occupied or engaged, but the doubt itself is not occupied or engaged. Meanwhile, (D) *cherish* adds a sense of valuing the entertained thing, as if it were something desirable.

8. D

The author claims that the person who actually wrote the plays must have had *intimate knowledge of life within royal courts and palaces*, but that Shakespeare was just a commoner, without that kind of *firsthand experience* of the aristocracy. He wants to cast doubt on Shakespeare's *familiarity with the life of [aristocrats]*, or choice (D). Shakespeare's ability to (A) *write poetically* and his (C) *ability to support himself as a playwright* never come up in Passage 1. The *knowledge of foreign places* mentioned in (B) does come up, but being a commoner is not necessarily related to Shakespeare's apparent lack of travel. Choice (E) is the closest wrong choice, since the aristocracy was the *government* in Elizabethan England, but the issue is his knowledge of all aspects of aristocratic life.

9. E

Two Shakespearian plays—*Coriolanus* and *Love's Labour's Lost*—are mentioned in lines 28–31 in connection with the allegedly specialized knowledge they contain. They support the point that the educated aristocrat Bacon was a more likely author than was the undereducated commoner Shakespeare. (E) answers the question best. Choice (A) is a clever wrong choice, but it's too extreme. The author's not trying to prove that *only* Bacon could have written these plays, just that Bacon was far more likely than Shakespeare to have written them. The *deep understanding of human nature* mentioned in (B) is something brought up in Passage 2, not Passage 1. The author is not comparing the two plays to *works written by Bacon*, as (C) claims. And (D) is wrong since nothing about society is

mentioned with regard to *Coriolanus*. Also, it's not the *broad spectrum of society* the author alludes to with regard to *Love's Labour's Lost*, but rather the knowledge of just the upper range of society.

10. A

It's clear that Ms. Bacon is looking down on actors, of which Shakespeare was one, regarding them with the *disdain* expressed in correct choice (A). She's not *resentful* at how the *characters are portrayed*, choice (B), since she's talking about the characters themselves and what they tell us about real-life actors. Given her opinion of actors, she certainly doesn't *regret that their conditions weren't better*, choice (C). (D) is closer, but it's a distortion. She never doubts that anyone could *create such characters*; she doubts that the author of the plays could *be like* such a character. Finally, in (E), there's no evidence in the quote that Ms. Bacon thinks the actors are inept at their art, just that they are vulgar and lowly persons.

11. B

This question sends you back to paragraph 4 of Passage 1, where Bacon's preference for anonymity is explained. The author claims that, because the plays were controversial, Bacon felt that associating himself with them would have been politically and personally damaging. So, *he wished to protect himself from the effects of controversy*, choice (B). (A) is wrong because Bacon did publish a lot of writing under his own name. (C) is plausible, but it's not the reason given in paragraph 4 or anywhere else in the first passage. (D) tries to confuse us by introducing the subject of *lowly actors* from the preceding paragraph, and (E) is a fabrication since we know that Bacon was already famous from his other writings.

12. C

This question takes us to the first paragraph of Passage 2, where the emphasis is on language ability. The author doubts that Bacon, a writer primarily of academic Latin, would have had the ability to produce the exalted English in which the plays were written. That makes (C) the best answer. (A) is a distortion. Just because Bacon wrote most of his own work in another language doesn't mean that he was *unfamiliar* with English. (B)'s emphasis on the difficult switch from *scientific writing* to *writing plays* is close, but language rather than the type of writing is the focus. There's no reason to surmise that the author doubts Bacon's ability to *cooperate* on a *committee,* choice (D). Finally, (E) is wrong because there is no evidence in the first paragraph that the author has doubts about Bacon's ability to produce that amount of work.

13. D

This question asks about *premier* as it is used in the phrase *premier stylist in the English language.* The author definitely wants to indicate the sublime language of the plays here, so *premier* is being used in the sense of *of the first rank,* or, as choice (D) has it, *greatest.* (A), (C), and (E) all play on the sense of premier as *first in sequence* (*inaugural,* by the way, means *marking the commencement or beginning*), but the author is not referring here to *when* Shakespeare wrote. He's writing about how *well* Shakespeare wrote. On the other hand, (B) *influential* misses on two counts—first, it's not a definition of *premier* in any context, and second, the issue of influence on other writers is not brought up here.

14. B

This question concerns the adjective *encyclopedic* in Passage 2, line 75, where it's used to modify the noun *knowledge.* The author says that Shakespeare's genius was one of common sense and perceptive intuition, not encyclopedic knowledge, which is related to great book-learning. So the knowledge described as *encyclopedic* is wide-ranging and in-depth—*comprehensive,* in other words, choice (B). (A) *technical* is close to the sense of the context, but it's not a synonym of *encyclopedic,* so it really won't work here. (C) won't work either, since *abridged* (meaning *condensed*) cannot describe the kind of exhaustive knowledge the author is describing here. While it may take discipline to gain encyclopedic knowledge, *encyclopedic* itself cannot be defined as *disciplined,* so cut (D). Finally, (E) *specialized* isn't quite right, since it implies a narrowness of focus.

15. E

The reference to Shakespeare's status as a landowner comes in the third paragraph of Passage 2, where it is brought up to show that Shakespeare would have been *knowledgeable about legal matters related to . . . real estate.* That makes (E) the best answer, *legal matters* being equivalent to *the law.* (A) is interesting, since the author does say that owning land was quite an

accomplishment for a playwright, but it has nothing to do with his knowledge of the law. (B) is off, since owning land doesn't make one automatically friendly with the highborn set. (C) is wrong, because Shakespeare's financial state is just a side issue; it's not the point of bringing up Shakespeare's landowning status. And (D) doesn't fit, since no one doubts that Shakespeare was a commoner.

16. A

This question directs us to Passage 2, lines 101–102, where the author claims that literary genius *can flower in any socioeconomic bracket.* That implies that genius has little to do with a person's social and financial position—or, as correct choice (A) has it—genius doesn't depend *on a writer's external circumstances.* (B) fails by bringing in the notion of *comprehension of human nature* from elsewhere in the passage. (C) is a common cliché, but there's no evidence here that the author felt that Shakespeare's genius was *enhanced by poverty.* In fact, this author implies that Shakespeare wasn't even all that poor. (D) may be a true statement, but recognition of genius isn't really under discussion here; it's the simple existence of genius. (E) is a distortion; the author claims that at least one kind of genius does not *stem* from *book-learning and academic training,* but that doesn't mean that those things would *stifle literary genius.*

17. C

Go back to the fourth paragraph of Passage 1, where our first author claims that Bacon may have *hired a lowly actor* like Shakespeare to put his name to the plays and take the heat of controversy. How would our second author respond to this claim? The second author, remember, writes in the concluding paragraph of Passage 2 that *no elaborate theories of intrigue and secret identity are nec-. essary to explain the accomplishment of William Shakespeare.* Surely author 2 would regard the *scenario* described in Passage 1 as just this kind of *unnecessary* theory, so (C) is the best guess for how author 2 would react. As for choice (A), author 2 may or may not agree that the plays were *controversial* in their time, so (A) won't work. (B) gets the thrust of author 2's argument wrong. Author 2 denigrates the notion that Bacon wrote the plays *not* by arguing that Bacon wasn't a great scholar, but by arguing that it didn't require a great scholar to write the plays. (D) tries to turn author 1's argument on its head. A nice idea, perhaps, but author 2 shows no hint of doing anything of the kind. (E) brings up the notion of Shakespeare's social *respectability,* which really isn't of much concern to author 2.

18. C

What would be author 1's reaction to author 2's skepticism that Bacon, the author of Latin treatises, could be the "premier stylist in the English language"? Well, author 1's repeated assertions of Bacon's scholarly genius and Shakespeare's lack of education are both reflected in choice (C), which makes it a good bet as the correct answer. (A)'s mention of the *similarities between Latin and English* is enough to kill this choice, since author 1 mentions no such similarities in the passage. (B) is a true statement, perhaps, but it doesn't really address the issue. (D) is fairly nonsensical, since it would weaken author 1's entire theory about why Bacon hired Shakespeare. Finally, (E) makes a good point, but again, there is no hint of this sentiment in author 1's statements.

19. D

Always check back to the passage to figure out the meaning of a Vocabulary-in-Context word. Here, the word *observation* refers to the phrase that *Shakespeare, in short, was Shakespeare*—a jokey comment on the author's part. None of the other choices fits the context of an informal remark, so (D) is correct here.

SECTION 8

1. B

Plug in −2 for p and 3 for q: $p^3q^2 + p^2q = (-2)^3 3^2 + (-2)^2 3 = (-8)(9) + 4(3)$, or $(-72) + 12 = -60$. (Note that a negative number raised to an even power becomes positive, but raised to an odd power stays negative.)

2. A

Keep track of the lengths you know on the diagram. B is the midpoint of AC so $AB = BC$. Since $AB = 5$, $BC = 5$. $BD = 8$, so $BC + CD = 8$. $BC = 5$, so $5 + CD = 8$, $CD = 3$. D is the midpoint of CE, so $CD = DE = 3$.

3. D

Try each answer choice until you find one that works for all of the pairs of numbers.

Choice (A), $P = N + 5$ works for 2 and 7, but not for 4 and 13.

Choice (B), $P = 2N + 3$ also works for 2 and 7, but not for 4 and 13.

Choice (C), $P = 2N + 5$, doesn't work for 2 and 7.

Choice (D), $P = 3N + 1$, works for all four pairs of numbers, so that's the answer.

4. A

$\angle PNM$ is supplementary to $\angle PNQ$, so $\angle PNM + 105° = 180°$, and $\angle PNM = 75°$. Since $PM = PN$, triangle MPN is an isosceles and $\angle PMN = \angle PNM = 75°$. The interior angles of a triangle sum to 180°, so $75 + 75 + x = 180$, and $x = 30$.

5. D

Probability is defined as the number of desired events divided by the total number of possible events. There are $5 + 6 + 4 = 15$ pens in the knapsack. If he pulls out 1 pen, there are 15 different pens he might pick, or 15 possible outcomes. The desired outcome is that the pen be either red or black. The group of acceptable pens consists of $4 + 6$, or 10 pens. So the probability that one of these pens will be picked is 10 of 15, or $\frac{10}{15}$, which we can reduce to $\frac{2}{3}$.

6. C

Pick variables for the two items and translate the given information into algebraic equations. Let $h =$ the price of a hot dog and $s =$ the price of a soda. The first statement is translated as $2h + s = \$3.25$, and the second as $3h + s = \$4.50$. If you subtract the first equation from the second, the s is eliminated so you can solve for h:

$$3h + s = \$4.50$$
$$\underline{-2h + s = \$3.25}$$
$$h = \$1.25$$

Plug this value for h into the first equation to solve for s:

$$2(\$1.25) + s = \$3.25$$
$$\$2.50 + s = \$3.25$$
$$s = \$0.75$$

So two sodas would cost $2 \times \$0.75 = \$1.50$.

7. C

$a = f$, since all the obtuse angles formed when two parallel lines are cut by a transversal are equal. f is an exterior angle of the small triangle containing angles c, d, and e, so it is equal to the sum of the two nonadjacent interior angles, c and d. Since $a = f$ and $f = c + d$, $a = c + d$, answer choice (C).

8. D

The first 3 minutes of the phone call cost 75 cents or 0.75 dollars. If the entire call lasted x minutes, the rest of the call lasted $x - 3$ minutes. Each minute after the first 3 cost 15 cents or $0.15, so the rest of the call cost $0.15(x - 3)$. Thus, the cost of the entire call is $0.75 + 0.15(x - 3)$ dollars.

If this isn't clear, pick numbers. Let $x = 5$. The first 3 minutes cost $0.75 and the additional $5 - 3 = 2$ minutes are $0.15 each. So the entire call costs $\$0.75 + 2(\$0.15) = \$1.05$. Plug 5 for x into all the answer choices to see which ones give you 1.05:

(A) $0.75(3) + 0.15x = 2.25 + 0.15(5) = 2.25 + 0.75 = 3.00$. Eliminate.

(B) $0.75(3) + 0.15(x + 3) = 2.25 + 0.15(5 + 3) = 2.25 + 1.20 = 3.45$. Eliminate.

(C) $0.75 + 0.15(3 - x) = 0.75 + 0.15(3 - 5) = 0.75 - 0.30 = 0.45$. Eliminate.

(D) $0.75 + 0.15(x - 3) = 0.75 + 0.15(5 - 3) = 0.75 + 0.30 = 1.05$. Works!

(E) $0.75 + 0.15(5) = 0.75 + 0.75 = 1.50$. Eliminate.

The only choice that yields the desired result is (D), so it must be correct.

9. B

Before you can find the area of the circle, you need to find the length of the wire. The wire is in the shape of a semi-circle with diameter 12. Since circumference $= \pi d$, the length of a semicircle is half of that, $\frac{\pi d}{2}$. So the length of the wire is $\frac{\pi(12)}{2}$, or 6π. When this wire is bent to form a circle, the circumference of this circle will equal 6π. So the length of the circle's diameter must equal 6, and the radius must be 3. Now you can find the area of the circle:

$$\begin{aligned}\text{Area} &= \pi r^2 \\ &= \pi(3)^2 \\ &= 9\pi\end{aligned}$$

10. C

If $a^2 - a = 72$, then $a^2 - a - 72 = 0$. Factoring this quadratic equation: $(a - 9)(a + 8) = 0$. So $a - 9 = 0$ or $a + 8 = 0$, and $a = 9$ or $a = -8$. b to the nth power equals a, so b must be a root of either 9 or -8. Look through the answer choices to find the choice that is not a root of either 9 or -8:

(A) $(-8)^1 = -8$, so this can be a value for b.

(B) $(-2)^3 = -8$, so this can be a value for b.

(C) $2^3 = 8$, not -8, so this *cannot* be a value for b.

(D) $3^2 = 9$, so this can be a value for b.

(E) $9^1 = 9$, so this can be a value for b.

So (C) is the only answer choice that cannot be a value for b.

11. C

The most efficient way to answer this question is to use the midpoint formula: the midpoint of points (x_1, y_1) and (x_2, y_2) is $\left(\dfrac{x_1 + x_2}{2}, \dfrac{y_1 + y_2}{2}\right)$. You'll use the formula more skillfully if, rather than merely memorize it, you think about what it means, namely, that the midpoint of two points is merely the average of their x- and y-coordinates:

$$\left(\frac{(0 + x_2)}{2} = 3, \frac{(2 + y_2)}{2} = 4\right)$$

$(x_2 = 6, y_2 = 6)$

12. D

$4\sqrt{2x} - 2 = 16$

$4\sqrt{2x} = 18$

$\sqrt{2x} = \dfrac{18}{4}$

$\left(\sqrt{2x}\right)^2 = \left(\dfrac{18}{4}\right)^2$

$x = \dfrac{18 \times 18}{4 \times 4 \times 2} = \dfrac{9 \times 9}{2 \times 2 \times 2} = \dfrac{81}{8}$

13. E

If you can't visualize a graph, plug points in and graph it yourself. If doing so is helpful, use your calculator.

Plug in 2 for x:

$y = -3x^2$

$y = -3(2)^2$

$y = -3(4)$

$y = -12$

Eliminate (A) and (B).

Plug in -2 for x:

$y = -3x^2$

$y = -3(-2)^2$

$y = -3(4)$

$y = -12$

Eliminate (C) and (D), leaving only (E).

14. C

Think backward. If the person now weighs w pounds, then his or her weight before losing 8 pounds was 8 pounds more than w, or $w + 8$. The person's weight before gaining p pounds was $w + 8 - p$, which can also be written as $w - p + 8$.

15. B

The surface area of a cube is $6e^2$, where e = the length of an edge of the cube. Since the surface area is $36n^2$:

$6e^2 = 36n^2$

$e^2 = 6n^2$

$e = n\sqrt{6}$

The volume of a cube is e^3. To solve for the volume in terms of n, plug in the value for an edge that you just found: Volume $= e^3 = (n\sqrt{6})^3 = 6n^3\sqrt{6}$, answer choice (B).

16. C

Since the ratio of x to y to z is 3:6:8, if $y = 24$ or 4×6, x and z must also be multiplied by 4 for the ratio to hold. So $x = 4 \times 3 = 12$ and $z = 4 \times 8 = 32$, and $x + z = 44$.

SECTION 9

1. E

The pronoun in the sentence must correspond with *teacher shortage* (not *salaries*). Therefore, the pronoun should be *it*. (E) is the only answer choice with this pronoun.

2. A

Items in a series must have the same structure, which is the case for the original sentence. The other answer choices break the parallelism.

3. D

(A) is a run-on, so it cannot be correct. (B), (C), and (E) are awkward and confusing. Be wary of sentences with nonessential clauses separated by commas. (D) has the cleanest structure and is the best answer choice.

4. A

(C) does not use a semicolon correctly. (B), (D), and (E) all unnecessarily add extra words. Be suspicious of answer choices that make the sentence more complex.

5. D

Idiomatically, *the same* should be followed by the preposition *as*, not *than*. There is also a problem of parallelism here; the two things being compared should be in the same grammatical form. Since *talking* is a gerund, the thing it's being compared to should also be a gerund: *driving*.

6. C

This run-on sentence is best corrected by (C), which is grammatically correct and doesn't include extra verbiage. (B) and (E) use the semicolon improperly, and (D) is wordy.

7. E

The sentence is unclear because it doesn't use the correct sequence of tenses. Since the client had already been waiting for fifteen minutes *before* the moment when the receptionist looked up, the first verb must be in the past perfect: *had been waiting*.

8. C

This run-on sentence is a comma splice. A good prediction is to exchange the comma for a semicolon. (B) does this, but (B) also removes *they* and with it the second independent clause. (C) is the only choice with correct sentence structure.

9. E

Because the second part of the sentence is an independent clause, the underlined portion must be altered to create a dependent clause. (C) and (E) do this, but (E) is clearer and better constructed.

10. D

(D) is the only answer choice that creates a complete sentence. Also, the words *rare enough to honor the spiritual essence of the Buddha* is descriptive of *stones*. Therefore, (D) makes sense.

11. D

The two independent clauses in this sentence must be separated by either a semicolon or a coordinating conjunction. (D) uses the semicolon correctly, so it is correct. (C) is close to being correct, but the nonessential information *on the other hand* needs to be set apart with commas.

12. C

The original sentence does not contain a verb. (C) and (E) insert *are* to create a working verb structure. However, (E) incorrectly creates a dependent clause with *these are*.

13. B

The word *that* at the beginning of the sentence makes this sentence incomplete. Simply removing *that*, as in (B), makes the sentence correct.

14. D

The coordinating conjunction *but* makes this sentence incorrect. (D) removes the word to make an independent clause that makes sense with *although* at the beginning of the sentence.

SAT Practice Test Two
Answer Sheet

Remove (or photcopy) the answer sheet and use it to complete the practice test. See the answer key following the test when finished. The "Compute Your Score" section on page 611 will show you how to find your score.

Start with number 1 for each section. If a section has fewer questions than answer spaces, leave the extra spaces blank.

SECTION 1

Section One is the writing section's essay component.
Lined pages on which you will write your essay can be found in that section.

SECTION 2

1. Ⓐ Ⓑ Ⓒ Ⓓ Ⓔ   11. Ⓐ Ⓑ Ⓒ Ⓓ Ⓔ   21. Ⓐ Ⓑ Ⓒ Ⓓ Ⓔ   31. Ⓐ Ⓑ Ⓒ Ⓓ Ⓔ
2. Ⓐ Ⓑ Ⓒ Ⓓ Ⓔ   12. Ⓐ Ⓑ Ⓒ Ⓓ Ⓔ   22. Ⓐ Ⓑ Ⓒ Ⓓ Ⓔ   32. Ⓐ Ⓑ Ⓒ Ⓓ Ⓔ
3. Ⓐ Ⓑ Ⓒ Ⓓ Ⓔ   13. Ⓐ Ⓑ Ⓒ Ⓓ Ⓔ   23. Ⓐ Ⓑ Ⓒ Ⓓ Ⓔ   33. Ⓐ Ⓑ Ⓒ Ⓓ Ⓔ
4. Ⓐ Ⓑ Ⓒ Ⓓ Ⓔ   14. Ⓐ Ⓑ Ⓒ Ⓓ Ⓔ   24. Ⓐ Ⓑ Ⓒ Ⓓ Ⓔ   34. Ⓐ Ⓑ Ⓒ Ⓓ Ⓔ

right in Section 2

5. Ⓐ Ⓑ Ⓒ Ⓓ Ⓔ   15. Ⓐ Ⓑ Ⓒ Ⓓ Ⓔ   25. Ⓐ Ⓑ Ⓒ Ⓓ Ⓔ   35. Ⓐ Ⓑ Ⓒ Ⓓ Ⓔ
6. Ⓐ Ⓑ Ⓒ Ⓓ Ⓔ   16. Ⓐ Ⓑ Ⓒ Ⓓ Ⓔ   26. Ⓐ Ⓑ Ⓒ Ⓓ Ⓔ   36. Ⓐ Ⓑ Ⓒ Ⓓ Ⓔ
7. Ⓐ Ⓑ Ⓒ Ⓓ Ⓔ   17. Ⓐ Ⓑ Ⓒ Ⓓ Ⓔ   27. Ⓐ Ⓑ Ⓒ Ⓓ Ⓔ   37. Ⓐ Ⓑ Ⓒ Ⓓ Ⓔ
8. Ⓐ Ⓑ Ⓒ Ⓓ Ⓔ   18. Ⓐ Ⓑ Ⓒ Ⓓ Ⓔ   28. Ⓐ Ⓑ Ⓒ Ⓓ Ⓔ   38. Ⓐ Ⓑ Ⓒ Ⓓ Ⓔ
9. Ⓐ Ⓑ Ⓒ Ⓓ Ⓔ   19. Ⓐ Ⓑ Ⓒ Ⓓ Ⓔ   29. Ⓐ Ⓑ Ⓒ Ⓓ Ⓔ   39. Ⓐ Ⓑ Ⓒ Ⓓ Ⓔ

wrong in Section 2

10. Ⓐ Ⓑ Ⓒ Ⓓ Ⓔ   20. Ⓐ Ⓑ Ⓒ Ⓓ Ⓔ   30. Ⓐ Ⓑ Ⓒ Ⓓ Ⓔ   40. Ⓐ Ⓑ Ⓒ Ⓓ Ⓔ

SECTION 3

1. Ⓐ Ⓑ Ⓒ Ⓓ Ⓔ   11. Ⓐ Ⓑ Ⓒ Ⓓ Ⓔ   21. Ⓐ Ⓑ Ⓒ Ⓓ Ⓔ   31. Ⓐ Ⓑ Ⓒ Ⓓ Ⓔ
2. Ⓐ Ⓑ Ⓒ Ⓓ Ⓔ   12. Ⓐ Ⓑ Ⓒ Ⓓ Ⓔ   22. Ⓐ Ⓑ Ⓒ Ⓓ Ⓔ   32. Ⓐ Ⓑ Ⓒ Ⓓ Ⓔ
3. Ⓐ Ⓑ Ⓒ Ⓓ Ⓔ   13. Ⓐ Ⓑ Ⓒ Ⓓ Ⓔ   23. Ⓐ Ⓑ Ⓒ Ⓓ Ⓔ   33. Ⓐ Ⓑ Ⓒ Ⓓ Ⓔ
4. Ⓐ Ⓑ Ⓒ Ⓓ Ⓔ   14. Ⓐ Ⓑ Ⓒ Ⓓ Ⓔ   24. Ⓐ Ⓑ Ⓒ Ⓓ Ⓔ   34. Ⓐ Ⓑ Ⓒ Ⓓ Ⓔ

right in Section 3

5. Ⓐ Ⓑ Ⓒ Ⓓ Ⓔ   15. Ⓐ Ⓑ Ⓒ Ⓓ Ⓔ   25. Ⓐ Ⓑ Ⓒ Ⓓ Ⓔ   35. Ⓐ Ⓑ Ⓒ Ⓓ Ⓔ
6. Ⓐ Ⓑ Ⓒ Ⓓ Ⓔ   16. Ⓐ Ⓑ Ⓒ Ⓓ Ⓔ   26. Ⓐ Ⓑ Ⓒ Ⓓ Ⓔ   36. Ⓐ Ⓑ Ⓒ Ⓓ Ⓔ
7. Ⓐ Ⓑ Ⓒ Ⓓ Ⓔ   17. Ⓐ Ⓑ Ⓒ Ⓓ Ⓔ   27. Ⓐ Ⓑ Ⓒ Ⓓ Ⓔ   37. Ⓐ Ⓑ Ⓒ Ⓓ Ⓔ
8. Ⓐ Ⓑ Ⓒ Ⓓ Ⓔ   18. Ⓐ Ⓑ Ⓒ Ⓓ Ⓔ   28. Ⓐ Ⓑ Ⓒ Ⓓ Ⓔ   38. Ⓐ Ⓑ Ⓒ Ⓓ Ⓔ

wrong in Section 3

9. Ⓐ Ⓑ Ⓒ Ⓓ Ⓔ   19. Ⓐ Ⓑ Ⓒ Ⓓ Ⓔ   29. Ⓐ Ⓑ Ⓒ Ⓓ Ⓔ   39. Ⓐ Ⓑ Ⓒ Ⓓ Ⓔ
10. Ⓐ Ⓑ Ⓒ Ⓓ Ⓔ   20. Ⓐ Ⓑ Ⓒ Ⓓ Ⓔ   30. Ⓐ Ⓑ Ⓒ Ⓓ Ⓔ   40. Ⓐ Ⓑ Ⓒ Ⓓ Ⓔ

Remove (or photocopy) this answer sheet and use it to complete the practice test.

Start with number 1 for each section. If a section has fewer questions than answer spaces, leave the extra spaces blank.

SECTION

4

1. Ⓐ Ⓑ Ⓒ Ⓓ Ⓔ
2. Ⓐ Ⓑ Ⓒ Ⓓ Ⓔ
3. Ⓐ Ⓑ Ⓒ Ⓓ Ⓔ
4. Ⓐ Ⓑ Ⓒ Ⓓ Ⓔ
5. Ⓐ Ⓑ Ⓒ Ⓓ Ⓔ
6. Ⓐ Ⓑ Ⓒ Ⓓ Ⓔ
7. Ⓐ Ⓑ Ⓒ Ⓓ Ⓔ
8. Ⓐ Ⓑ Ⓒ Ⓓ Ⓔ
9. Ⓐ Ⓑ Ⓒ Ⓓ Ⓔ
10. Ⓐ Ⓑ Ⓒ Ⓓ Ⓔ

11. Ⓐ Ⓑ Ⓒ Ⓓ Ⓔ
12. Ⓐ Ⓑ Ⓒ Ⓓ Ⓔ
13. Ⓐ Ⓑ Ⓒ Ⓓ Ⓔ
14. Ⓐ Ⓑ Ⓒ Ⓓ Ⓔ
15. Ⓐ Ⓑ Ⓒ Ⓓ Ⓔ
16. Ⓐ Ⓑ Ⓒ Ⓓ Ⓔ
17. Ⓐ Ⓑ Ⓒ Ⓓ Ⓔ
18. Ⓐ Ⓑ Ⓒ Ⓓ Ⓔ
19. Ⓐ Ⓑ Ⓒ Ⓓ Ⓔ
20. Ⓐ Ⓑ Ⓒ Ⓓ Ⓔ

21. Ⓐ Ⓑ Ⓒ Ⓓ Ⓔ
22. Ⓐ Ⓑ Ⓒ Ⓓ Ⓔ
23. Ⓐ Ⓑ Ⓒ Ⓓ Ⓔ
24. Ⓐ Ⓑ Ⓒ Ⓓ Ⓔ
25. Ⓐ Ⓑ Ⓒ Ⓓ Ⓔ
26. Ⓐ Ⓑ Ⓒ Ⓓ Ⓔ
27. Ⓐ Ⓑ Ⓒ Ⓓ Ⓔ
28. Ⓐ Ⓑ Ⓒ Ⓓ Ⓔ
29. Ⓐ Ⓑ Ⓒ Ⓓ Ⓔ
30. Ⓐ Ⓑ Ⓒ Ⓓ Ⓔ

31. Ⓐ Ⓑ Ⓒ Ⓓ Ⓔ
32. Ⓐ Ⓑ Ⓒ Ⓓ Ⓔ
33. Ⓐ Ⓑ Ⓒ Ⓓ Ⓔ
34. Ⓐ Ⓑ Ⓒ Ⓓ Ⓔ
35. Ⓐ Ⓑ Ⓒ Ⓓ Ⓔ
36. Ⓐ Ⓑ Ⓒ Ⓓ Ⓔ
37. Ⓐ Ⓑ Ⓒ Ⓓ Ⓔ
38. Ⓐ Ⓑ Ⓒ Ⓓ Ⓔ
39. Ⓐ Ⓑ Ⓒ Ⓓ Ⓔ
40. Ⓐ Ⓑ Ⓒ Ⓓ Ⓔ

 # right in Section 4

 # wrong in Section 4

If section 4 of your test book contains math questions that are not multiple choice, continue to item 9 below. Otherwise, continue to item 9 above.

9.
10.
11.
12.
13.

14.
15.
16.
17.
18.

Remove (or photocopy) this answer sheet and use it to complete the practice test.

Start with number 1 for each section. If a section has fewer questions than answer spaces, leave the extra spaces blank.

SECTION 5

1. Ⓐ Ⓑ Ⓒ Ⓓ Ⓔ   11. Ⓐ Ⓑ Ⓒ Ⓓ Ⓔ   21. Ⓐ Ⓑ Ⓒ Ⓓ Ⓔ   31. Ⓐ Ⓑ Ⓒ Ⓓ Ⓔ
2. Ⓐ Ⓑ Ⓒ Ⓓ Ⓔ   12. Ⓐ Ⓑ Ⓒ Ⓓ Ⓔ   22. Ⓐ Ⓑ Ⓒ Ⓓ Ⓔ   32. Ⓐ Ⓑ Ⓒ Ⓓ Ⓔ
3. Ⓐ Ⓑ Ⓒ Ⓓ Ⓔ   13. Ⓐ Ⓑ Ⓒ Ⓓ Ⓔ   23. Ⓐ Ⓑ Ⓒ Ⓓ Ⓔ   33. Ⓐ Ⓑ Ⓒ Ⓓ Ⓔ
4. Ⓐ Ⓑ Ⓒ Ⓓ Ⓔ   14. Ⓐ Ⓑ Ⓒ Ⓓ Ⓔ   24. Ⓐ Ⓑ Ⓒ Ⓓ Ⓔ   34. Ⓐ Ⓑ Ⓒ Ⓓ Ⓔ   # right in Section 5
5. Ⓐ Ⓑ Ⓒ Ⓓ Ⓔ   15. Ⓐ Ⓑ Ⓒ Ⓓ Ⓔ   25. Ⓐ Ⓑ Ⓒ Ⓓ Ⓔ   35. Ⓐ Ⓑ Ⓒ Ⓓ Ⓔ
6. Ⓐ Ⓑ Ⓒ Ⓓ Ⓔ   16. Ⓐ Ⓑ Ⓒ Ⓓ Ⓔ   26. Ⓐ Ⓑ Ⓒ Ⓓ Ⓔ   36. Ⓐ Ⓑ Ⓒ Ⓓ Ⓔ
7. Ⓐ Ⓑ Ⓒ Ⓓ Ⓔ   17. Ⓐ Ⓑ Ⓒ Ⓓ Ⓔ   27. Ⓐ Ⓑ Ⓒ Ⓓ Ⓔ   37. Ⓐ Ⓑ Ⓒ Ⓓ Ⓔ
8. Ⓐ Ⓑ Ⓒ Ⓓ Ⓔ   18. Ⓐ Ⓑ Ⓒ Ⓓ Ⓔ   28. Ⓐ Ⓑ Ⓒ Ⓓ Ⓔ   38. Ⓐ Ⓑ Ⓒ Ⓓ Ⓔ   # wrong in Section 5
9. Ⓐ Ⓑ Ⓒ Ⓓ Ⓔ   19. Ⓐ Ⓑ Ⓒ Ⓓ Ⓔ   29. Ⓐ Ⓑ Ⓒ Ⓓ Ⓔ   39. Ⓐ Ⓑ Ⓒ Ⓓ Ⓔ
10. Ⓐ Ⓑ Ⓒ Ⓓ Ⓔ   20. Ⓐ Ⓑ Ⓒ Ⓓ Ⓔ   30. Ⓐ Ⓑ Ⓒ Ⓓ Ⓔ   40. Ⓐ Ⓑ Ⓒ Ⓓ Ⓔ

SECTION 6

1. Ⓐ Ⓑ Ⓒ Ⓓ Ⓔ   11. Ⓐ Ⓑ Ⓒ Ⓓ Ⓔ   21. Ⓐ Ⓑ Ⓒ Ⓓ Ⓔ   31. Ⓐ Ⓑ Ⓒ Ⓓ Ⓔ
2. Ⓐ Ⓑ Ⓒ Ⓓ Ⓔ   12. Ⓐ Ⓑ Ⓒ Ⓓ Ⓔ   22. Ⓐ Ⓑ Ⓒ Ⓓ Ⓔ   32. Ⓐ Ⓑ Ⓒ Ⓓ Ⓔ
3. Ⓐ Ⓑ Ⓒ Ⓓ Ⓔ   13. Ⓐ Ⓑ Ⓒ Ⓓ Ⓔ   23. Ⓐ Ⓑ Ⓒ Ⓓ Ⓔ   33. Ⓐ Ⓑ Ⓒ Ⓓ Ⓔ
4. Ⓐ Ⓑ Ⓒ Ⓓ Ⓔ   14. Ⓐ Ⓑ Ⓒ Ⓓ Ⓔ   24. Ⓐ Ⓑ Ⓒ Ⓓ Ⓔ   34. Ⓐ Ⓑ Ⓒ Ⓓ Ⓔ   # right in Section 6
5. Ⓐ Ⓑ Ⓒ Ⓓ Ⓔ   15. Ⓐ Ⓑ Ⓒ Ⓓ Ⓔ   25. Ⓐ Ⓑ Ⓒ Ⓓ Ⓔ   35. Ⓐ Ⓑ Ⓒ Ⓓ Ⓔ
6. Ⓐ Ⓑ Ⓒ Ⓓ Ⓔ   16. Ⓐ Ⓑ Ⓒ Ⓓ Ⓔ   26. Ⓐ Ⓑ Ⓒ Ⓓ Ⓔ   36. Ⓐ Ⓑ Ⓒ Ⓓ Ⓔ
7. Ⓐ Ⓑ Ⓒ Ⓓ Ⓔ   17. Ⓐ Ⓑ Ⓒ Ⓓ Ⓔ   27. Ⓐ Ⓑ Ⓒ Ⓓ Ⓔ   37. Ⓐ Ⓑ Ⓒ Ⓓ Ⓔ
8. Ⓐ Ⓑ Ⓒ Ⓓ Ⓔ   18. Ⓐ Ⓑ Ⓒ Ⓓ Ⓔ   28. Ⓐ Ⓑ Ⓒ Ⓓ Ⓔ   38. Ⓐ Ⓑ Ⓒ Ⓓ Ⓔ   # wrong in Section 6
9. Ⓐ Ⓑ Ⓒ Ⓓ Ⓔ   19. Ⓐ Ⓑ Ⓒ Ⓓ Ⓔ   29. Ⓐ Ⓑ Ⓒ Ⓓ Ⓔ   39. Ⓐ Ⓑ Ⓒ Ⓓ Ⓔ
10. Ⓐ Ⓑ Ⓒ Ⓓ Ⓔ   20. Ⓐ Ⓑ Ⓒ Ⓓ Ⓔ   30. Ⓐ Ⓑ Ⓒ Ⓓ Ⓔ   40. Ⓐ Ⓑ Ⓒ Ⓓ Ⓔ

SECTION 7

1. Ⓐ Ⓑ Ⓒ Ⓓ Ⓔ   11. Ⓐ Ⓑ Ⓒ Ⓓ Ⓔ   21. Ⓐ Ⓑ Ⓒ Ⓓ Ⓔ   31. Ⓐ Ⓑ Ⓒ Ⓓ Ⓔ
2. Ⓐ Ⓑ Ⓒ Ⓓ Ⓔ   12. Ⓐ Ⓑ Ⓒ Ⓓ Ⓔ   22. Ⓐ Ⓑ Ⓒ Ⓓ Ⓔ   32. Ⓐ Ⓑ Ⓒ Ⓓ Ⓔ
3. Ⓐ Ⓑ Ⓒ Ⓓ Ⓔ   13. Ⓐ Ⓑ Ⓒ Ⓓ Ⓔ   23. Ⓐ Ⓑ Ⓒ Ⓓ Ⓔ   33. Ⓐ Ⓑ Ⓒ Ⓓ Ⓔ
4. Ⓐ Ⓑ Ⓒ Ⓓ Ⓔ   14. Ⓐ Ⓑ Ⓒ Ⓓ Ⓔ   24. Ⓐ Ⓑ Ⓒ Ⓓ Ⓔ   34. Ⓐ Ⓑ Ⓒ Ⓓ Ⓔ   # right in Section 7
5. Ⓐ Ⓑ Ⓒ Ⓓ Ⓔ   15. Ⓐ Ⓑ Ⓒ Ⓓ Ⓔ   25. Ⓐ Ⓑ Ⓒ Ⓓ Ⓔ   35. Ⓐ Ⓑ Ⓒ Ⓓ Ⓔ
6. Ⓐ Ⓑ Ⓒ Ⓓ Ⓔ   16. Ⓐ Ⓑ Ⓒ Ⓓ Ⓔ   26. Ⓐ Ⓑ Ⓒ Ⓓ Ⓔ   36. Ⓐ Ⓑ Ⓒ Ⓓ Ⓔ
7. Ⓐ Ⓑ Ⓒ Ⓓ Ⓔ   17. Ⓐ Ⓑ Ⓒ Ⓓ Ⓔ   27. Ⓐ Ⓑ Ⓒ Ⓓ Ⓔ   37. Ⓐ Ⓑ Ⓒ Ⓓ Ⓔ
8. Ⓐ Ⓑ Ⓒ Ⓓ Ⓔ   18. Ⓐ Ⓑ Ⓒ Ⓓ Ⓔ   28. Ⓐ Ⓑ Ⓒ Ⓓ Ⓔ   38. Ⓐ Ⓑ Ⓒ Ⓓ Ⓔ   # wrong in Section 7
9. Ⓐ Ⓑ Ⓒ Ⓓ Ⓔ   19. Ⓐ Ⓑ Ⓒ Ⓓ Ⓔ   29. Ⓐ Ⓑ Ⓒ Ⓓ Ⓔ   39. Ⓐ Ⓑ Ⓒ Ⓓ Ⓔ
10. Ⓐ Ⓑ Ⓒ Ⓓ Ⓔ   20. Ⓐ Ⓑ Ⓒ Ⓓ Ⓔ   30. Ⓐ Ⓑ Ⓒ Ⓓ Ⓔ   40. Ⓐ Ⓑ Ⓒ Ⓓ Ⓔ

Remove (or photocopy) this answer sheet and use it to complete the practice test.

Start with number 1 for each section. If a section has fewer questions than answer spaces, leave the extra spaces blank.

SECTION

8

1. Ⓐ Ⓑ Ⓒ Ⓓ Ⓔ	11. Ⓐ Ⓑ Ⓒ Ⓓ Ⓔ	21. Ⓐ Ⓑ Ⓒ Ⓓ Ⓔ	31. Ⓐ Ⓑ Ⓒ Ⓓ Ⓔ
2. Ⓐ Ⓑ Ⓒ Ⓓ Ⓔ	12. Ⓐ Ⓑ Ⓒ Ⓓ Ⓔ	22. Ⓐ Ⓑ Ⓒ Ⓓ Ⓔ	32. Ⓐ Ⓑ Ⓒ Ⓓ Ⓔ
3. Ⓐ Ⓑ Ⓒ Ⓓ Ⓔ	13. Ⓐ Ⓑ Ⓒ Ⓓ Ⓔ	23. Ⓐ Ⓑ Ⓒ Ⓓ Ⓔ	33. Ⓐ Ⓑ Ⓒ Ⓓ Ⓔ
4. Ⓐ Ⓑ Ⓒ Ⓓ Ⓔ	14. Ⓐ Ⓑ Ⓒ Ⓓ Ⓔ	24. Ⓐ Ⓑ Ⓒ Ⓓ Ⓔ	34. Ⓐ Ⓑ Ⓒ Ⓓ Ⓔ
5. Ⓐ Ⓑ Ⓒ Ⓓ Ⓔ	15. Ⓐ Ⓑ Ⓒ Ⓓ Ⓔ	25. Ⓐ Ⓑ Ⓒ Ⓓ Ⓔ	35. Ⓐ Ⓑ Ⓒ Ⓓ Ⓔ
6. Ⓐ Ⓑ Ⓒ Ⓓ Ⓔ	16. Ⓐ Ⓑ Ⓒ Ⓓ Ⓔ	26. Ⓐ Ⓑ Ⓒ Ⓓ Ⓔ	36. Ⓐ Ⓑ Ⓒ Ⓓ Ⓔ
7. Ⓐ Ⓑ Ⓒ Ⓓ Ⓔ	17. Ⓐ Ⓑ Ⓒ Ⓓ Ⓔ	27. Ⓐ Ⓑ Ⓒ Ⓓ Ⓔ	37. Ⓐ Ⓑ Ⓒ Ⓓ Ⓔ
8. Ⓐ Ⓑ Ⓒ Ⓓ Ⓔ	18. Ⓐ Ⓑ Ⓒ Ⓓ Ⓔ	28. Ⓐ Ⓑ Ⓒ Ⓓ Ⓔ	38. Ⓐ Ⓑ Ⓒ Ⓓ Ⓔ
9. Ⓐ Ⓑ Ⓒ Ⓓ Ⓔ	19. Ⓐ Ⓑ Ⓒ Ⓓ Ⓔ	29. Ⓐ Ⓑ Ⓒ Ⓓ Ⓔ	39. Ⓐ Ⓑ Ⓒ Ⓓ Ⓔ
10. Ⓐ Ⓑ Ⓒ Ⓓ Ⓔ	20. Ⓐ Ⓑ Ⓒ Ⓓ Ⓔ	30. Ⓐ Ⓑ Ⓒ Ⓓ Ⓔ	40. Ⓐ Ⓑ Ⓒ Ⓓ Ⓔ

□ # right in Section 8

□ # wrong in Section 8

SECTION

9

1. Ⓐ Ⓑ Ⓒ Ⓓ Ⓔ	11. Ⓐ Ⓑ Ⓒ Ⓓ Ⓔ	21. Ⓐ Ⓑ Ⓒ Ⓓ Ⓔ	31. Ⓐ Ⓑ Ⓒ Ⓓ Ⓔ
2. Ⓐ Ⓑ Ⓒ Ⓓ Ⓔ	12. Ⓐ Ⓑ Ⓒ Ⓓ Ⓔ	22. Ⓐ Ⓑ Ⓒ Ⓓ Ⓔ	32. Ⓐ Ⓑ Ⓒ Ⓓ Ⓔ
3. Ⓐ Ⓑ Ⓒ Ⓓ Ⓔ	13. Ⓐ Ⓑ Ⓒ Ⓓ Ⓔ	23. Ⓐ Ⓑ Ⓒ Ⓓ Ⓔ	33. Ⓐ Ⓑ Ⓒ Ⓓ Ⓔ
4. Ⓐ Ⓑ Ⓒ Ⓓ Ⓔ	14. Ⓐ Ⓑ Ⓒ Ⓓ Ⓔ	24. Ⓐ Ⓑ Ⓒ Ⓓ Ⓔ	34. Ⓐ Ⓑ Ⓒ Ⓓ Ⓔ
5. Ⓐ Ⓑ Ⓒ Ⓓ Ⓔ	15. Ⓐ Ⓑ Ⓒ Ⓓ Ⓔ	25. Ⓐ Ⓑ Ⓒ Ⓓ Ⓔ	35. Ⓐ Ⓑ Ⓒ Ⓓ Ⓔ
6. Ⓐ Ⓑ Ⓒ Ⓓ Ⓔ	16. Ⓐ Ⓑ Ⓒ Ⓓ Ⓔ	26. Ⓐ Ⓑ Ⓒ Ⓓ Ⓔ	36. Ⓐ Ⓑ Ⓒ Ⓓ Ⓔ
7. Ⓐ Ⓑ Ⓒ Ⓓ Ⓔ	17. Ⓐ Ⓑ Ⓒ Ⓓ Ⓔ	27. Ⓐ Ⓑ Ⓒ Ⓓ Ⓔ	37. Ⓐ Ⓑ Ⓒ Ⓓ Ⓔ
8. Ⓐ Ⓑ Ⓒ Ⓓ Ⓔ	18. Ⓐ Ⓑ Ⓒ Ⓓ Ⓔ	28. Ⓐ Ⓑ Ⓒ Ⓓ Ⓔ	38. Ⓐ Ⓑ Ⓒ Ⓓ Ⓔ
9. Ⓐ Ⓑ Ⓒ Ⓓ Ⓔ	19. Ⓐ Ⓑ Ⓒ Ⓓ Ⓔ	29. Ⓐ Ⓑ Ⓒ Ⓓ Ⓔ	39. Ⓐ Ⓑ Ⓒ Ⓓ Ⓔ
10. Ⓐ Ⓑ Ⓒ Ⓓ Ⓔ	20. Ⓐ Ⓑ Ⓒ Ⓓ Ⓔ	30. Ⓐ Ⓑ Ⓒ Ⓓ Ⓔ	40. Ⓐ Ⓑ Ⓒ Ⓓ Ⓔ

□ # right in Section 9

□ # wrong in Section 9

 GO ONLINE

Be sure to add your scores to your syllabus.

Practice Test Two

SECTION 1
Time—25 Minutes
ESSAY

The essay gives you an opportunity to show how effectively you can develop and express ideas. You should, therefore, take care to develop your point of view, present your ideas logically and clearly, and use language precisely.

Your essay must be written in your Answer Grid Booklet—you will receive no other paper on which to write. You will have enough space if you write on every line, avoid wide margins, and keep your handwriting to a reasonable size. Remember that people who are not familiar with your handwriting will read what you write. Try to write or print so that what you are writing is legible to those readers.

You have twenty-five minutes to write an essay on the topic assigned below.
DO NOT WRITE ON ANOTHER TOPIC. AN OFF-TOPIC ESSAY WILL RECEIVE A SCORE OF ZERO.

Think carefully about the issue presented in the following excerpt and the assignment below.

> "Life without memory is no life at all, just as an intelligence without the possibility of expression is not really an intelligence. Our memory is our coherence, our reason, our feeling, even our action. Without it, we are nothing."
> –Luis Buñuel, *An Unspeakable Betrayal*
>
> "Many a man fails to become a thinker for the sole reason that his memory is too good."
> –Friedrich Nietzsche, *Maxims*

Assignment: Is memory as central as Buñuel believes, or does it merely hold us back? Plan and write an essay in which you develop your point of view on this issue. Support your position with reasoning and examples taken from your reading, studies, experience, or observations.

DO NOT WRITE YOUR ESSAY IN YOUR TEST BOOK.
You will receive credit only for what you write in your Answer Grid Booklet.

_____

_____

_____

_____

_____

_____

_____

_____

_____

_____

_____

_____

_____

_____

_____

_____

_____

_____

_____

_____

_____

_____

_____

_____

_____

_____

_____

_____

_____

_____

_____

_____

_____

_____

_____

_____

_____

_____

_____

_____

_____

_____

_____

IF YOU FINISH BEFORE TIME IS CALLED, YOU MAY CHECK YOUR WORK ON THIS SECTION ONLY. DO NOT TURN TO ANY OTHER SECTION IN THE TEST.

SECTION 2

Time—25 Minutes

20 Questions

Directions: For this section, solve each problem and decide which is the best of the choices given. Fill in the corresponding oval on the answer sheet. You may use any available space for scratchwork.

Notes:

(1) Calculator use is permitted.

(2) All numbers used are real numbers.

(3) Figures are provided for some problems. All figures are drawn to scale and lie in a plane UNLESS otherwise indicated.

(4) Unless otherwise specified, the domain of any function f is assumed to be the set of all real numbers x for which $f(x)$ is a real number.

Information

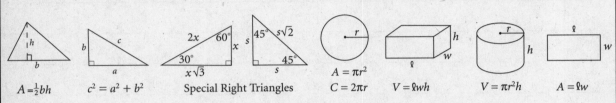

$A = \frac{1}{2}bh$ $\qquad$ $c^2 = a^2 + b^2$ $\qquad$ Special Right Triangles $\qquad$ $A = \pi r^2$ $\qquad$ $V = \ell wh$ $\qquad$ $V = \pi r^2 h$ $\qquad$ $A = \ell w$

$\qquad\qquad\qquad\qquad\qquad\qquad\qquad\qquad\qquad\qquad\qquad\qquad$ $C = 2\pi r$

The sum of the degree measures of the angles in a triangle is 180.

The number of degrees of arc in a circle is 360.

A straight angle has a degree measure of 180.

---

1. $\left(\dfrac{1}{5} + \dfrac{1}{3} \right) \div \dfrac{1}{2} =$

   (A) $\dfrac{1}{8}$

   (B) $\dfrac{1}{4}$

   (C) $\dfrac{4}{15}$

   (D) $\dfrac{1}{2}$

   (E) $\dfrac{16}{15}$

2. What is the value of $x^2 - 2x$ when $x = -2$?

   (A) -8
   (B) -4
   (C) 0
   (D) 4
   (E) 8

3. Vito read 96 pages in 2 hours and 40 minutes. What was Vito's average rate of pages per hour?

   (A) 24

   (B) 30

   (C) 36

   (D) 42

   (E) 48

GO ON TO THE NEXT PAGE ⟩

KAPLAN

4. For how many integer values of x will $\frac{7}{x}$ be greater than $\frac{1}{4}$ and less than $\frac{1}{3}$?

   (A) 6

   (B) 7

   (C) 12

   (D) 28

   (E) infinitely many

5. What is the average (arithmetic mean) of $2x + 5$, $5x - 6$, and $-4x + 2$?

   (A) $x + \frac{1}{3}$

   (B) $x + 1$

   (C) $3x + \frac{1}{3}$

   (D) $3x + 3$

   (E) $3x + 3\frac{1}{3}$

6. In a group of 25 students, 16 are female. What percent of the group is female?

   (A) 16%

   (B) 40%

   (C) 60%

   (D) 64%

   (E) 75%

7. In the triangle above, what is the degree measure of angle B?

   (A) 45

   (B) 60

   (C) 65

   (D) 75

   (E) 80

8. For all $x \neq 0$, $\dfrac{x^2 + x^2 + x^2}{x^2} =$

   (A) 3

   (B) $3x$

   (C) x^2

   (D) x^3

   (E) x^4

9. The equation $x^2 = 5x - 4$ has how many distinct real solutions?

   (A) 0

   (B) 1

   (C) 2

   (D) 3

   (E) infinitely many

GO ON TO THE NEXT PAGE

KAPLAN

10. Which of the following sets of numbers has the property that the sum of any two numbers in the set is also a number in the set?

    I. The set of even integers
    II. The set of odd integers
    III. The set of prime numbers

    (A) I only
    (B) III only
    (C) I and II only
    (D) I and III only
    (E) I, II, and III

11. Martin's average (arithmetic mean) score after 4 tests is 89. What score on the 5th test would bring Martin's average up to exactly 90?

    (A) 90
    (B) 91
    (C) 92
    (D) 93
    (E) 94

12. The price s of a sweater is reduced by 25% for a sale. After the sale, the reduced price is increased by 20%. Which of the following represents the final price of the sweater?

    (A) $.80s$
    (B) $.85s$
    (C) $.90s$
    (D) $.95s$
    (E) $1.05s$

13. How many distinct prime factors does the number 36 have?

    (A) 2
    (B) 3
    (C) 4
    (D) 5
    (E) 6

14. If the area of a triangle is 36 and its base is 9, what is the length of the altitude to that base?

    (A) 2
    (B) 4
    (C) 6
    (D) 8
    (E) 12

15. Let a ♣ be defined for all positive integers a by the equation a ♣ $= \dfrac{a}{4} - \dfrac{a}{6}$. If x ♣ $= 3$, what is the value of x?

    (A) 18
    (B) 28
    (C) 36
    (D) 40
    (E) 54

16. Joan has q quarters, d dimes, n nickels, and no other coins in her pocket. Which of the following represents the total number of coins in Joan's pocket?

    (A) $q + d + n$
    (B) $5q + 2d + n$
    (C) $.25q + .10d + .05n$
    (D) $(25 + 10 + 5)(q + d + n)$
    (E) $25q + 10d + 5n$

GO ON TO THE NEXT PAGE

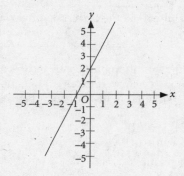

17. Which of the following is an equation for the graph above?

(A) $y = -2x + 1$

(B) $y = x + 1$

(C) $y = x + 2$

(D) $y = 2x + 1$

(E) $y = 2x + 2$

18. If an integer is divisible by 6 and by 9, then the integer must be divisible by which of the following?

    I. 12

    II. 18

    III. 36

(A) I only

(B) II only

(C) I and II only

(D) II and III only

(E) I, II, and III

19. A wooden cube with volume 64 is sliced in half horizontally. The two halves are then glued together to form a rectangular solid which is not a cube. What is the surface area of this new solid?

(A) 48

(B) 56

(C) 96

(D) 112

(E) 128

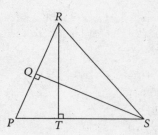

20. In $\triangle PRS$ above, RT is the altitude to side PS, and QS is the altitude to side PR. If $RT = 7$, $PR = 8$, and $QS = 9$, what is the length of PS?

(A) $5\frac{1}{7}$

(B) $6\frac{2}{9}$

(C) $7\frac{7}{8}$

(D) $10\frac{2}{7}$

(E) $13\frac{4}{9}$

IF YOU FINISH BEFORE TIME IS CALLED, YOU MAY CHECK YOUR WORK ON THIS SECTION ONLY. DO NOT TURN TO ANY OTHER SECTION IN THE TEST.

STOP

KAPLAN

SECTION 3

Time—25 Minutes
24 Questions

Directions: For each of the following questions, choose the best answer and darken the corresponding oval on the answer sheet.

Each sentence below has one or two blanks, each blank indicating that something has been omitted. Beneath the sentence are five words or sets of words labeled A through E. Choose the word or set of words that, when inserted in the sentence, best fits the meaning of the sentence as a whole.

EXAMPLE:

Today's small, portable computers contrast markedly with the earliest electronic computers, which were -------.

(A) effective
(B) invented
(C) useful
(D) destructive
(E) enormous

---

1. Finding an old movie poster that is still ------- usually proves difficult because such posters were meant to be used and then -------.

   (A) recognizable . . returned
   (B) relevant . . discarded
   (C) intact . . destroyed
   (D) immaculate . . restored
   (E) displayed . . maintained

2. The Kemp's Ridley turtle, long considered one of the most ------- creatures of the sea, finally appears to be making some headway in its battle against extinction.

   (A) elusive
   (B) prevalent
   (C) combative
   (D) voracious
   (E) imperiled

3. Before the invention of the tape recorder, quotes from an interview were rarely -------; journalists usually paraphrased the words of their subject.

   (A) verbatim
   (B) misconstrued
   (C) pragmatic
   (D) extensive
   (E) plagiarized

4. Batchelor's reputation as ------- novelist encouraged hopes that his political thriller would offer more ------- characterizations than are usually found in the genre.

   (A) a serious . . subtle
   (B) a maturing . . sweeping
   (C) a prolific . . accurate
   (D) an accomplished . . fictional
   (E) a reclusive . . authentic

5. Aristotle espoused a ------- biological model in which all extant species are unchanging and eternal and no new species ever come into existence.

   (A) paradoxical
   (B) morbid
   (C) static
   (D) holistic
   (E) homogeneous

GO ON TO THE NEXT PAGE

KAPLAN

6. The agency's failure to ------- policies that it has acknowledged are flawed is a potent demonstration of its ------- approach to correcting its problems.

   (A) support . . ambiguous

   (B) institute . . earnest

   (C) rescind . . lackadaisical

   (D) amend . . devoted

   (E) chasten . . meticulous

7. The inconsistency of the educational policies adopted by various schools across the state has been greatly ------- by the rapid turnover of school superintendents.

   (A) counteracted

   (B) stabilized

   (C) criticized

   (D) exacerbated

   (E) understated

8. The journalist's claim of ------- is belied by her record of contributing to the campaign funds of only one party's candidates.

   (A) innocence

   (B) corruption

   (C) impartiality

   (D) affluence

   (E) loyalty

GO ON TO THE NEXT PAGE

KAPLAN

Directions: The passages below are followed by questions based on their content; questions following a pair of related passages may also be based on the relationship between the paired passages. Answer the questions on the basis of what is <u>stated</u> or <u>implied</u> in the passages and in any introductory material that may be provided.

Questions 9–12 refer to the following passage.

Passage 1

Recently, a disturbing practice has developed among book publishers. They have hired contemporary authors to write sequels to the novels of long-dead authors. If these sequels were being
(5) written for the works of relatively untalented or unknown authors, then no one would pay much attention. Unfortunately, this has not been the case. One author wrote a sequel to Margaret Mitchell's *Gone with the Wind*, for example. It's
(10) clear that these sequels are written in order to entice an author's or a literary work's fans to spend money. Since these counterfeits can never equal the original, however, disappointment is the only possible outcome for the reader.

Passage 2

(15)   What unalloyed delight for those who have read all of Sir Arthur Conan Doyle's stories of Sherlock Holmes to discover Nicholas Meyer's 1989 novel, *The Seven Percent Solution*. In it, the violin-playing detective and his faithful sidekick, Dr. Watson,
(20) roam the moors in search of evil-doers. Once again, readers can get lost in the cozy, yet often terrifying world of Victorian England. While Meyer's style, informed as it is by modern civilization and sensibilities, is not Sir Arthur's, the book
(25) nonetheless contains many pleasures for the avid Sherlockian. One can only hope that Meyer will continue to write novels about Watson and Holmes so that devoted followers will get lasting pleasure from reading them.

9. The author of Passage 1 would most likely agree with which of the following statements?

(A) It is easier to write a sequel to the work of an unknown author than it is to write a sequel to the work of a famous author.

(B) Modern sequels to old works should be regarded as pale imitations of the originals.

(C) Although many modern sequels to older books are of poor quality, *The Seven Percent Solution* is an exception to that rule.

(D) The works of Margaret Mitchell have caused indignation among many readers.

(E) Readers who buy sequels rarely read the original works on which the sequels are based.

10. The author of Passage 1 most likely regards Margaret Mitchell as an author

(A) who is well-known

(B) who wrote only one novel

(C) whose skills are comparable to those of Sir Arthur Conan Doyle

(D) whose book is more famous than its author

(E) who will disappoint her readers

GO ON TO THE NEXT PAGE

11. In Passage 2, line 15, the word "unalloyed" most nearly means

   (A) metallic
   (B) effervescent
   (C) plentiful
   (D) pure
   (E) bland

12. The author of Passage 2 would most likely respond to the contention that "disappointment is the only possible outcome for the reader" (Passage 1, lines 13–14) of sequels by

   (A) reconsidering his own thesis
   (B) countering that *The Seven Percent Solution* is superior to the sequel to *Gone with the Wind*
   (C) mocking the author's rigid views in Passage 1
   (D) agreeing that while some readers will be disappointed, some will be very pleased
   (E) emphasizing the pleasure an ardent fan gets from reading a sequel to the work of an admired author

GO ON TO THE NEXT PAGE

KAPLAN

Questions 13–24 refer to the following passage.

The following passage is an excerpt from a book about wolves, written by a self-taught naturalist who studied them in the wild.

My precautions against disturbing the wolves were superfluous. It had required me a week to get their measure, but they must have taken mine at our first meeting; and while there was nothing dis-
(5) dainful in their evident assessment of me, they managed to ignore my presence, and indeed my very existence, with a thoroughness which was somehow disconcerting.

Quite by accident I had pitched my tent within
(10) ten yards of one of the major paths used by the wolves when they were going to, or coming from, their hunting paths to the westward; and only a few hours after I had taken up my residence one of the wolves came back from a trip and discov-
(15) ered me and my tent.

He was at the end of a hard night's work and was clearly tired and anxious to go home to bed. He came over a small rise fifty yards from me with his head down, his eyes half-closed, and a preoc-
(20) cupied air about him. Far from being the preter-naturally alert and suspicious beast of fiction, this wolf was so self-engrossed that he came straight on to within fifteen yards of me, and might have gone right past the tent without seeing it at all,
(25) had I not banged an elbow against the teakettle, making a resounding clank. The wolf's head came up and his eyes opened wide, but he did not stop or falter in his pace. One brief, sidelong glance was all he vouchsafed to me as he continued on his
(30) way.

By the time this happened, I had learned a great deal about my wolfish neighbors, and one of the facts which had emerged was that they were not nomadic roamers, as is almost universally
(35) believed, but were settled beasts and the posses-sors of a large permanent estate with very definite boundaries. The territory owned by my wolf fam-ily comprised more than a hundred square miles, bounded on one side by a river but otherwise not
(40) delimited by geographical features. Nevertheless there were boundaries, clearly indicated in wolfish fashion.

Once a week, more or less, the clan made the rounds of the family lands and freshened up the
(45) boundary markers—a sort of lupine* beating of the bounds. This careful attention to property rights was perhaps made necessary by the pres-ence of two other wolf families whose lands abutted on ours, although I never discovered any
(50) evidence of bickering or disagreements between the owners of the various adjoining estates. I sus-pect, therefore, that it was more of a ritual activity.

In any event, once I had become aware of this strong feeling of property among the wolves, I
(55) decided to use this knowledge to make them at least recognize my existence. One evening, after they had gone off for their regular nightly hunt, I staked out a property claim of my own, embracing perhaps three acres, with the tent at the middle,
(60) and including a hundred yard long section of the wolves' path. This took most of the night and required frequent returns to the tent to consume copious quantities of tea; but before dawn brought the hunters home, the task was done and
(65) I retired, somewhat exhausted, to observe the results.

I had not long to wait. At 0814 hours, according to my wolf log, the leading male of the clan appeared over the ridge behind me, padding
(70) homeward with his usual air of preoccupation. As usual, he did not deign to look at the tent; but when he reached the point where my property line intersected the trail, he stopped as abruptly as if he had run into an invisible wall. His attitude of
(75) fatigue vanished and was replaced by one of bewilderment. Cautiously he extended his nose and sniffed at one of my marked bushes. After a minute of complete indecision he backed away a few yards and sat down. And then, finally, he
(80) looked directly at the tent and me. It was a long, considering sort of look.

Having achieved my object—that of forcing at least one of the wolves to take cognizance of my existence—I now began to wonder if, in my igno-
(85) rance, I had transgressed some unknown wolf law

GO ON TO THE NEXT PAGE ▷

of major importance and would have to pay for
my temerity. I found myself regretting the absence
of a weapon as the look I was getting became
longer, more thoughtful, and still more intent. In
(90) an effort to break the impasse I loudly cleared my
throat and turned my back on the wolf to indicate
as clearly as possible that I found his continued
scrutiny impolite, if not actually offensive.

    He appeared to take the hint. Briskly, and with
(95) an air of decision, he turned his attention away
from me and began a systematic tour of the area,
sniffing each boundary marker once or twice, and
carefully placing his mark on the outside of each
clump of grass or stone. In fifteen minutes he
(100) rejoined the path at the point where it left my
property and trotted off towards his home, leaving
me with a good deal to occupy my thoughts.

    lupine: relating to wolves

13. According to the author, why were his precautions
against disturbing the wolves "superfluous"
(line 2)?

    (A) It was several weeks before he encountered
his first wolf.

    (B) Other wild animals posed a greater threat to
his safety.

    (C) The wolves noticed him but were not inter-
ested in harming him.

    (D) He was not bothered by the wolves until he
started interfering with them.

    (E) The wolves were unable to detect him
because of their poor eyesight.

14. The author mentions the wolves' "assessment" of
him (line 5) in order to

    (A) account for their strange behavior towards
him

    (B) convey his initial fear of being attacked

    (C) emphasize his ignorance on first encountering
them

    (D) indicate the need for precautions against
disturbing them

    (E) suggest his courage in an unfamiliar situation

15. In the third paragraph, the author is primarily
surprised to find that the wolf

    (A) is traveling alone

    (B) lacks the energy to respond

    (C) is hunting at night

    (D) is not more on its guard

    (E) does not attack him

16. In line 17, the word "anxious" most nearly means

    (A) distressed

    (B) afraid

    (C) eager

    (D) uneasy

    (E) worried

17. In line 35, the word "settled" most nearly means

    (A) decided

    (B) resolute

    (C) stable

    (D) inflexible

    (E) confident

18. Lines 31–37 provide

    (A) a contradiction of popular myth

    (B) an explanation of a paradox

    (C) a rebuttal of established facts

    (D) an exception to a general rule

    (E) a summary of conclusions

GO ON TO THE NEXT PAGE >

19. The author suggests that boundary marking was a "ritual activity" (line 52) because

    (A) the wolves marked their boundaries at regular intervals

    (B) no disputes over territory ever seemed to occur

    (C) the boundaries were marked by geographical features

    (D) the boundaries were marked at the same time each week

    (E) the whole family of wolves participated in the activity

20. Which of the following discoveries would most weaken the author's thesis concerning the wolves' "strong feeling of property" (line 54)?

    (A) Disputes over boundaries are a frequent occurrence.

    (B) Wolf territories are typically around one hundred square miles in area.

    (C) Wolf families often wander from place to place to find food.

    (D) Territorial conflicts between wolves and human beings are rare.

    (E) Wolves are generally alert when encountering other animals.

21. The author most likely mentions an "invisible wall" (line 74) in order to emphasize

    (A) his delight in attracting the wolf's attention

    (B) the wolf's annoyance at encountering a challenge

    (C) the high speed at which the wolf was traveling

    (D) the sudden manner in which the wolf stopped

    (E) the wolf's exhaustion after a night of hunting

22. The wolf's first reaction on encountering the author's property marking is one of

    (A) combativeness

    (B) confusion

    (C) anxiety

    (D) wariness

    (E) dread

23. In line 87, "temerity" means

    (A) discourtesy

    (B) rashness

    (C) courage

    (D) anger

    (E) discretion

24. The author turns his back on the wolf (lines 91–92) primarily in order to

    (A) demonstrate his power over the wolf

    (B) bring about some change in the situation

    (C) compel the wolf to recognize his existence

    (D) look for a suitable weapon

    (E) avoid the wolf's hypnotic gaze

IF YOU FINISH BEFORE TIME IS CALLED, YOU MAY CHECK YOUR WORK ON THIS SECTION ONLY. DO NOT TURN TO ANY OTHER SECTION IN THE TEST.  STOP

KAPLAN

SECTION 4

Time—25 Minutes
18 Questions

Directions: For this section, solve each problem and decide which is the best of the choices given. Fill in the corresponding oval on the answer sheet. You may use any available space for scratchwork.

Notes:

(1) Calculator use is permitted.

(2) All numbers used are real numbers.

(3) Figures are provided for some problems. All figures are drawn to scale and lie in a plane UNLESS otherwise indicated.

(4) Unless otherwise specified, the domain of any function f is assumed to be the set of all real numbers x for which $f(x)$ is a real number.

  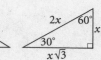

$A = \frac{1}{2}bh$ $c^2 = a^2 + b^2$ Special Right Triangles $A = \pi r^2$ $V = \ell wh$ $V = \pi r^2 h$ $A = \ell w$
$C = 2\pi r$

The sum of the degree measures of the angles in a triangle is 180.
The number of degrees of arc in a circle is 360.
A straight angle has a degree measure of 180.

1. If $r = 3$ and $s = 1$, then $r^2 - 2s =$

 (A) 2
 (B) 4
 (C) 6
 (D) 7
 (E) 9

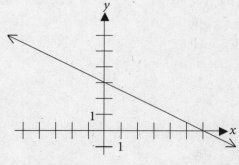

2. Which of the following equations best describes the line shown in the graph above?

 (A) $y = -2x + 6$

 (B) $y = \frac{1}{2}x + 6$

 (C) $y = -2x + 3$

 (D) $y = \frac{-1}{2}x + 3$

 (E) $y = 2x + 3$

GO ON TO THE NEXT PAGE

KAPLAN

3. If q is 4 less than r and r is 6 more than s, what is the value of q when $s = 2$?

   (A) −8
   (B) −4
   (C) −2
   (D) 4
   (E) 8

4. On a certain planet, if each year has 9 months and each month has 15 days, how many full years have passed after 700 days on this planet?

   (A) 1
   (B) 2
   (C) 3
   (D) 5
   (E) 7

5. If $f(x) = x^2$ for all real values of x, which of the following is *not* a possible value of $f(x)$?

      I. −4
     II.   0
     III. 2.3

   (A) I only
   (B) II only
   (C) III only
   (D) I and II only
   (E) II and III only

Questions 6–8 refer to the following table, which shows the amount of trash collected by 30 participants in a litter clean-up drive.

Trash Collected in Litter Clean-up Drive

Pieces of trash	10	15	20	25	30
Number of participants	12	9	4	4	1

6. What is the mode of the number of pieces of trash collected by the participants in the litter clean-up drive?

   (A) 10
   (B) 15
   (C) 20
   (D) 25
   (E) 30

7. The goal of the litter clean-up drive was to collect 500 pieces of trash. What percent of this goal did the 30 participants achieve?

   (A)   8%
   (B) 20%
   (C) 56%
   (D) 93%
   (E) 100%

8. What was the average amount of trash collected by the 30 participants in the litter clean-up drive?

   (A) between 10 and 11 pieces
   (B) between 11 and 12 pieces
   (C) between 15 and 16 pieces
   (D) between 19 and 20 pieces
   (E) between 20 and 21 pieces

GO ON TO THE NEXT PAGE

Directions: For Student-Produced Response questions 9–18, use the grids at the bottom of the answer sheet page on which you have answered questions 1–8.

Each of the remaining 10 questions requires you to solve the problem and enter your answer by marking the ovals in the special grid, as shown in the example below. You may use any available space for scratch work.

Answer: 1.25 or $\frac{5}{4}$ or 5/4

Write answer in → boxes.

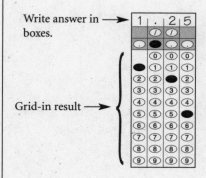

Grid-in result →

Fraction line
Decimal point

Either position is correct.

You may start your answers in any column, space permitting. Columns not needed should be left blank.

- It is recommended, though not required, that you write your answer in the boxes at the top of the columns. However, you will receive credit only for darkening the ovals correctly.

- Grid only one answer to a question, even though some problems have more than one correct answer.

- Darken no more than one oval in a column.

- No answers are negative.

- Mixed numbers cannot be gridded. For example: the number $1\frac{1}{4}$ must be gridded as 1.25 or 5/4.

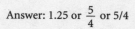

(If | 1 | 1 | / | 4 | is gridded, it will be interpreted as $\frac{11}{4}$ not $1\frac{1}{4}$.)

- <u>Decimal Accuracy:</u> Decimal answers must be entered as accurately as possible. For example, if you obtain an answer such as 0.1666..., you should record the result as .166 or .167. **Less accurate values such as .16 or .17 are not acceptable.**

Acceptable ways to grid $\frac{1}{6}$ = .1666...

10. What is $\frac{1}{4}$ percent of 16?

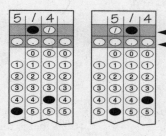

9. In the figure above, if line p is parallel to line q, what is the value of y?

GO ON TO THE NEXT PAGE →

KAPLAN

$$\frac{3}{a}, \frac{5}{a}, \frac{14}{a}$$

11. Each of the fractions above is in its simplest reduced form, and a is an integer greater than 1 and less than 50. Grid-in one possible value of a.

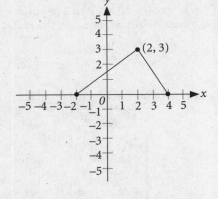

12. If there are 36 men and 24 women in a group, women make up what fraction of the entire group?

16. What is the area of the triangle in the figure above?

13. What is the value of $\frac{3s + 5}{4}$ when $s = 9$?

17. A square is divided in half to form two congruent rectangles, each with perimeter 24. What is the area of the original square?

14. If the positive integer x leaves a remainder of 2 when divided by 6, what will the remainder be when $x + 8$ is divided by 6?

18. The formula for converting a Fahrenheit temperature reading to a Celsius temperature reading is $C = \frac{5}{9}(F - 32)$, where C is the reading in degrees Celsius and F is the reading in degrees Fahrenheit. What is the Fahrenheit equivalent to a reading of 95° Celsius?

15. Pat deposited 15% of last week's take-home pay into a savings account. If she deposited $37.50, what was last week's take-home pay?

IF YOU FINISH BEFORE TIME IS CALLED, YOU MAY CHECK YOUR WORK ON THIS SECTION ONLY. DO NOT TURN TO ANY OTHER SECTION IN THE TEST. **STOP**

KAPLAN

SECTION 5
Time—25 Minutes
35 Questions

Directions: For each question in this section, select the best answer from among the choices given and fill in the corresponding oval on the answer sheet.

The following sentences test correctness and effectiveness of expression. Part of each sentence or the entire sentence is underlined; beneath each sentence are five ways of phrasing the underlined material. Choice A repeats the original phrasing; the other four choices are different. If you think the original phrasing produces a better sentence than any of the alternatives, select choice A; if not, select one of the other choices.

In making your selection, follow the requirements of standard written English; that is, pay attention to grammar, choice of words, sentence construction, and punctuation. Your selection should result in the most effective sentence—clear and precise, without awkwardness or ambiguity.

EXAMPLE: ANSWER:

Every apple in the baskets <u>are ripe and labeled according to the date it was picked</u>.   Ⓐ ● Ⓒ Ⓓ Ⓔ

(A) are ripe and labeled according to the date it was picked
(B) is ripe and labeled according to the date it was picked
(C) are ripe and labeled according to the date they were picked
(D) is ripe and labeled according to the date they were picked
(E) are ripe and labeled as to the date it was picked

---

1. Trekking into the deep, inactive crater, we suddenly realized that all outside sound <u>blocked by the dense rock walls</u> of the volcano.

   (A) blocked by the dense rock walls
   (B) blocked as a result of the dense rock walls
   (C) was blocked by the dense rock walls
   (D) was blocking the dense rock walls
   (E) was going to be blocking the dense and rocky walls

2. Tessa, after several lengthy phone conversations <u>who occupied most of her afternoon</u>, confirmed debate practice, an African dance class, and a part-time babysitting job.

   (A) who occupied most of her afternoon
   (B) whom occupied most of her afternoon
   (C) that occupied most afternoons
   (D) which occupied most of her afternoon
   (E) which became her afternoon occupation

3. <u>Perhaps no person was most crucial</u> to the success of the film "On the Waterfront" than the young actor Marlon Brando, who mesmerized audiences with his talent.

   (A) Perhaps no person was most crucial
   (B) Perhaps no person was crucialer
   (C) Perhaps every person was more crucial
   (D) Perhaps the most crucial person
   (E) Perhaps no person was more crucial

4. During the Renaissance, artists such as Michelangelo and Fra Angelico, <u>who have worked</u> for the Church, did not have to search far for subject matter.

   (A) who have worked
   (B) which worked
   (C) who worked
   (D) who worked mostly
   (E) who have always worked

GO ON TO THE NEXT PAGE

KAPLAN

5. As we waited for the Haunted House ride to begin, we heard strange sounds that seemed to be <u>neither of human or mechanical origin</u>.

    (A) neither of human or mechanical origin

    (B) neither of human nor mechanical origin

    (C) either of human nor mechanical origin

    (D) neither of human nor was it mechanical in origin

    (E) either of human origin or that of mechanical

6. Artists during World War I created performances and paintings that reflected the chaos of war, the anxiety of the people, and <u>they showed the irrational behavior that was escalating</u> in the cities of Europe.

    (A) they showed the irrational behavior that was escalating

    (B) the irrational behavior that is escalating

    (C) they showed the irrational escalation of behavior

    (D) the irrational behavior that was escalating

    (E) the irrational behavior that should have been escalating

7. Known as one of the group of existential French writers, Simone Weil is respected as much for her philosophical ideas <u>as she was for her writing</u>.

    (A) as she was for her writing

    (B) as she was for writing them down

    (C) as she is for having written

    (D) and she was for her writing

    (E) as she is for her writing

8. The professor, after distributing samples of igneous rock, explained that this type of rock is formed under intense heat and pressure <u>deep down there within the crust of the Earth</u>.

    (A) deep down there within the crust of the Earth

    (B) deep within Earth's crust

    (C) deeper down there within the crust of Earth

    (D) deep within the Earth

    (E) deep down there within the Earth's crust

9. Three women in the booth of the Swan Diner <u>were angrily discussing the terms of the lease, and arguing about</u> the level of commitment expected from each of them.

    (A) were angrily discussing the terms of the lease, and arguing about

    (B) were angrily discussing the terms of the lease, but they argued about

    (C) were discussing angrily the terms of the lease, and arguing for

    (D) was angrily discussing the terms of the lease, and arguing with

    (E) had been angrily in discussion about the terms of the lease, and arguing about

10. Although talent may be a crucial element on the road to fame, it will be <u>difficult to get very far</u> without a highly developed work ethic.

    (A) difficult to get very far

    (B) difficult to travel there

    (C) hard to get going

    (D) difficult to get farther

    (E) difficult to become well known

11. Unlike a root canal, which is the preferred method for saving a diseased tooth, <u>chewing problems can result from extraction</u>.

    (A) chewing problems can result from extraction

    (B) problems with chewing can result from an extraction

    (C) an extraction is resulting in chewing problems

    (D) an extraction can result in chewing problems

    (E) an extraction is the result of chewing problems

GO ON TO THE NEXT PAGE

Directions: The following sentences test your ability to recognize grammar and usage errors. Each sentence contains either a single error or no error at all. No sentence contains more than one error. The error, if there is one, is underlined and lettered. If the sentence contains an error, select the one underlined part that must be changed to make the sentence correct. If the sentence is correct, select choice E. In choosing answers, follow the requirements of standard written English.

EXAMPLE:

Whenever one is driving late at night, you must take extra precautions against
  A   B   C

falling asleep at the wheel. No error
             D   E

---

12. In the <u>original</u> Star Trek series, the crew <u>defied</u> the
         A   B
    laws <u>of nature</u>, because they could breathe as
         C
    easily on other planets <u>as humans</u> could breathe
                             D
    on Earth. <u>No error</u>
            E

13. Thomas <u>was</u> so proud of his <u>younger</u> brother,
          A   B
    <u>who was graduating</u> <u>from</u> college last month.
            C   D
    <u>No error</u>
      E

14. <u>Outside the barn</u>, a commotion <u>involving</u> three
         A   B
    hens and a rooster <u>woke</u> the twins, who were
                  C
    sleeping <u>deep</u>. <u>No error</u>
          D   E

15. <u>When</u> we <u>looked</u> at the photograph of the
     A   B
    lightning bolt hitting the tree, we noticed a
    <u>more smaller</u> bolt of electricity also <u>emanating</u>
       C   D
    from the ground. <u>No error</u>
                 E

16. Our Monthly Club seasonal fruits are <u>such a</u>
                                    A
    popular gift item that it <u>has become</u> necessary
                        B
    <u>to find ways</u> to accelerate the growth of <u>its</u> trees.
       C   D
    <u>No error</u>
      E

GO ON TO THE NEXT PAGE

KAPLAN

17. He could have easily <u>completed</u> the <u>unusually</u> long
                    A   B

    and complicated assignment before it was due, if

    only <u>he had started</u> it <u>earlier</u> in the week. <u>No error</u>
           C   D   E

18 Concerned <u>about</u> the playoff game <u>on</u> Saturday,
          A   B

    each of the team members <u>spent</u> most of the week
                         C

    practicing <u>their</u> plays. <u>No error</u>
           D   E

19. Studies indicate that the environment in schools

    <u>where</u> there are <u>less</u> adults on staff <u>is</u> often not
    A   B   C
    conducive <u>to</u> learning. <u>No error</u>
          D   E

20. At breakfast, Dad asked <u>Hilary and I</u> if we <u>wanted</u>
                        A   B
    to attend <u>my cousin Noah's</u> university graduation
                 C
    ceremony in Nebraska <u>next spring</u>. <u>No error</u>
                   D   E

21. Only after the water in the river had <u>rose</u>
                             A
    <u>to dangerous</u> levels <u>did</u> the governor order the
        B   C
    <u>evacuation of</u> the city. <u>No error</u>
        D   E

22. The list of concert-goers <u>who waited</u> hours for
                        A

    the entrance of their favorite music group, <u>include</u>
                                         B

    <u>more than</u> one hundred fans from European
    C
    countries, <u>who</u> traveled long distances for the
              D
    show. <u>No error</u>
        E

23. Because the university's math department was

    reconsidering <u>its</u> degree requirements it
              A
    <u>announced</u> that the schedule of classes <u>would be</u>
        B   C
    delayed for an <u>indecisive</u> period. <u>No error</u>
               D   E

24. Grant Parson's new book <u>is</u> more a compilation of
                    A
    stories <u>than like</u> a novel; characters and plot lines
          B
    appear <u>and</u> disappear <u>from chapter to</u> chapter.
          C   D
    <u>No error</u>
      E

25. If one <u>is interested</u> <u>in learning</u> <u>even more</u> about
          A   B   C
    Eleanor and Franklin Roosevelt, <u>you</u> should read
                                   D
    Goodwin's biography of the couple. <u>No error</u>
                            E

GO ON TO THE NEXT PAGE

26. Learning stations <u>in</u> elementary school classrooms
        A
<u>allow</u> students to personalize <u>their</u> education by
  B   C
reading extra-curricular books that <u>interests</u> them.
                                      D

<u>No error</u>
  E

27. The guidance counselor's recommendation

<u>included</u> a plan <u>where</u> each student was <u>to visit</u>
  A   B   C
colleges <u>throughout</u> the spring of junior year.
            D

<u>No error</u>
  E

28. <u>From 1607 until</u> 1698, Jamestown, now an
        A
<u>excavation site</u> in Virginia, was the capital of the
  B
state; <u>however</u>, by 1750 it <u>will be</u> privately owned.
        C   D

<u>No error</u>
  E

29. Throughout history, <u>both literary scholars</u> as well
                        A
as Greek historians <u>have been obsessed</u>
                      B
<u>with discovering</u> if the lost city of Atlantis,
  C
<u>described</u> by Plato, is real or mythological.
  D

<u>No error</u>
  E

GO ON TO THE NEXT PAGE >

KAPLAN

Directions: The following passage is an early draft of an essay. Some parts of the passage need to be rewritten.

Read the passage and select the best answer for each question that follows. Some questions are about particular sentences or parts of sentences and ask you to improve sentence structure or word choice. Other questions ask you to consider organization and development. In choosing answers, follow the conventions of standard written English.

Questions 30–35 are based on the following passage.

(1) Most people seem to find the winter season dreary. (2) It is true that it is cold and snows a lot. (3) But I don't see this as bleak; I see it as beautiful. (4) Winter is my favorite season of the year for three reasons.

(5) First, I think white snow and icicles all around are magical and make winter exceptional. (6) The snow puts a beautiful blanket on the outdoors, with a certain shimmer and shine. (7) Most days, when it doesn't snow, are very bright and sunny, not bleak.

(8) Second, winter weather provides them with the opportunity for so many activities. (9) It allows us to ski down mountains, skate on frozen ponds, and sled down hills. (10) When we complain that Americans don't exercise enough, people are saying that they don't take advantage of the outdoors. (11) But winter sport are the perfect opportunity to exercise outdoors.

(12) Third, winter weather allows families to gather together and connect. (13) On winter nights my family, is always enjoying a fire in the fireplace, hot chocolate, and board games. (14) And throughout the evening we can look outside and see the beautiful white snow fall on the trees and the ground. (15) The winter weather makes us more aware of the protection our home provides, and of the companionship we can provide each other, than the rest of the year.

30. Which sentence would be most appropriate to follow sentence 1?

(A) They see it as cold, snowy, and bleak.

(B) There are three months in winter.

(C) I think they are right.

(D) People prefer the warmth of summer

(E) In winter they don't get enough exercise.

31. In context, which is the best way to revise and combine the underlined portions of sentences 8 and 9 (reproduced below)?

Second, winter weather provides them with the opportunity for so many activities. It allows us to ski down mountains, skate on frozen ponds, sled down hills.

(A) winter weather provides them with the opportunity for so many activities, allowing us to

(B) winter weather provides the opportunity for so many activities, allowing people to

(C) providing the opportunity for so many activities, in winter weather it is allowed to

(D) winter weather provides many activities and allows them to

(E) winter weather is the opportunity for so many activities, it allows them to

GO ON TO THE NEXT PAGE ⟩

KAPLAN

32. Which of the following is the best version of the underlined portion of sentence 10 (reproduced below)?

    When we complain that Americans don't exercise enough, people *are saying that they don't take advantage of the outdoors.*

    (A) (As it is now)

    (B) In fact, Americans don't exercise enough; we however

    (C) Therefore, by our complaints that Americans don't exercise enough, people

    (D) However, when Americans don't exercise enough, it is because people,

    (E) When people complain that Americans don't exercise enough, they

33. In context, which of the following revisions is necessary in sentence 13 (reproduced below)?

    On winter nights my family, for instance, is always enjoying a fire in the fireplace, hot chocolate, and board games.

    (A) replace "and board games" with "and playing board games"

    (B) replace "is always" with "are always"

    (C) replace "is always enjoying" with "always enjoys"

    (D) replace "on" with "during"

    (E) replace "for instance" with "as an example"

34. Which of the following is the best version of the underlined portion of sentence 15 (reproduced below)?

    The winter weather makes us more aware of the protection our home provides, and of the companionship we can provide each other, than the rest of the year.

    (A) (As it is now)

    (B) than the rest of the year of the protection of our home and companionship of our family.

    (C) of the protection and companionship which is provided by our home and family than the rest of the year

    (D) than we are during the rest of the year of the protection our home provides, and of the companionship we can provide each other.

    (E) of home protection and companionship than we are during the rest of the year.

35. Which of the following would make the most logical final sentence for the essay?

    (A) However, in the summertime I can't enjoy hot beverages.

    (B) The snow even seems to magnify the sunlight.

    (C) Most people prefer the spring or autumn months.

    (D) Increased outdoor activity improves both mental and physical health.

    (E) Winter deserves a better reputation.

IF YOU FINISH BEFORE TIME IS CALLED, YOU MAY CHECK YOUR WORK ON THIS SECTION ONLY. DO NOT TURN TO ANY OTHER SECTION IN THE TEST.

STOP

SECTION 6

Time—25 Minutes
24 Questions

Directions: For each of the following questions, choose the best answer and darken the corresponding oval on the answer sheet.

Each sentence below has one or two blanks, each blank indicating that something has been omitted. Beneath the sentence are five words or sets of words labeled A through E. Choose the word or set of words that, when inserted in the sentence, best fits the meaning of the sentence as a whole.

EXAMPLE:

Today's small, portable computers contrast markedly with the earliest electronic computers, which were -------.

(A) effective
(B) invented
(C) useful
(D) destructive
(E) enormouss

1. The band has courted controversy before in order to get attention, and the ------- lyrics on their new album demonstrate that they found the strategy -------.

(A) sedate . . plausible
(B) vacuous . . rewarding
(C) belligerent . . counterproductive
(D) scandalous . . effective
(E) provocative . . comparable

2. James Joyce regarded ------- as central to the creative process, which is evident in the numerous scribbled edits that cover even his supposedly final drafts.

(A) contrivance
(B) revision
(C) inspiration
(D) obsession
(E) disavowal

3. Fans who believe that the players' motivations are not ------- would be ------- to learn that they now charge for their signatures.

(A) self-serving . . vindicated
(B) venal . . chagrined
(C) altruistic . . unsurprised
(D) atypical . . disillusioned
(E) tainted . . gratified

4. Though the film ostensibly deals with the theme of -------, the director seems to have been more interested in its absence—in isolation and the longing for connection.

(A) reliance
(B) fraternity
(C) socialism
(D) privation
(E) levity

5. Everything the candidate said publicly was -------; he manipulated the media in order to present the image he wanted.

(A) incendiary
(B) calculated
(C) facetious
(D) scrupulous
(E) impromptu

GO ON TO THE NEXT PAGE

KAPLAN

Directions: The passages below are followed by questions based on their content; questions following a pair of related passages may also be based on the relationship between the paired passages. Answer the questions on the basis of what is <u>stated</u> or <u>implied</u> in the passages and in any introductory material that may be provided.

Questions 6–7 refer to the following passage.

The discovery of helium required the combined efforts of several scientists. Pierre-Jules Cesar Janssen first obtained evidence for the existence of helium during a solar eclipse in 1868 when he
(5) detected a new yellow line on his spectroscope while observing the sun. This experiment was repeated by Norman Lockyer who concluded that no known element produced such a line. However, other scientists were dubious, finding it unlikely
(10) that an element existed only on the sun. Then, in 1895, William Ramsay discovered helium on Earth after treating clevite, a uranium mineral, with mineral acids. After isolating the resulting gas, Ramsay sent samples to William Crookes and
(15) Norman Lockyer who identified it conclusively as the missing element helium.

6. The passage indicates that Ramsay's chief contribution to the discovery of helium was to

(A) prove the validity of Janssen's experiment

(B) find helium in uranium minerals

(C) identify the element discovered by Crookes as helium

(D) detect helium on the sun without using a spectroscope

(E) discover that helium naturally occurs on Earth

7. The author of the passage suggests that the results of the work of Janssen and Lockyer were

(A) repeated incorrectly by other scientists

(B) thought by others to be the result of flawed methodologies

(C) met with skepticism by other scientists

(D) only valid during solar eclipses

(E) obtained using outdated equipment

Questions 8–9 refer to the following passage.

July 19: Loretta arrives tomorrow, and I'll pick her up at the airport. We'll spend the week exploring the city together, but first we'll visit Grandmama. It's been years since Loretta has seen
(5) her. The rift that began for reasons lost in the mists of family lore has continued to this day. I'll wager that Loretta can't even remember why she and Grandmama haven't spoken in all this time. The truth is, I think that Grandmama is angry
(10) with Uncle Martin, not his daughter. Now she seems ready for reconciliation—perhaps this is because she's getting older.

8. Based on the passage, the reason that Loretta and Grandmama have not seen each other in years is most likely

(A) due to Grandmama's treatment of Uncle Martin

(B) the sole purpose of Loretta's visit to the city

(C the impetus for their reunion

(D) that Loretta has been too busy to visit

(E) forgotten by both of them

9. In line 5, "rift" is best understood as meaning

(A) motion

(B) break

(C) revelry

(D) clarity

(E) discussion

GO ON TO THE NEXT PAGE

KAPLAN

Questions 10–16 refer to the following passage.

The following passage is from a discussion of the origin of the Cold War between the United States and the Soviet Union.

Revisionist historians maintain that it was within the power of the United States, in the years during and immediately after the Second World War, to prevent the Cold War with the Soviet Union.
(5) Revisionists suggest that the prospect of impending conflict with the Soviets could have been avoided in several ways. The U.S. could have officially recognized the new Soviet sphere of influence in Eastern Europe instead of continuing to
(10) call for self-determination in those countries. A much-needed reconstruction loan could have helped the Soviets recover from the war. The Americans could have sought to assuage Soviet fears by giving up the U.S. monopoly of the atomic
(15) bomb and turning the weapons over to an international agency (with the stipulation that future nuclear powers do the same).

This criticism of the post-war American course of action fails to take into account the political
(20) realities in America at the time and unfairly condemns the American policy-makers who did consider each of these alternatives and found them to be unworkable. Recognition of a Soviet Eastern Europe was out of the question. Roosevelt had
(25) promised self-determination to the Eastern European countries, and the American people, having come to expect this, were furious when Stalin began to shape his spheres of influence in the region. The President was in particular acutely
(30) conscious of the millions of Polish-Americans who would be voting in the upcoming election.

Negotiations had indeed been conducted by the administration with the Soviets about a reconstruction loan, but the Congress refused to
(35) approve it unless the Soviets made enormous concessions tantamount to restructuring their system and withdrawing from Eastern Europe. This, of course, made Soviet rejection of the loan a foregone conclusion. As for giving up the bomb—the
(40) elected officials in Washington would have been in deep trouble with their constituents had that plan been carried out. Polls showed that 82 percent of the American people understood that other nations would develop bombs eventually, but that
(45) 85 percent thought that the U.S. should retain exclusive possession of the weapon. Policy-makers have to abide by certain constraints in deciding what is acceptable and what is not. They, and not historians, are in the best position to perceive
(50) those constraints and make the decisions.

Revisionist historians tend to eschew this type of political explanation of America's supposed failure to reach a peaceful settlement with the Soviets in favor of an economic reading of events.
(55) They point to the fact that in the early post-war years, American businessmen and government officials cooperated to expand American foreign trade vigorously and to exploit investment opportunities in many foreign countries. In order to
(60) sustain the lucrative expansion, revisionists assert, American policy-makers were obliged to maintain an "Open Door" foreign policy, the object of which was to keep all potential trade opportunities open. Since the Soviets could jeopardize such
(65) opportunities in Eastern Europe and elsewhere, they had to be opposed. Hence, the Cold War. But if American policy-makers were simply pawns in an economic game of expansionist capitalism, as the revisionists seem to think, why do the revi-
(70) sionists hold them responsible for not attempting to reach an accord with the Soviets? The policy-makers, swept up by a tidal wave of capitalism, clearly had little control and little choice in the matter.
(75) Even if American officials had been free and willing to make conciliatory gestures toward the Soviets, the Cold War would not have been prevented. Overtures of friendship would not have been reciprocated (as far as we can judge; infor-
(80) mation on the inner workings of the Kremlin during that time is scanty). Soviet expert George F. Kennan concluded that Russian hostility could not be dampened by any effort on the part of the United States. The political and ideological differ-
(85) ences were too great, and the Soviets had too long

GO ON TO THE NEXT PAGE ⟶

a history of distrust of foreigners—exacerbated at the time by Stalin's rampant paranoia, which infected his government—to embark on a process of establishing trust and peace with the United
(90) States, though it was in their interest to do so.

10. The primary purpose of the passage is to

 (A) explode a popular myth
 (B) criticize historical figures
 (C) refute an argument
 (D) analyze an era
 (E) reconcile opposing views

11. In line 8, the word "recognized" most nearly means

 (A) identified
 (B) noticed
 (C) acknowledged
 (D) distinguished
 (E) remembered

12. The author refers to the Polish-Americans (lines 29–31) chiefly to illustrate that

 (A) the president had an excellent rapport with ethnic minorities
 (B) immigrants had fled from Eastern European countries to escape communism
 (C) giving up the idea of East European self-determination would have been costly in political terms
 (D) the Poles could enjoy self-determination only in America
 (E) the political landscape of the United States had changed considerably since the president was elected

13. A fundamental assumption underlying the author's argument in the second and third paragraphs is that

 (A) the Soviets were largely to blame for the failure of conciliatory U.S. initiatives
 (B) the American public was very well-informed about the incipient Cold War situation
 (C) none of the proposed alternatives would have had its intended effect
 (D) the American public was overwhelmingly opposed to seeking peace with the Soviets
 (E) the government could not have been expected to ignore public opinion

14. The phrase "certain constraints" in line 47 most likely refers to the

 (A) etiquette of international diplomacy
 (B) danger of leaked information about atomic bombs
 (C) views of the electorate
 (D) potential reaction of the enemy
 (E) difficulty of carrying out a policy initiative

GO ON TO THE NEXT PAGE

15. Which statement best summarizes the revisionist argument concerning the origin of the Cold War (lines 51–66)?

    (A) The United States started the Cold War in order to have a military cover for illegal trading activities.

    (B) The Soviets were oblivious to the negative impact they had on the American economy.

    (C) The economic advantage of recognizing Soviet Europe outweighed the disadvantage of an angry public.

    (D) America could trade and invest with foreign countries only if it agreed to oppose the Soviet Union.

    (E) American economic interests abroad would have been threatened by any Soviet expansion.

16. The question at the end of the fourth paragraph (lines 66–71) serves to

    (A) point out an inconsistency in a position

    (B) outline an area that requires further research

    (C) contrast two different historical interpretations

    (D) sum up a cynical view of post-war economic activity

    (E) restate the central issue of the passage

GO ON TO THE NEXT PAGE

Questions 17–24 refer to the following passage.

James Weldon Johnson was a poet, diplomat, composer, and historian of black culture who wrote around the turn of the century. In this narrative passage, Johnson recalls his first experience of hearing rag-time jazz.

When I had somewhat collected my senses, I realized that in a large back room into which the main room opened, there was a young fellow singing a song, accompanied on the piano by a
(5) short, thickset black man. After each verse, he did some dance steps, which brought forth great applause and a shower of small coins at his feet. After the singer had responded to a rousing encore, the stout man at the piano began to run
(10) his fingers up and down the keyboard. This he did in a manner which indicated that he was a master of a good deal of technique. Then he began to play; and such playing! I stopped talking to listen. It was music of a kind I had never heard before. It
(15) was music that demanded physical response, patting of the feet, drumming of the fingers, or nodding of the head in time with the beat. The dissonant harmonies, the audacious resolutions, often consisting of an abrupt jump from one key to
(20) another, the intricate rhythms in which the accents fell in the most unexpected places, but in which the beat was never lost, produced a most curious effect . . .

This was rag-time music, then a novelty in New
(25) York, and just growing to be a rage, which has not yet subsided. It was originated in the questionable resorts about Memphis and St. Louis by Negro piano-players who knew no more of the theory of music than they did of the theory of the universe,
(30) but were guided by natural musical instinct and talent. It made its way to Chicago, where it was popular some time before it reached New York. These players often improvised simple and, at times, vulgar words to fit the melodies. This was
(35) the beginning of the rag-time song . . .

American musicians, instead of investigating rag-time, attempt to ignore it, or dismiss it with a contemptuous word. But that has always been the course of scholasticism in every branch of art.
(40) Whatever new thing the *people* like is pooh-poohed; whatever is *popular* is spoken of as not worth the while. The fact is, nothing great or enduring, especially in music, has ever sprung full-fledged and unprecedented from the brain of any
(45) master; the best that he gives to the world he gathers from the hearts of the people, and runs it through the alembic* of his genius. In spite of the bans which musicians and music teachers have placed upon it, the people still demand and enjoy
(50) rag-time. One thing cannot be denied; it is music which possesses at least one strong element of greatness: it appeals universally; not only the American, but the English, the French, and even the German people find delight in it. In fact, there
(55) is not a corner of the civilized world in which it is not known, and this proves its originality; for if it were an imitation, the people of Europe, anyhow, would not have found it a novelty . . .

I became so interested in both the music and
(60) the player that I left the table where I was sitting, and made my way through the hall into the back room, where I could see as well as hear. I talked to the piano player between the musical numbers and found out that he was just a natural musician,
(65) never having taken a lesson in his life. Not only could he play almost anything he heard, but he could accompany singers in songs he had never heard. He had, by ear alone, composed some pieces, several of which he played over for me;
(70) each of them was properly proportioned and balanced. I began to wonder what this man with such a lavish natural endowment would have done had he been trained. Perhaps he wouldn't have done anything at all; he might have become, at best, a
(75) mediocre imitator of the great masters in what they have already done to a finish, or one of the modern innovators who strive after originality by seeing how cleverly they can dodge about through the rules of harmony and at the same time avoid
(80) melody. It is certain that he would not have been so delightful as he was in rag-time.

alembic: scientific apparatus used in the process of distillation

GO ON TO THE NEXT PAGE

17. In relating his initial impression of rag-time music to the reader, the narrator makes use of

    (A) comparison with the improvisations of classical music

    (B) reference to the audience's appreciative applause

    (C) description of the music's compelling rhythmic effect

    (D) evocation of poignant visual images

    (E) allusion to several popular contemporary tunes

18. In the first paragraph, the narrator portrays rag-time as a type of music that

    (A) would be a challenge to play for even the most proficient musician

    (B) satisfied the narrator's expectations regarding the genre

    (C) violated all of the accepted rules governing musical composition

    (D) made up for a lack of melody with a seductive rhythm

    (E) contained several surprises for the discerning listener

19. In line 26, "questionable" most nearly means

    (A) disreputable

    (B) ambiguous

    (C) doubtful

    (D) approachable

    (E) unconfirmed

20. The narrator's perspective during the second and third paragraphs is that of

    (A) an impartial historian of events in the recent past

    (B) a mesmerized spectator of a musical spectacle

    (C) a knowledgeable critic of the contemporary musical scene

    (D) a commentator reflecting on a unique experience

    (E) an adult reminiscing fondly about his youth

21. The discussion in the third paragraph of the refusal of American musicians to investigate rag-time suggests that they

    (A) have little or no interest in pleasing people with their music

    (B) need to be made aware of the popularity of rag-time in Europe

    (C) are misguided in their conservative and condescending attitude

    (D) attack rag-time for being merely an imitation of an existing style

    (E) know that it would be difficult to refine rag-time as a musical form

22. Which statement best summarizes the author's argument in the third paragraph?

    (A) Any type of music that is extremely popular should be considered great.

    (B) The two criteria for musical greatness are popularity and originality.

    (C) Music that has become popular overseas cannot be ignored by American musicians.

    (D) Rag-time must be taken up by a musical master and purified to earn critical acclaim.

    (E) Mass appeal in music can be a sign of greatness rather than a stigma.

GO ON TO THE NEXT PAGE ▷

KAPLAN

23 The statement in lines 73–74 ("Perhaps he wouldn't have done anything at all") is best interpreted as conveying

(A) doubt about the depth of the piano player's skill

(B) understanding that no amount of talent can compensate for a lack of discipline

(C) cynicism about the likelihood that a man can live up to his potential

(D) a recognition that the piano player might have wasted his talent

(E) frustration at the impossibility of knowing what might have been

24. The author's view (lines 71–80) about the rag-time piano player's lack of formal training can best be summarized as which of the following?

(A) The piano player's natural talent had allowed him to develop technically to the point where formal training would have been superfluous.

(B) Formal lessons would have impaired the piano player's native ability to play and compose by ear alone.

(C) More would have been lost than gained if the piano player had been given formal lessons.

(D) The piano player's potential to be a truly innovative rag-time artist had been squandered because he had not been formally trained.

(E) Although dazzling when improvising rag-time, the piano player could never have been more than mediocre as a classical pianist.

IF YOU FINISH BEFORE TIME IS CALLED, YOU MAY CHECK YOUR WORK ON THIS SECTION ONLY. DO NOT TURN TO ANY OTHER SECTION IN THE TEST.

STOP

SECTION 7

Time—20 Minutes
16 Questions

Directions: For this section, solve each problem and decide which is the best of the choices given. Fill in the corresponding oval on the answer sheet. You may use any available space for scratchwork.

Notes:

(1) Calculator use is permitted.

(2) All numbers used are real numbers.

(3) Figures are provided for some problems. All figures are drawn to scale and lie in a plane UNLESS otherwise indicated.

(4) Unless otherwise specified, the domain of any function f is assumed to be the set of all real numbers x for which $f(x)$ is a real number.

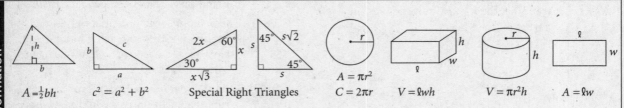

$A = \frac{1}{2}bh$ $c^2 = a^2 + b^2$ Special Right Triangles $A = \pi r^2$ $V = \ell wh$ $V = \pi r^2 h$ $A = \ell w$
                                                                    $C = 2\pi r$

The sum of the degree measures of the angles in a triangle is 180.
The number of degrees of arc in a circle is 360.
A straight angle has a degree measure of 180.

1. For all values of x, $(3x + 4)(4x - 3) =$

   (A) $7x + 1$
   (B) $7x - 12$
   (C) $12x^2 - 12$
   (D) $12x^2 - 25x - 12$
   (E) $12x^2 + 7x - 12$

2. In a certain set of numbers, the ratio of integers to nonintegers is 2:3. What percent of the numbers in the set are integers?

   (A) 20%
   (B) $33\frac{1}{3}$%
   (C) 40%
   (D) 60%
   (E) $66\frac{2}{3}$%

3. If $xyz \neq 0$, which of the following is equivalent to $\dfrac{x^2 y^3 z^4}{(xyz^2)^2}$?

   (A) $\dfrac{1}{y}$

   (B) $\dfrac{1}{z}$

   (C) y

   (D) $\dfrac{x}{yz}$

   (E) xyz

4. When the positive integer p is divided by 7, the remainder is 5. What is the remainder when $5p$ is divided by 7?

   (A) 0
   (B) 1
   (C) 2
   (D) 3
   (E) 4

GO ON TO THE NEXT PAGE

KAPLAN

5. What is the *y*-intercept of the line with the equation $2x - 3y = 18$?

   (A) −9
   (B) −6
   (C) −3
   (D) 6
   (E) 9

6. Jan types at an average rate of 12 pages per hour. At that rate, how long will it take Jan to type 100 pages?

   (A) 8 hours and 3 minutes
   (B) 8 hours and 15 minutes
   (C) 8 hours and 20 minutes
   (D) 8 hours and 30 minutes
   (E) 8 hours and $33\frac{1}{3}$ minutes

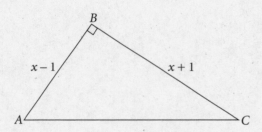

7. In the figure above, *AB* is perpendicular to *BC*. The lengths of *AB* and *BC* are given in terms of *x*. Which of the following represents the area of $\triangle ABC$ for all $x > 1$?

   (A) x
   (B) $2x$
   (C) x^2
   (D) $x^2 - 1$
   (E) $\dfrac{x^2 - 1}{2}$

8. If Jim and Bill have less than 15 dollars between them, and Bill has 4 dollars, which of the following could be the number of dollars that Jim has?

   I. 10
   II. 11
   III. 15

   (A) I only
   (B) II only
   (C) I and II only
   (D) II and III only
   (E) I, II, and III

9. Angelo makes *x* dollars for *y* hours of work. Sarah makes the same amount of money for 1 less hour of work. Which of the following expressions represents the positive difference between the two people's hourly wage?

   (A) $\dfrac{x}{y-1} - \dfrac{x}{y}$
   (B) $\dfrac{x}{y} - \dfrac{x}{y-1}$
   (C) $\dfrac{x}{y-1} + \dfrac{x}{y}$
   (D) $\dfrac{y-1}{x} - \dfrac{y}{x}$
   (E) $\dfrac{y}{x} - \dfrac{y-1}{x}$

10. Erica has 8 squares of felt, each with area 16. For a certain craft project she cuts the largest circle possible from each square of felt. What is the combined area of the excess felt left over after cutting out all the circles?

   (A) $4(4 - \pi)$
   (B) $8(4 - \pi)$
   (C) $8(\pi - 2)$
   (D) $32(4 - \pi)$
   (E) $16(16 - \pi)$

GO ON TO THE NEXT PAGE

11. In the sequence 2, 6, 18, x, 162 ... , what is the most likely value of x?

   (A) 36

   (B) 48

   (C) 54

   (D) 81

   (E) 98

12. What is the remainder when $5x^3 - 2x^2 + x + 1$ is divided by $x - 3$?

   (A) −121

   (B) −60

   (C) 65

   (D) 120

   (E) 121

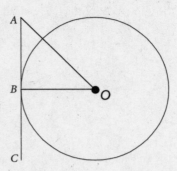

13. In the diagram above, the circle's center is at point O. $\overline{AC}$ is tangent to the circle at point B, which is the midpoint of $\overline{AC}$. If $AC = 4$ and the area of the circle is 4π, what is the length of $\overline{AO}$?

   (A) 2

   (B) $2\sqrt{2}$

   (C) 3

   (D) 4

   (E) $4\sqrt{2}$

GO ON TO THE NEXT PAGE

KAPLAN

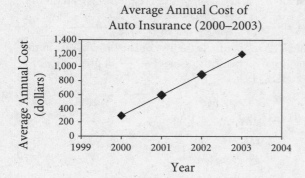

Average Annual Cost of
Auto Insurance (2000–2003)

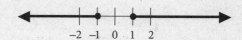

14. The graph above represents the average annual cost of automobile insurance in a certain state from 2000 to 2003. Assuming that the cost of insurance increases at the same average (arithmetic mean) rate depicted in the graph, what is the expected cost of automobile insurance in 2004?

(A) $200
(B) $550
(C) $875
(D) $1,000
(E) $1,500

15. Which of the following expressions describes the indicated values on the number line above?

(A) $x \leq 1$
(B) $x \geq 1$
(C) $|x| \leq 1$
(D) $|x| \geq 1$
(E) $x \geq |1|$

16. There are 3 routes from Bay City to Riverville. There are 4 routes from Riverville to Straitstown. There are 3 routes from Straitstown to Frog Pond. If a driver must pass through Riverville and Straitstown exactly once, how many possible ways are there to go from Bay City to Frog Pond?

(A)   6
(B) 10
(C) 12
(D) 24
(E) 36

IF YOU FINISH BEFORE TIME IS CALLED, YOU MAY CHECK YOUR WORK ON THIS SECTION ONLY. DO NOT TURN TO ANY OTHER SECTION IN THE TEST.

STOP

KAPLAN

SECTION 8

Time—20 Minutes
19 Questions

Directions: For each of the following questions, choose the best answer and darken the corresponding oval on the answer sheet.

Each sentence below has one or two blanks, each blank indicating that something has been omitted. Beneath the sentence are five words or sets of words labeled A through E. Choose the word or set of words that, when inserted in the sentence, <u>best</u> fits the meaning of the sentence as a whole.

EXAMPLE

Today's small, portable computers contrast markedly with the earliest electronic computers, which were -------.

(A) effective
(B) invented
(C) useful
(D) destructive
(E) enormouss

---

1. Although Sub-Saharan Africa encompasses a large number of ------- cultures, its music is often considered an essentially ------- mass.

   (A) disparate . . homogeneous
   (B) impoverished . . inimitable
   (C) warring . . concrete
   (D) interwoven . . distinctive
   (E) proud . . languid

2. His face was -------, his features pulled downward by the weight of heavy thoughts.

   (A) morose
   (B) onerous
   (C) contorted
   (D) ossified
   (E) inscrutable

3. The unfortunate demise of the protagonist in the final scene of the movie ------- all possibility of a sequel.

   (A) entertained
   (B) dissembled
   (C) raised
   (D) exacerbated
   (E) precluded

4. The repeated breakdown of negotiations only ------- the view that the two sides were not truly committed to the goal of ------- a military confrontation.

   (A) established . . escalating
   (B) undermined . . avoiding
   (C) distorted . . financing
   (D) strengthened . . initiating
   (E) reinforced . . averting

5. Duncan was a modest and cooperative worker; he demonstrated none of his colleague's -------.

   (A) geniality
   (B) influence
   (C) arrogance
   (D) reluctance
   (E) humility

6. When the election results were announced, the victorious candidate's exhilaration temporarily ------- the recognition of the forthcoming ------- to improve the economic climate of the city.

   (A) accepted . . . promise
   (B) illuminated . . . campaign
   (C) admitted . . . hostility
   (D) eclipsed . . . struggle
   (E) blocked . . . inauguration

GO ON TO THE NEXT PAGE

Questions 7–19 refer to the following passages.

These passages present two critics' perspectives on the topic of design museums.

Passage 1

City museums are places where people can learn about various cultures by studying objects of particular historical or artistic value. The increasingly popular "design museums" that are opening today

(5) perform quite a different function. Unlike most city museums, the design museum displays and assesses objects that are readily available to the general public. These museums place ignored household appliances under spotlights, breaking

(10) down the barriers between commerce and creative invention.

Critics have argued that design museums are often manipulated to serve as advertisements for new industrial technology. But their role is not

(15) simply a matter of merchandising—it is the honoring of impressive, innovative products. The difference between the window of a department store and the showcase in a design museum is that the first tries to sell you something, while the second

(20) informs you of the success of the attempt.

One advantage that the design museum has over other civic museums is that design museums are places where people feel familiar with the exhibits. Unlike the average art gallery patron, design mu-

(25) seum visitors rarely feel intimidated or disoriented. Partly this is because design museums clearly illustrate how and why mass-produced consumer objects work and look as they do and show how design contributes to the quality of our lives. For

(30) example, an exhibit involving a particular design of chair would not simply explain how it functions as a chair. It would also demonstrate how its various features combine to produce an artistic effect or redefine our manner of performing the basic act of

(35) being seated. The purpose of such an exhibit would be to present these concepts in ways that challenge, stimulate, and inform the viewer. An art gallery

exhibit, on the other hand, would provide very little information about the chair and charge the visitor

(40) with understanding the exhibit on some abstract level.

Within the past decade, several new design museums have opened their doors. Each of these museums has responded in totally original ways to

(45) the public's growing interest in the field. London's Design Museum, for instance, displays a collection of mass-produced objects ranging from Zippo lighters to electric typewriters to a show of Norwegian sardine-tin labels. The options open to

(50) curators of design museums seem far less rigorous, conventionalized, and pre-programmed than those applying to curators in charge of public galleries of paintings and sculpture. The humorous aspects of our society are better represented in the

(55) display of postmodern playthings or quirky Japanese vacuum cleaners in pastel colors than in an exhibition of Impressionist landscapes.

Passage 2

The short histories of some of the leading technical and design museums make clear an

(60) underlying difficulty in this area. The tendency everywhere today is to begin with present machines and technological processes and to show how they operate and the scientific principles on which they are based without paying much atten-

(65) tion to their historical development, to say nothing of the society that produced them. Only a few of the oldest, largest and best-supported museums collect historical industrial objects. Most science centers put more emphasis on mock-ups, graphs,

(70) and multimedia devices. This approach of "presentism" often leads the museum to drop all attempts at study and research; if industry is called upon to design and build the exhibits, curators may be entirely dispensed with, so that impartial and scien-

(75) tific study disappears, and emphasis is placed on the idea that progress automatically follows technology.

GO ON TO THE NEXT PAGE

Industrialization and the machine have, of
course, brought much progress; a large portion of
humankind no longer works from sun-up to sun-
(80) down to obtain the bare necessities of life. But
industrialization also creates problems—harm to
the environment and ecology, neglect of social,
cultural, and humanistic values, depletion of
resources, and even threats of human extinction.
(85) Thus, progress needs to be considered critically—
from a wider social and humanitarian point of
view. Unfortunately, most museums of science and
technology glorify machines. Displayed in pristine
condition, elegantly painted or polished, they can
(90) make the observer forget the noise, dirt, danger,
and frustration of machine-tending. Mines,
whether coal, iron, or salt, are a favorite museum
display but only infrequently is there even a hint
of the dirt, the damp, the smell, the low head-
(95) room, or the crippling and destructive accidents
that sometimes occur in industry.

Machinery also ought to be operated to be mean-
ingful. Consequently, it should not be shown in
sculptured repose but in full, often clattering,
(100) action. This kind of operation is difficult to obtain,
and few museums can command the imagination,
ingenuity, and manual dexterity it requires.
Problems also arise in providing adequate safety
devices for both the public and the machine opera-
(105) tors. These, then, are some of the underlying problems of the technical museum—problems not
solved by the usual push buttons, cranks, or multimedia gimmicks. Yet attendance figures show that
technical museums outdraw all the others; the pub-
(110) lic possesses lively curiosity and a real desire to
understand science and technology.

7. In Passage 1, line 7, the word "readily" most nearly
means

(A) easily
(B) willingly
(C) instantly
(D) cheaply
(E) constantly

8. The author of Passage 1 refers to objects displayed
in design museums as "ignored" (line 8) to
emphasize that these objects were

(A) unsuccessful commercially
(B) generally unused in the household
(C) never the subject of conversation in the
household
(D) allowed to fall into disrepair
(E) not treated as objects of beauty

9. In lines 16–20, the author of Passage 1 suggests
that design museums are different from store windows in that

(A) design museums display more technologically
advanced products
(B) store window displays are not created with as
much concern to the visual quality of the
display
(C) design museums are not concerned with the
commercial aspects of a successful product
(D) design museums focus on highlighting the
artistic qualities that help sell products
(E) the objects in store displays are more commercially successful than those in design
museums

10. From Passage 1, lines 24–29, it can be inferred that
the author believes that most museum visitors

(A) are hostile toward the concept of abstract art
(B) prefer to have a context in which to understand museum exhibits
(C) are confused when faced with complex technological exhibits
(D) are unfamiliar with the exhibits in design
museums
(E) undervalue the artistic worth of household
items

GO ON TO THE NEXT PAGE

11. The third paragraph of Passage 1 suggests that one important difference between design museums and the art galleries is

    (A) the low price of admission at design museums

    (B) the amount of information presented with design museum exhibits

    (C) the intelligence of the average museum visitor

    (D) that art galleries feature exhibits that have artistic merit

    (E) the contribution that design museums make to our quality of life

12. In Passage 1, line 49, the word "options" most likely refers to the ability of curators of design museums to

    (A) afford large collections of exhibits

    (B) attract a wide range of visitors

    (C) put together unconventional collections

    (D) feature rare objects that interest the public

    (E) satisfy their own personal whims in planning exhibitions

13. In Passage 1, line 57, the author most likely mentions "Impressionist landscapes" in order to

    (A) provide an example of a typical design museum exhibit

    (B) compare postmodern exhibits to 19th century art

    (C) point out a decline in the sophistication of the museum-going public

    (D) refute the notion that postmodern art is whimsical

    (E) emphasize the contrast between two different types of exhibits

14. Which of the following best describes the "underlying difficulty" mentioned in lines 59–60 of Passage 2?

    (A) Design museums rarely mention the historical origin of objects they display.

    (B) Industrial involvement often forces curators out of their jobs.

    (C) Design museums appropriate technology that is essential for study and research.

    (D) Technology almost never leads to progress.

    (E) Industry places too much emphasis on impartial research.

15. The author of Passage 2 most likely mentions "harm to the environment and ecology" (lines 82–83) in order to

    (A) encourage a critical response to the technological age

    (B) discourage the reader from visiting technology museums

    (C) describe the hazardous conditions in coal, iron, and salt mines

    (D) dissuade museum visitors from operating the machinery on display

    (E) praise museums that present an accurate depiction of technology

16. The author uses the phrase "sculptured repose" (Passage 2, line 99) in order to

    (A) condemn the curators of design museums for poor planning

    (B) illustrate the greatest problem inherent in design museums

    (C) present an idealized vision of a type of exhibit

    (D) describe the unrealistic way in which machinery is generally displayed

    (E) compare the shape of a machine to a work of art

GO ON TO THE NEXT PAGE

KAPLAN

17. The word "command" (Passage 2, line 101) most nearly means

    (A) oversee
    (B) direct
    (C) control
    (D) summon
    (E) order

18. The author of Passage 2 would probably object to the statement in Passage 1 that design "contributes to the quality of our lives" (lines 28–29) on the grounds that

    (A) technical innovation has historically posed threats to our physical and social well-being
    (B) the general public would benefit more from visiting art galleries
    (C) machinery that is not shown in action is meaningless to the viewer
    (D) industry has made a negligible contribution to human progress
    (E) few people have a genuine interest in the impact of science and technology

19. The authors of both passages would probably agree that

    (A) machinery is only enjoyable to watch when it is moving
    (B) most people are curious about the factors behind the design of everyday objects
    (C) the public places a higher value on packaging than it does on quality
    (D) the very technology that is displayed in the museums is likely to cost curators their jobs
    (E) design museums are flawed because they fail to accurately portray the environmental problems that technology sometimes causes

IF YOU FINISH BEFORE TIME IS CALLED, YOU MAY CHECK YOUR WORK ON THIS SECTION ONLY. DO NOT TURN TO ANY OTHER SECTION IN THE TEST. **STOP**

KAPLAN

SECTION 9

Time—10 Minutes
14 Questions

Directions: For each question in this section, select the best answer from among the choices given and fill in the corresponding oval on the answer sheet.

The following sentences test correctness and effectiveness of expression. Part of each sentence or the entire sentence is underlined; beneath each sentence are five ways of phrasing the underlined material. Choice A repeats the original phrasing; the other four choices are different. If you think the original phrasing produces a better sentence than any of the alternatives, select choice A; if not, select one of the other choices.

In making your selection, follow the requirements of standard written English; that is, pay attention to grammar, choice of words, sentence construction, and punctuation. Your selection should result in the most effective sentence—clear and precise, without awkwardness or ambiguity.

EXAMPLE: ANSWER:

Every apple in the baskets <u>are ripe and labeled according to the date it was picked</u>.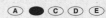

(A) are ripe and labeled according to the date it was picked
(B) is ripe and labeled according to the date it was picked
(C) are ripe and labeled according to the date they were picked
(D) is ripe and labeled according to the date they were picked
(E) are ripe and labeled as to the date it was picked

---

1. A spokesman for the car company boasted that the new model was lightweight, effective, <u>and virtually indistinguishable from the expensive model commonly used in movies</u>.

   (A) and virtually indistinguishable from the expensive model commonly used in movies

   (B) and the expensive model commonly used in movies could not distinguish it

   (C) and virtually indistinguishable by the expensive model commonly used in movies

   (D) and had gone virtually indistinguished by the expensive model commonly used in movies

   (E) and the expensive model commonly used in movies virtually unable to distinguish it

2. <u>Because the polar ice caps are melting, therefore many</u> scientists and environmentalists fear that several small island nations will be completely covered by water in only a few decades.

   (A) Because the polar ice caps are melting, therefore many

   (B) Because the polar ice caps are melting, many

   (C) The polar ice caps are melting, therefore many

   (D) Because the polar ice caps are melting; many

   (E) The polar ice caps are melting; and many

GO ON TO THE NEXT PAGE

KAPLAN

3. One of the great literary artists of the nineteenth <u>century was Gustave Flaubert known for his obsession with the writer's craft</u>.

   (A) century was Gustave Flaubert known for his obsession with the writer's craft

   (B) century, Gustave Flaubert's obsession with the writer's craft was well known

   (C) century, Gustave Flaubert was known for his obsession with the writer's craft

   (D) century, Gustave Flaubert, known for his obsession with the writer's craft

   (E) century was Gustave Flaubert: known for his obsession with the writer's craft

4. David Hockney created <u>images and they converge</u> the art of photography with the craft of collages, giving his works a cubist effect.

   (A) images and they converge

   (B) images, being the convergence of

   (C) images, they converge

   (D) images that converge

   (E) images, and converging in them

5. The dean of students argued that although the university's professors have raised students' interest in continuing in academia, <u>the failure is in their not preparing</u> the students for the real world outside of textbooks and calculators.

   (A) the failure is in their not preparing

   (B) the failure they have is in their not preparing

   (C) they failed not to prepare

   (D) they have failed to prepare

   (E) failing in their preparation of

6. The amount of water used by Americans can be reduced by turning off faucets when not in use, decreasing time spent in showers, <u>and running washing machines</u> less frequently.

   (A) and running washing machines

   (B) and if they run washing machines

   (C) also by running washing machines

   (D) and washing machines being run

   (E) and if there ran washing machines

GO ON TO THE NEXT PAGE

KAPLAN

7. <u>Having exceptionally clear waters and active underwater life, the directors chose Cozumel</u> as a prospective site for their next documentary on scuba diving.

   (A) Having exceptionally clear waters and active underwater life, the directors chose Cozumel

   (B) Directors who chose Cozumel for its exceptionally clear waters and active underwater life seeing it

   (C) Cozumel's exceptionally clear waters and active underwater life led to its choice by directors

   (D) Because its waters are clear and it has active underwater life, directors chose Cozumel

   (E) Based on its clear waters and active underwater life, Cozumel, which was chosen by directors,

8. Several of Salvador Dali's <u>paintings were inspired by his wife, featured</u> beauty, grace, and femininity.

   (A) paintings were inspired by his wife, featured

   (B) paintings had their inspiration from his wife, with features

   (C) paintings, inspired by his wife, featured

   (D) paintings, which were inspired by his wife, and which featured

   (E) paintings, being inspired by his wife, featuring

9. <u>The fire, once close to destroying another forest, had</u> trickled to a small flame.

   (A) The fire, once close to destroying another forest, had

   (B) The fire was once close to destroying another forest, it had

   (C) The fire that once having been close to destroying another forest had

   (D) The fire, because it was once close to destroying a forest, had

   (E) The fire was once close to destroying a forest, and it had

10. Michael Ondaatje collected the anecdotes and memories of his family in Ceylon, his native country, and <u>these are stories that are told</u> in his memoir.

    (A) these are stories that are told

    (B) the telling of these stories is

    (C) these stories having been told

    (D) his telling of these stories

    (E) told these stories

GO ON TO THE NEXT PAGE

11. The idea that women should not vote or express
    their political opinions prevailed in nineteenth-
    century America.

    (A) The idea that women should not vote or
        express their political opinions prevailed in
        nineteenth-century America.

    (B) The idea that prevailed about women during
        nineteenth-century America was that of
        not voting and not expressing their political
        opinions.

    (C) During most of nineteenth-century America,
        they had a prevalent idea that women
        should not vote or express political
        opinions.

    (D) Prevalent as the idea during nineteenth-
        century America was for women to not
        vote or express their political opinions.

    (E) Prevalent during nineteenth-century
        America, they thought that women should
        not vote or express political opinions.

12. The peace conference that was being mediated by
    the president, but now the countries are adamantly
    refusing to compromise their positions.

    (A) The peace conference that was being mediated
        by the president, but now the countries are
        adamantly refusing to compromise their
        positions.

    (B) The president had mediated the peace confer-
        ence, but the countries are now adamantly
        refusing to compromise their positions.

    (C) The peace conference was mediated by the
        president, and so now the countries are
        adamantly refusing to compromise their
        positions.

    (D) Though the president mediated the peace
        conference, the countries now adamantly
        refusing to compromise their beliefs.

    (E) Now adamantly refusing to compromise their
        beliefs, the president mediated the peace
        conference.

GO ON TO THE NEXT PAGE ▷

13. For many an inspirational writer, <u>being free to create is more important</u> than having a lot of money.

    (A) being free to create is more important
    (B) having freedom of creation is more important
    (C) there is more importance in the freedom to create
    (D) freedom to create has more importance
    (E) to have the freedom to create is more important

14. Although Internet traffic often occurs during the evening hours, <u>causing it to delay connection no more</u> than 2 minutes.

    (A) causing it to delay connection no more
    (B) and yet it delays connection no more
    (C) it does not delay connection more
    (D) and it does not delay connection more
    (E) yet causing it to delay no more

IF YOU FINISH BEFORE TIME IS CALLED, YOU MAY CHECK YOUR WORK ON THIS SECTION ONLY. DO NOT TURN TO ANY OTHER SECTION IN THE TEST.

STOP

KAPLAN

Practice Test Two: **Answer Key**

SECTION 1

Essay

SECTION 2

1. E
2. E
3. C
4. A
5. A
6. D
7. C
8. A
9. C
10. A
11. E
12. C
13. A
14. D
15. C
16. A
17. E
18. B
19. D
20. D

SECTION 3

1. C
2. E
3. A
4. A
5. C
6. C
7. D
8. C
9. B

10. A
11. D
12. E
13. C
14. A
15. D
16. C
17. C
18. A
19. B
20. C
21. D
22. B
23. B
24. B

SECTION 4

1. D
2. D
3. D
4. D
5. A
6. A
7. D
8. C
9. 115
10. .04
11. 11, 13, 17, 19, 23, 29, 31, 37, 41, 43, or 47
12. 2/5 or .4
13. 8
14. 4
15. 250
16. 9

17. 64
18. 203

SECTION 5

1. C
2. D
3. E
4. C
5. B
6. D
7. E
8. B
9. A
10. A
11. D
12. E
13. C
14. D
15. C
16. D
17. E
18. D
19. B
20. A
21. A
22. B
23. D
24. B
25. D
26. D
27. B
28. D
29. A
30. A
31. B

32. E
33. C
34. D
35. E

SECTION 6

1. D
2. B
3. B
4. B
5. B
6. E
7. C
8. E
9. B
10. C
11. C
12. C
13. E
14. C
15. E
16. A
17. C
18. E
19. A
20. C
21. C
22. E
23. D
24. C

SECTION 7

1. E
2. C
3. C
4. E

5. B
6. C
7. E
8. A
9. A
10. D
11. C
12. E
13. B
14. E
15. D
16. E

SECTION 8

1. A
2. A
3. E
4. E
5. C
6. D
7. A
8. E
9. D
10. B
11. B
12. C
13. E
14. A
15. A
16. D
17. D
18. A
19. B

SECTION 9

1. A
2. B
3. C
4. D
5. D
6. A
7. C
8. C
9. A
10. E
11. A
12. B
13. A
14. C

Answers and Explanations

SECTION 1

6 Essay

Luis Buñuel hits truth with this statement, bringing up one of the human condition's greatest dilemmas. I think that without memory, we would know nothing, absorb nothing, feel nothing, and be nothing. The only reason humans care about anything, feel anything, or are anything, is because of memories from their own lives.

Memories play a large role in shaping our societies, because we learn from the events of history, and we even shape our governments based on the ideas of ancient Greeks.

And most importantly, memories are exactly what make us individuals. For example, our childhood shapes who we are for our whole lives, from things as vital as the thinking process, to things as trivial as eating habits and music taste. We have to remember words in order to speak and we have to remember how to walk as well as the names and faces of our parents.

I have found that love, hate, anger, happiness, sadness, are all caused by remembering what just happened to us. And these emotions would mean nothing if we forgot them an instant after we had them, because they would seem to never existed. Even the greatest suffering would mean nothing if we forgot it seconds later, and if I fell in love with someone, but I forgot about them a second later, it would mean absolutely nothing to me. It's just like the "If a tree falls in the forest and no one sees it, does it make a sound" dilemma. If we experience something and forget it instantly, we can never know and will never know if it existed.

Memory is vital to human existence. In fact, it is human existence. To quote Luis Buñuel, …*Memory is our coherence, our reason… Without it we are nothing*.

Grader's Comments

The essay is scored based on 4 basic criteria: Topic, Support, Organization, and Language. This essay does well on all counts, so it has earned a 6. It demonstrates an especially strong grasp of the writing assignment, earning high points for topic, support, and organization. The author states a thesis in paragraph 1, and then provides specific, relevant examples in each paragraph that support the idea of memory shaping the individual life. The examples are explained clearly and follow logically.

The writing stays on track, using the writer's previous knowledge to discuss the topic comfortably. The writer uses key phrases such as *and most importantly, for example,* and *I have found* to link and explain connected ideas. Vocabulary is strong (*dilemmas,* and *absorb* for example). The brief discussion of philosophy in the fourth paragraph shows the writer's attempt to connect the argument to literature. The closing paragraph sums up the writer's opinion. The opening sentence of the fourth paragraph is unnecessarily passive but this does not detract from the overall high quality of the essay.

4 Essay

Without memory, we are basically nothing. For instance, during the war in 2003, if we had remembered that Saddam Hussein hadn't cooperated last time, we could have gone in and removed him without the hassle of waiting for the weapons inspectors and things might have gone easier.

Another is example is to eat chocolate. Everyone knows that it tastes good. But I would never buy chocolate if I didn't remember how it tasted. In history, as well, such as the French revolution, memory is also vital. The French would not have fought for their freedom in the Revolution unless they remembered what freedom was like or what it would be like as well. Also, scientists wouldn't be able to make new discoveries without the memory, because how else would they remember complicated formulas or even their experiments? They wouldn't. Also, I remember that when I was about three years old, I burned my hand on the stove, and because then I have not placed my hand on a hot stove again. if I had no memory, I would still be burning myself. I believe people learn from their mistakes and this is because of memory.

There is another experience that tells me memory is vital. My grandfather had Alscizmers's disease. He completely lost his memory and didn't even recognize my mother, his own daughter. And this was disturbing because she was his own daughter. My mother said it was like her dad had disappeared completely because he has no memory. He also forgot how to brush his teeth and asked the same question over and over again. It was the opposite of when I burned myself. So memory is vital to human life, and so I agree with Bunuel's idea.

Grader's Comments

The essay is scored based on 4 basic criteria: Topic, Support, Organization, and Language. This author attempted with some success to fulfill the assignment, and the arguments make sense overall. However, no one idea is sufficiently developed and many opinions are lacking supporting examples. The essay presents several logical arguments in the third paragraph, but organization is lacking. The final argument is the most successful as it shows the writer's understanding of the essay topic. However the organization is confused and this detracts from the strength of the argument.

The language and vocabulary in the essay could be improved. Phrases like *as well, and how else* and *this is because of* distract the reader from the author's meaning. The tone of the question and answer in the third paragraph is not appropriate for the essay. Many sentences could have been written with more clarity.

Overall, the essay looks like the writer is able to think about difficult issues but unable to express his or her ideas clearly. It would have been a better essay if the writer had spent a few minutes reviewing the completed essay to clarify sentences, add supporting ideas, and improve the vocabulary.

1 Essay

I remember songs in my head all the time and there is nothing I can do about it. My favorite songs are not the ones I remember but more than likely some advertisement I heard on the way to school this morning. It seems like things are like that. You have to remember so. Everyone does and then if we didn't remember things we wouldn't really have much thoughts or people who live wouldn't really have very much reasons to make decesions.

Once my fish died and when the fish buried, we didn't like the part when the fish didn't remind us of things. It was sad, like when Roger moved to Dallas. But memory is a funny thing, the way you can't control it or nothing when you really want to.

Grader's Comments

The essay is scored based on 4 basic criteria: Topic, Support, Organization, and Language. In this essay, the author mentions memory, but does not answer the assignment. Nearly every sentence has a grammatical error (*there is nothing I can do about it, we didn't like the part when the fish didn't remind us*) and there are many spelling errors. The story about remembering songs might have been used to create an argument about memory, but the story about the fish makes no sense. The essay lacks a thesis statement and a closing summary. It might have been a better essay if the writer had focused on one story and developed a single basic argument about how memory shapes our lives.

SECTION 2

1. E

Do what's in parentheses first:

$$\left(\frac{1}{5} + \frac{1}{3}\right) \div \frac{1}{2} = \left(\frac{3}{15} + \frac{5}{15}\right) \div \frac{1}{2}$$

$$= \frac{8}{15} \div \frac{1}{2}$$

Then, to divide fractions, invert the one after the division sign and multiply:

$$\frac{8}{15} \div \frac{1}{2} = \frac{8}{15} \times \frac{2}{1} = \frac{16}{15}$$

2. E

Plug in $x = -2$ and see what you get:

$$x^2 - 2x = (-2)^2 - 2(-2)$$

$$= 4 - (-4)$$

$$= 4 + 4$$

$$= 8$$

3. C

To get Vito's rate in pages per hour, take the 96 pages and divide by the time in hours. The time is given as "2 hours and 40 minutes." Forty minutes is $\frac{2}{3}$ of an hour, so you can express Vito's time as $2\frac{2}{3}$ hours, or $\frac{8}{3}$ hours:

$$\text{Pages per hour} = \frac{96 \text{ pages}}{\frac{8}{3} \text{ hours}}$$

$$= 96 \times \frac{3}{8} = 36$$

4. A

For $\frac{7}{x}$ to be greater than $\frac{1}{4}$, the denominator x has to be less than 4 times the numerator, or 28. And for $\frac{7}{x}$ to be less than $\frac{1}{3}$, the denominator x has to be greater than 3 times the numerator, or 21. Thus, x could be any of the integers 22 through 27, of which there are 6.

5. A

To find the average of three numbers—even if they're algebraic expressions—add them up and divide by 3:

$$\text{Average} = \frac{(2x + 5) + (5x - 6) + (-4x + 2)}{3}$$

$$= \frac{3x + 1}{3}$$

$$= x + \frac{1}{3}$$

6. D

$$\text{Percent} \times \text{Whole} = \text{Part:}$$

$$(\text{Percent}) \times 25 = 16$$

$$\text{Percent} = \frac{16}{25} \times 100\% = 64\%$$

7. C

The measures of the interior angles of a triangle add up to 180, so add the two *given* measures and subtract the sum from 180. The difference will be the measure of the third angle:

$$45 + 70 = 115$$

$$180 - 115 = 65$$

8. A

$$\frac{x^2 + x^2 + x^2}{x^2} = \frac{3x^2}{x^2} = 3$$

9. C

To solve a quadratic equation, put it in the "$ax^2 + bx + c = 0$" form, factor the left side (if you can), and set each factor equal to 0 separately to get the two solutions. To solve $x^2 = 5x - 4$, first, rewrite it as $x^2 - 5x + 4 = 0$. Then factor the left side:

$$x^2 - 5x + 4 = 0$$

$$(x - 1)(x - 4) = 0$$

$$x = 1 \text{ or } 4$$

10. A

Picking numbers is the easiest, fastest way to do this problem. Choose a pair of numbers from each set and add them together. If you are unable to prove immediately that a set does not have the property described in the question stem, you may want to choose another pair. In set I, if we add 2 and 4, we get 6. Adding 12 and 8 gives us 20. Adding −2 and 8 gives us 6. Since each sum is a member of the set of even integers, set I seems to be true. For set II, adding 3 and 5 yields 8, which is not an odd integer. Therefore, II is not true. Finally, if we add two primes, say 2 and 3, we get 5. That example is true. If we add 3 and 5, however, we get 8, and 8 is not a prime number. Therefore, only set I has the property, and the answer is (A).

11. E

The best way to deal with changing averages is to use the sum. Use the old average to figure out the total of the first 4 scores:

$$\text{Sum of first 4 scores} = (4)(89) = 356$$

Use the new average to figure out the total he needs after the 5th score:

Sum of 5 scores = (5)(90) = 450

To get his sum from 356 to 450, Martin needs to score 450 − 356 = 94.

12. C

Don't fall for the trap choice (D): You can't add or subtract percents of different wholes. Let the original price $s = 100$. Reducing s by 25% gives you a sale price of $75. This price is then increased by 20%, so the final price is $90. Since $s = 100$, it's easy to see that this is equal to choice (C), .90s.

13. A

The prime factorization of 36 is $2 \times 2 \times 3 \times 3$. That factorization includes 2 distinct prime factors, 2 and 3.

14. D

The area of a triangle is equal to one-half the base times the height:

$$\text{Area} = \frac{1}{2}(\text{base})(\text{height})$$

$$36 = \frac{1}{2}(9)(\text{height})$$

$$36 = \frac{9}{2}h$$

$$h = \frac{2}{9} \times 36 = 8$$

15. C

According to the definition, $x \clubsuit = \frac{x}{4} - \frac{x}{6}$. Set that equal to 3 and solve for x:

$$\frac{x}{4} - \frac{x}{6} = 3$$

$$12\left(\frac{x}{4} - \frac{x}{6}\right) = 12(3)$$

$$3x - 2x = 36$$

$$x = 36$$

16. A

Read carefully. This question's a lot easier than you might think at first. It's asking for the total number of coins, not the total value. q quarters, d dimes, and n nickels add up to a total of $q + d + n$ coins.

17. E

Use the points where the line crosses the axes—$(-1, 0)$ and $(0, 2)$—to find the slope:

$$\text{Slope} = \frac{y_2 - y_1}{x_2 - x_1} = \frac{2 - 0}{0 - (-1)} = 2$$

The y-intercept is 2. Now plug $m = 2$ and $b = 2$ into the slope-intercept equation form:

$$y = mx + b$$

$$y = 2x + 2$$

18. B

An integer that's divisible by 6 has at least one 2 and one 3 in its prime factorization. An integer that's divisible by 9 has at least two 3s in its prime factorization. Therefore, an integer that's divisible by both 6 and 9 has at least one 2 and two 3s in its prime factorization. That means it is divisible by 2 and 3: $2 \times 3 = 6$, $3 \times 3 = 9$, and $2 \times 3 \times 3 = 18$. It's not necessarily divisible by 12 or 36, each of which includes two 2s in its prime factorization.

You could also do this one by picking numbers. Think of a common multiple of 6 and 9 and use it to eliminate some options. $6 \times 9 = 54$ is an obvious common multiple—and it's not divisible by 12 or 36, but it is divisible by 18. The least common multiple of 6 and 9 is 18, which is also divisible by 18. It looks like every common multiple of 6 and 9 is also a multiple of 18.

19. D

The volume of a cube is equal to an edge cubed, so $e^3 = 64$, and each edge of the cube has length 4. If the cube is sliced horizontally in two, each of the resulting solids will have two sides of length 4 and one of length 2. So when they are glued together, the resulting figure will have one edge of length 2, one of length 4, and one of length 4 + 4 or 8.

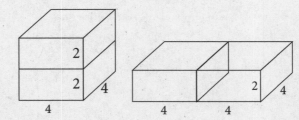

The surface area is the sum of the areas of the solid's six faces. The top and bottom each have area $8 \times 4 = 32$, the front and back each have area $8 \times 2 = 16$, and each side has area $4 \times 2 = 8$. So the surface area of the new solid is $2(32) + 2(16) + 2(8) = 64 + 32 + 16 = 112$.

20. D

The area of a triangle is equal to one-half the base times the height. You can use any of the 3 sides of a triangle for the base—each side has a height to go along with it. It doesn't make any difference which base-height pair you use—a triangle has the same area no matter how you figure it. Thus, one-half times PR times QS will be the same as one-half times PS times RT:

$$\frac{1}{2}(PR)(QS) = \frac{1}{2}(PS)(RT)$$

$$\frac{1}{2}(8)(9) = \frac{1}{2}(PS)(7)$$

$$(8)(9) = (PS)(7)$$

$$PS = \frac{72}{7} = 10\frac{2}{7}$$

SECTION 3

1. C

The phrase *proves difficult* is a clue: the two missing words have to be nearly opposite in meaning. Choice (C) is correct, because few posters would be *intact* if they were meant to be *destroyed*. None of the other choices makes sense: being (A) *returned* would not stop something from being *recognizable*, being (B) *discarded* would not necessarily stop something from being *relevant*, and so on.

2. E

The phrases *long considered* and *finally* suggest contrast. The missing word is probably the opposite of *making some headway in its battle against extinction*. (E) *imperiled, in danger*, is the best answer. (A) *elusive* means *hard to find*; (B) *prevalent* means *common*; (C) *combative* means *eager to fight*; (D) *voracious* means *having a huge appetite*.

3. A

The sentence sets up a contrast between the situation before the invention of the tape recorder and the situation after. We need a word that's the opposite of *paraphrased*, which means *expressed in different words*. The answer is *verbatim*, *word-for-word*.

4. A

The phrase *encouraged hopes* suggests that the two missing words will be somewhat related in meaning. Choice (A) is the best answer, because we expect a *serious* novelist to use *subtle* characterizations. The other choices make less sense; in fact, it's not clear what (C) *accurate*, (D) *fictional*, or (E) *authentic* characterizations would be. (C) *prolific* means *highly productive*; (D) *accomplished* means *skillful, experienced*; (E) *reclusive* means *unsociable*.

5. C

Words like *unchanging* and *eternal* provide a definition of the missing word, (C) *static*. (D) *holistic* means *functioning as a whole*, and (E) *homogeneous* means *all of one kind*; neither word implies species being unchanging and no new species coming into existence.

6. C

The phrase *failure to* establishes the negative tone of the sentence. An agency ought to *fix* or *get rid of* flawed policies. Possible answers for the first blank are (C) *rescind* or *remove, cancel*, and (D) *amend* or *fix*. Failure to do this is a bad thing, so we need a negative word for the second blank. The best choice is *lackadaisical, careless, sloppy*.

7. D

Rapid turnover would tend to increase *inconsistency*, so we need a word that means *increased* or *worsened*. *Exacerbated* means *made worse*.

8. C

What claim would be *belied* or contradicted by a record of contributing to only one party? A claim of *impartiality*, of not favoring one side over the other.

Book Sequels

9. B

When asked for information about one author, eliminate choices that discuss the other author. Be sure that you have each author's position clear in your mind before you tackle the questions. The author of Passage 1 is hostile to the idea of sequels, so you should look for an answer that reflects this attitude. (B) fits well and follows directly from the last sentence. The author of Passage 1 is not concerned with the ease of writing a sequel (A)—she considers all sequels a bad idea. Author 1 never discusses *The Seven Percent Solution*, so (C) is out. Although the author is indignant, you don't have any information that other readers feel that way. (E) is actually the opposite of the truth, since the author states that sequels are written to entice readers of the original books.

10. A

The author uses Margaret Mitchell as an example of a group of authors who've had sequels written to their books. The author states that if the authors and the books that are the subjects of sequels were untalented or unknown, this practice wouldn't be so bad. But, the author goes on to state, that's not the case. From this, you can infer that the author regards Margaret Mitchell as talented or well-known (A). While the author mentions only one novel, *Gone with the Wind*, you can't infer that Mitchell only wrote one book (B). The passage doesn't discuss the relative skills of the authors she mentions (C), or the relative fame of the author and her book (D). (E) might be tempting for the unwary test taker; the passage says that the authors of sequels, rather than of the original books, will disappoint readers.

11. D

Always read the context in which the vocabulary word appears—the context for this word is: *What unalloyed delight for those who have read* . . . You can tell immediately that the adjective unalloyed must have a positive connotation, since it modifies a positive noun—delight. It wouldn't make sense to say, *awful delight*, or *unpleasant delight*. Even something neutral won't work with delight, *middling delight*, or *moderate delight*, for example. Since delight means high satisfaction or great pleasure, you need an adjective of equal intensity to modify it. Therefore, you can eliminate all negative or neutral words, like (A) and

(E). (B), (C), and (D) are all positive, but (D) is the best match here. Unalloyed means not mixed with anything else. (You might be familiar with the term *alloy* to refer to a blend of metals.) So, unalloyed means pure.

12. E

Remember, author 1 is against sequels; author 2 contends that fans will be delighted that there's a sequel to Arthur Conan Doyle's Sherlock Holmes stories. So author 2 would almost certainly disagree with author 1's comments that sequels are always disappointing. (E) captures this by noting the delight that readers will get when they read a sequel to a book they love. You don't have any reason to believe that author 1 will change her mind (A), or even concede that some readers will be disappointed (D). Since author 2 never discusses *Gone with the Wind*, there's no support for (B). Finally, you can rule out (C) since the tone is so extreme.

The Wolves Passage

This Science passage is written by a naturalist who recounts how he went into the wilderness and, through trial and error experimentation and observation, learned some new and surprising things about the way wolves live. For example, wolves are a lot less suspicious and aggressive than people think they are, and contrary to popular belief, wolf families are not nomadic—they live and stay in territories with very definite boundaries.

13. C

In the first paragraph, the author explains how the wolves were aware of his presence but ignored him. That's why the author's precautions were superfluous. (C) basically paraphrases that idea: the author's precautions were unnecessary because the wolves weren't interested in him. (A) doesn't work because the author never really says how long it was before he encountered the wolves. (B) is out because the author never mentions any wild animals other than wolves. Contrary to (D), even after the author interfered with the wolves' boundaries, they never bothered him. (E) is out because it's never suggested that the wolves have poor eyesight.

14. A

The author's basic point in paragraph 1 is that he was surprised at the way the wolves behaved toward him: they sized him up quickly right at the beginning and, from then on, ignored him. He found this behavior disconcerting, or *strange*, as (A) puts it. (B) sounds exaggerated—the author never really suggests that he was fearful of attack. With (C), the author says that he took longer to assess the wolves than they took to assess him, but his basic point is not to emphasize his own ignorance. (D) doesn't work because the wolves left the author alone—precautions weren't necessary. (E), like (B), isn't suggested—that the author thinks he has a lot of courage.

15. D

In paragraph 3, the author describes how the wolf was so preoccupied that he came within 15 yards of his tent without seeing it. It wasn't until the author made noise that the wolf suddenly became aware of its surroundings. (D) paraphrases this idea: that the wolf was not *on its guard*—it was self-absorbed. The author expresses no surprise about the wolf traveling alone (A) or hunting at night (C). As for (B), the point is not that the wolf lacks energy—it does respond when the author startles it. (E) is out because the author doesn't really mention any fear of attack.

16. C

The first sentence of paragraph 3 describes the wolf as *anxious to go home to bed*. The idea is that he was *eager* to get home (C). *Distressed* (A), *afraid* (B), *uneasy* (D), and *worried* (E) are other definitions of anxious, but they don't fit the idea in the sentence.

17. C

In paragraph 4, the author explains that one of the things he learned is that, contrary to popular belief, the wolves were *settled beasts* rather than *nomadic hunters*. The idea, in other words, is that the wolves were *stable*—they had established homes. *Decided* (A) and *resolute* (B) are other meanings of *settled*, but they don't work in the sentence. Neither *inflexible* (D) nor *confident* (E) fits when plugged in.

18. A

The idea at the beginning of paragraph 4 is that the wolves, contrary to what people generally think, are not nomadic. (A) catches the idea: the author is countering a popular myth or belief about the behavior of wolves. (B) is tricky, but there's really no paradox or ambiguity: the idea is that the wolves are NOT nomadic. (C) is tricky too, but the passage never says that the idea that wolves are nomadic is an established fact. As for (D), there's no indication that what the author observed—that the wolves live in established territories—is an exception to a general rule. (E) doesn't work because there's really no summary of any conclusions in the quoted lines. (A) is the best choice.

19. B

In the middle of paragraph 5, the author describes how the wolf family regularly made the rounds of their lands and *freshened up the boundary markers*. He guessed that this was done because there were other wolves living in adjacent areas, although he never saw any sign of trouble between the neighboring wolf families. Then you get the quoted idea: since he never witnessed any disputes, he figured that it was all basically a ritual activity. (B) catches the idea. The idea that the activity was a ritual isn't related to the fact that it was repeated (A), that the boundaries were marked by geographic features (C), that they were marked at the same time each week (D)—that's never suggested—or that the whole family participated (E). The wrong choices miss the point.

20. C

One of the author's discoveries is that the wolves live in territories with clearly marked boundaries. So, contrary to what most people think, they aren't nomadic—they don't travel endlessly from place to place looking for food and sleeping in new areas. The idea in (C), if it were true, would contradict or weaken that idea. The idea in (A) would strengthen the thesis—if there were disputes over boundaries, that would suggest that the wolves are protective of their territory. The idea in (B)—the particular size of the wolves' territory—is irrelevant—it doesn't really relate to the question. (D) is tricky, but it doesn't work: the author finds that the wolves are territorial even though they actually don't have conflicts with their neighbors. The idea in (E) is irrelevant: the passage never discusses whether or not wolves are alert when encountering other animals.

21. D

The phrase *invisible wall* occurs in paragraph 7, and the point is that the wolf, who was plodding home as preoccupied as usual, was suddenly stopped in its tracks when it encountered the spot where the author had left his own markings. So the idea about the invisible wall is that the wolf was stopped suddenly (D), as if it had suddenly banged up against it. The idea of an invisible wall has nothing to do with delight in getting the wolf's attention (A), annoyance on the part of the wolf (B), high speed (C)—the wolf was *padding*, not running—or exhaustion after a night of hunting (E).

22. B

In the very same sentence in paragraph 7, the author says that the wolf, upon finding the author's marks, immediately became bewildered. (B) restates that. The passage says nothing about *combativeness* (A), *anxiety* (C), *wariness* (D), or *dread* (E).

23. B

Temerity is a tough vocabulary word—it means *impetuousness* or *rashness* (B). But you really didn't have to know that definition to pick the right answer. All you have to do with Vocabulary-in-Context questions is plug in each of the answer choices, and eliminate the ones that don't fit the sentence's meaning. If you do that here, none of the other choices works. With (A), it's not that the author's being discourteous. That sounds strange. Rather, he's being too bold—only (B) makes sense. Remember, if you're stumped with any hard question, work backward by eliminating any wrong choices you can—and then guess.

24. B

At the end of paragraph 8, the author states that he turned his back on the wolf *in an effort to break the impasse.* In other words, he did it to bring about a change in the situation (B). Nothing suggests that he did it to show his power over the wolf (A); make the wolf recognize his existence (C)—the wolf already did; look for a weapon (D); or avoid the wolf's *hypnotic* gaze (E).

SECTION 4

1. D

This is a straightforward substitution problem. Plug in the given values and remember your order of operations (PEMDAS). $3^2 - 2(1) = 9 - 2(1) = 9 - 2 = 7$

2. D

The answer choices are given in the form $y = mx + b$, where m is the slope and b is the y-intercept. The y-intercept is clearly 3, so the answer must be (C), (D), or (E). You can either estimate the slope by looking at the graph, or calculate it. To calculate it, you first need the x and y values of two points on the graph, for instance (0, 3) and (6, 0). $\frac{0-3}{6-0} = \frac{-3}{6} = \frac{-1}{2}$, so the slope of the graph must be $\frac{-1}{2}$.

3. D

First translate the question into a system of equations. $q = r - 4$ and $r = 6 + s$. Now plug $s = 2$ into the second equation to get $r = 6 + 2 = 8$, and plug this into the first equation to find $q = 8 - 4 = 4$.

4. D

Each month has 15 days, so 700 days is $\frac{700}{15}$ months.

Each year has 9 months, so $\frac{700}{15}$ months is $\frac{\frac{700}{15}}{9} = \frac{700}{135}$

$= 5\frac{5}{27}$. This means 5 full years have gone by.

5. A

The square of a positive number is positive. The square of a negative number is positive. The square of zero is zero. Therefore, statement I, which presents a negative number, cannot be the square of any real number x. I cannot be the value of $f(x)$ for any real value of x. II is the result of $f(0)$. III is the result of $f(\pm\sqrt{2.3})$.

6. A

The mode is the number that appears most often in a set of data. The largest number of people who collected the same amount of trash was the 12 people who collected 10 pieces of trash, so 10 is the mode of this set of data.

7. D

The total amount of trash collected by the 30 participants was $12(10) + 9(15) + 4(20) + 4(25) + 1(30) = 120 + 135 + 80 + 100 + 30 = 465$ pieces of trash. The goal of the drive was to collect 500 pieces of trash, so we need to figure out what percent 465 is of 500. $\frac{465}{500} = .93$, so the participants reached 93% of the goal.

8. C

The total amount of trash collected by the 30 participants was $12(10) + 9(15) + 4(20) + 4(25) + 1(30) = 120 + 135 + 80 + 100 + 30 = 465$ pieces of trash. Since there were 30 participants, the average amount of trash collected by each one was $\frac{465}{30} = 15.5$ pieces.

9. 115

Since lines p and q are parallel, we can use the rule about alternate interior angles to fill in the following:

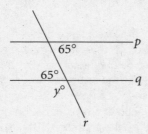

Since the angle marked $y°$ is adjacent and supplementary to a 65° angle, $y = 180 - 65 = 115$.

10. .04

Be careful. The question is not asking: "What is $\frac{1}{4}$ of 16?" It's asking: "What is $\frac{1}{4}$ *percent* of 16?" One-fourth of 1 percent is 0.25%, or 0.0025:

$$\frac{1}{4}\% \text{ of } 16 = 0.0025 \times 16 = .04$$

11. 11, 13, 17, 19, 23, 29, 31, 37, 41, 43, or 47

In order for each of these fractions to be in its simplest form, a would have to be a number that has no prime factors in common with 3, 5, or 14 . So, find a value between 2 and 50 that fits that description. Your best bet is to use a prime number, such as 11. That's one of 11 acceptable answers.

12. $\frac{2}{5}$ or .4

If there are 36 men and 24 women in the group, then the total number of group members is 60. The women make up $\frac{24}{60}$ of the group. Since this fraction cannot be gridded, reduce it or turn it into a decimal. To reduce it, divide both the numerator and denominator by 12, and you end up with $\frac{2}{5}$. To turn it into a decimal, divide 60 into 24, and you end up with .4.

13. 8

To evaluate this expression when $s = 9$, simply plug 9 in for s. Substituting 9 into the expression yields:

$$\frac{3(9) + 5}{4} = \frac{27 + 5}{4} = \frac{32}{4} = 8$$

14. 4

The easiest way to get the answer here is to pick numbers. Pick a number for x that has a remainder of 2 when divided by 6, such as 8. Increase the number you picked by 8. In this case, $8 + 8 = 16$. Now divide 16 by 6, which gives you 2 remainder 4. Therefore, the answer is 4.

15. 250

$$\text{Percent} \times \text{Whole} = \text{Part:}$$
$$(15\%) \times (\text{take-home pay}) = \$37.50$$
$$(0.15) \times (\text{take-home pay}) = \$37.50$$
$$\text{take-home pay} = \frac{\$37.50}{0.15} = \$250.00$$

16. 9

The area of a triangle is equal to one-half the base times the height. Here the base (along the x-axis) is 6 and the height (perpendicular to the base—i.e., parallel to the y-axis) is 3, so the area is $\frac{1}{2}bh = \frac{1}{2}(6)(3) = 9$.

17. 64

You cannot find the area of the square without finding the length of a side, so use the information you are given about the rectangles to find the length of the square's sides. Since the rectangles have the same dimensions, we know that the side of the square must be twice the length of the shorter side of either rectangle. The side of the square must also be the longer side of either rectangle. Call the length of a side of the square, which is also the length of a longer side of either rectangle, x. Then the shorter side of either rectangle is $\frac{x}{2}$. Now use the formula for the perimeter:

$$P = 2l + 2w$$

For either rectangle, you have

$$24 = 2x + 2\left(\frac{x}{2}\right)$$
$$24 = 2x + x$$
$$24 = 3x$$
$$8 = x$$

To find the area of the square, simply multiply 8 by 8. The answer is 64.

18. 203

This looks like a physics question, but in fact it's just a "plug-in-the-number-and-see-what-you-get" question. Be sure you plug 95 in for C (not F):

$$C = \frac{5}{9}(F - 32)$$

$$95 = \frac{5}{9}(F - 32)$$

$$\frac{9}{5} \times 95 = F - 32$$

$$F - 32 = 171$$

$$F = 171 + 32 = 203$$

SECTION 5

1. C

In this sentence the subject *sound* lacks a verb. The word *blocked* is not a verb; it's the past participle of the verb, which is used as an adjective. Look for choices that offer, *was blocked*. (B) keeps the original problem. It also unnecessarily changes the preposition *by* to the longer *as a result of*. In general, the SAT prefers sentences that are more concise. (C) matches your prediction. (D) gives you *was*, but makes a mess of the meaning of the sentence. (E) has the same problem as (D), even though it's expressed a little differently.

2. D

Here, the pronoun *who* is incorrectly used to refer to phone conversations. For this clause, look for choices that replace *who* with *which*. (C), (D), and (E) are all possibilities. (B) uses *whom* which should refer to people, incorrectly. (C) uses *that* but changes the meaning of the sentence. (D) matches your prediction. (E) changes the meaning of the sentence.

3. E

Because the error in this sentence occurs before you have enough information to know it is wrong, a majority of students get this type of question wrong. The comparative adjective *more* is used to compare two people, places, or things; *most* is used to compare more than two. Here, you are comparing Brando to any other person on the set individually. (E) matches the prediction. (B) tries to form the comparative by adding the suffix *-er* to crucial. This is incorrect. (C) changes the meaning of the sentence. (D) is grammatically incorrect and distorts the meaning.

4. C

Be sure that each verb tense is the appropriate choice in the context of the sentence. Because this sentence talks about the Renaissance, which is long over, it requires simple past tenses. Look for a choice that provides it. (B) uses the incorrect pronoun to refer to people. You need the correct form of *who*. (C) This choice provides the simple past tense that you were looking for. (D) changes the meaning of the sentence. (E) has a similar problem to (D).

5. B

Remember that *neither ... nor* and *either ... or* work in pairs. In this sentence you have *neither ... or*, so you need to find a choice that gives you *neither ... nor*. Two choices start with *neither*—(B) and (D). (B) correctly pairs *neither ... nor* and maintains the meaning of the sentence. (D) correctly pairs *neither ... nor*, but it adds unnecessary wordiness. While (E) gives you *either ... or*, when you read it into the sentence you see that it makes the sentence grammatically incorrect. In (C), the incorrect pairing of *either ... nor* makes this an easy choice to eliminate.

6. D

In this sentence you have a series that should be written the same way to maintain parallelism—*the chaos of war, the anxiety of the people*, and *the irrational behavior*. Look for that parallel structure among the choices. (B) corrects the parallelism but adds the incorrect present tense verb *is*. Because choice (C) maintains the incorrect, *they showed*, you know it's wrong. It also changes the meaning of the sentence, because here it's the escalation and not the behavior that is irrational. Choice (D) does what you predicted you'd need—it fixes the parallelism problem while keeping the meaning of the sentence intact. (E) uses an incorrect verb tense.

7. E

In this sentence the comparison is between *is respected ... as she was*. You need to find a choice that changes *was* to *is*. Only (C) and (E) make this change. (C) uses the passive voice which should be avoided, if possible, in the SAT Writing section. (B), in addition to not correcting the error, slightly changes the meaning of the sentence. (D) maintains *was*, and destroys the comparison by changing *as* to *and*.

8. B

Be on the lookout for words and phrases that are acceptable in speech but not in writing. The expression, *deep down there* is too colloquial for written English. (B) eliminates the colloquialism and also cleans up the possessive to make it less wordy. (C) uses the incorrect comparative form of the adjective. (D) changes the meaning of the sentence. (E) cleans up the possessive, but doesn't correct the colloquialism.

9. A

If you think there are no errors in a sentence, there's at least a 20% chance that you're right. Check the sentence for common errors if you're not sure—subject-verb, pronoun agreement, parallelism, logical comparisons. If this all checks out, choose (A). (B) substitutes the incorrect conjunction, *but*, for the correct one. It also incorrectly changes the past progressive tense to the simple past. (C) changes the correct preposition, *about*, to *for*. (D) The subject , *three women*, is plural so you need the plural verb, *were*, not *was*. (E) uses the wrong verb tense and changes the meaning of the sentence by changing *discussing* to *in discussion*.

10. A

Be sure that idioms are expressed clearly and precisely. In (B), *there* is used without any proper antecedent—what place is referred to? (C) expresses a different idea. (D) makes no sense; what is *farther* a comparison to? (E) also expresses a different meaning.

11. D

This sentence meant to compare two dental procedures— root canal and extraction, instead it compares root canals to chewing problems. Only (C), (D), and (E) correctly begin with *an extraction*, eliminating (A) and (B). (B) is also wordy. (C) uses the incorrect verb tense. (D) is what you were looking for. (E) reverses the cause/effect—an extraction can lead to chewing problems according to the original sentence. This choice has chewing problems leading to an extraction.

12. E

What are the possible issues? An adjective, a past-tense verb, a prepositional phrase, and a phrase completing a comparison are underlined. (A) uses an appropriate adjective to describe the noun *series*. (B) is a verb that agrees in tense and number with its subject. (C) uses the idiomatically correct preposition. (D) correctly completes the comparison begun with *as easily*. Therefore, (E) is the right answer: no error.

13. C

You have a clear indication of time in this sentence—last month. Make sure that the verb or verbs that refer to this event are in the simple past tense. (D) is in the progressive

past tense and needs to be changed to the simple past—
graduated. (A) uses the correct, simple past tense form of
the verb. (B) is the correct comparative form of the adjective. (D) is the correct preposition to use with *graduate*.

14. D

The adjective *deep* is incorrectly used to modify *sleeping*.
Remember adjectives modify nouns and adverbs modify
verbs, adjectives, and other adverbs. (A) is an idiomatically
correct prepositional phrase that explains where the commotion took place. (B) is correctly used to indicate that the
hens and the rooster were part of an ongoing ruckus. In
(C), the past tense verb, *woke* is correct.

15. C

The general rule for forming comparatives is to use *more* if
the adjective has more than one syllable, and the suffix *-er*
if the adjective has one syllable. In this sentence (C) does
both things—it places *more* in front of *small and* adds the
suffix *-er* to it. Because *small* has one syllable, the correct
comparative form is *smaller*. In (A), *when* is used correctly
to refer to time. (B) correctly uses the past tense form of
the verb *to look*. (D) is a good vocabulary word, correctly
used. It means *to come forth*.

16. D

Note that the subject is *fruits* not *item*. The singular pronoun
its incorrectly refers to the plural subject *fruits*. *Its* should
be *their*. (A) is idiomatically correct. (B) is in the correct
tense and in (C) *necessary* correctly takes the preposition
to.

17. E

The sentence is correct as written. In (A), *completed* is the
correct form to complete the verb *could have completed*.
(B) correctly modifies the adjective *long*. (C) is in the
correct tense because it happened before *he might have
succeeded*. (D) is the correct form of the adverb,
modifying *started*.

18. D

The pronoun *their* is plural, but it refers to the pronoun
each which is singular. If you were correcting this sentence,
you would replace *their* with *his* or *her* depending on who
is on the team. In (A), *about* is one of the prepositions

that can be used with *concerned*. In (B), the preposition
on is used correctly. In (C), the past tense verb correctly
expresses the time indicated in the sentence.

19. B

Use *fewer* for countable nouns and *less* for uncountable
nouns. *Adults* is a countable noun, so (B) is incorrect. (A)
is the correct adverb. (C) agrees with the singular subject,
environment. (D) The preposition *to* is correctly used with
conducive.

20. A

(A) is a compound object using a noun, *Hilary*, and a
pronoun, *I*. Read the sentence without *Hilary*. You would
never say: *Dad asked I* so you need the objective pronoun, *me*. (B) uses the correct simple past tense. (C) uses
the possessive correctly. (D) is idiomatically correct.

21. A

This sentence needs a verb in the past perfect tense, to
indicate that an action was completed at some point in the
past before something else happened. Here the water
rose and then governor ordered the evacuation. The
correct form of the irregular verb *rise* is *had risen*. (B) is
idiomatically correct usage. (C) is correctly the past tense,
(D) is idiomatically correct.

22. B

The phrase and clause *of concert-goers who waited hours
for the entrance of their favorite music group* comes
between the subject and verb. The singular subject *list*
needs a singular verb and so (B) should be *includes*. (A)
is the right relative pronoun to refer to people correctly
uses the past tense. (C) is idiomatically correct and *who*
(D) is the correct pronoun.

23. D

Make sure that all underlined words are used correctly. In
this sentence the author meant to use *indeterminate* or
undetermined which mean *not yet decided*. Instead he
used *indecisive* which means *uncertain* or *vague*. (A) is
the correct possessive pronoun to refer to the university.
(B) is correctly the past tense. (C) is the correct verb form.

24. B

Remember that certain words go together. For example, *not only . . . but also; more . . . than*. The addition of *like* is incorrect and it has to be omitted to make this sentence correct. (A) is correct in the present singular tense. (C) is the right conjunction. (D) is idiomatically correct.

25. D

The sentence begins with the impersonal pronoun *one* and then switches to the personal pronoun *you*. You have to change *you* to *one* for consistency. (A) is correctly in the present progressive. (B) uses the idiomatically correct preposition. (C) is idiomatically correct.

26. D

Make sure all subjects and verbs agree. *Books* is plural, so *interests* needs to be changed to *interest* to agree with the plural subject. Don't be confused by the relative pronoun *that*. (A) is the right preposition. (B) is correctly the present tense. (C) is the right plural pronoun to refer to *students*.

27. B

If you're not sure there's an error, check each underlined part of the sentence. The adverb *where* means *in what place*. A plan is not a place, so you need to change *where* to *in which* to make this sentence correct. (A) is appropriately in the past tense. (C) is idiomatically correct. (D) is the right preposition.

28. D

Each verb must accurately express time. Something that happened in 1750 needs a past tense verb. In this sentence, the verb *will be* is the future tense. (A) idiomatically expresses the time period. (B) uses the correct words. (C) is an appropriate transition word.

29. A

If you find two elements in the sentence that are expressing the same thought, you need to eliminate one of them. In this sentence *both* and *as well as* are saying the same thing, creating a redundancy. You need to eliminate one and the only one that is underlined is *both* (A). (B) is correctly in the perfect tense, since it is an ongoing obsession. (C) uses the idiomatically correct preposition. (D) is properly in the past tense.

30. A

To determine what logically follows the first sentence, read through the first paragraph to see what ideas are introduced. The paragraph goes on to describe how winter is viewed by some as cold, snowy, and bleak. (A) introduces this. (B) is true, but irrelevant here. (C) is opposite in meaning to the passage; the author clearly likes winter. (D) is out of scope; the author never states what season people prefer. And, this sentence doesn't introduce the ideas that follow in the paragraph. (E) brings in an idea from paragraph 3 which is out of place here.

31. B

To combine the sentences, you must determine their relationship. (B) combines the sentences by subordinating the second clause and replacing the ambiguous pronouns *them* and *us*. (A) doesn't correct the ambiguity or the inconsistency between *them* and *us*. (C) badly distorts the meaning. (D) omits the idea that the *opportunity* for activity is provided. (E) is a run-on sentence with a comma splice.

32. E

Sentence 10 starts with the pronoun *we* and then switches to *people*. (E) correctly uses *people* as the subject of the sentence. (B) changes the meaning by stating a fact instead of stating that people *complain* about this fact. (C) inserts the transition word *therefore* which incorrectly sets up a causal relationship with sentence 9. (D) incorrectly sets up a causal relationship within sentence 10.

33. C

Paragraph 4 generally uses present tense, but sentence 13 uses present progressive. (C) correctly uses the present tense. (A) eliminates the parallelism in the list of nouns (*a fire, hot chocolate,* and *board games*). (B) is incorrect—*family* is a singular noun. (D) and (E) make unnecessary changes.

34. D

The original sentence is unclear about what is being compared: how aware we are in winter compared to how aware we are the rest of the year. (D) clarifies this by moving the "than..." closer to "more…" and by adding "we are during" to complete the second half of that thought. (B) starts to correct the problem, but "protection of our home" is ambiguous. (C) mixes the ideas of protection and companionship together, making them less clear. (E) is another partial correction, but it loses part of the original meaning.

35. E

The essay claims most other people don't appreciate winter as much as they should, and details three reasons why the writer prefers winter. (E) is a logical conclusion to this reasoning. (A) is a change of subject. (B) might be added in the second paragraph, but not here, where evening snowfall is discussed. (C) could be appropriate close to the first sentence, and (D) in the third paragraph.

SECTION 6

1. D

The word in the first blank has to be similar in meaning to *controversy*: (C) *belligerent*, (D) *scandalous*, and (E) *provocative* would fit. The band wouldn't do this if they didn't find that the strategy worked, so (B) *rewarding* and (D) *effective* fit for the second blank. Only (D) fits for both blanks.

2. B

The correct answer is implied by *numerous scribbled edits that cover even his supposed final drafts*. In other words, Joyce attached great importance to (B) *revision*.

3. B

The key is that the players *now charge for their signatures*. Either the fans who believe that the players are not *greedy* would be *surprised* or *disappointed*, or the fans who believe that the players are not *ungreedy* would be *confirmed*. Choice (B) fits the former prediction.

4. B

The words *though* and *absence* indicate contrast, so the missing word has to be nearly opposite in meaning to *isolation and the longing for connection*. *Fraternity*—brotherhood or fellowship—is the best choice. Choice (D) may be tempting, but the term *socialism* refers to a specific set of political and economic doctrines, not just to any sort of society.

5. B

The part of the sentence after the semicolon basically defines the missing word. The word is *calculated*, consciously planned. (A) *incendiary* means *inflaming*; (C) *facetious* means *joking*; (D) *scrupulous* means *honest*; (E) *impromptu* means *unplanned*.

Discovery of Helium

6. E

Ramsay appears toward the middle of the passage after the author mentions that scientists doubted that helium exists only on the sun. Since Ramsay's experiment with naturally occurring Earth minerals occurs in the next sentence, the correct answer will probably be something that cites discovering helium on Earth, and (E) fits this well. The wrong answers here all misuse details from other parts of the passage. Ramsay did not repeat Janssen's experiment, Lockyer did (A). Ramsay's chief contribution was to find helium on Earth; the fact that it was found in uranium minerals is secondary to this larger concern (B). Ramsay did not identify the gas as being helium, Crookes did (C). Finally, Ramsay was not involved with detecting helium on the sun; Janssen and Lockyer were (D).

7. C

The passage states that Janssen and Lockyer observed the sun using their spectroscopes and discovered a new yellow line that belonged to an unknown element. Reading the next sentence reveals that Janssen and Lockyer's work was doubted by many other scientists (C). Watch out for incorrectly used details: Lockyer repeated Janssen's experiment, but it is not stated that other scientists repeated the experiment incorrectly (A). Other scientists were skeptical, but this doesn't mean they thought the methodology behind the experiments was unsound (B); for example, perhaps they thought the results were interpreted incorrectly. Although it is mentioned that Janssen did his experiment during a solar eclipse, the author does not mention that this was necessary for the experiment (D). (E) is pretty far out-of-scope; using outdated equipment is never mentioned in the passage.

Loretta's Visit

8. E

In the fourth sentence, we learn that the reasons for their separation is *lost in the mists of family lore*. In other words, no one knows the original cause of the estrangement (E). The author doesn't tell us how Grandmama treated Uncle Martin (A). (B) is too extreme, since Loretta is also visiting the city to spend time exploring it with the author. The author doesn't tell us what led to the impending reunion between Loretta and Grandmama (C), or anything about how busy Loretta is (D).

9. B

The context for this word is: *The rift that began for reasons lost in the mists of family lore has continued to this day*. Reading the sentence following this one is helpful: *I'll wager that Loretta can't even remember why she and Grandmama haven't spoken in all this time*. So there's been a *break* in relations between Grandmama and Loretta (B). A *motion* (A) between the two doesn't make sense. *Revelry* (C) and *clarity* (D) are both too positive for this situation. *Discussion* also doesn't fit for people that are angry with one another.

The Cold War Passage

The author of this passage has one overarching strategy: Set up the arguments of the revisionist historians and then knock them down. Paragraph 1 explains the things that, according to the revisionists, could have been done to avoid the Cold War, which are 1) the U.S. could have just accepted Soviet domination in Eastern Europe, 2) the U.S. could have given them money for reconstruction, and 3) the U.S. could have given up its monopoly of the bomb. Paragraphs 2 and 3 outline the author's refutation of these arguments; he concentrates on the American political atmosphere as the main reason that the revisionists' ideas were not really workable at the time. Revisionists, he then asserts in paragraph 4, would reject this politics-based argument and claim instead that it was the economic situation that forced American policy makers to oppose the Soviets. The author of course then knocks down this new argument; it is contradictory, he says, to say that American officials were caught in an economic tide and then to blame them for not doing things differently. The author concludes in the final paragraph by stating that there was essentially no way, given the climate in the Soviet Union, that the Cold War could have been avoided.

10. C

As we noted above, the author of this passage is primarily engaged in setting up and knocking down the arguments of the revisionist historians of the Cold War. This makes (C) correct and (E) wrong (the author is definitely not interested in reconciling his view with that of the revisionists). (A) is wrong because the ideas of the revisionists are not, as far as we know, a popular myth. (B) is out because the author is defending historical figures—the policy makers—for what they did, not criticizing them. (D) is too neutral a choice for this passage; the author does engage in analysis of the era of the beginning of the Cold War, but his purpose is to do far more than just analyze events. He wants to poke holes in revisionist theories.

11. C

When revisionists say that the U.S. could have *recognized* the Soviet influence in Eastern Europe, they mean that the U.S. could have formally *acknowledged* this Soviet presence. (C) is correct.

12. C

Look back to the second half of the second paragraph. The author says there that Roosevelt could never have recognized a Soviet Eastern Europe because the American people did not like the idea of the Soviets holding sway in that region. In particular, the president would have lost the votes of the Polish Americans who, you can infer, did not want the Soviets controlling their *old country*. (C) spells out this point. Each of the other choices is a misreading of the context of the sentence about the Polish American voters.

13. E

In the second and third paragraphs, the author refutes the suggestions of the revisionists primarily by saying that the policy-makers couldn't do what was necessary to avoid the Cold War because the American people were against it. The assumption the author makes is that the policy makers *could not have been expected to ignore public opinion* (E). The author never says in the second and third paragraphs that the Soviets were to blame for failed U.S. peace initiatives (A), or that none of the alternatives would work (C)—what he does say, in a later paragraph, is that if peace initiatives had not run aground due to American politics, then they would have run aground due to the Soviet climate. The author also does not say in the second and third paragraphs that the American public was *well-informed* (B) or *overwhelmingly opposed to seeking peace* (D); all we know is that they opposed Soviet influence in Eastern Europe as well as the idea of giving up the atom bomb monopoly.

14. C

This question is closely linked to the previous one. The author refers to the *certain constraints* at the end of the third paragraph, in the midst of the discussion on the impact of public opinion on the policy-makers. From context, then, you know that the constraints the author is talking about are the opinions of the people—in other words, *the views of the electorate* (C). If you didn't put the sentence about *constraints* in context, any of the other choices might have looked appealing.

15. E

This question centers on the fourth paragraph, which is where the author explains the revisionists' view that American policy makers decided to oppose the Soviet Union because Soviet expansion could jeopardize U.S. trade and investment opportunities in Eastern Europe and elsewhere. (E) captures this idea. The author says nothing about illegal trading activities (A), nor does he indicate whether or not the Soviets knew about the negative impact they could have on the American economy (B). (C) is out because the Soviet Union was not recognized by the United States, so this could not possibly have had anything to do with the origin of the Cold War. (D) is wrong because there is no evidence in the paragraph to support it.

16. A

The author poses the question in order to show that there is a problem with the revisionists' economic interpretation of the Cold War: you can't blame the policy-makers if they didn't have any control. Thus, the question serves to *point out an inconsistency* (A) in the revisionists' position. (D) might be tempting since the revisionists' view is pretty cynical, but the author is questioning that view here, not summing it up.

The James Weldon Johnson Passage

Johnson, the author of this autobiographical piece, does not just describe the experience he had watching the piano-player playing rag-time; he also uses the scene as a jumping-off point from which to comment on the origin of rag-time (second paragraph), to disparage American musicians for refusing to accept rag-time (third paragraph), and to speculate on what the piano player could have amounted to under different circumstances (fourth paragraph).

17. C

The author's initial impression of rag-time can be found in the first paragraph. He emphasizes how the beat demanded a physical response and meshed with the *dissonant harmonies*, etc., to produce a *curious effect*. (C) is the correct answer. The only other choice that has anything to do with the first paragraph is (B). (B) is wrong because the audience is said to have applauded the singer's dance steps, not the rag-time music.

18. E

Let's go through the choices one-by-one, keeping in mind that we're focusing exclusively on the first paragraph. Although the piano player is *master of a good deal of technique*, choice (A) is too extreme to be correct. We know nothing in the first paragraph of the author's expectations of rag-time, so (B) is out too. (C), (D), and (E) are different interpretations of the author's description of the piano player's playing. While it is certainly true that rag-time has dissonant harmonies and jumps from one key to another, you cannot infer from this that rag-time violates every rule of musical composition (C) or that it has no melody at all (D). (E) is correct since the narrator notes that *the accents fell in the most unexpected places*.

19. A

In the context of the phrase *questionable resorts about Memphis and St. Louis*, the word questionable means *disreputable* (A).

20. C

Choice (B) might have jumped right out at you since the narrator's perspective in paragraph 1 is that of a mesmerized spectator, but his perspective in paragraphs 2 and 3 changes. He steps back from the description of his first encounter with rag-time and begins to discuss rag-time's history, appeal, and impact on the contemporary musical scene. Therefore, (C) is the correct answer. (A) is wrong because the author is not impartial; he thinks highly of rag-time. Watching rag-time playing is not a *unique experience*, which eliminates (D). As for (E), the narrator says nothing about his youth in the second and third paragraphs.

21. C

The narrator argues in the third paragraph that rag-time should not be ignored or dismissed by American musicians just because it is popular. All great music, he states, comes from the hearts of the people. In other words, he is saying that the *conservative and condescending attitude* of the American musicians is misguided (C). There is no evidence in the third paragraph to support any of the other choices. (B) is perhaps the most tempting since the author talks in the third paragraph about rag-time's popularity in Europe, but it seems as though American musicians do know about rag-time's popularity and find it distasteful.

22. E

This question is a follow-up on the previous one. As we've said, the author's argument in the third paragraph is that music should not be dismissed by serious musicians just because it happens to be popular. (E) paraphrases this idea. (A) stretches the author's argument way too far. (B) is wrong because the author does not try to establish criteria for musical greatness. (C) focuses too narrowly on the author's mention of the fact that rag-time was popular abroad. (D) is clearly wrong since rag-time gained popularity even though it had not been *taken up by a musical master*.

23. D

The narrator poses to himself the question about what might have become of the piano player had he been properly trained and then answers himself by saying *perhaps he wouldn't have done anything at all*. The narrator goes on to say that even if the piano player achieved some success as an imitator of the greats or as an innovator, he still would not have been as *delightful* as he was playing rag-time. Thus, the statement that *perhaps he wouldn't have done anything at all* can best be interpreted as a *recognition that the piano player might have wasted*

his talent (D) had he been formally trained. (A) and (B) are wrong because the narrator thinks highly of the piano player's skill even if that skill is not genius-level or particularly disciplined. (C) and (E) are both far too broad and too negative to be the correct answer.

24. C

The correct answer here is going to be a paraphrase of the idea that no matter how far the piano player would have gone if trained, he would not have been as delightful as he was as a rag-time player. (C) is the choice you're looking for. (E) is the most tempting wrong answer since the author's statements at the end of the passage can easily be misconstrued to mean that the piano player could never have been more than mediocre as a classical artist. However, *never* is too strong a word here—the narrator is not, and cannot be, as sure as that—so this choice is wrong.

SECTION 7

1. E

Use FOIL:

$$(3x + 4)(4x - 3)$$
$$= (3x \times 4x) + [3x \times (-3)] + (4 \times 4x) + [4 \times (-3)]$$
$$= 12x^2 - 9x + 16x - 12$$
$$= 12x^2 + 7x - 12$$

2. C

When you know that the given parts add up to the whole, then you can turn a part-to-part ratio into two part-to-whole ratios—put each term of the ratio over the sum of the terms. In this case, since all the numbers in the set must be either integers or nonintegers, the parts do add up to the whole. The sum of the terms in the ratio 2:3 is 5, so the two part-to-whole ratios are 2:5 and 3:5.

$$\frac{integers}{numbers} = \frac{2}{5}(100\%) = \frac{200\%}{5} = 40\%$$

3. C

Get rid of the parentheses in the denominator, and then cancel factors the numerator and denominator have in common:

$$\frac{x^2y^3z^4}{(xyz^2)^2} = \frac{x^2y^3z^4}{x^2y^2z^4}$$

$$= \frac{x^2}{x^2} \times \frac{y^3}{y^2} \times \frac{z^4}{z^4}$$

$$= y$$

4. E

If p divided by 7 leaves a remainder of 5, you can say that $p = 7n + 5$, where n represents some integer. Multiply both sides by 5 to get $5p = 35n + 25$. The remainder when you divide 7 into $35n$ is 0. The reminder when you divide 7 into 25 is 4, so the remainder when you divide $5p$ by 7 is $0 + 4 = 4$.

For most people this one's a lot easier to do by picking numbers. Think of an example for p and try it out. p could be 12, for example, because when you divide 12 by 7, the remainder is 5. (p could also be 19, 26, 33, or any of infinitely many more possibilities.) Now multiply your chosen p by 5: $12 \times 5 = 60$. Divide 60 by 7 and see what the remainder is: 60 by $7 = 8$, remainder 4.

5. B

To find the y-intercept of a line from its equation, put the equation in slope-intercept form:

$$2x - 3y = 18$$

$$-3y = -2x + 18$$

$$y = \frac{2}{3}x - 6$$

In this form, the y-intercept is what comes after the x. In this case, it's −6.

6. C

Set up a proportion:

$$\frac{12 \text{ pages}}{1 \text{ hour}} = \frac{100 \text{ pages}}{x \text{ hours}}$$

$$12x = 100$$

$$x = \frac{100}{12} = 8\frac{1}{3}$$

One-third of an hour is $\frac{1}{3}$ of 60 minutes, or 20 minutes.

So $8\frac{1}{3}$ hours is 8 hours and 20 minutes.

7. E

With a right triangle you can use the two legs as the base and the height to figure out the area. Here, the two leg lengths are expressed algebraically. Just plug the two expressions in for b and h in the triangle area formula:

$$\text{Area} = \frac{1}{2}(x - 1)(x + 1)$$

$$= \frac{1}{2}(x^2 - 1) = \frac{x^2 - 1}{2}$$

8. A

The easiest way to do this problem is to subtract Bill's money from the total of the money that Jim and Bill have. Doing this gives you $15 - 4 = 11$. However, the problem states that they have LESS THAN 15 dollars. Therefore, Jim must have less than 11 dollars. Of I, II, and III, the only value that is less than 11 is I, so the answer must be (A).

To solve this problem algebraically, set up an inequality where J is Jim's money and B is Bill's money:

$$J + B < 15 \text{ where } B = 4$$

$$J + 4 < 15$$

$$J < 11$$

Again, be wary of the fact that this is an inequality, NOT an equation.

9. A

Pick numbers for x and y. For instance, say that Angelo makes $20 for working 5 hours and Sarah makes $20 for working 4 hours. In this case, Angelo makes $4 per hour and Sarah makes $5. The difference between their wages is $1 per hour. Now plug 20 in for x and 5 in for y in each of the answer choices. Which ones give you a result of 1? Only (A), which is the answer.

10. D

A square with area 16 has sides of length 4. Therefore, the largest circle that could possibly be cut from such a square would have a diameter of 4.

Such a circle would have a radius of 2, making its area 4π. So the amount of felt left after cutting such a circle from one of the squares of felt would be $16 - 4\pi$, or $4(4 - \pi)$. There are 8 such squares, so the total area of the leftover felt is $8 \times 4(4 - \pi) = 32(4 - \pi)$.

11. C

When you see a question like this one on test day, look for patterns in the differences between terms. Is each term a result of adding some number to the previous term? Is each term a result of multiplying the previous term by some number? In this case, each term is the result of multiplying the previous term by 3.

$x = 18(3) = 54$

You can check this result by comparing it to later terms:

$54(3) = 162$

12. E

$$\begin{array}{r} 5x^2 + 13x + 40 \\ x - 3 \overline{)\ 5x^3 - 2x^2 + x + 1} \\ \underline{-(5x^3 - 15x^2)} \\ 13x^2 + x \\ \underline{-(13x^2 - 39x)} \\ 40x + 1 \\ \underline{-(40x - 120)} \\ 121 \end{array}$$

13. B

This problem requires you to put together several different pieces of information. If you don't see all the steps you need to follow at first, just write down what information you can get from the problem and that may help you figure out what to do next. Since B is the midpoint of $\overline{AC}$, which is 4 units long, $\overline{AB}$ and $\overline{BC}$ are each 2 units long.

Since the area of the circle is $4\pi = \pi r^2 = \pi 2^2$, its radius is 2. $\overline{BO}$ is a radius of the circle, so it is 2 units long. $\overline{AC}$ is tangent to the circle at point B, so $\angle OBA$ is 90 degrees. The following diagram summarizes this information:

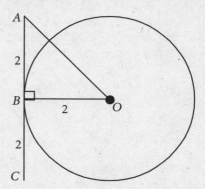

Since BO and AB both equal 2 and $\angle ABO$ is 90 degrees, triangle ABO is a 45-45-90 special triangle, and $AO = 2\sqrt{2}$.

14. E

Learning how to interpret a graph can be challenging. Practice this skill before test day, so you have mastered it by then. Each year, the cost increases. In 2003, insurance was $1,200. So you know that in 2004 it should be more; the only option is (E).

15. D

Be sure not to be tempted by answers that are partly right. $x \geq 1$ describes the right half of the values on the number line but leaves out the left half. The selected values on the number line consist of 1, everything greater than 1, −1, and everything less than −1. The easiest way to describe this set is that the absolute value of x, or its distance from zero on the number line, is greater than or equal to 1. This can be written in mathematical notation as $|x| \geq 1$.

16. E

In order to find the number of possibilities, multiply the number of possibilities in each step. In other words, there are 3 routes from Bay City to Riverville and 4 routes from Riverville to Straitstown. There are 3 more routes from Straitstown to Frogs Pond, so there are $12 \times 3 = 36$ total routes from Bay City to Frog Pond.

SECTION 8

1. A

The word *although* indicates contrast, and the words *large number* and *mass* provide a clue to what's missing. We need something that means *different* for the first blank, and something that means *the same* for the second blank. This is basically what *disparate* and *homogeneous* mean.

2. A

We need something here that goes with *heavy thoughts*. *Morose*, or *gloomy*, is the best choice.

3. E

The *demise* or death of the protagonist presumably *eliminated* all possibility of a sequel. That's what *precluded* means.

4. E

Repeated breakdown of negotiations would tend to *support* or *reinforce* the view that the sides *were not truly committed to preventing* or *averting* a military confrontation. In (A) and (D), *established* and *strengthened* fit the first blank, but *escalating* and *initiating* are wrong for the second. In (B), *avoiding* fits the second blank, but *undermined* is wrong for the first.

5. C

The sentence contrasts Duncan with his coworker. You can, therefore, predict that the colleague is neither *modest* nor *cooperative*. (C) meaning "proud contempt for others," matches the prediction. (A) meaning "pleasantness, friendliness" and (E) meaning "the quality of being humble," have the wrong charge. You could use those words to describe Duncan perhaps, but not the colleague. The remaining two choices do not contrast with the modest and cooperative qualities of Duncan.

6. D

Start with the second blank where you are looking for a word to suggest the effort needed to improve the economic climate. (B) and (D) both fit. (A) may be tempting because the candidate may very well have made a *promise* about the economic climate before the election. You do not, however, recognize a forthcoming ("approaching, upcoming") *promise*. Note that an *inauguration* ("formal acceptance into office) may be forthcoming for the candidate, but it will not improve the economic climate. (C) is too extreme for the second blank. Now look at the first blank for (B) and (D). The candidate's exhilaration ("joy, elation") temporarily *illuminated* ("clarified, brought to light") or *eclipsed* ("surpassed, outshone") the recognition of the coming effort. (D) is the best fit.

The Design Museums Passages

Passage 1: The position of the author of this passage starts to become clear in the second paragraph: she likes design museums and is willing to defend them against critics. She thinks design museums are not just advertisements for new technology but places where new products can be honored. Design museums, she asserts, are comfortable for visitors because the exhibits provide a lot of information about the objects displayed—information you wouldn't get in an art gallery. Another advantage of design museums, she says, is that their curators have more freedom than do the curators of public art galleries.

Passage 2: Author 2 does not hold technical and design museums in the same high regard as author 1 does. Author 2 complains about several things: 1) technical museums concentrate on present technology and ignore historical study and research; 2) they glorify machines and industrialization when these things do harm as well as good; and 3) they do not (and cannot safely and imaginatively) show machinery in action. Author 2 does admit at the very end, however, that the public has shown a healthy curiosity about science and technology.

7. A

To say that something is *readily available to the general public* is to say that it is *easily* available. (A) is the correct answer.

8. E

Although the question is not "vocab-in-context," you must still be careful not to assume the word is used in its most common sense. Look at the context. Since these appliances are in design museums, they must have been very popular and successful. It's only as "design" that they have been ignored. (C) might have been tempting, but it's not to the point and outside the scope. People may or may not have had conversations about, say, a toaster—it's never mentioned. But the conversations might have been about how well it worked, or how little it cost, not about its design attributes—the focus of the passage.

9. D

Author 1 says that department store windows try to sell you something whereas design exhibits try to give you an appreciation of the aesthetic value of something. (D) paraphrases this idea. (A), (B), and (E) can be readily eliminated. Be careful with (C), though. Even though design museums focus on the artistic qualities of products, it does not automatically follow from this that design museums are not concerned at all with the commercial aspects of a successful product. (C) is wrong.

10. B

In the third paragraph of Passage 1, the author argues that design museums make visitors feel comfortable because the exhibits illustrate the purpose behind the look and function of the displayed object; art gallery exhibits, by contrast, provide no such information. From this argument you can infer that author 1 thinks that visitors want to be informed about the object they are viewing. This makes (B) correct. There is no evidence to support any of the other choices, all of which are misreadings of paragraph 3. (A) can be eliminated as soon as you see *hostile toward . . . abstract art*. (C) and (D) contradict the author, who says that visitors are not confused by technological exhibits since they are familiar and informative. (E) is an unwarranted inference based on the author's statement that design exhibits point out the artistic qualities of the displayed items; you cannot conclude from this that most museum visitors undervalue the artistic worth of household items.

11. B

Since you just reviewed paragraph 3 for the last question, the answer to this one should jump right out at you. The difference between a design museum exhibit and an art gallery exhibit is that a design museum exhibit provides you with information about the object being displayed, whereas the art gallery exhibit does not. (B) is correct. None of the other choices has any basis in the passage.

12. C

After mentioning the collection of Zippo lighters, etc., in London's Design Museum, author 1 says that curators of design museums have options that are far less rigorous, conventionalized, and pre-programmed than those open to curators of art galleries. This is a fancy way of saying that the curators of design museums have more freedom to put together unconventional collections (C). (E) is the tempting wrong answer to this question. It's wrong because it goes too far: the design curators have freedom, but not, as far as we know, the freedom to satisfy *their own personal whims*.

13. E

In the very last sentence of Passage 1, the author says that design museums (*the display of postmodern playthings or quirky Japanese vacuum cleaners*) are better able to represent humor than art galleries (*an exhibition of Impressionist landscapes*). The author is emphasizing the contrast between design museum and art gallery exhibits (E). (B) is the trickiest wrong answer. It misses the point of the last sentence because the author is not comparing *postmodern playthings* with Impressionist art; she is comparing the different ways these two things are exhibited.

14. A

The answer to this question will be the choice that summarizes paragraph 1. Since the author spends paragraph 1 complaining that design museums ignore the historical aspect of technology, choice (A) is the best answer. (B) focuses too narrowly on the last part of the paragraph, where the author says that since industry builds the exhibits, curators may be dispensed with. This is not the underlying difficulty referred to at the beginning of the paragraph. The other choices have nothing to do with the first paragraph.

15. A

Author 2's point in the second paragraph is that industrialization and *progress* have not been all good and should be considered critically, but technology museums just glorify them. He mentions industrialization's harm to the environment and ecology to support this point and to encourage a *critical response* to technology, so (A) is correct. (B) is wrong because it's too negative, even for this author. (C) is a distortion of a detail at the end of the second paragraph, whereas (D) is a distorted idea from the third paragraph. (E) is out because author 2 doesn't do any praising in the second paragraph.

16. D

Put the phrase in context. Author 2 says that displayed machinery should be in action, not in *sculptured repose*, as is the case with the machinery in technology museums. To author 2, you can infer, the *sculptured repose* is meaningless and *unrealistic* (D). (A) is out because the author is not condemning the curators for poor planning; in fact, the author admits that displaying operating machinery would be extremely difficult. (B) can be eliminated because it's too extreme. The author never says which—if any—of the problems he discusses is the *greatest problem*. (C) and (E) miss the author's point and the context in which the phrase *sculptured repose* is found.

17. D

Choices (A), (B), (C), and (E) are common synonyms for *command*, but none of them works in the context of the phrase *command the imagination, ingenuity, and manual dexterity it requires*. Only choice (D) can do the job.

18. A

Predict the answer to the question before you go looking through the choices. You know that author 2 thinks that technology has had a lot of negative consequences, so you can assume that he would point this out in response to author 1's optimistic statement. This makes (A) the best answer. We don't know what author 2's position on art galleries is, so (B) is out. (C) comes from Passage 2 but is irrelevant to the question asked in the stem. (D) and (E) contradict specific things author 2 says in the course of his passage.

19. B

In questions like this one, wrong answer choices are often statements that one author, but not both, would agree with. For example, author 2 would probably agree with choice (A) and would definitely agree with (D) and (E), but author 1 would most likely not agree with any of these three. That narrows the field to (B) and (C). (C) is a very general statement that really has no basis in either passage. (B), on the other hand, is an idea that can be found in both passages, so it is the correct answer.

SECTION 9

1. A

The sentence is correct and conforms to the rules of parallelism; all three items in the list are adjectives describing the new model.

2. B

There is an error of subordination here. To express the causal relationship between melting ice caps and flooding of islands, you need only one conjunction: *because* or *therefore*. To have both is redundant. (Furthermore, the word therefore should be preceded by a semicolon, not a comma.)

3. C

This sentence fragment is best corrected by moving the verb *was* and inserting a comma after the introductory phrase describing *Flaubert*.

4. D

In order for (A) to be grammatically correct, a comma is needed before the coordinating conjunction *and*. (C) adds the comma but takes away the conjunction, so it is incorrect. (B) and (E) are extremely awkward. (D) is the clearest and most concise answer

5. D

Eliminate the excessively wordy answer choices—(A), (B), and (E). (C) might be tempting, but *failed* not creates a double negative. (D) is correct because it is clear and concise; (D) also continues the structure established in the first part of the sentence: *have raised…have failed*.

6. A

Make sure that all three items in the series are parallel. The first two begin with gerunds (verbs ending in *–ing*), so (A) is correct. Do not be confused by the word *washing*. It is part of the noun *washing machine* and cannot be called upon to function in any other way in this sentence

7. C

First, eliminate any answer choices that begin with misplaced modifiers. (A) and (D) both say the *directors* have *exceptionally clear waters and active underwater life*. Next, eliminate answer choices that do not create complete sentences. (B) and (E) are long sentence fragments. (C) is correct because it is the only choice with grammatically correct structure.

8. C

(A) is a run-on; the phrase beginning with *featured* makes the sentence incorrect. (B) is nonsensical—the phrase *with features beauty* makes it incorrect. The remaining answer choices set apart the nonessential information with commas, so look for the choice that does this best. That choice is (C)—it is the clearest (and shortest).

9. A

(A) is the clearest answer choice because it sets apart the nonessential information with commas. (D) also uses this structure, but it unnecessarily adds *because it was*. The other answer choices are wordy.

10. E

Eliminate the answer choices that change the underlined portion to an incomplete sentence—(C) and (D). The other answer choices are technically correct, but (E) is the clearest and most concise.

11. A

(C) and (E) have vague pronouns with the word *they*. (B) is very awkward with the words *that* and *not* repeated. (D) is also awkward because of the word *as* toward the beginning of the sentence. (A), the original sentence, is the most concise answer choice.

12. B

Some of the answer choices violate the rules of independent and dependent clauses. For example, (A) uses a comma and coordinating conjunction, calling for two independent clauses. However, the first clause is dependent because of the word *that*. In (D), the first clause is dependent, so the second should be independent, but it is not. (E) introduces a misplaced modifier, and (C) has an illogical connection between the two clauses. (B) has correct structure and makes the most sense.

13. A

The correct answer will have to be parallel with *having a lot of money*. In other words, the underlined portion should contain a gerund (a word ending in *–ing*). The only answer choices with this structure are (A) and (B). (A) is much clearer and more concise, so it is the correct answer.

14. C

The introductory phrase is a dependent clause, so the underlined portion must create an independent clause. The word *causing* in (A) and (E) does not make an independent clause, so eliminate these choices. (B) and (D) insert the coordinating conjunction *and*, which is incorrect when connecting a dependent clause and an independent clause. (The coordinating conjunction and comma are only used for connecting two independent clauses.) (C) is the only answer choice to set up a correct independent clause.

SAT Practice Test Three
Answer Sheet

Remove (or photocopy) the answer sheet and use it to complete the practice test. See the answer key following the test when finished. The "Compute Your Score" section on page 611 will show you how to find your score.

Start with number 1 for each section. If a section has fewer questions than answer spaces, leave the extra spaces blank.

SECTION

1

Section One is the writing section's essay component.
Lined pages on which you will write your essay can be found in that section.

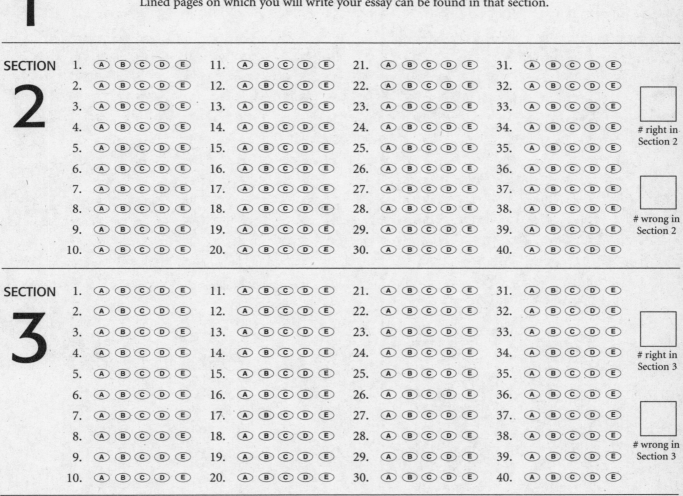

SECTION

2

SECTION

3

Remove (or photocopy) this answer sheet and use it to complete the practice test.

Start with number 1 for each section. If a section has fewer questions than answer spaces, leave the extra spaces blank.

SECTION 4

1. Ⓐ Ⓑ Ⓒ Ⓓ Ⓔ   11. Ⓐ Ⓑ Ⓒ Ⓓ Ⓔ   21. Ⓐ Ⓑ Ⓒ Ⓓ Ⓔ   31. Ⓐ Ⓑ Ⓒ Ⓓ Ⓔ
2. Ⓐ Ⓑ Ⓒ Ⓓ Ⓔ   12. Ⓐ Ⓑ Ⓒ Ⓓ Ⓔ   22. Ⓐ Ⓑ Ⓒ Ⓓ Ⓔ   32. Ⓐ Ⓑ Ⓒ Ⓓ Ⓔ
3. Ⓐ Ⓑ Ⓒ Ⓓ Ⓔ   13. Ⓐ Ⓑ Ⓒ Ⓓ Ⓔ   23. Ⓐ Ⓑ Ⓒ Ⓓ Ⓔ   33. Ⓐ Ⓑ Ⓒ Ⓓ Ⓔ
4. Ⓐ Ⓑ Ⓒ Ⓓ Ⓔ   14. Ⓐ Ⓑ Ⓒ Ⓓ Ⓔ   24. Ⓐ Ⓑ Ⓒ Ⓓ Ⓔ   34. Ⓐ Ⓑ Ⓒ Ⓓ Ⓔ
5. Ⓐ Ⓑ Ⓒ Ⓓ Ⓔ   15. Ⓐ Ⓑ Ⓒ Ⓓ Ⓔ   25. Ⓐ Ⓑ Ⓒ Ⓓ Ⓔ   35. Ⓐ Ⓑ Ⓒ Ⓓ Ⓔ
6. Ⓐ Ⓑ Ⓒ Ⓓ Ⓔ   16. Ⓐ Ⓑ Ⓒ Ⓓ Ⓔ   26. Ⓐ Ⓑ Ⓒ Ⓓ Ⓔ   36. Ⓐ Ⓑ Ⓒ Ⓓ Ⓔ
7. Ⓐ Ⓑ Ⓒ Ⓓ Ⓔ   17. Ⓐ Ⓑ Ⓒ Ⓓ Ⓔ   27. Ⓐ Ⓑ Ⓒ Ⓓ Ⓔ   37. Ⓐ Ⓑ Ⓒ Ⓓ Ⓔ
8. Ⓐ Ⓑ Ⓒ Ⓓ Ⓔ   18. Ⓐ Ⓑ Ⓒ Ⓓ Ⓔ   28. Ⓐ Ⓑ Ⓒ Ⓓ Ⓔ   38. Ⓐ Ⓑ Ⓒ Ⓓ Ⓔ
9. Ⓐ Ⓑ Ⓒ Ⓓ Ⓔ   19. Ⓐ Ⓑ Ⓒ Ⓓ Ⓔ   29. Ⓐ Ⓑ Ⓒ Ⓓ Ⓔ   39. Ⓐ Ⓑ Ⓒ Ⓓ Ⓔ
10. Ⓐ Ⓑ Ⓒ Ⓓ Ⓔ   20. Ⓐ Ⓑ Ⓒ Ⓓ Ⓔ   30. Ⓐ Ⓑ Ⓒ Ⓓ Ⓔ   40. Ⓐ Ⓑ Ⓒ Ⓓ Ⓔ

☐ # right in Section 4

☐ # wrong in Section 4

SECTION 5

1. Ⓐ Ⓑ Ⓒ Ⓓ Ⓔ   11. Ⓐ Ⓑ Ⓒ Ⓓ Ⓔ   21. Ⓐ Ⓑ Ⓒ Ⓓ Ⓔ   31. Ⓐ Ⓑ Ⓒ Ⓓ Ⓔ
2. Ⓐ Ⓑ Ⓒ Ⓓ Ⓔ   12. Ⓐ Ⓑ Ⓒ Ⓓ Ⓔ   22. Ⓐ Ⓑ Ⓒ Ⓓ Ⓔ   32. Ⓐ Ⓑ Ⓒ Ⓓ Ⓔ
3. Ⓐ Ⓑ Ⓒ Ⓓ Ⓔ   13. Ⓐ Ⓑ Ⓒ Ⓓ Ⓔ   23. Ⓐ Ⓑ Ⓒ Ⓓ Ⓔ   33. Ⓐ Ⓑ Ⓒ Ⓓ Ⓔ
4. Ⓐ Ⓑ Ⓒ Ⓓ Ⓔ   14. Ⓐ Ⓑ Ⓒ Ⓓ Ⓔ   24. Ⓐ Ⓑ Ⓒ Ⓓ Ⓔ   34. Ⓐ Ⓑ Ⓒ Ⓓ Ⓔ
5. Ⓐ Ⓑ Ⓒ Ⓓ Ⓔ   15. Ⓐ Ⓑ Ⓒ Ⓓ Ⓔ   25. Ⓐ Ⓑ Ⓒ Ⓓ Ⓔ   35. Ⓐ Ⓑ Ⓒ Ⓓ Ⓔ
6. Ⓐ Ⓑ Ⓒ Ⓓ Ⓔ   16. Ⓐ Ⓑ Ⓒ Ⓓ Ⓔ   26. Ⓐ Ⓑ Ⓒ Ⓓ Ⓔ   36. Ⓐ Ⓑ Ⓒ Ⓓ Ⓔ
7. Ⓐ Ⓑ Ⓒ Ⓓ Ⓔ   17. Ⓐ Ⓑ Ⓒ Ⓓ Ⓔ   27. Ⓐ Ⓑ Ⓒ Ⓓ Ⓔ   37. Ⓐ Ⓑ Ⓒ Ⓓ Ⓔ
8. Ⓐ Ⓑ Ⓒ Ⓓ Ⓔ   18. Ⓐ Ⓑ Ⓒ Ⓓ Ⓔ   28. Ⓐ Ⓑ Ⓒ Ⓓ Ⓔ   38. Ⓐ Ⓑ Ⓒ Ⓓ Ⓔ
9. Ⓐ Ⓑ Ⓒ Ⓓ Ⓔ   19. Ⓐ Ⓑ Ⓒ Ⓓ Ⓔ   29. Ⓐ Ⓑ Ⓒ Ⓓ Ⓔ   39. Ⓐ Ⓑ Ⓒ Ⓓ Ⓔ
10. Ⓐ Ⓑ Ⓒ Ⓓ Ⓔ   20. Ⓐ Ⓑ Ⓒ Ⓓ Ⓔ   30. Ⓐ Ⓑ Ⓒ Ⓓ Ⓔ   40. Ⓐ Ⓑ Ⓒ Ⓓ Ⓔ

☐ # right in Section 5

☐ # wrong in Section 5

If section 5 of your test book contains math questions that are not multiple choice, continue to item 9 below. Otherwise, continue to item 9 above.

9. [grid-in]   10. [grid-in]   11. [grid-in]   12. [grid-in]   13. [grid-in]

14. [grid-in]   15. [grid-in]   16. [grid-in]   17. [grid-in]   18. [grid-in]

Remove (or photocopy) this answer sheet and use it to complete the practice test.

Start with number 1 for each section. If a section has fewer questions than answer spaces, leave the extra spaces blank.

SECTION

6

1. Ⓐ Ⓑ Ⓒ Ⓓ Ⓔ 11. Ⓐ Ⓑ Ⓒ Ⓓ Ⓔ 21. Ⓐ Ⓑ Ⓒ Ⓓ Ⓔ 31. Ⓐ Ⓑ Ⓒ Ⓓ Ⓔ
2. Ⓐ Ⓑ Ⓒ Ⓓ Ⓔ 12. Ⓐ Ⓑ Ⓒ Ⓓ Ⓔ 22. Ⓐ Ⓑ Ⓒ Ⓓ Ⓔ 32. Ⓐ Ⓑ Ⓒ Ⓓ Ⓔ
3. Ⓐ Ⓑ Ⓒ Ⓓ Ⓔ 13. Ⓐ Ⓑ Ⓒ Ⓓ Ⓔ 23. Ⓐ Ⓑ Ⓒ Ⓓ Ⓔ 33. Ⓐ Ⓑ Ⓒ Ⓓ Ⓔ
4. Ⓐ Ⓑ Ⓒ Ⓓ Ⓔ 14. Ⓐ Ⓑ Ⓒ Ⓓ Ⓔ 24. Ⓐ Ⓑ Ⓒ Ⓓ Ⓔ 34. Ⓐ Ⓑ Ⓒ Ⓓ Ⓔ
5. Ⓐ Ⓑ Ⓒ Ⓓ Ⓔ 15. Ⓐ Ⓑ Ⓒ Ⓓ Ⓔ 25. Ⓐ Ⓑ Ⓒ Ⓓ Ⓔ 35. Ⓐ Ⓑ Ⓒ Ⓓ Ⓔ

 # right in Section 6

6. Ⓐ Ⓑ Ⓒ Ⓓ Ⓔ 16. Ⓐ Ⓑ Ⓒ Ⓓ Ⓔ 26. Ⓐ Ⓑ Ⓒ Ⓓ Ⓔ 36. Ⓐ Ⓑ Ⓒ Ⓓ Ⓔ
7. Ⓐ Ⓑ Ⓒ Ⓓ Ⓔ 17. Ⓐ Ⓑ Ⓒ Ⓓ Ⓔ 27. Ⓐ Ⓑ Ⓒ Ⓓ Ⓔ 37. Ⓐ Ⓑ Ⓒ Ⓓ Ⓔ
8. Ⓐ Ⓑ Ⓒ Ⓓ Ⓔ 18. Ⓐ Ⓑ Ⓒ Ⓓ Ⓔ 28. Ⓐ Ⓑ Ⓒ Ⓓ Ⓔ 38. Ⓐ Ⓑ Ⓒ Ⓓ Ⓔ
9. Ⓐ Ⓑ Ⓒ Ⓓ Ⓔ 19. Ⓐ Ⓑ Ⓒ Ⓓ Ⓔ 29. Ⓐ Ⓑ Ⓒ Ⓓ Ⓔ 39. Ⓐ Ⓑ Ⓒ Ⓓ Ⓔ
10. Ⓐ Ⓑ Ⓒ Ⓓ Ⓔ 20. Ⓐ Ⓑ Ⓒ Ⓓ Ⓔ 30. Ⓐ Ⓑ Ⓒ Ⓓ Ⓔ 40. Ⓐ Ⓑ Ⓒ Ⓓ Ⓔ

 # wrong in Section 6

SECTION

7

1. Ⓐ Ⓑ Ⓒ Ⓓ Ⓔ 11. Ⓐ Ⓑ Ⓒ Ⓓ Ⓔ 21. Ⓐ Ⓑ Ⓒ Ⓓ Ⓔ 31. Ⓐ Ⓑ Ⓒ Ⓓ Ⓔ
2. Ⓐ Ⓑ Ⓒ Ⓓ Ⓔ 12. Ⓐ Ⓑ Ⓒ Ⓓ Ⓔ 22. Ⓐ Ⓑ Ⓒ Ⓓ Ⓔ 32. Ⓐ Ⓑ Ⓒ Ⓓ Ⓔ
3. Ⓐ Ⓑ Ⓒ Ⓓ Ⓔ 13. Ⓐ Ⓑ Ⓒ Ⓓ Ⓔ 23. Ⓐ Ⓑ Ⓒ Ⓓ Ⓔ 33. Ⓐ Ⓑ Ⓒ Ⓓ Ⓔ
4. Ⓐ Ⓑ Ⓒ Ⓓ Ⓔ 14. Ⓐ Ⓑ Ⓒ Ⓓ Ⓔ 24. Ⓐ Ⓑ Ⓒ Ⓓ Ⓔ 34. Ⓐ Ⓑ Ⓒ Ⓓ Ⓔ

 # right in Section 7

5. Ⓐ Ⓑ Ⓒ Ⓓ Ⓔ 15. Ⓐ Ⓑ Ⓒ Ⓓ Ⓔ 25. Ⓐ Ⓑ Ⓒ Ⓓ Ⓔ 35. Ⓐ Ⓑ Ⓒ Ⓓ Ⓔ
6. Ⓐ Ⓑ Ⓒ Ⓓ Ⓔ 16. Ⓐ Ⓑ Ⓒ Ⓓ Ⓔ 26. Ⓐ Ⓑ Ⓒ Ⓓ Ⓔ 36. Ⓐ Ⓑ Ⓒ Ⓓ Ⓔ
7. Ⓐ Ⓑ Ⓒ Ⓓ Ⓔ 17. Ⓐ Ⓑ Ⓒ Ⓓ Ⓔ 27. Ⓐ Ⓑ Ⓒ Ⓓ Ⓔ 37. Ⓐ Ⓑ Ⓒ Ⓓ Ⓔ
8. Ⓐ Ⓑ Ⓒ Ⓓ Ⓔ 18. Ⓐ Ⓑ Ⓒ Ⓓ Ⓔ 28. Ⓐ Ⓑ Ⓒ Ⓓ Ⓔ 38. Ⓐ Ⓑ Ⓒ Ⓓ Ⓔ
9. Ⓐ Ⓑ Ⓒ Ⓓ Ⓔ 19. Ⓐ Ⓑ Ⓒ Ⓓ Ⓔ 29. Ⓐ Ⓑ Ⓒ Ⓓ Ⓔ 39. Ⓐ Ⓑ Ⓒ Ⓓ Ⓔ

 # wrong in Section 7

10. Ⓐ Ⓑ Ⓒ Ⓓ Ⓔ 20. Ⓐ Ⓑ Ⓒ Ⓓ Ⓔ 30. Ⓐ Ⓑ Ⓒ Ⓓ Ⓔ 40. Ⓐ Ⓑ Ⓒ Ⓓ Ⓔ

SECTION

8

1. Ⓐ Ⓑ Ⓒ Ⓓ Ⓔ 11. Ⓐ Ⓑ Ⓒ Ⓓ Ⓔ 21. Ⓐ Ⓑ Ⓒ Ⓓ Ⓔ 31. Ⓐ Ⓑ Ⓒ Ⓓ Ⓔ
2. Ⓐ Ⓑ Ⓒ Ⓓ Ⓔ 12. Ⓐ Ⓑ Ⓒ Ⓓ Ⓔ 22. Ⓐ Ⓑ Ⓒ Ⓓ Ⓔ 32. Ⓐ Ⓑ Ⓒ Ⓓ Ⓔ
3. Ⓐ Ⓑ Ⓒ Ⓓ Ⓔ 13. Ⓐ Ⓑ Ⓒ Ⓓ Ⓔ 23. Ⓐ Ⓑ Ⓒ Ⓓ Ⓔ 33. Ⓐ Ⓑ Ⓒ Ⓓ Ⓔ
4. Ⓐ Ⓑ Ⓒ Ⓓ Ⓔ 14. Ⓐ Ⓑ Ⓒ Ⓓ Ⓔ 24. Ⓐ Ⓑ Ⓒ Ⓓ Ⓔ 34. Ⓐ Ⓑ Ⓒ Ⓓ Ⓔ

 # right in Section 8

5. Ⓐ Ⓑ Ⓒ Ⓓ Ⓔ 15. Ⓐ Ⓑ Ⓒ Ⓓ Ⓔ 25. Ⓐ Ⓑ Ⓒ Ⓓ Ⓔ 35. Ⓐ Ⓑ Ⓒ Ⓓ Ⓔ
6. Ⓐ Ⓑ Ⓒ Ⓓ Ⓔ 16. Ⓐ Ⓑ Ⓒ Ⓓ Ⓔ 26. Ⓐ Ⓑ Ⓒ Ⓓ Ⓔ 36. Ⓐ Ⓑ Ⓒ Ⓓ Ⓔ
7. Ⓐ Ⓑ Ⓒ Ⓓ Ⓔ 17. Ⓐ Ⓑ Ⓒ Ⓓ Ⓔ 27. Ⓐ Ⓑ Ⓒ Ⓓ Ⓔ 37. Ⓐ Ⓑ Ⓒ Ⓓ Ⓔ
8. Ⓐ Ⓑ Ⓒ Ⓓ Ⓔ 18. Ⓐ Ⓑ Ⓒ Ⓓ Ⓔ 28. Ⓐ Ⓑ Ⓒ Ⓓ Ⓔ 38. Ⓐ Ⓑ Ⓒ Ⓓ Ⓔ

 # wrong in Section 8

9. Ⓐ Ⓑ Ⓒ Ⓓ Ⓔ 19. Ⓐ Ⓑ Ⓒ Ⓓ Ⓔ 29. Ⓐ Ⓑ Ⓒ Ⓓ Ⓔ 39. Ⓐ Ⓑ Ⓒ Ⓓ Ⓔ
10. Ⓐ Ⓑ Ⓒ Ⓓ Ⓔ 20. Ⓐ Ⓑ Ⓒ Ⓓ Ⓔ 30. Ⓐ Ⓑ Ⓒ Ⓓ Ⓔ 40. Ⓐ Ⓑ Ⓒ Ⓓ Ⓔ

Remove (or photocopy) this answer sheet and use it to complete the practice test.

Start with number 1 for each section. If a section has fewer questions than answer spaces, leave the extra spaces blank.

SECTION

9

1. Ⓐ Ⓑ Ⓒ Ⓓ Ⓔ	11. Ⓐ Ⓑ Ⓒ Ⓓ Ⓔ	21. Ⓐ Ⓑ Ⓒ Ⓓ Ⓔ	31. Ⓐ Ⓑ Ⓒ Ⓓ Ⓔ
2. Ⓐ Ⓑ Ⓒ Ⓓ Ⓔ	12. Ⓐ Ⓑ Ⓒ Ⓓ Ⓔ	22. Ⓐ Ⓑ Ⓒ Ⓓ Ⓔ	32. Ⓐ Ⓑ Ⓒ Ⓓ Ⓔ
3. Ⓐ Ⓑ Ⓒ Ⓓ Ⓔ	13. Ⓐ Ⓑ Ⓒ Ⓓ Ⓔ	23. Ⓐ Ⓑ Ⓒ Ⓓ Ⓔ	33. Ⓐ Ⓑ Ⓒ Ⓓ Ⓔ
4. Ⓐ Ⓑ Ⓒ Ⓓ Ⓔ	14. Ⓐ Ⓑ Ⓒ Ⓓ Ⓔ	24. Ⓐ Ⓑ Ⓒ Ⓓ Ⓔ	34. Ⓐ Ⓑ Ⓒ Ⓓ Ⓔ
5. Ⓐ Ⓑ Ⓒ Ⓓ Ⓔ	15. Ⓐ Ⓑ Ⓒ Ⓓ Ⓔ	25. Ⓐ Ⓑ Ⓒ Ⓓ Ⓔ	35. Ⓐ Ⓑ Ⓒ Ⓓ Ⓔ
6. Ⓐ Ⓑ Ⓒ Ⓓ Ⓔ	16. Ⓐ Ⓑ Ⓒ Ⓓ Ⓔ	26. Ⓐ Ⓑ Ⓒ Ⓓ Ⓔ	36. Ⓐ Ⓑ Ⓒ Ⓓ Ⓔ
7. Ⓐ Ⓑ Ⓒ Ⓓ Ⓔ	17. Ⓐ Ⓑ Ⓒ Ⓓ Ⓔ	27. Ⓐ Ⓑ Ⓒ Ⓓ Ⓔ	37. Ⓐ Ⓑ Ⓒ Ⓓ Ⓔ
8. Ⓐ Ⓑ Ⓒ Ⓓ Ⓔ	18. Ⓐ Ⓑ Ⓒ Ⓓ Ⓔ	28. Ⓐ Ⓑ Ⓒ Ⓓ Ⓔ	38. Ⓐ Ⓑ Ⓒ Ⓓ Ⓔ
9. Ⓐ Ⓑ Ⓒ Ⓓ Ⓔ	19. Ⓐ Ⓑ Ⓒ Ⓓ Ⓔ	29. Ⓐ Ⓑ Ⓒ Ⓓ Ⓔ	39. Ⓐ Ⓑ Ⓒ Ⓓ Ⓔ
10. Ⓐ Ⓑ Ⓒ Ⓓ Ⓔ	20. Ⓐ Ⓑ Ⓒ Ⓓ Ⓔ	30. Ⓐ Ⓑ Ⓒ Ⓓ Ⓔ	40. Ⓐ Ⓑ Ⓒ Ⓓ Ⓔ

☐ # right in Section 9

☐ # wrong in Section 9

 GO ONLINE

Be sure to add your scores to your syllabus.

Practice Test Three

SECTION 1
Time—25 Minutes
ESSAY

The essay gives you an opportunity to show how effectively you can develop and express ideas. You should, therefore, take care to develop your point of view, present your ideas logically and clearly, and use language precisely.

Your essay must be written in your Answer Grid Booklet—you will receive no other paper on which to write. You will have enough space if you write on every line, avoid wide margins, and keep your handwriting to a reasonable size. Remember that people who are not familiar with your handwriting will read what you write. Try to write or print so that what you are writing is legible to those readers.

You have twenty-five minutes to write an essay on the topic assigned below.
DO NOT WRITE ON ANOTHER TOPIC. AN OFF-TOPIC ESSAY WILL RECEIVE A SCORE OF ZERO.

Think carefully about the issue presented in the following excerpt and the assignment below.

> "Nothing in the world can take the place of persistence. Talent will not; nothing is more common than unsuccessful men with talent. Genius will not; unrewarded genius is almost a proverb. Education will not; the world is full of educated derelicts. Persistence and determination are omnipotent. The slogan, "Press on!" has solved and always will solve the problems of the human race."
>
> –Calvin Coolidge, *Autobiography*

Assignment: Do you agree that persistence is the major factor in success, and that talent, genius, and education play, at best, secondary roles? Plan and write an essay in which you develop your point of view on this issue. Support your position with reasoning and examples taken from your reading, studies, experience, or observations.

DO NOT WRITE YOUR ESSAY IN YOUR TEST BOOK.
You will receive credit only for what you write in your Answer Grid Booklet.

GO ON TO THE NEXT PAGE

KAPLAN

_____

_____

_____

_____

_____

_____

_____

_____

_____

_____

_____

_____

_____

_____

_____

_____

_____

_____

_____

_____

_____

IF YOU FINISH BEFORE TIME IS CALLED, YOU MAY CHECK YOUR WORK ON
THIS SECTION ONLY. DO NOT TURN TO ANY OTHER SECTION IN THE TEST.

SECTION 2

Time—25 Minutes
24 Questions

Directions: For each of the following questions, choose the best answer and darken the corresponding oval on the answer sheet.

Each sentence below has one or two blanks, each blank indicating that something has been omitted. Beneath the sentence are five words or sets of words labeled A through E. Choose the word or set of words that, when inserted in the sentence, <u>best</u> fits the meaning of the sentence as a whole.

EXAMPLE:

Today's small, portable computers contrast markedly with the earliest electronic computers, which were -------.

(A) effective
(B) invented
(C) useful
(D) destructive
(E) enormous

1. Despite their fierce appearance, caymans are rarely -------, and will not attack humans unless provoked.

   (A) extinct
   (B) timid
   (C) domesticated
   (D) amphibious
   (E) aggressive

2. Some historians claim that the concept of courtly love is a ------- that dates from the age of chivalry, while others believe it has more ------- origins.

   (A) relic . . simultaneous
   (B) notion . . ancient
   (C) memento . . discovered
   (D) period . . documented
   (E) doctrine . . amorous

3. In Shakespeare's day, ------- theater audiences would often throw fruits and vegetables at actors who failed to live up to their expectations.

   (A) doting
   (B) ravenous
   (C) jingoistic
   (D) boisterous
   (E) stagnant

4. Although they physically resemble each other, the brothers could not be more ------- temperamentally; while the one is quiet and circumspect, the other is brash and -------.

   (A) inimical . . timid
   (B) passionate . . superficial
   (C) dissimilar . . audacious
   (D) different . . forgiving
   (E) alike . . respectful

5. The retreat of Napoleon's army from Moscow quickly turned into a rout, as French soldiers, already ------- in the snow were ------- by Russian troops.

   (A) replenishing . . ravaged
   (B) pursuing . . joined
   (C) sinking . . camouflaged
   (D) floundering . . assaulted
   (E) tottering . . upbraided

GO ON TO THE NEXT PAGE

6. The Morgan Library in New York provides a -------
   environment in which scholars work amidst costly
   tapestries, paintings, stained-glass windows, and
   hand-crafted furniture.

   (A) realistic
   (B) frugal
   (C) sumptuous
   (D) friendly
   (E) practical

7. The lecturer's frustration was only ------- by the
   audience's ------- to talk during her presentation.

   (A) compounded . . propensity
   (B) alleviated . . invitation
   (C) soothed . . authorization
   (D) increased . . inability
   (E) supplanted . . desire

8. The proposal to build a nuclear power plant was
   the most ------- issue ever to come up at a council
   meeting; it is astonishing, therefore, that the
   members' vote was unanimous.

   (A) popular
   (B) contentious
   (C) concise
   (D) exorbitant
   (E) inconsequential

GO ON TO THE NEXT PAGE

KAPLAN

Directions: The passages below are followed by questions based on their content; questions following a pair of related passages may also be based on the relationship between the paired passages. Answer the questions on the basis of what is <u>stated</u> or <u>implied</u> in the passages and in any introductory material that may be provided.

Questions 9–10 refer to the following passage.

While it is often helpful to think of humans as simply another successful type of mammal, a vital distinction remains. When a pride of lions enjoys a surfeit of food, they are likely to hunt quickly,
(5) eat all they can, then spend the remainder of the day sleeping. When people enjoy such easy living, we see a markedly different pattern—our big brains cause us to be restless, and we engage in play. This takes the form of art, philosophy, sci-
(10) ence, even government. So the intelligence and curiosity that allowed early humans to develop agriculture, and thus a caloric surplus, also led to the use of that surplus as a foundation for culture.

9. The author most likely cites the behavior of lions in order to

(A) provide an example of an even more success-ful mammalian species

(B) question the efficiency of the lion's feeding behavior

(C) provide a contrast to the image of humans as industrious and resourceful

(D) help illustrate the distinguishing characteris-tic of humans that led to the development of culture

(E) explore the range of hunting behaviors in different successful species

10. The final sentence ("So, the intelligence … for culture.") primarily serves to

(A) illustrate the significance of a distinction

(B) counter a likely objection

(C) provide an alternative explanation

(D) suggest future implications of a phenomenon

(E) condone a future investigation

Questions 11–12 refer to the following passage.

Eugene O'Neill is truly a playwright of ideas, ideas that speak to a fundamental aspect of humanity. Many of O'Neill's plays are set firmly on American soil at a particular time in history,
(5) and it is easy to imagine that since the characters on stage are American, the only viable audience for such a play must be American as well. While a logical conclusion, this does not allow for the con-sistently strong record of production of O'Neill
(10) plays in Europe. His plays encompass ideas rele-vant to everyone, not just Americans.

11. The "logical conclusion" (line 8) is contradicted by O'Neill's

(A) primarily American audiences

(B) knowledge of American humanity

(C) mastery of playwriting

(D) authentically American characters

(E) popularity in Europe

12. Which of the following, if true, would most seriously undermine the conclusion of the passage?

(A) O'Neill's plays, once popular in American theaters, are rarely performed there today.

(B) In order to be a successful playwright, it is important to cultivate a specific and loyal following.

(C) When O'Neill's plays are staged in Europe, they are generally performed in English.

(D) The audiences attending O'Neill's plays in Europe are, for the most part, Americans traveling or living in Europe.

(E) O'Neill never traveled to Europe.

GO ON TO THE NEXT PAGE ▷

Questions 13–24 refer to the following passage.

In the following passage, a famous zoologist discusses the origins of the domesticated animal.

The relationship between humans and animals dates back to the misty morning of history. The caves of southern France and northern Spain are full of wonderful depictions of animals. Early

(5) African petroglyphs depict recognizable mammals and so does much American Indian art. But long before art, we have evidence of the closeness of humans and animals. The bones of dogs lie next to those of humans in the excavated villages of

(10) northern Israel and elsewhere. This unity of death is terribly appropriate. It marks a relationship that is the most ancient of all, one that dates back at least to the Mesolithic Era.* With the dog, the hunter acquired a companion and ally very early

(15) on, before agriculture, and long before the horses and the cat. The companion animals were followed by food animals, and then by those that provided enhanced speed and range, and those that worked for us.

(20) How did it all come about? A dog of some kind was almost inevitable. Consider its essence: a social carnivore, hunting larger animals across the broad plains it shared with our ancestors. Because of its pack structure it is susceptible to domina-

(25) tion by, and attachment to, a pack leader—the top dog. Its young are born into the world dependent, rearable, without too much skill, and best of all, they form bonds with the rearers. Dogs have a set of appeasement behaviors that elicit affective reac-

(30) tions from even the most hardened and unsophisticated humans. Puppies share with human babies the power to transform cynics into cooing softies. Furthermore, the animal has a sense of smell and hearing several times more acute than our own,

(35) great advantages to a hunting companion and intrusion detector. The dog's defense behavior makes it an instinctive guard animal.

No wonder the dog was first and remains so close to us. In general, however, something else

(40) was probably important in narrowing the list— the candidates had to be camp followers or cohabitants. When humankind ceased to be continually nomadic, when we put down roots and established

semi-permanent habitations, hut clusters, and

(45) finally villages, we created an instant, rich food supply for guilds of opportunistic feeders. Even today, many birds and mammals parasitize our wastes and feed from our stores. They do so because their wild behaviors provide the mecha-

(50) nisms for opportunistic exploitation. A striking example occurred in Britain during the 1940s and '50s. In those days, milk was delivered to the homeowners' doorstep in glass bottles with aluminum foil caps. Rich cream topped the milk, the

(55) paradise before homogenization. A chickadee known as the blue tit learned to puncture the cap and drink the cream. The behavior soon spread among the tits, and soon milk bottles were being raided in the early morning throughout Britain. If

(60) the birds had been so specialized that they only fed in deep forest, it never would have happened. But these were forest-edge opportunists, pioneers rather than conservatives. It is from animals of this ilk that we find our allies and our foes.

(65) Returning to the question of how it all came about, my instincts tell me that we first domesticated those individual animals that were orphaned by our hunting ancestors. In my years in the tropics, I have seen many wild animals raised by sim-

(70) ple people in their houses. The animals were there, without thought of utility or gain, mainly because the hunter in the family had brought the orphaned baby back for his wife and children. In Panama it was often a beautiful small, spotted cat

(75) that bounced friskily out of a peasant's kitchen to play at my feet. The steps from the home-raised wolfling to the domestic dog probably took countless generations. I bet it started with affection and curiosity. Only later did it become useful.

(80) When we consider that there are more than 55 million domestic cats and 50 million dogs in this country, and that they support an industry larger than the total economy of medieval Europe, we must recognize the strength of the ancient bond.

GO ON TO THE NEXT PAGE ⟩

KAPLAN

(85) Without the "aid" of goats, sheep, pigs, cattle, and horses we would never have reached our present population densities. Our parasitization of some species and symbiosis with others made civilization possible. That civilization, in turn, is increas-
(90) ingly causing the extinction of many animals and plant species—an ironic paradox indeed.

*Mesolithic Era: the Middle Stone Age, between 8,000 and 3,000 years B.C.

13. The author most likely describes the archeological discoveries mentioned in lines 8–10 as "terribly appropriate" because

    (A) dogs were always buried next to their owners in the Mesolithic Era
    (B) few animals were of religious significance in prehistoric cultures
    (C) they illustrate the role of dogs on a typical hunting expedition
    (D) our relationship with dogs goes back farther than with any other animal
    (E) they indicate the terrible speed of natural disasters

14. According to the first paragraph, the first animals that humans had a close relationship with were those that

    (A) acted as companions
    (B) provided a source of food
    (C) helped develop agriculture
    (D) enabled humans to travel farther
    (E) raided our food supply

15. According to the author, why was some kind of dog "inevitable" (line 21) as a companion animal for humans?

    (A) It survived by maintaining its independence.
    (B) It was stronger than other large animals.
    (C) It shared its prey with our ancestors.
    (D) It was friendly to other carnivores.
    (E) It was suited for human domination.

16. In line 21, "essence" means

    (A) history
    (B) nature
    (C) scent
    (D) success
    (E) aggression

17. Judging from lines 29–30, "affective reactions" most probably means

    (A) callous decisions
    (B) rational judgements
    (C) emotional responses
    (D) juvenile behavior
    (E) cynical comments

18. The author most likely compares puppies with human babies in lines 31–32 in order to

    (A) criticize an uncaring attitude toward animals
    (B) point out ways in which animals dominate humans
    (C) support the idea that dogs form bonds with their owners
    (D) dispel some misconceptions about the innocence of puppies
    (E) show how rewarding the ownership of a dog can be

19. In line 40, "the list" most likely refers to the

    (A) types of birds that scavenge human food supplies
    (B) number of animals that developed relationships with humans
    (C) group of species that are able to communicate with dogs
    (D) variety of attributes that make dogs good hunters
    (E) range of animals depicted in cave paintings

GO ON TO THE NEXT PAGE

20. The author most likely discusses the case of the British blue tit (lines 55–59) in order to

    (A) highlight a waste of valuable food supplies

    (B) indicate the quality of milk before homoge-nization

    (C) explain how unpredictable animal behavior can be

    (D) point out the disadvantages of living in rural areas

    (E) provide one example of an opportunistic feeder

21. In lines 63–64, "animals of this ilk" refers to animals that are

    (A) good companions

    (B) forest inhabitants

    (C) adaptable feeders

    (D) efficient hunters

    (E) persistent pests

22. The author most likely describes his experience in the tropics (lines 68–76) in order to

    (A) portray the simple life led by a hunter's family

    (B) show how useful animals can be in isolated places

    (C) underline the effort involved in training a wild animal

    (D) illustrate how the first domesticated animals were created

    (E) indicate the curious nature of the domestic cat

23. In line 85, the use of "aid" in quotation marks emphasizes the point that

    (A) the animals' help was involuntary

    (B) population levels are dangerously high

    (C) the contribution of animals is rarely recognized

    (D) many animals benefited from the relationship

    (E) livestock animals are not as loyal as dogs

24. Which of the following best describes the "ironic paradox" mentioned in line 91?

    (A) More money is now spent on domestic ani-mals than on animal livestock.

    (B) Pet ownership will become impractical if population density continues to increase.

    (C) The pet care industry in the U.S. today is larger than the total economy of medieval Europe.

    (D) Many parasitical species have a beneficial effect on the human population.

    (E) Human civilization is currently making extinct many of the other life forms that enabled it to grow.

IF YOU FINISH BEFORE TIME IS CALLED, YOU MAY CHECK YOUR WORK ON THIS SECTION ONLY. DO NOT TURN TO ANY OTHER SECTION IN THE TEST.   **STOP**

SECTION 3

Time—25 Minutes
20 Questions

Directions: For this section, solve each problem and decide which is the best of the choices given. Fill in the corresponding oval on the answer sheet. You may use any available space for scratchwork.

Notes:

(1) Calculator use is permitted.

(2) All numbers used are real numbers.

(3) Figures are provided for some problems. All figures are drawn to scale and lie in a plane UNLESS otherwise indicated.

(4) Unless otherwise specified, the domain of any function f is assumed to be the set of all real numbers x for which $f(x)$ is a real number.

Information

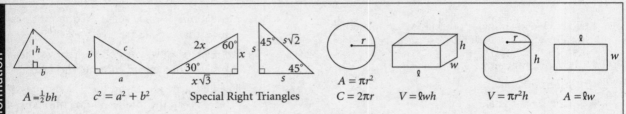

$A = \frac{1}{2}bh$ $\qquad c^2 = a^2 + b^2$ $\qquad$ Special Right Triangles $\qquad$ $A = \pi r^2$ $\qquad$ $V = \ell wh$ $\qquad$ $V = \pi r^2 h$ $\qquad$ $A = \ell w$
$\qquad\qquad\qquad\qquad\qquad\qquad\qquad\qquad\qquad\qquad\qquad\qquad C = 2\pi r$

The sum of the degree measures of the angles in a triangle is 180.
The number of degrees of arc in a circle is 360.
A straight angle has a degree measure of 180.

1. If $2(x + y) = 8 + 2y$, then $x =$

   (A) 1
   (B) 2
   (C) 3
   (D) 4
   (E) 8

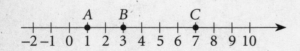

2. On the number line above, what is the distance from point B to the midpoint of AC?

   (A) 1
   (B) 2
   (C) 3
   (D) 4
   (E) 5

3. A certain machine caps 5 bottles every 2 seconds. At this rate, how many bottles will be capped in 1 minute?

   (A) 10
   (B) 75
   (C) 150
   (D) 225
   (E) 300

4. If $2n + 3 = 5$, then $4n =$

   (A) 1
   (B) 2
   (C) 4
   (D) 8
   (E) 16

GO ON TO THE NEXT PAGE

KAPLAN

5. If $a + b < 5$, and $a - b > 6$, which of the following pairs could be the values of a and b?

   (A) $(1, 3)$

   (B) $(3, -2)$

   (C) $(4, -2)$

   (D) $(4, -3)$

   (E) $(5, -1)$

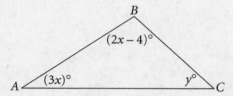

Note: Figure not drawn to scale.

6. In the triangle above, if the measure of angle B is 60 degrees, then what is the value of y?

   (A) 24

   (B) 26

   (C) 28

   (D) 30

   (E) 32

7. In a certain building, there are 10 floors and the number of rooms on each floor is R. If each room has exactly C chairs, which of the following gives the total number of chairs in the building?

   (A) $10R + C$

   (B) $10R + 10C$

   (C) $\dfrac{10}{RC}$

   (D) $10RC$

   (E) $100RC$

8. If a "sump" number is defined as one in which the sum of the digits of the number is greater than the product of the digits of the same number, which of the following is a "sump" number?

   (A) 123

   (B) 234

   (C) 332

   (D) 411

   (E) 521

9. If 4 percent of r is 6.2, then 20 percent of $r =$

   (A) 25

   (B) 26

   (C) 30

   (D) 31

   (E) 35

10. At a certain school, if the ratio of teachers to students is 1 to 10, which of the following could be the total number of teachers and students?

    (A) 100

    (B) 121

    (C) 144

    (D) 222

    (E) 1,011

11. If $x \wedge y$ is defined by the expression $(x - y)^x + (x + y)^y$, what is the value of $4 \wedge 2$?

    (A) 16

    (B) 20

    (C) 28

    (D) 44

    (E) 52

GO ON TO THE NEXT PAGE

KAPLAN

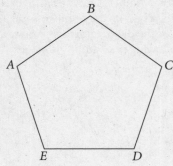

12. In pentagon *ABCDE* shown above, each side is 1 centimeter. If a particle starts at point *A* and travels clockwise 723 centimeters along *ABCDE*, the particle will stop on which point?

(A) *A*

(B) *B*

(C) *C*

(D) *D*

(E) *E*

13. Which of the following values of *s* would yield the smallest value for $4 + \frac{1}{s}$?

(A) $\frac{1}{4}$

(B) $\frac{1}{2}$

(C) 1

(D) 2

(E) 4

14. The first and seventh terms in a sequence are 1 and 365 respectively. If each term after the first in the sequence is formed by multiplying the preceding term by 3 and subtracting 1, what is the sixth term?

(A) 40

(B) 41

(C) 121

(D) 122

(E) 123

15. If an integer is randomly chosen from the first 50 positive integers, what is the probability that an integer with a digit of 3 is selected?

(A) $\frac{7}{25}$

(B) $\frac{3}{10}$

(C) $\frac{8}{25}$

(D) $\frac{2}{5}$

(E) $\frac{3}{5}$

16. In a certain triangle, the measure of the largest angle is 40 degrees more than the measure of the middle-sized angle. If the measure of the smallest angle is 20 degrees, what is the degree measure of the largest angle?

(A) 60

(B) 80

(C) 100

(D) 120

(E) 160

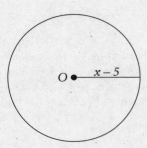

17. In the circle with center *O* above, for what value of *x* does the circle have a circumference of 20π?

(A) 5

(B) 10

(C) 15

(D) 20

(E) 25

GO ON TO THE NEXT PAGE

18. In a coordinate plane, if points $A(p, 3)$ and $B(6, p)$ lie on a line with a slope of 2, what is the value of p?

(A) 1

(B) 2

(C) 3

(D) 4

(E) 5

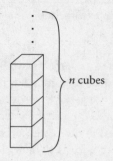

n cubes

20. In the figure above, there is a total of n cubes, each with an edge of 1 inch, stacked directly on top of each other. If $n > 1$, what is the total surface area, in square inches, of the resulting solid, in terms of n?

(A) $2n$

(B) $2n^2 + 2$

(C) $4n + 2$

(D) $4n^2$

(E) $5n$

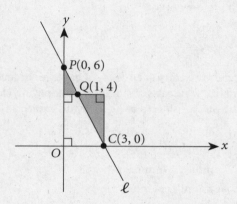

19. In the coordinate plane above, points $P(0, 6)$, $Q(1, 4)$, and $C(3, 0)$ are on line ℓ. What is the sum of the areas of the shaded triangular regions?

(A) $\dfrac{7}{2}$

(B) 4

(C) $\dfrac{9}{2}$

(D) 5

(E) $\dfrac{11}{2}$

IF YOU FINISH BEFORE TIME IS CALLED, YOU MAY CHECK YOUR WORK ON THIS SECTION ONLY. DO NOT TURN TO ANY OTHER SECTION IN THE TEST.

STOP

KAPLAN

SECTION 4

Time—25 Minutes
24 Questions

Directions: For each of the following questions, choose the best answer and darken the corresponding oval on the answer sheet.

Each sentence below has one or two blanks, each blank indicating that something has been omitted. Beneath the sentence are five words or sets of words labeled A through E. Choose the word or set of words that, when inserted in the sentence, best fits the meaning of the sentence as a whole.

EXAMPLE:

Today's small, portable computers contrast markedly with the earliest electronic computers, which were -------.

(A) effective
(B) invented
(C) useful
(D) destructive
(E) enormous   Ⓐ Ⓑ Ⓒ Ⓓ ●

---

1. Ozone in the upper layers of Earth's atmosphere is beneficial, ------- animal and plant life from dangerous ultraviolet radiation.

   (A) reflecting
   (B) withdrawing
   (C) displacing
   (D) thwarting
   (E) protecting

2. While George Balanchine's choreography stayed within a classical context, he challenged convention by recombining ballet idioms in ------- ways.

   (A) unexpected
   (B) familiar
   (C) redundant
   (D) naive
   (E) awkward

3. All of today's navel oranges are ------- of a single mutant tree that began bearing seedless fruit 200 years ago.

   (A) progenitors
   (B) combinations
   (C) descendants
   (D) conglomerations
   (E) spores

4. Because he consumed ------- quantities of food and drink at feasts given in his honor, King Henry VIII was considered a ------- by his subjects.

   (A) enormous . . glutton
   (B) prodigious . . peer
   (C) minute . . luminary
   (D) unhealthy . . fraud
   (E) unknown . . dolt

5. The prime minister ordered the cabinet to stay on as ------- administration until a new government could be formed.

   (A) an interim
   (B) a political
   (C) an invalid
   (D) a premature
   (E) a civilian

GO ON TO THE NEXT PAGE

> <u>**Directions:**</u> The passages below are followed by questions based on their content; questions following a pair of related passages may also be based on the relationship between the paired passages. Answer the questions on the basis of what is <u>stated</u> or <u>implied</u> in the passages and in any introductory material that may be provided.

Questions 6–9 refer to the following passages.

Passage 1

Miles Davis, though noteworthy as a jazz trumpet player, can best be understood instead as the ultimate musical iconoclast—a constant defier of popular and critical expectations. He first came to
(5) prominence as the young trumpeter in Charlie Parker's quintet in the late 1940s. In the early 50s, however, Davis led his own band in a completely different direction, using elaborate and original arrangements to explore a cool, subdued sound
(10) more in keeping with Davis's own personality. Characteristically, Davis soon abandoned this increasingly popular sound, pioneering the less harmonically sophisticated "modal" movement. Each decade brought more surprises, as Davis was
(15) at the forefront of free jazz, Fusion, and electronic instrumentation.

Passage 2

Great art often comes from limitations, and one can find no better example of this maxim than jazz great Miles Davis. Davis entered the jazz
(20) world when bebop music was at its peak. This style, pioneered by alto saxophonist Charlie Parker, demanded acrobatic facility, as soloists improvised dizzying melodies at break-neck speeds. Davis, though supremely expressive, didn't
(25) have the range or technique to play convincingly in this style. Rather than giving up, or continuing his career as a second-rate footnote, Davis evolved a unique style in which a few well-chosen notes were surrounded by artful silences that spoke
(30) volumes.

6. The author of Passage 1 most likely uses the word "characteristically" (line 11) in order to convey that

(A) like many artists, Davis creatively overcame technical limitations to create original art

(B) Davis's development of the new "modal" sound was part of a larger pattern of innovation

(C) Davis's inability to dedicate himself to a single style of jazz compromised his ultimate contribution to the art form

(D) Davis's skill as an instrumentalist is secondary to his role as a stylistic pioneer

(E) the modal movement, like Davis's other innovations, occurred about a decade after his previous stylistic advance

7. As used in Passage 2, line 27, "footnote" most nearly means

(A) unexpressive technician

(B) bibliographic citation

(C) unskilled artist

(D) stylistic innovator

(E) incidental participant

GO ON TO THE NEXT PAGE

8. Which of the following is most like Davis's "unique style" as described in Passage 2, lines 27–30?

   (A) a writer who explores poetry, short stories, and novels over the course of her career

   (B) a chef who carefully selects ingredients to create a balanced flavor

   (C) a photographer who purposely leaves his subject unfocused

   (D) a painter who uses a simple background to highlight her subject

   (E) a playwright who writes fast-paced, witty dialogue to advance the play's plot

9. The author of Passage 1 would most likely regard the description of Davis's departure from "bebop music" described in Passage 2, as

   (A) illustrative of Davis's ability to overcome technical obstacles

   (B) an example of limitations facilitating artistic progress

   (C) characteristic of Davis's stylistic innovations

   (D) a surprising though important development in Davis's career

   (E) the most significant of Davis's contributions to jazz music

Questions 10–17 refer to the following passage.

The passage below is adapted from a short story set in the wilderness of Alaska.

Day had broken cold and gray, exceedingly cold and gray, when the man turned away from the main Yukon trail and climbed the high earthbank, where a dim and little-traveled trail led east-
(5) ward through the spruce timberland. It was a steep bank, and he paused for breath at the top, excusing the act to himself by looking at his watch. It was nine o'clock. There was no hint of sun, though there was not a cloud in the sky. It
(10) was a clear day, and yet there seemed an intangible pall over the face of things that made the day dark. This fact did not worry the man.

In fact, all this—the dim trail, the absence of sun from the sky, the tremendous cold, and the
(15) strangeness and weirdness of it all—made no impression on the man. It was not because he was used to it. He was a newcomer in the land, and this was his first winter. The trouble was that he was without imagination. He was young and quick
(20) and alert in the things of life, but only in the things, and not in the significances. It was fifty degrees below zero, he judged. That impressed him as being cold and uncomfortable, but it did not lead him to meditate upon his frailty as a
(25) creature of temperature, and upon human frailty in general, able only to live within narrow limits of heat and cold; and from there on it did not lead him to the conjectural field of immortality and humanity's place in the universe. Fifty degrees
(30) below zero stood for a bite of frost that hurt and that must be guarded against. Nothing more than that entered his head.

He plunged in among the trees with determination. The trail was faint. A foot of snow had fallen
(35) since the last sled had passed, and he was glad he was traveling light. In fact, he carried nothing but the lunch wrapped in his handkerchief. He was surprised, however, at the cold. It certainly was cold, he concluded, as he rubbed his numb nose
(40) and cheekbones with his mittened hand. He was bearded, but that did not protect the high cheekbones and the eager nose that thrust itself aggressively into the frosty air.

GO ON TO THE NEXT PAGE

At his heels walked a dog, a big native husky,
(45) gray-coated, without any visible or temperamental
difference from its close relative, the wild wolf.
The animal was depressed by the tremendous
cold. It knew that it was no time for traveling. Its
instinct told it a truer tale than was told by the
(50) man's judgment. In reality, it was not merely colder
than fifty below zero; it was colder than sixty
below, than seventy below. It was seventy-five
below zero. The dog knew nothing of thermometers. Possibly in its brain there was no sharp con-
(55) sciousness of a condition of very cold such as was
in the human brain. But the brute had its instinct.
It experienced a vague but menacing apprehension that subdued it and made it slink along at the
man's heels, and that made it question every
(60) unusual movement of the man as if expecting him
to go into camp or to seek shelter somewhere and
build a fire. The dog had learned fire, and it wanted fire, or else to burrow under the snow and
cuddle its warmth away from the air.

10. By using the phrase "excusing the act to himself"
(line 7), the author suggests that the man

(A) is annoyed that it is already nine o'clock in
the morning

(B) distrusts his own intuitive reactions to things

(C) finds fault with others more readily than with
himself

(D) doubts that the time of day has any real bearing on things

(E) dislikes admitting to personal weaknesses

11. The author identifies the man as "a newcomer in
the land" (line 17) most likely in order to suggest
that the man was

(A) excited at being in a new place with many
opportunities

(B) nervous about being alone in an unfamiliar
place

(C) lacking in knowledge and experience about
the things around him

(D) trying hard to forget something in his past

(E) unsure about why he chose to come to the
new place

12. In lines 24–25, the phrase "a creature of
temperature" refers to

(A) the man's preference for cold climates

(B) the innate human ability to judge
temperature

(C) the fact that one's personality is shaped by the
environment

(D) the human body's physical vulnerability in
extreme climates

(E) the man's unfamiliarity with wilderness
survival techniques

13. Judging from lines 18–29, the man does not
see that

(A) he should appreciate the immense beauty of
nature

(B) humans cannot survive in the Alaskan
wilderness

(C) there is no way to accurately judge the
temperature

(D) the extreme cold could potentially be fatal

(E) he has undertaken to do something which
most people could not

14. The man's opinion of the temperature
(lines 29–32) reveals which aspect of his
character?

(A) determination to succeed against all odds

(B) lack of concern about personal welfare

(C) pragmatic approach to travel

(D) absence of insight and understanding

(E) apprehension about the extreme cold

GO ON TO THE NEXT PAGE

KAPLAN

15. In lines 47–56, by discussing the dog's reaction to the "tremendous cold," the author suggests that

    (A) animal instinct can prove to be superior to human intelligence

    (B) animals can judge temperature more accurately than humans can

    (C) humans are ill-equipped to survive in the wilderness

    (D) there is little difference between animal instinct and human judgment

    (E) animals and humans have different reactions to extreme temperatures

16. The statement "the dog knew nothing of thermometers" (lines 53–54) means that

    (A) dogs need not be as concerned about temperature as humans do

    (B) the dog's awareness of its environment is on a different level from the man's

    (C) a dog's mental faculties are not very well developed

    (D) the dog's experience of humans had been rather limited

    (E) the dog could not rely on the technological devices that the man could

17. Which of the following best explains why the dog would "question every unusual movement of the man" (lines 59–60)?

    (A) The dog senses that it cannot rely on the man for survival.

    (B) The man is beginning to be visibly affected by the cold.

    (C) The dog recognizes the need for protection from the cold.

    (D) The dog worries that the man intends to leave it behind.

    (E) The dog understands that the man does not realize how cold it is.

Questions 18–24 refer to the following passage.

The social science passage below was adapted from an article written by a health scientist.

For people in Southeast Asian refugee families, the experience of aging in America is very different from what they had expected for their second half of life. Older Southeast Asian refugees must
(5) cope with their rapidly acculturating younger family members, while taking on new roles and expectations in a foreign culture.

Many Southeast Asian immigrants are surprised to find that by American standards, they are not
(10) even considered elderly. Migration to a new culture often changes the definition of life stages. In the traditional Hmong culture of Vietnam, one can become an elder at 35 years of age when one becomes a grandparent. With grandparent status,
(15) elder Hmong can retire and expect their children to take financial responsibility for the family. Retiring at 35, of course, is not common in the United States.

There is a strong influence of Confucianism in
(20) traditional Vietnamese society. Confucianism, an ancient system of moral and religious thought, fosters strong filial piety and respect for family elders. In many Southeast Asian societies, age roles are hierarchical, with strict rules for social interac-
(25) tion. In America, however, because older refugees lack facility with the English language and knowledge of American culture, their credibility decreases when advising younger family members about important decisions. As younger family
(30) members take on primary roles as family mediators with American institutions—schools, legal systems, and social service agencies, for example— the leadership position of elders within the family is gradually eroded.

(35) Refugee elders must also cope with differences in gender roles in the United States. Even before migration, traditional gender roles were changing in Southeast Asia. During the Vietnam War, when men of military age were away, women took
(40) responsibility for tasks normally divided along gender lines. When Vietnamese families came to

GO ON TO THE NEXT PAGE

KAPLAN

this country, these changes became more pronounced. There were more employment opportunities for younger refugees and middle-
(45) aged refugee women because their expectations often fit with the lower status jobs that were among the few opportunities open to refugees. Many middle-aged women and younger refugees of both sexes became family breadwinners. This
(50) was a radical change for middle-aged men, who had been the major breadwinners of the family.

Although the pattern for long-term adaptation of middle-aged and older Southeast Asian refugees is still unknown, there are indications that the
(55) outlook for women is problematic. Many older women provide household and childcare services in order to allow younger family members to hold jobs or go to school. While these women are help-ing younger family members to succeed in
(60) America, they themselves are often isolated at home and cut off from learning English or other new skills, or becoming more familiar with American society. Thus, after the immigrant family passes through the early stages of meeting basic
(65) survival needs, older women may find that they are strangers in their own families as well as in their new country.

18. The major purpose of the passage is to discuss

(A) the reasons why Southeast Asian people move to the United States

(B) educational challenges facing young refugees in America today

(C) problems that elderly Southeast Asian people encounter in America

(D) the influence of Confucianism in Southeast Asian cultures

(E) changing gender relationships in Southeast Asian refugee families

19. In lines 4-6, "older Southeast Asian refugees must cope with their rapidly acculturating younger family members" refers to

(A) middle-aged men's embarrassment at not being the principal breadwinner

(B) middle-aged women's isolation in the home

(C) the high crime rate among younger refugees

(D) younger refugees' better educational and social opportunities in America

(E) the tendency of younger refugees to join non-Asian gangs

20. The author mentions "the traditional Hmong culture" (lines 11–12) in order to

(A) show that social expectations may vary greatly from one country to another

(B) suggest the lessening importance of traditional values in Vietnamese society

(C) indicate that modern Vietnam encompasses a number of ancient cultures

(D) illustrate the growing influence of Confucianism in Vietnamese society

(E) compare the religious beliefs of the Vietnamese to those of other Southeast Asian peoples

21. The author uses the term "family mediators" (lines 30–31) to mean the

(A) traditional role of elders in Vietnamese families

(B) responsibilities which young refugees assume in a new country

(C) help that newly arrived refugees get from friends who migrated earlier

(D) professional help available to refugee families in U.S. communities

(E) benefits that American society derives from immigrant people

GO ON TO THE NEXT PAGE

KAPLAN

22. The word "pronounced" in line 43 most nearly means

    (A) delivered
    (B) noticeable
    (C) famous
    (D) acceptable
    (E) declared

23. The phrase "radical change" (line 50) refers to the fact that

    (A) older refugees find that retirement ages are very different in America
    (B) women filled men's jobs during the Vietnam War
    (C) the education of their children is considered crucial by refugee parents
    (D) refugee men are often displaced as primary income earners in their families
    (E) it is difficult for young refugees of both sexes to find jobs in America

24. The author's point about the problematic long-term outlook for refugee women is made primarily through

    (A) personal recollection
    (B) historical discussion
    (C) case study analysis
    (D) philosophical commentary
    (E) informed speculation

IF YOU FINISH BEFORE TIME IS CALLED, YOU MAY CHECK YOUR WORK ON THIS SECTION ONLY. DO NOT TURN TO ANY OTHER SECTION IN THE TEST.   STOP

SECTION 5

Time—25 Minutes
18 Questions

Directions: For this section, solve each problem and decide which is the best of the choices given. Fill in the corresponding oval on the answer sheet. You may use any available space for scratchwork.

Notes:

(1) Calculator use is permitted.

(2) All numbers used are real numbers.

(3) Figures are provided for some problems. All figures are drawn to scale and lie in a plane UNLESS otherwise indicated.

(4) Unless otherwise specified, the domain of any function f is assumed to be the set of all real numbers x for which $f(x)$ is a real number.

$A = \frac{1}{2}bh$ $\qquad$ $c^2 = a^2 + b^2$ $\qquad$ Special Right Triangles $\qquad$ $A = \pi r^2$ $\qquad$ $V = \ell wh$ $\qquad$ $V = \pi r^2 h$ $\qquad$ $A = \ell w$

$\qquad\qquad\qquad\qquad\qquad\qquad\qquad\qquad\qquad\qquad\qquad\qquad C = 2\pi r$

The sum of the degree measures of the angles in a triangle is 180.
The number of degrees of arc in a circle is 360.
A straight angle has a degree measure of 180.

---

1. If $r = 3$, then $(r^2 - 2)(4 + r) =$

    (A) 5
    (B) 7
    (C) 49
    (D) 77
    (E) 91

2. If $f(x) = x^2 + x$, what is the value of $f(3)$?

    (A) 12
    (B) 9
    (C) 6
    (D) 3
    (E) 0

3. If Set A is the set of prime numbers between 10 and 20, Set B is the set of integers between −10 and 15, and Set C is the intersection of Set A and Set B, then how many elements does Set C contain?

    (A) 2
    (B) 4
    (C) 25
    (D) 29
    (E) 30

4. What is the greatest prime factor of 87?

    (A) 3
    (B) 17
    (C) 29
    (D) 43
    (E) 87

GO ON TO THE NEXT PAGE

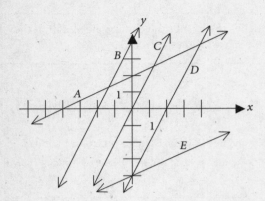

5. The graph above shows five lines, lettered A through E. Which of these lines can be represented as $y = 2x - 4$?

(A) A

(B) B

(C) C

(D) D

(E) E

6. The statement $(y - 3)^2 = (y + 1)^2$ is true for which of the following values of y?

(A) -1 only

(B) 1 only

(C) 3 and 1

(D) -3 and -1

(E) $\sqrt{3}$ only

7. A circular frame with a width of 2 inches surrounds a circular photo with a diameter of 8 inches. Assuming that the area of the frame does not overlap the area of the photo, what is the area of the frame?

(A) 4π

(B) 12π

(C) 16π

(D) 20π

(E) 36π

8. A business is owned by 4 women and 1 man, each of whom owns an equal share. If one of the women sells $\frac{1}{2}$ of her share to the man, and another woman keeps $\frac{1}{4}$ of her share and sells the rest to the man, what fraction of the business will the man own?

(A) $\frac{1}{3}$

(B) $\frac{9}{20}$

(C) $\frac{11}{20}$

(D) $\frac{2}{3}$

(E) $\frac{4}{5}$

GO ON TO THE NEXT PAGE

Directions: For Student-Produced Response questions 9–18, use the grids at the bottom of the answer sheet page on which you have answered questions 1–8.

Each of the remaining 10 questions requires you to solve the problem and enter your answer by marking the ovals in the special grid, as shown in the example below. You may use any available space for scratch work.

Answer: 1.25 or $\frac{5}{4}$ or 5/4

Write answer in boxes.

Grid-in result

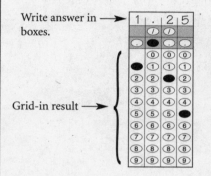

Fraction line
Decimal point

You may start your answers in any column, space permitting. Columns not needed should be left blank.

Either position is correct.

- It is recommended, though not required, that you write your answer in the boxes at the top of the columns. However, you will receive credit only for darkening the ovals correctly.

- Grid only one answer to a question, even though some problems have more than one correct answer.

- Darken no more than one oval in a column.

- No answers are negative.

- Mixed numbers cannot be gridded. For example: the number $1\frac{1}{4}$ must be gridded as 1.25 or 5/4.

(If $\boxed{1\,|\,1\,|\,/\,|\,4}$ is gridded, it will be interpreted as $\frac{11}{4}$ not $1\frac{1}{4}$.)

- Decimal Accuracy: Decimal answers must be entered as accurately as possible. For example, if you obtain an answer such as 0.1666…, you should record the result as .166 or .167. **Less accurate values such as .16 or .17 are not acceptable.**

Acceptable ways to grid $\frac{1}{6}$ = .1666…

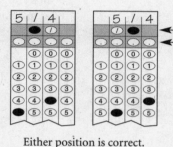

9. If $y = 2$, then $(5 - y)(y + 3) =$

10. At a certain car rental company, the daily rental rate for a mid-size car is $18.99. If the weekly rental rate for the same car is $123.50, how much money, in dollars, is saved by renting this car by the week instead of renting daily for seven days? (Exclude the $ when gridding your answer.)

GO ON TO THE NEXT PAGE ⟩

KAPLAN

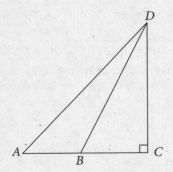

Note: Figure not drawn to scale.

11. In the figure above, $AB = 4$, $BC = 5$, and $DC = 12$. If point E lies somewhere between points A and B on line segment AB, what is one possible length of DE?

12. If $\frac{3}{4}$ of a cup of a certain drink mix is needed for every 2 quarts of water, how many cups of this drink mix is needed for 10 quarts of water?

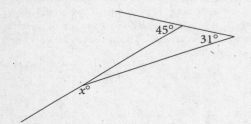

13. In the figure above, what is the value of x?

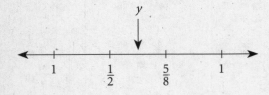

Note: Figure not drawn to scale.

14. On the number line above, what is one possible value for y?

15. Melanie drove at an average rate of 40 miles per hour for two hours and then increased her average rate by 25% for the next 3 hours. Her average rate of speed for the 5 hours was t miles per hour. What is the value of t?

16. At a convention of 500 dealers, each dealer sold coins or stamps or both. If 127 dealers sold both coins and stamps, and 198 dealers sold *only* stamps, how many dealers sold only coins?

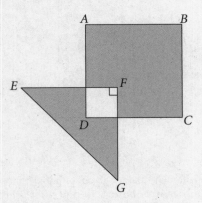

Note: Figure not drawn to scale.

17. In the figure above, square $ABCD$ and right triangle EFG overlap to form a smaller square. The length of each side of the smaller square is 2. If $AB = EF = FG = 6$, what is the sum of the areas of the shaded regions?

$$
\begin{array}{r}
NR \\
+RN \\
\hline
ABC
\end{array}
$$

18. The addition problem above is correct. If N, R, A, B, and C are different digits, what is the greatest possible value of $B + C$?

KAPLAN

SECTION 6

Time—25 Minutes
35 Questions

Directions: For each question in this section, select the best answer from among the choices given and fill in the corresponding oval on the answer sheet.

The following sentences test correctness and effectiveness of expression. Part of each sentence or the entire sentence is underlined; beneath each sentence are five ways of phrasing the underlined material. Choice A repeats the original phrasing; the other four choices are different. If you think the original phrasing produces a better sentence than any of the alternatives, select choice A; if not, select one of the other choices.

In making your selection, follow the requirements of standard written English; that is, pay attention to grammar, choice of words, sentence construction, and punctuation. Your selection should result in the most effective sentence—clear and precise, without awkwardness or ambiguity.

EXAMPLE: ANSWER:

Every apple in the baskets <u>are ripe and labeled according to the date it was picked</u>.   Ⓐ ● Ⓒ Ⓓ Ⓔ

(A) are ripe and labeled according to the date it was picked
(B) is ripe and labeled according to the date it was picked
(C) are ripe and labeled according to the date they were picked
(D) is ripe and labeled according to the date they were picked
(E) are ripe and labeled as to the date it was picked

---

1. By the time I graduate from college three years from now, my brother <u>has practiced</u> law for five years.

   (A) has practiced
   (B) has been practicing
   (C) will have been practicing
   (D) would have practiced
   (E) is practicing

2. The historians at the university who are researching the Napoleonic Wars from the Russian <u>perspective includes more than two professors who emigrated from Russia</u> to the United States.

   (A) perspective includes more than two professors who emigrated from Russia
   (B) perspective included more than two professors who emigrated from Russia
   (C) perspective include more than two professors who emigrated from Russia
   (D) perspective include more than two professors whom emigrated from Russia
   (E) perspective includes at least two professors who emigrated from Russia

3. In her Comparative Literature class, Nancy enjoyed reading Marcel Proust's groundbreaking novel, <u>which she considered to be more brilliant than the other writers we read</u>.

   (A) which she considered to be more brilliant than the other writers we read
   (B) whom she considered to have been more brilliant than the other writers we read
   (C) which she considered to be more brilliant than the other novels we read
   (D) which she considered to be brilliant opposed to the other novels we read
   (E) whom she considered to be more brilliant than the other novels we read

GO ON TO THE NEXT PAGE ⟶

KAPLAN

4. Many people <u>watching the baseball series seen the hometown hero arriving</u> at the stadium before the game.

   (A) watching the baseball series seen the hometown hero arriving

   (B) watching the baseball series saw the hometown hero arriving

   (C) who watch the baseball series seen the hometown hero arriving

   (D) watching the baseball series saw the hometown hero have arrived

   (E) who watch the baseball series seen the hometown hero arrived

5. The oxygen tank's increased capacity allows divers <u>to discover new species that congregate and feed close to</u> the bottom of the ocean.

   (A) to discover new species that congregate and feed close to

   (B) to have discovered new species that congregate and feed close to

   (C) to discover new species that congregate in and feed close to

   (D) to discover new species that congregate in and feed from close to

   (E) to discover new species who congregate and feed close to

6. The referee halted play in an effort <u>at avoiding serious altercations in the stadium between fans of</u> the opposing teams.

   (A) at avoiding serious altercations in the stadium between fans of

   (B) at avoiding a serious altercation in the stadium between fans of

   (C) to avoid serious altercations in the stadium between fans of

   (D) to avoid serious altercations in the stadium between fans on

   (E) to avoid serious altercations between fans in the stadium of

7. <u>Primarily a strategy to attract the votes of the elderly</u>, the social security adjustment carried great weight among the entire voting public of the day.

   (A) Primarily a strategy to attract the votes of the elderly

   (B) Primarily a strategy of attracting the votes of the elderly

   (C) Primarily the strategy to attract the votes of the elders

   (D) Primarily strategic to attracting the votes of the elderly

   (E) Primarily elderly voters' votes were attracted

8. A group of experts researching the bizarre occurrences theorized that the configuration of bright lights <u>were rather unusual but probably due to optical illusion</u>.

   (A) were rather unusual but probably due to optical illusion

   (B) were hardly unusual but probably due to optical illusion

   (C) were rather unusual and probably due to optical illusion

   (D) was rather unusual but probably due to optical illusion

   (E) was rather unusual probably due to optical illusion

GO ON TO THE NEXT PAGE

KAPLAN

9. The school's new retro rock-and-roll band has drawn such huge crowds that an entirely new team has been hired <u>to determine new methods of providing security for their concerts</u>.

   (A) to determine new methods of providing security for their concerts

   (B) to determine new methods of providing security for its concerts

   (C) to determine new methods for providing security for its concerts

   (D) to determining new methods for providing security for their concerts

   (E) to be determining new methods of providing security for their concerts

10. <u>If the concert had begun later, the conductor might have succeeded in giving the difficult last-minute corrections for the symphony to the orchestra.</u>

    (A) If the concert had begun later, the conductor might have succeeded in giving the difficult last-minute corrections for the symphony to the orchestra.

    (B) If the concert had began later, the conductor might have succeeded in giving the difficult last-minute corrections for the symphony to the orchestra.

    (C) If the concert had begun later, the conductor will succeed in giving last-minute corrections to the difficult orchestra for the symphony.

    (D) If the concert had begun afterwards, the conductor might have succeeded in having given last-minute corrections for the difficult symphony to the orchestra.

    (E) If the concert had begun later, the orchestra would have succeeded in having difficulty last-minute corrections for the symphony from the conductor.

11. Igor Stravinsky created innovative musical <u>works and they superimposed</u> beautiful melodies over discordant harmonies.

    (A) works and they superimposed

    (B) works, which superimposing

    (C) works, they superimposed

    (D) works that superimposed

    (E) works, and superimposed

GO ON TO THE NEXT PAGE

KAPLAN

Directions: The following sentences test your ability to recognize grammar and usage errors. Each sentence contains either a single error or no error at all. No sentence contains more than one error. The error, if there is one, is underlined and lettered. If the sentence contains an error, select the one underlined part that must be changed to make the sentence correct. If the sentence is correct, select choice E. In choosing answers, follow the requirements of standard written English.

EXAMPLE:

<u>Whenever</u> one is driving late at night, <u>you</u> must take extra precautions <u>against</u>
   A   B   C

falling asleep <u>at the wheel</u>. <u>No error</u>
          D   E

---

12. The great blue heron, perhaps the most elegant species among birds, <u>live</u> in <u>most</u> parts of the
                    A   B
United States, <u>at home</u> in wetland habitats in <u>both</u>
         C   D
inland and coastal regions. <u>No error</u>
                      E

13. At the football stadium, Susan <u>liked watching</u> the
                             A
home team's pre-game warm-ups, <u>which she</u>
                             B
considered <u>more interesting</u>
           C
<u>than the visiting team</u>. <u>No error</u>
     D   E

14. <u>By tracing</u> the source of artifacts found in Europe,
   A
researchers <u>determined</u> that the pattern of Viking
           B
settlements <u>were</u> <u>generally</u> similar, but varied in
          C   D
response to different climates. <u>No error</u>
                      E

15. The cake recipe <u>actually called</u> for a generous
               A
amount of sugar, <u>and</u> Chad used a sugar substitute
                B
instead <u>since</u> he wanted to <u>lower</u> the cake's calorie
        C   D
count. <u>No error</u>
       E

16. <u>Although</u> Luther Burbank <u>conducted</u> experiments
   A   B
that led to many new or improved plants, <u>such as</u>
                               C
the blight-resistant potato, his attempt <u>to develop</u>
                          D
a spineless cactus was not a success. <u>No error</u>
                          E

17. <u>They</u> were relieved <u>when</u> monsoons <u>carried</u> rain
   A   B   C
from the southern seas <u>and</u> replenished India's
                  D
drought-stricken water supply. <u>No error</u>
                     E

GO ON TO THE NEXT PAGE ⇒

18. All of the children <u>waiting</u> for the school bus <u>seen</u>
                     A   B
    the crossing guard <u>walking out</u> into the street
                        C
    <u>to stop traffic</u>. <u>No error</u>
        D   E

19. Arthur Miller's moral viewpoint allows him

    <u>to produce</u> plays <u>that</u> uniquely and dramatically
       A   B
    <u>expresses</u> the damaging effect modern life <u>has had</u>
     C   D
    on Americans. <u>No error</u>
                 E

20. <u>While</u> many small children <u>claim hearing</u> Santa
     A   B
    and his reindeer on the roof, few teenagers believe

    that <u>such a person</u> <u>truly</u> exists. <u>No error</u>
            C   D   E

21. This week, the company <u>initiated</u> Hawaiian Shirt
                         A
    Day in an attempt <u>at creating</u> a higher degree
                 B
    <u>of team spirit</u> <u>in the office</u>. <u>No error</u>
        C   D   E

22. <u>As</u> Shirin Abadi <u>was awarded</u> the Nobel Peace
    A   B
    Prize, many of her colleagues <u>praised</u> her
                       C
    exceptional efforts <u>about</u> democracy and human
                 D
    rights in Iran. <u>No error</u>
              E

23. Although the San Francisco Earthquake

    <u>in the spring</u> of 1906 <u>was leveling</u> many buildings,
       A   B
    the subsequent <u>series of fires</u> actually <u>destroyed</u>
                C   D
    most of the city. <u>No error</u>
              E

24. The quarterback, after his startling <u>failure to</u>
                             A
    throw a complete pass, <u>went about</u>
                   B
    <u>absolute shamefaced</u> and was available to
           C
    <u>only a few</u> of his teammates. <u>No error</u>
       D   E

25. <u>While</u> the effect of disease-causing agents on
    A
    cigarette smokers <u>has been known</u> for years, only
                  B
    recently <u>has</u> the damaging effects of cigarette
          C
    smoke on second-hand smokers <u>become</u> widely
                          D
    recognized. <u>No error</u>
           E

GO ON TO THE NEXT PAGE ▷

KAPLAN

26. The FBI <u>maintains</u> strict <u>requirements for</u> citizens
             A   B
when <u>they are</u> <u>interested in</u> joining the Bureau.
         C   D
<u>No error</u>
  E

27. <u>Although</u> James Joyce, Samuel Beckett, and
   A
Seamus Deane <u>drew on similar</u> aspects of Irish
              B
culture in their novels, Beckett <u>was</u> <u>more abstract</u>
                  C   D
in his interpretations. <u>No error</u>
             E

28. José Limón, <u>assuredly</u> one of the today's
            A
<u>most inventive</u> modern dance choreographers,
  B
<u>brought</u> to the stage a startling <u>approach to</u>
  C   D
movement and musicality. <u>No error</u>
                E

29. Among the great moments in twentieth century

history, the toppling of the Berlin Wall by East

Germans <u>are</u> <u>probably seen</u> by <u>them</u> as one of the
       A   B   C
<u>most felicitous</u>. <u>No error</u>
    D   E

GO ON TO THE NEXT PAGE

Directions: The following passage is an early draft of an essay. Some parts of the passage need to be rewritten.

Read the passage and select the best answer for each question that follows. Some questions are about particular sentences or parts of sentences and ask you to improve sentence structure or word choice. Other questions ask you to consider organization and development. In choosing answers, follow the conventions of standard written English.

Questions 30–35 refer to the following passage.

(1) When I visited England last year, I wanted to attend a football match (football in England is what is called soccer in the U.S.). (2) My mother wouldn't let me. (3) She tells me, "the fans are much too violent." (4) I really wanted to go so I did some research on English fans' violence.

(5) Through my research I realized that my mother would never let me go to a game. (6) But beyond that, I felt sad that hooliganism was such a reality in the English game. (7) They cause riots, and innocent football fans are sometimes injured by them when football-related fights get out of control.

(8) England had tried all sorts of remedies to stop the violence, but they couldn't stop hooliganism from increasing. (9) The officials tried creating lists of people banned from stadiums. (10) At international matches some known hooligans weren't even allowed into the country. (11) Some say that the older generation of hooligans was teaching the younger. (12) It is just human nature and crowd mentality. (13) But there was an argument that rang even more true for me: poverty was an underlying cause. (14) Economic data indicating that the football teams with the highest rate of violence were situated in the poorest areas.

30. In context, which is the best version of the underlined portion of sentence 3 (reproduced below)?

    She tells me, "the fans are much too violent."

    (A) (As it is now)
    (B) My mother tells me,
    (C) This was because she tells me,
    (D) She told me,
    (E) She suggested:

31. In context, which is the best version of the underlined portion of sentence 7 (reproduced below)?

    They cause riots, and innocent football fans are sometimes injured by them when football-related fights get out of control.

    (A) (As it is now)
    (B) They caused riots and innocent football fans were sometimes injured by them
    (C) Causing riots and injuring innocent football fans, the hooligans caused problems
    (D) The hooligans cause riots and sometimes injure innocent football fans
    (E) Innocent football fans sometimes cause riots and are injured

GO ON TO THE NEXT PAGE

KAPLAN

32. In context, which of the following words are the most logical to insert at the beginning of sentence 12 (reproduced below)?

    It is just human nature and crowd mentality.

    (A) I see that
    (B) They say that
    (C) Others say that
    (D) However,
    (E) As a result,

33. In context, which is the best version of the underlined portion of sentence 14 (reproduced below)?

    Economic data indicating that the football teams with the highest rate of violence were situated in the poorest areas.

    (A) (As it is now)
    (B) seeming to indicate that the football teams
    (C) are indicating that the football teams
    (D) indicated that the football teams
    (E) had indicated that the football teams

34. Which of the following best describes the relationship between sentences 13 and 14?

    (A) Sentence 14 provides the conclusion supported by evidence in sentence 13.
    (B) Sentence 14 adds to information reported in sentence 13.
    (C) Sentence 14 poses an argument that contradicts the point made in sentence 13.
    (D) Sentence 14 provides supporting evidence for the conclusion in sentence 13.
    (E) Sentence 14 concludes that the theory proposed in sentence 13 is wrong.

35. Where is the best place to insert the following sentence?

    Instead of just punishing acts of hooliganism, England should attack its source, poverty.

    (A) after sentence 5
    (B) after sentence 7
    (C) after sentence 9
    (D) after sentence 12
    (E) after sentence 14

IF YOU FINISH BEFORE TIME IS CALLED, YOU MAY CHECK YOUR WORK ON THIS SECTION ONLY. DO NOT TURN TO ANY OTHER SECTION IN THE TEST.   STOP

KAPLAN

SECTION 7

Time—20 Minutes
19 Questions

Directions: For each of the following questions, choose the best answer and darken the corresponding oval on the answer sheet.

Each sentence below has one or two blanks, each blank indicating that something has been omitted. Beneath the sentence are five words or sets of words labeled A through E. Choose the word or set of words that, when inserted in the sentence, <u>best</u> fits the meaning of the sentence as a whole.

EXAMPLE:

Today's small, portable computers contrast markedly with the earliest electronic computers, which were -------.

(A) effective
(B) invented
(C) useful
(D) destructive
(E) enormous

1. The itinerary set by their travel agent included so many stops in ------- amount of time that they received only the most ------- impressions of places visited.

   (A) a limited . . lasting
   (B) a brief . . cursory
   (C) a generous . . favorable
   (D) a sufficient . . fleeting
   (E) an unnecessary . . preliminary

2. Many formerly ------- peoples have moved into ------- settlements as urban areas have encroached upon their land.

   (A) roving . . vulnerable
   (B) despondent . . stable
   (C) transitory . . covert
   (D) fervid . . enduring
   (E) nomadic . . permanent

3. The ------- effect of the sleeping tablets was so ------- that she still felt groggy the next day.

   (A) toxic . . erratic
   (B) soporific . . pronounced
   (C) salubrious . . dependable
   (D) pharmaceutical . . peculiar
   (E) stimulating . . unreliable

4. For many years Davis had difficulty in accepting those who were in positions of authority; in fact, when he was in high school his teachers described him as a ------- student.

   (A) compliant
   (B) slothful
   (C) conscientious
   (D) model
   (E) recalcitrant

5. Although the actress had lived in a large city all her life, she was such a ------- performer that she became the virtual ------- of the humble farm girl she portrayed in the play.

   (A) versatile . . opposite
   (B) melodramatic . . understudy
   (C) natural . . nemesis
   (D) consummate . . incarnation
   (E) drab . . caricature

6. The chairman ------- the decision of the board members, describing it as a ------- of every worthy ideal that the organization had hitherto upheld.

   (A) defended . . denial
   (B) lamented . . negation
   (C) criticized . . fulfillment
   (D) endorsed . . renunciation
   (E) applauded . . repudiation

GO ON TO THE NEXT PAGE

Directions: The passages below are followed by questions based on their content; questions following a pair of related passages may also be based on the relationship between the paired passages. Answer the questions on the basis of what is <u>stated</u> or <u>implied</u> in the passages and in any introductory material that may be provided.

Questions 7–19 refer to the following passages.

The two excerpts below are from speeches that were made by outstanding American leaders of the nineteenth century. The first excerpt is from Thomas Jefferson's first Inaugural Address in 1801; the second was delivered by Frederick Douglass during the Fourth of July celebration in Rochester, New York, in 1852.

Passage 1

Let us then, with courage and confidence, pursue our own federal and republican principles; our attachment to union and representative government. Kindly separated by nature and a wide
(5) ocean from the exterminating havoc of one quarter of the globe; too high-minded to endure the degradation of others, possessing a chosen country, with room enough for our descendants to the thousandth and thousandth generation, entertain-
(10) ing a due sense of our equal right to the use of our own faculties, to the acquisition of our own industry, to honor and confidence from our fellow-citizens, resulting not from birth, but from our actions and their sense of them, enlightened
(15) by a benign religion, professed in deed and practiced in various forms, yet all of them inculcating honesty, truth, temperance, gratitude, and the love of man.... Still one thing more, fellow citizens, a wise and frugal government, which shall restrain
(20) men from injuring one another, shall leave them otherwise free to regulate their own pursuits of industry and improvement, and shall not take from the mouth of labor the bread it has earned. This is the sum of good government; and this is
(25) necessary to close the circle of our felicities.

About to enter, fellow citizens, upon the exercise of duties which comprehend everything dear and valuable to you, it is proper you should understand what I deem the essential principles of our
(30) government, and consequently, those which ought to shape its administration. I will compress them within the narrowest compass they will bear, stating the general principle, but not all its limitations. Equal and exact justice to all men, of what-
(35) ever state or persuasion, religious or political...

Passage 2

I say it with a sad sense of disparity between us. I am not included within the pale of this glorious anniversary! Your high independence only reveals the immeasurable distance between us. The bless-
(40) ings in which you this day rejoice are not enjoyed in common. The rich inheritance of justice, liberty, prosperity, and independence bequeathed by your fathers is shared by you, not by me. The sunlight that brought life and healing to you has
(45) brought stripes and death to me. This Fourth of July is yours, not mine. You may rejoice, I must mourn. To drag a man in fetters into the grand illuminated temple of liberty, and call upon him to join you in joyous anthems, were inhuman
(50) mockery and sacrilegious irony. Do you mean, citizens, to mock me by asking me to speak today?

...Fellow citizens, above your national, tumultuous joy, I hear the mournful wail of millions, whose chains, heavy and grievous yesterday, are
(55) today rendered more intolerable by the jubilant shouts that reach them. If I do forget, if I do not remember those bleeding children of sorrow this day, "may my right hand forget her cunning, and may my tongue cleave to the roof of my mouth!"
(60) To forget them, to pass lightly over their wrongs, and to chime in with the popular theme, would be treason most scandalous and shocking, and would make me a reproach before God and the world. My subject, then, fellow citizens, is "American
(65) Slavery..."

...Would you have me argue that man is entitled to liberty? That he is the rightful owner of his own body? You have already declared it. Must I argue the wrongfulness of slavery? Is that a ques-
(70) tion for republicans? Is it to be settled by the rules of logic and argumentation, as a matter beset with great difficulty, involving a doubtful application of the principle of justice, hard to understand? ...

GO ON TO THE NEXT PAGE ⟹

…What to the American slave is your Fourth of
(75) July? I answer, a day that reveals more to him than
all other days of the year, the gross injustice and
cruelty to which he is the constant victim. To him
your celebration is a sham; your boasted liberty an
unholy license; your national greatness, swelling
(80) vanity; your sounds of rejoicing are empty and
heartless; your denunciation of tyrants, brass-
fronted impudence; your shouts of liberty and
equality, hollow mockery; your prayers and
hymns, your sermons and thanksgivings, with all
(85) your religious parade and solemnity, are to him
mere bombast, fraud, deception, impiety, and
hypocrisy—a thin veil to cover up crimes which
would disgrace a nation of savages. There is not a
nation of the earth guilty of practices more shock-
(90) ing and bloody than are the people of the United
States at this very hour.

7. By "our equal right . . . to honor and confidence
from our fellow-citizens, resulting not from birth,
but from our actions and their sense of them"
(Passage 1, lines 10–14), Jefferson means that

   (A) members of all nations are welcome to come
to America

   (B) citizens have the right to demand respect
from each other

   (C) citizens should judge each other by their
accomplishments rather than their ancestry

   (D) one can build trust by doing things for others

   (E) one should rely not only on one's family but
also on other citizens

8. In Passage 1, line 27, the word "comprehend" most
nearly means

   (A) include

   (B) understand

   (C) perceive

   (D) outline

   (E) realize

9. By "I will compress them within the narrowest
compass they will bear" Passage 1, (lines 31–32),
Jefferson means that

   (A) he intends to limit the role of government

   (B) those who oppose justice will be imprisoned

   (C) the general principles of government have
boundaries

   (D) he will speak concisely about the principles of
government

   (E) government bureaucracy has become too
inflated

10. The word "persuasion" in Passage 1, line 35 most
nearly means

   (A) enticement

   (B) influence

   (C) cajolery

   (D) authority

   (E) opinion

11. The statement "To drag a man . . . sacrilegious
irony" Passage 2, (lines 47–50) conveys a sense of

   (A) indignation at the hypocrisy of Fourth of July
celebrations

   (B) sorrow over the way the slaves had been
treated

   (C) anger that slavery had not yet been abolished

   (D) disbelief that Fourth of July celebrations
could even take place

   (E) amazement that slaves were being forced to
join in the celebration

GO ON TO THE NEXT PAGE

12. In Passage 2, the references to the "mournful wail" and the "jubilant shouts" (lines 53–56) serve to

(A) remind the audience of difficulties in the past that have been overcome

(B) indicate the importance of commemorating the Fourth of July

(C) warn that the future of the country looks deceptively bright

(D) emphasize the different outlooks of two groups in the country

(E) suggest that some are faced with an unsolvable problem

13. In Passage 2, line 62, the author uses the word "treason" to refer to the act of

(A) rebelling against authority

(B) betraying the needs of a social group

(C) renouncing one's own principles

(D) expressing unpopular views

(E) acting upon irrational impulses

14. The author of Passage 2 most likely describes "American Slavery" as "my subject" (lines 64–65) in order to

(A) underline an unexpected new direction in his argument

(B) indicate the broad historical scope of his address

(C) emphasize his intent to discuss an apparent contradiction

(D) highlight the answer to a problem facing the United States

(E) underscore his eagerness to learn more about the topic of slavery

15. In lines 81–82 of Passage 2, the phrase "brass-fronted impudence" is primarily used to convey the author's

(A) outrage at the contrast between political speeches and social reality

(B) exasperation at the many obstacles to racial equality

(C) resentment at the number of people excluded from July Fourth celebrations

(D) belief that resistance to authority is ultimately futile

(E) anger at the acts of tyrants throughout the world

16. The author of Passage 1 would most likely react to the questions at the beginning of the third paragraph of Passage 2 (lines 66–73) by commenting that

(A) a nation's political ideals are not always consistent with its actions

(B) the doctrine of equality is necessary for good government

(C) political views must be expressed through the proper democratic channels

(D) the goal of liberty for all may not be practical to attain

(E) the degradation of others must sometimes be endured

GO ON TO THE NEXT PAGE

17. The author of Passage 2 would most likely react to the general principle of government in the last sentence of Passage 1 by pointing out that

    (A) this general principle is hopelessly naive

    (B) the real situation strongly contradicts this principle

    (C) experience has proven this principle to be unattainable

    (D) this principle is meaningless because it is vaguely worded

    (E) the government never intended to adhere to this principle

18. Which statement is best supported by a comparison of the excerpts from the two speeches?

    (A) Both excerpts denounce the degradation of some men and women in America.

    (B) The purpose of both excerpts is to urge citizens to critically evaluate themselves.

    (C) Both excerpts emphasize the necessity of justice for all citizens.

    (D) Both excerpts argue that slavery is a violation of human rights.

    (E) Both excerpts present a hopeful vision of the future.

19. The attitudes expressed in Passage 1 and Passage 2 towards equality in the United States might best be described as

    (A) cautious versus angry

    (B) disappointed versus adulated

    (C) optimistic versus critical

    (D) hopeful versus promising

    (E) indulgent versus prudent

IF YOU FINISH BEFORE TIME IS CALLED, YOU MAY CHECK YOUR WORK ON THIS SECTION ONLY. DO NOT TURN TO ANY OTHER SECTION IN THE TEST.

STOP

SECTION 8

Time—20 Minutes
16 Questions

Directions: For this section, solve each problem and decide which is the best of the choices given. Fill in the corresponding oval on the answer sheet. You may use any available space for scratchwork.

Notes:

(1) Calculator use is permitted.

(2) All numbers used are real numbers.

(3) Figures are provided for some problems. All figures are drawn to scale and lie in a plane UNLESS otherwise indicated.

(4) Unless otherwise specified, the domain of any function f is assumed to be the set of all real numbers x for which $f(x)$ is a real number.

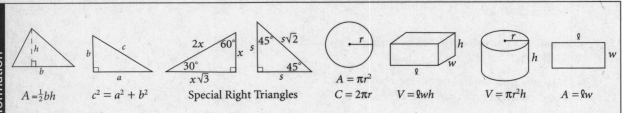

$A = \frac{1}{2}bh$ $c^2 = a^2 + b^2$ Special Right Triangles $A = \pi r^2$ $C = 2\pi r$ $V = \ell wh$ $V = \pi r^2 h$ $A = \ell w$

The sum of the degree measures of the angles in a triangle is 180.
The number of degrees of arc in a circle is 360.
A straight angle has a degree measure of 180.

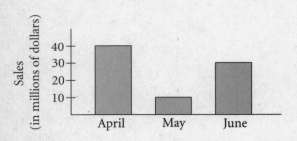

1. According to the graph above, April sales accounted for approximately what percent of the total sales?

(A) $12\frac{1}{2}$

(B) 25

(C) $37\frac{1}{2}$

(D) 50

(E) 60

2. If xy is negative, which of the following CANNOT be negative?

(A) $y - x$

(B) $x - y$

(C) $x^2 y$

(D) xy^2

(E) $x^2 y^2$

3. If 1 bora = 2 fedis and 1 fedi = 3 glecks, how many boras are equal to 48 glecks?

(A) 4

(B) 8

(C) 16

(D) 48

(E) 96

GO ON TO THE NEXT PAGE

4. A college class is made up of f freshman and s sophomores. If 5 freshman drop this class, then the number of sophomores in the class is 3 times the number of freshman. Which of the following equations represents s in terms of f?

(A) $s = \dfrac{f-5}{3}$

(B) $s = \dfrac{f+5}{3}$

(C) $s = 3(f-5)$

(D) $s = 3(f+5)$

(E) $s = 5(f-3)$

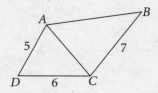

5. In the figure above, if the perimeter of triangle ABC is 4 more than the perimeter of triangle ACD, what is the perimeter of quadrilateral $ABCD$?

(A) 20

(B) 22

(C) 24

(D) 25

(E) 26

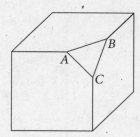

6. The figure above shows a cube-shaped stone with edges of 3 centimeters. Points A, B, and C are on three different edges of the cube, each 1 centimeter away from the same vertex. A jeweler slices off the corner with a straight cut through A, B, and C, as shown, and slices pieces of the same size off all the other corners of the stone. What is the total number of faces on the resulting stone?

(A) 7

(B) 10

(C) 12

(D) 14

(E) 16

7. What is the average of the first 30 positive integers?

(A) 14

(B) 14.5

(C) 15

(D) 15.5

(E) 16

GO ON TO THE NEXT PAGE

KAPLAN

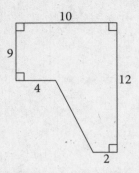

Note: Figure not drawn to scale.

8. What is the area of the figure above?

    (A)   96
    (B)   102
    (C)   104
    (D)   108
    (E)   110

9. Sixty cookies were to be equally distributed to x campers. When 8 campers did not want the cookies, the other campers each received 2 more cookies. Which of the following equations could be used to find the number of campers x?

    (A) $x^2 - 8x - 240 = 0$
    (B) $x^2 - 8x + 240 = 0$
    (C) $x^2 + 8x - 240 = 0$
    (D) $x^2 + 8x + 240 = 0$
    (E) $x^2 - 4x - 120 = 0$

10. If 6 students are eligible for 2 scholarships worth $1,000 each how many different combinations of 2 students winning the 2 scholarships are possible?

    (A)   6
    (B)   9
    (C)   12
    (D)   15
    (E)   30

11. If $q \neq 0$ and $q = q^{-2}$, what is the value of q?

    (A) -1
    (B) 0
    (C) $\dfrac{1}{2}$
    (D) 1
    (E) 2

Price of One Can	Projected Number of Cans Sold
$0.75	10,000
$0.80	9,000
$0.85	8,000
$0.90	7,000
$0.95	6,000
$1.00	5,000

12. The chart above describes how many cans of a new soft drink a company expects to sell at a number of possible prices per can. Which of the following equations best describes the relationship shown in the chart, where n indicates the number of cans sold and p represents the price in dollars of one can?

    (A) $n = -20,000p - 25,000$
    (B) $n = -20,000p + 25,000$
    (C) $n = -200p - 250$
    (D) $n = 200p + 250$
    (E) $n = 20,000p - 25,000$

GO ON TO THE NEXT PAGE

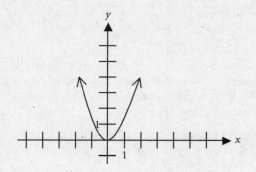

13. Which of the following equations best describes the curve shown in the graph?

    (A) $y = x$
    (B) $y = x^2$
    (C) $y = x^3$
    (D) $y = \sqrt{x}$
    (E) $y = \dfrac{1}{2}x$

14. In a game, all tokens of the same color are worth the same number of points. If one player won 4 green tokens and 8 yellow tokens for a total score of 48 points, and another player won 6 green tokens and 4 yellow tokens for a total score of 32 points, how many points is a yellow token worth?

    (A) 2
    (B) 4
    (C) 5
    (D) 8
    (E) 10

15. Pablo has c grams of cherries. He uses 30 percent of the cherries to make muffins, each of which requires m grams of cherries. He uses the rest of the cherries to make preserves, each pint of which requires p grams of cherries. Which of the following describes the number of pints of preserves Pablo can make?

    (A) $\dfrac{3c}{10m}$

    (B) $\dfrac{3c}{10p}$

    (C) $\dfrac{7c}{10p}$

    (D) $\dfrac{7c}{10m}$

    (E) $\dfrac{3cp}{10}$

16. At a fruit stand, the price of one pound of cherries is twice the price of one pound of grapes. If 32 pounds of cherries and 8 pounds of grapes were sold and sales totaled $90.00, how much more money was made on the cherries than on the grapes?

    (A) $75.00
    (B) $70.00
    (C) $65.00
    (D) $60.00
    (E) $55.00

IF YOU FINISH BEFORE TIME IS CALLED, YOU MAY CHECK YOUR WORK ON THIS SECTION ONLY. DO NOT TURN TO ANY OTHER SECTION IN THE TEST.

STOP

KAPLAN

SECTION 9

Time—10 Minutes
14 Questions

Directions: For each question in this section, select the best answer from among the choices given and fill in the corresponding oval on the answer sheet.

The following sentences test correctness and effectiveness of expression. Part of each sentence or the entire sentence is underlined; beneath each sentence are five ways of phrasing the underlined material. Choice A repeats the original phrasing; the other four choices are different. If you think the original phrasing produces a better sentence than any of the alternatives, select choice A; if not, select one of the other choices.

In making your selection, follow the requirements of standard written English; that is, pay attention to grammar, choice of words, sentence construction, and punctuation. Your selection should result in the most effective sentence—clear and precise, without awkwardness or ambiguity.

EXAMPLE:

Every apple in the baskets <u>are ripe and labeled according to the date it was picked</u>.

ANSWER:

(A) are ripe and labeled according to the date it was picked
(B) is ripe and labeled according to the date it was picked
(C) are ripe and labeled according to the date they were picked
(D) is ripe and labeled according to the date they were picked
(E) are ripe and labeled as to the date it was picked

---

1. Lost items can be found <u>at the admissions booth they can be picked up until one hour after the museum's closing</u>.

   (A) at the admissions booth they can be picked up until one hour after the museum's closing

   (B) at the admissions booth; they can be picked up until one hour after the museum's closing

   (C) until one hour after the museum's closing, they can be picked up at the admissions booth

   (D) and that can be picked up at the admissions booth until one hour after the museum's closing

   (E) at the admissions booth, until one hour after the museum's closing is when they can be picked up

2. By utilizing cacophony and inconsistent rhythms, <u>the shock value of postmodern music was raised by Webern to a higher level</u> than ever before.

   (A) the shock value of postmodern music was raised by Webern to a higher level

   (B) Webern raised the shock value of postmodern music to a higher level

   (C) a higher level of postmodern music was reached by Webern

   (D) postmodern music's shock value was raised to a higher level by Webern

   (E) Webern's postmodern music shock value rose to a higher level

GO ON TO THE NEXT PAGE

3. The electric fan was an ingenious invention for keeping people cool during the <u>summer; it was popular only briefly, however</u>, until the air conditioner made it old-fashioned.

   (A) summer; it was popular only briefly, however

   (B) summer, for it was popular only briefly, however

   (C) summer; however, popular only briefly

   (D) summer, having been popular only briefly

   (E) summer, but was popular only briefly

4. Even the play's most tragic characters are delivered with a comic touch, <u>this dramatic effect results in a very unconventional story</u>.

   (A) this dramatic effect results in a very unconventional story

   (B) with this dramatic effect resulting in a very unconventional story

   (C) and a very unconventional story being the result of this dramatic effect

   (D) and this dramatic effect results in a very unconventional story

   (E) a very unconventional story results from this dramatic effect

5. The strict training schedule allowed the marathon runner to eventually run for 20 miles <u>and she could scale</u> steep hills without stopping for rest.

   (A) and she could scale

   (B) as well as scale

   (C) so she could scale

   (D) and a scaling

   (E) and to scale

6. Joseph Campbell espoused definitive ideas about the art of storytelling and <u>the heroes and villains were defined</u> through his work.

   (A) the heroes and villains were defined

   (B) the heroes and villains were defined by him

   (C) had defined the heroes and villains

   (D) defined the heroes and villains

   (E) the definition of the heroes and villains

7. In the past, many renowned singers wrote their own songs, <u>a trademark of originality that is now rarely found</u>.

   (A) a trademark of originality that is now rarely found

   (B) inasmuch as they displayed trademark of originality, it is now rarely found

   (C) this found rarely now in displaying their trademarks of originality

   (D) a trademark that is now rarely found in displaying their originality

   (E) which is now rarely found and it displays a trademark of originality

8. Thomas Jefferson was known as a brilliant <u>politician and he was also known as an accomplished architect</u>.

   (A) politician and he was also known as an accomplished architect

   (B) politician, and he was also an accomplished architect

   (C) politician; also he was known as an accomplished architect

   (D) politician and, furthermore, he was known as an accomplished architect

   (E) politician and an accomplished architect

GO ON TO THE NEXT PAGE

KAPLAN

9. <u>Although liquor companies are now introducing low-alcohol and alcohol-free beverages, litigation against distillers continues to increase year after year.</u>

(A) Although liquor companies are now introducing low-alcohol and alcohol-free beverages, litigation against distillers continues to increase year after year.

(B) Litigation against distillers year after year continues to increase even though liquor companies are now introducing low-alcohol and alcohol-free beverages.

(C) Although introducing low-alcohol and alcohol-free beverages are liquor companies now, litigation against distillers continues to increase year after year.

(D) Increasing year after year, liquor companies are now introducing low-alcohol and alcohol-free beverages, but litigation against distillers continues.

(E) Liquor companies are now introducing low-alcohol and alcohol-free beverages, litigation against distillers continues to increase year after year.

10. The domestic <u>cat of which there are more than 40 breeds,</u> is a member of the feline family.

(A) cat being that there are more than 40 breeds

(B) cat, of which there are more than 40 breeds

(C) cat to which there belongs more than 40 breeds

(D) cat, which there are more than 40 breeds of

(E) cat, of which more than 40 breeds in existence

11. The Nobel Foundation <u>was established in 1900; since then</u> it has awarded prizes for achievements in literature and science.

(A) was established in 1900; since then

(B) was established in 1900, since then

(C) was established in 1900, then

(D) established in 1900; since then

(E) was established in 1900; and since then

12. Women are not rejecting the idea of raising children, but <u>many taking jobs</u> as well.

(A) many taking jobs

(B) many are taking jobs

(C) jobs are taken by many of them

(D) jobs are being taken

(E) many having taken jobs

13. Changing over from a military to a peace-time economy means producing tractors rather than tanks, radios rather than rifles, and <u>to produce running shoes rather than combat boots.</u>

(A) to produce running shoes rather than combat boots

(B) to the production of running shoes rather than combat boots

(C) running shoes rather than combat boots

(D) replacing combat boots with running shoes

(E) to running shoes rather combat boots

14. The protest movement's impact will depend on both how many people it touches and <u>its durability.</u>

(A) its durability

(B) is it going to endure

(C) if it has durability

(D) how long it endures

(E) the movement's ability to endure

Practice Test Three: **Answer Key**

SECTION 1

Essay

SECTION 2

1. E
2. B
3. D
4. C
5. D
6. C
7. A
8. B
9. D
10. A
11. E
12. D
13. D
14. A
15. E
16. B
17. C
18. C
19. B
20. E
21. C
22. D
23. A
24. E

SECTION 3

1. D
2. A
3. C
4. C
5. D

6. A
7. D
8. D
9. D
10. B
11. E
12. D
13. E
14. D
15. A
16. C
17. C
18. E
19. D
20. C

SECTION 4

1. E
2. A
3. C
4. A
5. A
6. B
7. E
8. D
9. C
10. E
11. C
12. D
13. D
14. D
15. A
16. B
17. C
18. C

19. D
20. A
21. B
22. B
23. D
24. E

SECTION 5

1. C
2. A
3. A
4. C
5. D
6. B
7. D
8. B
9. 15
10. 9.43
11. $13 < length < 15$
12. 15/4 or 3.75
13. 166
14. $0.5 < y < 0.625$
15. 46
16. 175
17. 46
18. 11

SECTION 6

1. C
2. C
3. C
4. B
5. A

6. C
7. A
8. D
9. B
10. A
11. D
12. A
13. D
14. C
15. B
16. E
17. A
18. B
19. C
20. B
21. B
22. D
23. B
24. C
25. C
26. E
27. D
28. E
29. A
30. D
31. D
32. C
33. D
34. D
35. E

SECTION 7

1. B
2. E
3. B

4. E
5. D
6. B
7. C
8. A
9. D
10. E
11. A
12. D
13. B
14. C
15. A
16. B
17. B
18. C
19. C

SECTION 8

1. D
2. E
3. B
4. C
5. E
6. D
7. D
8. B
9. A
10. D
11. D
12. B
13. B
14. C
15. C
16. B

SECTION 9

1. B
2. B
3. A
4. D
5. E
6. D
7. A
8. E
9. A
10. B
11. A
12. B
13. C
14. D

KAPLAN

Answers and Explanations

SECTION 1

6 Essay

The first time I encountered a thought similar to the one expressed above by Calvin Coolidge was when I read a quote by Benjamin Franklin: "Energy and persistence conquer all things." The truth that Franklin expressed continues to affect me. I agree, therefore, that persistence is the major factor in someone's success. In fact, I know it's true because I've witnessed it first hand.

When I was 10 years old, my mother was in a car accident that left her a paraplegic; she is paralyzed from the waist down. I have watched her struggle from that day to this to reclaim a normal life and to be a mother to me and a wife to my father. She has come so far because she never gives up. She is a model of persistence. After the initial trauma she suffered from the accident faded she had to begin a long period of training to strengthen her upper body and to gain whatever strength she could in her legs. It was hard work. I used to go with her to the training room in the hospital and watch her sweat through the routines the therapist gave her.

Even today, almost 7 years since the accident, she trains three times a week. She also had to learn to use a wheelchair and how to drive a car using hand controls. She had to re-learn things she knew how to do before the accident like cooking and gardening. In fact, she had to learn how to do almost everything all over again, and she did.

I once asked her how she did all this and she said she did it because she was grateful that she survived the accident and could still be part of my father's and my life. So, Coolidge was right, and so was Franklin; persistence pays off. My mother is persistent and I'm so proud of her and so happy that her persistence means that she is still part of my life.

Grader's Comments

All essays are evaluated on 4 basic criteria: Topic, Support, Organization, and Language. This is a strongly written essay in which the writer sticks to the assigned topic and develops it in a creative way. She has a stirring story to tell and she tells it very well. She never strays from her main idea which is that persistence pays off and her mother is living proof of that. The author's clear recounting of her mother's heroic actions since the accident offers much support for her thesis.

The essay has an interesting and strong organization. The first paragraph offers another quote that is similar to the statement given. The author whets the reader's appetite by not jumping immediately into her main point. The last sentence keeps the reader's interest going. The remaining three paragraphs support her thesis.

The essay exhibits a high degree of skill with language. Both the sentence structure and the vocabulary indicate that the essay is written by an adept writer. The sentence structure is varied and even long, complex sentences are correctly punctuated. This is particularly apparent throughout the second paragraph. Some words that indicate the author's solid vocabulary: reclaim; initial; trauma; encountered; witnessed; factor.

4 Essay

I think that Pres. Coolidge is right. It seems to me that if your persistent you do well in life. An example I can think of is Albert Einstein who said something like 99% of genius was hard work and the remaining 1% was because you are a genius. This shows that Einstein agreed that you need more persistence than genius to succeed. Of course, Albert Einstein was a genius, too, but as the quote above says a lot of geniuses don't get rewarded. Einstein is famous because he was a persistent genius.

When Einstein was young he failed some math tests and he didn't always get great grades. He didn't let this stop him, though. He knew he wanted to be a mathematician and a physics professor and he worked hard to get to these goals. His persistence paid off. He became a teacher and later he won the Nobel Prize.

Later on Einstein came to America where he taught at Princeton University. In this way he fulfilled his dream of being a teacher of physics and mathematics. This was what he said he wanted to do when he was young and he did it because he persisted until he reached his goal. I believe that his persistence more than his genius is what brought Einstein the things he wanted.

In conclusion, Einstein is a great example of why I agree with Calvin Coolidge that persistence is the most important quality a person can have to be successful.

Grader's Comments

All essays are evaluated on 4 basic criteria: Topic, Support, Organization, and Language. This writer sticks to the topic, agreeing with the quote. The writer's use of Einstein's life is great support for his agreement. Note, however: the writer misattributes the quote about genius. Thomas Edison actually said that, not Einstein. But the essay is not testing for content; a mistake like this won't hurt the score.

The essay is well organized with an introduction, body, and conclusion. The writer's use of "In conclusion" in the last paragraph helps the sense of organization. Using words and phrases that indicate to the reader what your intentions are is a good technique for SAT essays.

The writer's language is generally good, though not very challenging. He makes a common error in the second sentence of the first paragraph—using "your" when he meant "you're." He also should not have abbreviated "President."

2 Essay

It's good to be persistent as the statement above says. I seen this many times. For example, my brother was not very good at basketball but he kept on shooting hoops in our backyard and after a while he got better he made the team. He not good enough to be on the varsity but he plays intrmurels.

I think persistent is importent but I also think being a genius is pretty cool. I'd like to be a genius but I guess its not gonna happen. I guess I will have to just be persistent and see if that works. I think it will because as I said above I agree with the statement of Calvin Coolidge.

Grader's Comments

All essays are evaluated on 4 basic criteria: Topic, Support, Organization, and Language. The author starts out pretty strongly by agreeing with the statement and using her brother as an example. However, she strays in the first part of the second paragraph and then returns to the topic at the end. The development of the topic is rudimentary. This contributed to her loss of points. The writer's example is good support for her opinion. She doesn't, however, develop her support enough. The essay meanders on and off topic, making the organization too loose.

The writer's language is generally below standard. There are grammatical and spelling errors. The grammar is particularly poor. There are numerous verb tense errors, run-on sentences, and slang words. Here's a sampling: "I seen" instead of "I've seen;" "He not good enough" instead of "He's not good enough;" "persistent" for "persistence;" "gonna" instead of "going to." The second sentence of the first paragraph is a long run-on. *Intramurals* and *important* are misspelled.

SECTION 2

1.   E

Despite is our first clue word, signaling a contrast coming up. Despite their fierce appearance, caymans are actually rarely -------, to the point at which they won't attack humans unless provoked. So for the blank we need a word that means the same as *fierce*. The closest word here is choice (E), *aggressive*. Choice (B) was the exact opposite of what we wanted. Choice (C), *domesticated*, means tame, and usually refers to animals treated as house pets.

2.   B

There are two different schools of thought competing in this sentence. One group believes one thing *while* another believes something else. So, clearly we want words that help create a sense of the opposition between these two viewpoints. Let's start with the second blank. One group argues that courtly love *dates from the age of chivalry*. In other words, they think it's a fairly old idea, dating back from the days of knights and fair maidens. Another group thinks something else though, so they must feel it's either an even older idea or a more recent idea. A quick check through the answer choices for the second blank leads us to choice (B) *ancient*. *Notion*, or idea, fits quite nicely into the first blank, fitting with the word *concept* in the first half of the sentence.

3.   D

Here we want a word that would describe the sort of people who might throw fruits and vegetables at those whose performance dissatisfied them. People like this are surely not *doting* (A), overindulgent or excessively fond, nor are they *ravenous* (B), or extremely hungry. If they were hungry, they'd eat the food instead of throwing it at the stage. There's nothing to imply that the audience is (C) *jingoistic*, or excessively nationalistic. However, the audience might certainly be described as (D) *boisterous*, or rowdy. (E) *stagnant* means dead or lifeless, which is illogical in the blank.

4.   C

Although two brothers look alike, they could not be more ------- in terms of their personalities. *Not alike* or *different* or some such word must go into this first blank, something that helps convey that they look alike, but their behavior is not alike. The semicolon is our hint that the information following it will be more or less in line with what preceded it. So, *while* one is circumspect, or cautious, the other is brash, or the opposite of cautious. For this second blank, you should predict something that means the opposite of quiet, something that's sort of synonymous with brash. The best answer is choice (C), because *dissimilar* fits our prediction for the first blank, while *audacious* means bold—it's kind of a synonym for brash. (A) *inimical* is related to the word *enemy*. *Inimical* means hostile.

5.   D

Napoleon's army was hightailing it out of Moscow. The retreat *quickly turned into a rout*, a state of wild confusion, a disastrous defeat. Why did it turn into an even bigger defeat? Probably because the French were stuck or struggling in the snow—if they were doing well traveling through snow, it's unlikely they'd end up being such big losers. Then, something was done to them by Russian troops. Well, if you know that Napoleon's army was routed by the opposing side, then it seems that we want a second-blank word that means something like *clobbered*. Choices (A) and (D) come close to that prediction. *Ravage* means to

violently destroy. Now, going back to the first blank, we know we want something that implies the troops were stuck or struggling in the snow. Only choice (D) fits both blanks: the retreat of Napoleon's army turned into a rout as French troops, already *floundering* in the snow, were *assaulted* by Russian soldiers. To flounder is to struggle awkwardly and stumble about. In (A), *replenishing* in the snow sounds a bit weird—*replenishing* means replacing something that was used up. In (E), *tottering* means walking unsteadily, and *upbraided* means scolded or reprimanded—a little mild-mannered for our purposes here.

6.   C

The word that will fill in the blank is defined here in the sentence—we want a word that describes an environment composed of tapestries, paintings, stained glass windows, and hand-crafted furniture. A quick survey of the answer choices leads us to choice (C), because *sumptuous* means costly or lavish, particularly with regard to furnishings and decor. While you might have been tempted to think that *friendly* in choice (D) was a plausible answer, it's hard to say to sure that an environment filled with rich, arty items is a *friendly* environment. For some people, such surroundings might be quite intimidating. *Frugal*, in choice (B), means thrifty or careful with money, which is quite the opposite of what we wanted here.

7.   A

In this question, a lecturer is frustrated by something her audience has done. This frustration was only ------- by some connection between the audience and talking. It sounds like the lecturer was frustrated by her audience's desire or tendency to talk during her presentation. Lecturers want to be heard; an audience's inability or lack of desire to talk would not frustrate a lecturer. So, for the second blank, we want something like desire—choice (A) *propensity*, or tendency, and choice (E) *desire* could work. (C) makes no sense. What's an audience's *authorization*? To choose between (A) and (E), let's look at the second blank. (E) *supplanted*, or replaced, is illogical. So (A)'s got to be correct. In fact, it makes the most sense: The lecturer's frustration was *compounded*, or increased, by the audience's *propensity*, or tendency, to talk.

8. B

There's something about the issue of the nuclear power plant that makes it surprising the council all voted in agreement. If it was shocking that there was agreement, the issue must have been divisive or controversial. The answer here is (B), because *contentious* means causing controversy and disagreement. *Concise* in (C) means brief and to the point, while *exorbitant* in (D) means extravagant or excessive.

Humans vs. Other Mammals

9. D

The author says that there's a difference between humans and other mammals, and uses the lions to illustrate this point. Lions sit around or nap after they eat a lot. People get bored and do stuff. Why is this important? Because this led to the ultimate development of culture. (C) and (D) both look OK, but only (D) includes the author's larger point about culture. Also, the language of (C) is not quite in keeping with the tone of the passage. *Industrious* means hard-working, but the actions of people are described as play, not work. (A) is the opposite of what you're looking for—the author seems to regard the achievements of humans as pretty positive, and so wouldn't think that lions are more successful. The author never introduces the idea of efficiency (B). (E) is too broad; the passage focuses on what animals and humans do after they eat, and never discusses the hunting that precedes the eating.

10. A

The general purpose of the passage is to explain something, so look for this direction. (A) and (C) both look feasible. On further consideration, (C) doesn't quite work, since only one thesis is presented—the author is not providing an *alternative* to anything. (A), however, fits well. The author shows a *distinction* between the behavior of people and other mammals, and then shows the *significance* of this distinction (it led to culture). (B) is off base, since the author never indicates that there might be an objection to the thesis. (D) and (E) are out of the scope of the passage—what will (or should) happen in the future is never discussed.

Eugene O'Neill

11. E

First, you need to identify the *logical conclusion*—O'Neill's plays are very American, so the audience must also be American. The author then goes on to say that this is not true. The plays are also quite popular in Europe. This matches (E) quite well. (A) actually expresses the opposite of what you're looking for. It describes the *logical conclusion* rather than the contradiction of that conclusion. (B) is a distortion of several ideas in the passage, but does nothing to contradict the *logical assumption*. (C) is in keeping with the tone of the passage, but is also not offered as a contradiction of the *logical assumption*. (D) is a detail from the passage, but appears earlier, and doesn't disprove the assumption that Americans are the sole audience of O'Neill's plays.

12. D

The conclusion of the passage is that O'Neill's plays are relevant to everyone, including non-Americans, and we know this because the plays are popular with Europeans. (D) weakens the argument, because if it's mostly Americans going to the European performances, then there's no evidence that the plays are popular with non-Americans. (A) is out of scope, since the passage discusses European, not American productions. (B) could be tempting if you thought that O'Neill didn't have an American audience, and so couldn't be considered a successful playwright. This is going too far however, since there's no evidence that O'Neill is not also popular in America. (C) doesn't hurt the author's conclusion, since the plays could still be popular with non-Americans when performed in English. There's no reason that O'Neill couldn't be popular with Europeans, even if he'd never gone to Europe himself, so (E) doesn't affect the conclusion.

Domesticated Animals

If you're an animal lover you might enjoy this passage. Actually, it's not a bad passage, but it's long, so be sure to keep up a good pace. You should aim at getting the main points of paragraphs and moving on. Basically, the author says that the dog was the first domesticated animal, which makes sense because of the dog's nature (it comes from a pack and likes to have a leader; puppies are cute and trainable; and it has better senses of hearing and smell than humans do, which makes it a valuable hunting companion). Then the author wonders how domestication occurred, which sends him off on a tangent about animals that *parasitize* human wastes or food stores. He speculates that domestication began because baby animals were cute—only later did domesticated animals actually become useful. He concludes that it's ironic that human civilization is destroying many species, since our learning to live with them is what made civilization possible.

13. D

The *archaeological discoveries* mentioned in the question stem are human and dog bones lying next to each other in ancient burial sites. The reason the author feels it's *terribly appropriate* that these bones are found together comes a few lines later, when he says *it marks a relationship that is the most ancient of all.* (D) paraphrases that idea. You can see from this how important it is to read a few lines before and after the line reference in the stem. The author says nothing about burial habits in the Mesolithic Era (A), or the religious significance of animals in prehistoric cultures (B). He says nothing about *natural disasters* (E) either. He does mention hunting (C), but the bone finds are not *appropriate* because they *illustrate the role of dogs in hunting expeditions*. (D) is the only possibility.

14. A

The end of paragraph 1 provides the answer. The author says that the dog was the first domesticated animal because it served as *a companion and an ally* (A). Only *after* domesticating animals as companions did humans domesticate *food animals* (B) and then *those that provide enhanced speed and range* (D) and then those that helped us farm (C). The key thing is to see that all these other types of domesticated animals came after animals were domesticated as companions.

15. E

The line reference takes you to the beginning of paragraph 2. The author says that having a dog as a companion animal was almost *inevitable*, and then lists several reasons why. One of these is that the dog *is susceptible to domination by, and attachment to, a pack leader—the top dog*. The implication is that humans formed bonds with dogs because they could dominate them (E). None of the other choices gives characteristics that make sense in answer to the question.

16. B

As with all Vocabulary-in-Context questions, you should go back to the sentence to see how the word is used. The author asks us to consider the *essence* of the dog in order to understand why it became a companion. He then lists several of the dog's characteristics that made it easy to domesticate. In other words, we're looking at the dog's *nature* (B). The only other choice that might seem to make sense in this context is (A) *history*—but what follows the line *consider its essence* is not a history; rather, it's a list of characteristics that make up the dog's nature.

17. C

This is definitely a question you need to return to the passage to answer. Back in the second paragraph, the author lists the characteristics that made dogs *inevitable* companions for humans. In addition to being born dependent and forming bonds with their rearers, dogs *have a set of appeasement behaviors* that elicit *affective reactions* from even the most *hardened* humans. The author goes on to talk about puppies transforming *cynics* into *cooing softies*. Even if you weren't sure what *appeasement behaviors* were, you can see the gist of the author's point here: humans form bonds with dogs largely because dogs are cute and loveable. So would it make sense if *affective reactions* were *callous* (A), *rational* (B), or *cynical* (E)? No. (D) goes too far. The author isn't saying humans become childish around dogs, but that dogs arouse human emotions. (C) is the best answer.

18. C

The easiest way to understand the point of a comparison is to understand the context. What's the author saying in these lines? He's trying to show why it was inevitable that dogs became human companions. One reason is that dogs form bonds with their owners (C). That's the only reason he compares puppies with babies—to show how emotional people get about dogs. The author's point has nothing to do with *criticizing an uncaring attitude* (A), so that can't be the point of his comparing puppies and babies. The same is true for the rest of the choices, so (C) is correct.

19. B

Again, go back to the passage. Notice that the start of paragraph 3 actually refers back to the end of the *first* paragraph. Paragraph 1 ended with the author listing the dog as the first domesticated animal, followed by food animals, work animals, etc. Paragraph 2 talks about *why* the dog came first. So when paragraph 3 begins with *no wonder the dog was first*, it's referring to the dog's status as the first domesticated animal. Similarly, *the list* refers to other domesticated animals, or *the number of animals that developed relationships with humans* (B). The author hasn't yet mentioned *birds that scavenge human food supplies,* and when he does, he only mentions one, not many *types* (A). The passage never mentions species that are able to communicate with dogs (C), or the variety of attributes that make dogs good hunters (D). Finally, if you chose (E), you were losing track of the author's main points. Read over the first three paragraphs to see what's going on, and give a closer reading next time.

20. E

This question might seem more complicated than it really is. If you were confused by the digression the author made to talk about the blue tit, taking a look at the choices first probably would've saved you time. (A), (B), and (D) are fairly easy to eliminate—they have nothing to do with any of the author's main points. Good—now that you've eliminated three choices, you can always guess. But first let's go back to the passage. In line 46 the author mentions *opportunistic feeders*. He goes on, saying *even today, many birds . . . feed from our stores*. So (E) must be right; the blue tit is an example of an opportunistic feeder. The question doesn't go any more into depth than that, so you're done.

21. C

This is a clear reference question. Go back to the lines you're given to see what kind of animals are being referred to. You have to read above a little to find the answer. The author has just finished describing the blue tit as an example of an opportunistic feeder. He reinforces the idea that the tit is an animal that feeds when and where it can by saying, *If all birds had been so specialized that they only fed in deep forest, it never would have happened*. In other words, they are *not* so specialized—they'll eat wherever they find a food source (C). The author isn't talking here about companion animals (A). Forest inhabitants (B) is too broad. (D) is out because the birds are not hunting, they're feeding. And the point about the birds is not to give an example of *persistent pests* (E).

22. D

Go back to the passage to see in what context the author discusses his experiences in the tropics. At the beginning of paragraph 4, the author says that he thinks that the very first domesticated animals were orphaned as a result of hunting. He then tells how, in the tropics, he saw many instances of wild animals raised in homes of hunters. So his experiences illustrate his theory about how *the first domesticated animals were created* (D). None of the other choices relate to the author's argument here (or anywhere in the passage).

23. A

This one's a little tricky—if you thought so, you should've jumped ahead and come back later if you had time. Remember, reading questions don't go from easy to hard, so the next one could be easier. Check out the line *aid* is in to see what's going on. The author says that without domesticated animals—goats, sheep, pigs, cattle, and horses—we never would've achieved civilization. These animals helped or *aided* us—but they didn't have much choice in the matter. We dominated them, and then used them for food or labor. That's why *aid* is in quotes, and (A) is correct. The passage never says *population levels are dangerously high* (B). (C) is a better possibility—but it's not a point the author makes; you're inferring too much if you chose (C). It's not clear that animals benefited at all from domestication (D). (E) is really far-out, not supported by the passage.

24. E

The *ironic paradox* is found in the last four lines of the passage. The author says our living with other species—using them for food and labor—is what made our civilization possible. It is ironic then, that our civilization is presently wiping out many plant and animal species (E). Nowhere does the author say anything about (A) or (B). With (C), the author does talk about the pet care industry in the final paragraph, but not to say its size is *ironic*. His point is just to show how big it is. (D) twists the author's point. It's by being parasites on other species that humans benefit, not the other way around.

SECTION 3

1. D

We want the value of x. Let's begin by distributing the 2 over the terms inside the parentheses on the left side of the equation. This gives us $2x + 2y = 8 + 2y$. Subtracting $2y$ from both sides results in $2x = 8$. Dividing both sides by 2 gives us $x = 4$.

2. A

Since point A is at 1 on the number line and point C is at 7, the distance between them is $7 - 1$, or 6. Half the distance from A to C is $\frac{1}{2}$ of 6, or 3, and 3 units from either point A or point C is 4, since $1 + 3 = 4$ and $7 - 3 = 4$. Therefore, the point at 4 on the number line is the midpoint of AC, since a midpoint by definition divides a line in half. Point B is at 3 and the midpoint of AC is at 4, so the distance between them is 1, answer choice (A).

3. C

The machine caps 5 bottles every 2 seconds, and we want to know how many bottles it caps in 1 minute, or 60 seconds. Multiplying 2 seconds by 30 gives you 60 seconds. If the machine caps 5 bottles in 2 seconds, how many bottles does it cap in 30 times 2 seconds? 30×5, or 150 bottles, is answer choice (C).

4. C

All you have to do here is solve the equation, but instead of solving it for n, you have to solve it for $4n$. If $2n + 3 = 5$, then you can subtract 3 from both sides of the equation to get $2n = 2$. Multiplying both sides of this equation by 2 gives you $4n = 4$, choice (C).

5. D

The easiest way to do this problem is just to backsolve. Since each pair of numbers in the answer choices represents possible values of a and b, just add up each a and b to see if $a + b < 5$, and subtract each b from each a to see if $a - b > 6$. If you do this, you'll find that in all 5 cases $a + b < 5$, but in only 1 case, in choice (D), is $a - b > 6$. In choice (D), $a + b = 4 + (-3) = 1$ and $a - b = 4 - (-3) = 7$.

If you think about the properties of negative and positive numbers (drawing a number line can help) you'll probably realize that the only way $a - b$ could be larger than $a + b$ is if b is a negative number, but that would only eliminate choice (A). In some problems your knowledge of math only helps you a little bit. In those cases you just have to play with the given answer choices in order to solve.

6. A

In the figure angle B is labeled $(2x - 4)°$ and in the question stem you're told that angle B measures 60°. So, $2x - 4 = 60$, and $x = 32$. That means that angle A, which is labeled $(3x)°$, must measure 3×32, or 96°. Since the three angles of a triangle must add up to 180°, $60° + 96° + y° = 180°$, and $y = 24$.

7. D

This one is easier if you plug in numbers for C and R. Suppose R is 2. Then there would be 2 rooms on each floor, and since there are 10 floors in the building, there would be 2×10 or 20 rooms altogether. If $C = 3$, then there are 3 chairs in each room. Since there are 20 rooms and 3 chairs per room there are $20 \times 3 = 60$ chairs altogether. Which answer choices are 60 when R is 2 and C is 3? Only $10RC$, choice (D).

You don't have to plug in numbers here if you think about the units of each variable. There are 10 floors, R rooms per floor, and C chairs per room. If you multiply 10 floors by $R \frac{\text{rooms}}{\text{floor}}$, the unit "floors" will cancel out, leaving you with $10R$ rooms, and if you multiply $10R$ rooms by $C \frac{\text{chairs}}{\text{room}}$, the unit "rooms" will cancel out, leaving $10RC$ chairs in the building, again choice (D).

8. D

Here you have a strange word, *sump*, which describes a number that has a certain relationship between the sum and the product of its digits. To solve this one, just find the sum and the product of the digits for each answer choice. You're told that for a "sump" number, the sum should be greater than the product. Choice (D), 411, has a sum of 6 and a product of 4, so that's the one you're looking for.

9. D

In this question, if you think about the relationship

between the information you're given and the information

you have to find, it becomes very easy. You're given 4% of

a number and you have to find 20% of that same num-

ber. 4% of r is just a certain fraction, $\frac{4}{100}$ to be exact,

times r; and 20% of r is just $\frac{20}{100}$ times r. That means

that 20% of r is 5 times as great as 4% of r, since $\frac{4}{100}$

times 5 is $\frac{20}{100}$. So if you're given that 4% of r is 6.2,

then 20% of r must be 5 times 6.2, or 31, choice (D).

You could also have figured out the value of r and then

found 20% of that value, but this takes a bit longer. 4% of

r is the same as 4% times r, or $.04r$. If $.04r = 6.2$, then

$r = \frac{6.2}{.04} = 155$, and 20% of 155 is $.2 \times 155 = 31$, choice

(D) again.

10. B

The ratio of teachers to students is 1 to 10, so there might
be only 1 teacher and 10 students, or there might be 50
teachers and 500 students, or just about any number of
teachers and students that are in the ratio 1 to 10. That
means that the teachers and the students can be divided
into groups of 11: one teacher and 10 students in each
group. Think of it as a school with a large number of classrooms, all with 1 teacher and 10 students, for a total of 11
people in each room. So, the total number of teachers and
students in the school must be a multiple of 11. If you
look at the answer choices, you'll notice that 121, choice
(B), is the only multiple of 11, so (B) must be correct.

11. E

Since x and y with a funny symbol between them is equal
to $(x - y)^x + (x + y)^y$, to find 4 and 2 with a funny symbol
between them just plug 4 in for x and 2 in for y. That
gives you $(4 - 2)^4 + (4 + 2)^2$, or $2^4 + 6^2$, or $16 + 36$, or
52, answer choice (E).

12. D

If the particle travels from A to B to C to D to E and then
back to A it has traveled 5 centimeters, since each side of
the pentagon measures 1 centimeter. If it goes all the way
around the pentagon again it's traveled another 5 centimeters, for a total of 10 centimeters. In fact, every time the
particle makes a complete revolution around the pentagon
(from point A back to point A again) it travels an additional
5 centimeters. So if the number of centimeters the particle
has traveled is a multiple of 5, the particle must be at
point A. The number 723 is 3 more than a multiple of 5. If
the particle had gone 720 centimeters it would be at point
A; since it has gone 3 more centimeters it must be at
point D, answer choice (D).

13. E

When would $4 + \frac{1}{s}$ have the smallest possible value?

Certainly if s, and its reciprocal $\frac{1}{s}$, were negative, $4 + \frac{1}{s}$

would be smaller than 4, since adding a negative number

is like subtracting a positive number. However, none of the

answer choices is negative, so $4 + \frac{1}{s}$ will be greater than

4. However, it will be as small as possible when $\frac{1}{s}$ is as

small as possible. If you look at the answer choices, you

can find the values for $\frac{1}{s}$. If $s = \frac{1}{4}$, then $\frac{1}{s} = 4$, etc. If

you do that you'll probably notice that as s gets larger its

reciprocal gets smaller, so $\frac{1}{s}$ is smallest when s is largest,

in this case when $s = 4$, choice (E).

14. D

Since you're looking for the sixth term of the sequence, let's call the sixth term x. Every term in this sequence is formed by multiplying the previous term by 3 and then subtracting 1, so the seventh term must be formed by multiplying the sixth term, x, by 3 and then subtracting 1; in other words, the seventh term is equal to $3x - 1$. Since the seventh term is 365, $365 = 3x - 1$, and you can solve for x to get $x = 122$, choice (D).

15. A

If an integer is chosen randomly from the first 50 integers the probability of choosing any particular number is 1 divided by 50, and the probability of choosing an integer with a digit of 3 is the number of integers with a digit of 3 divided by 50. The integers 3, 13, 23, 30, 31, 32, 33, 34, 35, 36, 37, 38, 39, and 43 are the only integers with 3's in them, for a total of 14 different integers, so the probability is $\frac{14}{50}$, or $\frac{7}{25}$, choice (A).

16. C

Let's call the degree measure of the largest angle x. Since the degree measure of the middle-sized angle is 40 degrees less than the degree measure of the largest angle, the degree measure of the middle-sized angle is $x - 40$. We also know that the smallest angle is 20 degrees. We know that the sum of the measures of the three interior angles of any triangle is 180 degrees. So we can write an equation for our triangle: $x + (x - 40) + 20 = 180$.

Now let's solve for x:

$$x + x - 40 + 20 = 180$$
$$2x - 20 = 180$$
$$2x = 200$$
$$x = 100$$

17. C

The diagram tells you that the radius of the circle is $x - 5$ and the question stem tells you that the circumference of the circle is 20π. Since the circumference of a circle is 2π times the radius, 20π must equal 2π times $(x - 5)$, which gives you the equation $20\pi = 2\pi(x - 5)$. Solving this equation gives you $x = 15$, answer choice (C).

18. E

The slope of a line is defined as the change in the y-coordinate divided by the change in the x-coordinate. As you go from point A to point B, the x-coordinate goes from p to 6 and the y-coordinate goes from 3 to p, so the change in the x-coordinate is $6 - p$ and the change in the y-coordinate is $p - 3$. You can make this into an equation: $\frac{p - 3}{6 - p} = 2$, and solve this equation for p. That would give you $p = 5$, choice (E). You could also plug the 5 possible values for p into the expression $\frac{p - 3}{6 - p}$ to see which one gives you 2 as a result. Either way, choice (E) is correct.

19. D

In order to find the areas of the shaded triangles, you have to find the coordinates of all the vertices of the triangles. You know where points P, Q, and C are in the coordinate plane, but what about the rest of them? Well, first of all let's label all the other points that are vertices of the triangles. The triangle on top has 2 labeled vertices, P and Q. The third vertex of that triangle is on the y-axis between P and the origin. Let's call it point A. The other triangle has vertices Q, C, and an unlabeled point that is also the upper right-hand corner of the rectangle. Call that point B. Points A and B are both on the same horizontal line that point Q is on, so all 3 points must have the same y-coordinate of 4. The x-coordinate of point A is 0 since it is on the y-axis, and the x-coordinate of B must be 3, the same as point C's x-coordinate, since points B and C lie on the same vertical line. So point A's coordinates are (0, 4) and point B's coordinates are (3, 4). Since triangles PQA and QBC are right triangles, we just need to know the lengths of their legs in order to find their areas. In the coordinate plane, the length of a horizontal line segment is the difference of the x-coordinates of its endpoints and the length of a vertical line segment is the difference of the y-coordinates of its endpoints. So, the length of PA is $6 - 4$, or 2, and the length of AQ is $1 - 0$, or 1, so the area of triangle PQA is $\frac{1}{2} \times 2 \times 1 = 1$. The length of QB is $3 - 1$, or 2, and the length of BC is $4 - 0$, or 4, so the area of triangle QBC is $\frac{1}{2} \times 2 \times 4 = 4$. The sum of those areas is $1 + 4 = 5$, answer choice (D).

20. C

No matter what the value of n is, this figure will be a rectangular solid. All rectangular solids have 6 faces. You just have to figure out the area of each of the 6 faces. The face on the bottom, which is the face up against the table or whatever this stack of cubes is sitting on, is a square, and it will have an area of 1 square inch, since the edge of each cube has a length of 1 inch. The face on the top of the stack of cubes is also a square and it will also have a surface area of 1 square inch. The other 4 faces making up the stack are identical rectangles, each with dimensions of 1 inch by n inches. So the area of one of these rectangles is $1 \times n$ or n square inches and these four identical rectangular faces have a total area of $4 \times n$ or $4n$ square inches. So the total surface area of the solid is the sum of the areas of the square top, the square bottom, and the four identical rectangular faces, which is $1 + 1 + 4n$ or $4n + 2$ square inches.

If you found that confusing, it might be easier just to pick a value for n. Suppose $n = 4$ and there are 4 cubes, as in the figure shown. Then just add up the areas of the faces of the stack in the figure, but don't forget the faces that aren't shown in the drawing. Since each face of each cube has an area of 1, in square inches, the figure shown has an area of 4 in the front plus 4 on the right side plus 4 on the left side (not shown in the drawing) plus 4 in the back (not shown in the drawing) plus 1 on the top and finally 1 on the bottom (not shown in the drawing), for a total of 18. Only choice (C) has a value of 18 when $n = 4$, so choice (C) must be correct.

SECTION 4

1. E

The key here is the word *beneficial*, or helpful. If you don't know *beneficial*, a knowledge of word roots would help you. *Beneficial* contains the root BENE, meaning good, which indicates to you that it's a positive word. Well, if in one breath we are told that the ozone layer is positive, and in the next, that it does something for plant and animal life relating to dangerous ultraviolet radiation, we know we

need a fairly positive word in the blank. The only choice that fits this requirement is choice (E) *protecting*. (D), *thwarting*, means impeding or preventing.

2. A

While is our tip-off that this sentence will in some way contain a contrast. While George Balanchine's choreography stayed within a classical context, he challenged convention by recombining ballet idioms. (If you don't know exactly what this means, it doesn't matter—you just need to grasp that this is how he challenged convention.) He's challenging convention by recombining typical ballet moves or whatever in some ---- way. The word in the blank must mean something like unconventional. The best choice here is (A), *unexpected*. Choice (C), *redundant*, means needlessly repetitive or excessive.

3. C

All of today's navel oranges have some common relationship to a single mutant tree that produced seedless fruit 200 years ago. They must all be descended from this one mutant. So the word in the blank must mean *descended from*. Choice (C), *descendants*, jumps out as the correct choice. *Progenitors*, in choice (A) is meant to fool you since it has something to do with genetics. If you break *progenitor* down, PRO means *for* or *before* while the GENUS root is related to the word *gene*. So, *progenitors* are ancestors—people (or things) which are related but came before—like grandparents. *Progenitors* are the opposite of descendants. Choice (E) was another word trap—just because *spores* have something to do with plants doesn't mean this is right. A *spore* is a reproductive body found in simpler forms of life. But you don't need to know biology to figure this one out. Just use your reasoning skills. While a seed could be a spore, it makes no sense to say that all of today's navel oranges are the actual *spores* of a 200-year-old tree. But it is more plausible that this one tree produced a number of seeds, which in turn produced more of their own seeds, and so on.

4. A

In this sentence, there's a relationship between the quantities of food and drink Henry VIII consumed, and the type of person he was seen as. Either he consumed minimal quantities of food and drink, and was considered a spartan of sorts, or he consumed large amounts, and was considered a pig. Well, choice (A) is the only one that fits either one of these predictions. A *glutton* is one who overindulges in the consumption of food and drink. This option is the only one that fits, where there's a connection between the type of person his subjects saw him as, and the amount of food and drink he scarfed up. (C)'s first word, *minute,* or very small, fits okay, but a *luminary*, a famous or important person, doesn't. Consuming small quantities of food wouldn't make someone famous. In (B), *prodigious* means either extraordinary or enormous, while a *peer* is an equal, or a member of nobility.

5. A

You want a vocabulary word that means something like *transition* or *temporary*—some word that describes a government that no longer is in power, but is staying in power just until a new government is ready to take over the reins. Choice (A), *interim*, means temporary or provisional, so this is the answer. INTER is a root you should know—it means between.

Miles Davis

6. B

Author 1's point is that Davis was a musical innovator. So, when the author says that Davis's change of musical direction was *characteristic*, she's making the point that this change was typical of Davis's innovation. That matches (B) quite well. (A) is the thesis of Passage 2, not Passage 1. (C) is far too negative; author 1 thinks that the stylistic innovation was a positive attribute. (D) is a paraphrase of the first sentence, but that occurs earlier and is unrelated to the word *characteristically*. (E) is too literal. The author says that *each decade brought more surprises*, but that doesn't mean the innovations were spaced 10 years apart, and it certainly doesn't follow from the word *characteristically*.

7. E

Davis couldn't play in Charlie Parker's style very well, so he created a new one to avoid becoming a *second-rate footnote*. The term *footnote* usually means a note at the bottom of the page that supplements the body of a test. Here, it refers to a person who is not the main focus, an unimportant person (E).

The author says that Davis was *supremely expressive*, so the author wouldn't think that he was in danger of becoming *unexpressive* (A). (B) is a literal meaning of footnote, but doesn't refer to a person. Even though Davis was not as technically skilled as Parker, it seems unlikely that the author would refer to him as *unskilled* (C). (D) is the opposite of what you're looking for; Davis became a *stylistic innovator* in order to avoid being a *footnote*.

8. D

Right after the phrase *unique style*, the author offers a description: *a few well-chosen notes were surrounded by artful silences that spoke volumes*. So, you're looking for a description of someone who uses a little to say a lot. That matches (D) pretty well. The painter is surrounding her subject with empty space in the same way that Davis surrounded his notes with silence.

(A) might fit well with the description in Passage 1 of Davis as a stylistic innovator, but the question is asking about Passage 2, not Passage 1. (B) is not too bad, since we do get the sense that Davis carefully selected his notes, but (B) doesn't convey the sense that the chef was as spare as Davis. (Maybe the chef uses tons of different ingredients.) If anything, Davis was more focused than his predecessors, so (C) doesn't fit here. (E) sounds more like the description of the highly-technical Parker than the spare and elegant Davis, so it's the opposite of what you're looking for.

9. C

Author 1 characterizes Davis as an innovator, so he would see Davis's development of a new style as typical of his entire career. That's right in line with (C).

(A) and (B) both fit pretty well with Passage 2, but author 1 never discusses technique or technical limitations, so they don't work for this question. (D) is half right, because author 1 does think the development is important, but the word surprising makes this the opposite of what you're looking for. The development was typical, not *surprising*. There's no real evidence that author 1 would think this particular innovation was more important that the many others described in Passage 1 (E).

To Build a Fire Passage

This fiction passage shouldn't pose too many problems: it's short, clear, and straightforward. If you enjoy reading fiction, be careful not to relax too much while reading the passage—you may slow down and lose time. Save pleasure reading for when you're not taking the SAT! The passage describes a man and a dog entering a little-traveled path in Alaska. A comparison is set up between the man, who *lacks imagination* and isn't alarmed by the extreme cold, and his dog who, going on instinct, is alarmed.

10. E

Review the beginning of the passage to see what *act* the man is *excusing to himself*. It turns out he stopped because he was out of breath, but doesn't want to admit it (to himself, since he's alone), so he plays it off by looking at his watch. That makes choice (E) correct. He shows no reaction to what time it is (A). You may have been confused by choice (B) because the narrator (later in the passage) implies that the dog's instincts are more accurate than the man's. However, the man never shows distrust of himself (B). You're overinterpreting if you chose (C)—there's no evidence in the passage to support this inference. The point of the man's *excusing the act to himself* has nothing to do with *the time of day* (D); it has to do with him not admitting why he stopped in the first place.

11. C

Watch for the tone in the lines around the quote—it'll help you eliminate choices. For example, does the man seem at all *excited*? No, so (A) is out. He also doesn't seem *nervous* (B), although by the end of the passage there's an ominous feeling of danger in the air. (C) is right because it's a straightforward description of what's going on. There's no evidence in the passage to support choice (D). (E) is similarly wrong—there's no discussion of why the man is in the wilderness. Remember, most inferences (or *suggestions*, as the question phrases it) are very mild, and are always supported by the passage.

12. D

Reread the lines the quote appears in. The man's being a creature of temperature is the same *frailty* that all humans have: we're *able only to live within narrow limits of heat and cold*. In other words, if it's too cold, we'll freeze to death. Choice (D) is correct. *A creature of temperature* does not imply the man prefers cold climates (A), because

temperature includes hot and cold. The author shows later in the passage how wrong the man's judgment of the temperature is, so (B) is unlikely. There's no discussion of *personality being shaped by the environment* (C). The man may or may not know wilderness survival techniques (E), but in any case, that's not what *a creature of temperature* refers to.

13. D

This question refers you to a big chunk of text, so save time by scanning the choices before you go to the passage. Choice (A) implies the wrong thing. This wilderness must be immensely beautiful, but whether the man notices it or not is not the point. The point is the judgment the man makes about the temperature. (B) overstates the case. The author isn't flatly declaring, *humans can't survive in the Alaskan wilderness*. Instead, he's describing a man who is underestimating the potential danger. That makes (D) correct. Just because this character can't judge the temperature accurately doesn't mean *there's no way to accurately judge the temperature* (C). There's no evidence that *most people could not do* what this guy is doing, even though it's obviously a difficult thing (E).

14. D

All of paragraph 2 leads up to the four lines you're sent to for this question. After a discussion of the potential danger extreme temperatures pose to humans, the paragraph concludes by saying none of this entered the man's head. In other words, he lacks *insight and understanding* (D). The man thinks the cold *must be guarded against*, so (B) can't be right. At the same time, (A) is too strong—the man doesn't even acknowledge that there are *odds* to succeed against. (C) is too general. *Apprehension* in (E) means *fearfulness*, which we've already seen the man lacks.

15. A

Again, you have a lot of lines to review, so save time by scanning the answer choices before you check the passage. It's in these lines that the author introduces the dog and its *instinct*—which tells it to take shelter from the cold. Correct. Choice (A) restates what's in lines 47–56. The dog isn't judging the temperature (B), it's just reacting to an instinct of danger. Choice (C) is an inference that goes too far—it's too general for these lines. (D) contradicts the point the author's making. (E) is partially true, but it captures only a small part of what the author suggests.

16. B

This question doesn't require too much interpretation, so don't go digging for difficult answers. The passage says that the dog *knew nothing of thermometers*, but that it *had its instinct*. In other words, it didn't read the temperature with a device as humans do, and it didn't need to—it knew instinctively how cold it was. The answer is (B)—the dog's awareness of its environment is different from the man's. Nothing implies that dogs *need not be concerned about temperature* (A); the point is that they perceive it differently than people do. (C) is too negative. Although the author calls the dog a *brute* at one point, it is done with respect, since the dog's instincts prove to be more valuable than the man's intelligence. (D) is too literal, and the point is not that the dog *could not rely on technological devices* (E), but that the dog has no need of them.

17. C

Reread the lines at the end of the passage to see what's going on. We've seen that the dog fears the cold, and the end of the passage describes the dog watching the man for a sign that they are heading for protection (C). Choices (A) and (E) miss the mark because the author never says that the dog recognizes the man's mistaken estimation of the cold. There is also no sign that the man is being visibly affected by the cold (B). Choice (D) invents something not found in the passage.

Elderly Asians Passage

This is a passage about Southeast Asian immigrants' experience of aging in America. This passage may be a little dry, but it's not complex. The discussion focuses on the problems older immigrants have when they come to America. These include: different standards of what's considered *elderly*, not getting the kind of respect they would in their homelands, dealing with different gender roles, and elderly women being isolated in the home and becoming estranged from their families. Don't worry about any more detail than this until you get to the questions.

18. C

Remember this strategy for dealing with main idea questions: look for an answer that's not too broad or too narrow, but that encompasses the whole passage. In this case, (A) is too broad. From the first paragraph, you know that the focus is more specific than *the reasons why*

Southeast Asian people move to the United States. This helps you eliminate (B) as well: from the start you're told the passage is concerned with the problems of the elderly, not the young. (C) covers the whole passage, and is correct. (D) picks up on a detail—Confucianism—and expands it beyond the scope of the passage. And (E) is just one topic discussed in the passage, not the focus of it.

19. D

Even if the word "acculturating" was unfamiliar to you, the rest of the passage should have made it clear that the differences between generations, once the family came to America, had to do with differences in language ability, different cultural attitudes toward and definitions of age, better employment opportunities, and obstacles to older refugees mixing in their new society. The closest answer to capturing all that is (D). (A) and (B) are too narrow, focusing on single issues that affect only a portion of the refugees, while this quotation applies generally to older refugees. (C) and (E) are out of the scope of the passage.

20. A

Review paragraph 2 to understand why the author mentions the *traditional Hmong culture*. There, the author says that American and Asian cultures define *elderly* differently. In the Hmong culture, people become elders and retire at 35; obviously, in American culture, this is not the case. So Hmong culture is mentioned to illustrate the paragraph's main point—that *social expectations vary greatly from one country to another* (A). There's no mention of traditional values in Vietnamese society *lessening* (B). No other ancient cultures are mentioned in paragraph 2, so (C) is out. (D) is out because Confucianism isn't mentioned until paragraph 3. Likewise, no other Southeast Asian peoples are mentioned (E).

21. B

Go back to the line in which *family mediators* appears. This part of paragraph 3 says that younger members of immigrant families deal with schools and other institutions because they have better English language skills than older family members. So being a *family mediator* is a responsibility that young refugees assume in a new country (B). (A) might've confused you because a hasty reading of the passage makes it sound like this is a role older people used to fill—but in fact, it's not. The passage really says that in the traditional culture there are strict rules for social interaction based on age, which the new role of "family mediator" gradually erodes. The passage says nothing about getting help from friends (C) or professionals (D). The author doesn't write about the benefits American society derives from immigrant people (E).

22. B

After rereading the line that *pronounced* is in, the first thing you should do is eliminate the obvious choice. In this case, that's (E), *declared*. The author uses *pronounced* to mean (B) *noticeable*. Gender roles changed somewhat in Southeast Asia during the Vietnam War, but they changed even more drastically for families that emigrated to the United States. None of the other choices fits this context. The author doesn't imply that these changes became more *acceptable* (D); she implies that they happened out of necessity and says they were a *radical change*.

23. D

The *radical change* the author refers to is the fact that women often become the main source of income in immigrant families in the Unites States. This is a major change in gender roles, because in Southeast Asia men were usually the breadwinners. (D) is correct. (A) is an unlikely answer because retirement ages were discussed back in paragraph 2. (B) might've been tempting, because the Vietnam War is mentioned in paragraph 4, along with the answer. But the author says that while gender roles are changing in Southeast Asia due to the Vietnam War, the *radical change* occurs when families emigrate. Education (C) is not discussed in these lines. (E) is out because the author says there are more jobs for younger refugees, not that it's hard for young refugees to find them.

24. E

When you're not given a line reference, it makes sense to look in the passage where the previous question left off because Critical Reading questions are ordered sequentially. So that takes you to the last paragraph, which is indeed where the author makes a point about the *long-term outlook for refugee women*. The author starts off by saying that although the long-term outlook is *unknown*, there are *indications* about it. Now look at the choices. There's no evidence that this is a *personal recollection* (A), or a *historical discussion* (B). No specific *case* is mentioned or analyzed (C). The author isn't being *philosophical* (D); if

anything, she's being as scientific as possible, given the lack of data. That leaves (E), *informed speculation*. Since the author is knowledgeable about the subject matter, but has to go on *indications* to make her final point, (E) is the best answer.

SECTION 5

1. C

This is a straightforward substitution problem, but be sure to remember order of operations. First plug in 3 for *r* to get $(3^2 - 2)(4 + 3)$. Simplify the expressions within the parentheses to get $(9 - 2)(4 + 3)$, which is 7×7, or 49.

2. A

Work carefully and follow the order of operations, and problems like this one will be easy points. $f(3) = 3^2 + 3 = 9 + 3 = 12$

3. A

The intersection of two sets consists of all the elements that are common to both sets. Be sure to read the question carefully; there are many different questions that could be asked about these sets. Set *A* consists of the numbers 11, 13, 17, and 19. Only two of these are also in Set *B*.

4. C

The factors of 87 are 1, 3, 29, and 87; 87 is a factor of 87, but it is not prime, so (E) is incorrect. 29 and 3 are both factors of 87 and prime, so the greater of these, (C), is correct.

5. D

In equations of the form $y = mx + b$, *m* represents the slope of the line and *b* represents the *y*-intercept of the line. The slope of a line is the rise over the run, or the difference between the values of *y* at two different points on the line over the difference between the values of *x* at those same points—a shorthand way of expressing this is $\frac{\Delta Y}{\Delta X}$. A good way to double-check your answer is to plug the values of *x* and *y* at some point on your chosen line into the equation to see if they work. You need to figure out which line in the figure changes two units in the y-direction for every one it changes in the x-direction. Lines B, C, and D all do this, so they all have a slope of 2. However, only line D also has the correct y-intercept, -4.

6. B

Backsolving is a good strategy for this question. Plug in all the numbers in the choices for y, and see which ones work; -1 gives you $(-1 - 3)^2 = (-1 + 1)^2$, which simplifies to $(-4)^2 = (0)^2$ or $16 = 0$. This isn't true, so eliminate (A) and (D). 1 gives you $(1 - 3)^2 = (1 + 1)^2$, which is $(-2)^2 = (2)^2$ or $4 = 4$. This is true, so (B) or (C) must be the answer. Try 3: $(3 - 3)^2 = (3 + 1)^2$, $(0)^2 = (4)^2$ or $0 = 16$. This isn't true, so the answer must be (B).

7. D

First find the area of the frame and photo combined; then find the area of the photo alone. Then find the difference. Since we know that the diameter of the photo is 8, its radius must be 4, and the area of the photo is $\pi r^2 = \pi 4^2 = 16\pi$. We are given that the frame is 2 inches wide, so we can say that the radius of the frame and photo combined is $4 + 2 = 6$. So the area of the frame and photo combined must be $\pi r^2 = \pi 6^2 = 36\pi$. Finally, to get the area of only the frame, we subtract the area of the photo from the area of the frame and photo combined, giving us $36\pi - 16\pi = 20\pi$.

8. B

Picking numbers makes this problem easier to work with. Rather than dealing with fractions of the business, say that there are 100 total shares. At the beginning of the problem, the 4 women each own 20 shares and the man owns 20 shares. One woman sells $\frac{1}{2}$ of her part of the business, 10 shares, to the man, and another woman sells $1 - \frac{1}{4} = \frac{3}{4}$ of her part of the business, $20\left(\frac{3}{4}\right) = 15$ shares to the man. Now the man owns $20 + 10 + 15 = 45$ shares out of the total 100 shares in the business. $\frac{45}{100} = \frac{9}{20}$, so the man now owns $\frac{9}{20}$ of the business.

9. 15

This is a simple plug-in, but make sure you write out every step so as to avoid a careless error. This is especially important in the Grid-ins. If $y = 2$, the expression $(5 - y)(y + 3)$ becomes $(5 - 2)(2 + 3)$. Remember to do the calculations inside the parentheses first. $5 - 2$ is 3 and $2 + 3$ is 5 so $(5 - 2)(2 + 3) = 3 \times 5 = 15$, so put 15 in the grid.

10. 9.43

If the daily rate is \$18.99, then the price for a week, or 7 days, is $7 \times \$18.99 = \$132.93$. Since the weekly rate is less, only \$123.50, you can save $\$132.93 - \$123.50 = \$9.43$ by renting at the weekly rate.

11. 13 < length < 15

The first thing to do is to put the numbers 4, 5, and 12 in the appropriate places in the figure. Now you should see that you have the lengths of 2 sides of triangle BCD. Since BCD is a right triangle, you can use the Pythagorean theorem to figure out the length of the hypotenuse, but if you've memorized the common Pythagorean triplets you don't have to do that—you'll immediately recognize that this is a 5-12-13 right triangle, and so the length of BD is 13. The length of AC is $4 + 5 = 9$, so the triangle ACD has legs of lengths 9 and 12. Again, you can use the Pythagorean theorem to find the length of the hypotenuse, but you should notice that ACD is a multiple of the 3-4-5 right triangle, and AD has length 15. If you draw in point E in the figure between A and B, you'll see that DE will be longer than BD but shorter than AD, or greater than 13 but less than 15. So, any number between 13 and 15, such as 14, is a possible answer.

12. 15/4 or 3.75

If you need $\frac{3}{4}$ of a cup of drink mix for 2 quarts of water, then you need more than $\frac{3}{4}$ of a cup of drink mix for 10 quarts of water. How much more? Since $2 \times 5 = 10$, you have 5 times as much water, so you also need 5 times as much drink mix. $5 \times \frac{3}{4} = \frac{15}{4}$, so grid in $\frac{15}{4}$ (in the form of $\frac{15}{4}$).

KAPLAN

13. 166

The sum of the 3 angles of the triangle must be 180°. One angle measures 31°, but you don't know the measures of the other 2 angles in the triangle. However, the interior angle of the triangle on top lies on a straight line with an angle measuring 45°, so that interior angle must measure 180° − 45° = 135°. If 2 angles of a triangle measure 135° and 31°, then the third angle measures 180° − 135° − 31° = 14°. The 14° angle lies on a straight line with the x° angle, so 14° + x° = 180°, and x = 166.

If you remembered that any exterior angle of a triangle has the same measure as the sum of the 2 opposite interior angles, you could have saved a few steps. Once you figure out that the top angle of the triangle is 135°, you know that x° = 135° + 31°, and therefore x = 166.

14. 0.5 < y < 0.625

The only thing you know about y is that it is between $\frac{1}{2}$ and $\frac{5}{8}$. $\frac{1}{2}$ is the same as $\frac{4}{8}$, so y is between $\frac{4}{8}$ and $\frac{5}{8}$. You can't grid a fraction like $\frac{4\frac{1}{2}}{8}$, but you can change $\frac{4}{8}$ to $\frac{8}{16}$ and $\frac{5}{8}$ to $\frac{10}{16}$. That gives you an obvious value for y; since y is between $\frac{8}{16}$ and $\frac{10}{16}$, it could be $\frac{9}{16}$, so that's one possible number to grid in. You could also solve this question by converting $\frac{1}{2}$ and $\frac{5}{8}$ to decimals. If you convert $\frac{1}{2}$ to .5 and $\frac{5}{8}$ to .625, you can grid in any number greater .5 and less than .625. For example, you can grid in .6.

15. 46

The average rate of speed is the total distance traveled divided by the total hours traveled. Melanie drove at 40 miles per hour for 2 hours, for a total of 40 × 2 or 80 miles. If she increased her speed by 25%, then she increased her speed by 25% of 40, or 10, so her new speed was 40 + 10 = 50. So, she drove at 50 miles per hour for the next 3 hours, for a total of 50 × 3 = 150 miles. She went 80 miles and then 150 miles, for a total of 230 miles, and she drove for 2 hours and then for 3 hours, for a total of 5 hours. Her average rate for the trip was 230 miles divided by 5 hours, or 46 miles per hour.

16. 175

There are 3 types of dealers at this convention—dealers who sell only stamps, dealers who sell only coins, and dealers who sell both stamps and coins. The total number of dealers is 500. You're given the number of 2 out of the 3 types of dealers—there are 127 that sell both stamps and coins, and 198 that sell only stamps. Since there are only 3 types of dealers, 127 + 198 + the number of dealers who sell only coins = 500, and so the number of dealers who sell only coins is 500 − 198 − 127 = 175.

17. 46

Since the small square has a side of length 2, the area of the square must be 2^2, or 4. The larger square has a side of length 6, so its area is 6^2, or 36. The shaded part of square $ABCD$ is then 36 − 4, or 32. The triangle is a right triangle with both legs of length 6, so the area of the triangle is $\frac{1}{2}$ × 6 × 6, or 18. The shaded area of the triangle is then 18 − 4 = 14. The total shaded area is 32 + 14, or 46, so grid in 46.

18. 11

If *N* and *R* added up to a number less than 10, the problem would look different, something like:

$$NR$$
$$\underline{RN}$$
$$XX$$

Since it doesn't look like that, $N + R$ must be greater than 10. The best way to proceed from here is to try different pairs of numbers for *R* and *N*, and see what you get for *B* and *C* (keeping in mind that *N*, *R*, *A*, *B*, and *C* are different digits.) If you try setting either *N* or *R* equal to 9, you'll notice that you won't get different digits for all 5 variables. For example, if $R = 9$ and $N = 7$:

$$79$$
$$\underline{97}$$
$$176$$

Since there is always a 1 carried over into the tens' place, if $R = 9$ then the tens' column will add up to $9 + N + 1$, or $10 + N$. The sum $10 + N$ has the same units' digit as *N*, so *B* and *N* will be the same if $R = 9$. The same thing happens if $N = 9$, only *R* and *B* turn out to be the same. If you try the next largest combination of numbers for *N* and *R*, which is 7 and 8, *B* and *C* turn out to be 6 and 5, so *B* + *C* = 11. Any smaller values for *N* and *R* will result in smaller values for *B* and *C*, so the greatest possible value of *B* + *C* is 11.

SECTION 6

1. C

This sentence tests your knowledge of the sequence of tenses. By the time the speaker graduates from college in the future, her brother *will have been* practicing law—you need the future perfect tense. (C) expresses the sequence correctly. All the remaining choices have incorrect tenses. (B) places this action in the past. (D) makes it inappropriately conditional. (E) places it in the present.

2. C

The intervening phrase and clause make it difficult to see that the subject and verb don't agree. The plural subject *historians* needs a plural verb, so *includes* should be *include*. (B) incorrectly changes *includes* to the past tense. (C) and (D) both correct this problem, but only (C) keeps

the correct relative pronoun. (D) incorrectly changes the subjective *who* to the objective *whom*. (E) doesn't correct the subject-verb problem and changes the idiomatically correct *more than* to *at least*, which changes the meaning.

3. C

Nancy illogically compares Marcel Proust's novel with other writers. Nancy should compare Proust's novel with other novels, as in (C), (D) and (E). Only (C) makes that change without introducing new errors. (D) illogically changes the comparison *more brilliant* (which is correct because two things are compared) to *brilliant opposed to*. (E) changes the correct relative pronoun *which* to *whom*—perhaps thinking that the authors, not the books, are compared. (B) also introduces that mistake, and incorrectly changes the second clause to the past tense.

4. B

The past tense of the irregular verb *to see* is *saw*. (B) and (D) correct this problem, but (D) introduces another error by changing *arriving* to *have arrived*. (C) and (E) illogically change the correct *watching* to *who watch*. (C) also doesn't correct the original problem and (E) incorrectly changes *arriving* to *arrived*.

5. A

This sentence is correct as written. (B) illogically changes *to discover* to the past tense *to have discovered*. (C) incorrectly adds the preposition *in* (the species don't congregate in the floor). (D) needlessly adds the preposition *from*. (E) incorrectly changes *that* to *who*.

6. C

In this sentence we must sort through all the prepositions to see that *in an effort at avoiding* is not good, idiomatic English. The correct phrase is *in an effort to avoid*. (C), (D), and (E) all make this change. However, (D) and (E) distort the meaning. (D) is incorrect because fans are not on the team. (E) switches the phrases *in the stadium* and *between fans* which would mean that the altercations happen in more than one stadium.

7. A

Look through the answer choices: all except (E) focus on the phrase *a means to attract*. Is that idiomatically correct? Yes, *a strategy to attract* is correct. (B), (C) and (D) alter the phrase. (C) also changes the adjective *elderly* to *elder*. (E) rearranges the introductory phrase so that the votes incorrectly modify the social security adjustment.

8. D

The words *bright lights* interrupt the subject and verb, making the agreement problem difficult to see. The singular subject *configuration* agrees with the singular verb *was*. (D) and (E) make this change but (E) omits the transition word *but*. (B) and (C) don't address the agreement problem and (C) changes the contrasting transition word *but* to *and*.

9. B

The plural pronoun *their* actually refers to the singular subject *band*. (B) and (C) correctly change *their* to *its*. (C) incorrectly changes the preposition *of* to *for*. The expression *methods of providing* is idiomatically correct. Neither (D) nor (E) address the pronoun problem. They both also change the infinitive *to determine* to *to determining* which is not standard English.

10. A

This is a complex sentence, so break it down to see if it is correct. (B) changes *had begun* (which is correctly in the past perfect tense) to the incorrect form *had began*. (C) illogically puts the second clause in the future tense. (D) incorrectly changes *later* (which is good standard written English) to the illogical *afterwards*. (E) changes the subject of the sentence from the conductor to the orchestra, altering the meaning.

11. D

The sentence is a run-on. (B) and (C) are also run-ons. (E) fixes the run-on, but the comma is incorrect. (D) is clear and concise, and it is the correct answer.

12. A

It's especially important to check subject-verb agreement when a verb is separated from its subject. The subject is the singular *heron*, but the verb is the plural *live*. To correct this, you would change *live* to *lives*. *Most* (B) is correctly in the superlative form, since all parts of the United States are compared. (C) is a idiomatically correct. (D) uses *both* correctly with *and*.

13. D

Susan compares the home team's warm-ups to the visiting team. She should compare the warm-ups of both teams. (D) is your answer. The phrase *liked watching* in (A) is correctly in the past tense. (B) uses the correct relative pronoun. In (C), the phrase *more interesting* works because two things are compared.

14. C

The intervening phrase *of Viking settlements and lifestyles* interrupts the subject and verb. The singular subject *pattern* doesn't agree with the plural verb *were*. The phrase *by tracing* (A) is idiomatically correct. The verb *determined* (B) is correctly in the past tense. The adverb *generally* (D) correctly modifies the adjective *similar*.

15. B

This sentence sets up a contrast between what the recipe required and what Chad did. However, the conjunction *and* indicates an addition rather than a contrast and should be replaced with a word like *but*. In (A), *actually* is an adverb correctly used to modify the verb, and *called for* is an idiomatic expression meaning *needed in the circumstances*. (C) sets up the right causal relationship required by the meaning of the sentence. (D) is idiomatically correct.

16. E

Read all sentences carefully looking for common errors, but remember that about 20% will be error-free. (A) is the correct word to express the contrast that the sentence sets up. (B) is correctly the past tense. (C) is a phrase that indicates an example is being given. (D) is idiomatically correct after the verb *attempt*. (E) is the correct choice since this sentence is correct as written.

17. A

When there are underlined pronouns in a Usage question, check to see that they have clear antecedents. The pronoun *they* doesn't. You can guess that *they* are the people of India, but that would be only a guess since the sentence doesn't provide that information. (B) is correctly used here. In (C), the past tense verb is correct. In (D), the conjunction *and* correctly expresses a continuation of the idea that precedes it.

18. B

The action took place in the past, and should use the simple past tense *saw* instead of the past participle of the verb *to see* (*seen*). The verbs *waiting* (A) and *walking* (C) are in the correct form and the phrase *to stop traffic* (D) is idiomatically correct.

19. C

The plural subject *plays* doesn't agree with the singular verb *expresses*. (C) should read *express*. The infinitive verb *to produce* (A) is correct. The phrases *that expresses* (B) and *has had* (D) are in the correct tense and idiomatically correct.

20. B

The phrase *claim hearing* is not idiomatically correct. (B) should read *claim to have heard*. The contrasting transition word *while* (A) is used appropriately as is the adverb *truly* (D). The phrase *such a person* is idiomatically correct.

21. B

The preposition *to* should follow the phrase *in an attempt*: The phrase *at creating* (B) should read *to create*. The verb *initiated* (A) is correctly in the present tense. The phrases *of team spirit* (C) and *in the office* (D) use the correct prepositions.

22. D

Did efforts *about* democracy sound correct when you read this sentence? Probably not. What you would need is something like *efforts on behalf of*. In (A), the adverb *as* is correctly used to modify the verb. In (B), the verb tense is correct—past perfect, which indicates that something happened before something else happened. Abadi got the Nobel Prize before her colleagues praised her. (C) correctly uses the simple past.

23. B

Be sure that the verbs in the sentence correctly express the time of the action. This sentence contains a clear indication of time—1906, which is in the past. Anything that happened in 1906 is done. The verb tenses should express this completeness. (B) should be in the simple past tense—*leveled*. (A) is idiomatically correct. (C) uses the right words and the correct preposition. (D) uses the correct tense—the simple past.

24. C

The phrase *absolute shamefaced* has an adjective modifying an adjective (*shamefaced*). The phrase should read *absolutely shamefaced*. The phrases *failure to* (A), *went about* (B), and *only a few* (D) are all idiomatically correct.

25. C

Reversing the sentence order can help you find the error. Does it make sense to say *The damaging effects of ciga-rette smoking has become recognized*? No. The plural subject *effects* takes the plural verb *have*, rather than *has* (C). The transition word *while* (A) correctly sets up a contrast. The verb *has been known* (B) is in the correct tense because it takes place before the second part of the sentence. Therefore, the past participle *become* (D) is also in the correct tense (you can also reverse the order to say *the damaging effects have become known*).

26. E

The sentence is correct as written. The verb *maintains* (A) agrees with the singular subject *FBI* and is correctly in the present tense. The prepositions *for* (B) and *in* (D) correctly follow *maintains* and *interested*, respectively. The pronoun *they* (C) clearly refers to *citizens*.

27. D

When three people are being compared, the superlative phrase *most* should be used. (D) should read *most abstract*, rather than *more abstract*. The phrase *in many ways* (A) is idiomatically correct. (B) is an idiomatically cor-rect phrase, and *similar* is correctly used to modify *aspects*. The verb *was* (C) is correctly in the past tense.

28. E

The sentence is correct as written. (A) correctly uses the adverb. (B) correctly uses the superlative, since all chore-ographers are compared, and *inventive* correctly modifies the noun *choreographers*. (C) is correctly in the past tense and is the correct form of the irregular verb, and the noun *approach* takes the preposition *to* (D).

29. A

The plural noun *Germans* is close to the verb but is not the subject. The subject *toppling* is singular, and so (A) should be the singular *is*. The phrases *probably seen* (B)

and *most felicitous* (D) are idiomatically correct and the pronoun *them* (C) is correctly plural and in the objective case (*they* wouldn't work).

30. D

The paragraph is in the past tense but *She tells me* is present tense. The author is telling a story about what happened last year so the mother's action should be in past tense. (D) is correct. (B) and (C) don't address the tense issue. (B) unnecessarily substitutes *my mother* for *she* and (C) incorrectly uses the causal word *because*.

31. D

Sentence 7 introduces the ambiguous pronoun *they* and uses the passive voice. (D) correctly substitutes *the hooligans* for *they* and uses the present tense. (B) doesn't address the pronoun problem. (C) is redundant and uses the past tense. (E) substitutes the football fans, instead of the hooligans, for *they*.

32. C

The correct answer should clarify sentence 12's relationship with sentence 11. Sentence 11 offers one explanation offered by *some*. Sentence 12 is another possibility, and (C) indicates that. (A) is incorrect because there is no indication this is the author's opinion. (B) introduces the ambiguous pronoun *they*. (D) and (E) set up incorrect relationships: contrasting and causal, respectively.

33. D

Sentence 14 is a fragment, with no verb in an independent clause. (D) uses the past tense *indicated*, which agrees with the prior sentence. (B) is still a fragment. (C) incorrectly uses the present progressive tense and (E) incorrectly uses the past perfect tense.

34. D

In sentence 13, the words "one argument…rang…true" tell you the author is offering a conclusion. What is the conclusion? It's set off by the colon: *poverty was an underlying cause*. Sentence 14, adding data about the connection between poverty and violence, supports that conclusion.

35. E

The sentence offers a conclusion based on the economic data in sentence 14, so it should conclude the passage. (A) would interrupt the related ideas in sentences 5 and 6. (B) is too soon; the problem has just been introduced, but the ways England has tried to solve the problem haven't been discussed. (C) is still too early—poverty isn't mentioned again until sentence 13. (D) is incorrect because the next sentence begins with the contrasting transition word *but*; however, the inserted sentence and sentence 14 do not contrast.

SECTION 7

1. B

So many stops in some particular amount of time led to only the most ------- impression about the places the tour visited. There's a connection between the amount of time spent visiting, and the impression of the places visited. So the two words that will fill in the blanks here must be roughly synonymous. Only choice (B) works here. There were so many stops in such a *brief* amount of time that only a *cursory* (superficial or hasty) impression of places was gained. (D)'s second word fits the blank, but (D)'s first word, *sufficient*, isn't a rough synonym and doesn't fit. In (A), many stops probably wouldn't leave a *lasting* impression. Nor would a tour at breakneck speed necessarily leave (C) a *favorable* impression on travelers.

2. E

The peoples discussed in this sentence were formerly -------, but now they've lost their land. They're living in ------- settlements. So we need two adjectives that are roughly the opposite of each other. The answer here is (E). Peoples who were once *nomadic*, or roaming freely without a permanent home, have moved into *permanent* settlements as their land got swallowed up by growing cities. *Fervid*, in choice (D), means passionate.

3. B

For the first blank, we want something that describes sleeping tablets—rule out (E) right away, since *stimulating* is the one word here that most definitely would not describe sleeping tablets. For the second blank, we want a word that characterizes the effect of those sleeping tablets, an effect that resulted in a woman feeling groggy the day after taking them. Something like *strong* or *intense* would be good. The best choice here is (B), because *soporific* means sleep-inducing—what word could be better to describe sleeping pills? *Pronounced*, meaning unmistakable or obvious, fits closely with our prediction. *Salubrious* in choice (C) means healthful.

4.   E

Here we want a vocabulary word meaning something like *unable to accept the authority of others*. Choice (A), *compliant*, means the exact opposite of this; a *compliant* person is one who bends easily to the will of others. (B) *slothful* means lazy. In choice (C), *conscientious* means responsible, hardly a word to describe Davis. (E) is correct because *recalcitrant* describes someone who refuses to obey authority.

5.   D

Although tells us that there will be some sort of contrast with the fact that the actress has lived in a large city her whole life. The contrast will be that, despite her upbringing in a city, she still manages to be successful at portraying a humble farm girl. Therefore, she must be quite a good performer—the first blank will be a positive word, describing what a good actress she is. The second blank must be a word that explains how successfully she portrays the farm girl. The best choice here is (D), because a *consummate* actress is very skilled, while an *incarnation* is the embodiment of something or someone—you'd have to be a pretty good actress to become the embodiment of the character you're playing. In choice (C), *nemesis* means enemy.

6.   B

Notice the word *hitherto* in this sentence. It means *previously*. The board members had previously upheld worthy ideals. This implies that they no longer do. For the second blank, then, we need a word like *rejection*: the board's recent decision must be a rejection of the previous worthy ideals. In the first blank, we need a word to describe what the chairman was doing as he described the board's decision so negatively. So the first blank must mean something like *criticized*. (C) fits in the first blank, but not in the second. Remember to try both words in the blanks! Choice (B) works with both blanks: to *lament* is to

regret, while a *negation* is what it sounds like, a rejection. The chairman lamented the decision of the board, describing it as a *negation* of worthy ideals. This was the only choice with two negative words that fit the context. To *endorse*, in choice (D), is to offer one's support, while a *renunciation* is a giving up or casting off of something like values. Finally, in (E), a *repudiation* is similar to a *renunciation*—it is a denial or rejection of something or someone.

The Jefferson/Douglass Passages

These two passages may seem hard because of their old-fashioned language. But the main points should be clear on a quick read-through. Jefferson emphasizes the natural and social riches of the United States (paragraph 1), supports the idea of limited government (end of paragraph 1), and states the principle of equal justice for all (paragraph 2). Douglass, speaking as an escaped slave, stresses that slaves do not have the freedoms celebrated on the Fourth of July. (If you don't remember who Douglass was, you may not catch the point of his speech until the end of paragraph 2, where it is stated directly. Always be patient—the drift of a passage often becomes clearer as you go along.) In paragraph 2, Douglass says that the case against slavery should not have to be argued, because freedom and liberty are basic American principles. In paragraph 3, he concludes that as long as slavery exists, the Fourth of July is a *sham*.

Before going to the questions it can be helpful to think for a second about how the two passages relate—an important paired-passage strategy. You should come up with something like: Jefferson is stating American principles, but Douglass is saying they haven't been applied in practice. In a double passage, you'll have several questions on passage 1, followed by several on passage 2, followed by some asking for comparisons. Since answering the questions is the priority, be sure to read the first passage, do the questions that relate to it, then read the second passage and answer the rest of the questions.

7.   C

In the cited lines, Jefferson is saying that Americans feel entitled to respect, or *honor and confidence*, on the basis of *actions* rather than *birth*. (C) is a paraphrase of this idea. Remember that the United States didn't have a hereditary aristocracy like European countries—that's what Jefferson is talking about. (A), (D), and (E) bring in ideas not mentioned in the excerpt—immigration (A), mutual help (D), family (E). (B)'s idea of demanding respect is wrong; Jefferson feels respect has to be based on actions.

8. A

In this Vocabulary-in-Context question, choice (B) might've jumped out at you. But remember, the correct answer is probably not going to be the most common or familiar definition of the word, so don't be too hasty. Find the word in the passage and see how it's used there. In this case, Jefferson is talking about what his duties as president involve, or *include*. Choices (A), (C), and (E) give you other common synonyms for *comprehend*, but they don't fit the context. (D) does not mean "comprehend."

9. D

Again, look at the context. Read the rest of the sentence in question, and the sentence before it. This should clarify that Jefferson is about to state what he believes to be the essential principles of government. Further, he's going to state them in the most brief possible way, which is what choice (D) says. (A) and (C) refer to Jefferson's mention of *limitations*, but all Jefferson says is that he won't mention *limitations* or exceptions to the general principles. (B) is wrong because *them* in Jefferson's sentence refers to the principles of government, not to people who oppose the principles. Finally, Jefferson never mentions *bureaucracy*, choice (E).

10. E

Ignore the choices for the moment and look at the context: Jefferson is talking about equal justice for all, regardless of something religious or political. This suggests that Jefferson is talking about people's beliefs, creeds, opinions, or convictions. (E) gives you the word that fits this context. (A), (B), and (C) are all vocabulary-list meanings for *persuasion*, but they don't fit the context. *Authority* (D) is often seen as the opposite of persuasion; it has nothing to do with Jefferson's meaning here.

11. A

The next two questions take us through the Douglass excerpt. This one asks about paragraph 1, in which Douglass is contrasting the American celebration of independence and liberty with the bondage of slaves. The overall idea is that the celebrations are a *mockery* and an *irony* (line 50) because they don't apply to everyone. In

other words, they are hypocritical (A). (B) and (C) refer to emotions Douglass undoubtedly feels, but is not expressing here. (D) is an idea he never expresses at all. (E) interprets *drag a man in fetters* (chains) literally—force a slave to attend. Don't go for a simple paraphrase like this. Go back and get the meaning in context. Douglass is speaking figuratively; he doesn't mean he's actually being dragged to the celebration in chains.

12. D

In the cited sentence, the *millions* who are wailing are the slaves, while the *shouts* come from Fourth of July celebrants. Douglass uses this contrast to emphasize the differences between the lives and attitudes of slaves and free Americans (D). (A) and (C) twist the meaning of Douglass's mention of *yesterday* and *today* in these lines. Choice (B) goes against Douglass's overall point, which is to point out the hypocrisy of Fourth of July celebrations. And while the problem of slavery is not yet solved, Douglass doesn't imply it is *unsolvable* (E).

13. B

Always put the detail in context by rereading the surrounding lines. Here, the author's referring to the *treason* of betraying the American slaves by failing to protest during July 4th celebrations. Douglass is saying that he'd be committing *treason* to them by not speaking out. So in this example, *treason* refers to acting against the needs of a social group, i.e., the slaves. (A) and (D) may have sounded tempting as common definitions of *treason*, but they don't express what the author means in this context.

14. C

Rereading the context, you can see that Douglass is emphasizing throughout paragraph 2 the contradiction between July 4th celebrations and the condition of the slaves. When he describes *American Slavery* as *my subject*, he's highlighting this paradox, and also describing what he's about to talk about next—literally outlining what the subject of the rest of his speech is. (A)'s wrong because the topic of slavery is not unexpected—it's what Douglass has been discussing all along. (B)'s wrong because Douglass isn't talking about slavery through the ages. (D)'s wrong because Douglass suggests no immediate answer to the problem. Finally, there's no suggestion that Douglass has to learn more about his topic (E).

15. A

Again, put the detail in context—who or what is *impudent* here? Douglass is contrasting political speeches with the actual conditions that slaves endured, making (A) the correct answer. (B) is too general; (C) is off the point. (D) actually contradicts Douglass's explicit point of view. Finally, (E) is a distortion—according to the passage, it's the hypocritical speeches of politicians that railed against tyrants.

16. B

In passage 1, Jefferson deals with the themes of liberty and equality as the necessary principles of good government—he's describing these qualities as the bedrock of the Constitution. Based on passage 1, you can infer that he would respond to Douglass's questions about liberty in a similar manner—by agreeing that these are staples in any democracy. None of the other choices is consistent with any statement made in passage 1—remember, you've always got to find evidence for your answer in the passage.

17. B

The last three questions ask for comparisons. In this one, you're asked how Douglass would respond to Jefferson's stated principle, *equal and exact justice to all men*. Douglass gives the answer when he says slaves do not enjoy the liberties of other Americans (paragraph 1). So he would respond that the principle is not being carried out in reality (B). (A), (C), and (E) all imply that the principle is invalid. But Douglass's argument is that a principle that is valid in general isn't being followed for African Americans. (E) is a possible response, but (B) sums up Douglass's overall point better.

18. C

Since each of the answer choices uses the word *both*, you should be looking for a similarity between the speeches. Jefferson states a general principle; Douglass points out how it has been violated. The only point that both agree on is that equal justice is desirable, choice (C). Choices (A) and (D) describe Douglass's speech as a whole; (B) is implied in Douglass's final sentence—but Jefferson's speech never discusses these topics. (E), on the other hand, is true of Jefferson's speech, but not Douglass's.

19. C

Summarizing each passage's point of view, you'd probably argue that Jefferson was optimistic about equality in the United States (having just established the Constitution), but that Douglass was critical of United States standards on equality 50 years later. Choice (C) picks up this contrast. None of the other choices captures the appropriate positive/negative answer required.

SECTION 8

1. D

The graph shows you the sales of all the toys for the months April, May, and June. If you look at the sales for those 3 months, you'll see that the bar for April goes up to 40, the bar for May goes up to 10, and the bar for June goes up to 30. The title on the vertical axis says "Sales (in millions of dollars)" so that's what those numbers represent: $40 million in sales for April, $10 million for May, and $30 million for June, for a total of $40 + 10 + 30 = 80$ million dollars total in sales for those months. The total sales were $80 million and the April sales were $40 million, and you want to know what percent of the total the April sales were. Since it says "of the total," $80 million is the whole and the $40 million is the part, so using the formula *Percent × Whole = Part*, you get Percent × 80 = 40, or Percent $= \frac{40}{80} = \frac{1}{2} = 50$, answer choice (D).

2. E

If you remembered that any number squared is positive, a quick look at the answer choices would tell you that choice (E), x^2y^2, will be positive for any nonzero values of x and y. If you didn't remember that you should make a note of it, since it's a very important concept. You can also solve this one by picking numbers. If xy is negative, then either x or y is negative and the other is positive since a negative times a positive equals a negative. Picking a couple of pairs of numbers for x and y will tell you that both $x - y$

and $y - x$ can be either positive or negative depending on the exact values of x and y; x^2y can be negative if y is negative and xy^2 can be negative if x is negative. However, any values you pick for x and y will give you a positive number for x^2y^2, so again choice (E) is correct.

3. B

Don't get confused by the strange words! They're just symbols for an unknown quantity, the same as the letters x and y, which we usually use as symbols for unknown quantities. If 1 fedi = 3 glecks, then multiplying both sides by 2 tells you that 2 fedis = 6 glecks. You're given that 1 bora = 2 fedis, so 1 bora must be equal to 6 glecks. Now that we know the relationship between boras and glecks (whatever they are), the rest is easy. 1 bora is equal to 6 glecks, so how many boras equal 48 glecks? Since $6 \times 8 = 48$, just multiply both sides of the equation 1 bora = 6 glecks by 8 to get 8 boras = 48 glecks. So, the correct answer is 8, answer choice (B).

4. C

If algebra confuses you, try picking numbers. If $f = 10$ then there are 10 freshmen in the class. If 5 freshmen drop the class then there are $10 - 5 = 5$ freshmen left in the class. The number of sophomores is 3 times the number of freshmen left, or 3 times 5, = 15. So there are 15 sophomores in the class and $s = 15$. Which of the answer choices work with $f = 10$ and $s = 15$? All you have to do is plug those numbers into the 5 choices and you'll find that only choice (C) works and is therefore correct.

To do it algebraically, just translate one step at a time. There are f freshmen in the class, but if 5 freshmen drop the class there are $f - 5$ freshmen left. The number of sophomores is 3 times the number of freshmen left, or 3 times $f - 5$, or $3(f - 5)$. So $s = 3(f - 5)$, answer choice (C).

5. E

The perimeter of triangle ABC is $AC + AB + 7$, and the perimeter of triangle ACD is $AC + 5 + 6$. You can combine that with the given information that the perimeter of triangle ABC is 4 more than the perimeter of triangle ACD to get $AC + AB + 7 = AC + 5 + 6 + 4$. Adding the numbers on the right side of the equation gives you $AC + AB + 7 = AC + 15$ and subtracting 7 from both sides gives you

$AC + AB = AC + 8$. If you subtract AC from both sides you get $AB = 8$. That's all you need to find the perimeter of $ABCD$, which is $5 + 6 + 7 + 8$, or 26, answer choice (E).

6. D

Notice that at each corner of the cube, a triangular face like triangular face ABC is being made. How many corners are there? There are 8 corners; 4 of the corners are on the top and 4 of them are on the bottom. After all 8 triangular faces are made, a part of each of the original 6 faces of the cube remains. The total number of faces of the resulting stone must be $6 + 8$, or 14.

7. D

We want the average of the first 30 positive integers.

Whenever we want the average of a group of evenly spaced numbers, we just have to take the average of the smallest number and the largest number. If you have difficulty seeing this, consider a simpler problem. Consider the average of 1, 2, 3, and 4. The average of 1, 2, 3, and 4 is $\frac{1 + 2 + 3 + 4}{4} = \frac{10}{4} = \frac{5}{2} = 2\frac{1}{2}$, using the average formula: Average $= \frac{\text{Sum of the terms}}{\text{Numbers of terms}}$. What happens if we just take the average of the smallest number, 1, and the largest number, 4? We get $\frac{1 + 4}{2} = \frac{5}{2} = 2\frac{1}{2}$, which is what we got by finding the average the other way. So the average of the first 30 positive integers is just the average of 1 and 30, which is $\frac{1 + 30}{2} = \frac{31}{2} = 15\frac{1}{2}$. None of the answer choices is $15\frac{1}{2}$, but $15\frac{1}{2}$ is 15.5. The average is 15.5.

8. B

You may notice that the figure looks like a rectangle with a quadrilateral piece hanging off of it. That means that you can find the area of the figure by adding the area of the rectangle and the area of the quadrilateral. The quadrilateral piece can be divided into a rectangle and a triangle. It may help to draw in some dotted lines to represent this:

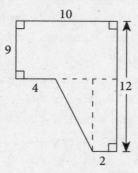

The larger rectangle on the top has length 10 and width 9. Since the vertical line segment on the right is labeled 12, the length of the part of that line that is not part of the larger rectangle must be 12 − 9, or 3, so write that on your figure. The short horizontal line in the middle of the figure has length 4, the small rectangle on the bottom has length 2, and the entire figure has a top horizontal length of 10, so the dotted horizontal line that is a leg of the right triangle must have length 10 − 4 − 2, or 4.

Now we've got the lengths of all the pieces of the figure:

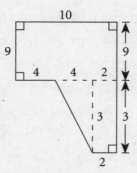

The rectangle on the top has an area of $9 \times 10 = 90$. The small rectangle on the bottom right has length 3 and width 2, so its area is 6, and the triangle has legs 4 and 3, so its area is also 6. The total area of the figure is $90 + 6 + 6 = 102$, answer choice (B).

9. A

If 60 cookies are distributed among x campers, then each camper gets $\frac{60}{x}$ cookies. When the same number of cookies is divided among fewer campers, then each camper gets 2 more than $\frac{60}{x}$ cookies, or $\frac{60}{x} + 2$. This number of cookies per camper is also equal to 60 cookies divided by 8 less than the original number of campers, or $\frac{60}{x - 8}$. This gives us the equation $\frac{60}{x} + 2 = \frac{60}{x - 8}$. Unfortunately, this equation is not in the same form as the equations in the answer choices, so you'll have to do some algebra:

$$\frac{60}{x} + 2 = \frac{60}{x - 8}$$

$$\frac{60 + 2x}{x} = \frac{60}{x - 8}$$

$$(60 + 2x)(x - 8) = 60x$$

$$60x - 480 + 2x^2 - 16x = 60x$$

$$2x^2 - 16x - 480 = 0$$

$$x^2 - 8x - 240 = 0, \text{ answer choice (A)}.$$

10. D

All they're asking here is—how many different pairs can you make from a group of 6? Let's call the 6 students A, B, C, D, E, and F; A can be joined with the others to make the 5 pairs AB, AC, AD, AE, and AF. Since you've already paired A and B you don't have to do it again, so just pair B up with the rest of the group to get BC, BD, BE, and BF. That's 4 new pairs. C has already been matched up with A and B, so the new pairs that involve C are CD, CE, and CF, for 3 new pairs. There are only 2 new pairs left for D, DE, and DF, and finally 1 more, EF. So, there's a total of $5 + 4 + 3 + 2 + 1 = 15$, choice (D).

11. D

$$q = q^{-2} = \frac{1}{q^2}$$

If $q = \frac{1}{q^2}$, then $q^3 = 1$ and $q = 1$.

12. B

Backsolving is a great way to answer this question. Pick a set of p and n from the chart; then, plug them in to each given equation to see whether the pair works. If you would rather see how the equation was derived, you can follow the steps below. On test day, follow whichever approach gets you to the answer faster. The relationship between n and p can be expressed in the form $n = -kp + b$, where k and b are constants. There is a negative sign before k to indicate that as the price increases, the number of expected sales decreases. Pick two points from the chart and insert those values of p and n into this equation, then solve for k and b:

First point:

$10,000 = -k(.75) + b$

Second point:

$5,000 = -k(1.00) + b$

$5,000 = -k + b$

$5,000 + k = b$

Substitute:

$10,000 = -k(.75) + 5,000 + k$

$5,000 = k - .75k$

$5,000 = .25k$

$20,000 = k$

$25,000 = b$

$n = -20,000p + 25,000$

13. B

It's a good idea to know what the graphs of common equations such as $y = x^2$ look like, but if you forget or would like to double-check your answer, you can plug the x and y values of a few points on the graph into the given equations to see which one works. Be careful of using points like $(0, 0)$, as they may work for several (or in this case, all) of the answer choices. In this case, some useful points to check are $(-2, 4)$ and $(2, 4)$: $4 = (-2)^2$ and $4 = 2^2$.

14. C

Let g = number of green tokens, and y = number of yellow tokens. The scores given in the problem can be written as $4g + 8y = 48$ and $6g + 4y = 32$. Both sides of the first equation can be divided by 4 to get $g + 2y = 12$.

Subtract $2y$ from both sides to find $g = 12 - 2y$. Substitute this into the second equation to get $6(12 - 2y) + 4y = 72 - 12y + 4y = 32$. Solving for y, you find that $40 = 8y$, and $y = 5$.

15. C

Since there are variables in the answer choices, picking numbers is a good strategy for solving this problem. Since the question deals with percentages, 100 is a good number to pick for c. Pablo uses 30% of 100 cherries, that is $100(.3) = 30$ grams of cherries to make muffins. You don't need to know how many grams of cherries it takes to make a muffin or how many muffins Pablo makes. All you need to know is how many grams of cherries are available to make preserves with. $100 - 30 = 70$ grams of cherries are available to make preserves with. If each pint of preserves requires 7 grams of cherries (that is, if $p = 7$), Pablo can make 10 pints of preserves. Plug $c = 100$ and $p = 7$ into the answer choices to see which yields 10. $\frac{7c}{10p} = \frac{7(100)}{10(7)} = \frac{700}{70} = 10$, so (C) is correct.

16. B

If C is the price of one pound of cherries and G is the price of one pound of grapes, then $C = 2G$. The total cost of 32 pounds of cherries and 8 pounds of grapes is $32C + 8G$, and is also equal to $90. You can use the equations $C = 2G$ and $32C + 8G = 90$ to solve for C and G. Plugging $2G$ for C into the equation $32C + 8G = 90$, we have $32(2G) + 8G = 90$, $64G + 8G = 90$, $72G = 90$, and $G = \frac{90}{72} = \frac{5}{4} = 1.25$. $C = 2G$, so $C = 2(1.25) = 2.50$. Since 32 pounds of cherries and 8 pounds of grapes were sold, $2.50 \times 32 = 80$ were made on the cherries, and $1.25 \times 8 = 10$ were made on the grapes. That means that $80 - 10 = 70$ more was made on the cherries than on the grapes, answer choice (B).

SECTION 9

1. B

This sentence is a run-on—the part beginning with *they* starts an entirely new sentence. Therefore, look for the answer choice that fixes the run-on. (B) does so by simply inserting a semicolon. The other answer choices are also run-ons.

2. B

All of the incorrect answer choices contain mis-placed modifiers. (A), (D), and (E) say the *shock value utilized cacophony*. (C) says *a higher level utilized cacophony*. Clearly, you want the sentence to say that Webern or Webern's music utilized cacophony— the only answer choice to accomplish this is (B).

3. A

The answer choices that utilize semicolons must have independent clauses on both sides of the semicolon. (A) is the only choice that meets the requirement. (D) and (E) exchange the semicolon for a comma, but they are both incorrect. (D) adds a tense shift with the words *having been*, and (E) incorrectly uses a coordinating conjunction and a comma to separate an independent clause and a dependent clause.

4. D

(A) and (E) are comma splices—two independent clauses separated only by a comma. (C) adds the coordinating conjunction *and*, but it also adds *being*, which makes the second clause dependent and incorrect. (B) becomes very awkward by adding *with*. (D) is the best choice because it simply fixes the comma splice by adding the coordinating conjunction *and*.

5. E

(A) and (C) are run-on sentences; a coordinating conjunction separates two independent clauses without a comma. Look for the answer choice that is parallel with to *eventually run*. That answer choice is (E) because of the word *scale*.

6. D

(A) and (B) are run-on sentences because they have two independent clauses separated by *and* but do not have a comma before that conjunction. (E) does not make sense because the verb *defined* was changed to a noun, *definition*. Between (C) and (D), (D) is correct. (C) adds the word *had*, indicating that the Campbell's definition of the heroes and villains happened before his espousal of definitive ideas. Without a broader context, this does not make sense. (D) is correct because it extends the simple past tense structure of *espoused* to *defined*.

7. A

Look for the simplest (and shortest) answer choice. As long as that choice is grammatically correct, you can be sure it is the correct answer. In this case, that choice is (A). The other answer choices are all too wordy or overly complex.

8. E

For (A) and (D) to be technically correct, there needs to be a comma before *and*, as in (B). However, (E) is the most clear and concise way of expressing the sentence. (C) uses the semicolon correctly, but there needs to be a comma after *also*.

9. A

The original sentence is the best choice because it has a dependent clause that is related to the complete independent clause. The other answer choices do not have as good sentence structure.

10. B

The phrase *of which there are more than 40 breeds* is nonessential information and should be set apart with commas on both sides. The words *of which* are correct in starting the phrase. The words *in existence* in (E) are unnecessary.

11. A

The semicolon is used correctly with two independent clauses on both sides of the punctuation mark. (B) and (C) are run-on sentences. (D) and (E) do not contain two independent clauses.

12. B

This sentence uses a *not...but* word pair, so it requires parallel blocks of words around each half of the pair. The first block is *are not rejecting*, so the second block must be *are taking*. Don't be misled because *are* and *rejecting* are separated by the word *not*. *Are* is still a helping verb that works together with *rejecting*.

13. C

This sentence presents a list of comparisons. All items in a list must have parallel construction. Only (C) gives the last comparison an appearance parallel to the previous two comparisons. The word *producing* could have been repeated in all three comparisons. But since it wasn't repeated in the second comparison, it can't be repeated in the third one either.

14. D

This sentence uses a *both...and* pair, so it requires parallel blocks of words following each half of the pair. Only (D) has a second block of words—*how long it endures*—similar to the first block—*how many people it touches*.

SAT Practice Test Four
Answer Sheet

Remove (or photocopy) the answer sheet and use it to complete the practice test. See the answer key following the test when finished. The "Compute Your Score" section on page 611 will show you how to find your score.

Start with number 1 for each section. If a section has fewer questions than answer spaces, leave the extra spaces blank.

SECTION

1

Section One is the writing section's essay component.
Lined pages on which you will write your essay can be found in that section.

SECTION

2

1. Ⓐ Ⓑ Ⓒ Ⓓ Ⓔ	11. Ⓐ Ⓑ Ⓒ Ⓓ Ⓔ	21. Ⓐ Ⓑ Ⓒ Ⓓ Ⓔ	31. Ⓐ Ⓑ Ⓒ Ⓓ Ⓔ
2. Ⓐ Ⓑ Ⓒ Ⓓ Ⓔ	12. Ⓐ Ⓑ Ⓒ Ⓓ Ⓔ	22. Ⓐ Ⓑ Ⓒ Ⓓ Ⓔ	32. Ⓐ Ⓑ Ⓒ Ⓓ Ⓔ
3. Ⓐ Ⓑ Ⓒ Ⓓ Ⓔ	13. Ⓐ Ⓑ Ⓒ Ⓓ Ⓔ	23. Ⓐ Ⓑ Ⓒ Ⓓ Ⓔ	33. Ⓐ Ⓑ Ⓒ Ⓓ Ⓔ
4. Ⓐ Ⓑ Ⓒ Ⓓ Ⓔ	14. Ⓐ Ⓑ Ⓒ Ⓓ Ⓔ	24. Ⓐ Ⓑ Ⓒ Ⓓ Ⓔ	34. Ⓐ Ⓑ Ⓒ Ⓓ Ⓔ
5. Ⓐ Ⓑ Ⓒ Ⓓ Ⓔ	15. Ⓐ Ⓑ Ⓒ Ⓓ Ⓔ	25. Ⓐ Ⓑ Ⓒ Ⓓ Ⓔ	35. Ⓐ Ⓑ Ⓒ Ⓓ Ⓔ
6. Ⓐ Ⓑ Ⓒ Ⓓ Ⓔ	16. Ⓐ Ⓑ Ⓒ Ⓓ Ⓔ	26. Ⓐ Ⓑ Ⓒ Ⓓ Ⓔ	36. Ⓐ Ⓑ Ⓒ Ⓓ Ⓔ
7. Ⓐ Ⓑ Ⓒ Ⓓ Ⓔ	17. Ⓐ Ⓑ Ⓒ Ⓓ Ⓔ	27. Ⓐ Ⓑ Ⓒ Ⓓ Ⓔ	37. Ⓐ Ⓑ Ⓒ Ⓓ Ⓔ
8. Ⓐ Ⓑ Ⓒ Ⓓ Ⓔ	18. Ⓐ Ⓑ Ⓒ Ⓓ Ⓔ	28. Ⓐ Ⓑ Ⓒ Ⓓ Ⓔ	38. Ⓐ Ⓑ Ⓒ Ⓓ Ⓔ
9. Ⓐ Ⓑ Ⓒ Ⓓ Ⓔ	19. Ⓐ Ⓑ Ⓒ Ⓓ Ⓔ	29. Ⓐ Ⓑ Ⓒ Ⓓ Ⓔ	39. Ⓐ Ⓑ Ⓒ Ⓓ Ⓔ
10. Ⓐ Ⓑ Ⓒ Ⓓ Ⓔ	20. Ⓐ Ⓑ Ⓒ Ⓓ Ⓔ	30. Ⓐ Ⓑ Ⓒ Ⓓ Ⓔ	40. Ⓐ Ⓑ Ⓒ Ⓓ Ⓔ

right in
Section 2

wrong in
Section 2

SECTION

3

1. Ⓐ Ⓑ Ⓒ Ⓓ Ⓔ	11. Ⓐ Ⓑ Ⓒ Ⓓ Ⓔ	21. Ⓐ Ⓑ Ⓒ Ⓓ Ⓔ	31. Ⓐ Ⓑ Ⓒ Ⓓ Ⓔ
2. Ⓐ Ⓑ Ⓒ Ⓓ Ⓔ	12. Ⓐ Ⓑ Ⓒ Ⓓ Ⓔ	22. Ⓐ Ⓑ Ⓒ Ⓓ Ⓔ	32. Ⓐ Ⓑ Ⓒ Ⓓ Ⓔ
3. Ⓐ Ⓑ Ⓒ Ⓓ Ⓔ	13. Ⓐ Ⓑ Ⓒ Ⓓ Ⓔ	23. Ⓐ Ⓑ Ⓒ Ⓓ Ⓔ	33. Ⓐ Ⓑ Ⓒ Ⓓ Ⓔ
4. Ⓐ Ⓑ Ⓒ Ⓓ Ⓔ	14. Ⓐ Ⓑ Ⓒ Ⓓ Ⓔ	24. Ⓐ Ⓑ Ⓒ Ⓓ Ⓔ	34. Ⓐ Ⓑ Ⓒ Ⓓ Ⓔ
5. Ⓐ Ⓑ Ⓒ Ⓓ Ⓔ	15. Ⓐ Ⓑ Ⓒ Ⓓ Ⓔ	25. Ⓐ Ⓑ Ⓒ Ⓓ Ⓔ	35. Ⓐ Ⓑ Ⓒ Ⓓ Ⓔ
6. Ⓐ Ⓑ Ⓒ Ⓓ Ⓔ	16. Ⓐ Ⓑ Ⓒ Ⓓ Ⓔ	26. Ⓐ Ⓑ Ⓒ Ⓓ Ⓔ	36. Ⓐ Ⓑ Ⓒ Ⓓ Ⓔ
7. Ⓐ Ⓑ Ⓒ Ⓓ Ⓔ	17. Ⓐ Ⓑ Ⓒ Ⓓ Ⓔ	27. Ⓐ Ⓑ Ⓒ Ⓓ Ⓔ	37. Ⓐ Ⓑ Ⓒ Ⓓ Ⓔ
8. Ⓐ Ⓑ Ⓒ Ⓓ Ⓔ	18. Ⓐ Ⓑ Ⓒ Ⓓ Ⓔ	28. Ⓐ Ⓑ Ⓒ Ⓓ Ⓔ	38. Ⓐ Ⓑ Ⓒ Ⓓ Ⓔ
9. Ⓐ Ⓑ Ⓒ Ⓓ Ⓔ	19. Ⓐ Ⓑ Ⓒ Ⓓ Ⓔ	29. Ⓐ Ⓑ Ⓒ Ⓓ Ⓔ	39. Ⓐ Ⓑ Ⓒ Ⓓ Ⓔ
10. Ⓐ Ⓑ Ⓒ Ⓓ Ⓔ	20. Ⓐ Ⓑ Ⓒ Ⓓ Ⓔ	30. Ⓐ Ⓑ Ⓒ Ⓓ Ⓔ	40. Ⓐ Ⓑ Ⓒ Ⓓ Ⓔ

right in
Section 3

wrong in
Section 3

Remove (or photocopy) this answer sheet and use it to complete the practice test.

Start with number 1 for each section. If a section has fewer questions than answer spaces, leave the extra spaces blank.

SECTION 4

1. Ⓐ Ⓑ Ⓒ Ⓓ Ⓔ	11. Ⓐ Ⓑ Ⓒ Ⓓ Ⓔ	21. Ⓐ Ⓑ Ⓒ Ⓓ Ⓔ	31. Ⓐ Ⓑ Ⓒ Ⓓ Ⓔ
2. Ⓐ Ⓑ Ⓒ Ⓓ Ⓔ	12. Ⓐ Ⓑ Ⓒ Ⓓ Ⓔ	22. Ⓐ Ⓑ Ⓒ Ⓓ Ⓔ	32. Ⓐ Ⓑ Ⓒ Ⓓ Ⓔ
3. Ⓐ Ⓑ Ⓒ Ⓓ Ⓔ	13. Ⓐ Ⓑ Ⓒ Ⓓ Ⓔ	23. Ⓐ Ⓑ Ⓒ Ⓓ Ⓔ	33. Ⓐ Ⓑ Ⓒ Ⓓ Ⓔ
4. Ⓐ Ⓑ Ⓒ Ⓓ Ⓔ	14. Ⓐ Ⓑ Ⓒ Ⓓ Ⓔ	24. Ⓐ Ⓑ Ⓒ Ⓓ Ⓔ	34. Ⓐ Ⓑ Ⓒ Ⓓ Ⓔ
5. Ⓐ Ⓑ Ⓒ Ⓓ Ⓔ	15. Ⓐ Ⓑ Ⓒ Ⓓ Ⓔ	25. Ⓐ Ⓑ Ⓒ Ⓓ Ⓔ	35. Ⓐ Ⓑ Ⓒ Ⓓ Ⓔ
6. Ⓐ Ⓑ Ⓒ Ⓓ Ⓔ	16. Ⓐ Ⓑ Ⓒ Ⓓ Ⓔ	26. Ⓐ Ⓑ Ⓒ Ⓓ Ⓔ	36. Ⓐ Ⓑ Ⓒ Ⓓ Ⓔ
7. Ⓐ Ⓑ Ⓒ Ⓓ Ⓔ	17. Ⓐ Ⓑ Ⓒ Ⓓ Ⓔ	27. Ⓐ Ⓑ Ⓒ Ⓓ Ⓔ	37. Ⓐ Ⓑ Ⓒ Ⓓ Ⓔ
8. Ⓐ Ⓑ Ⓒ Ⓓ Ⓔ	18. Ⓐ Ⓑ Ⓒ Ⓓ Ⓔ	28. Ⓐ Ⓑ Ⓒ Ⓓ Ⓔ	38. Ⓐ Ⓑ Ⓒ Ⓓ Ⓔ
9. Ⓐ Ⓑ Ⓒ Ⓓ Ⓔ	19. Ⓐ Ⓑ Ⓒ Ⓓ Ⓔ	29. Ⓐ Ⓑ Ⓒ Ⓓ Ⓔ	39. Ⓐ Ⓑ Ⓒ Ⓓ Ⓔ
10. Ⓐ Ⓑ Ⓒ Ⓓ Ⓔ	20. Ⓐ Ⓑ Ⓒ Ⓓ Ⓔ	30. Ⓐ Ⓑ Ⓒ Ⓓ Ⓔ	40. Ⓐ Ⓑ Ⓒ Ⓓ Ⓔ

right in Section 4

wrong in Section 4

SECTION 5

1. Ⓐ Ⓑ Ⓒ Ⓓ Ⓔ	11. Ⓐ Ⓑ Ⓒ Ⓓ Ⓔ	21. Ⓐ Ⓑ Ⓒ Ⓓ Ⓔ	31. Ⓐ Ⓑ Ⓒ Ⓓ Ⓔ
2. Ⓐ Ⓑ Ⓒ Ⓓ Ⓔ	12. Ⓐ Ⓑ Ⓒ Ⓓ Ⓔ	22. Ⓐ Ⓑ Ⓒ Ⓓ Ⓔ	32. Ⓐ Ⓑ Ⓒ Ⓓ Ⓔ
3. Ⓐ Ⓑ Ⓒ Ⓓ Ⓔ	13. Ⓐ Ⓑ Ⓒ Ⓓ Ⓔ	23. Ⓐ Ⓑ Ⓒ Ⓓ Ⓔ	33. Ⓐ Ⓑ Ⓒ Ⓓ Ⓔ
4. Ⓐ Ⓑ Ⓒ Ⓓ Ⓔ	14. Ⓐ Ⓑ Ⓒ Ⓓ Ⓔ	24. Ⓐ Ⓑ Ⓒ Ⓓ Ⓔ	34. Ⓐ Ⓑ Ⓒ Ⓓ Ⓔ
5. Ⓐ Ⓑ Ⓒ Ⓓ Ⓔ	15. Ⓐ Ⓑ Ⓒ Ⓓ Ⓔ	25. Ⓐ Ⓑ Ⓒ Ⓓ Ⓔ	35. Ⓐ Ⓑ Ⓒ Ⓓ Ⓔ
6. Ⓐ Ⓑ Ⓒ Ⓓ Ⓔ	16. Ⓐ Ⓑ Ⓒ Ⓓ Ⓔ	26. Ⓐ Ⓑ Ⓒ Ⓓ Ⓔ	36. Ⓐ Ⓑ Ⓒ Ⓓ Ⓔ
7. Ⓐ Ⓑ Ⓒ Ⓓ Ⓔ	17. Ⓐ Ⓑ Ⓒ Ⓓ Ⓔ	27. Ⓐ Ⓑ Ⓒ Ⓓ Ⓔ	37. Ⓐ Ⓑ Ⓒ Ⓓ Ⓔ
8. Ⓐ Ⓑ Ⓒ Ⓓ Ⓔ	18. Ⓐ Ⓑ Ⓒ Ⓓ Ⓔ	28. Ⓐ Ⓑ Ⓒ Ⓓ Ⓔ	38. Ⓐ Ⓑ Ⓒ Ⓓ Ⓔ
9. Ⓐ Ⓑ Ⓒ Ⓓ Ⓔ	19. Ⓐ Ⓑ Ⓒ Ⓓ Ⓔ	29. Ⓐ Ⓑ Ⓒ Ⓓ Ⓔ	39. Ⓐ Ⓑ Ⓒ Ⓓ Ⓔ
10. Ⓐ Ⓑ Ⓒ Ⓓ Ⓔ	20. Ⓐ Ⓑ Ⓒ Ⓓ Ⓔ	30. Ⓐ Ⓑ Ⓒ Ⓓ Ⓔ	40. Ⓐ Ⓑ Ⓒ Ⓓ Ⓔ

right in Section 5

wrong in Section 5

If section 5 of your test book contains math questions that are not multiple choice, continue to item 9 below. Otherwise, continue to item 9 above.

9. 10. 11. 12. 13.

14. 15. 16. 17. 18.

Remove (or photocopy) this answer sheet and use it to complete the practice test.

Start with number 1 for each section. If a section has fewer questions than answer spaces, leave the extra spaces blank.

SECTION

6

1. Ⓐ Ⓑ Ⓒ Ⓓ Ⓔ   11. Ⓐ Ⓑ Ⓒ Ⓓ Ⓔ   21. Ⓐ Ⓑ Ⓒ Ⓓ Ⓔ   31. Ⓐ Ⓑ Ⓒ Ⓓ Ⓔ
2. Ⓐ Ⓑ Ⓒ Ⓓ Ⓔ   12. Ⓐ Ⓑ Ⓒ Ⓓ Ⓔ   22. Ⓐ Ⓑ Ⓒ Ⓓ Ⓔ   32. Ⓐ Ⓑ Ⓒ Ⓓ Ⓔ
3. Ⓐ Ⓑ Ⓒ Ⓓ Ⓔ   13. Ⓐ Ⓑ Ⓒ Ⓓ Ⓔ   23. Ⓐ Ⓑ Ⓒ Ⓓ Ⓔ   33. Ⓐ Ⓑ Ⓒ Ⓓ Ⓔ
4. Ⓐ Ⓑ Ⓒ Ⓓ Ⓔ   14. Ⓐ Ⓑ Ⓒ Ⓓ Ⓔ   24. Ⓐ Ⓑ Ⓒ Ⓓ Ⓔ   34. Ⓐ Ⓑ Ⓒ Ⓓ Ⓔ
5. Ⓐ Ⓑ Ⓒ Ⓓ Ⓔ   15. Ⓐ Ⓑ Ⓒ Ⓓ Ⓔ   25. Ⓐ Ⓑ Ⓒ Ⓓ Ⓔ   35. Ⓐ Ⓑ Ⓒ Ⓓ Ⓔ

right in
Section 6

6. Ⓐ Ⓑ Ⓒ Ⓓ Ⓔ   16. Ⓐ Ⓑ Ⓒ Ⓓ Ⓔ   26. Ⓐ Ⓑ Ⓒ Ⓓ Ⓔ   36. Ⓐ Ⓑ Ⓒ Ⓓ Ⓔ
7. Ⓐ Ⓑ Ⓒ Ⓓ Ⓔ   17. Ⓐ Ⓑ Ⓒ Ⓓ Ⓔ   27. Ⓐ Ⓑ Ⓒ Ⓓ Ⓔ   37. Ⓐ Ⓑ Ⓒ Ⓓ Ⓔ
8. Ⓐ Ⓑ Ⓒ Ⓓ Ⓔ   18. Ⓐ Ⓑ Ⓒ Ⓓ Ⓔ   28. Ⓐ Ⓑ Ⓒ Ⓓ Ⓔ   38. Ⓐ Ⓑ Ⓒ Ⓓ Ⓔ
9. Ⓐ Ⓑ Ⓒ Ⓓ Ⓔ   19. Ⓐ Ⓑ Ⓒ Ⓓ Ⓔ   29. Ⓐ Ⓑ Ⓒ Ⓓ Ⓔ   39. Ⓐ Ⓑ Ⓒ Ⓓ Ⓔ
10. Ⓐ Ⓑ Ⓒ Ⓓ Ⓔ   20. Ⓐ Ⓑ Ⓒ Ⓓ Ⓔ   30. Ⓐ Ⓑ Ⓒ Ⓓ Ⓔ   40. Ⓐ Ⓑ Ⓒ Ⓓ Ⓔ

wrong in
Section 6

SECTION

7

1. Ⓐ Ⓑ Ⓒ Ⓓ Ⓔ   11. Ⓐ Ⓑ Ⓒ Ⓓ Ⓔ   21. Ⓐ Ⓑ Ⓒ Ⓓ Ⓔ   31. Ⓐ Ⓑ Ⓒ Ⓓ Ⓔ
2. Ⓐ Ⓑ Ⓒ Ⓓ Ⓔ   12. Ⓐ Ⓑ Ⓒ Ⓓ Ⓔ   22. Ⓐ Ⓑ Ⓒ Ⓓ Ⓔ   32. Ⓐ Ⓑ Ⓒ Ⓓ Ⓔ
3. Ⓐ Ⓑ Ⓒ Ⓓ Ⓔ   13. Ⓐ Ⓑ Ⓒ Ⓓ Ⓔ   23. Ⓐ Ⓑ Ⓒ Ⓓ Ⓔ   33. Ⓐ Ⓑ Ⓒ Ⓓ Ⓔ
4. Ⓐ Ⓑ Ⓒ Ⓓ Ⓔ   14. Ⓐ Ⓑ Ⓒ Ⓓ Ⓔ   24. Ⓐ Ⓑ Ⓒ Ⓓ Ⓔ   34. Ⓐ Ⓑ Ⓒ Ⓓ Ⓔ
5. Ⓐ Ⓑ Ⓒ Ⓓ Ⓔ   15. Ⓐ Ⓑ Ⓒ Ⓓ Ⓔ   25. Ⓐ Ⓑ Ⓒ Ⓓ Ⓔ   35. Ⓐ Ⓑ Ⓒ Ⓓ Ⓔ

right in
Section 7

6. Ⓐ Ⓑ Ⓒ Ⓓ Ⓔ   16. Ⓐ Ⓑ Ⓒ Ⓓ Ⓔ   26. Ⓐ Ⓑ Ⓒ Ⓓ Ⓔ   36. Ⓐ Ⓑ Ⓒ Ⓓ Ⓔ
7. Ⓐ Ⓑ Ⓒ Ⓓ Ⓔ   17. Ⓐ Ⓑ Ⓒ Ⓓ Ⓔ   27. Ⓐ Ⓑ Ⓒ Ⓓ Ⓔ   37. Ⓐ Ⓑ Ⓒ Ⓓ Ⓔ
8. Ⓐ Ⓑ Ⓒ Ⓓ Ⓔ   18. Ⓐ Ⓑ Ⓒ Ⓓ Ⓔ   28. Ⓐ Ⓑ Ⓒ Ⓓ Ⓔ   38. Ⓐ Ⓑ Ⓒ Ⓓ Ⓔ
9. Ⓐ Ⓑ Ⓒ Ⓓ Ⓔ   19. Ⓐ Ⓑ Ⓒ Ⓓ Ⓔ   29. Ⓐ Ⓑ Ⓒ Ⓓ Ⓔ   39. Ⓐ Ⓑ Ⓒ Ⓓ Ⓔ
10. Ⓐ Ⓑ Ⓒ Ⓓ Ⓔ   20. Ⓐ Ⓑ Ⓒ Ⓓ Ⓔ   30. Ⓐ Ⓑ Ⓒ Ⓓ Ⓔ   40. Ⓐ Ⓑ Ⓒ Ⓓ Ⓔ

wrong in
Section 7

Remove (or photocopy) this answer sheet and use it to complete the practice test.

Start with number 1 for each section. If a section has fewer questions than answer spaces, leave the extra spaces blank.

SECTION

8

1. Ⓐ Ⓑ Ⓒ Ⓓ Ⓔ	11. Ⓐ Ⓑ Ⓒ Ⓓ Ⓔ	21. Ⓐ Ⓑ Ⓒ Ⓓ Ⓔ	31. Ⓐ Ⓑ Ⓒ Ⓓ Ⓔ
2. Ⓐ Ⓑ Ⓒ Ⓓ Ⓔ	12. Ⓐ Ⓑ Ⓒ Ⓓ Ⓔ	22. Ⓐ Ⓑ Ⓒ Ⓓ Ⓔ	32. Ⓐ Ⓑ Ⓒ Ⓓ Ⓔ
3. Ⓐ Ⓑ Ⓒ Ⓓ Ⓔ	13. Ⓐ Ⓑ Ⓒ Ⓓ Ⓔ	23. Ⓐ Ⓑ Ⓒ Ⓓ Ⓔ	33. Ⓐ Ⓑ Ⓒ Ⓓ Ⓔ
4. Ⓐ Ⓑ Ⓒ Ⓓ Ⓔ	14. Ⓐ Ⓑ Ⓒ Ⓓ Ⓔ	24. Ⓐ Ⓑ Ⓒ Ⓓ Ⓔ	34. Ⓐ Ⓑ Ⓒ Ⓓ Ⓔ
5. Ⓐ Ⓑ Ⓒ Ⓓ Ⓔ	15. Ⓐ Ⓑ Ⓒ Ⓓ Ⓔ	25. Ⓐ Ⓑ Ⓒ Ⓓ Ⓔ	35. Ⓐ Ⓑ Ⓒ Ⓓ Ⓔ
6. Ⓐ Ⓑ Ⓒ Ⓓ Ⓔ	16. Ⓐ Ⓑ Ⓒ Ⓓ Ⓔ	26. Ⓐ Ⓑ Ⓒ Ⓓ Ⓔ	36. Ⓐ Ⓑ Ⓒ Ⓓ Ⓔ
7. Ⓐ Ⓑ Ⓒ Ⓓ Ⓔ	17. Ⓐ Ⓑ Ⓒ Ⓓ Ⓔ	27. Ⓐ Ⓑ Ⓒ Ⓓ Ⓔ	37. Ⓐ Ⓑ Ⓒ Ⓓ Ⓔ
8. Ⓐ Ⓑ Ⓒ Ⓓ Ⓔ	18. Ⓐ Ⓑ Ⓒ Ⓓ Ⓔ	28. Ⓐ Ⓑ Ⓒ Ⓓ Ⓔ	38. Ⓐ Ⓑ Ⓒ Ⓓ Ⓔ
9. Ⓐ Ⓑ Ⓒ Ⓓ Ⓔ	19. Ⓐ Ⓑ Ⓒ Ⓓ Ⓔ	29. Ⓐ Ⓑ Ⓒ Ⓓ Ⓔ	39. Ⓐ Ⓑ Ⓒ Ⓓ Ⓔ
10. Ⓐ Ⓑ Ⓒ Ⓓ Ⓔ	20. Ⓐ Ⓑ Ⓒ Ⓓ Ⓔ	30. Ⓐ Ⓑ Ⓒ Ⓓ Ⓔ	40. Ⓐ Ⓑ Ⓒ Ⓓ Ⓔ

☐ # right in Section 8

☐ # wrong in Section 8

SECTION

9

1. Ⓐ Ⓑ Ⓒ Ⓓ Ⓔ	11. Ⓐ Ⓑ Ⓒ Ⓓ Ⓔ	21. Ⓐ Ⓑ Ⓒ Ⓓ Ⓔ	31. Ⓐ Ⓑ Ⓒ Ⓓ Ⓔ
2. Ⓐ Ⓑ Ⓒ Ⓓ Ⓔ	12. Ⓐ Ⓑ Ⓒ Ⓓ Ⓔ	22. Ⓐ Ⓑ Ⓒ Ⓓ Ⓔ	32. Ⓐ Ⓑ Ⓒ Ⓓ Ⓔ
3. Ⓐ Ⓑ Ⓒ Ⓓ Ⓔ	13. Ⓐ Ⓑ Ⓒ Ⓓ Ⓔ	23. Ⓐ Ⓑ Ⓒ Ⓓ Ⓔ	33. Ⓐ Ⓑ Ⓒ Ⓓ Ⓔ
4. Ⓐ Ⓑ Ⓒ Ⓓ Ⓔ	14. Ⓐ Ⓑ Ⓒ Ⓓ Ⓔ	24. Ⓐ Ⓑ Ⓒ Ⓓ Ⓔ	34. Ⓐ Ⓑ Ⓒ Ⓓ Ⓔ
5. Ⓐ Ⓑ Ⓒ Ⓓ Ⓔ	15. Ⓐ Ⓑ Ⓒ Ⓓ Ⓔ	25. Ⓐ Ⓑ Ⓒ Ⓓ Ⓔ	35. Ⓐ Ⓑ Ⓒ Ⓓ Ⓔ
6. Ⓐ Ⓑ Ⓒ Ⓓ Ⓔ	16. Ⓐ Ⓑ Ⓒ Ⓓ Ⓔ	26. Ⓐ Ⓑ Ⓒ Ⓓ Ⓔ	36. Ⓐ Ⓑ Ⓒ Ⓓ Ⓔ
7. Ⓐ Ⓑ Ⓒ Ⓓ Ⓔ	17. Ⓐ Ⓑ Ⓒ Ⓓ Ⓔ	27. Ⓐ Ⓑ Ⓒ Ⓓ Ⓔ	37. Ⓐ Ⓑ Ⓒ Ⓓ Ⓔ
8. Ⓐ Ⓑ Ⓒ Ⓓ Ⓔ	18. Ⓐ Ⓑ Ⓒ Ⓓ Ⓔ	28. Ⓐ Ⓑ Ⓒ Ⓓ Ⓔ	38. Ⓐ Ⓑ Ⓒ Ⓓ Ⓔ
9. Ⓐ Ⓑ Ⓒ Ⓓ Ⓔ	19. Ⓐ Ⓑ Ⓒ Ⓓ Ⓔ	29. Ⓐ Ⓑ Ⓒ Ⓓ Ⓔ	39. Ⓐ Ⓑ Ⓒ Ⓓ Ⓔ
10. Ⓐ Ⓑ Ⓒ Ⓓ Ⓔ	20. Ⓐ Ⓑ Ⓒ Ⓓ Ⓔ	30. Ⓐ Ⓑ Ⓒ Ⓓ Ⓔ	40. Ⓐ Ⓑ Ⓒ Ⓓ Ⓔ

☐ # right in Section 9

☐ # wrong in Section 9

GO ONLINE

Be sure to add your scores to your syllabus.

Practice Test Four

SECTION 1
Time—25 Minutes
ESSAY

The essay gives you an opportunity to show how effectively you can develop and express ideas. You should, therefore, take care to develop your point of view, present your ideas logically and clearly, and use language precisely.

Your essay must be written in your Answer Grid Booklet—you will receive no other paper on which to write. You will have enough space if you write on every line, avoid wide margins, and keep your handwriting to a reasonable size. Remember that people who are not familiar with your handwriting will read what you write. Try to write or print so that what you are writing is legible to those readers.

You have twenty-five minutes to write an essay on the topic assigned below.
DO NOT WRITE ON ANOTHER TOPIC. AN OFF-TOPIC ESSAY WILL RECEIVE A SCORE OF ZERO.

Think carefully about the issue presented in the following excerpt and the assignment below.

> "I don't know the key to success, but the key to failure is to try to please everyone."
> –Bill Cosby

Assignment: Is trying to please people a way to achieve success or a route to failure? Plan and write an essay in which you develop your point of view on this issue. Support your position with reasoning and examples taken from your reading, studies, experience, or observations.

DO NOT WRITE YOUR ESSAY IN YOUR TEST BOOK.
You will receive credit only for what you write in your Answer Grid Booklet.

GO ON TO THE NEXT PAGE ⟶

KAPLAN

_____

_____

_____

_____

_____

_____

_____

_____

_____

_____

_____

_____

_____

_____

_____

_____

_____

_____

_____

IF YOU FINISH BEFORE TIME IS CALLED, YOU MAY CHECK YOUR WORK ON
THIS SECTION ONLY. DO NOT TURN TO ANY OTHER SECTION IN THE TEST.

SECTION 2

Time—25 Minutes

20 Questions

Directions: For this section, solve each problem and decide which is the best of the choices given. Fill in the corresponding oval on the answer sheet. You may use any available space for scratchwork.

Notes:

(1) Calculator use is permitted.

(2) All numbers used are real numbers.

(3) Figures are provided for some problems. All figures are drawn to scale and lie in a plane UNLESS otherwise indicated.

(4) Unless otherwise specified, the domain of any function f is assumed to be the set of all real numbers x for which $f(x)$ is a real number.

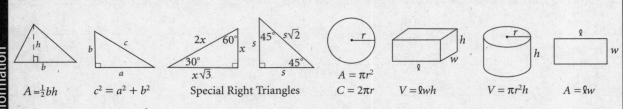

$A = \frac{1}{2}bh$ $\qquad$ $c^2 = a^2 + b^2$ $\qquad$ Special Right Triangles $\qquad$ $A = \pi r^2$ $\qquad$ $C = 2\pi r$ $\qquad$ $V = \ell wh$ $\qquad$ $V = \pi r^2 h$ $\qquad$ $A = \ell w$

The sum of the degree measures of the angles in a triangle is 180.
The number of degrees of arc in a circle is 360.
A straight angle has a degree measure of 180.

1. If $x^6 + 4 = x^6 + w$, then $w =$

   (A) -4

   (B) $-\sqrt[6]{4}$

   (C) $\sqrt[6]{4}$

   (D) 4

   (E) 4^6

2. Depending on the cycle, washing a load of clothes takes from 22 to 28 minutes. Drying takes an additional 20 to 30 minutes. What are the minimum and maximum total times to complete a load of laundry?

   (A) 22 minutes and 28 minutes

   (B) 28 minutes and 48 minutes

   (C) 28 minutes and 58 minutes

   (D) 42 minutes and 48 minutes

   (E) 42 minutes and 58 minutes

3. If $\frac{a}{b} = 4$, $\frac{a}{c} = 8$, and $c = 9$, what is the value of b?

   (A) 2

   (B) 8

   (C) 18

   (D) 36

   (E) 72

4. Between which two digits of 4567890 should a decimal point be placed so that the value of the resulting number is 4.567890×10^2?

   (A) 5 and 6

   (B) 6 and 7

   (C) 7 and 8

   (D) 8 and 9

   (E) 9 and 0

GO ON TO THE NEXT PAGE

5. Set *A* is the set of all prime numbers. Set *B* is the set of all numbers equal to a prime number plus 2. Which of the following are in the intersection of set *A* and set *B*?

   I. 2
   II. 4
   III. 5

   (A) I only
   (B) II only
   (C) III only
   (D) I and III only
   (E) II and III only

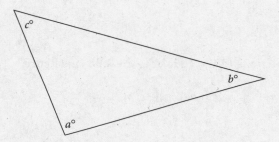

Note: Figure not drawn to scale

6. In the figure above, if $a = 7c$ and $b = 2c$, what is the value of *c*?

   (A) 18
   (B) 20
   (C) 28
   (D) 34
   (E) 36

7. After 21 kids were added to a class, there were 4 times as many students as before. How many kids were in the class before the addition?

   (A) 3
   (B) 7
   (C) 11
   (D) 14
   (E) 17

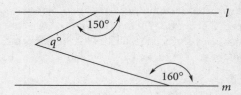

8. In the figure above, $l \parallel m$. What is the value of *q*?

   (A) 40°
   (B) 50°
   (C) 60°
   (D) 70°
   (E) 80°

9. The value of $3x + 9$ is how much more than the value of $3x - 2$?

   (A) 7
   (B) 11
   (C) $3x + 7$
   (D) $3x + 11$
   (E) $6x + 7$

10. If $a < b < 0 < c$, which of the following must be true?

    I. $-b > -a$
    II. $a + c < b + c$
    III. $a + b < c$

    (A) I only
    (B) II only
    (C) III only
    (D) II and III only
    (E) I, II, and III

GO ON TO THE NEXT PAGE

KAPLAN

11. If set C includes all numbers between 0 and 5, inclusive. Set D includes all numbers between 3 and 7, inclusive. Which of the following sets of inequalities correctly describes x, where x is the union of set C and set D?

(A) $0 \le x \le 3$

(B) $0 \le x \le 5$

(C) $0 \le x \le 7$

(D) $3 \le x \le 5$

(E) $3 \le x \le 7$

12. If $\dfrac{10}{a+b} = \dfrac{4}{a}, \dfrac{b^2}{18} = \dfrac{a}{2}$, and $ab \ne 0$, what is the value of b?

(A) 0

(B) 2

(C) 4

(D) 6

(E) 8

13. If $c^{-\frac{1}{2}} = 3$, what is the value of c^2?

(A) -9

(B) -3

(C) $\dfrac{1}{81}$

(D) $\dfrac{1}{9}$

(E) $\dfrac{1}{\sqrt{3}}$

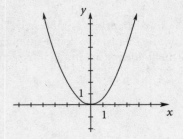

14. Which of the following equations best describes the curve in the figure above?

(A) $y = -2x^2$

(B) $y = -x^2$

(C) $y = |x|$

(D) $y = \dfrac{1}{2}x^2$

(E) $y = 2x^2$

Questions 15 and 16 refer to the following figure:

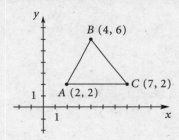

15. What is the area of triangle ABC?

(A) 5

(B) 6

(C) 8

(D) 9

(E) 10

16. What is the perimeter of triangle ABC?

(A) 10

(B) 11

(C) $10 + \sqrt{5}$

(D) 13

(E) $10 + 2\sqrt{5}$

GO ON TO THE NEXT PAGE

17. Which of the following represents the statement "When the sum of the squares of $2a$ and $3b$ are added to the difference between $8c$ and $7d$, the result is 3 more than e"?

    (A) $(2a)^2 + (3b)^2 + (8c - 7d) = e + 3$

    (B) $(2a)^2 + (3b)^2 + (8c - 7d) + 3 = e$

    (C) $(2a + 3b)^2 + (8c - 7d) + 3 = e$

    (D) $(2a + 3b)^2 + (8c - 7d) = e + 3$

    (E) $2a^2 + 3b^2 + (8c - 7d) + 3 = e$

18. Line l has an undefined slope and contains the point $(-2, 3)$. Which of the following points is also on line l?

    (A) $(0, 3)$

    (B) $(5, 5)$

    (C) $(0, 0)$

    (D) $(3, -2)$

    (E) $(-2, 5)$

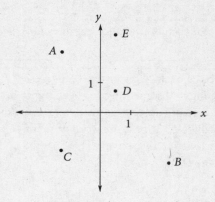

19. In the figure above, for which point (x, y) is the product xy the greatest?

    (A) A

    (B) B

    (C) C

    (D) D

    (E) E

20. If $a = 3n + 4$ and $b = 7 + 9n^2$, what is b in terms of a?

    (A) $a^2 + 8a + 23$

    (B) $a^2 - 8a + 23$

    (C) $9a^2 - 108a + 144$

    (D) $9a^2 - 108a + 148$

    (E) $9a^2 + 108a + 148$

IF YOU FINISH BEFORE TIME IS CALLED, YOU MAY CHECK YOUR WORK ON THIS SECTION ONLY. DO NOT TURN TO ANY OTHER SECTION IN THE TEST. **STOP**

KAPLAN

SECTION 3

Time—25 Minutes
25 Questions

Directions: For each of the following questions, choose the best answer and darken the corresponding oval on the answer sheet.

Each sentence below has one or two blanks, each blank indicating that something has been omitted. Beneath the sentence are five words or sets of words labeled A through E. Choose the word or set of words that, when inserted in the sentence, <u>best</u> fits the meaning of the sentence as a whole.

Example:

Today's small, portable computers contrast markedly with the earliest electronic computers, which were -------.

(A) effective
(B) invented
(C) useful
(D) destructive
(E) enormous

1. Leonardo Da Vinci was a ------- artist; he was a painter, sculptor, draftsman, architect, and inventor.

   (A) demonstrative
   (B) nebulous
   (C) meticulous
   (D) versatile
   (E) metaphoric

2. Although the class was told by their math teacher that the exercises in the chapter review were -------, the students knew that some questions on the exam would be the same as those found in the review.

   (A) pivotal
   (B) ritualistic
   (C) salient
   (D) supplementary
   (E) solemn

3. Renowned buildings such as "Fallingwater" and the eminent Solomon R. Guggenheim Museum in New York City ------- Frank Lloyd Wright as one of the most ------- architects of the 20th century.

   (A) buoyed . . irrelevant
   (B) established . . prominent
   (C) surrendered . . prolific
   (D) decried . . cynical
   (E) categorized . . mundane

4. Although he was not particularly talented, his years of experience as a plumber at least solidified his status as a ------- of the profession.

   (A) novice
   (B) neighbor
   (C) interpreter
   (D) practitioner
   (E) detractor

5. Known as a skilled mediator, Ms. Poole was able to ------- the couple's relationship by carefully ------- their numerous differences.

   (A) reinforce . . strengthening
   (B) preserve . . bridging
   (C) convey . . widening
   (D) overcome . . plugging
   (E) disregard . . destroying

GO ON TO THE NEXT PAGE

KAPLAN

6. The ------- that plagued the once venerable institution was so entrenched and highly publicized that few imagined its reputation could ever be -------.

   (A) integrity . . discredited
   (B) conviction . . justified
   (C) corruption . . redeemed
   (D) dignity . . excused
   (E) degradation . . convicted

7. The waiter performs his job with ------- and hopes that if he continues to work ------- he will eventually be promoted to maitre'd.

   (A) sagacity . . unscrupulously
   (B) leniency . . decorously
   (C) nonchalance . . tenaciously
   (D) acrimony . . cheerfully
   (E) ardor . . assiduously

8. Even though we are supposed to be more evolved than animals, the human tendency toward ------- and egocentrism, shows that sometimes people can carry a narrow view of the universe.

   (A) irrationality
   (B) humanity
   (C) temerity
   (D) serendipity
   (E) anthropocentrism

GO ON TO THE NEXT PAGE

KAPLAN

Directions: The passages below are followed by questions based on their content; questions following a pair of related passages may also be based on the relationship between the paired passages. Answer the questions on the basis of what is <u>stated</u> or <u>implied</u> in the passages and in any introductory material that may be provided.

Questions 9–10 refer to the following passage.

With my months of anticipation finally satisfied and the long-awaited bundle of fur fast asleep in my lap, I could not have then imagined the trials to come. Yet, by the time I arrived home from the
(5) breeder's with slightly scored shins and puppy urine coating my shoes, I had some idea. I suppose my mother had provided something of a warning with her constant refrain that came every time I crossed another day off my calendar: "Just
(10) make sure he stays your responsibility, not mine." But looking back, with that once tiny menace now a snoring beast asleep at my feet, I feel a hint of what must be parental satisfaction.

9. In line 5, "scored" most nearly means

(A) counted
(B) indented
(C) acquired
(D) scratched
(E) slashed

10. The author uses the words "snoring beast" (line 12) in order to

(A) suggest that her puppy grew to be too large
(B) imply that her once-energetic puppy is now rather lazy
(C) indicate that her decision to get a puppy was a mistake
(D) emphasize how much she has grown to love her puppy
(E) underscore how much her puppy has matured

Questions 11–12 refer to the following passage.

When the revolutionary American chocolate-maker Milton Hershey enthusiastically opened his first candy shop in Philadelphia at the age of 18, he knew little of the business, and his inexperience
(5) caused his endeavor to fold six years later. Nonetheless, getting his feet wet in the industry proved enough to keep him hooked on it, for he went on to work as an intern for a local caramel manufacturer. There he learned that superior
(10) results could only be achieved when the freshest milk was used, and thus was born a lifelong dedi-cation to quality ingredients upon which he would later build his chocolate empire.

11. As indicated in the first sentence of the passage, Milton Hershey was

(A) quite industrious
(B) something of a child prodigy
(C) an untalented entrepreneur
(D) a groundbreaking candy producer
(E) committed to using high-quality ingredients

12. The passage implies that Hershey

(A) was the first to make candy from quality ingredients
(B) had a persisting interest in candy manufacturing
(C) tried to apply caramel-making techniques to chocolate production
(D) was well-suited for a career only in candy making
(E) had been fascinated by candy-making since early childhood

GO ON TO THE NEXT PAGE

Questions 13–25 refer to the following passage.

The following passage is from a 2004 essay that discusses the decline in artistic awareness, appreciation, and taste in America.

While many of us express disdain at the declining condition of artistic awareness, let alone appreciation, in this country, we cannot honestly express surprise. This general decline in tastes has
(5) not escaped the commentary and analysis of cultural critics who have warned us that we may be turning into a nation of Philistines. These same critics have pointed to a pair of causes for this cultural decline. Perhaps, they note, the decline is
(10) due to the crumbling state of our educational system, or to the media's focus on pop culture and the general decline of taste this breeds. Nevertheless, this type of scholarly discussion about the roots of the decline, while relevant to
(15) sociological and cultural historical analysis, does nothing to solve the problem. Understanding the causes does not change the sad fact that the same country that gave the world film noir, jazz, and abstract expressionism now mostly concerns itself
(20) with teen movies and boy bands. We must use our understanding and analysis of the causes to address the problem of artistic decline in America.

Before we can begin a discussion of artistic decline, we must first define the word "art," an
(25) endeavor that has proven problematic, especially after the introduction of modern art forms during the twentieth century. Indeed, some may argue that the entire debate about artistic decline in this country is flawed due to our exclusion of modern
(30) forms of art such as pop music. Many claim that such discussion can be seen as snobby, even culturally imperious. Without entering the debate on the validity of the post-modern conception of art as an idea, the question of "what is art" must
(35) be addressed. But it should be addressed expeditiously. Far too much time has been spent arguing over whether a teen movie is more or less art than *Citizen Kane* is, or whether the music of a boy band is more or less art than are the works of
(40) Sondheim. To be fair, society should not adopt an exclusionary definition or attitude. Indeed, history has proven that today's pop music can be tomorrow's great art in retrospect. Thus, we should accept all artistic endeavors as art. Individuals and
(45) critics should judge the quality of such endeavors. But this does not change the fact that today, people are unaware of and uneducated about the classics, or even about recent movements in art apart from cinema, television, and pop music.
(50) Imagine a United States of America in which artistic education, and thus appreciation, flourishes, a place where parents read books on art and listen to classical music and opera, as well as pop music. Children observe these adult activities and
(55) mimic them. Parents read to their children and educate them. These parents also give their children art books, classical recordings, and plays as gifts. These parents underwrite, with their tax dollars, public art, public broadcasting, and
(60) community art groups. In school, students receive an education in art history, classical music, and opera. This curriculum can also include pop culture such as the music videos, teen movies, and pop music students enjoy in their free time. In
(65) fact, a better education in art will better equip them to judge the artistic merit of these newer, more trendy art forms, or at least place these art forms in historical context and analyze them as an outgrowth of societal and sociological trends—an
(70) important aspect of artistic knowledge that has been lost by the general public. When these children grow up, some may produce their own art, which would likely be higher in quality than the pop music and movies produced today. Imagine a
(75) land of such developed artistic production and taste! How can we achieve such a society?

Having noted that the proliferation of low quality art in pop culture can be addressed effectively by education, there remains one fundamental
(80) cause for the decline in artistic taste: the crumbling state of our educational system. The society dreamed of above can only be achieved by sustained efforts to improve the American educational system. Unfortunately, with tightening
(85) budgets due to increased levels of government

GO ON TO THE NEXT PAGE ⇒

debt, often the first programs cut are those that provide art and music classes. Often these cuts are viewed as easy ones by the public since they do not compromise the fundamentals supposedly (90) required for an adequate education: reading, writing, history, science, and math. However, what the public often misses is that art, music, and culture are inextricably tied to literary and historical developments that themselves stem from changes (95) in society and culture. A holistic approach to the arts would both redefine their role in education (thereby subsuming the argument of those who want to focus on fundamentals) and improve the state of artistic education by teaching students in (100) an intertextual and multidisciplinary manner. The first step in improving artistic awareness and taste in this country will be not only to reinstate and improve art, music, and other cultural classes but also to restructure the curriculum to provide a (105) more holistic education in which art, music, and culture become a part of the fundamental education in history, literature, and society. This system would require more funding and most likely higher taxes. However, such an investment would (110) pay dividends by ensuring a more educated populace, one which is better equipped to analyze its surroundings in an analytically balanced manner and one which appreciates all forms of human artistic endeavor.

13. According to the author, which endeavor has proven problematic?

(A) Improving the education system
(B) Making art seem relevant
(C) Defining the word "art"
(D) Deciding what students should learn in school
(E) Deciding whether or not to teach art

14. In the second paragraph of the passage (lines 23–49), the author suggests that too much time has been spent

(A) debating the artistic merits of so-called "classics"
(B) debating the artistic merits of modern works
(C) debating whether or not art education can be improved
(D) debating whether or not a historical perspective should be used in art education
(E) comparing the artistic merits of different works traditionally considered classics

15. The author mentions "film noir, jazz, and abstract expressionism" (lines 18–19) chiefly in order to

(A) appeal to the reader's sense of nostalgia
(B) introduce a historical parallel
(C) examine the history of art
(D) remind the reader how tastes change over time
(E) suggest that current artistic works are inferior to older ones

16. In line 32, "imperious" most nearly means

(A) imperative
(B) arbitrary
(C) regal
(D) urgent
(E) arrogant

GO ON TO THE NEXT PAGE

17. According to the author, which important aspect of artistic knowledge has been lost by the general public?

    (A) the ability to place art works in a historical context

    (B) the ability to define the word "art"

    (C) the ability to produce art that rivals the classics

    (D) the ability to judge the merits of current art works

    (E) the ability to value all forms of art

18. In lines 50–58 ("Imagine… gifts"), the hypothetical United States described is noteworthy because

    (A) people have allowed new interests to develop

    (B) parents share their interest in and enjoyment of art

    (C) children learn about art in school

    (D) children and parents share many activities

    (E) artistic knowledge is viewed as a valuable skill

19. Lines 60–64 ("In school… time ") present a model of education where students learn to

    (A) value artistic diversity over tradition

    (B) respect the views of all artists

    (C) reflect critically on the nature of artistic education

    (D) appreciate classic art works over contemporary ones

    (E) encounter art through a wide-ranging exploration

20. The author includes the third paragraph (lines 50–76) primarily in order to

    (A) propose a vision of a utopian society

    (B) propose a vision of an artistically educated society

    (C) argue that pop culture leaves no lasting impact on society

    (D) observe that classic literature has great appeal for even reluctant students

    (E) indicate that contemporary and classical works are interchangeable

21. In lines 91–107 ("However… society"), the education illustrated is best described as

    (A) elitist

    (B) philanthropic

    (C) eclectic

    (D) comprehensive

    (E) rudimentary

22. In lines 107–114, the author describes an education system that would be

    (A) more expensive than the current system

    (B) more celebrated than the current system

    (C) more controversial than the current system

    (D) more interesting than the current system

    (E) more likely to inspire than the current system

GO ON TO THE NEXT PAGE

23. The main purpose of the passage is to

    (A) shift the focus of a debate from causes to effects

    (B) outline a debate and support one side

    (C) present a problem and suggest a solution

    (D) revive a discredited idea that might be able to solve a current problem

    (E) promote certain kinds of art

24. In the hypothetical United States the author discusses, why does the author imply that children will grow up to produce art that may be higher in quality than the pop music and movies produced today?

    (A) they would not want to disappoint their parents

    (B) society would not accept low quality art

    (C) their education would provide them with more artistic knowledge

    (D) they would have more free time to experiment with their art

    (E) critics would judge the merits of the art more harshly

25. The author's attitude toward pop music is that

    (A) he admires it

    (B) he has no feelings about it

    (C) he is not a fan

    (D) he wants to see more pop-influenced education

    (E) he believes it is more important than classical music

IF YOU FINISH BEFORE TIME IS CALLED, YOU MAY CHECK YOUR WORK ON THIS SECTION ONLY. DO NOT TURN TO ANY OTHER SECTION IN THE TEST.

STOP

KAPLAN

SECTION 4

Time—25 Minutes
35 Questions

Directions: For each question in this section, select the best answer from among the choices given and fill in the corresponding oval on the answer sheet.

The following sentences test correctness and effectiveness of expression. Part of each sentence or the entire sentence is underlined; beneath each sentence are five ways of phrasing the underlined material. Choice A repeats the original phrasing; the other four choices are different. If you think the original phrasing produces a better sentence than any of the alternatives, select choice A; if not, select one of the other choices.

In making your selection, follow the requirements of standard written English; that is, pay attention to grammar, choice of words, sentence construction, and punctuation. Your selection should result in the most effective sentence—clear and precise, without awkwardness or ambiguity.

EXAMPLE:

Every apple in the baskets <u>are ripe and labeled according to the date it was picked</u>.

ANSWER:

(A) are ripe and labeled according to the date it was picked
(B) is ripe and labeled according to the date it was picked
(C) are ripe and labeled according to the date they were picked
(D) is ripe and labeled according to the date they were picked
(E) are ripe and labeled as to the date it was picked

---

1. <u>Nora would like to fly to Egypt, but flying is unable to be afforded by her.</u>

   (A) Nora would like to fly to Egypt, but flying is unable to be afforded by her.

   (B) Nora would like to fly to Egypt, but she cannot afford to do so.

   (C) Nora would like to fly to Egypt, but she is unable to afford that.

   (D) Flying to Egypt is what Nora would like to do, but she cannot afford it.

   (E) Flying to Egypt appeals to Nora, but she cannot afford to buy the plane ticket.

2. The state of New Jersey <u>is one of the smallest states in the union, being also</u> the most densely populated.

   (A) is one of the smallest states in the union, being also

   (B) although one of the smallest states in the union, is

   (C) being one of the smallest states in the union makes it

   (D) which is one of the smallest states in the union, although it is

   (E) whose size is the smallest in the union, makes it

GO ON TO THE NEXT PAGE

KAPLAN)

3. The love story of Romeo and Juliet was the subject of a teen movie, being popular among high school students in the 90s.

   (A) The love story of Romeo and Juliet was the subject of a teen movie, being popular among high school students in the 90s.

   (B) The love story of Romeo and Juliet was popular among high school students in the 90s, where it is being made the subject of a teen movie.

   (C) The love story of Romeo and Juliet was popular among high school students in the 90s, when it was the subject of a teen movie.

   (D) Romeo and Juliet, whose love story was the subject of a popular teen movie among high school students in the 90s.

   (E) Being the subject of a teen movie, the love story of Romeo and Juliet having been popular among high school students in the 90s.

4. One consequence of the University's new bylaws is that they can no longer pay reduced wages to lecturers.

   (A) One consequence of the University's new bylaws is that they can no longer pay reduced wages to lecturers.

   (B) As a result of its new bylaws, the University can no longer pay reduced wages to lecturers.

   (C) One consequence of the University's new bylaws is that reduced wages to lecturers can no longer be paid by them.

   (D) The University's new bylaws result in their no longer being able to pay lecturers reduced wages.

   (E) One consequence of the University's new bylaws are that paying reduced wages to lecturers is no longer possible.

5. Photographer Andrea Valerai permitted only a few friends to view her work because her strict standards caused her to doubt that her pictures were worth looking at.

   (A) because her strict standards caused her to doubt

   (B) her standards being strict, she doubted

   (C) because of her standards being strict, which she doubted

   (D) from having strict standards causing her to doubt

   (E) having strict standards causing her doubting

6. It is hard for me to imagine that 100 years ago this area was undeveloped swamp land, but it has since become high-rise apartment buildings.

   (A) land, but it has since become high-rise apartment buildings

   (B) land, but it is now high-rise apartment buildings

   (C) land, and has since become high-rise apartment buildings

   (D) land that has since become high-rise apartment buildings

   (E) land, since becoming high-rise apartment buildings

7. Gorbachev started the opening of Soviet society and he was raised in the relative freedom of thought under Khrushchev.

   (A) Gorbachev started the opening of Soviet society and he

   (B) Gorbachev, who started the opening of Soviet society,

   (C) Starting the opening of Soviet society was Gorbachev, and he

   (D) Gorbachev started the opening of Soviet society and that is why he

   (E) A start of the opening of Soviet society, Gorbachev

GO ON TO THE NEXT PAGE ⇨

KAPLAN

8. The cost of attending college has been affected by an increase in scholarships and <u>because there has been a decrease in large alumni donations</u>.

    (A) because there has been a decrease in large alumni donations

    (B) because of the decrease in large alumni donations

    (C) by alumni who have decreased large donations

    (D) decreasing large alumni donations

    (E) a decrease in large alumni donations

9. Airlines such as *Ryan Air* and *Easy Jet* are able to find alternative, cheap landing strips <u>and are therefore able to pass savings on to their customers</u>.

    (A) and are therefore able to pass savings on to their customers

    (B) and savings are passed on as a result to their customers

    (C) so that their customers could have savings passed to them

    (D) so, therefore, savings would be gained by their customers

    (E) and therefore have savings gained in their customers

10. The first hand transplant was performed in 1998, made possible <u>by their fuller understanding of</u> immunobiology.

    (A) by their fuller understanding of

    (B) by their understanding more fully

    (C) by their more fully understanding

    (D) by a fuller understanding of

    (E) by its fuller understanding of

11. Some speedometers register <u>high speeds as</u> two hundred miles per hour, even though few cars will ever go faster than one hundred.

    (A) high speeds as

    (B) speeds as high as

    (C) speeds that are high

    (D) high speeds that are capable of exceeding

    (E) a speed as

GO ON TO THE NEXT PAGE

KAPLAN

Directions: The following sentences test your ability to recognize grammar and usage errors. Each sentence contains either a single error or no error at all. No sentence contains more than one error. The error, if there is one, is underlined and lettered. If the sentence contains an error, select the one underlined part that must be changed to make the sentence correct. If the sentence is correct, select choice E. In choosing answers, follow the requirements of standard written English.

EXAMPLE:

<u>Whenever</u> one is driving late at night, <u>you</u> must take extra precautions <u>against</u>
   A   B   C

falling asleep <u>at the wheel</u>. <u>No error</u>
             D   E

12. <u>That</u> the team with the worst record won the
    A

    game <u>easily</u> using players <u>whom</u> had previously
           B   C

    scored only two goals <u>came</u> as a shock to the
                      D

    sportscasters. <u>No error</u>
                E

13. Acknowledging that her performance in class

    <u>was</u> not up to her usual standards, Stacy
    A

    <u>had worked</u> <u>to raise</u> her test score average
       B   C

    <u>for the third marking period</u>. <u>No error</u>
            D   E

14. <u>Although</u> he <u>knows</u> his own life was <u>in danger</u>,
    A   B   C

    the Mayor insisted on going downtown to see

    the site of the attack <u>for himself</u>. <u>No error</u>
                    D   E

15. The director was <u>annoyed by</u> Tom's inability
                A

    <u>to learn</u> his lines, <u>because</u> his lack of preparation
      B   C

    forced her to schedule an extra rehearsal

    <u>for the next day</u>. <u>No error</u>
          D   E

16. The professor wanted <u>to be sure that</u> his students
                        A

    <u>come</u> to class <u>on time</u>, so he posted a <u>schedule on</u>
       B   C   D

    the Spanish department's bulletin board. <u>No error</u>
                                    E

17. Henley decorated her plain white kitchen walls

    <u>with</u> colorful posters <u>because</u> she knew she
    A   B

    <u>would enjoy</u> looking at the bright reds, blues,
        C

    and yellows <u>every morning</u>. <u>No error</u>
               D   E

18. Paula, <u>who</u> loved <u>to see</u> new places but
        A   B

    <u>had never enjoyed</u> flying, grew <u>increasing</u>
        C   D

    nervous as the day of her first overseas

    vacation approached. <u>No error</u>
                   E

19. In the <u>anticipatory</u> hush of the dark theater,
          A

    we <u>could hear</u> the <u>rustling of</u> the costumes as
        B   C

    the dancers took <u>their place</u> on the stage. <u>No error</u>
                 D   E

GO ON TO THE NEXT PAGE

KAPLAN

20. The neighbors got <u>into their car</u> and <u>driving</u>
                   A   B

off toward the main street as Katie <u>looked</u> out
                                  C

the window, <u>sipping her hot chocolate</u>. <u>No error</u>
                    D   E

21. The <u>heroine of</u> Dorothy Parker's short story
     A

"The Telephone Call" waits <u>feverishly</u> for the
                        B

telephone to ring, <u>refuses</u> to face her knowledge
                 C

that the boy <u>will never call</u>. <u>No error</u>
             D   E

22. As we walked <u>through</u> the South Philadelphia
         A

neighborhood <u>known as</u> the Italian Market,
          B

a <u>number of</u> appetizing smells <u>greeting</u> our
    C   D

nostrils. <u>No error</u>
      E

23. Kyoko took <u>every opportunity</u> to practice <u>speaking</u>
          A   B

English, <u>even though</u> her friends <u>prefer</u> to speak
       C   D

Japanese together. <u>No error</u>
        E

24. The Berlin Wall, <u>which</u> became the <u>most potent</u>
         A   B

symbol <u>of the Cold War</u>, <u>constructed</u> in 1961.
        C   D

<u>No error</u>
 E

25. Larry McMurtry's <u>short</u> novel *The Last Picture Show*
          A

<u>perfectly</u> captures the atmosphere of a small Texas
 B

town <u>and</u> the loneliness <u>of its inhabitants</u>. <u>No error</u>
    C   D   E

26. Mrs. Ramsay told us that, since only one <u>slice of</u>
                               A

apple pie was left, <u>she</u> <u>would not be able</u> <u>to offer</u>
             B   C   D

us any desert. <u>No error</u>
        E

27. Today's student <u>frequently choose</u> a college degree
            A

program <u>that</u> <u>leads to</u> a <u>specific</u> career. <u>No error</u>
      B   C   D   E

28. This Tibetan restaurant <u>serving</u> several varieties
               A

stuffed dumplings <u>as well as</u> some <u>excellent</u>
            B   C

and hearty soups, unlike the restaurant

<u>around the corner</u>. <u>No error</u>
    D   E

29. In the 1950s, painters Jackson Pollock and

James Brooks <u>developed</u> <u>the idea of</u> automatism:
        A   B

<u>to drip</u> and throwing paint <u>spontaneously</u> across
 C   D

an unprimed canvas. <u>No error</u>
          E

GO ON TO THE NEXT PAGE ▷

KAPLAN

Directions: The following passage is an early draft of an essay. Some parts of the passage need to be rewritten.

Read the passage and select the best answer for each question that follows. Some questions are about particular sentences or parts of sentences and ask you to improve sentence structure or word choice. Other questions ask you to consider organization and development. In choosing answers, follow the conventions of standard written English.

---

(1) It is generally accepted as a theory among scientists that a change in atmospheric phenomena may signal pending changes to the Earth's climate. (2) Consequently, when NASA began to document increased sightings of noctilucent clouds in the latter half of the twentieth century, the agency institutes plans for a study to determine the cause, and to learn what effect, if any, this may have on future weather patterns. (3) Noctilucent, or night-shining, clouds are virtually unknown to most people, even those that star-gaze on a regular basis. (4) This is because NCLs (as they are known in the scientific community) generally occur north of 50° latitude, above the polar region. (5) These clouds, however, are becoming increasingly visible in areas farther south. (6) In 1999, a dramatic display of NCLs appearing over Colorado and Utah, nearly 10° below the latitudes where scientists have come to expect them. (7) Sightings in Europe have also become more frequent in the past 50 years, for reasons that remain unclear. (8) Ordinary clouds occur approximately 10 kilometers from the Earth's surface. (9) Noctilucent clouds are found at about 82 kilometers. (10) This is more than seven times higher than commercial airlines fly. (11) Although most scientists believe NCLs are formed of ice crystals, but some are convinced that they are composed of cosmic or volcanic dust. (12) This theory is most likely attributable to the fact that the first NCL sightings were documented following a large volcanic explosion in Indonesia.

30. In context, what is the best version of sentence 1 (reproduced below)?

    It is generally accepted as a theory among scientists that a change in atmospheric phenomena may signal pending changes to the Earth's climate.

    (A) (As it is now)
    (B) Generally accepted by scientists as a theory, a change in atmospheric phenomena may signal pending changes to the Earth's climate.
    (C) Scientists generally accepting the theory that a change in atmospheric phenomena may signal pending changes to the Earth's climate.
    (D) Scientists generally accept the theory that a change in atmospheric phenomena may signal pending changes to the Earth's climate.
    (E) Scientists, having generally accepted the theory that a change in atmospheric phenomena may signal pending changes to the Earth's climate.

GO ON TO THE NEXT PAGE

KAPLAN

31. In context, what revision is required in sentence 2 (reproduced below)?

    Consequently, when NASA began to document increased sightings of noctilucent clouds in the latter half of the twentieth century, the agency institutes plans for a study to determine the cause, and to learn what effect, if any, this may have on future weather patterns.

    (A) Eliminate "Consequently."

    (B) Change "institutes" to "instituted."

    (C) Change "for a study" to "for studying."

    (D) Change "and" to "but."

    (E) Change "may have" to "may have had."

32. Which of the following is the best version of the underlined portion of sentence 3 (reproduced below)?

    Noctilucent, or night-shining, clouds are virtually unknown to <u>most people, even those that star-gaze on a regular basis</u>.

    (A) (As it is now)

    (B) more people, even those that star-gaze on a regular basis

    (C) most people, even them that star-gaze on a regular basis

    (D) most people, even them who star-gaze on a regular basis

    (E) most people, even those who star-gaze on a regular basis

33. In context, which of the following is the best way to phrase the underlined portion of sentence 6 (reproduced below)?

    In 1999, <u>a dramatic display of NCLs appearing over Colorado and Utah</u>, nearly 10° below the latitudes where scientists have come to expect them.

    (A) (As it is now)

    (B) a dramatic display of NCLs appears over Colorado and Utah

    (C) a dramatic display of NCLs appeared over Colorado and Utah

    (D) appearing over Colorado and Utah was a dramatic display of NCLs

    (E) over Colorado and Utah there appeared a dramatic display of NCLs

GO ON TO THE NEXT PAGE

34. Which of the following is the best way to combine sentences 8, 9, and 10 (reproduced below)?

    Ordinary clouds occur approximately 10 kilometers from the Earth's surface. Noctilucent clouds are found at about 82 kilometers. This is more than seven times higher than commercial airlines fly.

    (A) Ordinary clouds occur approximately 10 kilometers from the Earth's surface, noctilucent clouds are found at about 82 kilometers, and this is more than seven times higher than commercial airlines fly.

    (B) Ordinary clouds occur approximately 10 kilometers from the Earth's surface; while noctilucent clouds, being found at about 82 kilometers, which is more than seven times higher than commercial airlines fly.

    (C) Ordinary clouds occur approximately 10 kilometers from the Earth's surface, but noctilucent clouds are found at about 82 kilometers, which is more than seven times higher than commercial airlines fly.

    (D) Ordinary clouds occur approximately 10 kilometers from the Earth's surface, so noctilucent clouds are found at about 82 kilometer, which is more than seven times higher than commercial airlines fly.

    (E) Ordinary clouds occurring approximately 10 kilometers from the Earth's surface, and noctilucent clouds at about 82 kilometers, more than seven times higher than commercial airlines fly.

35. In context, what revision is necessary in sentence 11 (reproduced below)?

    Although most scientists believe NCLs are formed of ice crystals, but some are convinced that they are composed of cosmic or volcanic dust.

    (A) Eliminate "Although" and change "but" to "or."
    (B) Eliminate "Although" and change "but" to "because."
    (C) Change "but" to "or."
    (D) Change "but" to "while."
    (E) Eliminate "but."

IF YOU FINISH BEFORE TIME IS CALLED, YOU MAY CHECK YOUR WORK ON THIS SECTION ONLY. DO NOT TURN TO ANY OTHER SECTION IN THE TEST.   STOP

KAPLAN

SECTION 5
Time—25 Minutes
18 Questions

Directions: For this section, solve each problem and decide which is the best of the choices given. Fill in the corresponding oval on the answer sheet. You may use any available space for scratchwork.

Notes:

(1) Calculator use is permitted.

(2) All numbers used are real numbers.

(3) Figures are provided for some problems. All figures are drawn to scale and lie in a plane UNLESS otherwise indicated.

(4) Unless otherwise specified, the domain of any function f is assumed to be the set of all real numbers x for which $f(x)$ is a real number.

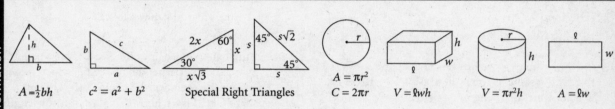

$A = \frac{1}{2}bh$ $c^2 = a^2 + b^2$ Special Right Triangles $A = \pi r^2$ $V = \ell wh$ $V = \pi r^2 h$ $A = \ell w$ $C = 2\pi r$

The sum of the degree measures of the angles in a triangle is 180.
The number of degrees of arc in a circle is 360.
A straight angle has a degree measure of 180.

1. If $3\sqrt{x} - 31 = -13$, what is x?

   (A) 6
   (B) 18
   (C) 36
   (D) 49
   (E) 72

2. Find the value of x if $\frac{3x-9}{2x+7} = 8$.

   (A) −5
   (B) −3
   (C) 1
   (D) 4
   (E) 5

3. Points P and Q are on the standard xy-plane. P has coordinates $(-2, 4)$, and Q has coordinates $(5, -2)$. What is the distance between P and Q?

   (A) 4
   (B) 7
   (C) $3\sqrt{5}$
   (D) $\sqrt{13}$
   (E) $\sqrt{85}$

4. For all u and v, let ∇ be defined by $u \nabla v = u - v + 2$. What is the value of $(2\nabla 3)\nabla 1$?

   (A) 0
   (B) 1
   (C) 2
   (D) 3
   (E) 4

GO ON TO THE NEXT PAGE

KAPLAN

5. If a and b are multiples of 3, which of the following CANNOT also be a multiple of 3?

    (A) $a + b$

    (B) $a - b$

    (C) $a + b + 1$

    (D) ab

    (E) $ab + 3$

6. If the length of one side of a triangle is 5, which of the following CANNOT be the lengths of the other two sides of the triangle?

    (A) 3 and 3

    (B) 3 and 5

    (C) 7 and 8

    (D) 7 and 3

    (E) 7 and 12

7. If k and s are positive integers and the ratio of $2k$ to $6s$ is the same as the ratio of $6k + 5$ to $18s + 10$, which of the following must be true?

    I. $k = s$
    II. $k = 1.5$
    III. $k = 1.5s$

    (A) None

    (B) I only

    (C) II only

    (D) III only

    (E) I and II

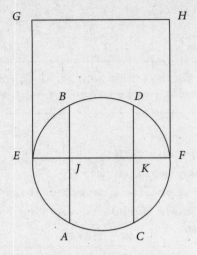

Note: Figure not drawn to scale

8. In the figure above lines $\overline{BA}$ and $\overline{DC}$ have equal length, and are perpendicular to $\overline{EF}$, which passes through the center of the circle. If the area of square $GEFH$ is 81, and $JK = 5$, what is the length of $\overline{EJ}$?

    (A) 2

    (B) 3

    (C) 4

    (D) 6

    (E) 9

GO ON TO THE NEXT PAGE

KAPLAN

Directions: For Student-Produced Response questions 9–18, use the grids at the bottom of the answer sheet page on which you have answered questions 1–8.

Each of the remaining 10 questions requires you to solve the problem and enter your answer by marking the ovals in the special grid, as shown in the example below. You may use any available space for scratch work.

Answer: 1.25 or $\frac{5}{4}$ or 5/4

Write answer in → boxes.

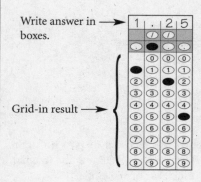

Grid-in result →

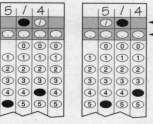

Fraction line
Decimal point

Either position is correct.

You may start your answers in any column, space permitting. Columns not needed should be left blank.

- It is recommended, though not required, that you write your answer in the boxes at the top of the columns. However, you will receive credit only for darkening the ovals correctly.

- Grid only one answer to a question, even though some problems have more than one correct answer.

- Darken no more than one oval in a column.

- No answers are negative.

- Mixed numbers cannot be gridded. For example: the number $1\frac{1}{4}$ must be gridded as 1.25 or 5/4.

  (If [1 | 1 | / | 4] is gridded, it will be interpreted as $\frac{11}{4}$ not $1\frac{1}{4}$.)

- **Decimal Accuracy:** Decimal answers must be entered as accurately as possible. For example, if you obtain an answer such as 0.1666…, you should record the result as .166 or .167. **Less accurate values such as .16 or .17 are not acceptable.**

Acceptable ways to grid $\frac{1}{6}$ = .1666…

9. The figure above shows $f(x)$, a quadratic function. What is one solution of this function?

10. To borrow a single book from a lending library, Mr. Brown was charged $2 for 2 weeks, plus a fine of $.15 per day for every day he was late returning it. If he paid a total of $4.55, how many days did he have the book?

GO ON TO THE NEXT PAGE

KAPLAN

11. Points V, W, X, Y and Z lie on a line in that order. VW is twice as long as WX and $\overline{XY}$ is half as long as YZ. If the length of segment $\overline{WY}$ is 6, what is the length of segment $\overline{VZ}$?

$\blacksquare -AA = AA$

12. In the equation above, AA represents a positive, two-digit number in which both digits are the same. If the number that has been covered by the box is a positive, three-digit number that is divisible by 3, what is one possible value of the covered number?

13. Kelly has 25 pairs of pants and 32 shirts in her closet. If she wants to pick out an outfit consisting of a pair of pants and a shirt, how many different outfits could she wear?

14. The last Monday of a 31-day month must be at least how many days after the first Friday of the same month?

15. For positive integers a and b, let a ~ b be defined by $a \sim b = a + (a-1) + (a-2) + \dots + b$. For example, $9 \sim 4 = 9 + 8 + 7 + 6 + 5 + 4 = 39$. What is the value of $(100 \sim 5) - (98 \sim 3)$?

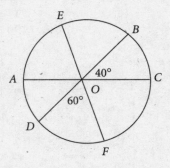

16. In the circle above, $\overline{AC}$, $\overline{BD}$, and $\overline{EF}$ pass through center O. The area of sector AOE is equal to what fraction of the total area of the circle?

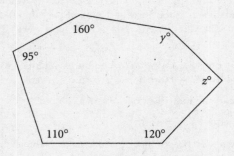

17. In the figure above, what is the sum of y and z?

18. Tameka cleans her house every 7 days and does laundry every 5 days. In the next 315 days, how many times will she have to clean her house <u>and</u> do laundry on the same day?

IF YOU FINISH BEFORE TIME IS CALLED, YOU MAY CHECK YOUR WORK ON THIS SECTION ONLY. DO NOT TURN TO ANY OTHER SECTION IN THE TEST.   STOP

KAPLAN

SECTION 6

Time—25 Minutes
24 Questions

Directions: For each of the following questions, choose the best answer and darken the corresponding oval on the answer sheet.

Each sentence below has one or two blanks, each blank indicating that something has been omitted. Beneath the sentence are five words or sets of words labeled A through E. Choose the word or set of words that, when inserted in the sentence, best fits the meaning of the sentence as a whole.

Example:

Today's small, portable computers contrast markedly with the earliest electronic computers, which were -------.

(A) effective
(B) invented
(C) useful
(D) destructive
(E) enormous

1. Jamal found the movie stubs lying on the counter to be ------- evidence that his friends had gone to the cinema without him; it was unquestionable that they had seen Spiderman.

(A) immaterial
(B) potential
(C) incriminating
(D) nominal
(E) indisputable

2. When training for a marathon, runners prepare themselves for a challenge that is both ------- and mentally -------.

(A) illusory . . taxing
(B) exaggerated . . balanced
(C) physically . . demanding
(D) appealing . . indulgent
(E) strenuous . . dubious

3. Healthy lifestyle choices such as exercising regularly and maintaining a nutritious diet can promote ------- yet are often ------- by the busy lives people today lead.

(A) extinction . . enhanced
(B) longevity . . hampered
(C) behavior . . belied
(D) mortality . . bolstered
(E) reproduction . . confirmed

4. Despite his apparent ------- lifestyle, the old man was known to drink to excess when visited by friends.

(A) temperate
(B) laconic
(C) duplicitous
(D) aesthetic
(E) voluble

5. Nostradamus gained a reputation for ------- as he accurately predicted events such as wars complete with descriptions of vehicles that were not invented until after the 16th century when he wrote about his presages.

(A) prescience
(B) sincerity
(C) avarice
(D) complicity
(E) mendacity

GO ON TO THE NEXT PAGE

KAPLAN

Directions: The passages below are followed by questions based on their content; questions following a pair of related passages may also be based on the relationship between the paired passages. Answer the questions on the basis of what is <u>stated</u> or <u>implied</u> in the passages and in any introductory material that may be provided.

Questions 6–9 refer to the following passages.

Passage 1

Acid rain clouds, formed by the release of gases from burning fossil fuels, join with existing weather patterns and eventually pour down toxic, highly acidic water droplets that can cause signifi-
(5) cant and often irreversible environmental damage. However, nuclear power and renewable energy technologies—those that take advantage of continuously-available resources such as the sea, sun, and various biofuels—can generate electricity
(10) without giving off the gases that contribute to acid rain, and there are even proven ways to effectively sequester the harmful gases generated by fossil fuel plants. Yet as acid rain continues to seriously damage countless waterways, forests, crops, and
(15) even to erode buildings, senselessly little is being done to take advantage of these new technologies.

Passage 2

While the world's most-developed nations have the luxury of squabbling over the political and environmental questions raised by those who
(20) actually have energy choices, the developing world usually has only one resource to turn to: coal. One of the cheapest and most plentiful sources of energy in the world, coal is used to generate nearly 40 percent of the world's electricity. But when
(25) burned, coal releases large amounts of carbon dioxide—a gas that, when present in excess, can cause a whole host of serious respiratory diseases. So while wealthy nations can complain about global warming and acid rain, the rest of the
(30) world must struggle to cope with the immediate human damage caused by the only natural resource they can afford.

6. In Passage 1, the author's attitude towards the continuing presence of acid rain is best described as

(A) astonishment that acid rain remains a
problem in the developed world

(B) frustration that the use of cleaner technologies
is not more widespread

(C) irritation that nothing is being done to curb
the creation of acid rain

(D) impatience towards plants that refuse to adopt
experimental technologies

(E) skepticism that irreversible damage is really
being done to the environment

7. In Passage 2, the author characterizes "the world's most-developed nations" (line 17) as which of the following?

(A) Insensitive
(B) Responsible
(C) Privileged
(D) Reckless
(E) Impoverished

GO ON TO THE NEXT PAGE ⟩

8. How would the author of Passage 2 most likely respond to the assertion in Passage 1 that "senselessly little" (line 15) is being done to take advantage of new and cleaner energy-generation technologies?

   (A) Wealthier nations have a responsibility to create opportunities for those less fortunate

   (B) Most countries would adopt these technologies if they were affordable

   (C) The environmental impact of an energy source is just as important as the cost of energy

   (D) Environmental damage is less significant than damage to humans

   (E) Not all countries can afford these technologies

9. The authors of both passages agree that

   (A) clean energy technologies are more expensive than conventional methods

   (B) acid rain is a problem inevitably created by energy generation

   (C) the burning of fossil fuels can release harmful gases

   (D) the environmental debate over energy generation is only intensifying

   (E) the human and environmental impacts of energy generation are equally important

Questions 10–15 refer to the following passage.

When I accepted a volunteer position as a social worker at a domestic violence shelter in a developing nation, I imagined the position for which my university experience had prepared me. I envi-
(5) sioned conducting intake interviews and traipsing around from organization to organization seeking the legal, psychological, and financial support that the women would need to rebuild their lives. When I arrived, I felt as if I already had months of experi-
(10) ence, experience garnered in the hypothetical situations I had invented and subsequently resolved single-handedly and seamlessly. I felt thoroughly prepared to tackle head-on the situation I assumed was waiting for me.
(15)   I arrived full of zeal, knocking at the shelter's door. Within moments, my reality made a sharp break from that which I had anticipated. The coordinator explained that the shelter's need for financial self-sufficiency had become obvious and acute.
(20) To address this, the center was planning to open a bakery. I immediately enthused about the project, making many references to the small enterprise case studies I had researched at the university. In response to my impassioned reply, the coordinator
(25) declared me in charge of the bakery and left in order to "get out of my way." At that moment, I was as prepared to bake bread as I was to run for political office. The bigger problem, however, was that I was completely unfamiliar with the for-profit
(30) business models necessary to run the bakery. I was out of my depth in a foreign river with only my coordinator's confidence to keep me afloat.
   They say that necessity is the mother of invention. I soon found that it is also the mother of initiative. I
(35) began finding recipes and appropriating the expertise of friends. With their help making bread, balancing books, printing pamphlets and making contacts, the bakery was soon running smoothly and successfully. After a short time it became a significant
(40) source of income for the house.
   In addition to funds, baking bread provided a natural environment in which to work with and get to know the women of the shelter. Kneading dough

GO ON TO THE NEXT PAGE

side by side, I shared in the camaraderie of the
(45) kitchen, treated to stories about their children and
the towns and jobs they had to leave behind to
ensure their safety. Baking helped me develop strong
relationships with the women and advanced my
understanding of their situations. It also improved
(50) the women's self-esteem. Their ability to master a
new skill gave them confidence in themselves, and
the fact that the bakery contributed to the upkeep of
the house gave the women, many of them newly
single, a sense of pride and the conviction that they
(55) had the capability to support themselves.

Baking gave me the opportunity to work in a
capacity I had not at all anticipated, but one that
proved very successful. I became a more sensitive
and skillful social worker, capable of making a
(60) mean seven-grain loaf. Learning to bake gave me
as much newfound self-confidence as it gave the
women, and I found that sometimes quality social
work can be as simple as kneading dough.

10. The primary purpose of the passage is to show
how the author

(A) was shocked by the discrepancy between her
earlier ideas about her work and the reality
she faced

(B) discovered a talent her overly-focused mind
had never allowed her to explore

(C) broadened how she defined the scope of
her work

(D) developed her abilities to orchestrate
a for-profit business enterprise

(E) was abroad when she encountered and
overcame a challenging situation

11. The statement that the author arrived "full of
zeal" (line 15) indicates that she was

(A) anxious and insecure

(B) eager and interested

(C) confident but uninformed

(D) cheerful but exhausted

(E) enthusiastic but incompetent

12. The author was initially enthusiastic about the
idea of the bakery because she

(A) considered it from a theoretical point of view

(B) hoped to obtain a leadership position in
the bakery

(C) wanted to demonstrate her baking knowledge
to her new coordinator

(D) believed it would be a good way to build the
women's self-esteem

(E) was a strong proponent of self-sufficiency
projects for non-profit organizations

13. The comparison in lines 26–28 ("At that
moment...political office") demonstrates the
author's belief that

(A) the bakery would never be a success

(B) social workers should not be involved in either
baking or politics

(C) it was unfair of the coordinator to ask the
author to run the bakery

(D) similar skills were involved in both baking
and politics

(E) she was unqualified for a job baking bread

GO ON TO THE NEXT PAGE

14. Lines 28–30 ("The bigger…models") suggest that the author believed that

(A) learning the necessary business practices would be a more daunting challenge than learning to bake bread

(B) good business practices are more important to running a successful bakery than is the quality of the bread

(C) her coordinator's confidence in for-profit business models was misplaced

(D) for-profit business models are significantly more complex than the non-profit models with which she was familiar

(E) her coordinator would be unwilling to help her

15. The last sentence ("Learning…dough") indicates that the author

(A) lacked self-confidence just as much as the women with whom she worked

(B) found that performing social work is surprisingly easy with no education

(C) underestimated her own ability to learn new skills

(D) discovered that social work is more effective when it includes tactile activities

(E) derived a benefit from her work while helping others

Questions 16–24 refer to the following passage.

This passage discusses some recreational options and reasons for making good use of leisure time.

Recreation is a vital aspect of human life, because it provides one with opportunities to recreate oneself. *Recreation* can be defined as the refreshment of mind or body through activity that

(5) stimulates or amuses. This definition invites one to both contemplate the myriad options for recreational activity and evaluate these options for their potential to enrich one's life and enhance personal growth and development.

(10)   The modern economic system has freed people from the necessity to relentlessly seek daily sustenance, and thus has augmented leisure, or recreational, time. Many choose to recreate by engaging in physical competition, namely sports. Former

(15) athletes cite their experiences in wrestling, tennis, football, or soccer by way of elucidating their successes in business, government, or academia. For instance, they commend coaches who taught them to gracefully handle conflict and disappoint-

(20) ment; or they vividly recount a specific moment of competition that transformed their lives forever.

Competition, proponents say, gives athletes a profound understanding of both their limits and their abilities. The ability to candidly analyze one's

(25) strengths and weaknesses confers resilience in the face of life's vicissitudes and thus the ability to overcome obstacles.

On the other hand, some athletes shun organized sports, preferring to test themselves physically with-

(30) out the element of competition. They may hike or bike, snowboard or ski, or run or ride alone or with companions. They contend that their bodies and spirits are best refreshed without the distraction of needless comparison with others.

(35)   Taking a different approach, many people engage in artistic and creative pursuits as a means of recreating themselves. In an academic environment of standardized testing, which directs minds down ever-narrowing avenues of thought, propo-

(40) nents of the arts point to the mental and

GO ON TO THE NEXT PAGE ⇒

KAPLAN

emotional flexibility developed by creative activity. For example, art teaches one how to exercise the exquisite faculty of judgment in the absence of rules. It sets forth dilemmas to be resolved, *(45)* demonstrating that every problem has more than one solution. Practitioners of the arts learn to swim in a turbulent sea of ambiguity and chance without the lifejacket of standard procedure; in other words, art prepares them for the exigencies *(50)* of life.

   Productive leisure activities amplify one's vocational efforts and increase chances of success. They enhance an understanding of one's place in the world. They facilitate full use of one's capacities *(55)* and provide pleasure that enhances all of life's experiences.

16. The author's primary purpose in writing this passage is to

   (A) describe the propensity of successful people for athletic participation

   (B) compare the theoretical benefits of physical versus artistic activities

   (C) convince the reader of the pleasurable nature of recreational pursuits

   (D) promote the tangible and intangible benefits of productive leisure activities

   (E) engage in speculation about the requisites for vocational success

17. The author's statement that "the modern economic system has freed people from the necessity to relentlessly seek daily sustenance" (lines 10–12) suggests that increased leisure time is

   (A) always preferable to work

   (B) a consequence of shortened work days

   (C) becoming more scarce, and hence more valuable

   (D) closely related to democratic forms of government

   (E) ideally engaged in on a daily basis

18. According to the second paragraph of the passage, which of the following is a lifelong benefit of engaging in competition?

   (A) increased persistence in surmounting difficulties

   (B) heightened sensitivity to inherent lack of ability

   (C) the capacity to always prevail in life's struggles

   (D) a lifelong engagement with physical activity

   (E) gratitude to those who help one, such as coaches

19. The concept of *competition* is mentioned in line 14 for which of the following reasons?

   (A) to strengthen the case for competition as an element of proper recreation

   (B) to distract the reader from the importance of comparative physical activities

   (C) to acknowledge that enjoyment is more important than competition in recreation

   (D) to contend that athletics without competition is meaningless

   (E) to emphasize that the benefits of physical recreation do not necessarily have to include competition

20. According to the passage, advantages of recreational pursuit of the arts include which of the following?

   I. Tolerance of uncertainty
   II. Ability to exercise independent judgment in unanticipated situations
   III. Appreciation of aesthetic presentation

   (A) I only

   (B) II only

   (C) I and II only

   (D) II and III only

   (E) I, II and III

GO ON TO THE NEXT PAGE

21. In line 50 "exigencies" most nearly means

    (A) crises

    (B) waves

    (C) situations

    (D) motivations

    (E) rules

22. The author's statement about standardized testing in schools "direct[ing] minds down ever-narrowing avenues of thought" suggests a conviction that such testing is

    (A) necessary

    (B) irrelevant

    (C) limiting

    (D) productive

    (E) creative

23. The author of this passage is primarily interested in which of the following aspects of recreation?

    (A) its benefits for society at large

    (B) the physical and emotional flexibility it confers

    (C) its role as requisite for vocational success

    (D) its benefits for the whole life of the individual

    (E) its ubiquitous position in the human psyche

24. The author uses the metaphor "learn to swim in a turbulent sea of ambiguity and chance without the lifejacket of standard procedure" (lines 46–49) for what purpose

    (A) to show that artists know how to swim

    (B) to show that artists live according to strict rules

    (C) to show that artists and athletes see the world the same way

    (D) to show that artists live without boundaries

    (E) to show the need for a life jacket

IF YOU FINISH BEFORE TIME IS CALLED, YOU MAY CHECK YOUR WORK ON THIS SECTION ONLY. DO NOT TURN TO ANY OTHER SECTION IN THE TEST. STOP

SECTION 7

Time—20 Minutes

16 Questions

Directions: For this section, solve each problem and decide which is the best of the choices given. Fill in the corresponding oval on the answer sheet. You may use any available space for scratchwork.

Notes:

(1) Calculator use is permitted.

(2) All numbers used are real numbers.

(3) Figures are provided for some problems. All figures are drawn to scale and lie in a plane UNLESS otherwise indicated.

(4) Unless otherwise specified, the domain of any function f is assumed to be the set of all real numbers x for which $f(x)$ is a real number.

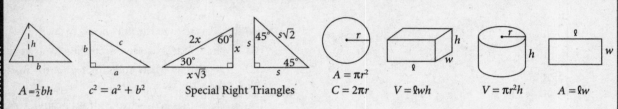

$A = \frac{1}{2}bh$ $c^2 = a^2 + b^2$ Special Right Triangles $A = \pi r^2$ $V = \ell wh$ $V = \pi r^2 h$ $A = \ell w$
$C = 2\pi r$

The sum of the degree measures of the angles in a triangle is 180.
The number of degrees of arc in a circle is 360.
A straight angle has a degree measure of 180.

---

1. If $8a < 3b$ and $3b < 10c$, which of the following must be true?

    (A) $8a < 10c$

    (B) $10c < 8a$

    (C) $c < a$

    (D) $8a = 10c$

    (E) $8a + 1 = 10c$

Department	Number of Teams	Employees per Team
Development	1	4
Marketing	2	3
Accounting	3	2
Public Relations	5	5

2. The chart above shows the distribution of employees at a company into different teams in different departments. According to the chart, how many total employees are there?

    (A) 14

    (B) 25

    (C) 41

    (D) 84

    (E) 154

GO ON TO THE NEXT PAGE

3. If the average (arithmetic mean) of 7 numbers is greater than 7 and less than 12, which of the following could be the sum of the 7 numbers?

(A) 84

(B) 77

(C) 49

(D) 42

(E) 35

4. Carmel is spinning a basketball on his finger so that it turns around completely every 1.5 seconds. How many degrees does the logo on the ball turn in 10 seconds, assuming it is not on the spinning axis?

(A) 54°

(B) 240°

(C) 720°

(D) 2,160°

(E) 2,400°

Questions 5 and 6 refer to the following figure:

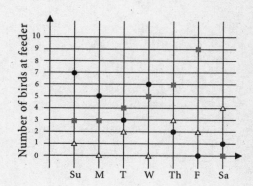

5. Joe kept a record of the birds that visited his backyard for one week. He set out three types of feeders and counted the number of birds that visited each feeder each day. In the graph above, each feeder is represented by a different colored dot. The black circles indicate the feeder with sunflower seeds. The gray squares represent the feeder with thistle seeds. The white triangles represent the feeder with suet. Approximately what percentage of the birds in Joe's yard on Thursday visited the suet feeder?

(A) 18%

(B) 27%

(C) 36%

(D) 48%

(E) 55%

6. On what day did the greatest number of birds eat sunflower seeds?

(A) Sunday

(B) Tuesday

(C) Wednesday

(D) Friday

(E) Saturday

GO ON TO THE NEXT PAGE

KAPLAN

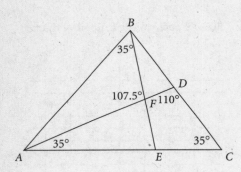

Note: Figure not drawn to scale

7. In triangle *ABC* above, $\overline{AD}$ and $\overline{BE}$ are line segments. All of the following are isosceles triangles, EXCEPT

(A) Triangle *AFE*

(B) Triangle *ABE*

(C) Triangle *ADC*

(D) Triangle *BFD*

(E) Triangle *ABC*

Questions 8–10 refer to the following sequence of steps.

Choose a number between 0 and 9.9.

Multiply the number from the previous step by 100.

Determine the smallest integer greater than or equal to the number obtained from the previous step.

Add 12 to the number found in the previous step.

Print the resulting number.

8. If 6.127 is the number chosen in step 1, what is the number printed in step 5?

(A) 12

(B) 74

(C) 624

(D) 624.7

(E) 625

9. Which of the following could be a number printed in step 5 after steps 1 through 4 are performed?

(A) −1

(B) 10

(C) 27.3

(D) 674

(E) 1,050

10. Which change, if any, could be made in the order of the steps without changing the number printed in step 5?

(A) Only steps 2 and 3 could be switched.

(B) Only steps 2 and 4 could be switched.

(C) Only steps 3 and 4 could be switched.

(D) Steps 2, 3, and 4 can be done in any order.

(E) None of the above changes can be made.

11. If $x = 3^5$, which of the following expressions is equal to 3^{11}?

(A) $243x$

(B) $3x^2$

(C) $9x^4$

(D) $27x^3$

(E) x^6

12. If $n - 3 = 7 + m$, what is the value of $2(n - m) + 4$?

(A) 8

(B) 12

(C) 17

(D) 24

(E) 29

13. If $x = -5$ satisfies the equation $x^2 + 3x + c = 0$, where c is a constant, what is another value of x that satisfies the equation?

(A) −2

(B) 2

(C) 5

(D) 7

(E) 10

GO ON TO THE NEXT PAGE

14. The sum of three consecutive odd integers is 1,089. What is the greatest integer of the three?

    (A) 185
    (B) 299
    (C) 317
    (D) 365
    (E) 423

15. Jan can mow her lawn in 60 minutes by herself. If she hires Wally to do it, he takes 30 minutes, while Peter can do it in 40 minutes. If Jan starts mowing the lawn for 15 minutes, then decides to hire Wally and Peter to help her finish, how long will it take (in hours), from when Jan started to when the three finished together?

    (A) $\frac{1}{6}$ hours

    (B) $\frac{5}{12}$ hours

    (C) $\frac{7}{12}$ hours

    (D) $\frac{3}{4}$ hours

    (E) $\frac{5}{6}$ hours

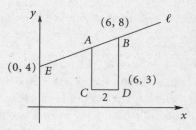

Note: Figure not drawn to scale

16. In the figure above, quadrilateral $ABDC$ has vertices A and B on line ℓ, point E is also on line ℓ, and the coordinates of B, D, and E are as indicated. What is the area of $ABDC$?

    (A) $\frac{1}{2}$

    (B) $\frac{4}{3}$

    (C) $\frac{11}{3}$

    (D) $\frac{22}{3}$

    (E) $\frac{26}{3}$

IF YOU FINISH BEFORE TIME IS CALLED, YOU MAY CHECK YOUR WORK ON THIS SECTION ONLY. DO NOT TURN TO ANY OTHER SECTION IN THE TEST.

STOP

KAPLAN

SECTION 8

Time—20 Minutes
18 Questions

> **Directions:** For each of the following questions, choose the best answer and darken the corresponding oval on the answer sheet.

Each sentence below has one or two blanks, each blank indicating that something has been omitted. Beneath the sentence are five words or sets of words labeled A through E. Choose the word or set of words that, when inserted in the sentence, <u>best</u> fits the meaning of the sentence as a whole.

Example:

Today's small, portable computers contrast markedly with the earliest electronic computers, which were -------.

(A) effective

(B) invented

(C) useful

(D) destructive

(E) enormous   Ⓐ Ⓑ Ⓒ Ⓓ ●

1. ------ two doses of the Hepatitis A vaccine over a period of six to twelve months is ------- providing protection from the disease for ten years.

   (A) Constraining .. required for

   (B) Distributing .. unsuccessful in

   (C) Reconstituting .. instrumental in

   (D) Administering .. effective in

   (E) Disseminating .. unverified for

2. After all of the passengers were safely aboard lifeboats, the crew of the King Cruiser made every attempt to ------- what scuba diving equipment they could off of the ------- dive boat before it sank.

   (A) qualify .. obsolete

   (B) salvage .. floundering

   (C) exacerbate .. defunct

   (D) revitalize .. prosperous

   (E) commandeer .. lucrative

3. Many towns bordering two different countries have a heterogeneous population and can boast of a ------- of different foods that incorporate a ------- of various ingredients.

   (A) multiplicity .. variety

   (B) proliferation .. moderation

   (C) ambivalence .. focus

   (D) dearth .. depletion

   (E) abridgment .. imitation

4. Despite the markings that ranked the trail as moderately difficult, the hikers found the trek to be challenging as the path was -------; it meandered ceaselessly around the riverbank for miles.

   (A) panoramic

   (B) precipitous

   (C) serpentine

   (D) circumscribed

   (E) retrograde

5. After the accident Jidapa's friends found that her behavior had changed drastically; once sprightly and friendly, she now seemed disheartened and unaffable, the ------- of her former self.

   (A) remnant

   (B) antithesis

   (C) consequence

   (D) extremity

   (E) mainstay

6. The detectives knew they had to act punctiliously because any mistakes, even the slightest -------, would compromise the stakeout.

   (A) query

   (B) gibe

   (C) gaffe

   (D) tryst

   (E) tribute

GO ON TO THE NEXT PAGE →

Directions: The passages below are followed by questions based on their content; questions following a pair of related passages may also be based on the relationship between the paired passages. Answer the questions on the basis of what is <u>stated</u> or <u>implied</u> in the passages and in any introductory material that may be provided.

Questions 7–18 refer to the following passages.

The following passages represent two points of view about the future of cinema. The first is by a screenwriter arguing for a change in methodology. The second is by a film critic expressing his views on the changing world of film.

Passage 1

Ancient Greek drama, often cited as the crucible of all Western drama, consisted of three types of plays. *Comedy* was a form greatly affected by changing times and fashions; *tragedy* was inspired
(5) by mythology and history. The ancient Greeks believed that the dark and brooding form of tragedy required a "relief." Still common today, a relief is designed to be a moment of respite from the seriousness of the tragic theme. *Satyr* plays
(10) fulfilled that function in ancient Greece. Of these three forms, tragedy has received the most critical and scholarly attention in modern times. It is the Satyr play, however, that will capture the imagination of the rising generation.
(15) A Satyr is a mythological creature—half-human and half-beast. This creature appears on stage in the Satyr plays as a character whose main function is to be part of the coterie of the god Dionysus, a central figure in the Greek theater. Even without
(20) the exact characters of Dionysus or the Satyrs, the ideas they embody can still be used in playwriting or screenwriting today. As ardent followers of their leader, the Satyrs in the plays display a curious mix of cowardice and boldness similar to what we
(25) see in Shakespeare's Falstaff.

The chorus is another dynamic element of the Satyr play that is full of potential. The chorus, sometimes dancing or singing, can be invisible to the central characters. In this mode, members of
(30) the chorus are free to engage the audience without interfering with the action of the play. At any moment, though, they can step into the world of the play and interact with the other characters. This fundamental boundary crossing is a central reason
(35) that this form lends itself to the modern cinema.

The Satyr form is widely ignored and has barely been acknowledged by critics and scholars. Screenwriters today persist in looking to tragic and comic forms for inspiration when there are
(40) volumes of untapped potential in the Satyr form. The example of the chorus, "unseen" by the central players at one moment and then jumping in to the center of the scene in the next, gives just a hint of what the Satyr form has to offer. If you
(45) seek an even more unpredictable inspiration, imagine the chorus jumping into the action singing and dancing.

Passage 2

Of the two primary forms of drama—comedy and tragedy—comedy is the more promising form
(50) for the future of cinema. Comedy has always been the more stylistically forward form, because it looks to current events for topics and is quick to respond to trends. While some subject matter has been consistent over the centuries (for example,
(55) the lampooning of leaders or the misadventures of husbands and wives), the forms employed in comedy today can only be described as sophisticated. Tragedy, on the other hand, has always looked to the past for subject matter and the form
(60) is consequently nostalgic.

In general, the forms of cinema have become predictable, to the point that the spoofing of some forms has become commonplace. Modern filmmakers' overuse of a small number of narrative devices
(65) has produced a generation of moviegoers who are compelled by twists and turns. Jaded by their overexposure to form, they seek out the new and surprising. It is a difficult task indeed to surprise this generation of media-saturated spectators. But
(70) the comedic form has the requisite flexibility.

GO ON TO THE NEXT PAGE ➜

KAPLAN

There is no limit to the ways in which comedy can transform and conform itself to the requirements of any generation. This assertion is confirmed by the fact that even in ancient Greece, (75) comedy responded to fashion and changing aesthetics. History has proven that comedy suits itself to all times and circumstances. The only theatrical tradition to survive the fall of Rome was comic. Even in the darkest times, or perhaps espe- (80) cially in the darkest times, comedy shines on. The basic human need for comedy and comic relief is one thing that has forced the form toward flexibility. Since people crave comedy, they do whatever they can, using form and structure, to create the (85) kind of comedy they need at the time.

All of this is not to say that making comedy is easy. Although the comic "form" is wildly loose, it is not the least bit forgiving. For this reason, the most impressive work is in the comic form. The discrimi- (90) nating viewer of today's cinema recognizes this fact and rewards successful filmmakers with loyalty. Today's audience seeks variety, excitement, and surprise. The filmmakers most likely to succeed in this market will be those skilled in the comic form (95) and willing to exploit all of its potential.

7. The overall tone of Passage 1 is

(A) muted

(B) strident

(C) whimsical

(D) grateful

(E) enthusiastic

8. As used in Passage 1, "engage" (line 30) most nearly means

(A) contract with

(B) propose marriage to

(C) hire

(D) lock together with

(E) hold the attention of

9. The statement that "there are volumes of untapped potential in the Satyr form" (lines 39–40) suggests that

(A) there are books of Satyr plays not yet translated

(B) numerous movies can be made about Greek drama

(C) many ideas in Satyr plays have not yet been explored

(D) the noise level in Satyr plays is extremely high

(E) there is dormant inspiration in music

10. The author of Passage 1 refers to the chorus in the fourth paragraph primarily in order to

(A) prove the superiority of the comic form

(B) underline the variety and surprise provided by the Satyr form

(C) emphasize the importance of dancing to the future of cinema

(D) contrast the Satyr character with the chorus

(E) explain why the Satyr form is widely ignored

11. In lines 55–56, "the misadventures of husbands and wives" is an example of

(A) a consistent form of Greek comedy

(B) sophisticated subject matter for comedy

(C) nostalgic subject matter for tragedy

(D) traditional subject matter for comedy

(E) a typical Satyric plot

12. As used in Passage 2, the word "Jaded" (line 66) most nearly means

(A) satisfied

(B) rocked

(C) conceited

(D) dulled

(E) surprised

GO ON TO THE NEXT PAGE

13. In Passage 2, the main purpose of the third paragraph is to

    (A) explain the flexibility of the comedic form

    (B) emphasize the importance of ancient Greek civilization

    (C) illustrate the tragedy of the fall of Rome

    (D) correct a general misunderstanding about the rigidity of comedy

    (E) illuminate the significance of intergenerational traditions

14. The word "form" (line 82) is in quotation marks primarily to

    (A) emphasize that the author is using the exact definition of the word

    (B) indicate that the structure of comedy is not as strict as the word suggests

    (C) show that the author intended to use another word

    (D) highlight the difference between theater and cinema

    (E) refer the reader to a previously mentioned definition of the word

15. Both authors would most likely agree that

    (A) ancient Greek theater is relevant to modern cinema

    (B) comedy is one of the most resilient forms of drama

    (C) tragedy is an irrelevant form in entertainment today

    (D) Satyr plays represent a more adaptable form than comedy

    (E) modern audiences are bored by the current cinema

16. Both authors would most likely agree on the value of the

    (A) chorus

    (B) audience

    (C) critic

    (D) screenwriter

    (E) characters

17. The main idea of Passage 2 is that

    (A) comedy and tragedy are superior to the Satyr form

    (B) American cinema has become too predictable

    (C) comedy is superior to tragedy as a form of drama

    (D) the comic form has the greatest promise for reinvigorating cinema

    (E) American moviegoers are anxious for the release of high-quality comedies

18. The author of Passage 2 might respond to the reference to "Shakespeare's Falstaff" (line 25) in Passage 1 by

    (A) criticizing the misuse of such a famous character in support of an unknown art form

    (B) highlighting the added relevance given to Falstaff by comic aspects Shakespeare accords to him

    (C) contending that characters of Greek and Roman drama are more applicable than those of Elizabethan drama

    (D) arguing that Falstaff would make an excellent template for the hero of a Satyr play

    (E) citing Falstaff as an example of the sophistication of the comic form

IF YOU FINISH BEFORE TIME IS CALLED, YOU MAY CHECK YOUR WORK ON THIS SECTION ONLY. DO NOT TURN TO ANY OTHER SECTION IN THE TEST.

STOP

SECTION 9

Time—10 Minutes
14 Questions

Directions: For each question in this section, select the best answer from among the choices given and fill in the corresponding oval on the answer sheet.

The following sentences test correctness and effectiveness of expression. Part of each sentence or the entire sentence is underlined; beneath each sentence are five ways of phrasing the underlined material. Choice A repeats the original phrasing; the other four choices are different. If you think the original phrasing produces a better sentence than any of the alternatives, select choice A; if not, select one of the other choices.

In making your selection, follow the requirements of standard written English; that is, pay attention to grammar, choice of words, sentence construction, and punctuation. Your selection should result in the most effective sentence—clear and precise, without awkwardness or ambiguity.

EXAMPLE: ANSWER:

Every apple in the baskets <u>are ripe and labeled according to the date it was picked</u>.   Ⓐ ● Ⓒ Ⓓ Ⓔ

(A) are ripe and labeled according to the date it was picked
(B) is ripe and labeled according to the date it was picked
(C) are ripe and labeled according to the date they were picked
(D) is ripe and labeled according to the date they were picked
(E) are ripe and labeled as to the date it was picked

---

1. For a hospital, a back-up generator is <u>invaluable so that it</u> provides power in the event of an emergency that disrupts local electrical service.

    (A) invaluable so that it
    (B) invaluable because it
    (C) invaluable, although it
    (D) invaluable in order that
    (E) invaluable because they

2. In his press release, the actor <u>asserted that the media had unfairly biased</u> potential jurors before his trial had even begun.

    (A) asserted that the media had unfairly biased
    (B) asserted of how the media had unfairly biased
    (C) made an assertion of the media having unfairly biased
    (D) made an assertion that the media had unfairly biased
    (E) asserted that unfair bias had been made by the media of

GO ON TO THE NEXT PAGE ⟩

3. During the harvest, French <u>vineyards hiring many temporary workers</u>, a large percentage of whom come from Spain.

   (A) vineyards hiring many temporary workers
   (B) vineyards hires many temporary workers
   (C) vineyards hiring many workers who are temporary
   (D) vineyards hire many temporary workers
   (E) vineyards hire many people who work temporarily

4. <u>In most cases, in the election of a president, the results are determined by a small number of "swing states."</u>

   (A) In most cases, in the election of a president, the results are determined by a small number of "swing states."
   (B) Generally, the results of a president election are determined by a small number of "swing states" most of the time.
   (C) A few "swing states" decide the results of most presidential elections.
   (D) A presidential election, as to results, is most often determined by "swing states," of which there are a small number.
   (E) Presidential elections generally have a small number of "swing states" that determine their results.

5. Vocational and technical schools offer teenagers the opportunity to start working as electricians, plumbers, auto mechanics, <u>and other jobs</u> immediately after graduation

   (A) and other jobs
   (B) and as other jobs
   (C) and working in other jobs
   (D) and other careers
   (E) and in other jobs

6. In a police lineup, witnesses see several people, <u>there is one who is</u> the suspect.

   (A) there is one who is
   (B) because one is
   (C) one is
   (D) one of whom is
   (E) of which one is

7. In the 19th century, European politicians sought to establish a balance of power in the hope that <u>this had prevented war on the continent</u>.

   (A) this had prevented war on the continent
   (B) this would prevent war on the continent
   (C) war on the continent will be prevented
   (D) the continent will find war prevented
   (E) this will prevent war on the continent

GO ON TO THE NEXT PAGE

8. <u>The Vatican City is one of the most visited
sites by tourists in Italy, since it is technically
its own country.</u>

   (A) The Vatican City is one of the most visited
   sites by tourists in Italy, since it is technically
   its own country.

   (B) The Vatican City, one of the most visited sites
   by tourists in Italy, is technically its own
   country.

   (C) Of the most visited sites by tourists in Italy,
   the Vatican City is technically its own
   country.

   (D) Since it is its own country, the Vatican City is
   technically one of the most visited sites by
   tourists in Italy.

   (E) Since it is technically its own country, one of
   the most visited sites by tourists in Italy is
   the Vatican City.

9. In the United States, a candidate must be 35 years
old before <u>you can run</u> for president.

   (A) you can run

   (B) it can run

   (C) he or she can run

   (D) one runs

   (E) he or she is running

10. Among the most complex musical composition of
the era, <u>Chopin wrote his Etudes to be performed
on the piano.</u>

   (A) Chopin wrote his Etudes to be performed on
   the piano

   (B) the piano is what Chopin wrote his Etudes to
   be performed on

   (C) Chopin's Etudes, written to be performed on
   the piano

   (D) Chopin's Etudes were written to be performed
   on the piano

   (E) Chopin, having written his Etudes to be
   performed on the piano

11. The defendant's lawyer told the jury that <u>he was
sorry for the damage he had caused and the
people he had hurt</u>.

   (A) he was sorry for the damage he had caused
   and the people he had hurt

   (B) his client was sorry for the damage he had
   caused and the people he had hurt

   (C) given the damage caused and the people hurt,
   he was sorry

   (D) his client, sorry for the damage he had caused
   and the people he had hurt

   (E) the damage he had caused and the people he
   had hurt were what his client was sorry for

12. <u>Although the first phase of construction was
completed last month and the new wing has
opened</u>, the hospital still suffers from a shortage of
rooms.

   (A) Although the first phase of construction was
   completed last month and the new wing has
   opened

   (B) Although the new wing has opened, following
   the completion of the first phase of
   construction which occurred last month

   (C) The first phase of construction was completed
   last month and the new wing has opened

   (D) The first phase of construction was completed
   last month, resulting in the new wing being
   open but, even so

   (E) The first phase of construction, being
   completed last month, and the new wing
   has opened

GO ON TO THE NEXT PAGE ▷

13. When washing a car, rinse it to remove excess dirt, wipe it with a soapy sponge, and <u>then the car is dried with a clean cloth</u>.

   (A) then the car is dried with a clean cloth
   (B) dry it with a clean cloth
   (C) then drying it with a clean cloth
   (D) finally, it is dried with a clean cloth
   (E) as a final step, then, you dry the car with a clean cloth

14. <u>Images transmitted by email, sharper and clearer than fax, are</u> quickly making obsolete technologies that were once considered state-of-the-art.

   (A) Images transmitted by email, sharper and clearer than fax, are
   (B) Sharper and clearer than the fax, images transmitted by email are
   (C) Images transmitted by email, sharper and clearer than those transmitted by fax, are
   (D) Images transmitted by email, which are sharper and clearer than fax, are
   (E) Email transmission of images, sharper and clearer than the fax, are

IF YOU FINISH BEFORE TIME IS CALLED, YOU MAY CHECK YOUR WORK ON THIS SECTION ONLY. DO NOT TURN TO ANY OTHER SECTION IN THE TEST.　STOP

KAPLAN

Practice Test Four: **Answer Key**

SECTION 1

Essay

SECTION 2
1. D
2. E
3. C
4. B
5. C
6. A
7. B
8. B
9. B
10. D
11. C
12. D
13. C
14. D
15. E
16. E
17. A
18. E
19. C
20. B

SECTION 3
1. D
2. D
3. B
4. D
5. B
6. C
7. E
8. E
9. D

10. E
11. D
12. B
13. C
14. B
15. E
16. E
17. A
18. B
19. E
20. B
21. D
22. A
23. C
24. C
25. C

SECTION 4
1. B
2. B
3. C
4. B
5. A
6. D
7. B
8. E
9. A
10. D
11. B
12. C
13. B
14. B
15. E
16. B
17. E

18. D
19. D
20. B
21. C
22. D
23. D
24. D
25. E
26. E
27. A
28. A
29. C
30. D
31. B
32. E
33. C
34. C
35. E

SECTION 5
1. C
2. A
3. E
4. C
5. C
6. E
7. D
8. A
9. 2
10. 31
11. 18
12. 132 or 198
13. 800
14. 24
15. 192

16. 8/36 or 2/19
17. 235°
18. 9

SECTION 6
1. E
2. C
3. B
4. A
5. A
6. B
7. C
8. E
9. C
10. C
11. B
12. A
13. E
14. A
15. E
16. D
17. B
18. A
19. E
20. C
21. A
22. C
23. D
24. D

SECTION 7
1. A
2. C
3. B

4. E
5. B
6. A
7. D
8. E
9. D
10. C
11. B
12. D
13. B
14. D
15. B
16. E

SECTION 8
1. D
2. B
3. A
4. C
5. B
6. C
7. E
8. E
9. C
10. B
11. D
12. D
13. A
14. B
15. A
16. B
17. D
18. B

SECTION 9
1. B
2. A
3. D
4. C
5. E
6. D
7. B
8. B
9. C
10. D
11. B
12. A
13. B
14. C

Answers and Explanations

SECTION 1

6 Essay

Most people are taught as children that it is important to do things to make other people happy. I remember how great I felt when I brought home the Valentine's Day card I made my mother in first grade. She was thrilled with the sparkly red heart and I was proud that my art project had made her so happy. This is just a small example of the positive reinforcement we receive when we make other people happy, but in the long run pleasing others can be have a negative effect on your life. If you are always guided by other people's desires, instead of discovering what makes you happy, you are more likely to fail than succeed.

I come from a football family, in a football town. My brother had been a star quarterback, and my whole family is very involved in the high school football team. My younger sister is a cheerleader; my mother works at the concession stand during games; and my father is good friends with the coach. I had played football since I was seven, and I was good enough to make the squad of our Division-A team. My parents were thrilled when I made the team in my sophomore year. My father took me aside to tell me how proud he was of me.

My decision to play football was completely motivated by my desire to please my family. What I really wanted to do was run for the cross country team. During football practice, I used to see the cross country team heading off on a long run and I felt so envious. I found the football drills boring, and I began to dread going to practice. During the season, the coach stopped playing me in games because he said I was not trying. He was right; my heart was not in the game. My father got very angry with the coach because he was not putting me in the games, and their friendship suffered. My grades even dropped because I found the situation with football so stressful.

At the end of the season I vowed that I would not play the following year. This summer when I told my parents that I

was not going out for football they were not as upset as I thought they might be. I joined the cross country team and have started winning races. I look forward to practice and have made some great friends on the team. My grades are better than they have ever been. My parents still love football, and I discovered that their interest in the local team does not revolve around me. They go to games and cheer as loudly as ever. I even enjoy going to the games, when I don't have a race.

When I was guided by what I thought would make my parents happy, I made myself miserable. When I followed my own interests, I not only succeeded, I think my family is actually happier than when I was trying to please them. You have to seek your own happiness first, as you can only truly succeed at something that you enjoy. Then, as I discovered, you will probably find that the people you are most interested in pleasing will take pleasure in your success.

Grader's Comments

All essays are evaluated on 4 basic criteria: Topic, Support, Organization, and Language. This is a very well written essay. The writer shows that he understood the topic and took the time to think about it before beginning to write. He sticks to the topic and uses a personal experience to support his stance. His argument is well developed and strongly supported. He never leaves the main point of his example by wandering into another story. He further completes his argument by referencing back to his opening remarks about making people happy in the conclusion. Furthermore, the essay has strong organization and is interesting.

The language used by the writer is straightforward and mature. He does not slip into slang or use awkward language to impress the reader. His writing style and vocabulary use indicate that he is educated and capable of expressing his position in a constructive manner. He uses different structures of his sentences and paragraphs, and despite a few minor errors, stays in the same tense throughout the essay.

4 Essay

To borrow a phrase from President Lincoln, "You can make some of the people happy all the time, and you can make all the people happy some of the time, but you can't make all the people happy all the time." This is especially true in politics. This fall I volunteered on the campaign of a man who was running for mayor of my town. It was the first time I had volunteered on a campaign and I was really excited by what the candidate wanted to accomplish. I really believed in his ideas. For example, he wanted to add money to the school budget so we can have arts classes again. He also wanted to improve public transportation, which was important to me because I have to take the bus.

When the campaign started, the candidate was very idealistic. He was very committed to his ideas. Later into the campaign, however, he started to compromise in order to win more votes. He stopped emphasizing public transportation in his campaign when it seemed unpopular with voters. He even backed away from his proposal for the school budget when it seemed that people weren't willing to support even the smallest increase in taxes. I was very disillusioned by his failure to stick by his ideas and principles. My candidate lost the mayoral race. I think his failure can be attributed to his attempt to please all the voters instead of sticking up for his own ideas.

Instead of trying to win people over to his platform, the candidate tried to accommodate everything all the voters wanted. Even though a politicians job is to represent the people, so in some ways, his or job is to make people happy, a politician has to stand for something otherwise nobody will vote for them. In politics, you cannot please everyone and if you try you will fail. To succeed in politics you have to stick by your own ideas and try to convince other people that you are right.

Grader's Comments

All essays are evaluated on 4 basic criteria: Topic, Support, Organization, and Language. The writer begins by using a quote to express his position on the topic and to preface his argument. However, the writer misquotes Lincoln. But the essay is not about content, so this mistake does not affect the score. The writer uses an example that covers the topic and supports his position. His personal account of the way political success is attributed to the candidate's desire to please all of the voters speaks directly to the heart of the question. The essay is well organized, with an introduction, a body, and a conclusion.

The writer's language is good and mostly grammatically correct; however, the description is very basic and uninteresting. The tone is often very standard and conversational. He could have used more expressive terminology to help prove his point, and the conclusion is not as strong as it could be.

2 Essay

It is not easy to be successful. If you are not going to try, you will never be successfull. You have to do things your own way. One time I was friends with a bunch of girls who did everything together. We would call each other everynight to see who was going to where what the next day so we would not wear the same stuff. If everyone was going to the mall then there was no way you could say you were going to go to the do something else. These girls were really into clothes and makeup and jewelry. This was not the only things I was interested in but I went along with the other girls because I wanted to fit in. Then one time I wanted to join the drama club and the other girls said that drama club was not cool and they would never join drama club. I really wanted to be in the play but I didn't want to make my friends mad so I never tried out. When I went to see the play it looked like so much fun I was mad at myself for listening to my friends. When we moved to high school we were not friends as much just some girls stayed friends. Now I do plays and I think it is really fun and even played the lead roll last year. I learned that you shouldn't not do things because of what other people say and you do what you want and then you will be successful.

Grader's Comments

All essays are evaluated on 4 basic criteria: Topic, Support, Organization, and Language. The writer is good about addressing the topic of the statement immediately in her opening sentence and using her friends as her example. However, the development of her example is not as descript as it needs to be, and her train of thought seems random and all over the place. The organization of the writer's thoughts is loose, and she never returns to her initial stance until the last sentence.

The writer's language is juvenile and against the principles of standard written English. She uses slang, such as "cool," and there are many spelling and diction errors. For example, she writes "where" when she meant "wear" and commits a double negative by using "shouldn't not." The last sentence is a run-on that goes nowhere.

SECTION 2

1.   D

Don't over think this one—the x^6 is on each side and can be subtracted from both sides. Subtract x^6 from both sides to get $4 = w$.

2.   E

To find the minimum total time, add the minimum times for each part; for the maximum total time, add the maximum times for each part.

Minimum = 22 + 20 = 42

Maximum = 28 + 30 = 58

3.   C

Systematically solve for the variables until you have what you're looking for. Start with c, since it's defined in the question stem. Use c to find a, then a to find b.

$$a = 8c = 8 \times 9 = 72$$
$$\frac{72}{b} = 4$$
$$72 = 4b$$
$$18 = b$$

4.   B

Convert the scientific notation into a simple number by multiplying it out. Then you can see where the decimal point should be.

$$4.567890 \times 10^2 = 4.567890 \times 100 = 456.7890$$

The decimal point should be between 6 and 7, choice (B).

5.   C

The intersection of two sets consists of the elements that are in both sets. In this case, the intersection contains numbers which are both prime and equal to a prime number plus 2.

2 is prime, but is not equal to a prime number plus 2. It is only in set A.

4 is equal to a prime number (2) plus 2, but is not itself prime. It is only in set B.

5 is both prime and equal to a prime number (3) plus 2. Choice (C) is correct.

6.   A

Whenever you see a triangle question about angles, remember that the sum of the interior angles of a triangle is 180 degrees

$$a + b + c = 180$$
$$7c + 2c + c = 180$$
$$10c = 180$$
$$c = 18$$

7.   B

Translate the words into algebra, and then let your algebra skills take you home!

Let x be the number of students at the beginning

After the addition there are $x + 21$ students, which is 4 times x.

So $x + 21 = 4x$
$$21 = 3x$$
$$x = 7$$

8.   B

Remember that you can always assume the diagram is drawn to scale, unless you're told otherwise. Use this to eliminate wrong answer choices if you get stuck.

Draw a third line parallel to l and m. Find the supplement of the given angles. The angle we want has been split into two angles, each of which is an alternate interior angle with one of the supplement, so $q = 30° + 20° = 50°$

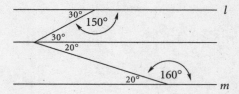

9.   B

When you find the language confusing, try to put it in concrete terms. If you wanted to know how much more 9 was than 7, what would you do? You would subtract: $9 - 7 = 2$ more. So you need to subtract these two algebraic expressions.

$$(3x + 9) - (3x - 2) = 3x + 9 - 3x + 2 = 11$$

10. D

Remember that you can always plug in numbers for the variables (being careful to follow all the rules you are given).

I. When you multiply by a negative, the inequality flips. If $b > a$, then $-b < -a$. So this statement is always false.

II. If $a < b$, you can add c to both sides to get $a + c < b + c$. Always true.

III. a and b are negative, so their sum will be negative, while c is positive. So this statement will be always true.

11. C

The union of two sets includes all the elements that appear in either set. In this case, that means all the numbers between 0 and 5 and all the numbers between 3 and 7. You can combine these ranges and say that the union includes all the numbers between 0 and 7.

$0 \leq x \leq 7$ includes all the numbers between 0 and 7, including both 0 and 7.

12. D

When you see fractions set equal to each other, as in this problem, you should cross-multiply to make the equations easier to work with. Next, you should solve one equation for a in terms of b and plug this into the other equation. Then solve this new equation for b. If you have extra time, you might want to double-check your answer by plugging the values you found for a and b back into the original equations.

$$\frac{10}{a+b} = \frac{4}{a}$$

$$10a = 4(a + b) = 4a + 4b$$

$$6a = 4b$$

$$a = \frac{4b}{6} = \frac{2b}{3}$$

$$\frac{b^2}{18} = \frac{a}{2} = \frac{\left(\frac{2b}{3}\right)}{2} = \frac{2b}{3} \times \frac{1}{2} = \frac{b}{3}$$

$$b^2 = 6b \quad \text{(Note that you can divide}$$
$$\text{by } b \text{ since you know } b \neq 0.)$$
$$b = 6$$

13. C

Most people find it easier to work with negative exponents if they are written as fractions. Once you've solved the given equation for c, don't forget to square it to find your answer!

$$c^{-\frac{1}{2}} = \frac{1}{\sqrt{c}} = 3$$

$$1 = 3\sqrt{c}$$

$$\frac{1}{3} = \sqrt{c}$$

$$\left(\frac{1}{3}\right)^2 = \frac{1^2}{3^2} = \frac{1}{9} = c$$

$$\left(\frac{1}{9}\right)^2 = \frac{1^2}{9^2} = \frac{1}{81} = c^2$$

14. D

If you're not familiar with transformations of x^2, you can try plugging some points from the graph into each equation to see which ones fit.

The point $(1, \frac{1}{2})$ is a great point to test—it only works for choice (D). (Even if you're not sure what the y-value of that point on the graph is, you can see that it is between 0 and 1. Choice (D) is the only equation that produces a y-value between 0 and 1 when $x = 1$.)

15. E

The area of a triangle is one-half the length of the base times the height. You need to find the base and height of this triangle. Since $\overline{AC}$ is a horizontal line (that is, A and C have the same y-coordinate) the length of the base is just the difference between the x-coordinates of A and C. The height is the vertical distance between B and the base. This is the difference between the y-coordinate of point B and the y-coordinate of the base.

Base: $7 - 2 = 5$

Height: $6 - 2 = 4$

Area: $\frac{1}{2}(5)(4) = 10$

16. E

The perimeter of this triangle is the sum of the lengths of its sides, $AB + BC + CA$. You can find these lengths by using the distance formula, $\sqrt{(x_1 - x_2)^2 + (y_1 - y_2)^2}$, or by sketching in the height of triangle ABC to create two right triangles, then using the Pythagorean theorem. In this case, both approaches take the same amount of time, so use whichever you prefer.

$$AB = \sqrt{(4-2)^2 + (6-2)^2}$$

$$= \sqrt{2^2 + 4^2} = \sqrt{4 + 16} = \sqrt{20} = 2\sqrt{5}$$

$$BC = \sqrt{(7-4)^2 + (2-6)^2}$$

$$= \sqrt{3^2 + (-4)^2} = \sqrt{9 + 16} = \sqrt{25} = 5$$

$CA = 7 - 2 = 5$ (Since this is a horizontal line, the distance between A and C is the difference between the x-coordinates of A and C. If you use the formula, you will get the same result.)

$$\text{Perimeter} = 2\sqrt{5} + 5 + 5 = 10 + 2\sqrt{5}$$

17. A

If you're stuck, focus on the differences between the answers; anything that's clearly wrong can be eliminated.

Squares of $2a$ and $3b$:

$$(2a)^2 \text{ and } (3b)^2$$

Sum of those squares:

$$(2a)^2 + (3b)^2$$

Difference between $8c$ and $7d$:

$$(8c - 7d)$$

Sum of squares added to the difference:

$$(2a)^2 + (9b)^2 + (8c - 7d)$$

3 more than e:

$$e + 3$$

Sum is 3 more than e:

$$(2a)^2 + (3b)^2 + (8c - 7d) = e + 3$$

18. E

Remember, slope is $\dfrac{rise}{run}$ or $\dfrac{y_2 - y_1}{x_2 - x_1}$, so a slope of zero

means the line is horizontal (rise $= 0$), and an undefined slope means the line is vertical (run $= 0$).

This line is vertical, so the x-coordinate stays the same. The only answer choice with the same x-coordinate is choice (E).

19. C

You should be able to immediately know where x and y are each positive and negative. Remember that a negative number times a negative number is positive.

The product will only be positive when either both coordinates are positive, or both are negative, so it must be C, D, or E. D clearly has a small product, so the answer is either C or E. Notice that E's x coordinate is less than one, which means its product, xy, is less than y. C's x and y coordinates both have large values, more than making up for its y being slightly smaller than E's y (thinking in terms of absolute value, since the product gets rid of the negatives). Thus, C will have the largest product. You could also use your answer sheet as a ruler to estimate and confirm this.

20. B

You're looking for a way to get a and b in the same equation, without n. So solve for n in terms of a, and substitute it into the equation for b.

$$a = 3n + 4$$

$$a - 4 = 3n$$

$$\frac{a - 4}{3} = n$$

$$b = 7 + 9n^2 = 7 + 9\,\frac{(a-4)^2}{3^2} = 7 + 9\,\frac{(a-4)^2}{9}$$

$$= 7 + (a-4)^2 = 7 + a^2 - 8a + 16 = a^2 - 8a + 23$$

KAPLAN

SECTION 3

1.   D

An artist who is proficient in many types of art forms is able to do many different things. Therefore, the prediction could be *adaptable* or maybe *"talented."* Although artists tend to be *"demonstrative"* (A) or *"uninhibited"* or *"unreserved,"* the sentence does not describe the emotional aspect of Da Vinci's work. (B) does not match the prediction. Nothing is said to indicate that he was "unique" or "obscure." The details of his artwork are not discussed here so there is no way of knowing if Da Vinci was *"meticulous"* (C), that is, *"careful"* or *"thorough."* There is no indication whether his artwork was *"metaphoric"* (E) or more straightforward and literal. (D) means *"adaptable"* or *"flexible"* and matches the prediction.

2.   D

We can assume that the questions on the exam will be required to be answered. Taking into consideration the contrast (exhibited by *although*) between the "required" exam and the word in the blank, a good prediction would be that the chapter review exercises are not required or additional questions. (A) can be eliminated because it is the opposite of the prediction. Only if the word *although* were eliminated and the word "and" was inserted after the blank would this word fit into the context of the sentence. If the students knew that these questions were to be found on the exam then doing the review may have already become *ritualistic* (B) for good students, but the teacher would not use this word to encourage the class to do extra studying. (C) doesn't make sense in the context of the question. (E) means "serious" but relates to demeanor or attitude, not to how the students are to treat the additional questions. (D) is the only answer that matches the prediction.

3.   B

Start with the second blank. The architect of well-known, famous buildings must have been well-known and acclaimed himself. The prediction for the first blank must support Wright's becoming so distinguished; a word such as "proved" works. (A) Although *buoyed* works in the first blank, *irrelevant* or inappropriate is the opposite of the prediction for the second blank. *Surrendered* (C) has a negative connotation and is a bit extreme; buildings

cannot surrender or give up a person as being either a good, bad, or prolific (productive) architect. Both words in (D) are negative; the predictions show they must be positive. (E), *categorized*, is not the best choice for the first blank, and *mundane*, or ordinary, does not fit as it is the opposite of the prediction. (B) is the best answer.

4.   D

The words *at least* are important here. If he was *not particularly talented* as a plumber but had some *years of experience*, then he must have been working as a plumber and at the very least would have been considered a professional practicing the profession. Look for a word that refers to one who simply practices a profession. If he had "years of experience", he could not have been a *novice* (A). One cannot really be a *neighbor* (B) of a profession. Nothing in the sentence indicates that he was merely interpreting, as (C) suggests, or performing his job as a plumber in a way that expressed his particular feelings about the profession. Nothing in the sentence indicates that he *devalued* (E) or spoke negatively of the profession. (D) is the best answer.

5.   B

Start with the second blank. As Ms. Poole is described as a *skilled mediator*, it would make sense that she found a way to "reconcile" or "resolve" their *numerous differences*. And if Ms. Poole were able to reconcile their differences, then she probably would have been able to save their relationship. Save and reconcile are great predictions for the two blanks. *Strengthening* (A) differences would not necessarily *reinforce* a relationship. *Widening* (C) their differences would not necessarily help Ms. Poole to express or give meaning to their relationship. *Plugging* (D) differences would not necessarily lead to a relationship being *overcome*. Again, *destroying* (E) numerous differences would not necessarily lead to their relationship being *disregarded* by Ms. Poole. (B) is the best choice.

6.   C

If the first blank refers to a bad problem at the company, then it would follow that the company's positive reputation would be difficult to *restore*. Look for a choice that fills the first blank with a problem and the second with a word that means *restore*.

Integrity (A) would not "plague" an institution. An institution with *conviction* (B) would not necessarily have trouble *justifying* its reputation. Whereas *dignity* (D) could potentially have a negative effect on an institution, such a quality would not necessarily make it difficult for that institution to *excuse* its reputation. *Degradation* (E) fits nicely into the first blank, but a reputation cannot really be *convicted*. (C) is the best answer.

7. E

If the waiter is hoping for a promotion, he is probably working hard and trying to smile about it. What words are synonyms for "hard work" and "a good attitude?" Anyone working *unscrupulously* (A) is surely on this way to getting fired. Approaching a job with *leniency* (B) is not really approaching it with a hard working ethic. If he approaches his job with *nonchalance* (C), then he's not working *tenaciously*. Having *acrimony* (D) or bitter feeling toward your job will not win you a promotion. (E) works. *Ardor* is a synonym for "strong enthusiasm," and doing something *assiduously* is doing it "diligently."

8. E

Think about the word *egocentrism*, which means to view one's own ego as a center. The fact that the blank is joined with egocentrism by "and" shows that the two words are linked in meaning. Look for a word that means something like human-centered. Although some would say that humans can display *irrationality* (A) at times, it does not mean the same thing as human-centered. A tendency toward humane acts does not match with egocentrism, thus (B) *humanity* is incorrect. To act with *temerity* (C) does not indicate a narrow view of the universe. (D), *serendipity,* would probably promote a larger or broader view of the universe. *Anthropocentrism*, (E), is a perfect fit. It puts humans at the center of the universe and works with egocentrism.

9. D

In the first two sentences of the passage, the author suggests that returning from the breeder's with "slightly scored shins" and "urine coating" her shoes gave her some idea of the trials to come. In this context, you can infer that "scored" refers to something negative that the puppy did to the author's shins, such as scratching them. (A) is a primary definition of the cited word and makes little sense in this context. (B) captures another meaning of scored—being grooved or gouged—but it's unclear

what it would mean to say that shins were indented by the puppy. Whereas (C) is another meaning of the word, as in scoring a pair of basketball tickets, it makes no sense in this context. (E) This choice is too extreme given the author's use of the word "slightly." (D) is the best choice.

10. E

The author says that her dog used to be a "tiny menace" but is now a "snoring beast." This comparison emphasizes how much the once-troublesome small puppy has grown and calmed down, giving the author a sense of "parental satisfaction." (A) is too extreme; the author indicates that her dog grew, but she does not suggest that the dog became *too* large. (B) does not match the positive tone of the sentence, and it undermines the statement that the author views her dog with pride or satisfaction. (C) is a distortion; the author's reference to "parental satisfaction" in the last sentence indicates that the dog has brought her some happiness. (D) is a misused detail; whereas the passage as a whole indicates that the author feels affection for her dog, the cited words themselves do not make this point. (E) is the best answer.

11. D

In the first sentence, the author refers to Hershey as a "revolutionary" chocolate-maker and suggests that he was enthusiastic, although his "inexperience" in the candy industry was the downfall of his first candy shop. You can expect the correct choice to match at least one of these characterizations. (A) is out of scope; this sentence does not say whether Hershey was particularly hard-working. (B) is a distortion; while the passage indicates that Hershey opened his own business when he was quite young, this information does not necessarily suggest he was exceptionally talented for his age. (C) is also a distortion; the passage describes Hershey as "inexperienced" but does not say that he lacked talent. (E) is an irrelevant detail; Hershey's commitment to using high-quality ingredients is mentioned in the last sentence, not the first. (D) is a good match for your prediction. "Groundbreaking" is a good synonym for "revolutionary."

12. B

Go through the choices one by one, comparing each with the evidence found in the text. Aim to work quickly, but not so quickly that you compromise accuracy. (A) is a distortion; the passage indicates that Hershey acquired this dedication from another candy maker. (C) is out of scope; the passage indicates that Hershey learned to use quality ingredients from the caramel manufacturer, but it does not say that he tried to apply the *techniques* he learned there to chocolate-making. (D) is too extreme; whereas the passage suggests that Hershey was successful and that he was dedicated to the candy industry from a young age, it does not imply that he could *only* have succeeded at candy making. (E) is also out of scope; the passage only begins describing Hershey at age 18 and does not say whether his interest in candy-making originated in early childhood. (B) is the best choice; the author indicates that Hershey was "enthusiastic" about candy-making when he opened his shop at age 19 and that he was still "hooked on it" after his shop closed six years later.

13. C

Your notes should list something like "a discussion of defining art" as the purpose of paragraph 2; if not, skim for the words *endeavor* and *problematic*. Either way, you should find the first sentence of paragraph 2 mentioning: "Before we can begin a discussion of artistic decline, we must first define the word 'art,' an endeavor that has proven problematic." (A), (B), (C), and (D) are all distortions; the author discusses improving the education system (A) in later paragraphs, but the author never characterizes this as a "problematic endeavor." The author discusses how education can make art more relevant (B) by linking it to historical and sociological developments, but the author never characterizes this as a "problematic endeavor." Likewise, in later paragraphs, the author discusses what students should learn in school (D), but the author never characterizes this as a "problematic endeavor." Finally, also in later paragraphs, the author discusses whether or not to teach art (E), but the author never characterizes this as a "problematic endeavor." (C) is exactly as the passage states and is correct.

14. B

Since you are given the part of the passage from which you must draw the inference, skim paragraph 2 to find evidence of what the author characterizes as "too much time spent." In. lines 36–40 the author says that, "far too much time has been spent arguing over whether a teen movie is more or less art than *Citizen Kane,* or whether a boy band is more or less art than Sondheim." Now examine the answer choices by comparing them to this information and eliminating those that do not necessarily have to be true based on it.

(A) is opposite; whereas the author discusses comparisons of "classics," the author does so in order to highlight the comparison of such classics to modern works, thereby judging the modern works' artistic merits. (C) and (D) are misused details; the author mentions them in later paragraphs. (E) is a distortion; the author never discusses comparisons of works traditionally considered classics to each other; the author discusses their comparison to newer works. (B) is the correct answer; the author states, "Far too much time has been spent arguing over whether a teen movie is more or less art than *Citizen Kane* is, or whether the music of a boy band is more or less art than the works of Sondheim are." Thus, the author implies that too much time has spent comparing modern works to more established works in order to judge the modern works' artistic merits.

15. E

Your task is to determine why the author included this detail in the passage. Your notes should tell you that the author uses most of paragraph 1 to bemoan or lament the decline of artistic appreciation and awareness in America. Since the author thinks that it is "sad" that America concerns itself with "teen movies and boy bands" then the author must think that film noir, jazz, and abstract expressionism are better. Thus, he must be mentioning them in order to draw a comparison and suggest their superiority. Look for that in the answer choices. (A) is a distortion; whereas the author does seem to be appealing to a sense of a lost golden age, the author uses that as part of the comparison to newer art to suggest their inferiority. (B) is opposite; far from making a historical parallel, this author suggests that newer works are inferior. (C) is out of scope; the author never examines the history of art. (D) is a misused detail; the author uses different details in a later paragraph to remind readers of this. (E) is just as we predicted.

16. E

The sentence in question states: "Many claim that our discussion can be seen as snobby, even culturally imperious." Since the author states that many people might think the discussion is "snobby" and then goes on to say "even culturally imperious" the author must be using imperious as a higher degree of the same meaning as snobby. (A), *imperative*, is not a higher degree of snobbery. (B) is opposite; when something is *arbitrary*, it is not carefully chosen which means that it cannot relay the meaning of snobbery. (C), *regal*, simply means elegant in a royal way. While this may be associated with snobbery, it does not convey the same meaning. (D), *urgent*, is a dictionary meaning of imperious but it makes no sense in the context of the original sentence. (E) is the answer; *arrogant* can be used as a higher degree of snobbery. When placed into the original sentence, it replaces imperious perfectly.

17. A

Both paragraphs 3 and 4 discuss aspects of artistic education. Skim for any language that might stand out of the text. In this case, the words "lost by the general public" should help you find the relevant detail in paragraph 3: "…a better education in art will better equip them to judge the artistic merit of these newer, more trendy art forms, or at least place these art forms in historical context and analyze them as an outgrowth of societal and sociological trends—an important aspect of artistic knowledge that has been lost by the general public." Now find the answer choice that matches an ability to place art works in a "historical context and analyze them as an outgrowth of societal and sociological trends."(B) is a misused detail; the definition of "art" is discussed earlier in the passage as a problematic endeavor for society, not an important aspect of artistic knowledge that has been lost. (C) is out of scope; the author never discusses the general public's ability to produce art that rivals the classics. (D) is a distortion; whereas the author does suggest ways the general public can better judge art works, the author never states that the general public has lost the ability to judge the merits of current art works. (E) is also a misused detail; the author discusses the value of all forms of art during the discussion of the definition of art. (A) is correct; this matches the first part of the author's detail.

18. B

Reread the lines in question in order to find evidence of what distinguishes the author's hypothetical United States. Parents read to their children and educate them. These parents also give their children art books, classical recordings, and plays as gifts." Now evaluate each answer choice, choosing the one that must be true based on the author's statements. (A) is out of scope; the author's statements deal with a new interest in art, not new interests in general. (C) is a misused detail; the author never mentions school in the piece of the paragraph mentioned by the question. (D) is out of scope; the author's statements discuss sharing

enthusiasm for art, not other activities. (E) is a distortion; in the referenced lines, the author never alludes to the value of artistic skill. (B) is correct; the lines in question describe a country in which parents share their interests in and enjoyment of art with their children, so it must be true that this what the author finds distinguishing about this hypothetical country.

19. E

Since you are given specific line numbers, your first step should be to reread the relevant lines, which state that "in school, students receive in education in art history, classical music, and opera. This curriculum can also include pop-culture such as the music videos, teen movies, and pop music students enjoy in their free time." Now use this information to evaluate the answer choices, choosing the one that must describe such an educational model. (A), (B), (C), and (D) are all distortions; whereas the author's statements describe an education that examines a diverse body of art forms, the author never mentions which, if any, are valued (A) over others or whether or not the students would learn to respect (B) the views of all artists. In fact, a critical examination might lead students to disrespect the views of certain art or artists. The author's statements describe an education that reflects upon art forms, but the author never describes an education that reflects on the nature of art education (C). Likewise, the author describes an education that examines both classical and contemporary art (D), but the author never describes whether one would be valued over the other. (E) is correct; the author describes an education that explores both classical and contemporary art, including pop-culture; such a model is wide-ranging in its exploration.

20. B

Your notes might indicate that in paragraph 3, the author advances a vision of an artistically educated society. If your notes do not indicate this, then simply revisit the paragraph by skimming it, and then evaluate what the author does in this paragraph. The author provides an example of a more artistically educated America. Thus, the author must have included the paragraph in order to propose or provide a vision of a more artistically educated society. (A) is a distortion; the author merely provides a vision of a more artistically educated society, not a utopian one. (C) and (D) are out of scope; in the third paragraph, the author never examines whether pop culture leaves a lasting impact on society (C), and the author never deals with classic literature and younger students (D). (E) is also a distortion; whereas the author proposes studying both, the author never states that contemporary and classical works are interchangeable. (B) is the best answer.

21. D

Use the line numbers to locate and reread the situation described by the author. The author states that since "art, music, and culture are inextricably tied to literary and historical developments which themselves stem from changes in society and culture" the educational system should focus on a more "holistic" approach that teaches "students in an intertextual and multi-disciplinary manner." Find the answer choice that must be characteristic of this education. (A) and (B) are distortions; the author describes an artistic education, not an *elitist* one (A) or a charitable one (B). (C) is the opposite; *eclectic* means mixed together from various elements. This might seem true, but eclectic implies a mismatching of items. The author argues that literature, art, and history are not mismatched at all. (E) is also opposite; *rudimentary* means basic; the education described by the author goes beyond the basics and fundamentals by contextualizing art within other developments in society, thus creating an overarching education. (D) is correct; the author describes an education that takes an overarching view. *Comprehensive* characterizes this.

22. A

In lines 107–114, the author states that "this system would require more funding, and most likely higher taxes." Find the answer choice that must be true based on this information.

(B), (C), (D), and (E) are all distortions; clearly, the author believes that the new system would be better, but the author's statements don't provide evidence that the new system would be more celebrated (B), more controversial (C), more interesting (D), or more likely to inspire (E) than the current system. (A) is correct; because the new system would require more funding and probably higher taxes, it must be true that the new system would be more expensive.

23. C

As you should have noted while reading the passage, the topic is the decline of artistic knowledge and appreciation in America. The author outlines causes for this decline then proposes a solution. Look for an answer choice that says something similar to this. (A) is a distortion; in the first paragraph, the author does shift the focus of the debate from analyzing causes to proposing solutions, but the author does not attempt to shift the focus of the debate from causes to effects. (B), (C) , and (D) are all out of scope; the author never supports a side in a debate (B), the author proposes a solution, nor does he revive a discredited idea (D), or promote certain types of art (E). The author promotes art education in general. (C) is the best answer.

24. C

Paragraph 3 contains the discussion of the author's hypothetical United States. Skim the passage for any facts regarding the production of higher quality art. The paragraph states that "when these children grow up, some may produce their own art, perhaps art that is higher in quality than the pop music and movies produced today." In a preceding line, the paragraph states that, "a better education in art will better equip them to judge the artistic merit of these newer, more trendy art forms, or at least place these art forms in historical context and analyze them as an outgrowth of societal and sociological trends…." Now compare each answer choice to this information. (A) is a distortion; the author never links parents to the production of better art. (B) is too extreme; the author presents a more artistically educated society, but the author never goes so far as to claim that this society would not accept lower quality art. (D) and (E) are also distortions; the author never mentions free time (D) or discusses how strictly critics would judge art in this hypothetical society (E). (C) is correct; the author presents children with better artistic educations, and then states that they would grow up to produce better art. Thus, their production of better art must stem from their artistic education.

25. C

In the first paragraph of the passage, the author states that the cultural decline in society has many causes, including "the media's focus on pop culture and the general decline of taste this breeds." (lines 11–12) . It is clear from this statement and the continuing tone of the passage that the author does not think much of popular music, making (C) the best choice. (A) and (B) are out of scope; there is not evidence in the passage to support either statement, and quite the contrary, there is plenty of evidence against both (A) and (B). (D) and (E) are misused details. The author discusses education, but he believes society would benefit from a more artistic and classically geared music education, and this would eliminate the possibility of his feeling that pop music was more important than classical music.

SECTION 4

1. B

Although the passive voice will not always be incorrect on the SAT, when you see a passive structure, look for an active version among the answer choices. *Flying is unable to be afforded by her* is a passive (and much wordier) version of *she cannot afford to fly.* Since the first clause already mentions flying, *to do so* is an acceptable variation; (B) is correct. *That* in (C) and *it* in (D) do not have clear antecedents. (E) is unnecessarily wordy.

2. B

Transition words must express the correct relationship between ideas. As written, this sentence does not use an appropriate transition to express the contrast between ideas. (B) corrects this with the transition word *although.* (C) and (E) express a cause-and-effect relationship between the clauses that is inappropriate in context. (D) is a sentence fragment.

3. C

Sentences should be structured so that any modifying words or phrases clearly refer to one specific item. As written, this sentence does not make clear what was *popular among high school students in the 90s*: *the love story* or the *teen movie.* (C) clarifies the sentence's meaning. (B) introduces a verb tense that is incorrect in context. (D) and (E) are sentence fragments.

4. B

Pronouns must always have clear antecedents. Here, the only plural antecedent for the pronoun *they* is *bylaws,* but *bylaws* don't *pay…wages.* (B) clarifies that it is *the University* that can no longer *pay reduced wages.* The pronoun *them* in (C) has no logical antecedent. (D) is unnecessarily in the passive voice, and the pronoun *their* has no logical antecedent. The plural verb *are* in (E) does not agree with the singular subject *consequence.*

5. A

Be methodical in eliminating wrong answer choices, but if you don't spot an error, don't be afraid to choose (A). This sentence is correct as written. (B) creates a run-on sentence. (C) and (D) have incorrect grammatical structure. (E) is awkward and not very clear.

6. D

Transition words must express the correct relationship between clauses. The transition word *but* indicates contrast. In this sentence the second clause expands on the information presented in the first, so *but* is incorrect. (D) corrects this error with an appropriate transition word, *that.* (B) does not address the error. Neither the conjunction *and* in (C) or the transition word *since* in (D) express the correct relationship between the clauses.

7. B

Choose the most concise answer that does not introduce any additional errors. Although not technically a run-on, this sentence consists of two independent clauses with no indication of how they are related. By making the first clause dependent, (B) indicates the relative importance of the two ideas. (C) does not address the error. (D) creates a cause-and-effect relationship between the clauses that is not present in the original. (E) is awkward and loses some of the meaning of the original.

8. E

Items in a series, list, or compound noun or verb must be parallel in structure. The object of the preposition *by* is the compound *an increase…and because there has been a decrease.* (E) makes the second part of the compound parallel to the first. None of the other choices makes the items parallel.

9. A

If you don't find an error, don't be afraid to choose (A). This sentence is correct as written. (B) and (C) unnecessarily introduce the passive voice. (E) has grammatically incorrect structure.

10. D

A pronoun must have a clear antecedent, and agree with that antecedent in gender and number. The problem here is the pronoun *their.* We don't know to whom *their* refers, since the sentence has no plural nouns. (D) is the only choice that eliminates the pronoun. (B) and (C) do not address the error. (E) replaces *their* with the singular pronoun *its,* but the pronoun's antecedent is still unclear.

11. B

Certain idioms appear regularly on the SAT; learn their proper structure. This question tests your knowledge of the idiom that compares two nouns using *as*; the correct construction is "as (adjective) as." Only (B) correctly completes the construction. (C) is grammatically incorrect, (D) is unnecessarily wordy, and (E) does not correct the error.

12. C

The pronoun *whom* is in the objective case and cannot be used as the subject of a verb. (C) should be in the subjective case ("who") because it is the subject of the verb phrase *had…scored.* (A) correctly uses *that* as a conjunction. (To check this, you can reverse the sentence order: "The sportscasters were shocked *that* the team with the worst record won…") The adverb in (B) correctly modifies the verb *won.* (D) is the appropriate verb tense in context.

13. B

The past perfect verb tense is only correct when used to refer to one completed action that precedes another. Since there is no other past action referred to in this sentence, (B) should simply be the past tense "worked." The verb in (A) agrees with its singular subject *performance.* In (C), the infinitive *to raise* is appropriate in context. (D) is a correctly used prepositional phrase.

14. B

All verbs within a sentence must agree in tense, unless more than one time frame is referenced. The present tense verb in (B) is not consistent with the rest of the sentence; it should be "knew." (A) correctly expresses the contrast between the two clauses in the sentence. (C) and (D) are properly used prepositional phrases.

15. E

The SAT writing sections will contain a total of 5–8 sentences that contain no errors. (A) uses an appropriate preposition in context. (B) is a correct use of the infinitive verb tense. (C) correctly shows the cause-and-effect relationship between the two clauses. (D) is a properly used prepositional phrase.

16. B

Unless context indicates that more than one time frame is referenced in a sentence, verb tenses should remain consistent. Since the rest of the sentence is in the past tense, (B) should be as well. (A) is a correct idiomatic usage. (C) and (D) use appropriate prepositions.

17. E

If you don't spot an obvious error, check each answer choice in turn. (A) is an appropriate preposition in context. (B) shows the cause-and-effect relationship between the two clauses in the sentence. (C) is the correct verb tense in context. (D) properly uses an adjective to modify a noun.

18. D

Adjectives (including participles) can only be used to modify nouns and pronouns. In (D), the participle verb form *increasing* is an adjective used to modify the adjective *nervous.* Adjectives cannot be used to modify other adjectives, however; (D) should be "increasingly." (A) is the proper relative pronoun to refer to a person. (B) is correct use of the infinitive. (C) is appropriate use of the past perfect tense, since it refers to an action completed before another stated past action (*grew…nervous*).

19. D

Related nouns in a sentence must agree in number. A plural number of *dancers* would have to take a plural number of "places"; the error is in (D). (A) properly uses an adjective to modify a noun. (B) is an appropriate verb phrase in context. (C) correctly uses the gerund *rustling* and the preposition *of.*

20. B

In a compound verb, the verbs must be in parallel form. The simple predicate of the main clause in this sentence is *got…and driving*; (B) should be "drove." (A) is a correctly used prepositional phrase. The verb in (C) is consistent in tense with the rest of the sentence. (D) is a correctly placed modifying phrase.

21. C

The correct verb form for a modifying phrase is the gerund (*-ing*) form. The verb *refuses* in (C) has no subject; without a conjunction to make it part of the predicate of the main clause, it would have to be changed to "refusing" to create a grammatically correct sentence. (A) uses the proper preposition in context. In (B), the adverb is used correctly to modify the verb *waits*. (D) is a correct verb phrase to describe a future action.

22. D

A sentence requires an independent clause that expresses a complete thought. Both clauses of this sentence are subordinate. Changing the gerund form in (D) to "greeted" would make the second clause independent, correcting the error. (A) is an appropriate preposition in context. (B) and (C) are idiomatically correct phrases.

23. D

All verbs within a sentence must agree in tense, unless a verb is included in a phrase that implies a different time from the rest of the sentence. The present tense verb in (D) is inconsistent with the rest of the sentence; "preferred" would be the correct form here. (A) properly uses an adjective to modify a noun. In (B), the gerund is correctly used. (C) correctly expresses the contrast between the two clauses in the sentence.

24. D

Even a sentence with numerous nouns and verbs can be a fragment, if there is no independent clause. As written, this sentence is a fragment. Changing (D) to "was constructed" would remedy this. (A) is appropriate use of the relative pronoun *which*. In (B), the superlative form is used correctly, since presumably there are more than two symbols of the Cold War. (C) is a correctly used prepositional phrase.

25. E

Expect some sentences to be correct as written. (A) and (B) are proper usages of an adjective and an adverb, respectively. (C) is the correct conjunction in context. The prepositional phrase in (D) is used correctly.

26. E

If you don't spot an obvious error, check each choice in turn. (A) is correct idiomatic usage. The pronoun in (B) clearly refers to *Mrs. Ramsay*. (C) is an appropriate verb phrase in context. (D) is proper use of the infinitive.

27. A

Verbs must agree in number with their subject nouns. (A) correctly uses an adverb to modify a verb, but the plural verb form *choose* does not agree with its singular subject *student.* (B) is the appropriate relative pronoun in context. (C) is consistent verb tense use, and uses the correct preposition. (D) properly uses an adjective to modify a noun.

28. A

Make sure each sentence has an independent clause that expresses a complete thought. As written, this sentence is a fragment, since neither clause is independent. Changing (A) to "serves" would correct the error. (B) is an appropriate conjunction in context. (C) correctly uses an adjective to modify the noun *soups*. (D) is a properly used prepositional phrase.

29. C

In a compound verb construction, all verbs must be in parallel form. *To drip and throwing* is grammatically incorrect; (C) should read "dripping." (A) is consistent verb tense usage. (B) is correct idiomatic usage. (D) properly uses an adverb to modify the compound verb.

30. D

By making *scientists* rather than *a theory* the subject, (D) puts the sentence in the active voice without changing its meaning. It also eliminates the pronoun *It,* which is used here with no antecedent. (B) eliminates the ambiguous pronoun, but does not address the passive problem. (C) and (E) correct the errors, but they are both sentence fragments.

31. B

Here, *institutes* is incorrectly in the present tense, since the sentence is talking about something that happened *in the latter half of the twentieth century.* (B) corrects the error.

Consequently, in (A), correctly relates this sentence to the previous one. (C) is not idiomatically correct English. (D) misrepresents the relationship between the two ideas. (E) introduces a verb tense that's incorrect in context.

32. E

The relative pronoun *who* is used when referring to people; *that* and *which* are used for things. Since *people* is the noun the pronoun *that* is referring to here, the pronoun should be replaced with *who.* (E) does this, without introducing any additional errors.

(B) misuses the comparative form *more.* (C) does not correct the error, and replaces the correct *those* with *them.* (D) corrects the error, but it also replaces *those* with *them,* which is incorrect.

33. C

As written, this sentence is a fragment, since neither of these clauses is independent. By changing the gerund (*-ing*) verb form, which can never be a predicate verb, to *appeared,* (C) corrects the error. (B) corrects the fragment error, but introduces an inappropriate verb tense. (D) does not address the error. (E) creates a complete sentence, but does so in the passive voice.

34. C

(C) combines the sentences, correctly using *but* to indicate the contrast between the first two clauses, and *while* to make the third clause subordinate. (A) merely strings the sentences together without relating their ideas. (B) misuses the semicolon splice, since the second clause is not independent. In (D), the transition word *so* indicates an inappropriate cause-and-effect relationship between the first and second clauses. (E) is a sentence fragment, with no predicate (main) verb in an independent clause.

35. E

The transition words *Although* and *but* both indicate contrast, so having one in each clause is unnecessary. The sentence could be corrected by eliminating either of them, but only (E) does this without introducing any additional errors.

(A) and (B) suggest eliminating *Although,* but they also involving changing *but* to another transition word, which alters the relationship of the ideas in the sentence. (C) creates a run-on sentence with two subordinate clauses. (D) simply replaces the second contrast transition word with a different one, but doesn't address the problem.

SECTION 5

1. C

Radical equations are not difficult, even though they may look complicated. Just remember to follow each step carefully, and you'll get the correct answer every time. Also, remember that Backsolving is often a good strategy for attacking radical equations.

$$3\sqrt{x} - 31 = -13$$
$$3\sqrt{x} = 18$$
$$\sqrt{x} = 6$$
$$x = 36$$

2. A

Rational equations can be solved just like any other equation. Just remember to follow the order of operations carefully, and you can solve these equations easily.

$$\frac{3x - 9}{2x + 7} = 8$$
$$3x - 9 = 8(2x + 7)$$
$$3x - 9 = 16x + 56$$
$$-13x = 65$$
$$x = -5$$

3. E

This question is a simple application of the distance formula. Keep track of which points you're using for x_1 and x_2, as well as y_1 and y_2, and this will be an easy question. Use P for (x_1, y_1), and Q for (x_2, y_2).

$$\text{Distance} = \sqrt{(x_1 - x_2)^2 + (y_1 - y_2)^2}$$
$$\sqrt{(-2 - 5)^2 + (4 - (-2))^2}$$
$$= \sqrt{(-7)^2 + 6^2} = \sqrt{49 + 36} = \sqrt{85}$$

4. C

Don't worry if you see a symbol you've never seen before—the operation will be defined in the problem. All you need to do is plug in the given values. Be sure to do anything in parentheses first.

$$2\nabla3 = 2 - 3 + 2 = 1$$
$$1\nabla1 = 1 - 1 + 2 = 2$$

5. C

You can use concrete numbers to get a handle on the situation.

> Try $a = 6$ and $b = 3$
> (A) $a + b = 9$, eliminate
> (B) $a - b = 3$, eliminate
> (C) $a + b + 1 = 10$
> (D) $ab = 18$, eliminate
> (E) $ab + 3 = 21$, eliminate

6. E

Any side of a triangle must be larger than the difference between than other two sides, and less than the sum of the other two sides

In choice (E), $12 = 5 + 7$, so the "triangle" would be totally flat.

7. D

Your task here is to translate English into math—what does "the ratio of $2k$ to $6s$" really mean?

The ratios described in the question can be written as:

$$\frac{2k}{6s} = \frac{6k + 5}{18s + 10}$$

Cross-multiply and simplify to get:

$$2k(18s + 10) = 6s(6k + 5)$$
$$36ks + 20k = 36ks + 30s$$
$$20k = 30s$$
$$k = 1.5s$$

You can see that statement I is never true, statement II is not necessarily true, and statement III must be true. If you're not sure about that, you can try plugging in numbers that fit each statement to see if they make the described ratios equivalent.

8. A

If two chords have equal length, they are the same distance from the center of the circle. Remember to add all the information from the question stem to the figure.

Because $GEFH$ is a square, its area is equal to the length of a side squared:

$$81 = EF^2$$
$$9 = EF$$

Since the chords are the same distance from the center of the circle, $EJ = KF$.

$$EF = EJ + JK + KF$$
$$9 = 5 + 2(EJ) + 4 = 2(EJ)$$
$$2 = EJ$$

9. 2

Remember that the solutions of a quadratic function are the values of x where the function equals zero. Where does this function equal zero?

The function equals zero at $x = 2$ and $x = -2$. Since you can't grid a negative number, grid in 2.

10. 31

You don't even have to turn this into algebra if you don't want to—just work backwards

> $2 for the first 14 days
> $4.55 - $2 = $2.55 for the rest of the days
> $\frac{\$2.55}{\$.15} = 17$ additional days
> $17 + 14 = 31$ days total

11. 18

Draw a diagram so you can see what's going on.

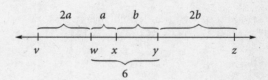

$\overline{WY} = 6 = a + b$ and $\overline{VZ} = 3a + 3b = 3(a + b) = 3(6) = 18$

12. 132 or 198

This question may look daunting, but we have two very useful pieces of information: $AA + AA$ is a 3-digit number that's divisible by 3, and it's also twice a 2-digit number where both digits are the same

> $2(AA) = $ covered number

Knowing 2(*AA*) is 3 digits narrows the possibilities down to
AA = 55, 66, 77, 88, or 99

But it also must be divisible by 3, which we can only get
from 66 or 99

So the covered number is 2 × 66 = 132 or 2 × 99 = 198

13. 800

Combinations are very similar to probabilities. How many
ways can she make the first choice? How many ways can
she make the second choice? Multiply these numbers to get
the number of combinations.

$$25 \times 32 = 800$$

14. 24

Think about what has to happen for them to be as close
together as possible—make the first Friday fall as late as
possible.

The latest the first Friday can be is the 7th, which makes the
last Friday the 28th and the last Monday the 31st. The last
Monday falls 31 − 7 = 24 days after the first Friday.

15. 192

Computing (100 ~ 5) would take forever, so there must be
an easier way. If a question on the SAT is taking a long time
or you find yourself setting up an extremely complicated
computation, you're probably missing a shortcut.

$$(100 \sim 5) = 100 + 99 + 98 + \dots + 6 + 5$$

$$(98 \sim 3) = 98 + 97 + \dots + 6 + 5 + 4 + 3$$

So when you subtract them, everything from 98 to 5
cancels out, leaving 100 + 99 − 4 − 3 = 192.

16. $\frac{8}{36} = \frac{2}{9}$

Don't forget that the fraction of 360 degrees a sector has
is also the fraction of the circle's area it contains, and the
fraction of the circumference that its arc takes up. Don't
stop too soon and grid the number of degrees in angle
AOE—remember to make it a fraction.

$$EOB = DOF = 60°$$

$$AOE = 180° − (60° + 40°) = 80°$$

$$\frac{80°}{360°} = \frac{8}{36} = \frac{2}{9}$$

17. 235°

If you ever forget the formula for the number of degrees
in a polygon, just divide it into triangles by drawing in
some diagonals.

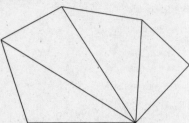

The sum of the interior angles in a polygon with *n* sides is
(*n* − 2) × 180° = (6 − 2) × 180° = 720°. Or, as shown
above, you can divide it into 4 triangles and deduce that the
sum of the angles is 4 × 180° = 720°

Since the known angles sum to
$$160° + 95° + 110° + 120° = 485°,$$
the remaining angles must sum to
$$720° − 485° = 235°.$$

18. 9

She will clean the house on days 7, 14, 21…(multiples of 7)
and do laundry on days 5, 10, 15…(multiples of 5). Think
about what has to be true of days where both happen.

The least common multiple of 7 and 5 is 35. So every 35th
day she will do both. This will happen $\frac{315}{35}$ = 9 times.

SECTION 6

1. E

If it was "unquestionable" that his friends had seen
Spiderman, then the evidence was "undeniable,"
"uncontestable," or "certain." Look for an answer choice that
matches this prediction. It may be helpful to break the
answer choices apart by looking at their prefixes and suffixes.
(A) is the opposite of the prediction; it means "not
important." (B) is too weak; it suggests that the movie stubs
are possible evidence that his friends had gone to the movies
without him. Possible is not as certain as "no denying."
Jamal's friends were not necessarily proven guilty. They had
seen a movie, and did not do anything that was incriminating
(C). (D) is the opposite of the prediction; "nominal" means

"very small" or "insignificant." (E) is the answer. Break the word apart if you are unsure of its meaning; "indisputable" means "not disputable" or "not questionable."

2. C

At least one of the blanks must describe why marathons are challenging. Think of a prediction for the second blank. Marathons are mentally "draining" or "strenuous." For the first blank, decide in what way marathons are primarily taxing; they are a challenge of fitness and bodily training. Although "taxing" or "difficult" works in the second blank, you can eliminate (A) based on the first blank. The challenge is not "illusory," or imagined. Neither word in (B) fits. The challenge of running a very long race is not "exaggerated," and describing a physical event as being "mentally balanced" does not make sense. Some runners may see the challenge as "appealing" (D), or interesting, but the process of preparing for a strenuous race is not in itself gratifying (although runners may feel a sense of satisfaction after the race has been completed). (E), "strenuous," works in the first blank, but "mentally dubious" or doubtful does not work. Only (C) fits both blanks.

3. B

What is "promoted" by "healthy lifestyle choices"? The first blank describes the benefits of healthy choices and must contain a positive word. A good prediction is "increased health" or "longer lifespan." The second blank must challenge this remark as busy lives reduce the time people have to exercise and eat right. For the second blank your prediction should be "prevented" or "challenged." Both words in (A) are the opposite of the predictions. (C), "behavior," is too general of a term. The blank is referring to the results of healthy behaviors, such as an increased lifespan. Although "belied" has a negative connotation, healthy lifestyles are not necessarily "contradicted" but rather challenged by busy lives. (D), "morality," is positive but out of scope and "bolstered" or "supported" is the opposite of the prediction. (E) can be eliminated based on the second blank; it is the opposite of the prediction. "Reproduction" may be enhanced by healthy choices but this isn't what the sentence is discussing. (B) is the best choice.

4. A

What word describes someone who does not "drink to excess"? A good prediction would be someone who leads an "abstinent" or "self-restrained" lifestyle. (B), "laconic,"

means brief or concise. The fact that the man is old and has therefore lived a long life is not what is being contrasted by the word in the blank. "Duplicitous," (C), means deceitful; who was the old man deceiving? He would only be deceptive if he were trying to hide his drinking habits. (D) can mean either artistic or tasteful. Whether or not his lifestyle was "aesthetic" is not related to his drinking habits. Being "voluble," (E), or talkative has nothing to do with drinking. (A) is the best choice.

5. A

The prediction should be a word that means Nostradamus had a knowledge of events before they occurred, such as "foresight." Eliminate all answer choices that do not match this prediction. (B) Nostradamus became known for his predictions, not for honesty or "sincerity." (C) is out of scope; nothing is said about Nostradamus being greedy. Be careful with (D); "complicity" does not mean "complicated;" it means involvement as an accomplice in a crime. (E) Because his predictions were accurate, Nostradamus was not being untruthful. (A) is the best choice.

6. B

What are the author's feelings or opinions about the fact that acid rain continues to exist despite the development of technologies that could eliminate it? An important clue comes in the final sentence, where the author uses the word "senselessly" to suggest that there seems to be no rational or understandable reason why the new technologies are not more widely used. (A) is a distortion; the author never expresses any *surprise* that acid rain continues to be a problem, and Passage 1 never mentions the "developed world" in particular. (C) is too extreme; the word "nothing" in this choice goes further than the author's "little." (D) is out of scope; although the cleaner technologies are new, the passage does not state that they are experimental. (E) is opposite; the author states that acid rain can produce "often irreversible environmental damage." (B) is the best choice.

7. C

The author of Passage 2 describes how the most-developed nations "have the luxury of squabbling over" questions that the poorer countries can't afford to consider, indicating that the wealthier nations have choices and advantages not shared by others. (A) is a distortion; that the author does not say whether developed nations are concerned about the energy choices available to poorer countries. (B) is out of scope; their degree of responsibility is not discussed in the passage. (D) is also a distortion; the passage does not mention any negative consequences resulting from blatant carelessness or the "squabbling" of developed nations. (E) is opposite; the author suggests that *less*-developed nations cannot afford cleaner fuels. (C) is the best answer.

8.   E

The scope of Passage 2 is limited to the difference between the developed world—which has the "luxury of squabbling" over a variety of energy issues—and poorer nations, who are forced to deal with the human damage caused by the "only natural resource they can afford." Therefore, the second author would probably reply that new and cleaner energy-generating technologies are not adopted by some countries because they can't afford them. (A) is out of scope; nowhere in Passage 2 does the author mention the responsibilities of wealthier nations. (B), (C), and (D) are distortions and are not supported by the text. (E) is the correct answer.

9.   C

Passage 1 focuses on the fact that there are cleaner alternatives to the conventional burning of fossil fuels, whereas Passage 2 focuses on the fact that poorer nations are stuck with the cheaper (but more damaging) coal. However, although their emphases are different, both authors recognize the basic point that burning fossil fuels can be harmful.

(A) is a distortion; only Passage 2 addresses the cost difference between clean and conventional technologies. (B) is too extreme; neither author makes such a strong statement, and the author of Passage 1 actually suggests that acid rain can be avoided. Both (D) and (E) are not supported by both passages.

10.   C

The passage begins with a description of what the author envisioned doing in her work at the shelter: "conducting intake interviews and traipsing around from organization to organization seeking the legal, psychological, and financial support that the women would need." At the end of the passage, she relates how her unanticipated baking endeavor made her "a more sensitive and skillful social worker." You are looking for a choice that expresses her changed view of social work. (A) is too extreme; although the author's "reality" did differ from what she expected, the passage does not focus on her shock, but rather on how

she responded to it. (B) is out of scope; the passage does not address the author's psychological constraints. (D) is a misused detail; although the bakery was for-profit, business abilities are not the focus of the passage. (E) is also a misused detail; the fact that the author was abroad in a "developing country" is not emphasized in the passage. (C) is correct; the author came to see social work as being more diverse than she originally envisioned.

11.   B

The paragraph preceding the citation indicates that the author had spent a significant amount of time imagining her work and felt "thoroughly prepared." It is thus likely that she arrived at the shelter with a positive, confident attitude. (A) is opposite; the last two sentences of the first paragraph indicate that the author felt self-assured. (C) is a misused detail; although she was uninformed about the actual content of her job, the author does not express this until later in the paragraph. (D) is also opposite; the author was energetic, not exhausted. (E) is a distortion; the author was not incompetent, only unprepared to run the bakery. (B) is the best choice.

12.   A

The author's enthusiasm at the beginning of the second paragraph contrasts with her shock a few sentences later, when she discovers she will be in charge of the bakery. Her references to the "case studies" she researched reveal that she was initially enthusiastic about the *concept* of the bakery, not necessarily about her practical involvement in it. (B) is opposite; initially, the author felt "out of her depth" at being put in charge of the bakery. (C) and (D) are distortions; initially the author had little knowledge of baking (C), and the author only later found that the bakery "improved the women's self-esteem" (D). (E) is out of scope; the passage does not address the author's beliefs about such projects in general.

13.   E

The author believed that starting the bakery presented a "problem," and she never mentions any political experience or ambitions. We can infer that the author feels she is equally unsuited to perform either activity. (A) is too extreme; the fact that the author feels "unprepared" does not mean she thinks the bakery will "never" work. (B) is a distortion; although the author did not expect the bakery to be part of her job, this doesn't mean she believes it should not be. (C) and (D) are out of scope; the author's feelings about her coordinator are not discussed (C), and no connection is made between the skills necessary for politics and those needed for baking bread (D). (E) is correct. The comparison makes the author's lack of preparation clear.

14. A

Just before the cited sentence, the author relates one problem: she was unprepared to bake bread. In the cited sentence, the author relates a second problem: she was "completely unfamiliar with" for-profit business models. This second problem, she suggests, was the "bigger" one that might pose more of a challenge. (B) is a distortion; the author is discussing her own comparative lack of preparation for each activity, not the relative importance of each. (C) and (E) are misused details; the coordinator's confidence is mentioned in the *next* sentence, and the author does not express a belief that confidence in for-profit business models is misplaced (C), nor does the fact that the coordinator "left" the author does not mean she was unwilling to help, only that she did not (E). (D) is out of scope; the passage does not compare the relative complexity of for-profit and non-profit business models. (A) is the correct answer.

15. E

The author makes two points in this sentence: baking improved her self-confidence as well as that of the shelter residents, and simple activities can be helpful in social work. Look for a choice that picks up on one or both of these ideas. (A) and (B) are distortions; the women's self-confidence and the author's increased together, but this does not mean that their self-confidence levels were initially equal. Also, although social work can be "as simple as kneading dough," this does not necessarily mean it is an easy profession for those who (unlike the author) have no education. (C) and (D) are out of scope; the author's prior expectations about learning new skills are not discussed, and (D) is too general because baking is the only hands-on activity discussed. (E) is the best answer. The "benefit" is increased self-confidence.

16. D

This passage has both introductory and concluding paragraphs. Reread those for an overview of the author's purpose. (A) is a misused detail; whereas the author says many successful people participate in athletics, it is not the purpose of the passage. (B) is a distortion; the author does not directly compare physical and artistic activities, nor is the passage theoretical in nature. (C) is a misused detail; pleasure is mentioned as a benefit of recreation but not as a major point of the passage. (E) is out of scope; the requisites for vocational success are not discussed in detail in this passage. (D) is the correct answer.

17. B

Limit your deliberations about meaning to the quoted clause and the sentence that contains it. (A), (D), and (E) are all out of scope; the author does not say that leisure time is preferable to work (A), does not refer to the democratic or any other form of government (D), and does not make a recommendation about frequency of recreational activities (E). (C) is opposite; the passage states that leisure time has been augmented or increased. (B) is the best answer.

18. A

Follow the logical chain of benefits mentioned in the second paragraph, to find the most important one. (B) is a distortion; this answer has a negative connotation that does not reflect either the question or the passage. (C) is too extreme; the word *always* exaggerates the expressed benefits of competition. (D) is out of scope; although this may be a true statement, it is not to be found in the passage. (E) is a misused detail; this relatively minor point is mentioned in passing. (A) is correct.

19. E

Match the tone of the answers to the tone of the words and sentences adjoining the word *competition*. (A) is opposite; note the words *without…competition* and, later in the paragraph, *needless comparison*. (B) is a distortion; the passage does not assign importance to comparative physical activities. (C) is a misused detail; whereas the author approves of enjoyment of recreation, the passage does not rank its importance. (D) is also opposite; this answer is basically a reworded version of (A) and should be eliminated for that reason alone. (E) is the best answer.

20. C

First, evaluate (for correctness) the advantage suggested after each roman numeral; then find the correct answer. (A) and (B) are limited; roman numeral I is correct but is not the only advantage mentioned in the passage, and roman numeral II is correct but is not the only advantage mentioned in the passage. (D) and (E) are out of scope; roman numerals I and II are correct, but aesthetic aspects of art are not mentioned in the passage. (C) is the best answer.

21. A

Carefully examine the context of the word, in this case, the comparison of life to a turbulent sea. (B) is a misused detail; the metaphor of the sea is not applicable in this part of the sentence. (C) is limited; *situations* is much too mild a term in this context of comparison to a sea where one might need a life jacket. (D) misconstrues the preceding metaphor of a turbulent sea. (E) counts on your being distracted by the previous mention of rules. (A) is the best answer.

22. C

Because the answer choices are adjectives, compare each one to the adjective in the quoted phrase. (A) is out of scope; the passage does not comment on the necessity of standardized testing. (B) is a misused detail; this answer could be justified by reference to the word *ever-narrowing,* but that is very different from *irrelevant.* (D) is also out of scope; the passage does not comment on whether or not standardized testing is productive. (E) is opposite; *ever-narrowing* is the opposite of *creative,* which implies expansive. (C) is the best answer.

23. D

Notice that each paragraph of the passage discusses positive aspects of productive leisure activities in terms of their benefits to individuals. (A) is opposite; the passage address the benefits of productive recreation for individuals, not for society. (B) is a misused detail; *emotional flexibility* is mentioned in connection with creative activity, but physical flexibility is not discussed. (C) and (E) are too extreme; the word *requisite* (C) means necessary, and this is an exaggeration of the author's position. Likewise, the word *ubiquitous* (E) means everywhere or always present, not a position taken by the author. (D) is the best choice.

24. D

The statement "learn to swim in a turbulent sea of ambiguity and chance without the lifejacket of standard procedure," is being used as a metaphor for the unorthodox world that artists often live in. The author is expressing the fact that those involved in this world often make decisions

and have experiences that those who live by the normal societal standards may not have, which is the opposite of (B). (A) and (E) have nothing to do with the passage, and (C) is never supported by the author. (D) is the best choice that expresses this idea.

SECTION 7

1. A

If $a < b$ and $b < c$, then $a < c$.

$8a < 3b < 10c$, so $8a < 10c$

2. C

If a problem at the beginning of a section seems easy, it probably is. All you have to do is be careful that you don't make a silly arithmetic error.

Employees by division:

Development $= 1 \times 4 = 4$

Marketing $= 2 \times 3 = 6$

Accounting $= 3 \times 2 = 6$

Public Relations $= 5 \times 5 = 25$

Overall total: $4 + 6 + 6 + 25 = 41$

3. B

You can rearrange the average formula to get whichever part you're missing.

For example, sum = (average) × (number of items).

$7 < \dfrac{sum}{7} < 12$

$49 < sum < 84$

4. E

We know that one revolution is 360°. Since this happens every 1.5 seconds, (A) and (B) are definitely too low.

The ball goes around $\dfrac{10}{1.5} = \dfrac{100}{15} = \dfrac{20}{3}$ times, for a total of

$\dfrac{20}{3}(360°) = 2{,}400°$

5. B

You need to find the total number of birds in Joe's yard on Thursday and the number of those birds that were at the suet feeder. Divide the number of birds at the suet feeder by the total number of birds, then multiply by 100 to convert this fraction into a percent.

There were 3 birds at the suet feeder on Thursday, and $6 + 3 + 2 = 11$ total birds. $\frac{3}{11} \times 100\% = 27.\overline{27}\%$. The nearest answer choice is (B), 27%.

6. A

Sunflower seeds are represented by the black circles. Find the black circle that is highest on the *y*-axis, and look down to see what day it belongs to.

The greatest number of birds at the sunflower seed feeder was 7, on Sunday. Choice (A) is correct.

7. D

This problem is testing two concepts: the sum of the angles in a triangle is 180 degrees, and the definition of an isosceles triangle. Remember that if two sides of a triangle have the same length, the angles opposite them have the same measurement.

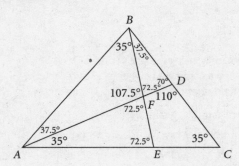

Use the facts that the interior angles of a triangle sum to 180 degrees and that angles along a line sum to 180 degrees to solve for the unknown angles, as in the figure above. Then you can see that *ABC*, *AFE*, *ADC,* and *ABE* are all isosceles; *BFD* is not.

8. E

This problem is designed to let you try out this procedure. Don't worry about having major insights—just plug in the given number and see what happens. This will help you gain the insight you need for the next two questions.

1. Choose 6.127
2. $6.127 \times 100 = 612.7$
3. The smallest integer greater than or equal to 612.7 is 613 (just round up)
4. $613 + 12 = 625$
5. Print 625

9. D

You can attack this by either trying to work backwards with each of the answers, or thinking about what kinds of results you can get from the procedure.

1. Choose a number 0–9.9
2. Result is between 0 and 990
3. Round up to nearest integer—now number is an integer between 0 and 990
4. Add 12—now number is an integer between 12 and 1002
5. Print the number from step 4

(A) Doesn't work because it's too small
(B) Doesn't work because it's too small
(C) Not an integer
(D) Correct
(E) Too large

10. C

Try plugging in a number into the reordered steps to see if you still get the same answer

We can try 6.127 again (the number doesn't change in step 5, so we'll only show 1–4)

(A) step 1. 6.127

   step 3. 7

   step 2. 700

   step 4. 712

   this does not match with what we found in #8, so it does not work

(B) step 1. 6.127

step 4. 18.127

step 3. 19

step 2. 1,900

this does not match with what we found in #8, so it does not work

(C) step 1. 6.127

step 2. 612.7

step 3. 624.7

step 4. 625

This seems to work. Notice that since we're adding an integer, it doesn't matter whether we add first or round first

(D) Doesn't work since (A) and (B) don't work

(E) Not true, since (C) works

11. B

Don't waste time trying to write fancy expressions for 3^{11} in terms of x—just convert the answer choices into powers of 3.

(A) $243x = 3^5(3^5) = 3^{10}$

(B) $3x^2 = 3(3^5)^2 = 3(3^{10}) = 3^{11}$

(C) $9x^4 = 3^2(3^5)^4 = 3^2(3^{20}) = 3^{22}$

(D) $27x^3 = 3^3(3^5)^3 = 3^3(3^{15}) = 3^{18}$

(E) $x^6 = (3^5)^6 = 3^{30}$

12. D

In many cases you can't solve for the variables individually, but you can solve for some expression in terms of them.

$n = 10 + m$

$n - m = 10$

$2(n - m) = 20$

$2(n - m) + 4 = 24$

13. B

Use the value of x to solve for c; then find the other value by factoring:

$(-5)^2 + 3(-5) + c = 0$

$25 - 15 + c = 0$

$c = -10$

$x^2 + 3x - 10 = 0$

$(x + 5)(x - 2) = 0$

$x = -5; x = 2$

14. D

Always make sure you're answering the right question. All the good algebra in the world doesn't help if you grid in the smallest or middle number.

$x + (x + 2) + (x + 4) = 1,089$

$3x + 6 = 1,089$

$3x = 1,083$

$x = 361$

$x + 2 = 363$

$x + 4 = 365$

numbers are 361, 363, 365

15. B

Work methodically, using the rate formula. Don't be discouraged by a somewhat higher level of complexity—if you understand rates then this is simply more steps.

Their respective mowing rates are:

Jan: 1 hour per lawn or 1 lawn per hour

Wally: $\frac{1}{2}$ hours per lawn or 2 lawns per hour

Peter: $\frac{2}{3}$ hour per lawn or $\frac{3}{2}$ lawns per hour

Jan mows for $\frac{1}{4}$ hours at 1 lawn per hour, so she finishes $\frac{1}{4} \times 1 = \frac{1}{4}$ of the lawn.

Together the three mow $1 + 2 + \frac{3}{2} = \frac{9}{2}$ lawns per hour, or $\frac{2}{9}$ hours per lawn.

The final part takes $\frac{3}{4}$ lawn $\times \frac{2}{9}$ hour per lawn $= \frac{1}{6}$ hours.

So the total time is $\frac{1}{4} + \frac{1}{6} = \frac{5}{12}$ hours.

16. E

Use the slope of the line to find *AB*, then split the quadrilateral into a triangle and a rectangle

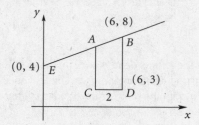

The slope of the line is $\frac{8-4}{6-0} = \frac{4}{6} = \frac{2}{3}$.

The coordinate of *C* is (4,3).

When we move from *E* to *A*, the *x*-coordinate changes by 4, so the *y*-coordinate changes by $4 \times \frac{2}{3} = \frac{8}{3}$, thus the coordinates of *A* are $(4, 4 + \frac{8}{3}) = (4, \frac{20}{3})$.

If you split the quadrilateral, the area of the triangle is $\left(\frac{1}{2}\right) \times (2) \times \left(8 - \frac{20}{3}\right) = \left(\frac{1}{2}\right) \times (2) \times \left(\frac{4}{3}\right) = \frac{4}{3}$.

The area of the rectangle is $2 \times \left(\frac{20}{3} - 3\right) = 2 \times \frac{11}{3} = \frac{22}{3}$.

So the total area is $\frac{4}{3} + \frac{22}{3} = \frac{26}{3}$.

SECTION 8

1. D

Start with the first blank. Vaccines can either be given or not given. If your prediction for the first blank is "giving," then the second blank should be positive in order to support this answer choice. A good prediction for the second blank would then be "successful" at providing protection. The first answer choice in (A) is the opposite of the prediction. "Unsuccessful in," (B), is the opposite of the prediction for the second blank. "Reconstituting," (C), or restoring, doses of the vaccine does not fit. Vaccines are not "restored" (although they may sometimes have to be re-administered). Both choices in (E) do not work; giving someone a dose of vaccine is not the same as "disseminating" or spreading it widely. "Unverified for" is the opposite of the prediction. (D) is the best answer.

2. B

Using the clue words to form a prediction for the blanks, the crew would be trying to *save* what equipment they could off of the *struggling* boat. The choices in (A) do not work. Although the boat may have been "obsolete" or "outdated," this does not describe the manner in which it sank or even why it sank. The boat was "defunct," (C), or no longer functioning, but the crew would not be "exacerbating" the equipment or making it worse. The words in (D) do not match the predictions; the crew would not try to "revitalize" or "invigorate" equipment, and a sinking dive boat is certainly not "prosperous." The first choice in (E) is too extreme. "Commandeer" means more along the lines of seizing or confiscating and suggests taking against the will of someone else. "Lucrative" does not work in the second blank as it means profitable. (B) is the best choice.

3. A

Start with a prediction for the first blank. A word such as *variety* or *diversity* would work. The second blank should support the first with a word such as a "range" of various ingredients. The first choice in (B) can be eliminated because the sentence says nothing about the size of the population growing. A growing population would imply an increasing amount of different foods would come to exist; however, nothing about growth is mentioned. The second choice is the opposite of the prediction. The first choice in (C) is out of scope; the town wouldn't have "mixed feelings towards" different foods. The second choice doesn't match the prediction. (D) Both blanks do not work. "Dearth" or "scarcity" is the opposite of the prediction and nothing is said about a reduction of ingredients available caused by using them. (E) The first blank does not fit because nothing is said about either the population or the amount of food increasing or decreasing. The second blank does not work; towns would not boast of artificial ingredients. (A) is the best answer.

4. C

If the path "meandered … for miles" then it must have "winded" and "twisted" around the riverbank. (A) is out of scope; the hiking trail may have afforded "panoramic" or "scenic" views but this is not mentioned in the sentence. Sentence completion questions will never ask you for information that is not presented in the question stem. There is no indication that the trail was "precipitous," (B), or steep. The trail did not necessarily "circumscribe," (D), the river or follow it in a circular path; the sentence describes a river, not a pond. If you did not know the meaning of this word, break it apart; circles by nature are round, so to "circumscribe" something means to go around it. There is no indication that the path twisted back on itself or went backwards, as (E) suggests. (C) is the best answer.

5.   B

Jidapa seemed to be the "opposite" of her former self. Check the answer choices to see if they match this prediction. (A) does not work. The sentence does not suggest that she became less of a certain way; she changed from behaving one way to acting quite the opposite. Her change in behavior was a result of the accident, but the sentence is comparing Jidapa to her former self and is not discussing the reasons for her change. Thus, (C) is incorrect. "The extremity of her former self," (D), does not make sense. Read back answer choices into the sentence to make sure that they fit. Even if the word were "extreme," the sentence does not suggest that she became an extreme version of her former self (i.e. more friendly or more sprightly). (E) does not fit; her behavior couldn't change to become "mainstay" or the "chief support" of herself. (B) is the best choice.

6.   C

What words describe a type of "mistake?" The blank could read *blunder*. Eliminate any answer choices that don't match this prediction. You can eliminate (A) because the sentence is not referring to a possible dispute between the detectives. (B) means jeer or laugh at and does not match the prediction. A "tryst" is a pact made between lovers and has nothing to do with detectives working on a case, thus (D) is incorrect. (E) A "tribute," (E), or praise, cannot compromise a stakeout. (C) is the best choice.

7.   E

Since the author is trying to convince or persuade the reader that the Satyr form is worthy of pursuit, you can expect the correct answer to have a positive charge. The author predicts that Satyr plays will "capture the imagination of the rising generation" and sees the chorus as a "dynamic element" that contributes to the "untapped potential" of the Satyr form. Together with the exclamation point ending the passage, this phrasing gives the passage a tone of *enthusiasm* or *excitement*. (A) is opposite; the tone is excited, not dull or faint. (B) is a distortion; the author's discussion does not have

a harsh tone overall. (C) is also a distortion; although the last paragraph is somewhat playful, overall the passage does not have a carefree or impulsive tone. (D) is out of scope; what the author hopes for has not taken place. He has nothing to be *grateful* for. (E) is the best answer.

8.   E

Read for context. The chorus dances and sings and although "invisible" to other characters, can "engage the audience without interfering" with the main action. Predict something like *draw the attention of the audience*.

(A), (B), (C), and (D) are all out of scope and relate to another meaning of the word that doesn't make sense in context. (E) is the best answer choice.

9.   C

The author's main point in the passage is that the Satyr form has not received as much attention as it deserves. The cited line supports this point by suggesting that screenwriters should seek inspiration in Satyr plays because these plays have "volumes of untapped potential." Look for a choice that notes the unexplored possibilities in Satyr plays. (A) and (B) are out of scope; translations are not discussed in the passage (A), and possible "movies about Greek drama," (B), are not mentioned. (D) is a distortion; in this context, volume is a matter of amount, not noise level. (E) is a misused detail; singing is mentioned elsewhere in the passage, but this is not related to the cited phrase.

10. B

The chorus is first mentioned in the third paragraph, but this question asks about the *fourth* paragraph. In the fourth paragraph, the author suggests that the chorus provides "a hint of what the Satyr form has to offer" and says that it can embody "unpredictable inspiration." This functions to reinforce the description from the third paragraph of the chorus as a "dynamic element…that is full of potential." Look for a choice that emphasizes the chorus's unpredictability or dynamic potential. (A) is opposite; the author is arguing that the Satyr form is worthy of more study. (C), (D), and (E) are misused details; the chorus dances, but this is not the point the author is making here (C), Satyrs, as creatures, are mentioned earlier in the passage, but this paragraph only mentions the Satyr *form* of drama (D), and although the author does say the form is *widely ignored*, the chorus is not mentioned in order to explain this fact (E). (B) is the best answer.

11. D

Along with "the lampooning of leaders," "the misadventures of husbands and wives" is given as an example of subject matter for comedy that has been "consistent over the centuries." Look for a choice that captures the long-term use of this subject matter. (A) is a distortion; whereas this may have been tempting, there is a distinction between *form* and "subject matter" that is important in this sentence and in the passage as a whole. Also, the consistency of use is not restricted to *Greek* comedy. (B) is also a distortion; again, this choice confuses form with subject matter. The form is described in the passage as sophisticated, not the *subject matter*. (C) is an example of subject matter for comedy, not tragedy. (E) is a misused detail; Satyr plays are discussed in Passage 1, not Passage 2. (D) is the best answer.

12. D

The gist of the paragraph is that, while moviegoers have become so used to common narrative devices that it's hard to surprise them, the comedic form is still flexible enough to do so. Since overexposure makes moviegoers "jaded" and unsurprised, you can infer that the word has a negative connotation. *Unsurprised* works fine as a prediction. (A) is opposite; this lacks the negative connotation required by the prediction. (B) is a distortion; this choice picks up on a similarity with jade, the mineral, but it is not the meaning in this passage. (C) is out of scope; this doesn't make sense in context. (E) is also opposite; moviegoers are *not* surprised by common narrative devices. (D) is the best answer.

13. A

The last sentence of the second paragraph leads you to anticipate more discussion of comedy's "flexibility," which is exactly what you get in the third paragraph. Look for a choice that mentions the changeable or *flexible nature of comedy*. (B) is a misused detail; although the comedic form originally came from ancient Greece, the purpose of this paragraph isn't to emphasize the importance of ancient Greek civilization as a whole. (C) is also a misused detail; the author mentions the fall of Rome in order to point out that comedy survived the fall, not to talk about the fall itself. (D) is a distortion; the author's focus is on the flexibility of comedy, but the passage does not suggest that there is a *general misunderstanding* of comedy as rigid. (E) is out of scope; the paragraph is about the flexibility of comedy for many generations, not intergenerational traditions beyond the sphere of comedy. (A) is the best choice.

14. B

A form is a structure, model, or mode. To say that a form is "wildly loose" is to create a contradiction. So, the author puts quotation marks around the word "form" to suggest that the word shouldn't be taken too literally. (A) is the opposite; if the author were using the exact definition, there would be no need for quotation marks. (C), (D), (E) are all distortions; if the author intended to use another word (C), presumably he would have; although the author discusses both theater and cinema (D), the quotation marks do not highlight a difference between them; and the author frequently uses the word earlier in the passage (E) but does not define it. (B) is the best answer.

15. A

The first author emphasizes the potential of Satyr plays, while the second author emphasizes the strengths of comedies. Despite these differences, however, both authors agree with the broad idea that current filmmakers and screenwriters can learn from the plays of antiquity. Even if this similarity doesn't occur to you right away, you can recognize it when you evaluate the choices. (B) is out of scope; the author of Passage 1 does not discuss comedy's flexibility or resilience as compared to other dramatic forms. (C) is too extreme; although neither author focuses on the potential value of tragedy, this choice is stronger than warranted by the text. (D) is also out of scope; the author of Passage 2 does not discuss Satyr plays. (E) is a distortion; both authors offer suggestions for making successful films, but they do not imply that audiences "are bored by the current cinema." (A) is correct; whereas the author of Passage 2 does not emphasize Greek theater as much as the first author does, he does reference it in the course of his argument.

16. B

Working by elimination is a good way to approach this question. The correct choice will be something discussed by both authors, and something both sees as valuable. The audience fits this bill. The first author describes the chorus's ability to "engage the audience" as a strength of Satyr plays, and the second author mentions how the audience "rewards successful filmmakers with loyalty." (A) is out of scope; the *chorus* is not mentioned in Passage 2. (C) is a distortion; the first author only mentions critics briefly in a negative light, and the second author does not directly discuss critics at all. (D) and (E) are also out of scope;

screenwriters (D) are mentioned in Passage 1, but the only job title mentioned in Passage 2 is that of filmmaker, and although this may initially seem tempting, a closer examination reveals that Passage 2 does not mention characters (E) at all. (B) is the best answer.

17. D

Sometimes the author will state the purpose right away, as in the first sentence here—"Of the two primary forms of drama…comedy is the more promising form for the future of cinema." The rest of the passage supports this thesis. Use this quote as your prediction. (A) is out of scope; Passage 2 does not discuss *the Satyr form*. (B) is a misused detail; whereas the author makes this point, it is not *the main idea* of the passage. (C) is too extreme; the author indicates that comedy is "more promising" for the cinema, not *superior* in every way. (E) is a distortion; this exaggerates points made in the text, and is hardly the author's main point. (D) is the best answer.

18. B

Passage 1 describes the "mix of cowardice and boldness" in Falstaff, but says little else. The author of Passage 2 is most concerned with advocating the comic form as the best way of breathing new life into the cinema. Look for a choice that incorporates that main idea in some way. (A) is out of scope; the author of Passage 2 does not comment on the Satyr form. (C) is a distortion; the author of Passage 2 does directly mention *Greek and Roman drama*, but says nothing about *Elizabethan drama*. (D) is also out of scope; the author of Passage 2 does not comment on Satyr plays. (E) is also a distortion; whereas the author of Passage 2 does mention *the sophistication of the comic form*, nothing indicates that Falstaff—based on the brief comment the first author makes about him—is *an example* of that sophistication. (B) is correct; this matches well with the main idea of Passage 2.

SECTION 9

1. B

This sentence presents a cause (providing emergency power) and its effect (being invaluable). *Because*, in (B), best reflects this relationship. The transitions in (C) and (D) do not properly relate the clauses. (E) uses a plural pronoun to refer to a singular antecedent, *generator*.

2. A

This sentence contains no error. The pronoun *of* in (B) is idiomatically incorrect with *assertive*. (C), (D), and (E) are unnecessarily wordy.

3. D

As written, this sentence as a fragment. (D) corrects this by replacing the gerund form with *hire*. The verb in (B) doesn't agree with its plural subject, *vineyards*. (C) does not address the error. (E) is unnecessarily wordy.

4. C

As written, this sentence is unnecessarily wordy. (C) is concise, yet contains all of the information in the original. Using both *Generally* and *most of the time*, as (B) does, is redundant. (D) and (E) are both unnecessarily wordy.

5. E

Technical school graduates work *in other jobs*, not *as…other jobs*. (E) is the correct choice here. None of the other choices is in parallel form.

6. D

As written, this is a run-on sentence. (D) corrects this by making the second clause dependent. (B) implies a causation that doesn't exist in the original. (C) does not address the error. (E) incorrectly uses the pronoun *which* to refer to a person.

7. B

The past tense is not correct for a result that had not yet happened at the time. *In the hope* indicates that the result may or may not occur, so *would prevent* is the appropriate verb phrase here; the correct choice is (B). *Will prevent* would only be appropriate if the rest of the sentence were in the present tense, so (C), (D), and (E) are incorrect; additionally, (C) unnecessarily introduces the passive voice.

8. B

As written, this sentence indicates that the Vatican City is visited frequently because it is its own country. (B) clarifies the relationship between the ideas. (C) is incorrect grammatical structure, (D) changes the meaning of the original sentence, and (E) fails to address the error.

9. C

The pronoun *you* cannot be used with the antecedent *candidate*. (C) replaces *you* with the appropriate third-person pronouns. (B) uses *it* to refer to a person. (D) and (E) use verb tenses that are inappropriate in context.

10. D

As written, this sentence says that Chopin was *Among the most complex musical composition of the era*. Both (C) and (D) place the correct noun, *Etudes*, after the modifying phrase (a possessive, such as *Chopin's* here, functions as an adjective), but (C) creates a sentence fragment. In (B), the introductory phrase modifies *piano*. (E) does not address the error; additionally, it creates a sentence fragment.

11. B

In this sentence, *he* could refer to either the defendant or the lawyer. (B) and (D) both make it clear about who *was sorry*, but (D) creates a sentence fragment. (C) and (E) do not address the ambiguity issue.

12. A

This sentence is correct as written. (B) and (D) are unnecessarily wordy. (C) creates a run-on sentence. (E) is incorrect grammatical structure.

13. B

The first two verbs in the series are *rinse* and *wipe*; "dry" would be the correct form for the third verb. None of the other choices make the third verb parallel.

14. C

The sentence as written compares what is being transmitted, *images*, to a method of transmission, *fax*. (C) corrects this by using the pronoun *those* to refer to *images*. (B), (D), and (E) fail to address the error.

Compute Your Score

These scores are intended to give you an approximate idea of your performance. There is no way to determine your exact score for the following reasons.

- Various statistical factors and formulas are taken into account on the real test.
- For each grade, the scaled score range changes from year to year.
- There is no way to accurately grade your essay on these practice tests. Additionally, there will be two graders reading your essay on the real test.

The official score range for each section of the SAT will be 200–800. Taken together, the perfect total score becomes 2400.

STEP 1: SCORE YOUR ESSAY.

Your essay will account for one-third of your writing grade, and the multiple-choice questions will account for two-thirds. Your essay is scored on a scale from 1–6, and that score is later calculated with the multiple-choice score into the 200–800 range.

Naturally, it will be difficult for you to score your own essay here. Ask someone whose opinion you respect to read it and assign it a value from 1 to 6, based on the following criteria:

6. **Outstanding essay**—Though it may have a few small errors, is well organized and fully developed with supporting examples. Displays consistent language facility, varied sentence structure, and range of vocabulary.

5. **Solid essay**—Though it has occasional errors or lapses in quality, it is generally organized and well-developed with appropriate examples. Displays language facility, with syntactic variety and a range of vocabulary.

4. **Adequate essay**—Though it has some flaws, it is organized and developed adequately with some examples. Displays adequate but inconsistent language facility.

3. **Limited essay**—Does not adequately fulfill the writing assignment and has many flaws. Has inadequate organization and development, along with many errors in grammar and/or diction. Has little variety.

2. **Flawed essay**—Demonstrates some incompetence with one or more weaknesses. Ideas are vague and thinly developed. Has frequent errors in grammar and diction and has no variety.

1. **Deficient essay**—Demonstrates incompetence, with serious flaws. Has no organization, no development, and severe grammar and diction errors. Is so seriously flawed that basic meaning is obscured.

STEP 2: FIGURE OUT YOUR RAW SCORE FOR EACH PRACTICE TEST.

First, check your answers to the multiple-choice questions against the answer keys on the previous pages. Count up the number of answers you got right and the number you got wrong for each section. Remember, do not count questions left blank as wrong. Round up to the nearest whole number. Now, plug them in below.

Note: Grid-in questions do not have a wrong-answer penalty. So, do not deduct anything for wrong answers.

PRACTICE TEST ONE

Critical Reading

	Number Right	Number Wrong	Raw Score
Section 2:	□	− (.25 × □) =	□
Section 4:	□	− (.25 × □) =	□
Section 7:	□	− (.25 × □) =	□
		Critical Reading Raw Score =	□ (rounded up)

Writing

	Number Right	Number Wrong	Raw Score
Section 1:	□ (ESSAY GRADE)	× 3.17 =	□
Section 6:	□	− (.25 × □) =	□
Section 9:	□	− (.25 × □) =	□
		Writing Raw Score =	□ (rounded up)

Math

	Number Right	Number Wrong	Raw Score
Section 3:	□	− (.25 × □) =	□
Section 5A: (QUESTIONS 1–8)	□	− (.25 × □) =	□
Section 5B: (QUESTIONS 9–18)	□	(no wrong answer penalty) =	□
Section 8:	□	− (.25 × □) =	□
		Math Raw Score =	□ (rounded up)

PRACTICE TEST TWO

Critical Reading

	Number Right	Number Wrong	Raw Score
Section 3:	☐	− (.25 × ☐)	= ☐
Section 6:	☐	− (.25 × ☐)	= ☐
Section 8:	☐	− (.25 × ☐)	= ☐
	Critical Reading Raw Score		= ☐
			(rounded up)

Writing

	Number Right	Number Wrong	Raw Score
Section 1:	☐ (ESSAY GRADE)	× 3.17	= ☐
Section 5:	☐	− (.25 × ☐)	= ☐
Section 9:	☐	− (.25 × ☐)	= ☐
	Writing Raw Score		= ☐
			(rounded up)

Math

	Number Right	Number Wrong	Raw Score
Section 2:	☐	− (.25 × ☐)	= ☐
Section 4A: (QUESTIONS 1–8)	☐	− (.25 × ☐)	= ☐
Section 4B: (QUESTIONS 9–18)	☐	(no wrong answer penalty)	= ☐
Section 7:	☐	− (.25 × ☐)	= ☐
	Math Raw Score		= ☐
			(rounded up)

KAPLAN

PRACTICE TEST THREE

Critical Reading

	Number Right		Number Wrong		Raw Score
Section 2:	☐	− (	.25 × ☐)	=	☐
Section 4:	☐	− (	.25 × ☐)	=	☐
Section 7:	☐	− (	.25 × ☐)	=	☐
		Critical Reading Raw Score		=	☐
					(rounded up)

Writing

	Number Right		Number Wrong		Raw Score
Section 1:	☐ (ESSAY GRADE)	×	3.17	=	☐
Section 6:	☐	− (	.25 × ☐)	=	☐
Section 9:	☐	− (	.25 × ☐)	=	☐
		Writing Raw Score		=	☐
					(rounded up)

Math

	Number Right		Number Wrong		Raw Score
Section 3:	☐	− (	.25 × ☐)	=	☐
Section 5A: (QUESTIONS 1–8)	☐	− (	.25 × ☐)	=	☐
Section 5B: (QUESTIONS 9–18)	☐	(no wrong answer penalty)		=	☐
Section 8:	☐	− (	.25 × ☐)	=	☐
		Math Raw Score		=	☐
					(rounded up)

PRACTICE TEST FOUR

Critical Reading

	Number Right	Number Wrong	Raw Score
Section 3:	☐	− (.25 × ☐) =	☐
Section 6:	☐	− (.25 × ☐) =	☐
Section 8:	☐	− (.25 × ☐) =	☐
	Critical Reading Raw Score	=	☐
			(rounded up)

Writing

	Number Right	Number Wrong	Raw Score
Section 1:	☐ (ESSAY GRADE) ×	3.17 =	☐
Section 4:	☐	− (.25 × ☐) =	☐
Section 9:	☐	− (.25 × ☐) =	☐
	Writing Raw Score	=	☐
			(rounded up)

Math

	Number Right	Number Wrong	Raw Score
Section 2:	☐	− (.25 × ☐) =	☐
Section 5A: (QUESTIONS 1–8)	☐	− (.25 × ☐) =	☐
Section 5B: (QUESTIONS 9–18)	☐	(no wrong answer penalty) =	☐
Section 7:	☐	− (.25 × ☐) =	☐
	Math Raw Score	=	☐
			(rounded up)

KAPLAN

STEP 3: CONVERT YOUR RAW SCORE TO A SCALED SCORE.

For each subject area in the practice test, convert your raw score to your scaled score using the table below.

| RAW | SCALED* | | | | | | | | |
	Critical Reading	Math	Writing 0	Writing 1	Writing 2	Writing 3	Writing 4	Writing 5	Writing 6
67	800								
66	800								
65	790								
64	770								
63	750								
62	740								
61	730								
60	720								
59	700								
58	690								
57	690								
56	680								
55	670								
54	660	800							
53	650	790							
52	650	760							
51	640	740							
50	630	720							
49	620	710	670	700	720	740	780	790	800
48	620	700	660	680	700	730	760	780	790
47	610	680	650	670	690	720	750	770	780
46	600	670	640	660	680	710	740	750	770
45	600	660	630	650	670	700	740	750	770
44	590	650	620	640	660	690	730	750	760
43	590	640	600	630	650	680	710	740	750
42	580	630	600	620	640	670	700	730	750
41	570	620	590	610	630	660	690	730	740
40	570	620	580	600	620	650	690	720	740
39	560	610	570	590	610	640	680	710	740
38	550	600	560	590	610	630	670	700	730
37	550	590	550	580	600	630	660	690	720
36	540	580	540	570	590	620	650	680	710
35	540	580	540	560	580	610	640	680	710
34	530	570	530	550	570	600	640	670	700
33	520	560	520	540	560	590	630	660	690
32	520	550	510	540	560	580	620	650	680
31	520	550	500	530	550	580	610	640	670
30	510	550	490	520	540	570	600	630	660
29	510	540	490	510	530	560	590	630	650

*These are not official College Board scores. They are rough estimates to help you get an idea of your performance.

RAW	Critical Reading	Math	Writing 0	Writing 1	Writing 2	Writing 3	Writing 4	Writing 5	Writing 6
28	500	540	480	500	520	550	590	620	640
27	490	530	470	490	510	540	580	610	640
26	480	520	460	490	500	530	570	600	630
25	470	510	450	480	500	520	560	590	620
24	460	500	440	470	490	510	550	580	610
23	460	500	430	460	480	510	540	570	600
22	450	490	430	450	470	500	530	570	590
21	450	490	430	450	470	500	530	570	590
20	440	480	420	440	460	490	520	560	580
19	430	470	410	430	450	480	520	550	570
18	420	460	400	420	440	470	510	540	570
17	410	460	390	420	430	460	500	530	560
16	400	450	380	410	430	450	490	520	550
15	390	440	370	400	420	450	480	510	540
14	380	430	360	390	410	440	470	500	530
13	360	420	360	380	400	430	460	500	520
12	340	400	340	370	390	420	450	490	510
11	330	390	340	360	380	410	450	480	510
10	320	380	330	350	370	400	440	470	500
9	310	370	320	350	360	390	430	460	490
8	300	360	310	340	360	390	420	450	480
7	290	350	300	330	350	380	410	440	470
6	270	340	290	320	340	370	400	430	460
5	270	330	290	310	330	360	390	430	450
4	260	300	280	300	320	350	390	420	450
3	240	280	270	290	310	340	380	410	440
2	230	260	260	280	300	330	370	400	430
1	210	240	250	270	290	320	340	380	410
0	200	220	250	260	280	310	340	370	400
neg 1	200	200	240	260	270	290	320	360	380
neg 2	200	200	230	250	260	270	310	340	370
neg 3	200	200	220	240	250	260	300	330	360
neg 4	200	200	220	230	240	250	290	320	350
neg 5	200	200	200	220	230	240	280	310	340
neg 6	200	200	200	210	220	240	280	310	340
neg 7	200	200	200	210	220	230	270	300	330
neg 8	200	200	200	210	220	230	270	300	330
neg 9	200	200	200	210	220	230	270	300	330
neg 10	200	200	200	210	220	230	270	300	330

Resources

RESOURCES OVERVIEW

The Kaplan Premier SAT Program prepares you for taking the SAT and helps you get your highest score. The following six resources are for students who want to make sure they have left no stone unturned when it comes to prepping for this important test.

We suggest you read Resource One if you need help calming down and focusing on the test. Resources Two, Three, and Four will help round and strengthen your SAT vocabulary. Resource Five is a good refresher course on the grammar tested on the SAT. Resource Six is a good refresher course on the Math tested on the SAT.

Resource One: **SAT Mindset**

You read the book. You took the practice tests. You know the SAT better than you know yourself. Wonderful. Give yourself a hug.

The next most important part of taking the SAT is having a cool, calm, and collected brain when you are prepping and on the day you take the test. That's what we teach you to do in this resource, because on SAT day, few things can hurt your score more than being:

- Fried out of your brain on Mountain Dew
- In deep denial over your lack of preparation
- Clueless as to what to expect from the test
- Clueless as to what to expect from yourself

This resource teaches you:

- How to relax
- How to visualize success
- How to build your physical and mental strength

DEALING WITH TEST STRESS

The SAT is scary because it is *the unknown*. You don't know the exact questions that are going to be on it. You don't know how you are going to do. You don't know how your score will stand up at your favorite college (is a 1950 good or bad for State Tech U?).

But we are here to ease that fear. We will focus on minimizing your SAT unknowns so you can focus on one single thing—getting the most points that you can possibly get out of each SAT section.

The main point of this book is to help you exert control over your SAT experience. You can control your anxiety the same way you can control how you answer a multiple-choice Math question—by knowing what to expect beforehand and developing strategies to deal with it.

We will show you how to relieve stress and mentally prepare for the SAT in seven specific ways:

1. Identifying sources of stress
2. Identifying strengths and weaknesses
3. Visualizing success
4. Exercising away anxiety
5. Eating right
6. Doing isometric exercises

SOURCES OF SAT STRESS

The following list contains some of the most common sources of SAT stress. Take a moment to read through them.

- I always freeze up on tests.
- I'm nervous about the essay (or the paragraph corrections, the sentence corrections, etc.).
- I need a good/great score to get into my first-choice college.
- My older brother/sister/best friend/girlfriend/boyfriend did really well. I must match their scores or do better.
- My parents, who are paying for school, will be quite disappointed if I don't do well.
- I'm afraid of losing my focus and concentration.
- I'm afraid I'm not spending enough time preparing.
- I study like crazy, but nothing seems to stick in my mind.
- I always run out of time and get panicky.
- The simple act of thinking, for me, is like wading through refrigerated syrup.

Now, grab a pencil and some scratch paper. You are going to take five to ten minutes to write down your sources of test-related stress. Feel free to use any of our examples that apply to you. The idea is to pin down your sources of anxiety so you can deal with them one by one. Start now.

Finished? Great. Now read through the list. Take another two or three minutes. Cross out things or add things. Now rewrite the list in order of most bothersome to least bothersome. Start now.

What was your number one stress source? Chances are, the top of the list is a fairly accurate description of exactly what you need to tackle. Taking care of the top 2–3 items on the list should go a long way toward relieving your overall test anxiety. So, circle your top 3 sources.

The rest of this chapter will help you eliminate them.

STRENGTHS AND WEAKNESSES

On the back of the same sheet of paper you used to identify your sources of stress take 60 seconds to list the areas of the SAT or any other test that you are good at. They can be general (math) or specific (addition of even numbers). Time yourself. Put down as many as you can think of. Write for the entire time. Go.

Now, take 60 seconds to list areas of the test you need to improve on, are just plain bad at, have failed at, or keep failing at. Write until you reach the cutoff. Go.

Taking stock of your strengths and weaknesses lets you know the areas you don't have to worry about and the ones that will demand extra attention and effort.

As you work through the book, refer back to your *weaknesses* list. Check off your weaknesses (Math? Uncontrollable nerves? Essay writing?) as you tackle each one of them.

Now we're going to focus on what you're good at. Sharpen your pencil. Go to your *strengths* list. You're going to make them more specific.

For example, if you listed *vocabulary* as a broad topic you feel strong in, you would get specific by including areas of this subject about which you are particularly knowledgeable. Your areas of strength might include Sentence Completion questions and Vocabulary-in-Context question types in the Reading Comprehension section. If any new strengths come to mind, jot them down, but don't list strengths you don't really have. You'll only be fooling yourself.

Check your watch. You have five minutes. Go.

You just took an active step toward helping yourself. Increased feelings of confidence work wonders on the SAT. For the rest of this chapter, we are going to focus on building on these good feelings. We are going to help you increase your feelings of confidence and put them toward taking and preparing for the SAT.

RELAXATION AND VISUALIZATION

Put away your pencil. Sit in a comfortable chair in a quiet setting. Really. Do it. If you wear glasses, take them off. Close your eyes and breathe in a deep, satisfying breath of air. Really fill your lungs until your rib cage is fully expanded and you can't take in anymore.

Now exhale the air completely. Imagine you're blowing out a candle with your last little puff of air. Do this two or three more times, filling your lungs to their maximum and emptying them totally.

With your eyes shut, you're no longer dealing with the worries of the outside world. Now you can concentrate on what happens inside. The more you recognize your own physical reactions to stress and anxiety, the more you can do about them. You may not realize it, but you've begun to regain a sense of being in control.

Now, visualize a relaxing situation. It might be in a special place you've visited before or one you've read about. It can be a fictional location that you create in your imagination, but a real-life memory of a place or situation you know is usually better.

Make it as detailed as possible, and notice as much as you can. Stay focused on the images as you sink farther into your chair. Breathe easily and naturally. You might have the sensation of any stress or tension draining from your muscles and flowing downward, out your feet, and away from you. Do this for five minutes or so.

When you are done, slowly open your eyes. Take a moment to check how you're feeling. Notice how comfortable you've become. Imagine how much easier it would be if you could take the SAT feeling this relaxed and in this state of ease. You've coupled the images of your special place with sensations of comfort and relaxation. You've also found a way to become relaxed simply by visualizing your own safe, special place.

Visualize Success

This next part reinforces your *strengths* list. It takes visualization one step further. Close your eyes and remember a situation in which you did something that you were really proud of—a genuine accomplishment.

Make the memory as detailed as possible. Think about the sights, the sounds, the smells, even the tastes associated with this remembered experience. Remember how confident you felt as you accomplished your goal.

Now start thinking about the SAT as an extension of this successful feeling. Don't make comparisons between them. Just imagine taking the SAT with the same feelings of confidence and relaxed control. This exercise is a great way to bring the test down to earth and to replace feelings of dread you may have associated with the SAT with feelings of accomplishment.

Practice your general relaxation technique and this specific relaxation technique together at least three times a week, especially when you feel burned out on SAT prep. The more you practice relaxation and visualization, the more effective the exercise will be for you.

EXERCISE AWAY YOUR ANXIETY

The SAT is like a marathon. Finishing a marathon strong is just as important as being quick early on. In fact, it's more important. Same goes with the 3-hour 45-minute SAT. If you can't sustain your energy level in the last sections of the exam, you could be in trouble.

Prepping for the SAT is like a marathon, too. You are going to be spending a lot of hours with this book. You are going to need stamina for those late nights, those early mornings, and those long study halls. Thus, you've got to get in shape.

Lots of students get out of the habit of regular exercise when they're prepping for the exam. But physical exercise is a very effective way to stimulate both your mind and body and to improve your ability to think and concentrate.

When you take a study break, do something active. Take a 5–10 minute exercise break for every 50 or 60 minutes that you study. The physical exertion helps keep your mind and body in sync.

Exercise also develops your mental stamina and increases the oxygen transfer to your brain. Sedentary people get less oxygen to the blood (and hence to the brain) than active people. You can watch TV with a little less oxygen, but you can't think as well.

Another advantage of exercise is that it releases your brain's endorphins. Endorphins have no side effects, and they're free! It just takes some exercise to release them and help them occupy the happy spots in your brain's neural synapses.

However, we do have one warning about exercise. It's not a good idea to exercise vigorously right before you go to bed. This could easily cause sleep-onset problems. For the same reason, it's not a good idea to study right up to bedtime. Make time for a buffer period before you go to bed.

SQUEEZE YOUR BODY

Here's a fast, natural route to relaxation and invigoration. You can do it whenever you get stressed out, including during the test. The entire process takes five minutes from start to finish (maybe a couple of minutes during the test). Starting with your eyes and—while breathing slowly and easily—gradually tighten every muscle in your body in the following sequence:

- Close your eyes tightly.
- Squeeze your nose and mouth together so that your whole face is scrunched up.
- Pull your chin into your chest, and pull your shoulders together.
- Tighten your arms to your body, then clench your fists.
- Pull in your stomach. Squeeze your thighs together, and tighten your calves.
- Stretch your feet, then curl your toes (watch out for cramping in this part).

At this point, every muscle should be tightened. Now, relax your body, one part at a time, in reverse order, starting with your toes. Let the tension drop out of each muscle. This clenching and unclenching exercise will feel silly at first, but, you will feel very relaxed.

SAY NO TO DRUGS, YES TO EATING RIGHT

Using drugs to prepare for a big test is not a good idea. Don't take uppers to stay alert. Amphetamines make it hard to retain information. Mild stimulants, such as coffee, cola, or over-the-counter caffeine pills can help you study longer because they keep you awake, but they can also lead to agitation, restlessness, and insomnia.

To reduce stress, eat fruits and vegetables (raw is best, or just lightly steamed or nuked), low-fat protein such as fish, skinless poultry, beans, and legumes (like lentils), and whole grains such as brown rice, whole wheat bread, and pasta (no bleached flour).

Don't eat sweet, high-fat snacks. Simple carbohydrates like sugar make stress worse, and fatty foods lower your immunity. Don't eat salty foods either. They can deplete potassium, which you need for nerve functions. You can go back to your Combos-and-Dew diet after the SAT.

GOOD STRESS

We haven't said this yet, but it bears mentioning. A *little* anxiety is a good thing. You want to be relaxed when you take and prepare for the SAT, but not too relaxed. The adrenaline that gets pumped into your bloodstream with anxiety helps you stay alert and think more clearly.

Resource Two: **Word Roots**

Knowing roots of words can help you in two ways. First, instead of learning one word at a time, you can learn a whole group of words that contain a certain root. They'll be related in meaning, so if you remember one, it will be easier for you to remember others. Second, roots can often help you decode an unknown SAT word. If you recognize a familiar root, you can get a good enough idea of the word to answer the question.

A, AN—not, without
amoral, atrophy, asymmetrical, anarchy, anesthetic

AB, A—from, away, apart
abnormal, abdicate, ablution, abnegate, absolve, abstemious, abstruse, annul, avert

AC, ACR—sharp, sour
acid, acerbic, exacerbate, acute, acrimony

AD, A—to, towards
adhere, adjacent, adjunct, admonish, adroit, adumbrate, accretion, accertion, alleviate, aspire, assail, assonance, attest

ALI, ALTR—another
alias, alienate, inalienable, altruism

AM, AMI—love
amorous, amicable, amiable, amity

AMBI, AMPHI—both
ambiguous, ambivalent, ambidextrous, amphibious

AMBL, AMBUL—walk
amble, ambulatory, perambulator, somnambulist

ANIM—mind, spirit, breath
animal, animosity, unanimous, magnanimous

ANN, ENN—year
annual, annuity, biennial, perennial

ANTE, ANT—before
antecedent, antediluvian, antiquated, anticipate

ANTHROP—human
anthropology, philanthropy

ANTI, ANT—against, opposite
antidote, antithesis, antacid, antagonist, antonym

AUD—hear
audio, audience, audition

AUTO—self
autobiography, autocrat, autonomous

BELLI, BELL—war
belligerent, bellicose, antebellum, rebellion

BENE, BEN—good
benevolent, benefactor, beneficent, benign

BI—two
bicycle, bisect, bilateral, bilingual, biped

BIBLIO—book
Bible, bibliography, bibliophile

BIO—life
biography, biology, amphibious, symbiotic, macrobiotics

BURS—money, purse
reimburse, disburse, bursar

KAPLAN

CAD, CAS, CID—happen, fall
accident, cadence, cascade, deciduous

CAP, CIP—head
captain, decapitate, precipitate, recapitulate

CARN—flesh
carnal, carnage, incarnate

CAP, CAPT, CEPT, CIP—take, hold, seize
capable, capacious, captivate, deception, intercept, inception, anticipate, emancipation

CED, CESS—yield, go
cease, cessation, incessant, cede, precede, accede

CHROM—color
chrome, chromatic, monochrome

CHRON—time
chronology, chronic, anachronism

CIDE—murder
suicide, homicide, regicide, patricide

CIRCUM—around
circumference, circumlocution, circumspect, circumvent

CLIN, CLIV—slope
incline, declivity, proclivity

CLUD, CLUS, CLAUS, CLOIS—shut, close
conclude, reclusive, claustrophobia, cloister, preclude, occlude

CO, COM, CON—with, together
coeducation, coagulate, coalesce, coerce, collateral, commodious, complaint, concord, congenial, congential

COGN, GNO—know
recognize, cognition, diagnosis, agnostic, prognosis

CONTRA—against
controversy, incontrovertible, contravene

CORP—body
corpse, corporeal, corpulence

COSMO, COSM—world
cosmopolitan, cosmos, microcosm, macrocosm

CRAC, CRAT—rule, power
democracy, bureaucracy, autocrat, aristocrat

CRED—trust, believe
incredible, credulous, credence

CRESC, CRET—grow
crescent, crescendo, accretion

CULP—blame, fault
culprit, culpable, inculpate, exculpate

CURR, CURS—run
current, concur, cursory, precursor, incursion

DE—down, out, apart
depart, debase, debilitate, defamatory, demur

DEC—ten, tenth
decade, decimal, decathlon, decimate

DEMO, DEM—people
democrat, demographics, demagogue, epidemic

DI, DIURN—day
diary, quotidian, diurnal

DIA—across
diagonal, diatribe, diaphanous

DIC, DICT—speak
abdicate, diction, indict, verdict

DIS, DIF, DI—not, apart, away
disaffected, disband, disbar, distend, differentiate, diffidence, diffuse, digress, divert

DOC, DOCT—teach
docile, doctrine, doctrinaire

DOL—pain
condolence, doleful, dolorous, indolent

DUC, DUCT—lead
seduce, induce, conduct, viaduct, induct

EGO—self
ego, egoist, egocentric

EN, EM—in, into
enter, entice, encumber, embroil, empathy

ERR—wander
erratic, aberration, errant

EU—well, good
eulogy, euphemism, eurythmics, euthanasia

EX, E—out, out of
exit, exacerbate, excerpt, excommunicate, elicit, egress, egregious

FAC, FIC, FECT, FY, FEA—make, do
factory, facility, benefactor, malefactor, fiction, fictive, rectify, vilify, feasible

FAL, FALS—deceive
infallible, fallacious, false

FERV—boil
fervent, fervid, effervescent

FID—faith, trust
confident, diffidence, perfidious, fidelity

FLU, FLUX—flow
fluent, affluent, superfluous, flux

FORE—before
forecast, foreboding, forestall

FRAG, FRAC—break
fragment, fracture, refract

FUS—pour
profuse, infusion, effusive, diffuse

GEN—birth, class, kin
generation, congenital, homogeneous, ingenious, engender

GRAD, GRESS—step
graduate, gradual, retrograde, ingress, egress

GRAPH, GRAM—writing
biography, bibliography, epigram

GRAT—pleasing
grateful, gratitude, gratuitous, gratuity

GRAV, GRIEV—heavy
grave, gravity, aggrieve, grievous

GREG—crowd, flock
segregate, gregarious, aggregate

HABIT, HIBIT—have, hold
habit, cohabit, habitat, inhibit

HAP—by chance
happen, haphazard, hapless, mishap

HELIO, HELI—sun
heliocentric, heliotrope, aphelion, perihelion, helium

HETERO—other
heterosexual, heterogeneous, heterodox

HOL—whole
holocaust, catholic, holistic

HOMO—same
homosexual, homogenize, homogeneous, homonym

HOMO—man
homo sapiens, homicide, bonhomie

HYDR—water
hydrant, hydrate, dehydration

HYPER—too much, excess
hyperactive, hyperbole, hyperventilate

HYPO—too little, under
hypodermic, hypothermia, hypochondria

IN, IG, IL, IM, IR—not
incorrigible, insomnia, interminable, incessant, ignorant, ignominious, ignoble, illicit, illimitable, immaculate, immutable, impertinent, improvident, irregular

IN, IL, IM, IR—in, on, into
invade, inaugurate, incandescent, illustrate, imbue, immerse, implicate, irrigate, irritate

INTER—between, among
intercede, intercept, interdiction, interject

INTRA, INTR—within
intrastate, intravenous, intramural, intrinsic

IT, ITER—between, among
transit, itinerant, transitory, reiterate

JECT, JET—throw
eject, interject, abject, trajectory, jettison

JOUR—day
journal, adjourn, sojourn

JUD—judge
judge, judicious, prejudice, adjudicate

JUNCT, JUG—join
junction, adjunct, injunction

JUR—swear, law
jury, abjure, perjure, jurisprudence

LAT—side
lateral, collateral, unilateral

LAV, LAU, LU—wash
lavatory, laundry, ablution, antediluvian

LEG, LEC, LEX—read, speak
legible, lecture, lexicon

LEV—light
elevate, levitate, levity, alleviate

LIBER—free
liberty, liberal, libertarian, libertine

LIG, LECT—choose, gather
eligible, elect, select

LIG, LI, LY—bind
ligament, oblige, religion, liable, liaison, lien, ally

LING, LANG—tongue
lingo, language, linguistics, bilingual

LITER—letter
literate, alliteration, literal

LITH—stone
monolith, lithograph, megalith

LOQU, LOC, LOG—speech, thought
eloquent, loqucaious, colloquial, circumlocution,
monologue, dialogue

LUC, LUM—light
lucid, elucidate, pellucid, translucent, illuminate

LUD, LUS—play
ludicrous, allude, delusion

MACRO—great
macrocosm, macrobiotics

MAG, MAJ, MAS, MAX—great
magnify, magnanimous, magnate, magnitude, majesty,
master, maximum

MAL—bad
malady, maladroit, malevolent, malodorous

MAN—hand
manual, manuscript, manifest

MAR—sea
submarine, marine, maritime

MATER, MATR—mother
maternal, matron, matrilineal

MEDI—middle
intermediary, medieval, mediate

MEGA—great
megaphone, megalomania, megaton, megalith

MEM, MEN—remember
memory, memento, memorabilia, reminisce

METER, METR, MENS—measure
meter, thermometer, commensurate

MICRO—small
microscope, microorganism, microcosm, microbe

MIS—wrong, bad, hate
misunderstand, misapprehension, misconstrue, mishap

MIT, MISS—send
transmit, emit, missive

MOLL—soft
mollify, emollient, mollusk

MON, MONIT—warn
admonish, monitor, premonition

MONO—one
monologue, monotonous, monogamy

MOR—custom, manner
moral, mores, morose

MOR, MORT—dead
morbid, moribund, mortal, amortize

MORPH—shape
amorphous, anthropomorphic, morphology

MOV, MOT, MOB, MOM—move
remove, motion, mobile, momentum, momentous

MUT—change
mutate, mutability, immutable, commute

NAT, NASC—born
native, nativity, cognate, nascent, renascent, renaissance

NAU, NAV—ship, sailor
nautical, nauseous, navy, circumnavigate

NEG—not, deny
negative, abnegate, renege

NEO—new
neoclassical, neophyte, neologism, neonate

NIHIL—none, nothing
annihilation, nihilism

NOM, NYM—name
nominate, nomenclature, nominal, synonym, anonymity

NOX, NIC, NEC, NOC—harm
obnoxious, internecine, innocuous

NOV—new
novelty, innovation, novitiate

NUMER—number
numeral, numerous, innumerable, enumerate

OB—against
obstruct, obdurate, obsequious, obtrusive

OMNI—all
omnipresent, omnipotent, omniscient, omnivorous

ONER—burden
onerous, exonerate

OPER—work
operate, cooperate, inoperable

PAC—peace
pacify, pacifist, pacific

PALP—feel
palpable, palpitation

PAN—all
panorama, panacea, pandemic, panoply

PATER, PATR—father
paternal, paternity, patriot, compatriot, expatriate

PATH, PASS—feel, suffer
sympathy, antipathy, pathos, impassioned

PEC—money
pecuniary, impecunious, peculation

PED, POD—foot
pedestrian, pediment, quadruped, tripod

PEL, PULS—drive
compel, compelling, expel, propel, compulsion

PEN—almost
peninsula, penultimate, penumbra

PEND, PENS—hang
pendant, pendulous, suspense, propensity

PER—through, by, for, throughout
perambulator, percipient, perfunctory, pertinacious

PER—against, destruction
perfidious, pernicious, perjure

PERI—around
perimeter, periphery, perihelion, peripatetic

PET—seek, go towards
petition, impetus, impetuous, petulant, centripetal

PHIL—love
philosopher, philanderer, philanthropy, philology

PHOB—fear
phobia, claustrophobia, xenophobia

PHON—sound
phonograph, megaphone, phonics

PLAC—calm, please
placate, implacable, placid, complacent

PON, POS—put, place
postpone, proponent, juxtaposition, depose

PORT—carry
portable, deportment, rapport

POT—drink
potion, potable

POT—power
potential, potent, impotent, potentate, omnipotence

PRE—before
precede, precipitate, premonition, preposition

PRIM, PRI—first
prime, primary, primordial, pristine

PRO—ahead, forth
proceed, proclivity, protestation, provoke

PROTO—first
prototype, protagonist, protocol

PROX, PROP—near
approximate, propinquity, proximity

PSEUDO—false
pseudoscientific, pseudonym

PYR—fire
pyre, pyrotechnics, pyromania

QUAD, QUAR, QUAT—four
quadrilateral, quadrant, quarter, quarantine

QUES, QUER, QUIS, QUIR—question
quest, inquest, query, querulous, inquisitive, inquiry

QUIE—quiet
disquiet, acquiesce, quiescent, requiem

QUINT, QUIN—five
quintuplets, quintessence

RADI, RAMI—branch
radiate, radiant, eradicate, ramification

RECT, REG—straight, rule
rectangle, rectitude, rectify, regular

REG—king, rule
regal, regent, interregnum

RETRO—backward
retrospective, retroactive, retrograde

RID, RIS—laugh
ridiculous, deride, derision

ROG—ask
interrogate, derogatory, arrogant

RUD—rough, crude
rude, erudite, rudimentary

RUPT—break
disrupt, interrupt, rupture

SACR, SANCT—holy
sacred, sacrilege, sanction, sacrosanct

SCRIB, SCRIPT, SCRIV—write
scribe, ascribe, script, manuscript, scrivener

SE—apart, away
separate, segregate, secede, sedition

SEC, SECT, SEG—cut
sector, dissect, bisect, intersect, segment, secant

SED, SID—sit
sedate, sedentary, supersede, reside, residence

SEM—seed, sow
seminar, seminal, disseminate

SEN—old
senior, senile, senescent

SENT, SENS—feel, think
sentiment, nonsense, consensus, sensual

SEQU, SECU—follow
sequence, sequel, subsequent, consecutive

SIM, SEM—similar, same
similar, verisimilitude, semblance, dissemble

SIGN—mark, sign
signal, designation, assignation

SIN—curve
sine curve, sinuous, insinuate

SOL—sun
solar, parasol, solarium, solstice

SOL—alone
solo, solitude, soliloquy, solipsism

SOMN—sleep
insomnia, somnolent, somnambulist

SON—sound
sonic, consonance, sonorous, resonate

SOPH—wisdom
philosopher, sophistry, sophisticated, sophomoric

SPEC, SPIC—see, look
spectator, retrospective, perspective, perspicacious

SPER—hope
prosper, prosperous, despair, desperate

SPERS, SPAR—scatter
disperse, sparse, aspersion, disparate

SPIR—breathe
respire, inspire, spiritual, aspire, transpire

STRICT, STRING—bind
stricture, constrict, stringent, astringent

STRUCT, STRU—build
structure, obstruct, construe

SUB—under
subconscious, subjugate, subliminal, subpoena

SUMM—highest
summit, summary, consummate

SUPER, SUR—above
supervise, supercilious, superfluous, insurmountable,
surfeit

SURGE, SURRECT—rise
surge, resurgent, insurgent, insurrection

SYN, SYM—together
synthesis, sympathy, symposium, symbiosis

TACIT, TIC—silent
tacit, taciturn, reticent

TACT, TAG, TANG—touch
tact, tactile, contagious, tangent, tangential, tangible

TEN, TIN, TAIN—hold, twist
detention, tenable, pertinacious, retinue, retain

TEND, TENS, TENT—stretch
intend, distend, tension, tensile, ostensible, contentious

TERM—end
terminal, terminus, terminate, interminable

TERR—earth, land
terrain, terrestrial, extraterrestrial, subterranean

TEST—witness
testify, attest, testimonial, protestation

THE—god
atheist, theology, apotheosis, theocracy

THERM—heat
thermometer, thermal, thermonuclear, hypothermia

TIM—fear, frightened
timid, intimidate, timorous

TOP—place
topic, topography, utopia

TORT—twist
distort, extort, tortuous

TORP—stiff, numb
torpedo, torpid, torpor

TOX—poison
toxic, toxin, intoxication

TRACT—draw
tractor, intractable, protract

TRANS—across, over, through, beyond
transport, transgress, transient, transitory, translucent

TREM, TREP—shake
tremble, tremor, trepidation, intrepid

TURB—shake
disturb, turbulent, perturbation

UMBR—shadow
umbrella, umbrage, adumbrate, penumbra

UNI, UN—one
unify, unilateral, unanimous

URB—city
urban, suburban, urbane

VAC—empty
vacant, evacuate, vacuous

VAL, VAIL—value, strength
valid, valor, ambivalent, convalescence, avail

VEN, VENT—come
convene, intervene, venue, convention, adventitious

VER—true
verify, verity, verisimilitude, verdict

VERB—word
verbal, verbose, verbiage, verbatim

VERT, VERS—turn
avert, convert, revert, incontrovertible, divert, aversion

VICT, VINC—conquer
victory, conviction, evict, evince, invincible

VID, VIS—see
evident, vision, visage, supervise

VIL—base, mean
vile, vilify, revile

VIV, VIT—life
vivid, vital, convivial, vivacious

VOC, VOK, VOW—call, voice
vocal, equivocate, invoke, avow

VOL—wish
voluntary, malevolent, benevolent, volition

VOLV, VOLUT—turn, roll
revolve, evolve, convoluted

VOR—eat
devour, carnivore, omnivorous, voracious

Resource Three: **Word Families**

Learning words in families is an efficient way of increasing your SAT vocabulary, since the SAT often tests only that you have a general sense of what a word means. Just remember, the categories in which these words are listed are GENERAL and not to be taken for the exact definitions of the words.

BOLD

audacious	courageous	dauntless

CHANGING QUICKLY

capricious	mercurial	volatile

HESITATE

dither	oscillate	teeter
vacillate	waver	

ACT QUICKLY

apace	abrupt	headlong
impetuous	precipitate	

INNOCENT/INEXPERIENCED

credulous	gullible	naive
ingenuous	novitiate	tyro

DIFFICULT TO UNDERSTAND

abstruse	ambiguous	arcane
bemusing	cryptic	enigmatic
esoteric	inscrutable	obscure
opaque	paradoxical	perplexing
recondite	turbid	

EASY TO UNDERSTAND

articulate	cogent	eloquent
evident	limpid	lucid
pellucid		

SMART/LEARNED

astute	canny	erudite
perspicacious		

CRITICIZE/CRITICISM

aspersion	belittle	berate
calumny	castigate	decry
defamation	denounce	deride/derisive
diatribe	disparage	excoriate
gainsay	harangue	impugn
inveigh	lambaste	obloquy
objurgate	opprobrium	pillory
remonstrate	rebuke	reprehend
reprove	revile	tirade
vituperate		

CAROUSAL

bacchanalian	depraved	dissipated
iniquity	libertine	libidinous
licentious	reprobate	ribald
salacious	sordid	turpitude

TRUTH

candor/candid	fealty	frankness
indisputable	indubitable	legitimate
probity	sincere	veracious
verity		

FALSEHOOD

apocryphal	canard	chicanery
dissemble	duplicity	equivocate
erroneous	ersatz	fallacious
feigned	guile	mendacious
mendacity	perfidy	prevaricate
specious	spurious	

BITING (as in wit or temperament)

acerbic	acidulous	acrimonious
asperity	caustic	mordant
mordacious	trenchant	

PRAISE

acclaim	accolade	aggrandize
encomium	eulogize	extol
fawn	laud/laudatory	venerate

HARMFUL

baleful	baneful	deleterious
inimical	injurious	insidious
minatory	perfidious	pernicious

TIMID/TIMIDITY

craven	diffident	pusillanimous
recreant	timorous	trepidation

BORING

banal	fatuous	hackneyed
insipid	mundane	pedestrian
platitude	prosaic	quotidian
trite		

WEAKEN

adulterate	enervate	exacerbate
inhibit	obviate	stultify
undermine	vitiate	

ASSIST

abet	advocate	ancillary
bolster	corroborate	countenance
espouse	mainstay	munificent
proponent	stalwart	sustenance

HOSTILE

antithetic	churlish	curmudgeon
irascible	malevolent	misanthropic
truculent	vindictive	

STUBBORN

implacable	inexorable	intractable
intransigent	obdurate	obstinate
recalcitrant	refractory	renitent
untoward	vexing	

BEGINNING/YOUNG

burgeoning	callow	engender
inchoate	incipient	nascent

GENEROUS/KIND

altruistic	beneficent	clement
largess	magnanimous	munificent
philanthropic	unstinting	

GREEDY

avaricious	covetous	mercenary
miserly	penurious	venal
rapacious		

TERSE

compendious	curt	laconic
pithy	succinct	taciturn

OVERBLOWN/WORDY

bombastic	circumlocution	garrulous
grandiloquent	loquacious	periphrastic
prolix	rhetoric	turgid
verbose		

DICTATIONAL

dogmatic	authoritarian	despotic
hegemonic	hegemony	imperious
peremptory	tyrannical	

HATRED

abhorrence	antagonism	anathema
antipathy	detestation	enmity
loathing	malice	odium
rancor		

BEGINNER/AMATEUR

dilettante	fledgling	neophyte
novitiate	proselyte	tyro

LAZY/SLUGGISH

indolent	inert	lackadaisical
languid	lassitude	lethargic
phlegmatic	quiescent	slothful
torpid		

PACIFY/SATISFY

ameliorate	appease	assuage
defer	mitigate	mollify
placate	propitiate	satiate
slake		

FORGIVE

absolve	acquit	exculpate
exonerate	expiate	palliate
redress	vindicate	

POOR

destitute	esurient	indigent
impecunious		

FAVORING/NOT IMPARTIAL

ardor/ardent	doctrinaire	fervid
partisan	tendentious	zealot

DENYING OF SELF

abnegate	abstain	ascetic
Spartan	stoic	temperate

WALKING ABOUT

ambulatory	itinerant	peripatetic

INSINCERE

disingenuous	dissemble	fulsome
ostensible	unctuous	

PREVENT/OBSTRUCT

discomfit	encumber	fetter
forfend	hinder	impede
inhibit	occlude	

ECCENTRIC/DISSIMILAR

aberrant	anomalous	anachronism
eclectic	esoteric	discrete
iconoclast		

FUNNY

chortle	droll	facetious
flippant	gibe	jocular
levity	ludicrous	raillery
riposte	simper	

SORROW

disconsolate	doleful	dolor
elegiac	forlorn	lament
lugubrious	melancholy	morose
plaintive	threnody	

DISGUSTING/OFFENSIVE

defile	fetid	invidious
noisome	odious	putrid
rebarbative		

WITHDRAWAL/RETREAT

abeyance	abjure	abnegation
abortive	abrogate	decamp
demur	recant	recidivism
remission	renege	rescind
retrograde		

DEATH/MOURNING

bereave	cadaver	defunct
demise	dolorous	elegy
knell	lament	macabre
moribund	obsequies	sepulchral
wraith		

COPY

counterpart	emulate	facsimile
factitious	paradigm	precursor
quintessence	simulated	vicarious

EQUAL

equitable	equity	tantamount

UNUSUAL

aberration	anomaly	iconoclast
idiosyncrasy		

WANDERING

discursive	expatiate	forage
itinerant	peregrination	peripatetic
sojourn		

GAPS/OPENINGS

abatement	aperture	fissure
hiatus	interregnum	interstice
lull	orifice	rent
respite	rift	

HEALTHY

beneficial	salubrious	salutary

ABBREVIATED COMMUNICATION

abridge	compendium	cursory
curtail	syllabus	synopsis
terse		

WISDOM

adage	aphorism	apothegm
axiom	bromide	dictum
epigram	platitude	sententious
truism		

FAMILY

conjugal	consanguine	distaff
endogamous	filial	fratricide
progenitor	scion	

NON A STRAIGHT LINE

askance	awry	careen
carom	circuitous	circumvent
gyrate	labyrinth	meander
oblique	serrated	sidle
sinuous	undulating	vortex

INVESTIGATE

appraise	ascertain	assay
descry	peruse	

TIME/ORDER/DURATION

anachronism	antecede	antedate
anterior	archaic	diurnal
eon	ephemeral	epoch
fortnight	millennium	penultimate
synchronous	temporal	

BAD MOOD

bilious	dudgeon	irascible
petulant	pettish	pique
querulous	umbrage	waspish

EMBARRASS

abash	chagrin	compunction
contrition	diffidence	expiate
foible	gaucherie	rue

HARDHEARTED

asperity	baleful	dour
fell	malevolent	mordant
sardonic	scathing	truculent
vitriolic	vituperation	

NAG

admonish	cavil	belabor
enjoin	exhort	harangue
hector	martinet	remonstrate
reproof		

PREDICT

augur	auspice	fey
harbinger	portentous	presage
prescient	prognosticate	

LUCK

adventitious	amulet	auspicious
fortuitous	kismet	nemesis
optimum	portentous	propitiate
propitious	providential	talisman

NASTY

fetid	noisome	noxious

HARSH-SOUNDING

assonance	cacophony	din
dissonant	raucous	strident

PLEASANT-SOUNDING

euphonious	harmonious	melodious
sonorous		

Resource Four: **Vocabulary Word List**

This Word List includes about 500 frequently tested SAT words. The more of these you know, the better. No one can predict exactly which words will show up on your SAT test. But there are certain words that the test makers favor.

MEMORIZING SAT WORDS

In general, the very best way to improve your vocabulary is to read. Choose challenging, college-level material. If you encounter an unknown word, put it on a flashcard or in your vocabulary notebook. If you are mainly concerned with honing your knowledge of SAT words, memorizing the words on the following list can help. Here are some techniques for memorizing words.

1. Learn words in groups. You can group words by a common root they contain (see the Root List for some examples), or you can group words together if they are related in meaning (i.e. word families). Memorizing words this way may help you to remember them.

2. Use flashcards. Write down new words or word groups and run through them when you have a few minutes to spare. Put one new word or word group on one side of a 3×5 card and put a short definition or definitions on the back.

3. Make a vocabulary notebook. List words in one column and their definitions in another. Test yourself. Cover up the meanings, and see which words you can define from memory. Make a sample sentence using each word in context.

4. Think of hooks that lodge a new word in your mind—create visual images of words.

5. Use rhymes, pictures, songs, and any other devices that help you remember words.

To get the most out of your remaining study time, use the techniques that work for you, and stick with them.

ABANDON

noun (uh <u>baan</u> duhn)

total lack of inhibition

With her strict parents out of town, Kelly danced all night with *abandon*.

ABATE

verb (uh <u>bayt</u>)

to decrease, to reduce

My hunger *abated* when I saw how filthy the chef's hands were.

ABET

verb (uh <u>beht</u>)

to aid; to act as an accomplice

While Derwin robbed the bank, Marvin *abetted* his friend by pulling up the getaway car.

ABJURE

verb (aab <u>joor</u>)

to renounce under oath; to abandon forever; to abstain from

After having been devout for most of his life, he suddenly *abjured* his beliefs, much to his family's disappointment.

ABNEGATE

verb (<u>aab</u> nih gayt)

to give up; to deny to oneself

After his retirement, the former police commissioner found it difficult to *abnegate* authority.

ABORTIVE

adj (uh <u>bohr</u> tihv)

ending without results

Her *abortive* attempt to swim the full five miles left her frustrated.

ABROGATE

verb (<u>aab</u> ruh gayt)

to annul; to abolish by authoritative action

The president's job is to *abrogate* any law that fosters inequality among citizens.

ABSCOND

verb (aab <u>skahnd</u>)

to leave quickly in secret

The criminal *absconded* during the night with all of his mother's money.

ABSTEMIOUS

adj (aab <u>stee</u> mee uhs)

done sparingly; consuming in moderation

The spa served no sugar or wheat, but the clients found the retreat so calm that they didn't mind the *abstemious* rules.

ACCEDE

verb (aak <u>seed</u>)

to express approval, to agree to

Once the mayor heard the reasonable request, she happily *acceded* to the proposal.

ACCLIVITY

noun (uh <u>klihv</u> ih tee)

an incline or upward slope, the ascending side of a hill

We were so tired from hiking that by the time we reached the *acclivity*, it looked more like a mountain than a hill.

ACCRETION

noun (uh <u>kree</u> shuhn)

a growth in size, an increase in amount

The committee's strong fund-raising efforts resulted in an *accretion* in scholarship money.

ACME

noun (<u>aak</u> mee)

the highest level or degree attainable

Just when he reached the *acme* of his power, the dictator was overthrown.

ACTUATE

verb (<u>aak</u> choo ayt)

to put into motion, to activate; to motivate or influence to activity

The leaders rousing speech *actuated* the crowd into a peaceful protest.

ACUITY

noun (uh <u>kyoo</u> ih tee)

sharp vision or perception characterized by the ability to resolve fine detail

With unusual *acuity*, she was able to determine that the masterpiece was a fake.

ACUMEN

noun (<u>aak</u> yuh muhn) (uh <u>kyoo</u> muhn)

sharpness of insight, mind, and understanding; shrewd judgment

The investor's financial *acumen* helped him to select high-yield stocks.

ADAMANT

adj (<u>aad</u> uh muhnt) (<u>aad</u> uh mihnt)

stubbornly unyielding

She was *adamant* about leaving the restaurant after the waiter was rude.

ADEPT

adj (uh <u>dehpt</u>)

extremely skilled

She is *adept* at computing math problems in her head.

ADJUDICATE

verb (uh <u>jood</u> ih kayt)

to hear and settle a matter; to act as a judge

The principal *adjudicated* the disagreement between two students.

ADJURE

verb (uh <u>joor</u>)

to appeal to

The criminal *adjured* to the court for mercy.

ADMONISH

verb (aad <u>mahn</u> ihsh)

to caution or warn gently in order to correct something

My mother *admonished* me about my poor grades.

ADROIT

adj (uh <u>droyt</u>)

skillful; accomplished; highly competent

The *adroit* athlete completed even the most difficult obstacle course with ease.

ADULATION

noun (<u>aaj</u> juh lay shuhn)

excessive flattery or admiration

The *adulation* she showed her professor seemed insincere; I suspected she really wanted a better grade.

ADUMBRATE

verb (<u>aad</u> uhm brayt) (uh <u>duhm</u> brayt)

to give a hint or indication of something to come

Her constant complaining about the job *adumbrated* her intent to leave.

AERIE

noun (<u>ayr</u> ee) (<u>eer</u> ee)

a nest built high in the air; an elevated, often secluded, dwelling

Perched high among the trees, the eagle's *aerie* was filled with eggs.

AFFECTED

adj (uh <u>fehk</u> tihd)

phony, artificial

The *affected* hairdresser spouted French phrases, though she had never been to France.

AGGREGATE

noun (<u>aa</u> grih giht)

a collective mass, the sum total

An *aggregate* of panic-stricken customers mobbed the bank, demanding their life savings.

ALGORITHM

noun (<u>aal</u> guh rith uhm)

an established procedure for solving a problem or equation

The accountant uses a series of *algorithms* to determine the appropriate tax bracket.

ALIMENTARY

adj (aal uh <u>mehn</u> tuh ree) (aal uh <u>mehn</u> tree)

pertaining to food, nutrition, or digestion

After a particularly good meal, Sherlock turned to his companion and exclaimed, "I feel quite good, very well fed. It was *alimentary* my dear Watson."

ALLAY

verb (uh <u>lay</u>)

to lessen, ease, reduce in intensity

Trying to *allay* their fears, the nurse sat with them all night.

AMITY

noun (<u>aa</u> mih tee)

friendship, good will

Correspondence over the years contributed to a lasting *amity* between the women.

AMORPHOUS

adj (<u>ay</u> <u>mohr</u> fuhs)

having no definite form

The Blob featured an *amorphous* creature that was constantly changing shape.

ANIMUS

noun (<u>aan</u> uh muhs)

a feeling of animosity or ill will

Though her teacher had failed her, she displayed no *animus* toward him.

ANODYNE

noun (<u>aan</u> uh dyen)

a source of comfort; a medicine that relieves pain

The sound of classical music is usually just the *anodyne* I need after a tough day at work.

ANOMALY

noun (uh <u>nahm</u> uh lee)

a deviation from the common rule, something that is difficult to classify

Among the top-ten albums of the year was one *anomaly*—a compilation of polka classics.

ANTHROPOMORPHIC

adj (aan thruh poh <u>mohr</u> fihk)

suggesting human characteristics for animals and inanimate things

Many children's stories feature *anthropomorphic* animals such as talking wolves and pigs.

ANTIQUATED

adj (<u>aan</u> tih kway tihd)

too old to be fashionable or useful

Next to her coworker's brand-new model, Marisa's computer looked *antiquated*.

APHORISM

noun (<u>aa</u> fuhr ihz uhm)

a short statement of a principle

The country doctor was given to such *aphorisms* as "Still waters run deep."

APLOMB

noun (uh <u>plahm</u>) (uh <u>pluhm</u>)

self-confident assurance; poise

For such a young dancer, she had great *aplomb*, making her perfect to play the young princess.

APOSTATE

noun (uh pahs tayt)

one who renounces a religious faith

So that he could divorce his wife, the king scoffed at the church doctrines and declared himself an *apostate*.

APPOSITE

adj (aap puh ziht)

strikingly appropriate or well adapted

The lawyer presented an *apposite* argument upon cross-examining the star witness.

APPRISE

verb (uh priez)

to give notice to, inform

"Thanks for *apprising* me that the test time has been changed," said Emanuel.

APPROPRIATE

verb (uh proh pree ayt)

to assign to a particular purpose, allocate

The fund's manager *appropriated* funds for the clean-up effort.

ARABLE

adj (aa ruh buhl)

suitable for cultivation

The overpopulated country desperately needed more *arable* land.

ARCANE

adj (ahr kayn)

secret, obscure; known only to a few

The *arcane* rituals of the sect were passed down through many generations.

ARCHIPELAGO

noun (ahr kuh pehl uh goh)

a large group of islands

Between villages in the Stockholm *archipelago*, boat taxis are the only form of transportation.

ARREARS
noun (uh <u>reerz</u>)

unpaid, overdue debts or bills; neglected obligations

After the expensive lawsuit, Dominic's accounts were in *arrears*.

ARROGATE
verb (<u>aa</u> ruh gayt)

to claim without justification; to claim for oneself without right

Lynn watched in astonishment as her boss *arrogated* the credit for her brilliant work on the project.

ASKANCE
adv (uh <u>skaans</u>)

with disapproval; with a skeptical sideways glance

She looked *askance* at her son's failing report card as he mumbled that he had done all the schoolwork.

ASSENT
verb (uh <u>sehnt</u>)

to agree, as to a proposal

After careful deliberation, the CEO *assented* to the proposed merger.

ATAVISTIC
adj (aat uh <u>vihs</u> tik)

characteristic of a former era, ancient

After spending three weeks on a desert island, Roger became a survivalist with *atavistic* skills that helped him endure.

AUTOCRAT
noun (<u>aw</u> toh kraat)

a dictator

Mussolini has been described as an *autocrat* who tolerated no opposition.

AVER
verb (uh <u>vuhr</u>)

to declare to be true, to affirm

"Yes, he was wearing a mask," the witness *averred*.

AVUNCULAR

adj (ah <u>vuhng</u> kyuh luhr)

like an uncle in behavior, especially in kindness and warmth

The coach's *avuncular* style made him well-liked.

AWRY

adv (uh <u>rie</u>)

crooked, askew, amiss

Something must have gone *awry* in the computer system because some of my files are missing.

BALK

verb (bawk)

to stop short and refuse to go on

When the horse *balked* at jumping over the high fence, the rider was thrown off.

BALLAST

noun (<u>baal</u> uhst)

a structure that helps to stabilize or steady

Communication and honesty are the true *ballasts* of a good relationship.

BEATIFIC

adj (bee uh <u>tihf</u> ihk)

displaying calmness and joy, relating to a state of celestial happiness

After spending three months in India, she had a *beatific* peace about her.

BECALM

verb (bih <u>kahm</u>)

to stop the progress of, to soothe

The warm air *becalmed* the choppy waves.

BECLOUD

verb (bih <u>klowd</u>)

to make less visible, to obscure, or blur

Her ambivalence about the long commute *beclouded* her enthusiasm about the job.

BEDRAGGLE

adj (bih <u>draag</u> uhl)

soiled, wet and limp; dilapidated

The child's *bedraggled* blanket needed a good cleaning.

BEGET

verb (bih geht)

to produce, especially as an effect or outgrowth; to bring about

The mayor believed that finding petty offenders would help reduce serious crime because, he argued, small crimes *beget* big crimes.

BEHEMOTH

noun (buh hee muhth)

something of monstrous size or power; huge creature

The budget became such a *behemoth* that observers believed the film would never make a profit.

BENEFICENT

adj (buh nehf ih sent)

pertaining to an act of kindness

The *beneficent* man donated the money anonymously.

BERATE

verb (bih rayt)

to scold harshly

When my manager found out I had handled the situation so insensitively, he *berated* me.

BILIOUS

adj (bihl yuhs)

ill-tempered, sickly, ailing

The party ended early when the *bilious* 5-year-old tried to run off with the birthday girl's presents.

BLASPHEMOUS

adj (blaas fuh muhs)

cursing, profane; extremely irreverent

The politician's offhanded comments seemed *blasphemous*, given the context of the orderly meeting.

BLATANT

adj (blay tnt)

completely obvious and conspicuous, especially in an offensive, crass manner

Such *blatant* advertising within the bounds of the school drew protest from parents.

BLITHELY

adv (<u>blieth</u> lee)

merrily, lightheartedly cheerful; without appropriate thought

Wanting to redecorate the office, she *blithely* assumed her co-workers wouldn't mind and moved the furniture in the space.

BOMBASTIC

adj (bahm <u>baast</u> ihk)

high-sounding but meaningless; ostentatiously lofty in style

The lawyer's speeches were mostly *bombastic*; his outrageous claims had no basis in fact.

BOVINE

adj (<u>boh</u> vien)

relating to cows; having qualities characteristic of a cow, such as sluggishness or dullness

His *bovine* demeanor did nothing to engage me.

BRAGGART

noun (<u>braag</u> uhrt)

a person who brags or boasts in a loud and empty manner

Usually the biggest *braggart* at the company party, Susan's boss was unusually quiet at this year's event.

BROACH

verb (brohch)

to mention or suggest for the first time

Sandy wanted to go to college away from home, but he didn't know how to *broach* the topic with his parents.

BUCOLIC

adj (byoo <u>kah</u> lihk)

pastoral, rural

My aunt likes the hustle and bustle of the city, but my uncle prefers a more *bucolic* setting.

BURNISH

verb (<u>buhr</u> nihsh)

to polish; to make smooth and bright

Mr. Frumpkin loved to stand in the sun and *burnish* his luxury car.

BURSAR

noun (<u>buhr</u> suhr) (<u>buhr</u> sahr)

a treasurer or keeper of funds

The *bursar* of the school was in charge of allocating all scholarship funds.

CACHE

noun (caash)

a hiding place; stockpile

It's good to have a *cache* where you can stash your cash.

CACOPHONY

noun (kuh <u>kah</u> fuh nee)

a jarring, unpleasant noise

As I walked into the open-air market after my nap, a *cacophony* of sounds surrounded me.

CALUMNY

noun (<u>kaa</u> luhm nee)

a false and malicious accusation; misrepresentation

The unscrupulous politician used *calumny* to bring down his opponent in the senatorial race.

CANTANKEROUS

adj (kaan <u>taang</u> kuhr uhs)

having a difficult, uncooperative, or stubborn disposition

The most outwardly *cantankerous* man in the nursing home was surprisingly sweet and loving with his grandchildren.

CAPTIOUS

adj (<u>kaap</u> shuhs)

marked by the tendency to point out trivial faults; intended to confuse in an argument

I resent the way he asked that *captious* question.

CATACLYSMIC

adj (<u>kaat</u> uh <u>klihz</u> mihk)

severely destructive

By all appearances, the storm seemed *cataclysmic*, though it lasted only a short while.

CATALYST

noun (<u>kaat</u> uhl ihst)

something that provokes or speeds up significant change, especially without being affected by the consequences

Technology has been a *catalyst* for the expansion of alternative education, such as home schooling and online courses.

CAUCUS

noun (<u>kaw</u> kuhs)

a closed committee within a political party; a private committee meeting

The president met with the delegated *caucus* to discuss the national crisis.

CAUSTIC

adj (<u>kah</u> stihk)

biting, sarcastic

Writer Dorothy Parker gained her reputation for *caustic* wit, and her tombstone is inscribed with a fittingly clever "Excuse my dust."

CEDE

verb (seed)

to surrender possession of something

Argentina *ceded* the Falkland Islands to Britain after a brief war.

CELERITY

noun (seh <u>leh</u> rih tee)

speed, haste

The celebrity ran past his fans with great *celerity*.

CENSORIOUS

adj (sehn <u>sohr</u> ee uhs)

critical; tending to blame and condemn

Closed-minded people tend to be *censorious* of others.

CERTITUDE

noun (<u>suhr</u> tih tood)

assurance, freedom from doubt

The witness' *certitude* about the night in question had a big impact on the jury.

CESSATION

noun (seh <u>say</u> shuhn)

a temporary or complete halt

The cessation of hostilities ensured that soldiers were able to spend the holidays with their families.

CHARY

adj (<u>chahr</u> ee)

watchful, cautious; extremely shy

Mindful of the fate of the Titanic, the captain was *chary* of navigating the iceberg-filled sea.

CHIMERICAL

adj (kie <u>mehr</u> ih kuhl) (kie <u>meer</u> ih kuhl)

fanciful; imaginary, impossible

The inventor's plans seemed *chimerical* to the conservative businessman from whom he was asking for financial support.

CIRCUITOUS

adj (suhr <u>kyoo</u> ih tuhs)

indirect, roundabout

The venue was only a short walk from the train station, but a roadblock meant I had to take a *circuitous* route.

CIRCUMVENT

verb (suhr kuhm <u>vehnt</u>)

to go around; avoid

Laura was able to *circumvent* the hospital's regulations, slipping into her mother's room long after visiting hours were over.

CLOYING

adj (<u>kloy</u> ing)

sickly sweet; excessive

When Dave and Liz were together their *cloying* affection towards one another often made their friends ill.

COAGULATE

verb (koh <u>aag</u> yuh layt)

to clot; to cause to thicken

Hemophiliacs can bleed to death from a minor cut because their blood does not *coagulate*.

COGENT

adj (<u>koh</u> juhnt)

logically forceful; compelling, convincing

Swayed by the *cogent* argument of the defense, the jury had no choice but to acquit the defendant.

COLLOQUIAL

adj (kuh <u>loh</u> kwee uhl)

characteristic of informal speech

The book was written in a *colloquial* style so it would be user-friendlier.

COMMUTE

verb (kuh <u>myoot</u>)

to change a penalty to a less severe one

In exchange for cooperating with detectives on another case, the criminal had his charges *commuted*.

COMPLACENT

adj (kuhm <u>play</u> sihnt)

self-satisfied, smug

Alfred always shows a *complacent* smile whenever he wins the spelling bee.

COMPLIANT

adj (kuhm <u>plie</u> uhnt)

submissive, yielding

The boss was unused to an assistant who spoke her mind, but he grew to respect the fact that she wasn't *compliant*.

CONCOMITANT

adj (kuh <u>kahm</u> ih tuhnt)

existing concurrently

A double-major was going to be difficult to pull off, especially since Lucy would have to juggle two papers and two exams *concomitantly*.

CONCORD

noun (<u>kahn</u> kohrd)

agreement

The sisters are now in *concord* about the car they had to share.

CONDOLE

verb (kuhn <u>dohl</u>)

to grieve; to express sympathy

My hamster died when I was in third grade, and my friends *condoled* with me and helped bury him in the yard.

CONFLAGRATION

noun (kahn fluh <u>gray</u> shuhn)

big, destructive fire

After the *conflagration* had finally died down, the city center was nothing but a mass of blackened embers.

CONFLUENCE

noun (<u>kahn</u> floo uhns)

the act of two things flowing together; the junction or meeting place where two things meet

At the political meeting, while planning a demonstration, there was a moving *confluence* of ideas between members.

CONSANGUINEOUS

adj (kahn saang <u>gwihn</u> ee uhs)

having the same lineage or ancestry; related by blood

After having a strange feeling about our relationship for years, I found out that my best friend and I are *consanguineous*.

CONSTERNATION

noun (kahn stuhr <u>nay</u> shuhn)

an intense state of fear or dismay

One would never think that a seasoned hunter would display such *consternation* when a grizzly bear lumbered too close to camp.

CONSTITUENT

noun (kuhn <u>stih</u> choo uhnt)

component, part; citizen, voter

A machine will not function properly if one of its *constituents* is defective.

CONSTRAINT

noun (kuhn <u>straynt</u>)

something that restricts or confines within prescribed bounds

Given the *constraints* of the budget, it was impossible to accomplish my goals.

CONTEMPTUOUS

adj (kuhn <u>tehmp</u> choo uhs)

scornful; expressing contempt

The diners were intimidated by the waiter's *contemptuous* manner.

CONTENTIOUS

adj (kuhn <u>tehn</u> shuhs)

quarrelsome, disagreeable, belligerent

The *contentious* gentleman ridiculed anything anyone said.

CONTIGUOUS

adj (kuhn <u>tihg</u> yoo uhs)

sharing a boundary; neighboring

The two houses had *contiguous* yards so the families shared the landscaping expenses.

CONTINENCE

noun (<u>kahn</u> tih nihns)

self-control, self-restraint

Lucy exhibited impressive *continence* in steering clear of fattening foods, and she lost 50 pounds.

CONVALESCE

verb (kahn vuhl <u>ehs</u>)

to recover gradually from an illness

After her bout with malaria, Tatiana needed to *convalesce* for a whole month.

CONVERGENCE

noun (kuhn <u>vehr</u> juhns)

the state of separate elements joining or coming together

A *convergence* of factors led to the tragic unfolding of World War I.

COQUETTE

noun (koh <u>keht</u>)

a flirtatious woman

The normally serious librarian could turn into a *coquette* just by letting her hair down.

COTERIE

noun (<u>koh</u> tuh ree)

an intimate group of persons with a similar purpose

Judith invited a *coterie* of fellow stamp enthusiasts to a stamp-trading party.

COUNTERVAIL

verb (kown tuhr <u>vayl</u>)

to act or react with equal force

In order to *countervail* the financial loss the school suffered after the embezzlement, the treasurer raised the price of room and board.

COVERT

adj (koh <u>vuhrt</u>)

secretive, not openly shown

The *covert* military operation wasn't disclosed until after it was determined to be a success.

CULL

verb (kuhl)

to select, weed out

You should *cull* the words you need to study from all the flash cards.

CUMULATIVE

adj (<u>kyoom</u> yuh luh tihv)

increasing, collective

The new employee didn't mind her job at first, but the daily, petty indignities had a *cumulative* demoralizing effect.

CURT

adj (kuhrt)

abrupt, short with words

The grouchy shop assistant was *curt* with one of her customers, which resulted in a reprimand from her manager.

DEARTH

noun (duhrth)

a lack, scarcity, insufficiency

The *dearth* of supplies in our city made it difficult to survive the blizzard.

DEBACLE

noun (dih <u>baa</u> kuhl)

a sudden, disastrous collapse or defeat; a total, ridiculous failure

It was hard for her to show her face in the office after the *debacle* of spilling coffee on her supervisor—three times.

DECLAIM

verb (dih <u>klaym</u>)

to speak loudly and vehemently

At Thanksgiving dinner, our grandfather always *declaims* his right, as the eldest, to sit at the head of the table.

DEFAMATORY

adj (dih <u>faam</u> uh tohr ee)

injurious to the reputation

The tabloid was sued for making *defamatory* statements about the celebrity.

DEMAGOGUE

noun (<u>deh</u> muh gahg) (<u>deh</u> muh gawg)

a leader, rabble-rouser, usually appealing to emotion or prejudice

The dictator began his political career as a *demagogue*, giving fiery speeches in town halls.

DENIZEN

noun (<u>dehn</u> ih zihn)

an inhabitant, a resident

The *denizens* of the state understandably wanted to select their own leaders.

DERIDE

verb (dih <u>ried</u>)

to laugh at contemptuously, to make fun of

As soon as Jorge heard the others *deriding* Anthony, he came to his defense.

DIFFUSE

verb (dih <u>fyooz</u>)

to spread out widely, to scatter freely, to disseminate

They turned on the fan, but all that did was *diffuse* the cigarette smoke throughout the room.

DIGRESS

verb (die <u>grehs</u>)

to turn aside, especially from the main point; to stray from the subject

The professor repeatedly *digressed* from the topic, boring his students.

DILAPIDATED

adj (dih <u>laap</u> ih dayt ihd)

in disrepair, run down

Rather than get discouraged, the architect saw great potential in the *dilapidated* house.

DILUVIAL

adj (dih <u>loo</u> vee uhl)

pertaining to a flood

After she left the water running in the house all day, it looked simply *diluvial*.

DISCOMFIT

verb (dihs <u>kuhm</u> fiht)

to disconcert, to make one lose one's composure

The class clown enjoyed *discomfiting* her classmates whenever possible.

DISCRETE

adj (dih <u>skreet</u>)

individually distinct, separate

What's nice about the CD is that each song functions as a *discrete* work and also as part of the whole compilation.

DISINGENUOUS

adj (<u>dihs</u> ihn <u>jehn</u> yoo uhs)

giving a false appearance of simple frankness; misleading

It was *disingenuous* of him to suggest that he had no idea of the requests made by his campaign contributors.

DISINTERESTED

adj (dihs <u>ihn</u> trih stihd) (dihs <u>ihn</u> tuh reh stihd)

fair-minded, unbiased

A fair trial is made possible by the selection of *disinterested* jurors.

DISPASSIONATE

adj (dihs <u>paash</u> ih niht)

unaffected by bias or strong emotions; not personally or emotionally involved in something

Ideally, photographers should be *dispassionate* observers of what goes on in the world.

DISSIDENT

adj (<u>dihs</u> ih duhnt)

disagreeing with an established religious or political system

The *dissident* had been living abroad and writing his criticism of the government from an undisclosed location.

DOCTRINAIRE

adj (dahk truh <u>nayr</u>)

rigidly devoted to theories without regard for practicality; dogmatic

The professor's manner of teaching was considered *doctrinaire* for such a liberal school.

DOGGED

adj (<u>daw</u> guhd)

stubbornly persevering

The police inspector's *dogged* determination helped him catch the thief.

DOLEFUL

adj (<u>dohl</u> fuhl)

sad, mournful

Looking into the *doleful* eyes of the lonely pony, the girl yearned to take him home.

DOUR

adj (<u>doo</u> uhr) (<u>dow</u> uhr)

sullen and gloomy; stern and severe

The *dour* hotel concierge demanded payment for the room in advance.

EFFLUVIA

noun (ih <u>floo</u> vee uh)

waste; odorous fumes given off by waste

He took out the garbage at 3 A.M. because the *effluvia* had begun wafting into the bedroom.

ELEGY

noun (<u>eh</u> luh jee)

a mournful poem, usually about the dead

A memorable *elegy* was read aloud for the spiritual leader.

ELUDE

verb (ee <u>lood</u>)

to avoid cleverly, to escape the perception of

Somehow, the runaway *eluded* detection for weeks.

EMOLLIENT

adj (ih <u>mohl</u> yuhnt)

soothing, especially to the skin

After being out in the sun for so long, the *emollient* cream was a welcome relief on my skin.

EMULATE

verb (<u>ehm</u> yuh layt)

to strive to equal or excel, to imitate

Children often *emulate* their parents.

ENCUMBER

verb (ehn <u>kuhm</u> buhr)

to weigh down, to burden

The distractions of the city *encumbered* her attempts at writing.

ENJOIN

verb (ehn <u>joyn</u>)

to direct or impose with urgent appeal, to order with emphasis; to forbid

Patel is *enjoined* by his culture from eating beef.

EPOCHAL

adj (<u>ehp</u> uh kuhl) (ehp <u>ahk</u> uhl)

momentous, highly significant

The Supreme Court's *epochal* decision will no doubt affect generations to come.

EPONYMOUS

adj (ih <u>pahn</u> uh muhs)

giving one's name to a place, book, restaurant

Macbeth was the *eponymous* protagonist of Shakespeare's play.

EQUIVOCATE

verb (ih <u>kwihv</u> uh kayt)

to avoid committing oneself in what one says, to be deliberately unclear

Not wanting to implicate himself in the crime, the suspect *equivocated* for hours.

ERSATZ

adj (uhr <u>sahtz</u>)

being an artificial and inferior substitute or imitation

The *ersatz* strawberry shortcake tasted more like plastic than like real cake.

ESCHEW

verb (ehs <u>choo</u>)

to shun; to avoid (as something wrong or distasteful)

The filmmaker *eschewed* artifical light for her actors, resulting in a stark movie style.

ESPOUSE

verb (ih <u>spowz</u>)

to take up and support as a cause; to marry

Because of his beliefs, he could not *espouse* the use of capital punishment.

ESPY

verb (ehs <u>peye</u>)

to catch sight of, glimpse

Amidst a crowd in black clothing, she *espied* the colorful dress that her friend was wearing.

EUPHEMISM

noun (<u>yoo</u> fuh mihz uhm)

an inoffensive and agreeable expression that is substituted for one that is considered offensive

The funeral director preferred to use the *euphemism* "passed away" instead of the word "dead."

EUTHANASIA

noun (yoo thun <u>nay</u> zhuh)

the practice of ending the life of terminally ill individuals; assisted suicide

Euthanasia has always been the topic of much moral debate.

EXCORIATE

verb (ehk <u>skohr</u> ee ayt)

to censure scathingly; to express strong disapproval of

The three-page letter to the editor *excoriated* the publication for printing the rumor without verifying the source.

EXPONENT

noun (<u>ehk</u> spoh nuhnt)

one who champions or advocates

The vice president was an enthusiastic *exponent* of computer technology.

EXPOUND

verb (ihk <u>spownd</u>)

to explain or describe in detail

The teacher *expounded* on the theory of relativity for hours.

EXPUNGE

verb (ihk <u>spuhnj</u>)

to erase, eliminate completely

The parents' association *expunged* the questionable texts from the children's reading list.

EXTIRPATE

verb (<u>ehk</u> stuhr payt)

to root out, eradicate, literally or figuratively; to destroy wholly

The criminals were *extirpated* after many years of investigation.

EXTRAPOLATION

noun (ihk <u>strap</u> uh lay shuhn)

using known data and information to determine what will happen in the future, prediction

Through the process of *extrapolation*, we were able to determine which mutual funds to invest in.

EXTRINSIC

adj (ihk <u>strihn</u> sihk) (ihk <u>strihn</u> zihk)

external, unessential; originating from the outside

"Though they are interesting to note," the meeting manager claimed, "those facts are *extrinsic* to the matter under discussion."

EXTRUDE

verb (ihk <u>strood</u>)

to form or shape something by pushing it out, to force out, especially through a small opening

We watched in awe as the volcano *extruded* molten lava.

FACETIOUS

adj (fuh <u>see</u> shuhs)

witty, humorous

Her *facetious* remarks made the uninteresting meeting more lively.

FACILE

adj (<u>faa</u> suhl)

easily accomplished; seeming to lack sincerity or depth; arrived at without due effort

Given the complexity of the problem, it seemed a rather *facile* solution.

FALLACIOUS

adj (fuh <u>lay</u> shuhs)

tending to deceive or mislead; based on a fallacy

The *fallacious* statement "the Earth is flat" misled people for many years.

FEBRILE

adj (<u>fehb</u> ruhl) (<u>fee</u> bruhl)

feverish, marked by intense emotion or activity

Awaiting the mysterious announcement, there was a *febrile* excitement in the crowd.

FECKLESS

adj (<u>fehk</u> lihs)

ineffective, worthless

Anja took on the responsibility of caring for her aged mother, realizing that her *feckless* sister was not up to the task.

FEIGN

verb (fayn)

to pretend, to give a false appearance of

Though she had discovered they were planning a party, she *feigned* surprise so as not to spoil the festivities.

FERAL

adj (<u>fehr</u> uhl)

suggestive of a wild beast, not domesticated

Though the animal-rights activists did not want to see the *feral* dogs harmed, they offered no solution to the problem.

FICTIVE

adj (<u>fihk</u> tihv)

fictional, relating to imaginative creation

She found she was more productive when writing *fictive* stories rather than autobiographical stories.

FILIBUSTER

verb (<u>fihl</u> ih buhs tuhr)

to use obstructionist tactics, especially prolonged speech making, in order to delay something

The congressman read names from the phonebook in an attempt to *filibuster* a pending bill.

FITFUL

adj (<u>fiht</u> fuhl)

intermittent, lacking steadiness; characterized by irregular bursts of activity

Her *fitful* breathing became cause for concern, and eventually, she phoned the doctor.

FLIPPANT

adj (<u>flihp</u> uhnt)

marked by disrespectful lightheartedness or casualness

Her *flippant* response was unacceptable and she was asked again to explain herself.

FLOUT

verb (flowt)

to scorn, to disregard with contempt

The protestors *flouted* the committee's decision and hoped to sway public opinion.

FODDER

noun (<u>fohd</u> uhr)

raw material, as for artistic creation, readily abundant ideas or images

The governor's hilarious blunder was good *fodder* for the comedian.

FOREGO

verb (fohr <u>goh</u>)

to precede, to go ahead of

Because of the risks of the expedition, the team leader made sure to *forego* the climbers.

FORGO

verb (fohr <u>goh</u>)

to do without, to abstain from

As much as I wanted to *forgo* statistics, I knew it would serve me well in my field of study.

FORMIDABLE

adj (<u>fohr</u> mih duh buhl) (fohr <u>mih</u> duh buhl)

fearsome, daunting; tending to inspire awe or wonder

The wrestler was not very big, but his skill and speed made him a *formidable* opponent.

FORTITUDE

noun (<u>fohr</u> tih tood)

strength of mind that allows one to encounter adversity with courage

Months in the trenches exacted great *fortitude* of the soldiers.

FORTUITOUS

adj (fohr <u>too</u> ih tuhs)

by chance, especially by favorable chance

After a *fortuitous* run-in with an agent, Roxy won a recording contract.

FRENETIC

adj (freh <u>neht</u> ihk)

frantic, frenzied

The employee's *frenetic* schedule left him little time to socialize.

FULSOME

adj (<u>fool</u> suhm)

abundant; flattering in an insincere way

The king's servant showered him with *fulsome* compliments in hopes of currying favor.

FURLOUGH

noun (<u>fuhr</u> loh)

a leave of absence, especially granted to soldier or a prisoner

After seeing months of combat, the soldier received a much-deserved *furlough*.

FURTIVE

adj (<u>fuhr</u> tihv)

sly, with hidden motives

The *furtive* glances they exchanged made me suspect they were up to something.

GALVANIZE

verb (<u>gaal</u> vuh niez)

to shock; to arouse awareness

The closing down of another homeless shelter *galvanized* the activist group into taking political action.

GAMELY

adj (<u>gaym</u> lee)

spiritedly, bravely

The park ranger *gamely* navigated the trail up the steepest face of the mountain.

GAUCHE

adv (gohsh)

lacking social refinement

Snapping one's fingers to get a waiter's attention is considered *gauche*.

GRANDILOQUENCE

noun (graan <u>dihl</u> uh kwuhns)

pompous talk; fancy but meaningless language

The headmistress was notorious for her *grandiloquence* at the lectern and her ostentatious clothes.

GREGARIOUS

adj (greh <u>gaar</u> ee uhs)

outgoing, sociable

Unlike her introverted friends, Susan was very *gregarious*.

GROTTO

noun (<u>grah</u> toh)

a small cave

Alone on the island, Philoctetes sought shelter in a *grotto*.

HARANGUE

verb (huh <u>raang</u>)

to give a long speech

Maria's parents *harangued* her when she told them she'd spent her money on magic beans.

HEDONIST

noun (<u>hee</u> duhn ihst)

one who pursues pleasure as a goal

Michelle, an admitted *hedonist*, lays on the couch eating cookies every Saturday.

HEGEMONY

noun (hih <u>jeh</u> muh nee)

the domination of one state or group over its allies

When Germany claimed *hegemony* over Russia, Stalin was outraged.

HERETICAL

adj (huh <u>reh</u> tih kuhl)

departing from accepted beliefs or standards, oppositional

Considering the conservative audience, her comments seemed *heretical*.

HIATUS

noun (hie <u>ay</u> tuhs)

a gap or interruption in space, time, or continuity

After a long *hiatus* in Greece, the philosophy professor returned to the university.

HISTRIONICS

noun (hihs tree <u>ahn</u> ihks)

deliberate display of emotion for effect; exaggerated behavior calculated for effect

With such *histrionics*, she should really consider becoming an actress.

HUBRIS

noun (<u>hyoo</u> brihs)

excessive pride or self-confidence

Nathan's *hubris* spurred him to do things that many considered insensitive.

HUSBAND

verb (<u>huhz</u> buhnd)

to manage economically; to use sparingly

The cyclist paced herself at the start of the race, knowing that if she *husbanded* her resources she'd have the strength to break out of the pack later on.

HYPOCRITE

noun (<u>hih</u> puh kriht)

one who puts on a false appearance of virtue; one who criticizes a flaw he in fact possesses

What a *hypocrite*: He criticizes those who wear fur, but then he buys a leather shearling coat.

IGNOBLE

adj (ihg <u>noh</u> buhl)

having low moral standards, not noble in character; mean

The photographer was paid a princely sum for the picture of the self-proclaimed ethicist in the *ignoble* act of pick-pocketing.

ILLUSORY

adj (ih <u>loo</u> suhr ee) (ih <u>loos</u> ree)

producing illusion, deceptive

The desert explorer was devastated to discover that the lake he thought he had seen was in fact *illusory*.

IMBIBE

verb (ihm <u>bieb</u>)

to receive into the mind and take in, absorb

If I always attend class, I can *imbibe* as much knowledge as possible.

IMPASSIVE

adj (ihm <u>pahs</u> sihv)

absent of any external sign of emotion, expressionless

Given his *impassive* expression, it was hard to tell whether he approved of my plan.

IMPERIOUS

adj (ihm <u>pihr</u> ee uhs)

commanding, domineering; urgent

Though the king had been a kind leader, his daughter was *imperious* and demanding during her rule.

IMPERTURBABLE

adj (<u>ihm</u> puhr <u>tuhr</u> buh buhl)

unshakably calm and steady

No matter how disruptive the children became, the babysitter remained *imperturbable*.

IMPLACABLE

adj (ihm <u>play</u> kuh buhl) (ihm <u>plaa</u> kuh buhl)

inflexible; not capable of being changed or pacified

The *implacable* teasing was hard for the child to take.

IMPORTUNATE

adj (ihm <u>pohr</u> chuh niht)

troublesomely urgent; extremely persistent in request or demand

Her *importunate* appeal for a job caused me to grant her an interview.

IMPRECATION

noun (ihm prih <u>kay</u> shuhn)

a curse

Spouting violent *imprecations*, Hank searched for the person who had vandalized his truck.

IMPUDENT

adj (<u>ihm</u> pyuh duhnt)

marked by cocky boldness or disregard for others

Considering the judge had been lenient in her sentence, it was *impudent* of the defendant to refer to her by her first name.

IMPUGN

verb (ihm <u>pyoon</u>)

to call into question; to attack verbally

"How dare you *impugn* my motives?" protested the lawyer, on being accused of ambulance chasing.

IMPUTE

verb (ihm <u>pyoot</u>)

to lay the responsibility or blame for, often unjustly

It seemed unfair to *impute* the accident on me, especially since they were the ones who ran the red light.

INCANDESCENT

adj (ihn kahn <u>dehs</u> uhnt)

shining brightly

The *incandescent* glow of the moon made it a night I'll never forget.

INCARNADINE

adj (ihn <u>kaar</u> nuh dien) (ihn <u>kaar</u> nuh dihn)

red, especially blood red

The *incarnadine* lipstick she wore made her look much older than she was.

INCHOATE

adj (ihn <u>koh</u> iht)

being only partly in existence; imperfectly formed

For every page of the crisp writing that made it into the final book, Jessie has 10 pages of *inchoate* rambling that made up the first draft.

INCIPIENT

adj (ihn <u>sihp</u> ee uhnt)

beginning to exist or appear; in an initial stage

The *incipient* idea seemed brilliant, but they knew it needed much more development.

INCORRIGIBLE

adj (ihn <u>kohr</u> ih juh buhl)

incapable of being corrected or amended; difficult to control or manage

"You're *incorrigible*," yelled the frustrated mother to her son, in the middle of his third tantrum of the day.

INCREDULOUS

adj (ihn <u>krehj</u> uh luhs)

unwilling to accept what is true, skeptical

The Lasky children were *incredulous* when their parents told them they were moving to Alaska.

INDOMITABLE

adj (ihn <u>dahm</u> ih tuuh buhl)

incapable of being conquered

Climbing Mount Everest would seem an *indomitable* task, but it has been done many times.

INGRATIATE

verb (ihn <u>gray</u> shee ayt)

to gain favor with another by deliberate effort, to seek to please somebody so as to gain an advantage

The new intern tried to *ingratiate* herself with the managers so that they might consider her for a future job.

INHERENT

adj (ihn <u>hehr</u> ehnt)

involving the essential character of something, built-in, inborn

The class was dazzled by the experiment and as a result more likely to remember the *inherent* scientific principle.

INQUEST

noun (<u>ihn</u> kwehst)

an investigation, an inquiry

The police chief ordered an *inquest* to determine what went wrong.

INSENSATE

adj (ihn <u>sehn</u> sayt) (ihn <u>sehn</u> siht)

lacking sensibility and understanding, foolish

The shock of the accident left him *insensate*, but after some time, the numbness subsided and he was able to tell the officer what had happened.

INSOLENT

adj (<u>ihn</u> suh luhnt)

insultingly arrogant, overbearing

After having spoken with three *insolent* customer service representatives, Shelly was relieved when the fourth one sympathized with her complaint.

INSULAR

adj (<u>ihn</u> suh luhr) (<u>ihn</u> syuh luhr)

characteristic of an isolated people, especially having a narrow viewpoint

It was a shock for Kendra to go from her small high school, with her *insular* group of friends, to a huge college with students from all over the country.

INSUPERABLE

adj (ihn <u>soo</u> puhr uh buhl)

incapable of being surmounted or overcome

Insuperable as our problems may seem, I'm confident we'll come out ahead.

INTER

verb (ihn <u>tuhr</u>)

to bury

After giving the masses one last chance to pay their respects, the leader's body was *interred*.

INTERLOCUTOR

noun (ihn tuhr <u>lahk</u> yuh tuhr)

ones who takes part in conversation

Though always the *interlocutor*, the professor actually preferred that his students guide the class discussion.

INTERNECINE

adj (ihn tuhr <u>nehs</u> een)

mutually destructive; equally devastating to both sides

Though it looked as though there was a victor, the *internecine* battle benefited no one.

INTERREGNUM

noun (ihn tuhr <u>rehg</u> nuhm)

a temporary halting of the usual operations of government or control

The new king began his reign by restoring order that the lawless *interregnum* had destroyed.

INTIMATION

noun (ihn tuh <u>may</u> shuhn)

a subtle and indirect hint

Abby chose to ignore Babu's *intimation* that she wasn't as good a swimmer as she claimed.

INTRACTABLE

adj (ihn <u>traak</u> tuh buhl)

not easily managed or manipulated

Intractable for hours, the wild horse eventually allowed the rider to mount.

INTRANSIGENT

adj (ihn <u>traan</u> suh juhnt) (ihn <u>traan</u> zuh juhnt)

uncompromising, refusing to abandon an extreme position

His *intransigent* positions on social issues cost him the election.

INTREPID

adj (ihn <u>trehp</u> ihd)

fearless, resolutely courageous

Despite freezing winds, the *intrepid* hiker completed his ascent.

INUNDATE

verb (<u>ihn</u> uhn dayt)

to cover with a flood; to overwhelm as if with a flood

The box office was *inundated* with requests for tickets to the award-winning play.

INVETERATE

adj (ihn <u>veht</u> uhr iht)

firmly established, especially with respect to a habit or attitude

An *inveterate* risk-taker, Lori tried her luck at bungee-jumping.

IRASCIBLE

adj (ih <u>raas</u> uh buhl)

easily angered, hot-tempered

One of the most *irascible* barbarians of all time, Attila the Hun ravaged much of Europe during his time.

IRONIC

adj (ie <u>rahn</u> ihk)

poignantly contrary or incongruous to what was expected

It was *ironic* to learn that shy Wendy from high school grew up to be the loud-mouth host of the daily talk show.

IRREVERENT

adj (ih <u>rehv</u> uhr uhnt)

disrespectful in a gentle or humorous way

Kevin's *irreverent* attitude toward the principal annoyed the teacher but amused the other children.

ITINERANT

adj (ie <u>tihn</u> uhr uhnt)

wandering from place to place; unsettled

The *itinerant* tomcat came back to the Johansson homestead every two months.

JETTISON

verb (<u>jeht</u> ih zuhn) (<u>jeht</u> ih suhn)

to discard, to get rid of as unnecessary or encumbering

The sinking ship *jettisoned* its cargo in a desperate attempt to reduce its weight.

JOCULAR

adj (<u>jahk</u> yuh luhr)

playful, humorous

The *jocular* old man entertained his grandchildren for hours.

JUNTA

noun (<u>hoon</u> tuh) (<u>juhn</u> tuh)

a small governing body, especially after a revolutionary seizure of power

Only one member of the *junta* was satisfactory enough to be elected once the new government was established.

KISMET

noun (<u>kihz</u> meht) (<u>kihz</u> miht)

destiny, fate

When Eve found out that Garret also played the harmonica, she knew their meeting was *kismet*.

LAMPOON

verb (laam <u>poon</u>)

to ridicule with satire

The mayor hated being *lampooned* by the press for his efforts to improve people's politeness.

LARGESS

noun (laar <u>jehs</u>)

generous giving (as of money) to others who may seem inferior

She'd always relied on her parent's *largess*, but after graduation, she had to get a job.

LAUDABLE

adj (<u>law</u> duh buhl)

deserving of praise

Kristin's dedication is *laudable*, but she doesn't have the necessary skills to be a good paralegal.

LAX

adj (laaks)

not rigid, loose; negligent

Because our delivery boy is *lax*, the newspaper often arrives sopping wet.

LEVITY

noun (<u>leh</u> vih tee)

an inappropriate lack of seriousness, overly casual

The joke added needed *levity* to the otherwise serious meeting.

LEXICON

noun (<u>lehk</u> sih kahn)

a dictionary; a stock of terms pertaining to a particular subject or vocabulary

The author coined the term Gen-X, which has since entered the *lexicon*.

LIBERTARIAN

noun (lih buhr <u>tehr</u> ee uhn)

one who advocates individual rights and free will

The *libertarian* was always at odds with the conservatives.

LIBERTINE

noun (<u>lihb</u> uhr teen)

a free thinker, usually used disparagingly; one without moral restraint

The *libertine* took pleasure in gambling away his family's money.

LICENTIOUS

adj (lih <u>sehn</u> shuhs)

immoral; unrestrained by society

Conservative citizens were outraged by the *licentious* exploits of the free-spirited artists living in town.

LILLIPUTIAN

adj (lihl ee <u>pyoo</u> shun)

very small

Next to her Amazonian roommate, the girl seemed *lilliputian*.

LIMBER

adj (<u>lihm</u> buhr)

flexible, capable of being shaped

After years of doing yoga, the elderly man was remarkably *limber*.

LITHE

adj (lieth)

moving and bending with ease; marked by effortless grace

The dancer's *lithe* movements proved her to be a rising star in the ballet corps.

LOQUACIOUS

adj (loh <u>kway</u> shuhs)

talkative

She was naturally *loquacious*, which was always a challenge when she was in a library or movie theater.

MACABRE

adj (muh <u>kaa</u> bruh) (muh <u>kaa</u> buhr)

having death as a subject; dwelling on the gruesome

Martin enjoyed *macabre* tales about werewolves and vampires.

MACROCOSM

noun (<u>maak</u> roh cahz uhm)

the whole universe; a large-scale reflection of a part of the greater world

Some scientists focus on a particular aspect of space, while others study the entire *macrocosm* and how its parts relate to one another.

MALAISE

noun (maa <u>layz</u>)

a feeling of unease or depression

During his presidency, Jimmy Carter spoke of a "national *malaise*" and was subsequently criticized for being too negative.

MALAPROPISM

noun (<u>maal</u> uh prahp ihz uhm)

the accidental, often comical, use of a word which resembles the one intended, but has a different, often contradictory meaning

Everybody laughed at the *malapropism* when instead of saying "public broadcasting" the announcer said "public boredcasting."

MALEDICTION

noun (maal ih <u>dihk</u> shun)

a curse, a wish of evil upon another

The frog prince looked for a princess to kiss him and put an end to the witch's *malediction*.

MALEVOLENT

adj (muh <u>lehv</u> uh luhnt)

exhibiting ill will; wishing harm to others

The *malevolent* gossiper spread false rumors with frequency.

MALFEASANCE

noun (maal <u>fee</u> zuhns)

wrongdoing or misconduct, especially by a public official

Not only was the deputy's *malfeasance* humiliating, it also spelled the end of his career.

MALLEABLE

adj (<u>maal</u> ee uh buhl)

easily influenced or shaped, capable of being altered by outside forces

The welder heated the metal before shaping it because the heat made it *malleable*.

MANNERED

adj (<u>maan</u> uhrd)

artificial or stilted in character

The portrait is an example of the *mannered* style that was favored in that era.

MAVERICK

noun (<u>maav</u> rihk) (<u>maav</u> uh rihk)

an independent individual who does not go along with a group

The senator was a *maverick* who was willing to vote against his own party's position.

MAWKISH

adj (<u>maw</u> kihsh)

sickeningly sentimental

The poet hoped to charm his girlfriend with his flowery poem, but its *mawkish* tone sickened her instead.

MEGALOMANIA

noun (<u>mehg</u> uh loh <u>may</u> nee uh)

obsession with great or grandiose performance

Many of the Roman emperors suffered from severe *megalomania*.

MELLIFLUOUS

adj (muh <u>lihf</u> loo uhs)

having a smooth, rich flow

She was so talented that her *mellifluous* flute playing transported me to another world.

MICROCOSM

noun (<u>mie</u> kruh kahz uhm)

a small scale representation of a larger system

This department is in fact a *microcosm* of the entire corporation.

MILIEU

noun (mihl <u>yoo</u>)

the physical or social setting in which something occurs or develops, environment

The *milieu* at the club wasn't one I was comfortable with, so I left right away.

MISANTHROPE

noun (<u>mihs</u> ahn throhp)

a person who hates or distrusts mankind

Scrooge was such a *misanthrope* that even the sight of children singing made him angry.

MISNOMER

noun (mihs <u>noh</u> muhr)

an error in naming a person or place

Iceland is a *misnomer* since it isn't really icy; the name means "island."

MISSIVE

noun (<u>mihs</u> ihv)

a written note or letter

Priscilla spent hours composing a romantic *missive* for Elvis.

MITIGATE

verb (<u>miht</u> ih gayt)

to make less severe, make milder

A judge may *mitigate* a sentence if it's decided that the crime was committed out of necessity.

MODICUM

noun (<u>mahd</u> ih kuhm)

a small portion, limited quantity

I expect at least a *modicum* of assistance from you on the day of the party.

MOLLIFY

verb (<u>mahl</u> uh fie)

to soothe in temper or disposition

A small raise and increased break time *mollified* the unhappy staff, at least for the moment.

MORDANT

adj (<u>mohr</u> dnt)

biting and caustic in manner and style

Roald Dahl's stories are *mordant* alternatives to bland stories intended for kids.

MORES

noun (<u>mawr</u> ayz)

fixed customs or manners; moral attitudes

In keeping with the *mores* of ancient Roman society, Nero held a celebration every weekend.

MOROSE

adj (muh <u>rohs</u>) (maw <u>rohs</u>)

gloomy, sullen

After hearing that the internship had been given to someone else, Lenny was *morose* for days.

MOTE

noun (moht)

a small particle, speck

Monica's eye watered, irritated by a *mote* of dust.

MUTABILITY

noun (myoo tuh <u>bihl</u> uh tee)

the quality of being capable of change, in form or character; susceptibility of change

The actress lacked the *mutability* needed to perform in the improvisational play.

MYOPIC

adj (mie <u>ahp</u> ihk) (mie <u>oh</u> pihk)

lacking foresight, having a narrow view or long-range perspective

Not wanting to spend a lot of money up front, the *myopic* business owner would likely suffer the consequences later.

NEBULOUS

adj (<u>neh</u> <u>byoo</u> luhs)

vague, undefined

The candidate's *nebulous* plans to fight crime made many voters skeptical.

NECROMANCY

noun (<u>nehk</u> ruh maan see)

the practice of communicating with the dead in order to predict the future

The practice of *necromancy* supposes belief in survival of the soul after death.

NEFARIOUS

adj (nih <u>fahr</u> ee uhs)

intensely wicked or vicous

Nefarious deeds are never far from an evil-doer's mind.

NEONATE

noun (<u>nee</u> uh nayt)

a newborn child

The *neonate* was born prematurely so she's still in the hospital.

NIHILISM

noun (<u>nie</u> hihl iz uhm)

the belief that traditional values and beliefs are unfounded and that existence is useless; the belief that conditions in the social organization are so bad as to make destruction desirable

Robert's *nihilism* expressed itself in his lack of concern with the norms of moral society.

NOMENCLATURE

noun (<u>noh</u> muhn klay chuhr)

a system of scientific names

In botany class, we learned the *nomenclature* used to identify different species of roses.

NON SEQUITUR

noun (nahn <u>sehk</u> wih tuhr)

a statement that does not follow logically from anything previously said

After the heated political debate, her comment about cake was a real *non sequitur*.

NOVEL

adj (<u>nah</u> vuhl)

new and not resembling anything formerly known

Piercing any part of the body other than the earlobes was *novel* in the 1950s, but now it is quite common.

OBDURATE

adj (<u>ahb</u> duhr uht)

stubbornly persistent, resistant to persuasion

The president was *obdurate* on the matter, and no amount of public protest could change his mind.

OBFUSCATE

verb (<u>ahb</u> fyoo skayt)

to confuse, make obscure

Benny always *obfuscates* the discussion by bringing in irrelevant facts.

OBSTINATE

adj (<u>ahb</u> stih nuht)

unreasonably persistent

The *obstinate* journalist would not reveal his source, and thus, was jailed for 30 days.

OLFACTORY

adj (ohl <u>faak</u> tuh ree)

relating to the sense of smell

Whenever she entered a candle store, her *olfactory* sense was awakened.

OLIGARCHY

noun (<u>oh</u> lih gaar kee)

a government in which a small group exercises supreme control

In an *oligarchy*, the few who rule are generally wealthier and have more status than the others.

ONUS

noun (<u>oh</u> nuhs)

a burden, an obligation

Antonia was beginning to feel the *onus* of having to feed her friend's cat for the month.

OPINE

verb (oh <u>pien</u>)

to express an opinion

At the "Let's Chat Talk Show," the audience member *opined* that the guest was in the wrong.

OPPORTUNIST

noun (aap ore <u>too</u> nist)

one who takes advantage of any opportunity to achieve an end, with little regard for principles

The *opportunist* wasted no time in stealing the idea and presenting it as his own.

OPPROBRIOUS

adj (uh <u>proh</u> bree uhs)

disgraceful, shameful

She wrote an *opprobrious* editorial in the newspaper about the critic who tore her new play to shreds.

ORNERY

adj (<u>ohr</u> nuh ree)

having an irritable disposition, cantankerous

My first impression of the taxi driver was that he was *ornery*, but then he explained that he'd just had a bad day.

OSCILLATE

verb (<u>ah</u> sihl ayt)

to swing back and forth like a pendulum; to vary between opposing beliefs or feelings

The move meant a new house in a lovely neighborhood, but she missed her friends, so she *oscillated* between joy and sadness.

OSSIFY

verb (<u>ah</u> sih fie)

to change into bone; to become hardened or set in a rigidly conventional pattern

The forensics expert ascertained the body's age based on the degree to which the facial structure had *ossified*.

OSTRACIZE

verb (<u>ahs</u> truh size)

to exclude from a group by common consent

Despite the fact that Tabatha had done nothing wrong, her friends *ostracized* her.

OUST

verb (owst)

to remove from position by force; eject

After President Nixon so offensively lied to the country during Watergate, he was *ousted* from office.

PAEAN

noun (<u>pee</u> uhn)

a tribute, a song or expression of praise

He considered his newest painting a *paean* to his late wife.

PALATIAL

adj (puh <u>lay</u> shuhl)

relating to a palace; magnificent

After living in a cramped studio apartment for years, Alicia thought the modest one bedroom looked downright *palatial*.

PALIMPSEST

noun (<u>pahl</u> ihmp sehst)

an object or place having diverse layers or aspects beneath the surface

Years ago, paper was very expensive, so the practice was to write over previous words, creating a *palimpsest* of writing.

PALPABLE

adj (<u>pahlp</u> uh buhl)

capable of being touched or felt; easily perceived

The tension was *palpable* as I walked into the room.

PALTRY

adj (<u>pawl</u> tree)

pitifully small or worthless

Bernardo paid the ragged boy the *paltry* sum of 25 cents to carry his luggage all the way to the hotel.

PANACHE

noun (puh <u>nahsh</u>)

flamboyance or dash in style and action

Leah has such *panache* when planning parties, even when they're last-minute affairs.

PANDEMIC

adj (paan <u>deh</u> mihk)

occurring over a wide geographic area and affecting a large portion of the population

Pandemic alarm spread throughout Colombia after the devastating earthquake.

PANEGYRIC

noun (paan uh <u>geer</u> ihk)

elaborate praise; formal hymn of praise

The director's *panegyric* for the donor who kept his charity going was heart-warming.

PARADIGM

noun (<u>paar</u> uh diem)

an outstandingly clear or typical example

The new restaurant owner used the fast-food giant as a *paradigm* for expansion into new locales.

PARAGON

noun (<u>paar</u> uh gon)

a model of excellence or perfection

She's the *paragon* of what a judge should be: honest, intelligent, and just.

PARAMOUNT

adj (<u>paar</u> uh mownt)

supreme, of chief importance

It's of *paramount* importance that we make it back to camp before the storm hits.

PARE

verb (payr)

to trim off excess, reduce

The cook's hands were sore after she *pared* hundreds of potatoes for the banquet.

PARIAH

noun (puh <u>rie</u> ah)

an outcast

Once he betrayed those in his community, he was banished and lived the life of a *pariah*.

PATENT

adj (<u>paa</u> tehnt)

obvious, evident

Moe could no longer stand Frank's *patent* fawning over the boss and so confronted him.

PATHOGENIC

adj (paa thoh <u>jehn</u> ihk)

causing disease

Bina's research on the origins of *pathogenic* microorganisms should help stop the spread of disease.

PATRICIAN

adj (puh <u>trih</u> shuhn)

aristocratic

Though he really couldn't afford an expensive lifestyle, Claudius had *patrician* tastes.

PATRONIZE

verb (<u>pay</u> troh niez)

to act as patron of, to adopt an air of condescension toward; to buy from

LuAnn *patronized* the students, treating them like simpletons, which they deeply resented.

PECULATE

verb (<u>pehk</u> yuh layt)

to embezzle

These days in the news, we read more and more about workers *peculating* the system.

PECUNIARY

adj (pih <u>kyoon</u> nee <u>ehr</u> ee)

relating to money

Michelle's official title was office manager, but she ended up taking on a lot of *pecuniary* responsibilities such as payroll duties.

PELLUCID

adj (peh <u>loo</u> sihd)

transparently clear in style or meaning, easy to understand

Though she thought she could hide her ulterior motives, they were *pellucid* to everyone else.

PENCHANT

noun (<u>pehn</u> chehnt)

an inclination, a definite liking

After Daniel visited the Grand Canyon, he developed a *penchant* for travel.

PENITENT

adj (<u>peh</u> nih tehnt)

expressing sorrow for sins or offenses, repentant

Claiming the criminal did not feel *penitent*, the victim's family felt his pardon should be denied.

PENURY

noun (<u>pehn</u> yuh ree)

an oppressive lack of resources (as money), severe poverty

Once a famous actor, he eventually died in *penury* and anonymity.

PEREGRINATE

verb (<u>pehr</u> ih gruh nayt)

to travel on foot

It has always been a dream of mine to *peregrinate* from one side of Europe to the other with nothing but a backpack.

PHALANX

noun (<u>fay</u> laanks)

a compact or close-knit body of people, animals, or things

A *phalanx* of guards stood outside the prime minister's home day and night.

PHILISTINE

noun (<u>fihl</u> uh steen)

a person who is guided by materialism and is disdainful of intellectual or artistic values

The *philistine* never even glanced at the rare violin in his collection but instead kept an eye on its value and sold it at a profit.

PHILOLOGY

noun (fih <u>lahl</u> uh jee)

the study of ancient texts and languages

Philology was the predecessor to modern-day linguistics.

PHLEGMATIC

adj (flehg <u>maa</u> tihk)

having a sluggish, unemotional temperament

His writing was energetic but his *phlegmatic* personality wasn't suited for television, so he turned down the interview.

PIQUE

verb (peek)

to arouse anger or resentment in; provoke

His continual insensitivity *piqued* my anger.

PLAINTIVE

adj (<u>playn</u> tihv)

expressive of suffering or woe, melancholy

The *plaintive* cries from the girl trapped in the tree were heard by all.

PLATITUDE

noun (<u>plaa</u> tuh tood)

overused and trite remark

Instead of the usual *platitudes*, the comedian gave a memorable and inspiring speech to the graduating class.

PLEBEIAN

adj (plee <u>bee</u> uhn)

crude or coarse; characteristic of commoners

After five weeks of rigorous studying, the graduate settled in for a weekend of *plebeian* socializing and television watching.

PLUCKY

adj (<u>pluh</u> kee)

courageous; spunky

The *plucky* young nurse dove into the foxhole, determined to help the wounded soldier.

POLITIC

adj (<u>pah</u> luh tihk)

shrewd and crafty in managing or dealing with things

She was wise to curb her tongue and was able to explain her problem to the judge in a respectful and *politic* manner.

POLYGLOT

noun (<u>pah</u> lee glaht)

a speaker of many languages

Ling's extensive travels have helped her to become a true *polyglot*.

PORE

verb (pohr)

to read studiously or attentively

I've *pored* over this text, yet I still can't understand it.

PORTENTOUS

adj (pohr <u>tehn</u> tuhs)

foreshadowing, ominous; eliciting amazement and wonder

Everyone thought the rays of light were *portentous* until they realized a nine-year-old was playing a joke on them.

POSIT

verb (<u>pohz</u> iht)

to assume as real or conceded; propose as an explanation

Before proving the math formula, we needed to *posit* that *x* and *y* were real numbers.

POTABLE

adj (<u>poh</u> tuh buhl)

suitable for drinking

Though the water was *potable*, it tasted terrible.

POTENTATE

noun (<u>poh</u> tehn tayt)

a ruler; one who wields great power

Alex was much kinder before he assumed the role of *potentate*.

PRECARIOUS

adj (prih <u>caa</u> ree uhs)

lacking in security or stability; dependent on chance or uncertain conditions

Given the *precarious* circumstances, I chose to opt out of the deal completely.

PRECIPITOUS

adj (pree <u>sih</u> puh tuhs)

steep

The *precipitous* cave was daunting for the first-time climber.

PRESAGE

noun (<u>preh</u> sihj)

something that foreshadows; a feeling of what will happen in the future

The demolition of the Berlin Wall was a *presage* to the fall of the Soviet Union.

PRESTIDIGITATION

noun (<u>prehs</u> tih <u>dihj</u> ih <u>tay</u> shuhn)

a cleverly executed trick or deception; sleight of hand

My hunch was that he won the contest not so much as a result of real talent, but rather through *prestidigitation*.

PRETERNATURAL

adj (pree tuhr <u>naach</u> uhr uhl)

existing outside of nature; extraordinary; supernatural

We were all amazed at her *preternatural* ability to recall smells from her early childhood.

PRIMEVAL

adj (priem <u>ee</u> vuhl)

ancient, primitive

The archaeologist claimed that the skeleton was of *primeval* origin, though in fact it was the remains of a modern-day monkey.

PRODIGAL

adj (<u>prah</u> dih guhl)

recklessly extravagant, wasteful

The *prodigal* expenditures on the military budget during a time of peace created a stir in the cabinet.

PROFFER

verb (<u>prahf</u> uhr)

to offer for acceptance

The deal *proffered* by the committee satisfied all those at the meeting, ending a month-long discussion.

PROGENITOR

noun (proh <u>jehn</u> uh tuhr)

an ancestor in the direct line, forefather; founder

Though he had been born here, his *progenitors* were from India.

PROLIFERATE

verb (proh <u>lih</u> fuhr ayt)

to grow by rapid production of new parts; increase in number

The bacteria *proliferated* so quickly that even the doctor was surprised.

PROMULGATE

verb (<u>prah</u> muhl gayt)

to make known by open declaration, proclaim

The publicist *promulgated* the idea that the celebrity had indeed gotten married.

PROPENSITY

noun (proh <u>pehn</u> suh tee)

a natural inclination or preference

She has a *propensity* for lashing out at others when stressed, so we leave her alone when she's had a rough day.

PROSAIC

adj (proh <u>say</u> ihk)

relating to prose (as opposed to poetry); dull, ordinary

Simon's *prosaic* style bored his writing teacher to tears, though he thought he had an artistic flair.

PROSCRIBE

verb (proh <u>skribe</u>)

to condemn or forbid as harmful or unlawful

Consumption of alcohol was *proscribed* in the country's constitution, but the ban was eventually lifted.

PROSTRATE

adj (<u>prah</u> strayt)

lying face downward in adoration or submission

My friends teased me for lying *prostrate* when I met my favorite musician.

PROVINCIAL

adj (pruh <u>vihn</u> shuhl)

limited in outlook, narrow, unsophisticated

Having grown up in the city, Anita sneered at the *provincial* attitudes of her country cousins.

PROXY

noun (<u>prahk</u> see)

a person authorized to act for someone else

In the event the shareholder can't attend the meeting, he'll send a *proxy*.

PSEUDONYM

noun (<u>soo</u> duh nihm)

a fictitious name, used particularly by writers to conceal identity

Though George Eliot sounds as though it's a male name, it was the *pseudonym* that Marian Evans used when she published her classic novel *Middlemarch*.

PUGILISM

noun (<u>pyoo</u> juhl ih suhm)

boxing

Pugilism has been defended as a positive outlet for aggressive impulses.

PUISSANT

adj (<u>pwih</u> sihnt) (<u>pyoo</u> sihnt)

powerful

His memoir was full of descriptions of *puissant* military heroics, but most were exaggerations or outright lies.

PUNCTILIOUS

adj (puhngk <u>tihl</u> ee uhs)

concerned with precise details about codes or conventions

The *punctilious* student never made spelling errors on her essays.

PUNDIT

noun (<u>puhn</u> diht)

one who gives opinions in an authoritative manner

The *pundits* on television are often more entertaining than the sitcoms.

PURLOIN

verb (<u>puhr</u> loyn)

to steal

His goal was to *purloin* the documents he felt belonged to him.

PURPORT

verb (puhr <u>pohrt</u>)

to profess, suppose, claim

Brad *purported* to be an opera lover, but he fell asleep at every performance he attended.

RANCOR

noun (<u>raan</u> kuhr)

bitter hatred

Having been teased mercilessly for years, Herb became filled with *rancor* toward those who had humiliated him.

RANKLE

verb (<u>raang</u> kuhl)

to cause anger and irritation

At first the kid's singing was adorable, but after 40 minutes it began to *rankle*.

RAPACIOUS

adj (ruh pay shuhs)

taking by force; driven by greed

Sea otters are so *rapacious* that they consumer 10 times their body weight in food every day.

RAPT

adj (raapt)

deeply absorbed

The story was so well performed that the usually rowdy children were *rapt* until the final word.

RAREFY

verb (rayr uh fie)

to make rare, thin, or less dense

The atmosphere *rarefies* as altitude increases, so the air atop a mountain is too thin to breathe.

RAZE

verb (rayz)

to tear down, demolish

The house had been *razed*; where it once stood, there was nothing but splinters and bricks.

REACTIONARY

adj (ree aak shuhn ayr ee)

marked by extreme conservatism, especially in politics

Her *reactionary* beliefs were misunderstood by her friends.

RECAPITULATE

verb (ree kuh pihch yoo layt)

to review by a brief summary

After the long-winded president had finished his speech, his assistant *recapitulated* for the press the points he had made.

RECIDIVISM

noun (rih sihd uh vih zihm)

a tendency to relapse into a previous behavior, especially criminal behavior

According to statistics, the *recidivism* rate for criminals is quite high.

REFRACT

verb (rih fraakt)

to deflect sound or light

The crystal *refracted* the rays of sunlight so they formed a beautiful pattern on the wall.

REFUTE

verb (rih fyoot)

to contradict, discredit

She made such a persuasive argument that nobody could *refute* it.

RELEGATE

verb (reh luh gayt)

to send into exile, banish; assign

Because he hadn't scored any goals during the season, Abe was *relegated* to the bench for the championship game.

REMISSION

noun (rih mih shuhn)

a lessening of intensity or degree

The doctor told me that the disease had gone into *remission*.

REMUNERATION

noun (rih myoo nuh ray shuhn)

payment for goods or services or to recompense for losses

You can't expect people to do this kind of boring work without some form of *remuneration.*

REPLETE

adj (rih pleet)

abundantly supplied, complete

The gigantic supermarket was *replete* with consumer products of every kind.

REPOSE

noun (rih pohz)

relaxation, leisure

After working hard every day in the busy city, Mike finds his *repose* on weekends playing golf with friends.

REPREHENSIBLE

adj (rehp ree hehn suh buhl)

blameworthy, disreputable

Lowell was thrown out of the restaurant because of his *reprehensible* behavior toward the other patrons.

REPROVE

verb (rih proov)

to criticize or correct, usually in a gentle manner

Mrs. Hernandez *reproved* her daughter for staying out late and not calling.

REQUITE

verb (rih kwiet)

to return or repay

Thanks for offering to lend me $1,000, but I know I'll never be able to *requite* your generosity.

RESCIND

verb (rih sihnd)

to repeal, cancel

After the celebrity was involved in a scandal, the car company *rescinded* its offer of an endorsement contract.

RESILIENT

adj (rih sihl yuhnt)

able to recover quickly after illness or bad luck; able to bounce back to shape

Psychologists say that being *resilient* in life is one of the keys to success and happiness.

RESOLUTE

adj (reh suh loot)

marked by firm determination

Louise was *resolute*: She would get into medical school no matter what.

RESPLENDENT

adj (rih splehn dihnt)

splendid, brilliant

The bride looked *resplendent* in her gown and sparkling tiara.

REVILE

verb (rih veye uhl)

to criticize with harsh language, verbally abuse

The artist's new installation was *reviled* by critics who weren't used to the departure from his usual work.

RHETORIC

noun (<u>reh</u> tuhr ihk)

the art of speaking or writing effectively; skill in the effective use of speech

Lincoln's talent for *rhetoric* was evident in his beautifully expressed Gettysburg Address.

RIFE

adj (rief)

abundant prevalent especially to an increasing degree; filled with

The essay was so *rife* with grammatical errors that it had to be rewritten.

ROSTRUM

noun (<u>rahs</u> truhm)

an elevated platform for public speaking

Though she was terrified, the new member of the debate club approached the *rostrum* with poise.

SACCHARINE

adj (<u>saa</u> kuh ruhn)

excessively sweet or sentimental

Geoffrey's *saccharine* poems nauseated Lucy, and she wished he'd stop sending them.

SACRILEGIOUS

adj (<u>saak</u> rih <u>lihj</u> uhs)

impious, irreverent toward what is held to be sacred or holy

It's considered *sacrilegious* for one to enter a mosque wearing shoes.

SALIENT

adj (<u>say</u> lee uhnt)

prominent, of notable significance

His most *salient* characteristic is his tendency to dominate every conversation.

SANCTIMONIOUS

adj (<u>saangk</u> tih <u>moh</u> nee uhs)

hypocritically devout; acting morally superior to another

The *sanctimonious* columnist turned out to have been hiding a gambling problem that cost his family everything.

SATIATE

verb (<u>say</u> shee ayt)

to satisfy (as a need or desire) fully or to excess

After years of journeying around the world with nothing but backpacks, the friends had finally *satiated* their desire to travel.

SATURNINE

adj (<u>saat</u> uhr nien)

cold and steady in mood, gloomy; slow to act

Her *saturnine* expression made her hard to be around.

SAVANT

noun (suh <u>vahnt</u>)

a person of learning; especially one with knowledge in a special field

The *savant* so impressed us with his knowledge that we asked him to come speak at our school.

SCRUPULOUS

adj (<u>skroop</u> yuh luhs)

acting in strict regard for what is considered proper; punctiliously exact

After the storm had destroyed their antique lamp, the Millers worked to repair it with *scrupulous* care.

SEAMY

adj (<u>see</u> mee)

morally degraded, unpleasant

The tour guide avoided the *seamy* parts of town.

SECULAR

adj (<u>seh</u> kyoo luhr)

not specifically pertaining to religion, relating to the world

Although his favorite books were religious, Ben also read *secular* works such as mysteries.

SEDITION

noun (seh <u>dih</u> shuhn)

behavior that promotes rebellion or civil disorder against the state

Li was arrested for *sedition* after he gave a fiery speech in the main square.

SEMINAL

adj (<u>seh</u> muhn uhl)

influential in an original way, providing a basis for further development; creative

The scientist's discovery proved to be *seminal* in the area of quantum physics.

SEQUESTER

verb (suh <u>kweh</u> stuhr)

to set apart, seclude

When juries are *sequestered*, it can take days, even weeks, to come up with a verdict.

SERAPHIC

adj (seh <u>rah</u> fihk)

angelic, sweet

Selena's *seraphic* appearance belied her nasty, bitter personality.

SIMIAN

adj (<u>sih</u> mee uhn)

apelike; relating to apes

Early man was more *simian* in appearance than is modern man.

SINECURE

noun (<u>sien</u> ih kyoor)

a well-paying job or office that requires little or no work

The corrupt mayor made sure to set up all his relatives in *sinecures* within the administration.

SOBRIQUET

noun (<u>soh</u> brih <u>kay</u>) (<u>soh</u> brih <u>keht</u>)

a nickname

One of former president Ronald Reagan's *sobriquets* was "The Gipper."

SOJOURN

noun (<u>soh</u> juhrn)

a temporary stay, visit

After graduating from college, Iliani embarked on a *sojourn* to China.

SOLICITOUS

adj (suh <u>lih</u> sih tuhs)

anxious, concerned; full of desire, eager

Overjoyed to see the pop idol in her presence, the *solicitous* store owner stood ready to serve.

SOPHOMORIC

adj (sahf <u>mohr</u> ihk)

exhibiting great immaturity and lack of judgment

After Sean's *sophomoric* behavior, he was grounded for weeks.

SPARTAN

adj (<u>spahr</u> tihn)

highly self-disciplined; frugal, austere

When he was in training, the athlete preferred to live in a *spartan* room so he could shut out all distractions.

SPECIOUS

adj (<u>spee</u> shuhs)

having the ring of truth but actually being untrue; deceptively attractive

After I followed up with some research on the matter, I realized that the charismatic politician's argument had been *specious*.

SPORTIVE

adj (<u>spohr</u> tihv)

frolicsome, playful

The lakeside vacation meant more *sportive* opportunities for the kids than the culinary tour through France.

SQUALID

adj (<u>skwa</u> lihd)

filthy and degraded as the result of neglect or poverty

The *squalid* living conditions in the building outraged the new tenants.

STALWART

adj (<u>stahl</u> wuhrt)

marked by outstanding strength and vigor of body, mind, or spirit

The 85-year old went to the market every day, impressing her neighbors with her *stalwart* routine.

STASIS

noun (<u>stay</u> sihs)

a state of static balance or equilibrium; stagnation

The rusty, ivy-covered World War II tank had obviously been in *stasis* for years.

STINT

verb (stihnt)

to be sparing or frugal; to restrict with respect to a share or allowance

Don't *stint* on the mayonnaise, because I don't like my sandwich too dry.

STIPULATE

verb (<u>stihp</u> yuh <u>layt</u>)

to specify as a condition or requirement of an agreement or offer

The contract *stipulated* that if the movie was never filmed, the actress got paid anyway.

STRATIFY

verb (<u>straa</u> tuh fie)

to arrange or divide into layers

Schliemann *stratified* the numerous layers of Troy, an archeological dig that remains legendary.

STRIDENT

adj (<u>strie</u> dehnt)

loud, harsh, unpleasantly noisy

The traveler's *strident* manner annoyed the flight attendant, but she managed to keep her cool.

STRINGENT

adj (<u>strihn</u> guhnt)

imposing severe, rigorous standards

Many employees found it difficult to live up to the *stringent* standards imposed by the company.

STYMIE

verb (<u>stie</u> mee)

to block or thwart

The police effort to capture the bank robber was *stymied* when he escaped through a rear window.

SUBTERRANEAN

adj (<u>suhb</u> tuh <u>ray</u> nee uhn)

hidden, secret; underground

Subterranean tracks were created for the trains after it was decided they had run out of room above ground.

SULLY

verb (suh lee)

to tarnish, taint

His outrageous gaffe *sullied* his public image.

SUPERFLUOUS

adj (soo puhr floo uhs)

extra, more than necessary

The extra recommendations Jake included in his application were *superfluous*, as only one was required.

SUPERSEDE

verb (soo puhr seed)

to cause to be set aside; to force out of use as inferior, replace

Her computer was still running version 2.0 of the software, which had been *superseded* by at least three more versions.

SUPPLANT

verb (suh plaant)

to replace (another) by force, to take the place of

The overthrow of the government meant a new leader would *supplant* the former one.

SURMOUNT

verb (suhr mownt)

to conquer, overcome

The blind woman *surmounted* great obstacles to become a well-known trial lawyer.

SYBARITE

noun (sih buh riet)

a person devoted to pleasure and luxury

A confirmed *sybarite*, the nobleman fainted at the thought of having to leave his palace and live in a small cottage.

TACTILE

adj (taak tihl)

producing a sensation of touch

The Museum of Natural History displays objects for people to touch so that they have a *tactile* understanding of how different peoples and animals lived.

TANTAMOUNT

adj (<u>taan</u> tuh mownt)

equal in value or effect

If she didn't get concert tickets to see her favorite band, it would be *tantamount* to a tragedy.

TAUTOLOGICAL

adj (<u>tawt</u> uh <u>lah</u> jih kuhl)

having to do with needless repetition, redundancy

I know he was only trying to clarify things, but his *tautological* statements confused me even more.

TAWDRY

adj (<u>taw</u> dree)

gaudy, cheap, showy

The performer changed into her *tawdry* costume and stepped onto the stage.

TEMERITY

noun (<u>teh</u> mehr ih tee)

unreasonable or foolhardy disregard for danger, recklessness

I offered her a ride since it was late at night, but she had the *temerity* to say she'd rather walk.

TEMPESTUOUS

adj (tehm <u>pehs</u> choo uhs)

stormy, turbulent

Our camping trip was cut short when the mild shower we were expecting turned into a *tempestuous* downpour.

TEMPORAL

adj (<u>tehmp</u> ore uhl)

having to do with time

The story lacked a *temporal* sense, so we couldn't figure out if the events took place in one evening or over the course of a year.

TENACIOUS

adj (teh <u>nay</u> shuhs)

tending to persist or cling; persistent in adhering to something valued or habitual

Securing women's right to vote required a *tenacious* fight.

TENET

noun (<u>teh</u> niht)

a principle, belief, or doctrine accepted by members of a group

One of the *tenets* of the school is that it is not acceptable to cheat.

TENUOUS

adj (<u>tehn</u> yoo uhs)

having little substance or strength; flimsy, weak

Francine's already *tenuous* connection to her cousins was broken when they moved away and left no forwarding address.

TERSE

adj (tuhrs)

concise, brief, free of extra words

Her *terse* style of writing was widely praised by the editors, who had been used to seeing long-winded material.

THWART

verb (thwahrt)

to block or prevent from happening; frustrate, defeat the hopes or aspirations of

The heavy lock *thwarted* his attempt to enter the building.

TITULAR

adj (<u>tihch</u> yoo luhr)

existing in title only; having a title without the functions or responsibilities

Carla was thrilled to be voted Homecoming Queen until somebody explained that the *titular* honor didn't mean she could boss anybody around.

TOADY

noun (<u>toh</u> dee)

one who flatters in the hope of gaining favors

The king was surrounded by *toadies* who rushed to agree with whatever outrageous thing he said.

TORTUOUS

adj (<u>tohr</u> choo uhs)

having many twists and turns; highly complex

To reach the remote inn, the travelers had to negotiate a *tortuous* path.

TOUT

verb (towt)

to praise or publicize loudly or extravagantly

She *touted* her skills as superior to ours, though in fact, we were all at the same level.

TRAJECTORY

noun (truh <u>jehk</u> tuh ree)

the path followed by a moving object, whether through space or otherwise; flight

The *trajectory* of the pitched ball was interrupted by an unexpected bird.

TRANSIENT

adj (<u>traan</u> see uhnt)

passing with time, temporary, short-lived

The reporter lived a *transient* life, staying in one place only long enough to cover the current story.

TRANSITORY

adj (<u>traan</u> sih <u>tohr</u> ee)

short-lived, existing only briefly

The actress' popularity proved *transitory* when her play folded within the month.

TREMULOUS

adj (<u>treh</u> myoo luhs)

trembling, timid; easily shaken

The *tremulous* kitten had been separated from her mother.

TROUNCE

verb (trowns)

to beat severely, defeat

The inexperienced young boxer was *trounced* in a matter of minutes.

TRUCULENT

adj (<u>truhk</u> yuh lehnt)

disposed to fight, belligerent

The bully was initially *truculent,* but eventually stopped picking fights at the least provocation.

TURGID

adj (<u>tuhr</u> jihd)

swollen as from a fluid, bloated

In the process of osmosis, water passes through the walls of *turgid* cells, ensuring that they never contain too much water.

TUTELAGE

noun (<u>toot</u> uh lihj)

guardianship, guidance

Under the *tutelage* of her older sister, the young orphan was able to persevere.

UNCANNY

adj (uhn <u>kaa</u> nee)

so keen and perceptive as to seem supernatural, peculiarly unsettling

Though they weren't related, their resemblance was *uncanny*.

UNCONSCIONABLE

adj (uhn <u>kahn</u> shuhn uh buhl)

unscrupulous; shockingly unfair or unjust

After she promised me the project, the fact that she gave it to someone else is *unconscionable*.

UNTOWARD

adj (uhn <u>tō rd</u>)

difficult to handle or work with

Charli's negative comments at work were a bit <u>untoward</u>.

USURY

noun (<u>yoo</u> zuh ree)

the practice of lending money at exorbitant rates

The moneylender was convicted of *usury* when it was discovered that he charged 50 percent interest on all his loans.

VARIEGATED

adj (<u>vaar</u> ee uh <u>gayt</u> ehd)

varied; marked with different colors

The *variegated* foliage of the jungle allows it to support thousands of animal species.

VEHEMENTLY

adv (<u>vee</u> ih mehnt lee)

marked by extreme intensity of emotions or convictions

She *vehemently* opposed the closing of the neighborhood garden, and was even arrested for protesting when the bulldozers came.

KAPLAN

VERACITY

noun (vuhr <u>aa</u> sih tee)

accuracy, truth

She had a reputation for *veracity*, so everyone believed her version of the story.

VERBOSE

adj (vuhr <u>bohs</u>)

wordy

The DNA analyst's answer was so *verbose* that the jury had trouble grasping his point.

VERITABLE

adj (<u>vehr</u> iht uh buhl)

being without question, often used figuratively

My neighbor was a *veritable* goldmine of information when I was writing my term paper on the Civil Rights era because she had been a student organizer and protester.

VERNACULAR

noun (vuhr <u>naa</u> kyoo luhr)

everyday language used by ordinary people; specialized language of a profession

Preeti could not understand the *vernacular* of the South, where she had recently moved.

VERNAL

adj (<u>vuhr</u> nuhl)

related to spring; fresh

Bea basked in the balmy *vernal* breezes, happy that winter was coming to an end.

VICARIOUSLY

adv (vie <u>kaar</u> ee uhs lee)

felt or undergone as if one were taking part in the experience or feelings of another

She lived *vicariously* through the characters in the adventure books she was always reading.

VILIFY

verb (<u>vih</u> lih fie)

to slander, defame

As gossip columnists often *vilify* celebrities, they're usually held in low regard.

VIM

noun (vihm)

vitality and energy

The *vim* with which she worked so early in the day explained why she was so productive.

VINDICATE

verb (<u>vihn</u> dih kayt)

to clear of blame; support a claim

Tess was *vindicated* when her prediction about the impending tornado came true.

VIRULENT

adj (<u>veer</u> yuh luhnt)

extremely poisonous; malignant; hateful

Alarmed at the *virulent* press he was receiving, the militant activist decided to go underground.

VISCERAL

adj (<u>vihs</u> uhr uhl)

instinctive, not intellectual; deep, emotional

When my twin was wounded many miles away, I had a *visceral* reaction.

VITUPERATE

verb (vih <u>too</u> puhr ayt)

to abuse verbally, berate

Vituperating someone is never a constructive way to effect change.

VOCIFEROUS

adj (voh <u>sih</u> fuhr uhs)

loud, noisy

Amid the *vociferous* protests of the members of parliament, the prime minister continued his speech.

VOLLEY

noun (<u>vah</u> lee)

a flight of missiles; round of gunshots

The troops fired a *volley* of bullets at the enemy, but they couldn't be sure how many hit their target.

VOLUBLE

adj (<u>vahl</u> yuh buhl)

talkative, speaking easily, glib

The *voluble* man and his reserved wife proved the old saying that opposites attract.

WAN

adj (wahn)

sickly pale

The sick child had a *wan* face, in contrast to her rosy-cheeked sister.

WANTON

adj (<u>wahn</u> tuhn)

undisciplined, unrestrained; reckless

The townspeople were outraged by the *wanton* display of disrespect when they discovered the statue of the town founder covered in graffiti.

WAX

verb (waaks)

to increase gradually; to begin to be

The moon was *waxing*, and would soon be full.

WIELD

verb (weeld)

to exercise authority or influence effectively

For such a young congressman, he *wielded* a lot of power.

WILY

adj (<u>wie</u> lee)

clever; deceptive

Yet again, the *wily* coyote managed to elude the ranchers who wanted it dead.

WINSOME

adj (<u>wihn</u> suhm)

charming, happily engaging

Dawn gave the customs officers a *winsome* smile, and they let her pass without searching her bags.

WORST

verb (wuhrst)

to gain the advantage over; to defeat

The North *worsted* the South in America's Civil War.

WRY

adj (rie)

bent or twisted in shape or condition; dryly humorous

Every time she teased him, she shot her friends a *wry* smile.

YEN

noun (yehn)

a strong desire, craving

Pregnant women commonly have a *yen* for pickles.

ZENITH

noun (zee nihth)

the point of culmination; peak

The diva considered her appearance at the Metropolitan Opera to be the *zenith* of her career.

ZEPHYR

noun (zeh fuhr)

a gentle breeze; something airy or unsubstantial

The *zephyr* from the ocean made the intense heat on the beach bearable for the sunbathers

Resource Five: **SAT English Basics**

GRAMMAR REVIEW

Subject-Verb Agreement
The form of a verb must match, or agree with, its subject in two ways: person and number.

1. Agreement of Person
When we talk about person, we're talking about whether the subject and verb of a sentence show that the author is making a statement about himself (first person), about the person he is speaking to (second person), or about some other person, place, or thing (third person).

- First Person Subjects: I, we.

  Example: I am going to Paris. We are going to Rome.
- Second Person Subject: you.

  Example: Are you sure you weren't imagining that flying saucer?
- Third Person Subjects: he, she, they, it, and names of people, places and things.

  Example: He is driving me crazy.

2. Agreement of Number
When we talk about number, we're talking about whether the subject and verb show that one thing is being discussed (singular) or that more than one thing is being discussed (plural). Subjects and verbs must agree in number. Subjects and verbs that don't agree in number appear very frequently on the SAT.

WRONG: The **children catches** the school bus every morning.

RIGHT: The **children catch** the school bus every morning.

Be especially careful of subject-verb agreement when the subject and verb are separated by a long string of words.

WRONG: **Wild animals** in jungles all over the world is endangered.

RIGHT: **Wild animals** in jungles all over the world **are** endangered.

Pronouns
A pronoun is a word that is used in place of a noun. The antecedent of a pronoun is the word to which the pronoun refers.

Example: <u>Mary</u> was late for work because
ANTECEDENT

<u>she</u> forgot to set the alarm.
PRONOUN

Occasionally, an antecedent will appear in a sentence after the pronoun.

Example: Because <u>he</u> sneezes so often, <u>Arthur</u>
PRONOUN   ANTECEDENT

always thinks <u>he</u> might have the flu.
PRONOUN

KAPLAN

1. Pronouns and Agreement

In clear, grammatical writing, a pronoun must clearly refer to and agree with its antecedent.

Number agreement of pronouns is more frequently tested on the SAT than person agreement, although you may see a question that tests person agreement.

Number and Person

	Singular	Plural
First Person	I, me	we, us
	my, mine	our, ours
Second Person	you	you
	your, yours	your, yours
Third Person	he, him	they, them
	she, her	
	it	
	one	
	his	their, theirs
	her, hers	
	its	
	one's	

Number Agreement

Pronouns must agree in number with their antecedents. A singular pronoun should stand in for a singular antecedent. A plural pronoun should stand in for a plural antecedent. Here's a typical SAT pronoun error.

> WRONG: The bank turned Harry down when he applied for a loan because **their** credit department discovered that he didn't have a job.

What does the plural possessive *their* refer to? The singular noun *bank*. The singular possessive *its* is what we need here.

> RIGHT: The bank turned Harry down for a loan because **its** credit department discovered that he didn't have a job.

Person Agreement

Pronouns must agree with their antecedents in person too. A first-person pronoun should stand in for a first-person antecedent, and so on. One more thing to remember

about *which* pronoun to use with which antecedent: Never use the relative pronoun *which* to refer to a human being. Use *who* or *whom* or *that*.

> WRONG: The woman **which** is standing at the piano is my sister.

> > RIGHT: The woman **who** is standing at the piano is my sister.

2. Pronouns and Case

A more subtle type of pronoun problem is one in which the pronoun is in the wrong case. Look at the following chart:

Case

	Subjective	Objective
First Person	I	me
	we	us
Second Person	you	you
Third Person	he	him
	she	her
	it	it
	they	them
	one	one
Relative Pronouns	who	whom
	that	that
	which	which

When to Use Subjective Case Pronouns

- Use the subjective case for the subject of a sentence.

Example: **She** is falling asleep.

WRONG: Nancy, Claire, and **me** are going to the ballet.

RIGHT: Nancy, Claire, and **I** are going to the ballet.

- Use the subjective case after a linking verb like *to be*.

Example: It is **I**.

- Use the subjective case in comparisons between the subject of verbs that are not stated, but understood.

Example: Gary is taller than **they** (are).

When to Use Objective Case Pronouns

- Use the objective case for the object of a verb.

Example: I called **her**.

- Use the objective case for the object of a preposition.

Example: I laughed at **him**.

- Use the objective case after gerunds and infinitives.

Example: Asking **him** to go was a big mistake.

Example: To give **him** the scare of his life, we all jumped out of his closet.

- Use the objective case in comparisons between objects of verbs that are not stated but understood.

Example: She calls you more than (she calls) **me**.

3. Who and Whom

Another thing you'll need to know is when to use the relative pronoun *who* (subjective case) and when to use the relative pronoun *whom* (objective case: *whom* goes with *him* and *them*). The following method is very helpful when you're deciding which one to use.

Example: Sylvester, (*who* or *whom*?) is afraid of the dark, sleeps with a Donald Duck night-light on.

- Look only at the relative pronoun in its clause. Ignore the rest of the sentence.

(Who or whom?) is afraid of the dark.

- Turn the clause into a question. Ask yourself:

Who or whom is afraid of the dark?

- Answer the question with an ordinary personal pronoun.

He is.

- If you've answered the question with a subjective case pronoun (as you have here), you need the subjective case *who* in the relative clause.

Sylvester, **who** is afraid of the dark, sleeps with a Donald Duck night-light on.

If you answer the question with an objective case pronoun, you need the objective case *whom* in the relative clause.

Try answering the question with *he* or *him*. *Who* goes with *he* (subjective case) and *whom* goes with *him* (objective case).

Sentence Structure

A sentence is a group of words that can stand alone because it expresses a complete thought. To express a complete thought, it must contain a subject, about which something is said, and a verb, which says something about the subject.

Example: Dogs bark.

Example: The explorers slept in yak-hide tents.

Example: Looking out of the window, John saw a flying saucer.

Every sentence consists of at least one clause. Many sentences contain more than one clause (and phrases, too).

A **clause** is a group of words that contains a subject and a verb. "Dogs bark," "The explorers slept in a yak-hide tent," and "John saw a flying saucer" are all clauses.

A **phrase** is a group of words that does not have both a subject and a verb.

Looking out of the window is a phrase.

1. Sentence Fragments

On the SAT, some of those innocent-looking groups of words beginning with capital letters and ending with periods are only masquerading as sentences. In reality, they're sentence fragments.

A sentence fragment is a group of words that seems to be a sentence but which is *grammatically* incomplete because it lacks a subject or a verb, **or** which is *logically* incomplete because other elements necessary for it to express a complete thought are missing.

WRONG: Eggs and fresh vegetables on sale at the farmers' market.

This is not a complete sentence because there's no verb to say something about the subject, *eggs and fresh vegetables.*

WRONG: Because Richard likes hippopotamuses.

Even though this contains a subject (Richard) and a verb (likes), it's not a complete sentence because it doesn't express a complete thought. We don't know what's true "*because* Richard likes hippopotamuses."

WRONG: Martha dreams about dinosaurs although.

This isn't a complete sentence because it doesn't express a complete thought. What makes Martha's dreaming about dinosaurs in need of qualification or explanation?

2. Run-On Sentences

Just as unacceptable as an incomplete sentence is a "too-complete" sentence, a run-on sentence.

A run-on sentence is actually two complete sentences stuck together either with just a comma or with no punctuation at all.

WRONG: The children had been playing in the park, they were covered with mud.

WRONG: The children had been playing in the park they were covered with mud.

There are a number of ways to fix this kind of problem. They all involve a punctuation mark or a connecting word that can properly connect two clauses.

- Join the clauses with a semicolon.

RIGHT: The children had been playing in the park; they were covered with mud.

- Join the clauses with a coordinating conjunction and a comma.

RIGHT: The children had been playing in the park, and they were covered with mud.

(Coordinating Conjunctions: *and, but, for, nor, or, so, yet*)

- Join the clauses with a subordinating conjunction.

   RIGHT: Because the children had been playing in the park, they were covered with mud.

OR

   RIGHT: The children were covered with mud because they had been playing in the park.

(Subordinating Conjunctions: *after, although, if, since, while*)

- And, of course, the two halves of a run-on sentence can be written as two separate, complete sentences.

RIGHT: The children had been playing in the park. They were covered with mud.

Verbs

On the SAT you'll find items that are wrong because a verb is in the wrong tense. To spot this kind of problem, you need to be familiar both with the way each tense is used and with the ways the tenses are used together. English has six tenses, and each has a simple form and a progressive form.

	<u>Simple</u>	<u>Progressive</u>
PRESENT	I work	I am working
PAST	I worked	I was working
FUTURE	I will work	I will be working
PRESENT PERFECT	I have worked	I have been working
PAST PERFECT	I had worked	I had been working
FUTURE PERFECT	I will have worked	I will have been working

1. Using the Present Tense

Use the present tense to describe a state or action occurring in the present time.

Example: I **am** a student.

Example: They **are studying** the Holy Roman Empire.

Use the present tense to describe habitual action.

Example: They **eat** at Joe's Diner every night.

Example: My father never **drinks** coffee.

Use the present tense to describe things that are always true.

> Example: The earth **is** round.
>
> Example: Grass **is** green.

2. Using the Past Tense

Use the simple past tense to describe an event or state that took place at a specific time in the past and is now over and done with.

> Example: Norman **broke** his toe when he tripped over his son's tricycle.

3. Using the Future Tense

> Use the future tense for actions expected in the future.
>
> Example: I **will call** you on Wednesday.

We often express future actions with the expression *to be going to:*

> Example: I **am going to move** to another apartment soon.

4. Using the Present Perfect Tense

Use the present perfect tense for actions and states that started in the past and continue up to and into the present time.

> Example: I **have been living** here for the last two years.

Use the present perfect for actions and states that happened a number of times in the past and may happen again in the future.

> Example: I **have heard** that song several times on the radio.

Use the present perfect for something that happened at an unspecified time in the past.

Example: Anna **has seen** that movie already.

5. Using the Past Perfect Tense

The past perfect tense is used to represent past actions or states that were completed before other past actions or states. The more recent past event is expressed in the simple past, and the earlier past event is expressed in the past perfect.

> Example: When I turned my computer on this morning, I realized that I **had exited** the program yesterday without saving my work.

6. Using the Future Perfect Tense

Use the future perfect tense for a future state or event that will take place before another future event.

> Example: By the end of the week, I **will have worked** four hours of overtime.

Adjectives and Adverbs

On the SAT, you may find an occasional item that's wrong because it uses an adjective where an adverb is called for, or vice versa.

An adjective modifies, or describes, a noun or pronoun.

> Example: A woman in a **white** dress stood next to the **old** tree.
>
> Example: The boat, **leaky** and **dirty**, hadn't been used in years.

An adverb modifies a verb, an adjective, or another adverb. Most, but not all, adverbs end in *-ly*. (Don't forget that some **adjectives**—*friendly, lovely*—also end in *-ly*.)

> Example: The interviewer looked *approvingly* at the *neatly* dressed applicant.

STYLE REVIEW

Pronouns and Reference

When we talk about pronouns and their antecedents, we say pronouns refer to or refer back to their antecedents. We talked earlier about pronouns that didn't agree in person or number with their antecedents. But a different kind of pronoun reference problem exists when a pronoun either doesn't refer to any antecedent at all or doesn't refer clearly to one, and only one, antecedent.

Sometimes an incorrectly used pronoun has no antecedent.

> POOR: Joe doesn't like what **they play** on this radio station.

Who are they? We can't tell, because there is no antecedent for *they*. On the SAT, this sort of usage is an error.

> RIGHT: Joe doesn't like what **the disc jockeys play** on this radio station.

Don't use pronouns without antecedents when doing so makes a sentence unclear. Sometimes a pronoun seems to have an antecedent until you look closely and see that the word that appears to be the antecedent is not a noun, but an adjective, a possessive form, or a verb. The antecedent of a pronoun must be a noun.

> WRONG: When you are painting, make sure you don't get **it** on the floor.

> RIGHT: When you are painting, make sure you don't get **paint** on the floor.

Other examples of pronoun reference problems:

> WRONG: I've always been interested in astronomy and finally have decided to become **one**.

> RIGHT: I've always been interested in astronomy and finally have decided to become an **astronomer**.

Don't use pronouns with remote references. A pronoun that is too far away from what it refers to is said to have a remote antecedent.

> WRONG: Jane quit smoking and, as a result, temporarily put on a lot of weight. **It** was very bad for her health.

> RIGHT: Jane quit smoking because **it** was very bad for her health, and, as a result, she temporarily gained a lot of weight.

Don't use pronouns with faulty broad reference. A pronoun with broad reference is one that refers to a whole idea instead of to a single noun.

> WRONG: He built a fence to stop people from looking into his backyard. **That's** not easy.

> RIGHT: He built a fence to stop people from looking into his backyard. The fence was not easy **to build**.

Redundancy

This type of style error is frequently tested on the SAT. Words or phrases are redundant when they have basically the same meaning as something already stated in the sentence. Don't use two phrases when one is sufficient.

> WRONG: The school was **established and founded** in 1906.

> RIGHT: The school was **established** in 1906.

Relevance

Irrelevant asides, even when set off in parentheses, are to be avoided on the SAT. Everything in the sentence should serve to get across the point in question. Something unrelated to that point should be cut.

> POOR: No one can say for sure just how successful the new law will be in the fight against crime (just as no one can be sure whether he or she will ever be a victim of a crime).

> BETTER: No one can say for sure just how successful the new law will be in the fight against crime.

Verbosity

Sometimes having extra words in a sentence results in a style problem. Conciseness is something that is valued on the SAT.

> WORDY: The supply of **musical instruments that are antique** is limited, so they become more valuable each year.

BETTER: The supply of **antique musical instruments** is limited, so they become more valuable each year.

> WORDY: We **were in agreement with each other** that Max was an unsuspecting old fool.

> BETTER: We **agreed** that Max was an unsuspecting old fool.

Resource Six: **100 Essential Math Concepts**

The math on the SAT covers a lot of ground—from arithmetic to algebra to geometry.

Don't let yourself be intimidated. We've highlighted the 100 most important concepts that you'll need for SAT Math and listed them in this chapter.

Use this list to remind yourself of the key areas you'll need to know. Do four concepts a day, and you'll be ready within a month. If a concept continually causes you trouble, circle it and refer back to it as you try to do the questions.

You've probably been taught most of these concepts in school already, so this list is a great way to refresh your memory.

NUMBER PROPERTIES

1. Number Categories

Integers are **whole numbers;** they include negative whole numbers and zero.

A **rational number** is a number that can be expressed as a **ratio of two integers. Irrational numbers** are real num- bers—they have locations on the number line—but they **can't be expressed precisely as a fraction or decimal.** For the purposes of the SAT, the most important **irrational numbers** are $\sqrt{2}$, $\sqrt{3}$, and π.

2. Adding/Subtracting Signed Numbers

To **add a positive and a negative,** first ignore the signs and find the positive difference between the number parts. Then attach the sign of the original number with the larger number part. For example, to add 23 and −34, first ignore the minus sign and find the positive difference between 23 and 34—that's 11. Then attach the sign of the number with the larger number part—in this case it's the minus sign from the −34. So, 23 + (−34) = −11.

Make **subtraction** situations simpler by turning them into addition. For example, you can think of −17 − (−21) as −17 + (+21).

To **add or subtract a string of positives and negatives,** first turn everything into addition. Then combine the posi- tives and negatives so that the string is reduced to the sum of a single positive number and a single negative number.

3. Multiplying/Dividing Signed Numbers

To multiply and/or divide positives and negatives, treat the number parts as usual and **attach a minus sign if there were originally an odd number of negatives**. For exam- ple, to multiply −2, −3, and −5, first multiply the number parts: 2 × 3 × 5 = 30. Then go back and note that there were *three*—an *odd* number—negatives, so the product is negative: (−2) × (−3) × (−5) = −30.

4. PEMDAS

When performing multiple operations, remember to perform them in the right order: **PEMDAS,** which means **Parentheses** first, then **Exponents,** then **Multiplication** and **Division** (left to right), and lastly **Addition** and **Subtraction** (left to right). In the expression $9 - 2 \times (5 - 3)^2 + 6 \div 3$, begin with the parentheses: (5 − 3) = 2. Then do the exponent: $2^2 = 4$. Now the expression is: $9 - 2 \times 4 + 6 \div 3$. Next do the multiplica- tion and division to get: 9 − 8 + 2, which equals 3. If you have difficulty remembering PEMDAS, use this sentence to recall it: **P**lease **E**xcuse **M**y **D**ear **A**unt **S**ally.

5. Counting Consecutive Integers

To count consecutive integers, **subtract the smallest from the largest and add 1.** To count the integers from 13 through 31, subtract: 31 − 13 = 18. Then add 1: 18 + 1 = 19.

NUMBER OPERATIONS AND CONCEPTS

6. Exponential Growth

If r is the ratio between consecutive terms, a_1 is the first term, a_n is the nth term, and S_n is the sum of the first n terms, then $a_n = a_1 r^{n-1}$ and $S_n = \dfrac{a_1 - a_1 r^n}{1 - r}$.

7. Union and Intersection of Sets

The things in a set are called elements or members. The union of Set A and Set B, sometimes expressed as $A \cup B$, is the set of elements that are in either or both of Set A and Set B. If Set $A = \{1, 2\}$ and Set $B = \{3, 4\}$, then $A \cup B = \{1, 2, 3, 4\}$. The intersection of Set A and Set B, sometimes expressed as $A \cap B$, is the set of elements com- mon to both Set A and Set B. If Set $A = \{1, 2, 3\}$ and Set $B = \{3, 4, 5\}$, then $A \cap B = \{3\}$.

DIVISIBILITY

8. Factor/Multiple

The **factors** of integer n are the positive integers that divide into n with no remainder. The **multiples** of n are the integers that n divides into with no remainder. For example, 6 is a factor of 12, and 24 is a multiple of 12. 12 is both a factor and a multiple of itself, since $12 \times 1 = 12$ and $12 \div 1 = 12$.

9. Prime Factorization

To find the prime factorization of an integer, just keep breaking it up into factors until **all the factors are prime.** To find the prime factorization of 36, for example, you could begin by breaking it into 4×9: $36 = 4 \times 9 = 2 \times 2 \times 3 \times 3$.

10. Relative Primes

Relative primes are integers that have no common factor other than 1. To determine whether two integers are relative primes, break them both down to their prime factorizations. For example: $35 = 5 \times 7$, and $54 = 2 \times 3 \times 3 \times 3$. They have **no prime factors in common,** so 35 and 54 are relative primes.

11. Common Multiple

A common multiple is a number that is a multiple of two or more integers. You can always get a common multiple of two integers by **multiplying** them, but, unless the two numbers are relative primes, the product will not be the *least* common multiple. For example, to find a common multiple for 12 and 15, you could just multiply: $12 \times 15 = 180$.

To find the **least common multiple**, check out the **multiples of the larger integer** until you find one that's **also a multiple of the smaller.** To find the LCM of 12 and 15, begin by taking the multiples of 15: 15 is not divisible by 12; 30 is not; nor is 45. But the next multiple of 15, 60, *is* divisible by 12, so it's the LCM.

12. Greatest Common Factor (GCF)

To find the greatest common factor, break down both integers into their prime factorizations and multiply **all the prime factors they have in common.** $36 = 2 \times 2 \times 3 \times 3$, and $48 = 2 \times 2 \times 2 \times 2 \times 3$. What they have in common is two 2s and one 3, so the GCF is $2 \times 2 \times 3 = 12$.

13. Even/Odd

To predict whether a sum, difference, or product will be even or odd, just **take simple numbers like 1 and 2 and see what happens.** There are rules—"odd times even is even," for example—but there's no need to memorize them. What happens with one set of numbers generally happens with all similar sets.

14. Multiples of 2 and 4

An integer is divisible by 2 (even) if the **last digit is even.** An integer is divisible by 4 if the **last two digits form a multiple of 4.** The last digit of 562 is 2, which is even, so 562 is a multiple of 2. The last two digits form 62, which is *not* divisible by 4, so 562 is not a multiple of 4. The integer 512, however is divisible by four because the last two digits form 12, which is a multiple of 4.

15. Multiples of 3 and 9

An integer is divisible by 3 if the **sum of its digits is divisible by 3.** An integer is divisible by 9 if the **sum of its digits is divisible by 9.** The sum of the digits in 957 is 21, which is divisible by 3 but not by 9, so 957 is divisible by 3 but not by 9.

16. Multiples of 5 and 10

An integer is divisible by 5 if the **last digit is 5 or 0.** An integer is divisible by 10 if the **last digit is 0.** The last digit of 665 is 5, so 665 is a multiple of 5 but *not* a multiple of 10.

17. Remainders

The remainder is the **whole number left over after division.** 487 is 2 more than 485, which is a multiple of 5, so when 487 is divided by 5, the remainder will be 2.

FRACTIONS AND DECIMALS

18. Reducing Fractions

To reduce a fraction to lowest terms, **factor out and cancel** all factors the numerator and denominator have in common.

$$\frac{28}{36} = \frac{4 \times 7}{4 \times 9} = \frac{7}{9}$$

19. Adding/Subtracting Fractions

To add or subtract fractions, first find a **common denominator,** then add or subtract the numerators.

$$\frac{2}{15} + \frac{3}{10} = \frac{4}{30} + \frac{9}{30} = \frac{4 + 9}{30} = \frac{13}{30}$$

20. Multiplying Fractions

To multiply fractions, **multiply** the numerators and **multiply** the denominators.

$$\frac{5}{7} \times \frac{3}{4} = \frac{5 \times 3}{7 \times 4} = \frac{15}{28}$$

21. Dividing Fractions

To divide fractions, **invert** the second one and **multiply.**

$$\frac{1}{2} \div \frac{3}{5} = \frac{1}{2} \times \frac{5}{3} = \frac{1 \times 5}{2 \times 3} = \frac{5}{6}$$

22. Mixed Numbers and Improper Fractions

To convert a mixed number to an improper fraction, **multiply** the whole number part by the denominator, then **add** the numerator. The result is the new numerator (over the same denominator). To convert $7\frac{1}{3}$, first multiply 7 by 3, then add 1, to get the new numerator of 22. Put that over the same denominator, 3, to get $\frac{22}{3}$.

To convert an improper fraction to a mixed number, divide the denominator into the numerator to get a **whole number quotient with a remainder.** The quotient becomes the whole number part of the mixed number, and the remainder becomes the new numerator—with the same denominator. For example, to convert $\frac{108}{5}$, first divide 5 into 108, which yields 21 with a remainder of 3. Therefore, $\frac{108}{5} = 21\frac{3}{5}$.

23. Reciprocal

To find the reciprocal of a fraction, **switch the numerator and the denominator.** The reciprocal of $\frac{3}{7}$ is $\frac{7}{3}$. The reciprocal of 5 is $\frac{1}{5}$. The product of reciprocals is 1.

24. Comparing Fractions

One way to compare fractions is to **re-express them with a common denominator.** $\frac{3}{4} = \frac{21}{28}$ and $\frac{5}{7} = \frac{20}{28}$. $\frac{21}{28}$ is greater than $\frac{20}{28}$, so $\frac{3}{4}$ is greater than $\frac{5}{7}$. Another method is to **convert them both to decimals.** $\frac{3}{4}$ converts to .75 , and $\frac{5}{7}$ converts to approximately .714.

25. Converting Fractions and Decimals

To convert a fraction to a decimal, **divide the bottom into the top.** To convert $\frac{5}{8}$, divide 8 into 5, yielding .625.

To convert a decimal to a fraction, set the decimal over 1 and **multiply the numerator and denominator by 10** raised to the number of digits to the right of the decimal point.

To convert .625 to a fraction, you would multiply $\frac{.625}{1}$ by $\frac{10^3}{10^3}$ or $\frac{1000}{1000}$. Then simplify: $\frac{625}{1000} = \frac{5 \times 125}{8 \times 125} = \frac{5}{8}$.

26. Repeating Decimal

To find a particular digit in a repeating decimal, note the **number of digits in the cluster that repeats.** If there are 2 digits in that cluster, then every second digit is the same. If there are 3 digits in that cluster, then every third digit is the same. And so on. For example, the decimal equivalent of $\frac{1}{27}$ is .037037037…, which is best written $.\overline{037}$. There are 3 digits in the repeating cluster, so every third digit is the same: 7. To find the 50th digit, look for the multiple of 3 just less than 50—that's 48. The 48th digit is 7, and with the 49th digit the pattern repeats with 0. The 50th digit is 3.

27. Identifying the Parts and the Whole

The key to solving most fractions and percents story problems is to identify the part and the whole. Usually you'll find the **part** associated with the verb *is/are* and the **whole** associated with the word *of.* In the sentence, "Half of the boys are blonds," the whole is the boys ("*of* the boys"), and the part is the blonds ("*are* blonds").

PERCENTS

28. Percent Formula

Whether you need to find the part, the whole, or the percent, use the same formula:

$$\textbf{Part} = \textbf{Percent} \times \textbf{Whole}$$

Example: What is 12 percent of 25?
Setup: Part = .12 × 25

Example: 15 is 3 percent of what number?
Setup: 15 = .03 × Whole

Example: 45 is what percent of 9?
Setup: 45 = Percent × 9

29. Percent Increase and Decrease

To increase a number by a percent, **add the percent to 100 percent,** convert to a decimal, and multiply. To increase 40 by 25 percent, add 25 percent to 100 percent, convert 125 percent to 1.25, and multiply by 40. 1.25 × 40 = 50.

30. Finding the Original Whole

To find the **original whole before a percent increase or decrease,** set up an equation. Think of the result of a 15 percent increase over *x* as 1.15*x*.

Example: After a 5 percent increase, the population was 59,346. What was the population before the increase?
Setup: 1.05*x* = 59,346

31. Combined Percent Increase and Decrease

To determine the combined effect of multiple percent increases and/or decreases, **start with 100 and see what happens.**

Example: A price went up 10 percent one year, and the new price went up 20 percent the next year. What was the combined percent increase?
Setup: First year: 100 + (10 percent of 100) = 110. Second year: 110 + (20 percent of 110) = 132. That's a combined 32 percent increase.

RATIOS, PROPORTIONS, AND RATES

32. Setting up a Ratio

To find a ratio, put the number associated with the word *of* **on top** and the quantity associated with the word *to* **on the bottom** and reduce. The ratio of 20 oranges to 12 apples is $\frac{20}{12}$, which reduces to $\frac{5}{3}$.

33. Part-to-Part Ratios and Part-to-Whole Ratios

If the parts add up to the whole, a part-to-part ratio can be turned into two part-to-whole ratios by putting **each number in the original ratio over the sum of the numbers.** If the ratio of males to females is 1 to 2, then the males-to-people ratio is $\frac{1}{1+2} = \frac{1}{3}$ and the females-to-people ratio is $\frac{2}{1+2} = \frac{2}{3}$. In other words, $\frac{2}{3}$ of all the people are female.

34. Solving a Proportion

To solve a proportion, **cross multiply:**

$$\frac{x}{5} = \frac{3}{4}$$

$$4x = 3 \times 5$$

$$x = \frac{15}{4} = 3.75$$

35. Rate

To solve a rates problem, **use the units** to keep things straight.

Example: If snow is falling at the rate of one foot every four hours, how many inches of snow will fall in seven hours?

Setup:

$$\frac{1 \text{ foot}}{4 \text{ hours}} = \frac{x \text{ inches}}{7 \text{ hours}}$$

$$\frac{12 \text{ inches}}{4 \text{ hours}} = \frac{x \text{ inches}}{7 \text{ hours}}$$

$$4x = 12 \times 7$$

$$x = 21$$

36. Average Rate

Average rate is *not* simply the average of the rates.

$$\text{Average } A \text{ per } B = \frac{\text{Total } A}{\text{Total } B}$$

$$\text{Average Speed} = \frac{\text{Total distance}}{\text{Total time}}$$

To find the average speed for 120 miles at 40 mph and 120 miles at 60 mph, **don't just average the two speeds.** First, figure out the total distance and the total time. The total distance is $120 + 120 = 240$ miles. The times are two hours for the first leg and three hours for the second leg, or five hours total. The average speed, then, is $\frac{240}{5} = 48$ miles per hour.

AVERAGES

37. Average Formula

To find the average of a set of numbers, **add them up and divide by the number of numbers.**

$$\text{Average} = \frac{\text{Sum of the terms}}{\text{Number of terms}}$$

To find the average of the 5 numbers 12, 15, 23, 40, and 40, first add them: $12 + 15 + 23 + 40 + 40 = 130$. Then, divide the sum by 5: $130 \div 5 = 26$.

38. Average of Evenly Spaced Numbers

To find the average of evenly spaced numbers, just **average the smallest and the largest.** The average of all the integers from 13 through 77 is the same as the average of 13 and 77:

$$\frac{13 + 77}{2} = \frac{90}{2} = 45$$

39. Using the Average to Find the Sum

$$\text{Sum} = (\text{Average}) \times (\text{Number of terms})$$

If the average of 10 numbers is 50, then they add up to 10×50, or 500.

40. Finding the Missing Number

To find a missing number when you're given the average, **use the sum.** If the average of 4 numbers is 7, then the sum of those 4 numbers is 4×7, or 28. Suppose that 3 of the numbers are 3, 5, and 8. These 3 numbers add up to 16 of that 28, which leaves 12 for the fourth number.

41. Median and Mode

The median of a set of numbers is the **value that falls in the middle of the set.** If you have 5 test scores, and they are 88, 86, 57, 94, and 73, you must first list the scores in increasing or decreasing order: 57, 73, 86, 88, 94.

The median is the middle number, or 86. If there is an even number of values in a set (6 test scores, for instance), simply take the average of the 2 middle numbers.

The mode of a set of numbers is the **value that appears most often.** If your test scores were 88, 57, 68, 85, 99, 93, 93, 84, and 81, the mode of the scores would be 93 because it appears more often than any other score. If there is a tie for the most common value in a set, the set has more than one mode.

POSSIBILITIES AND PROBABILITY

42. Counting the Possibilities

The fundamental counting principle: If there are **m ways** one event can happen and **n ways** a second event can happen, then there are **$m \times n$ ways** for the 2 events to happen. For example, with 5 shirts and 7 pairs of pants to choose from, you can have $5 \times 7 = 35$ different outfits.

43. Probability

$$\text{Probability} = \frac{\text{Favorable Outcomes}}{\text{Total Possible Outcomes}}$$

For example, if you have 12 shirts in a drawer and 9 of them are white, the probability of picking a white shirt at random is $\frac{9}{12} = \frac{3}{4}$. This probability can also be expressed as .75 or 75%.

KAPLAN

POWERS AND ROOTS

44. Multiplying and Dividing Powers

To multiply powers with the same base, **add the exponents and keep the same base:**

$$x^3 \times x^4 = x^{3+4} = x^7$$

To divide powers with the same base, **subtract the exponents and keep the same base:**

$$y^{13} \div y^8 = y^{13-8} = y^5$$

45. Raising Powers to Powers

To raise a power to a power, **multiply the exponents:**

$$(x^3)^4 = x^{3 \times 4} = x^{12}$$

46. Simplifying Square Roots

To simplify a square root, **factor out the perfect squares** under the radical, unsquare them, and put the result in front.

$$\sqrt{12} = \sqrt{4 \times 3} = \sqrt{4} \times \sqrt{3} = 2\sqrt{3}$$

47. Adding and Subtracting Roots

You can add or subtract radical expressions **when the part under the radicals is the same:**

$$2\sqrt{3} + 3\sqrt{3} = 5\sqrt{3}$$

Don't try to add or subtract when the radical parts are different. There's not much you can do with an expression like:

$$3\sqrt{5} + 3\sqrt{7}$$

48. Multiplying and Dividing Roots

The product of square roots is equal to the **square root of the product:**

$$\sqrt{3} \times \sqrt{5} = \sqrt{3 \times 5} = \sqrt{15}$$

The quotient of square roots is equal to the **square root of the quotient:**

$$\frac{\sqrt{6}}{\sqrt{3}} = \sqrt{\frac{6}{3}} = \sqrt{2}$$

49. Negative Exponent and Rational Exponent

To find the value of a number raised to a negative exponent, simply rewrite the number, without the negative sign, as the bottom of a fraction with 1 as the numerator of the fraction: $3^{-2} = \frac{1}{3^2} = \frac{1}{9}$. If x is a positive number and a is a nonzero number, then $x^{\frac{1}{a}} = \sqrt[a]{x}$. So $4^{\frac{1}{2}} = \sqrt[2]{4} = 2$. If p and q are integers, then $x^{\frac{p}{q}} = \sqrt[q]{x^p}$. So $4^{\frac{3}{2}} = \sqrt[2]{4^3} = \sqrt{64} = 8$.

ABSOLUTE VALUE

50. Determining Absolute Value

The absolute value of a number is the distance of the number from zero on the number line. Because absolute value is a distance, it is always positive. The absolute value of 7 is 7; this is expressed $|7| = 7$. Similarly, the absolute value of −7 is 7: $|-7| = 7$. Every positive number is the absolute value of 2 numbers: itself and its negative.

ALGEBRAIC EXPRESSIONS

51. Evaluating an Expression

To evaluate an algebraic expression, **plug in** the given values for the unknowns and calculate according to **PEMDAS**. To find the value of $x^2 + 5x - 6$ when $x = -2$, plug in −2 for x: $(-2)^2 + 5(-2) - 6 = -12$.

52. Adding and Subtracting Monomials

To combine like terms, **keep the variable part unchanged while adding or subtracting the coefficients:**

$$2a + 3a = (2 + 3)a = 5a$$

53. Adding and Subtracting Polynomials

To add or subtract polynomials, **combine like terms.**

$$(3x^2 + 5x - 7) - (x^2 + 12) =$$
$$(3x^2 - x^2) + 5x + (-7 - 12) =$$
$$2x^2 + 5x - 19$$

54. Multiplying Monomials

To multiply monomials, **multiply the coefficients and the variables separately:**

$$2a \times 3a = (2 \times 3)(a \times a) = 6a^2$$

55. Multiplying Binomials—FOIL

To multiply binomials, use **FOIL.** To multiply $(x + 3)$ by $(x + 4)$, first multiply the First terms: $x \times x = x^2$. Next the Outer terms: $x \times 4 = 4x$. Then the Inner terms: $3 \times x = 3x$. And finally the Last terms: $3 \times 4 = 12$. Then add and combine like terms:

$$x^2 + 4x + 3x + 12 = x^2 + 7x + 12$$

56. Multiplying Other Polynomials

FOIL works only when you want to multiply two binomials. If you want to multiply polynomials with more than two terms, make sure you **multiply each term in the first polynomial by each term in the second.**

$$(x^2 + 3x + 4)(x + 5) =$$
$$x^2(x + 5) + 3x(x + 5) + 4(x + 5) =$$
$$x^3 + 5x^2 + 3x^2 + 15x + 4x + 20 =$$
$$x^3 + 8x^2 + 19x + 20$$

After multiplying two polynomials together, the number of terms in your expression before simplifying should equal the number of terms in one polynomial multiplied by the number of terms in the second. In the example, you should have $3 \times 2 = 6$ terms in the product before you simplify like terms.

FACTORING ALGEBRAIC EXPRESSIONS

57. Factoring out a Common Divisor

A factor common to all terms of a polynomial can be **factored out.** All three terms in the polynomial $3x^3 + 12x^2 - 6x$ contain a factor of $3x$. Pulling out the common factor yields $3x(x^2 + 4x - 2)$.

58. Factoring the Difference of Squares

One of the test maker's favorite factorables is the **difference of squares.**

$$a^2 - b^2 = (a - b)(a + b)$$

$x^2 - 9$, for example, factors to $(x - 3)(x + 3)$.

59. Factoring the Square of a Binomial

Recognize polynomials that are squares of binomials:

$$a^2 + 2ab + b^2 = (a + b)^2$$
$$a^2 - 2ab + b^2 = (a - b)^2$$

For example, $4x^2 + 12x + 9$ factors to $(2x + 3)^2$, and $n^2 - 10n + 25$ factors to $(n - 5)^2$.

60. Factoring Other Polynomials—FOIL in Reverse

To factor a quadratic expression, **think about what binomials you could use FOIL on to get that quadratic expression.** To factor $x^2 - 5x + 6$, think about what First terms will produce x^2, what Last terms will produce $+6$, and what Outer and Inner terms will produce $-5x$. Some common sense—and a little trial and error—lead you to $(x - 2)(x - 3)$.

61. Simplifying an Algebraic Fraction

Simplifying an algebraic fraction is a lot like simplifying a numerical fraction. The general idea is to **find factors common to the numerator and denominator and cancel them.** Thus, simplifying an algebraic fraction begins with factoring.

For example, to simplify $\dfrac{x^2 - x - 12}{x^2 - 9}$, first factor the numerator and denominator:

$$\frac{x^2 - x - 12}{x^2 - 9} = \frac{(x - 4)(x + 3)}{(x - 3)(x + 3)}$$

Canceling $x + 3$ from the numerator and denominator leaves you with $\dfrac{x - 4}{x - 3}$.

SOLVING EQUATIONS

62. Solving a Linear Equation

To solve an equation, do whatever is necessary to both sides to **isolate the variable.** To solve the equation $5x - 12 = -2x + 9$, first get all the x's on one side by adding $2x$ to both sides: $7x - 12 = 9$. Then add 12 to both sides: $7x = 21$. Then divide both sides by 7: $x = 3$.

63. Solving "In Terms Of"

To solve an equation for one variable **in terms of** another means to **isolate the one variable on one side of the equation,** leaving an expression containing the other variable on the other side of the equation. To solve the equation $3x - 10y = -5x + 6y$ for x in terms of y, isolate x:

$$3x - 10y = -5x + 6y$$

$$3x + 5x = 6y + 10y$$

$$8x = 16y$$

$$x = 2y$$

64. Translating from English into Algebra

To translate from English into algebra, look for the key words and systematically turn phrases into algebraic expressions and sentences into equations. Be careful about order, especially when subtraction is called for.

Example: The charge for a phone call is r cents for the first 3 minutes and s cents for each minute thereafter. What is the cost, in cents, of a phone call lasting exactly t minutes? $(t > 3)$

Setup: The charge begins with r, and then something more is added, depending on the length of the call. The amount added is s times the number of minutes past 3 minutes. If the total number of minutes is t, then the number of minutes past 3 is $t - 3$. So the charge is $r + s(t - 3)$.

65. Solving a Quadratic Equation

To solve a quadratic equation, put it in the "$ax^2 + bx + c = 0$" form, **factor** the left side (if you can), and set each factor equal to 0 separately to get the two solutions. To solve $x^2 + 12 = 7x$, first rewrite it as $x^2 - 7x + 12 = 0$. Then factor the left side:

$$(x - 3)(x - 4) = 0$$

$$x - 3 = 0 \text{ or } x - 4 = 0$$

$$x = 3 \text{ or } 4$$

66. Solving a System of Equations

You can solve for 2 variables only if you have 2 distinct equations. 2 forms of the same equation will not be adequate. **Combine the equations** in such a way that **one of the variables cancels out.** To solve the 2 equations $4x + 3y = 8$ and $x + y = 3$, multiply both sides of the second equation by -3 to get: $-3x - 3y = -9$. Now add the 2 equations; the $3y$ and the $-3y$ cancel out, leaving: $x = -1$. Plug that back into either one of the original equations and you'll find that $y = 4$.

67. Solving an Inequality

To solve an inequality, do whatever is necessary to both sides to **isolate the variable.** Just remember that when you **multiply or divide both sides by a negative number,** you must **reverse the sign.** To solve $-5x + 7 < -3$, subtract 7 from both sides to get: $-5x < -10$. Now divide both sides by -5, remembering to reverse the sign: $x > 2$.

68. Radical Equations

A radical equation contains at least one radical expression. Solve radical equations by using standard rules of algebra. If $5\sqrt{x} - 2 = 13$, then $5\sqrt{x} = 15$ and $\sqrt{x} = 3$, so $x = 9$.

FUNCTIONS

69. Function Notation and Evaluation

Standard function notation is written $f(x)$ and read "f of 4." To evaluate the function $f(x) = 2x + 3$ for $f(4)$, replace x with 4 and simplify: $f(4) = 2(4) + 3 = 11$.

70. Direct and Inverse Variation

In direct variation, $y = kx$, where k is a nonzero constant. In direct variation, the variable y changes directly as x does. If a unit of Currency A is worth 2 units of Currency B, then $A = 2B$. If the number of units of B were to double, the number of units of A would double, and so on for halving, tripling, etc. In inverse variation, $xy = k$, where x and y are variables and k is a constant. A famous inverse relationship is *rate* × *time* = *distance*, where distance is constant. Imagine having to cover a distance of 24 miles. If you were to travel at 12 miles per hour, you'd need 2 hours. But if you were to halve your rate, you would have to double your time. This is just another way of saying that rate and time vary inversely.

71. Domain and Range of a Function

The domain of a function is the set of values for which the function is defined. For example, the domain of $f(x) = \dfrac{1}{1 - x^2}$ is all values of x except 1 and -1, because for

those values the denominator has a value of 0 and is therefore undefined. The range of a function is the set of outputs or results of the function. For example, the range of $f(x) = x^2$ is all numbers greater than all or equal to zero, because x^2 cannot be negative.

COORDINATE GEOMETRY

72. Finding the Distance Between Two Points

To find the distance between points, **use the Pythagorean theorem** or **special right triangles.** The difference between the x's is one leg and the difference between the y's is the other.

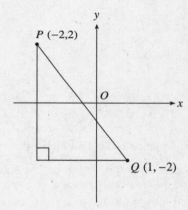

In the figure above, PQ is the hypotenuse of a 3-4-5 triangle, so $PQ = 5$.

You can also use the **distance formula:**

$$d = \sqrt{(x_1 - x_2)^2 + (y_1 - y_2)^2}$$

To find the distance between $R(3, 6)$ and $S(5, -2)$:

$$d = \sqrt{(3 - 5)^2 + [6 - (-2)^2]}$$

$$= \sqrt{(-2)^2 + (8)^2}$$

$$= \sqrt{68} = 2\sqrt{17}$$

73. Using Two Points to Find the Slope

$$\text{Slope} = \frac{\text{Change in } y}{\text{Change in } x} = \frac{\text{Rise}}{\text{Run}}$$

The slope of the line that contains the points $A(2, 3)$ and $B(0, -1)$ is:

$$\frac{y_A - y_B}{x_A - x_B} = \frac{3 - (-1)}{2 - 0} = \frac{4}{2} = 2$$

74. Using an Equation to Find the Slope

To find the slope of a line from an equation, put the equation into the **slope-intercept** form:

$$y = mx + b$$

The **slope is** m. To find the slope of the equation $3x + 2y = 4$, rearrange it:

$$3x + 2y = 4$$
$$2y = -3x + 4$$
$$y = -\frac{3}{2}x + 2$$

The slope is $-\frac{3}{2}$.

75. Using an Equation to Find an Intercept

To find the y-intercept, you can either put the equation into $y = mx + b$ (slope-intercept) form—in which case b **is the y-intercept**—or you can just **plug $x = 0$** into the equation and **solve for y**. To find the x-intercept, **plug $y = 0$** into the equation and **solve for x**.

76. Finding the Midpoint

The midpoint of two points on a line segment is the average of the x-coordinates of the endpoints and the average of the y-coordinates of the endpoints. If the endpoints are (x_1, y_1) and (x_2, y_2), the midpoint is

$\left(\frac{x_1 + x_2}{2}, \frac{y_1 + y_2}{2}\right)$. The midpoint of $(3, 5)$ and $(9, 1)$ is $\left(\frac{3 + 9}{2}, \frac{5 + 1}{2}\right)$.

LINES AND ANGLES

77. Intersecting Lines

When two lines intersect, **adjacent angles are supplementary and vertical angles are equal.**

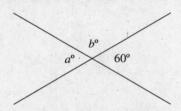

In the figure above, the angles marked $a°$ and $b°$ are adjacent and supplementary, so $a + b = 180$. Furthermore, the angles marked $a°$ and $60°$ are vertical and equal, so $a = 60$.

78. Parallel Lines and Transversals

A transversal across parallel lines forms **four equal acute angles and four equal obtuse angles.**

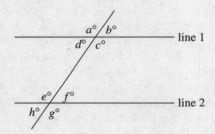

In the figure above, line 1 is parallel to line 2. Angles a, c, e, and g are obtuse, so they are all equal. Angles b, d, f, and h are acute, so they are all equal.

Furthermore, **any of the acute angles is supplementary to any of the obtuse angles.** Angles a and h are supplementary, as are b and e, c and f, and so on.

TRIANGLES—GENERAL

79. Interior and Exterior Angles of a Triangle

The 3 angles of any triangle **add up to 180 degrees.**

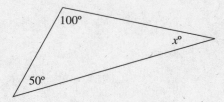

In the figure above, $x + 50 + 100 = 180$, so $x = 30$.

An exterior angle of a triangle is equal to the **sum of the remote interior angles.**

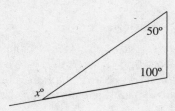

In the figure above, the exterior angle labeled $x°$ is equal to the sum of the remote angles: $x = 50 + 100 = 150$.

The 3 exterior angles of a triangle add up to 360 degrees.

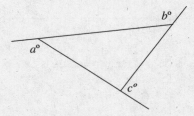

In the figure above, $a + b + c = 360$.

80. Similar Triangles

Similar triangles have the same shape: **corresponding angles are equal and corresponding sides are proportional.**

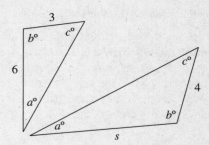

The triangles above are similar because they have the same angles. The 3 corresponds to the 4 and the 6 corresponds to the s.

$$\frac{3}{4} = \frac{6}{s}$$

$$3s = 24$$

$$s = 8$$

81. Area of a Triangle

$$\text{Area of Triangle} = \frac{1}{2}(\text{base})(\text{height})$$

The height is the perpendicular distance between the side that's chosen as the base and the opposite vertex.

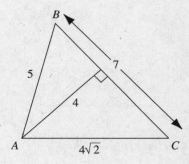

In the triangle above, 4 is the height when the 7 is chosen as the base.

$$\text{Area} = \frac{1}{2}bh = \frac{1}{2}(7)(4) = 14$$

82. Triangle Inequality Theorem

The length of one side of a triangle must be **greater than the difference and less than the sum** of the lengths of the other two sides. For example, if it is given that the length of one side is 3 and the length of another side is 7, then you know that the length of the third side must be greater than $7 - 3 = 4$ and less than $7 + 3 = 10$.

83. Isosceles and Equilateral Triangles

An isosceles triangle is a triangle that has **2 equal sides.** Not only are 2 sides equal, but the angles opposite the equal sides, called **base angles**, are also equal.

Equilateral triangles are triangles in which **all 3 sides are equal.** Since all the sides are equal, all the angles are also equal. All 3 angles in an equilateral triangle measure 60 degrees, regardless of the lengths of sides.

RIGHT TRIANGLES

84. Pythagorean Theorem

For all right triangles:

$$(\text{leg}_1)^2 + (\text{leg}_2)^2 = (\text{hypotenuse})^2$$

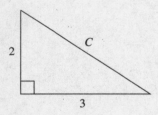

If one leg is 2 and the other leg is 3, then:

$$2^2 + 3^2 = c^2$$
$$c^2 = 4 + 9$$
$$c = \sqrt{13}$$

85. The 3-4-5 Triangle

If a right triangle's leg-to-leg ratio is 3:4, or if the leg-to-hypotenuse ratio is 3:5 or 4:5, it's a 3-4-5 triangle and you don't need to use the Pythagorean theorem to find the third side. Just figure out what multiple of 3-4-5 it is.

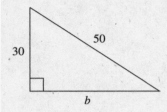

In the right triangle shown, one leg is 30 and the hypotenuse is 50. This is 10 times 3-4-5. The other leg is 40.

86. The 5-12-13 Triangle

If a right triangle's leg-to-leg ratio is 5:12, or if the leg-to-hypotenuse ratio is 5:13 or 12:13, then it's a 5-12-13 triangle and you don't need to use the Pythagorean theorem to find the third side. Just figure out what multiple of 5-12-13 it is.

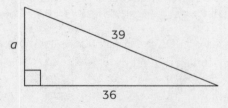

Here one leg is 36 and the hypotenuse is 39. This is 3 times 5-12-13. The other leg is 15.

87. The 30-60-90 Triangle

The sides of a 30-60-90 triangle are in a ratio of $x : x\sqrt{3} : 2x$. You don't need the Pythagorean theorem.

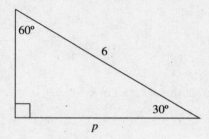

If the hypotenuse is 6, then the shorter leg is half that, or 3; and then the longer leg is equal to the short leg times $\sqrt{3}$, or $3\sqrt{3}$.

88. The 45-45-90 Triangle

The sides of a 45-45-90 triangle are in a ratio of $x : x : x\sqrt{2}$.

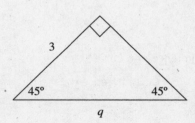

If one leg is 3, then the other leg is also 3, and the hypotenuse is equal to a leg times $\sqrt{2}$, or $3\sqrt{2}$.

OTHER POLYGONS

89. Characteristics of a Rectangle

A rectangle is a **four-sided figure with four right angles.** Opposite sides are equal. Diagonals are equal.

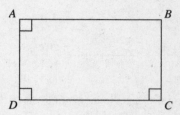

Quadrilateral *ABCD* above is shown to have three right angles. The fourth angle therefore also measures 90 degrees, and *ABCD* is a rectangle. The perimeter of a rectangle is equal to the sum of the lengths of the four sides, which is equivalent to 2(length + width).

Area of Rectangle = length × width

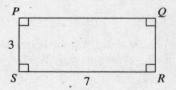

The area of a 7-by-3 rectangle is $7 \times 3 = 21$.

90. Characteristics of a Parallelogram

A parallelogram has **two pairs of parallel sides.** Opposite sides are equal. Opposite angles are equal. Consecutive angles add up to 180 degrees.

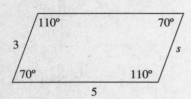

In the figure above, s is the length of the side opposite the 3, so $s = 3$.

Area of Parallelogram = base × height

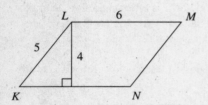

In parallelogram *KLMN* above, 4 is the height when *LM* or *KN* is used as the base. Base × height = 6 × 4 = 24.

91. Characteristics of a Square

A square is a **rectangle with four equal sides.**

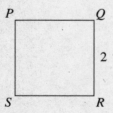

If *PQRS* is a square, all sides are the same length as *QR*. The perimeter of a square is equal to four times the length of one side.

Area of Square = (Side)²

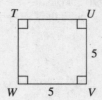

The square above, with sides of length 5, has an area of $5^2 = 25$.

92. Interior Angles of a Polygon

The **sum of the measures of the interior angles of a polygon = $(n - 2) \times 180$,** where n is the number of sides.

Sum of the Angles = $(n - 2) \times 180$

The eight angles of an octagon, for example, add up to $(8 - 2) \times 180 = 1,080$.

CIRCLES

93. Circumference of a Circle

Circumference = $2\pi r$

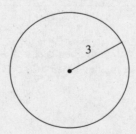

In the circle above, the radius is 3, and so the circumference is $2\pi(3) = 6\pi$.

94. Length of an Arc

An **arc** is a piece of the circumference. If n is the degree measure of the arc's central angle, then the formula is:

$$\text{Length of an Arc} = \left(\frac{n}{360}\right)(2\pi r)$$

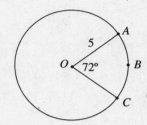

In the figure above, the radius is 5 and the measure of the central angle is 72 degrees. The arc length is $\frac{72}{360}$ or $\frac{1}{5}$ of the circumference:

$$\left(\frac{72}{360}\right)(2\pi)(5) = \left(\frac{1}{5}\right)(10\pi) = 2\pi$$

95. Area of a Circle

$$\text{Area of a Circle} = \pi r^2$$

The area of the circle is $\pi(4)^2 = 16\pi$.

96. Area of a Sector

A **sector** is a piece of the area of a circle. If n is the degree measure of the sector's central angle, then the formula is:

$$\text{Area of a Sector} = \left(\frac{n}{360}\right)(\pi r^2)$$

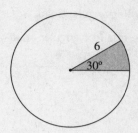

In the figure above, the radius is 6 and the measure of the sector's central angle is 30 degrees. The sector has $\frac{30}{360}$ or $\frac{1}{12}$ of the area of the circle:

$$\left(\frac{30}{360}\right)(\pi)(6^2) = \left(\frac{1}{12}\right)(36\pi) = 3\pi$$

97. Tangency

When a line is tangent to a circle, the radius of the circle is perpendicular to the line at the point of contact.

SOLIDS

98. Surface Area of a Rectangular Solid

The surface of a rectangular solid consists of three pairs of identical faces. To find the surface area, find the area of each face and add them up. If the length is l, the width is w, and the height is h, the formula is:

$$\text{Surface Area} = 2lw + 2wh + 2lh$$

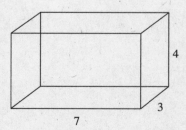

The surface area of the box above is:
$2 \times 7 \times 3 + 2 \times 3 \times 4 + 2 \times 7 \times 4 = 42 + 24 + 56 = 122$

99. Volume of a Rectangular Solid

Volume of a Rectangular Solid = *lwh*

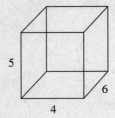

The volume of a 4-by-5-by-6 box is

$$4 \times 5 \times 6 = 120$$

A cube is a rectangular solid with length, width, and height all equal. If *e* is the length of an edge of a cube, the volume formula is:

Volume of a Cube = e^3

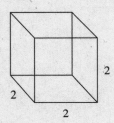

The volume of this cube is $2^3 = 8$.

100. Volume of a Cylinder

Volume of a Cylinder = $\pi r^2 h$

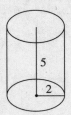

In the cylinder above, $r = 2$, $h = 5$, so:

$$\text{Volume} = \pi(2^2)(5) = 20\pi$$

A Note for International Students

If you are an international student considering attending an American university, you are not alone. Nearly 600,000 international students pursued academic degrees at the undergraduate, graduate, or professional school level at U.S. universities during the 2004–2005 academic year, according to the Institute of International Education's Open Doors report. Almost 50 percent of these students were studying for a bachelor's or first university degree. This number of international students pursuing higher education in the United States is expected to continue to grow. Business, management, engineering, and the physical and life sciences are particularly popular majors for students coming to the United States from other countries.

If you are not a U.S. citizen and you are interested in attending college or university in the United States, here is what you'll need to get started.

- If English is not your first language, you'll probably need to take the TOEFL® (Test of English as a Foreign Language) or provide some other evidence that you are proficient in English. Colleges and universities in the United States will differ on what they consider to be an acceptable TOEFL score. A minimum TOEFL score of 213 (550 on the paper-based TOEFL) or better is often required by more prestigious and competitive institutions. Because American undergraduate programs require all students to take a certain number of general education courses, all students—even math and computer science students—need to be able to communicate well in spoken and written English.

- You may also need to take the SAT® or the ACT®. Many undergraduate institutions in the United States require both the SAT and TOEFL for international students.

- There are over 3,400 accredited colleges and universities in the United States, so selecting the correct undergraduate school can be a confusing task for anyone. You will need to get help from a good advisor or at least a good college guide that gives you detailed information on the different schools available. Since admission to many undergraduate programs is quite competitive, you may want to select three or four colleges and complete applications for each school.

- You should begin the application process at least a year in advance. An increasing number of schools accept applications year round. In any case, find out the application deadlines and plan accordingly. Although September (the fall semester) is the traditional time to begin university study in the United States, you can begin your studies at many schools in January (the spring semester).

- In addition, you will need to obtain an I-20 Certificate of Eligibility from the school you plan to attend if you intend to apply for an F-1 Student Visa to study in the United States.

KAPLAN ENGLISH PROGRAMS*

If you need more help with the complex process of university admissions, assistance preparing for the SAT, ACT, or TOEFL, or help building your English language skills in general, you may be interested in Kaplan's programs for international students.

Kaplan English Programs were designed to help students and professionals from outside the United States meet their educational and career goals. At locations throughout the United States, international students take advantage of Kaplan's programs to help them improve their academic and conversational English skills, raise their scores on the TOEFL, SAT, ACT, and other standardized exams, and gain admission to the schools of their choice. Our staff and instructors give international students the individualized attention they need to succeed. Here is a brief description of some of Kaplan's programs for international students:

General Intensive English

Kaplan's General Intensive English course is the fastest and most effective way for students to improve their English. This full-time program integrates the four key elements of language learning—listening, speaking, reading and writing. The challenging curriculum and intensive schedule are designed for both the general language learner and the academically bound student.

TOEFL and Academic English

Our world-famous TOEFL course prepares you for the TOEFL and also teaches you the academic language and skills needed to succeed in a university. Designed for high-intermediate to advanced-level English speakers, our course includes TOEFL-focused reading, writing, listening, speaking, vocabulary, and grammar instruction.

General English

Our General English course is a semi-intensive program designed for students who want to improve their listening and speaking skills without the time commitment of an intensive program. With morning class time and flexible computer lab hours throughout the week, our General English course is perfect for every schedule.

OTHER KAPLAN PROGRAMS

Since 1938, more than 3 million students have come to Kaplan to advance their studies, prepare for entry to American universities, and further their careers. In addition to the above programs, Kaplan offers courses to prepare for the ACT, GMAT®, GRE®, MCAT®, DAT®, USMLE®, NCLEX®, and other standardized exams at locations throughout the United States.

Applying to Kaplan English Programs

To get more information, or to apply for admission to any of Kaplan's programs for international students and professionals, contact us at:

Kaplan English Programs

700 South Flower, Suite 2900
Los Angeles, CA 90017, USA
Phone (if calling from within the United States): 800-818-9128
Phone (if calling from outside the United States): 213-452-5800
Fax: 213-892-1364
Website: www.kaplanenglish.com
Email: world@kaplan.com

*Kaplan is authorized under federal law to enroll nonimmigrant alien students. Kaplan is accredited by ACCET (Accrediting Council for Continuing Education and Training).

FREE Services for International Students

Kaplan now offers international students many services online—*free of charge*!
Students may assess their TOEFL skills and gain valuable feedback on their English
language proficiency in just a few hours with Kaplan's TOEFL Skills Assessment.
Log onto www.kaplanenglish.com today.

NOTES

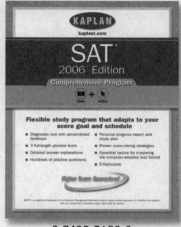

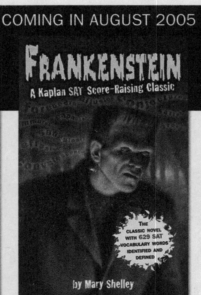
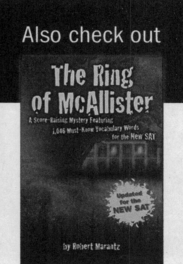

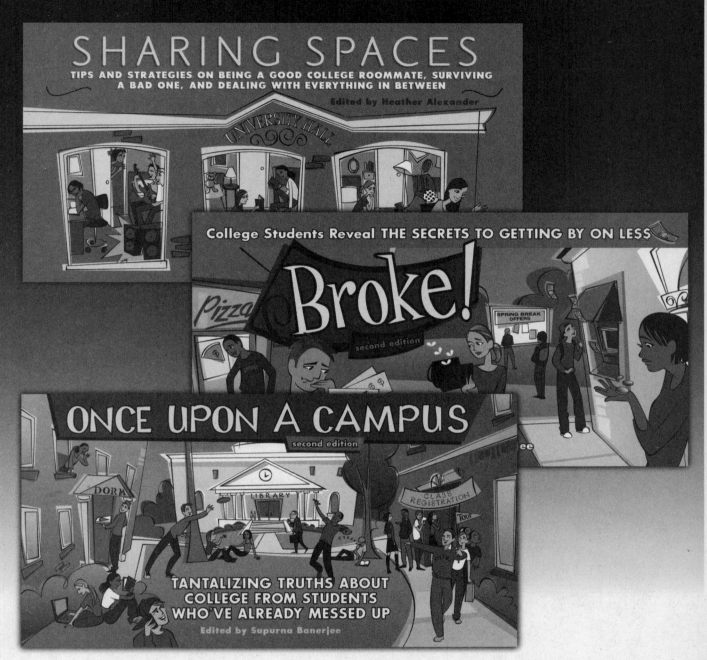